How to
Master Skills for the

Second Edition

TOEFL® iBT
READING Advanced

 DARAKWON

How to
Master Skills for the

Second Edition

TOEFL® iBT

READING Advanced

Publisher Kyudo Chung
Editor Sangik Cho
Authors Timothy Hall, Arthur H. Milch, Denise McCormack, E2K
Proofreaders Michael A. Putlack, Will Link
Designers Minji Kim, Kyuok Jeong

First Published in March 2007 By Darakwon, Inc.
Second edition first published in November 2024 by Darakwon, Inc.
Darakwon Bldg., 211, Munbal-ro, Paju-si, Gyeonggi-do 10881
Republic of Korea
Tel: 02-736-2031 (Ext. 250)
Fax: 02-732-2037

ISBN 978-89-277-8093-9 14740
        978-89-277-8084-7 14740 (set)

www.darakwon.co.kr

Photo Credits
Shutterstock.com

Components Main Book / Answer Key / Free MP3 Downloads
7 6 5 4 3 2 1   24 25 26 27 28

Table of
Contents

INTRODUCTION

1 Information on the TOEFL® iBT

A The Format of the TOEFL® iBT

Section	Number of Questions or Tasks	Timing	Score
Reading	**20 Questions** • **2 reading passages** – with 10 questions per passage – approximately 700 words long each	35 Minutes	30 Points
Listening	**28 Questions** • **2 conversations** – 5 questions per conversation – 3 minutes each • **3 lectures** – 6 questions per lecture – 3-5 minutes each	36 Minutes	30 Points
Speaking	**4 Tasks** • **1 independent speaking task** – 1 personal choice/opinion/experience – preparation: 15 sec. / response: 45 sec. • **2 integrated speaking tasks: Read-Listen-Speak** – 1 campus situation topic reading: 75-100 words (45 sec.) conversation: 150-180 words (60-80 sec.) – 1 academic course topic reading: 75-100 words (50 sec.) lecture: 150-220 words (60-120 sec.) – preparation: 30 sec. / response: 60 sec. • **1 integrated speaking task: Listen-Speak** – 1 academic course topic lecture: 230-280 words (90-120 sec.) – preparation: 20 sec. / response: 60 sec.	17 Minutes	30 Points
Writing	**2 Tasks** • **1 integrated writing task: Read-Listen-Write** – reading: 230-300 words (3 min.) – lecture: 230-300 words (2 min.) – a summary of 150-225 words (20 min.) • **1 academic discussion task** – a minimum 100-word essay (10 min.)	30 Minutes	30 Points

B What Is New about the TOEFL® iBT?

- The TOEFL® iBT is delivered through the Internet in secure test centers around the world at the same time.
- It tests all four language skills and is taken in the order of Reading, Listening, Speaking, and Writing.
- The test is about 2 hours long, and all of the four test sections will be completed in one day.
- Note taking is allowed throughout the entire test, including the Reading section. At the end of the test, all notes are collected and destroyed at the test center.
- In the Listening section, one lecture may be spoken with a British or Australian accent.
- There are integrated tasks requiring test takers to combine more than one language skill in the Speaking and Writing sections.
- In the Speaking section, test takers wear headphones and speak into a microphone when they respond. The responses are recorded and transmitted to ETS's Online Scoring Network.
- In the Writing section, test takers must type their responses. Handwriting is not possible.
- Test scores will be reported online. Test takers can see their scores online 4-8 business days after the test and can also receive a copy of their score report by mail.

2 Information on the Reading Section

The Reading section of the TOEFL® iBT measures test takers' ability to understand university-level academic texts. This section has 2 passages, and the length of each passage is about 700 words. Some passages may have underlined words or phrases in blue. Test takers can click on them to see a definition or explanation. Test takers have to answer 10 questions per passage. 35 minutes are given to complete this section, including the time spent reading the passages and answering the questions.

A Types of Reading Passages

- Exposition: Material that provides an explanation of a topic
- Argumentation: Material that presents a point of view about a topic and provides evidence to support it
- Historical narrative: An account of a past event or of a person's life, narrated or written by someone else

B Types of Reading Questions

- Basic Comprehension Questions
  - Vocabulary Question (1-3 questions per passage): This type of question asks you to identify the meanings of words and phrases in the reading passage.
  - Reference Question (0-1 questions per passage): This type of question asks you to identify the referential relationship between the words in the passage.
  - Factual Information Question (1-3 questions per passage): This type of question asks you to identify specific information that is explicitly stated in the passage.

- Negative Factual Information Question (0-2 questions per passage): This type of question asks you to check what information is NOT mentioned in the passage.
- Sentence Simplification Question (0-1 question per passage): This type of question asks you to choose the sentence that best paraphrases the essential information in the highlighted sentence.

- Inference Questions
  - Inference Question (0-2 questions per passage): This type of question asks you to identify an idea that is not explicitly stated in the passage.
  - Rhetorical Purpose Question (1-2 questions per passage): This type of question asks you why the author uses particular words, phrases, or sentences.
  - Insert Text Question (1 question per passage): This type of question provides an example sentence and asks you to decide where the best place for that sentence would be in the passage.

- Reading to Learn Questions
  - Prose Summary Questions (0-1 question per passage): This type of question asks you to complete a summary chart with major ideas from the passage. It is worth up to 2 points, and partial credit is given. This type of question does not occur with a Fill in a Table question in one passage.
  - Fill in a Table Question (0-1 question per passage): This type of question asks you to identify and organize the major ideas of the passage into table categories. It is worth up to 3 points for tables with 5 correct answers and 4 points for tables with 7 correct answers. Partial credit is given. This type of question does not occur with a Prose Summary question in one passage.

C Question Formats

- There are three question formats in the Reading section: Four-choice questions with a single answer in traditional multiple-choice format, four-choice questions with a single answer that ask test takers to insert a sentence where it fits best in a passage, and Reading to Learn questions with more than four choices and more than one answer

HOW TO USE THIS BOOK

How to Master Skills for the TOEFL® iBT Reading Advanced is designed to be used either as a textbook for a TOEFL® iBT reading preparation course or as a tool for individual learners who are preparing for the TOEFL® test on their own. With a total of ten units, this book is organized to prepare you for the test with a comprehensive understanding of the test and a thorough analysis of every question type. Each unit consists of six parts and provides a step-by-step program that provides question-solving strategies and the development of test-taking abilities. At the back of the book are three actual tests of the Reading section of the TOEFL® iBT.

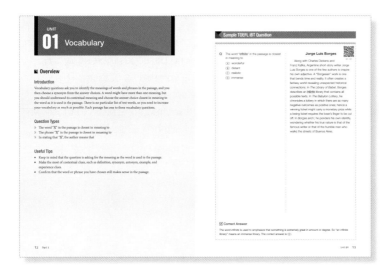

❶ Overview

This part is designed to prepare you for the type of question the unit covers. You will be given a full description of the question type and its application in the passage. You will also be given some useful tips as well as an illustrated introduction and sample.

❷ Basic Drill

The purpose of this section is to ensure that you understand the new types of questions that were described in the overview. You will be given a chance to confirm your understanding in brief texts before starting on the practice exercises. You will read some simple passages and answer questions of a particular type. This part will help you learn how to deal with each type of question on the Reading section of the TOEFL® iBT.

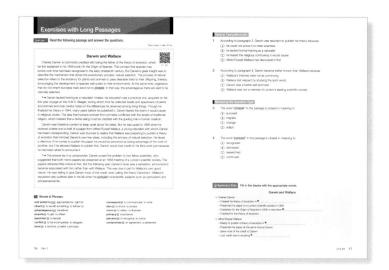

❸ Exercises with Long Passages

This section allows you to practice reading TOEFL® passages. Six long passages are provided, and a time limit is given for reading each passage. You first read the passage within a time limit and then solve general comprehension questions and the questions of the type that is mainly dealt with in the unit. A glossary of important words is listed in each passage to help increase your understanding. In addition, summary notes are provided to help you grasp the overall organization of each passage and understand important points.

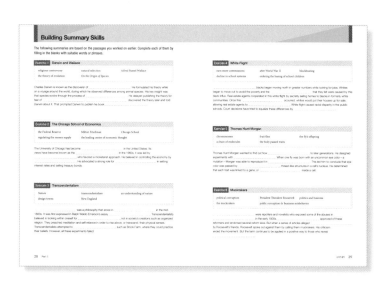

❹ Building Summary Skills

The purpose of this part is for you to understand the previous long passages thoroughly by completing the summaries of them. This will also help you enhance your paraphrasing skills, which are strongly recommended to those who are preparing for the TOEFL® iBT.

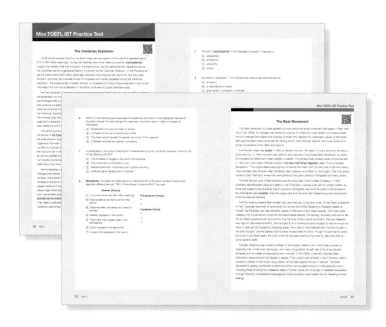

❺ Mini TOEFL iBT Practice Test

This part gives you a chance to experience an actual TOEFL® iBT test in a shortened form. You will be given two passages with 7-8 questions each. The topics are similar to those on the actual TOEFL® test, as are the questions.

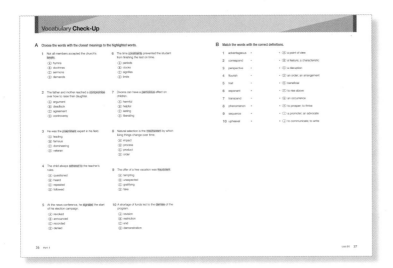

❻ Vocabulary Check-Up

This part offers you a chance to review some of the words you need to remember after finishing each unit. Vocabulary words for each unit are also provided at the back of the book to help you prepare for each unit.

❼ Actual Test

This part offers three full practice tests that are modeled on the Reading section of the TOEFL® iBT. This will familiarize you with the actual test format of the TOEFL® iBT.

PART I

Basic Comprehension

In this part, the reading comprehension questions include vocabulary, reference, factual information, negative factual information, and sentence simplification. The learning objectives of these reading comprehension questions are to identify individual words, referential relations between words in the passage, factual information, and essential sentences.

◤ Overview

Introduction

Vocabulary questions ask you to identify the meanings of words and phrases in the passage, and you then choose a synonym from the answer choices. A word might have more than one meaning, but you should understand its contextual meaning and choose the answer choice closest in meaning to the word as it is used in the passage. There is no particular list of test words, so you need to increase your vocabulary as much as possible. Each passage has one to three vocabulary questions.

Question Types

- The word "X" in the passage is closest in meaning to
- The phrase "X" in the passage is closest in meaning to
- In stating that "X", the author means that

Useful Tips

- Keep in mind that the question is asking for the meaning as the word is used in the passage.
- Make the most of contextual clues, such as definition, synonym, antonym, example, and experience clues.
- Confirm that the word or phrase you have chosen still makes sense in the passage.

Q   The word "infinite" in the passage is closest in meaning to

(A) wonderful

(B) distant

(C) realistic

(D) immense

Jorge Luis Borges

01-01

Along with Charles Dickens and Franz Kafka, Argentine short-story writer Jorge Luis Borges is one of the few authors to inspire his own adjective. A "Borgesian" work is one that bends time and reality. It often creates a fantasy world revealing unexpected historical connections. In *The Library of Babel*, Borges describes an infinite library that contains all possible texts. In *The Babylon Lottery*, he chronicles a lottery in which there are as many negative outcomes as positive ones; hence a winning ticket might carry a monetary prize while a losing ticket requires the loser's finger to be cut off. In *Borges and I*, he ponders his own identity, wondering whether his true nature is that of the famous writer or that of the humble man who walks the streets of Buenos Aires.

☑ **Correct Answer**

The word *infinite* is used to emphasize that something is extremely great in amount or degree. So "an infinite library" means an immense library. The correct answer is (D).

Basic Drill

Read the passages and answer the questions.

Drill 1

Rosalind Franklin

The Nobel Prize for finding the structure of the DNA molecule was shared by three men in 1962. But it was a woman, Rosalind Franklin, who made that discovery possible. Working with Maurice Wilkins, Franklin used the technique known as X-ray crystallography to show that the DNA had a helical, or spiral, shape. Her results gave James Watson and Francis Crick the key insight that led them to conclude in 1953 that the DNA molecule was shaped like a double helix. That breakthrough enabled scientists to deduce how genes are passed by heredity. Because female scientists in the early 1950s were often forced to work in the shadow of their male counterparts, Franklin's pivotal work has been relegated to a footnote in the history of science.

01-02

1. The word "breakthrough" in the passage is closest in meaning to
   - Ⓐ discovery
   - Ⓑ experiment
   - Ⓒ attempt
   - Ⓓ announcement

2. The word "pivotal" in the passage is closest in meaning to
   - Ⓐ difficult
   - Ⓑ essential
   - Ⓒ published
   - Ⓓ preliminary

Drill 2

Charter Schools

The charter-school movement in the United States developed in the 1990s as a reaction to the perceived failure of public schools, especially in the inner cities. The concept is that money which normally goes to public schools is given instead to private groups, who find their own buildings, hire their own teachers, and plan their own curriculums. Charter schools operate free from the control of the public schools and are expected to produce better academic results. The name charter refers to the statutorily defined performance contract that the schools are expected to meet. While there are many successful charter schools, many others have not achieved the desired improvements. Thus, the wisdom and the effectiveness of this innovation is still being debated.

01-03

1. The word "perceived" in the passage is closest in meaning to
   - Ⓐ costly
   - Ⓑ familiar
   - Ⓒ complete
   - Ⓓ apparent

2. The word "statutorily" in the passage is closest in meaning to
   - Ⓐ legally
   - Ⓑ adequately
   - Ⓒ strictly
   - Ⓓ specifically

Philip Roth

Often picked by critics as the best American novelist of the past fifty years, Philip Roth writes personal reflections on the experience of being a Jew in the United States as well as satiric looks at history. His first book, *Goodbye, Columbus*, won the National Book Award in 1960 and later became an influential movie. His 1969 novel, *Portnoy's Complaint*, won critical praise while triggering a storm of controversy due to some of its descriptions of adolescents. It was banned in some towns for many years. Roth often adopts a character as an alter ego and has that person reappear in several novels. For example, Nathan Zuckerman is the protagonist of five novels from 1979 to 1986 and again in three more from 1997 to 2000.

01-04

1 The word "triggering" in the passage is closest in meaning to

- (A) prompting
- (B) rejecting
- (C) advising
- (D) calming

2 The word "adopts" in the passage is closest in meaning to

- (A) recalls
- (B) develops
- (C) assumes
- (D) promises

The Malthusian Catastrophe

In 1798, English economist Thomas Malthus theorized that human populations tend to increase faster than food supplies. He predicted that much of the surplus population would be killed off by wars and diseases. Then, the remaining people would be condemned to catastrophe, that is, periods of starvation and misery. The Malthusian catastrophe has already occurred in isolated cultures that had no means of replenishing resources. For example, the original Easter Islanders died out after they deforested the entire island. This led to soil erosion and the demise of the animals and plants on which they depended for food. Some scientists see signs that a broader Malthusian catastrophe may be gaining momentum today. They cite the recent tragic histories of Haiti, Rwanda, and Ethiopia.

01-05

1 The word "theorized" in the passage is closest in meaning to

- (A) proved
- (B) learned
- (C) proposed
- (D) guessed

2 The word "replenishing" in the passage is closest in meaning to

- (A) renewing
- (B) protecting
- (C) creating
- (D) altering

Exercises with Long Passages

Exercise 1 Read the following passage and answer the questions.

Time Limit: 3 min. 40 sec.

Darwin and Wallace

01 - 06

Charles Darwin is commonly credited with being the father of the theory of evolution, which he first explained in his 1859 book *On the Origin of Species*. The concept that species may evolve over time had been recognized in the early nineteenth century. But Darwin's great insight was to describe the mechanism that drives the evolutionary process: natural selection. The process of natural selection refers to the tendency for plants and animals to pass desirable traits to their offspring, thereby encouraging the development of species well suited to their environments. At the same time, organisms that do not inherit favorable traits tend not to prosper. In that way, the advantageous traits are said to be naturally selected.

2 ➝ Darwin lacked training as a naturalist. Indeed, his education was a practical one, acquired on his five-year voyage on the *H.M.S. Beagle*, during which time he collected fossils and specimens of plants and animals and took careful notes on the differences he observed among living things. Though he finalized his theory in 1844, many years before he published it, Darwin feared the storm it would cause in religious circles. The idea that humans evolved from primates conflicted with the tenets of traditional religion, which insisted that a divine being must be credited with the guiding role in human creation.

Darwin was therefore content to keep quiet about his ideas. But he was upset in 1858 when he received a letter and a draft of a paper from Alfred Russel Wallace, a young naturalist with whom Darwin had been corresponding. Darwin was stunned to realize that Wallace was preparing to publish a theory of evolution that mirrored Darwin's own key ideas, including the primacy of natural selection. He faced a dilemma: If he hurried to publish his paper, he would be perceived as taking advantage of the work of another; but if he allowed Wallace to publish first, Darwin would lose credit for his life's work just because he had been afraid to announce it.

4 ➝ The answer lay in a compromise. Darwin posed the problem to two fellow scientists, who suggested that both men's papers be presented at an 1858 meeting of a London scientific society. The papers attracted little notice at first. But the following year, Darwin's book was a sensation, and evolution became associated with him rather than with Wallace. This was due in part to Wallace's own good nature. He was willing to give Darwin most of the credit, even calling the theory Darwinism. Wallace's reputation also suffered later in his life when he pursued nonscientific subjects such as spiritualism and extraterrestrial life.

📖 Words & Phrases

well suited to phr appropriate for; right for
inherit v to be left something; to fall heir to
advantageous adj beneficial
acquire v to get; to obtain
specimen n a sample
conflict v to be incompatible; to disagree
tenet n a doctrine; a belief; a principle

correspond v to communicate; to write
stun v to shock; to amaze
mirror v to reflect; to illustrate
primacy n importance
perceive v to recognize; to notice
compromise n an agreement; a settlement

1 According to paragraph 2, Darwin was reluctant to publish his theory because

    Ⓐ he could not prove it to other scientists

    Ⓑ he lacked formal training as a naturalist

    Ⓒ he feared the religious controversy it would cause

    Ⓓ Alfred Russel Wallace had discovered it first

2 According to paragraph 4, Darwin became better known than Wallace because

    Ⓐ Wallace's theories were not as convincing

    Ⓑ Wallace lost respect by studying the spirit world

    Ⓒ Darwin was a better self-promoter

    Ⓓ Wallace was not a member of London's leading scientific society

Mastering the Question Type

3 The word "prosper" in the passage is closest in meaning to

    Ⓐ succeed

    Ⓑ migrate

    Ⓒ change

    Ⓓ adapt

4 The word "pursued" in the passage is closest in meaning to

    Ⓐ recognized

    Ⓑ dismissed

    Ⓒ researched

    Ⓓ continued

Summary Note   Fill in the blanks with the appropriate words.

Darwin and Wallace

- Charles Darwin
  - Created his theory of evolution in ❶ ....
  - Presented his paper to a London scientific society in 1858
  - Published *On the Origin of Species* in 1859 → describes ❷ ....
  - Credited for the theory of evolution

- Alfred Russel Wallace
  - Ready to publish a theory of evolution in ❸ ....
  - Presented his paper at the same time as Darwin
  - Gave most of the credit to Darwin
  - Lost credit due to studying ❹ ....

Time Limit: 3 min. 40 sec.

The Chicago School of Economics

01 - 07

Over the past century, the University of Chicago's Department of Economics has been the preeminent source of economic thought in the United States. Its influence has been so pervasive that its theoretical approaches have come to be known in academic circles as the Chicago School. This refers not only to the university department but also to a broader economic worldview. Adherents of the Chicago School may be found in many universities and governmental institutions around the world.

2 ➡ The Chicago School has passed through several historical stages. Each is characterized by its own unique perspective. It began in the 1920s with Frank H. Knight and Jacob Viner. They rejected the reigning empirical approach of economics, which derived conclusions by analyzing data about the performance of economic indicators. Knight and Viner denounced economic imperialism, which viewed all social forces as having an economic explanation. They were also suspicious of a laissez-faire approach. Instead, they argued for activist governmental policies to avoid recessions. But they rejected a full-scale Keynesian policy that would grant government a role in all phases of economic life. Rather, they were confident in the ability of neoclassical paradigms, with their focus on individual and group choices to maximize self-interest, to solve all economic problems.

3 ➡ The second great flowering of the Chicago School began in the 1960s under George J. Stigler and Milton Friedman. The Second Chicago School adhered to neoclassical economics and rejected a Keynesian exaltation of government regulation. In the macroeconomic sphere, it is best known for its stress on monetarism. It was developed by Milton Friedman, with whom the Chicago School became most closely associated. Friedman's view, borrowed from the nineteenth-century quantity of money theory, was that price levels are directly related to the amount of money in circulation. Unlike Keynesianism, monetarism eschews direct government control by means of taxation and spending in favor of imposing limits on the nation's money supply. Friedman espoused a dominant role for the Federal Reserve. It can raise or lower interest rates as needed to put the brakes on inflation or to stimulate a stagnant economy. Another tool is the sale of United States treasury bonds. The government can use them to obtain funds by selling to citizens at stated interest rates.

On the microeconomic level, the Chicago School was led by George Stigler. He argued for preserving the neoclassical paradigm while extending it to new areas whenever possible. Resulting innovations in the microeconomic sphere include search theory, human capital theory, and property rights and transaction cost theory. The Chicago School's continued embrace of neoclassicism has led to criticisms that it encourages an imperialist view, in which all social and political phenomena are seen in terms of economic forces.

📖 Words & Phrases

preeminent adj leading
adherent n a supporter; an advocate; a follower
perspective n a point of view
reigning adj dominant
empirical adj experiential

denounce v to criticize; to attack
paradigm n a model
suspicious adj doubtful
adhere to phr to follow; to stick to
regulation n control; direction

espouse v to support; to advocate
stagnant adj motionless
preserve v to keep; to maintain
extend v to widen
embrace n acceptance; adoption

1 According to paragraphs 2 and 3, a difference between monetarism and Keynesian economics is that

Ⓐ Keynesian economics was taught in the Chicago School

Ⓑ monetarism preaches the merits of government regulation

Ⓒ monetarism favors controls over the money supply

Ⓓ Keynesian economics would limit the role of government

2 The word "them" in the passage refers to

Ⓐ the brakes

Ⓑ government bonds

Ⓒ funds

Ⓓ citizens

Mastering the Question Type

3 The word "pervasive" in the passage is closest in meaning to

Ⓐ harmful

Ⓑ celebrated

Ⓒ frequent

Ⓓ widespread

4 The word "eschews" in the passage is closest in meaning to

Ⓐ avoids

Ⓑ favors

Ⓒ preaches

Ⓓ involves

📝 Summary Note Fill in the blanks with the appropriate words.

The Chicago School of Economics

- First stage (1920s)
  - Frank H. Knight & Jacob Viner
    - → against economic imperialism, a ❶ _____ approach, and a full-scale Keynesian policy
    - → for ❷ _____ → the focus on individual and group choices to maximize self-interest
- Second stage (1960s)
  - Milton Friedman & George J. Stigler
  - adhered to neoclassical economics
  - Macroeconomics → ❸ _____ : emphasis on the role of the Federal Reserve
  - Microeconomics → extended the neoclassical paradigm to areas such as search theory,
    ❹ _____ , and property rights and transaction cost theory

Exercise 3 Read the following passage and answer the questions.

Time Limit: 3 min. 40 sec.

Transcendentalism

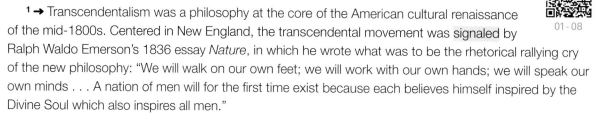
01-08

1 → Transcendentalism was a philosophy at the core of the American cultural renaissance of the mid-1800s. Centered in New England, the transcendental movement was signaled by Ralph Waldo Emerson's 1836 essay *Nature*, in which he wrote what was to be the rhetorical rallying cry of the new philosophy: "We will walk on our own feet; we will work with our own hands; we will speak our own minds . . . A nation of men will for the first time exist because each believes himself inspired by the Divine Soul which also inspires all men."

2 → In addition, in 1836, Emerson and his other transcendentalists sought a forum for their ideas by forming the Transcendental Club in Cambridge, Massachusetts. In 1840, the group began to publish their philosophy in a journal, *The Dial*. The term transcendentalism was derived from a concept of the German philosopher, Immanuel Kant, who said that knowledge was "transcendent" when it was concerned not with reality but with the mode of knowing reality. By meditating and communing with nature, through work and art, people can transcend their senses and arrive at an understanding of truth and beauty. The doctrine rejects the idea that people can rely on their senses and experiences to attain knowledge; rather, they must look to their inner spiritual essence as guideposts to the true nature of things.

The transcendentalists believed that the path to truth lay within themselves. Society was a necessary evil, one that gave humans useful goods and the means of physical survival. But in order to lead a just life, people must ignore customs and social conventions and rely on their own reason. They believed organized religion was an obstacle to this process because it interfered with people's personal relationships with God. Transcendentalism exercised a profound influence on American literature and intellectual history. In his essays, such as *Self Reliance*, Emerson became the leading exponent of the movement. Henry David Thoreau's *On Walden Pond* insisted on humankind's ability to survive and prosper outside the constraints of society. Poets Walt Whitman and Emily Dickinson revealed universal truths that could be uncovered by studying nature.

Emerson conceded that a true transcendental life was impossible to attain. Nonetheless, the movement spawned utopian communities like the one at Brook Farm near Boston. Founded by George Ripley in 1841, Brook Farm was inspired by the socialist views of George Fourier, who believed that people of like beliefs could live together in harmony by sharing their material goods and by growing food for all. But the farm was situated on poor soil that was not productive for agriculture. More successful were its schools, which gave the community its only income. A fire to the main building doomed the experiment, which ended in 1847.

📖 Words & Phrases

core n a center
rallying cry phr a slogan to gather support
divine adj godlike; sacred; holy
transcend v to rise above
meditate v to contemplate; to reflect
commune v to communicate
attain v to achieve; to obtain; to reach

obstacle n a hindrance; a barrier
interfere with phr to hinder; to harm
profound adj deep; heavy
prosper v to thrive; to flourish
constraint n a restriction; a limitation
exponent n a promoter; an advocate
doom v to destroy

1 According to paragraph 1, the event that started the transcendental movement was

Ⓐ the American cultural renaissance

Ⓑ Emerson's essay *Nature*

Ⓒ the formation of the Transcendental Club

Ⓓ the publication of *The Dial*

2 According to paragraph 2, transcendentalism's view of the physical senses is that

Ⓐ people achieve all knowledge through their senses

Ⓑ people's senses lead to sinful behavior

Ⓒ people cannot rely on their senses to understand nature

Ⓓ senses can lead to understanding only when guided by organized religion

Mastering the Question Type

3 The word "signaled" in the passage is closest in meaning to

Ⓐ indicated

Ⓑ noted

Ⓒ foretold

Ⓓ declared

4 The word "spawned" in the passage is closest in meaning to

Ⓐ discovered

Ⓑ inspired

Ⓒ described

Ⓓ produced

Summary Note Fill in the blanks with the appropriate words.

Transcendentalism

- The term → derived from a philosophical concept of ❶ ....

- A central philosophy of the American cultural renaissance of the mid-1800s in New England
  - physical senses do not lead to an understanding of nature
  - ❷ .... and reject organized religion
  - rely on oneself and seek personal connection to God

- Important publications and literature
  - *Nature and Self Reliance* by ❸ ....
  - *The Dial*, the journal published by the Transcendental Club
  - *On Walden Pond* by Henry David Thoreau
  - poems written by Walt Whitman and Emily Dickinson

- ❹ .... founded by George Ripley in 1841 and burned down in 1847

White Flight

01- 09

1 ➜ Large cities in the United States were founded and populated by whites. After the Civil War, blacks began moving to the northern cities for jobs in the factories. This black influx increased during World War II as blacks came seeking jobs in the war industries. A tight housing market resulted, and the birth of the Civil Rights Movement caused increased racial tension in the white-controlled cities. Whites with the economic means began moving away from these social problems into nearby suburban communities, a phenomenon known as white flight.

Americans had traditionally lived either in cities or on farms. But the spike in demand for post-World War II housing created the suburbs, which were residential communities often built on former farmland and from which people commuted by automobile to their jobs in the cities. The suburbs were perceived by some whites as peaceful havens, free from the urban turmoil caused by poor blacks and the decline of city schools.

3 ➜ Real estate agents played a crucial role in fostering white flight, often prying upon whites' negative attitudes toward blacks. The most pernicious technique used by realtors was blockbusting. Real estate agents would secretly sell a house in a white neighborhood, either buying the house themselves or using a white proxy and then reselling the house to a black family. When white homeowners saw a black family moving in, they would panic, thinking that the values of their homes would decline if the neighborhood were overtaken by blacks. Their fears were self-fulfilling; as soon as more homes were put on the market, the prices would decline. Often, the only willing buyers were the real estate agents, who would then resell the homes at higher prices to new black families. In that way, the realtors would reap not only their sales commissions but also the profits on their briefly owned houses.

In addition to altering the racial composition of cities, white flight profoundly impacted public education. In 1954, the Supreme Court ordered that public schools be desegregated so that schools would no longer be mostly black or mostly white. That order triggered social upheaval, especially in the South, which had a long tradition of requiring separate schools for blacks. To overcome this resistance, later court decisions mandated the busing of students, so blacks might be bused many miles to a formerly white school and white students many miles to a black school. White parents balked at having their children waste time riding on buses to a school that might not be as good as the one nearby. Their solution was to enroll their children in private schools, which, because they received no tax money, were free to operate without being subject to racial apportionment.

📖 Words & Phrases

populate v to inhabit; to live in
influx n arrival
phenomenon n an event; an occurrence
haven n a safe place
decline n deterioration; failing
crucial adj very important; critical
pry upon phr to take advantage of
pernicious adj harmful

proxy n a substitute; a surrogate
overtake v to outstrip
trigger v to cause
alter v to change
desegregate v to integrate
upheaval n a disruption
mandate v to command; to require
balk at phr to stop; to be unwilling to continue

1   According to paragraph 1, what event prompted a sudden increase in migration to the north?
    (A) The Civil War
    (B) The Civil Rights Movement
    (C) The Second World War
    (D) White flight

2   According to paragraph 3, blockbusting involved
    (A) using a white representative to buy a house
    (B) demolishing old houses and building new ones
    (C) advertising homes to whites only
    (D) offering less than the value of a house

Mastering the Question Type

3   The word "turmoil" in the passage is closest in meaning to
    (A) pollution
    (B) poverty
    (C) agitation
    (D) calm

4   The word "apportionment" in the passage is closest in meaning to
    (A) allocation
    (B) segregation
    (C) discrimination
    (D) controversy

Summary Note   **Fill in the blanks with the appropriate words.**

White Flight

- Refers to the phenomenon of whites moving out into ❶ _____ to avoid living with blacks
- Triggered by an increasing number of blacks moving into white cities during World War II
- Fostered by realtors using the ❷ _____ technique to sell houses at high prices
- Resulted in changes in ❸ _____ of cities
- Led to segregation in public schools
    – courts ordered desegregation and ❹ _____ regardless of their races
    – white parents sent their children to private schools

Exercise 5 Read the following passage and answer the questions.

Time Limit: 3 min. 40 sec.

Thomas Hunt Morgan

In the early part of the twentieth century, scientists were struggling to discover the physical basis of heredity. They knew that traits were inherited, but they did not know the mechanism by which the traits were passed to later generations. One candidate was the chromosome, the thread-like structure in the nucleus of a cell that had been discovered in 1888. But no one had performed the experiments needed to demonstrate the precise role of chromosomes in conveying genetic information.

2 ➜ A geneticist at Columbia University, Thomas Hunt Morgan, chose a tiny fly as the subject of his quest to understand the chromosome. Fruit flies, formally called the *Drosophila melanogaster*, were ideal for Morgan's project because they were inexpensive to keep and feed, they could be bred in large numbers in a small space, they became adults in just ten days, and they had only four chromosomes, which made them easy to study.

Working out of a small laboratory at Columbia, appropriately called the Fly Room, Morgan and his team began breeding fruit flies by the millions. The process was a painstaking one as each fly had to be captured with tweezers and examined under a magnifying glass for any variations in inherited traits. Morgan tried to produce variations, also called mutations, by exposing the flies to radiation, growing them in either bright light or total darkness, spinning them in centrifuges, and baking them in ovens. Morgan worked diligently for six years but had no success in finding mutations that he could try to reproduce in a fly's offspring.

4 ➜ Just as he was about to give up, in 1910, he found a fly with white eyes instead of the usual red ones. That mutation reappeared in later generations, implying that it had been passed on by inheritance. Morgan learned how to track traits from generation to generation, allowing him to show how particular traits were linked to particular chromosomes. In this way, he finally established that chromosomes were the carriers of hereditary factors. Those factors were later determined to be genes, or chain-like molecules of nucleic acid.

Morgan's results led him to explain sex-linked inheritance, meaning that some traits pass only to one or the other sex. He also discovered that genes are arranged on a chromosome in a fixed linear order, occupying a specific place on the chromosome. His insights made possible the recent success of the Human Genome Project, which successfully mapped out the sequence and location of all human genes. Armed with that knowledge, scientists can now work to identify the genes that carry certain diseases, and they may be able to remove defective genes and replace them with healthy ones.

📖 Words & Phrases

trait (n) a feature; a characteristic
mechanism (n) a means; a process
convey (v) to carry; to send
quest (n) a search; a pursuit
appropriately (adv) aptly; properly
breed (v) to reproduce
capture (v) to catch; to take

variation (n) a change
inherited (adj) received; handed down
offspring (n) children
track (v) to follow; to chase
linear (adj) arranged in a straight line
sequence (n) an order; an arrangement
defective (adj) flawed; imperfect

1 According to paragraph 2, which of the following is NOT true of the reasons Morgan experimented with fruit flies?

(A) They had four chromosomes.

(B) They did not require a large breeding area.

(C) They were available in his laboratory at Columbia.

(D) They did not cost much to care for.

2 According to paragraph 4, the appearance of a mutation that was passed on resulted in what key insight by Morgan?

(A) Most fruit flies have red eyes.

(B) Chromosomes carry hereditary traits.

(C) Mutations last for only one generation.

(D) A mutation is caused by an absence of genes.

Mastering the Question Type

3 The word "painstaking" in the passage is closest in meaning to

(A) harmful

(B) violent

(C) boring

(D) precise

4 The word "implying" in the passage is closest in meaning to

(A) suggesting

(B) proving

(C) announcing

(D) guessing

Summary Note Fill in the blanks with the appropriate words.

Thomas Hunt Morgan's Search for the Basis of Heredity

- Experimented with ❶ _____
  - inexpensive to keep and feed
  - can be bred in large numbers in a small space
  - become adults in just ❷ _____
  - have only ❸ _____, making them easy to study
- Succeeded in causing a ❹ _____ in 1910
  - white eyes passed to later generations by chromosomes
- Led to Human Genome Project

Exercise 6 Read the following passage and answer the questions.

Time Limit: 3 min. 30 sec.

Muckrakers

In the late 1800s and early 1900s, magazine writers and newspaper reporters began to write reports exposing the abuses and corruption in politics and business. Among their targets were child labor, unsafe practices in food processing plants, fraudulent claims by drug companies, prostitution, labor racketeering, and inhumane prison conditions.

2 ➔ One of the most famous of these reformers was the novelist Upton Sinclair, who, in *The Jungle*, dramatizes the unsanitary conditions in the meat-packing industry. Another was Jacob Riis, a newspaper reporter and photographer. He revealed the misery in the slums of New York City. The public's enthusiasm for these reports was inspired mainly by a 1903 series in *McClure's Magazine*. It published investigations of corruption in city government by Lincoln Steffens and of the Standard Oil Company by Ida M. Tarbell.

This brand of socially conscious journalism was originally embraced by President Theodore Roosevelt. He persuaded Congress to pass reform laws such as the Pure Food and Drugs Act and the Meat Inspection Act. But in 1906, David Graham Phillips wrote a series of articles in *Cosmopolitan* magazine that alleged political corruption by some of Roosevelt's allies. Roosevelt fought back. In a speech, he compared some of the journalists to the character in John Bunyan's *Pilgrim's Progress* who worked with a muck-rake. He was always looking down into the muck, or animal dung, and never looking up at the world around him. He praised writers who showed a genuine concern for correcting injustices. But he condemned those who were interested only in uncovering filth and sensationalizing the misbehavior they had found. He called them muckrakers.

4 ➔ Responsible investigative journalists felt betrayed by Roosevelt's unsavory label. Lincoln Steffens, one of the reformers respected by Roosevelt, was furious with the speech. The day after, he told Roosevelt, "Well, you have put an end to all these journalistic investigations that have made you." In fact, Roosevelt's verbal attack did lead to the demise of what was generally considered to be a positive movement that had drawn attention to and cured many of society's ills. Nonetheless, while it flourished, especially between 1900 and 1915, the muckraking movement achieved important successes. Among them were dissolving corporate monopolies, ending child labor, adopting workers' compensation laws, and improving food-processing safety.

Later in the twentieth century, the term muckraker became associated with any author or filmmaker who focused on public dangers that politicians were unwilling to confront. Recent muckrakers include Ralph Nader, the author of an exposé on unsafe automobiles, Bob Woodward and Carl Bernstein, the chroniclers of the Watergate scandal, and Morgan Spurlock, the maker of a film about the fast-food industry.

📖 Words & Phrases

expose v to uncover; to reveal
corruption n dishonesty; illegal behavior
fraudulent adj fake; phony
racketeering n threatening
inhumane adj cruel; brutal

enthusiasm n a strong interest
embrace v to welcome; to adopt
genuine adj real
condemn v to criticize; to blame
betray v to be disloyal; to be treacherous

demise n an end; death
flourish v to prosper; to thrive
dissolve v to end; to break up
monopoly n complete control
exposé n an exposure; a disclosure
chronicler n a storyteller; a reporter

1 According to paragraph 2, the public became interested in muckraking reports thanks to

- (A) the election of Theodore Roosevelt
- (B) poor prison conditions
- (C) a series of magazine articles in 1903
- (D) reform laws passed by Congress

2 According to paragraph 4, why did the muckraking movement end?

- (A) It succeeded in curing the problems it had uncovered.
- (B) President Roosevelt criticized the muckrakers.
- (C) It lost the support of many big corporations.
- (D) World War I made people lose interest in it.

Mastering the Question Type

3 The word "unsanitary" in the passage is closest in meaning to

- (A) dangerous
- (B) unclean
- (C) miserable
- (D) startling

4 The word "unsavory" in the passage is closest in meaning to

- (A) unfavorable
- (B) unsettled
- (C) unstable
- (D) unreasonable

Summary Note Fill in the blanks with the appropriate words.

Muckrakers

- Reporters & novelists in ❶ _____
  - Upton Sinclair → his novel, *The Jungle*
  - Jacob Riis → a newspaper reporter and photographer
  - Lincoln Steffens & Ida M. Tarbell → articles in ❷ _____
  - David Graham Phillips → articles in *Cosmopolitan* magazine
- Targets of muckrakers
  - drug companies, child labor, ❸ _____, prison conditions, and labor racketeering
- First approved by President Roosevelt but fell into decline due to his later verbal attack
  - a negative allusion to the character in ❹ _____ who raked animal waste
- Muckrakers in the 20th century
  - authors or filmmakers who focus on the public dangers
  - Ralph Nader, Bob Woodward and Carl Bernstein, and Morgan Spurlock

Building Summary Skills

The following summaries are based on the passages you worked on earlier. Complete each of them by filling in the blanks with suitable words or phrases.

Exercise 1 | Darwin and Wallace

religious controversy	natural selection	Alfred Russel Wallace
the theory of evolution	*On the Origin of Species*	

Charles Darwin is known as the discoverer of _____. He formulated his theory while on a voyage around the world, during which he observed differences among animal species. His key insight was that species evolve through the process of _____. He delayed publishing the theory for fear of _____. _____ discovered the theory later and told Darwin about it. That prompted Darwin to publish his book _____.

Exercise 2 | The Chicago School of Economics

the Federal Reserve	Milton Friedman	Chicago School
regulating the money supply	the leading center of economic thought	

The University of Chicago has become _____ in the United States. Its views have become known as the _____. In the 1960s, it was led by _____, who favored a monetarist approach. He believed in controlling the economy by _____. He advocated a strong role for _____ in setting interest rates and selling treasury bonds.

Exercise 3 | Transcendentalism

Nature	transcendentalism	an understanding of nature
design towns	New England	

_____ was a philosophy that arose in _____ in the mid-1800s. It was first expressed in Ralph Waldo Emerson's essay _____. Transcendentalists believed in looking within oneself for _____, not in society's creations such as organized religion. They preached meditation and self-reliance in order to rise above, or transcend, their physical senses. Transcendentalists attempted to _____, such as Brook Farm, where they could practice their beliefs. However, all these experiments failed.

Exercise 4　White Flight

earn more commissions	after World War II	blockbusting
decline in school systems	ordering the busing of school children	

_____, blacks began moving north in greater numbers while looking for jobs. Whites began to move out to avoid the poverty and the _____ that they felt were caused by this black influx. Real estate agents cooperated in this white flight by secretly selling homes to blacks in formerly white communities. Once this _____ occurred, whites would put their houses up for sale, allowing real estate agents to _____. White flight caused racial disparity in the public schools. Court decisions have tried to equalize these differences by _____.

Exercise 5　Thomas Hunt Morgan

chromosomes	fruit flies	the fly's offspring
a chain of molecules	the body passed traits	

Thomas Hunt Morgan wanted to find out how _____ to later generations. He designed experiments with _____. When one fly was born with an uncommon eye color—a mutation—Morgan was able to reproduce it in _____. This led him to conclude that eye color was passed by _____, thread-like structures in a cell's nucleus. He determined that each trait was linked to a gene, or _____ inside a cell.

Exercise 6　Muckrakers

political corruption	President Theodore Roosevelt	politics and business
the muckrakers	public corruption or business misbehavior	

_____ were reporters and novelists who exposed some of the abuses in _____ in the early 1900s. _____ approved of these reformers and endorsed several reform laws. But when a series of articles alleged _____ by Roosevelt's friends, Roosevelt spoke out against them by calling them muckrakers. His criticism ended the movement. But the term continues to be applied in a positive way to those who reveal _____.

The Cambrian Explosion

01-12

1 ➡ All animal species found on the Earth today can be traced to forms that first appeared about 570 to 530 million years ago. During that relatively short time, there occurred an unprecedented surge in the variety of life that is found in the fossil record. As this rapid evolution happened during the Cambrian period of geological history, it is known as the Cambrian Explosion. In the Precambrian period, before about 600 million years ago, evolution had produced few life forms, and they were simple in structure. But a sudden burst of complexity and variety appeared during the Cambrian Explosion. The evidence lies in fossils, remains or impressions of living things preserved in rock or soil. The reason for such an acceleration in evolution continues to puzzle scientists today.

2 ➡ The Cambrian Explosion posed a special problem for Charles Darwin, who, in 1859, published his explanation for how living things evolved. Darwin's theory proposes that the current diversity of life had emerged after a very long time. Natural selection needed a long period to work the small changes that produce the species alive today. That idea required that evolution occur gradually and that the fossil record show this gradual change. But the record in fact showed that the beings that arose during the Cambrian Explosion could not be found in the Precambrian period. Darwin himself conceded that this missing fossil record could be used as an argument against the validity of his theory. Indeed, that argument is asserted today by those who believe in Creationism or Intelligent Design, the view that life was created at one time by a divine being.

3 ➡ Darwin got around this objection by suggesting that Precambrian evolution did occur but is not shown in the fossil record. In other words, there may not have been an explosion at all. Rather, the phenomenon may be explained by the fact that the Precambrian stages of evolution involved organisms that were too fragile to be preserved as fossils. Not all organisms become fossilized. Two conditions must be met. First, the organisms must have parts that are hard enough to leave a trace in the rock and dirt in which they died. Precambrian life forms may not have developed such rigid parts, as did the shellfish that appeared in the Cambrian period. Second, the remains must be buried in a non-hostile environment, one in which the parts will not dissolve or decay. Thus, many Precambrian specimens may have simply disappeared.

4 ➡ Nonetheless, most scientists agree that the Cambrian period witnessed greater and faster changes than before. They have offered several explanations for this speeding up of the evolutionary process, some external and some internal to the organisms themselves. One theory points to the increase in the amount of oxygen in the Earth's atmosphere just before the Cambrian period. Low oxygen levels limit the capacity of animals to become more diverse and complex. Another external cause might have been radical movements of the Earth's crust, causing populations to be separated from one another and to evolve into different species. Internal explanations include gene development; animals cannot evolve into different forms until they achieve a certain minimum complexity of genes. They need a sufficient genetic toolbox to generate more diverse forms. Perhaps it was not until the Cambrian period that this toolbox became effective.

1 The word "unprecedented" in the passage is closest in meaning to

(A) unexpected

(B) unwelcome

(C) uneventful

(D) unique

2 According to paragraph 1, the Precambrian period was characterized by

(A) dinosaurs

(B) an abundance of fossils

(C) great genetic complexity in animals

(D) little variety of organisms

3 According to paragraph 2, why did the Cambrian explosion present a challenge to Darwin?

(A) He could find no evidence of it.

(B) It conflicted with his theory that evolution occurs gradually over a long period.

(C) It could not explain why there were no fossils before the explosion.

(D) He favored the theory of Intelligent Design.

4 The author discusses "the fossil record" in paragraph 3 in order to

(A) point out some interesting developments in some animals

(B) argue that many fossils are fragile and are easily destroyed

(C) note there are fossils for all animals that have lived on the Earth

(D) explain why the Cambrian Explosion may not have occurred

5 The word "fragile" in the passage is closest in meaning to

(A) delicate

(B) sturdy

(C) large

(D) complex

6 Which of the following best expresses the essential information in the highlighted sentence? *Incorrect* answer choices change the meaning in important ways or leave out essential information.

Ⓐ Simple life forms are not ready to evolve.

Ⓑ Complex forms cannot evolve any further.

Ⓒ The fossil record reveals the genetic structure of the organism.

Ⓓ Fossilized animals lack genetic complexity.

7 In paragraph 4, the author's description of explanations for the Cambrian Explosion mentions all of the following EXCEPT:

Ⓐ The increase of oxygen in the Earth's atmosphere

Ⓑ The movement of the Earth's crust

Ⓒ Massive extinction of animals due to global warming

Ⓓ Sufficient gene development in animals

8 **Directions:** Complete the table below by matching FIVE of the seven answer choices that describe different periods. TWO of the answer choices will NOT be used.

Answer Choices

1. It occurred more than 600 million years ago.

2. Fossil evidence can be found from this period.

3. There was little complexity and variety in animals.

4. Shellfish appeared in this period.

5. There were high oxygen levels in the atmosphere.

6. Darwin explained this period fully.

7. Humans first appeared in this period.

Precambrian Period

•

•

Cambrian Period

•

•

•

01-13

The Beat Movement

The Beat Generation is a label applied to a nonconformist social movement that began in New York City in the 1950s. Its message was carried by a group of writers who used stream-of-consciousness forms to express the insights and longings of those who rejected the mainstream values of the times. Although the Beat writers produced few lasting works, their attitudes inspired rock music artists and social movements of the 1960s and beyond.

2 → The term beat was coined in 1946 by Herbert Huncke. He meant it to be a synonym for tired or down and out. In 1948, the word was used by Jack Kerouac in his phrase Beat Generation, by which he changed the reference to mean upbeat or beatific. The phrase finally entered public consciousness in 1952 with John Clellon Holmes's article in the *New York Times Magazine* called "This is the Beat Generation." The original Beats were a group of friends from New York City who met in the mid-1940s. They included Jack Kerouac, Allen Ginsberg, Neal Cassady, and William S. Burroughs. That core group moved to San Francisco, where they were joined by the poet Lawrence Ferlinghetti and many others.

The first famous work of Beat literature was the long poem *Howl* by Allen Ginsberg. In 1955, Ginsberg read the poem aloud at a gallery in San Francisco, causing a stir with its content matter. Its fame was fueled by the obscenity trial of Lawrence Ferlinghetti, who sold the poem in his bookstore. But Ferlinghetti was acquitted when the judge ruled that the work had "redeeming social importance" and thus was not obscene.

4 → The most successful Beat novelist was Jack Kerouac. In his best novel, *On the Road*, published in 1957, Kerouac described an automobile trip around the United States by a character based on himself, Sal Paradise, and Dean Moriarty, based on Kerouac's friend Neal Cassady. The novel made Cassady into a cultural icon known for his irresponsible lifestyle, womanizing, amorality, and lust for life. *On the Road* became known as much for how Kerouac wrote it as for its content. Kerouac allegedly was high on pills while he wrote it, and he typed it on a continuous scroll of paper so that he would not have to interrupt his thoughts by changing paper. He is said to have believed that "the first thought is the best thought," and he claimed that he never revised what he wrote. Though he said that he wrote the book in just three weeks, the truth is that he had been planning the novel for years and that he wrote several drafts.

5 → Also influential was a novel by William S. Burroughs, *Naked Lunch*, which also survived an obscenity trial. In that work, Burroughs, who was a drug addict himself, tells of his drug-induced fantasies and his travels among addicts and criminals. In the 1960s, those who followed Beat philosophy became known as hippies or yippies. Their culture was centered in San Francisco, which became a center of rock music, drug culture, and protest against the war in Vietnam. The Beat Generation's lasting contribution to literature is that it encouraged writing on more personal topics, including those showing the unpleasant sides of human nature and of society. It validated expression through informal, conversational language and made profanity a permissible tool for revealing human feelings.

9   The word "coined" in the passage is closest in meaning to

    Ⓐ invented

    Ⓑ spread

    Ⓒ minted

    Ⓓ explained

10   Why does the author mention "the *New York Times Magazine*" in paragraph 2?

    Ⓐ To show the origin of the term Beat

    Ⓑ To identify when the term Beat Generation became widely known

    Ⓒ To name the *New York Times* as a Beat newspaper

    Ⓓ To give information about John Clellon Holmes

11   According to paragraph 2, all of the following were members of the original Beat group EXCEPT:

    Ⓐ Jack Kerouac

    Ⓑ Lawrence Ferlinghetti

    Ⓒ Allen Ginsberg

    Ⓓ William S. Burroughs

12   The word "acquitted" in the passage is closest in meaning to

    Ⓐ admitted

    Ⓑ honored

    Ⓒ arrested

    Ⓓ cleared

13   The word "it" in the passage refers to

    Ⓐ a cultural icon

    Ⓑ *On the Road*

    Ⓒ its content

    Ⓓ a continuous scroll of paper

14   According to paragraph 4, which of the following is true of *On the Road*?

    Ⓐ It portrays the reckless lifestyle of American youngsters in the late 1950s.

    Ⓑ It was completed in a short time while Jack Kerouac was on drugs.

    Ⓒ It made Neal Cassady an important symbol of a libertine lifestyle.

    Ⓓ It is based on two characters taking a road trip around North America.

15 In paragraph 5, the author implies that Beat literature

Ⓐ was almost always banned by the courts

Ⓑ had little lasting influence

Ⓒ addressed personal feelings in rebellion against society

Ⓓ expressed the conservative views of the 1950s

16 **Directions:** An introductory sentence for a brief summary of the passage is provided below. Complete the summary by selecting the THREE answer choices that express the most important ideas in the passage. Some answer choices do not belong in the summary because they express ideas that are not in the passage or are minor ideas in the passage.

The major writers of the Beat Movement created works that were very influential.

-
-
-

Answer Choices

1. The word beat originated in the *New York Times Magazine*.

2. The first major work was *Howl* by Allen Ginsberg.

3. Lawrence Ferlinghetti read *Howl* in his art gallery.

4. Jack Kerouac was the leading Beat novelist.

5. William S. Burroughs wrote about his addictions in *Naked Lunch*.

6. Most members of the Beat Generation were financially successful.

Vocabulary Check-Up

A Choose the words with the closest meanings to the highlighted words.

1 Not all members accepted the church's tenets.

(A) hymns
(B) doctrines
(C) sermons
(D) demands

2 The father and mother reached a compromise over how to raise their daughter.

(A) argument
(B) deadlock
(C) agreement
(D) controversy

3 He was the preeminent expert in his field.

(A) leading
(B) famous
(C) domineering
(D) veteran

4 The child always adhered to the teacher's rules.

(A) questioned
(B) heard
(C) repeated
(D) followed

5 At the news conference, he signaled the start of his election campaign.

(A) revoked
(B) announced
(C) recorded
(D) denied

6 The time constraints prevented the student from finishing the test on time.

(A) periods
(B) clocks
(C) signifies
(D) limits

7 Divorce can have a pernicious effect on children.

(A) harmful
(B) helpful
(C) lasting
(D) liberating

8 Natural selection is the mechanism by which living things change over time.

(A) impact
(B) process
(C) product
(D) order

9 The offer of a free vacation was fraudulent.

(A) tempting
(B) unexpected
(C) gratifying
(D) fake

10 A shortage of funds led to the demise of the program.

(A) revision
(B) restriction
(C) end
(D) demonstration

B Match the words with the correct definitions.

1 advantageous •		• Ⓐ a point of view
2 correspond •		• Ⓑ a feature; a characteristic
3 perspective •		• Ⓒ a disruption
4 flourish •		• Ⓓ an order; an arrangement
5 trait •		• Ⓔ beneficial
6 exponent •		• Ⓕ to rise above
7 transcend •		• Ⓖ an occurrence
8 phenomenon •		• Ⓗ to prosper; to thrive
9 sequence •		• Ⓘ a promoter; an advocate
10 upheaval •		• Ⓙ to communicate; to write

UNIT

02 Reference

◤ Overview

Introduction

Reference questions ask you to understand the relationship between a pronoun and the word to which the pronoun refers. Usually, personal pronouns such as *it, its, they, their,* and *them* are tested on the TOEFL iBT. Sometimes other reference words such as *which, this, one, the former,* and *the latter* are also asked.

Question Types

❯ The word "X" in the passage refers to

Useful Tips

- The referent, the word to which a pronoun refers, usually appears before the pronoun in the same sentence or shows up in an earlier sentence. Sometimes, however, the referent is found after the pronoun.
- Substitute your answer for the highlighted word or words in the passage.
- Make sure that your answer is the same number (singular or plural), gender (male or female), and case (first, second, or third person) as the highlighted pronoun.

Q The word "others" in the passage refers to

- Ⓐ characteristics
- Ⓑ particles
- Ⓒ waves
- Ⓓ conditions

The Wave Theory of Light

02-01

In 1666, Isaac Newton proposed that light consists of particles traveling only straight lines. But experiments showed that light can travel away from a source in all directions as well as around corners. So Robert Hooke and Christian Huygens proposed an opposing theory that light is a wave moving up and down in all directions through some substance, such as when a stone is dropped into water. Until the twentieth century, scientists did not know which theory was correct because light demonstrated characteristics of both particles and waves. Finally, in 1909, Albert Einstein reasoned that light has a double nature. It behaves like a particle under some conditions and like a wave under others. This insight led in the 1920s to an understanding of how electrons behave in the nucleus of an atom, creating a new field in physics known as quantum mechanics.

☑ Correct Answer

The highlighted word *others* corresponds to the phrase "some conditions" in the same sentence. So it can be easily noticed that *others* means other conditions. The correct answer is Ⓓ.

Basic Drill

Read the passages and answer the questions.

Drill 1

The French and Indian War

02-02

In the mid-1700s, the Ohio Country, the land west of the thirteen colonies, was disputed by the British and the French, each of whom had settled parts of that territory by constructing trading posts and forts. Both ignored the claims of the first inhabitants, the Native American Indians. In 1753, the British sent George Washington, then a twenty-one-year-old major, to negotiate with the French, who refused Washington's demand that they abandon their ownership claims. In 1754, the British launched an attack on the French in what was the first battle of the French and Indian War. Both sides enlisted the aid of Indian tribes, who sought to preserve their own rights to the land. The war continued until 1763, when a treaty was signed that granted all of Canada to England, gave Louisiana to Spain, and limited France's rights to some islands in the Caribbean and near Newfoundland.

1 The word "Both" in the passage refers to

- (A) The thirteen colonies
- (B) The British and the French
- (C) Parts of that territory
- (D) Trading posts and forts

2 The word "who" in the passage refers to

- (A) the French
- (B) the French and Indian War
- (C) both sides
- (D) Indian tribes

Drill 2

Development Economics

02-03

Development economics is the branch of economics that focuses on the special economic problems faced by poor and undeveloped countries. Unlike classical economics, development economics studies the social and political factors that affect economic growth. It addresses the problem of debt in the developing world and the role of the World Bank and International Monetary Fund in continuing that debt with strict repayment rules. Scholars in the field have proposed that the best long-term solution is to excuse much of the debt. Debtor nations also must be helped to establish stable governments and self-sustaining economies. The goal is to help them become trading partners with creditor nations. An important means to that end is to encourage the growth of a strong middle class. Some ways to do that include guaranteeing education for all, allowing free trade, and providing medical care. Governments must allow for elected representatives and independent court systems.

1 The word "It" in the passage refers to

- (A) Classical economics
- (B) Development economics
- (C) Economic growth
- (D) Debt in the developing world

2 The word "them" in the passage refers to

- (A) debtor nations
- (B) stable governments
- (C) self-sustaining economies
- (D) creditor nations

The Panic of 1873

The years following the Civil War saw a boom in railroad construction. But excessive investment by speculators and overbuilding by the railroads caused chaotic, uncontrolled growth. In that era, the federal government lacked the power to curb the abuses of private railroad owners. At the same time President Grant's restrictions on the money supply made it harder for investors to borrow the funds they needed to finance growth. The crisis culminated in the Panic of 1873, when the leading investment banking firm declared bankruptcy. That had a domino effect, causing railroads to close, unemployment to soar, and the New York Stock Exchange to plummet, ushering in a six-year depression. By 1877, wage cuts and poor working conditions prompted workers to go on strike. When a railroad strike stopped the trains from running, President Hayes sent in federal troops to end the work stoppage.

02-04

1 The word "they" in the passage refers to

   Ⓐ private railroad owners   Ⓑ restrictions on the money supply

   Ⓒ investors   Ⓓ the funds

2 The word "That" in the passage refers to

   Ⓐ The Panic of 1873   Ⓑ The leading investment banking firm

   Ⓒ Bankruptcy   Ⓓ A six-year depression

Lev Vygotsky's Theory of Zone of Proximal Development

Two competing theories have been advanced to explain how a child develops. One theory holds that a child is a product of his inherited traits—nature. The other maintains that a child is defined by environment—nurture. Russian psychologist Lev Vygotsky reconciled these by proposing the theory of zone of proximal development (ZPD). ZPD represents the gap between a child's current actual level of ability and his potential level. The baseline of ZPD is the child's ability to solve problems or perform tasks without help. The upper boundary of ZPD is the level the child can reach with aid from teachers and adults. Vygotsky proposed that a child rises through the zone by a process called scaffolding, in which a mentor provides guided step-by-step instruction. In that way, a child's ZPD constantly changes as the child's independent capacity improves and his potential capacity increases.

02-05

1 The word "these" in the passage refers to

   Ⓐ two competing theories

   Ⓑ his inherited traits

   Ⓒ a child's current actual level of ability and his potential level

   Ⓓ teachers and adults

2 The word "which" in the passage refers to

   Ⓐ a child

   Ⓑ the zone

   Ⓒ scaffolding

   Ⓓ guided step-by-step instruction

Exercise 1 Read the following passage and answer the questions.

Time Limit: 3 min. 40 sec.

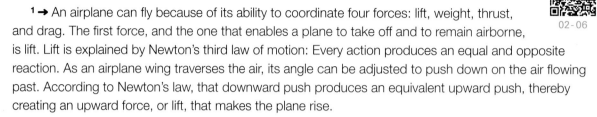

The Mechanics of Flight

02-06

1 → An airplane can fly because of its ability to coordinate four forces: lift, weight, thrust, and drag. The first force, and the one that enables a plane to take off and to remain airborne, is lift. Lift is explained by Newton's third law of motion: Every action produces an equal and opposite reaction. As an airplane wing traverses the air, its angle can be adjusted to push down on the air flowing past. According to Newton's law, that downward push produces an equivalent upward push, thereby creating an upward force, or lift, that makes the plane rise.

Lift also can be understood by using Bernoulli's Principle, which states that a fluid moving fast, like air, has lower pressure than a slower moving one. Because the top side of an airplane wing is curved, air has a greater distance to cover than air passing by the flat bottom side of the wing, but the air on both sides reaches the rear of the wing at the same time, meaning that the air passing on the top side moves faster than it does past the flat bottom side, lowering the pressure on the top and causing the wing to elevate.

A second force acting on a plane is weight. Weight offsets lift and therefore moves the plane in the opposite direction. A plane cannot achieve flight if its weight is greater than its lift. The challenge for airplane designers is to build a wing strong enough to lift a plane yet streamlined enough to fly at high speeds for long distances. Another force is thrust, the force that propels a plane forward, which is supplied either by a propeller or jet engine. Without sufficient thrust, air would stop moving over and under the wings, which would negate the lift and cause the plane to fall.

4 → Finally, airplanes must overcome the force of drag. When a plane moves through the air, it pushes air out of its way, creating friction when the metal contacts the air. That friction becomes drag, which tends to slow down the plane. To counteract drag, high-speed planes and missiles must have thin wings, which minimize drag, while slow-moving planes, like crop dusters, can have thick wings because lift is more important than drag.

All four forces must be precisely managed during a flight. The pilot manipulates his controls whenever he wants to take off, alter direction and speed, or land. The plane accelerates when thrust is greater than drag and climbs when lift is greater than weight. It slows when the pilot reduces thrust and increases drag by lowering landing gear or raising the wing flaps. By retracting landing gear and flaps, the pilot can make the plane climb or increase its speed.

📖 **Words & Phrases**

coordinate v to harmonize

traverse v to pass through; to move across

equivalent adj equal; corresponding

state v to say; to assert

offset v to counterbalance; to counteract; to neutralize

counteract v to neutralize; to offset

precisely adv exactly

manipulate v to control; to handle

accelerate v to speed up

reduce v to decrease

gear n equipment

retract v to withdraw

1 According to paragraph 1, which force does Newton's third law describe?

- Ⓐ Weight
- Ⓑ Drag
- Ⓒ Thrust
- Ⓓ Lift

2 According to paragraph 4, drag is caused by friction from

- Ⓐ metal moving through the air
- Ⓑ a spinning propeller
- Ⓒ the thrust of a plane
- Ⓓ downward pressure

3 The word "one" in the passage refers to

- Ⓐ lift
- Ⓑ a fluid
- Ⓒ air
- Ⓓ lower pressure

4 The word "It" in the passage refers to

- Ⓐ Speed
- Ⓑ The plane
- Ⓒ Thrust
- Ⓓ Lift

Summary Note Fill in the blanks with the appropriate words.

The Mechanics of Flight

- Lift
  - enables a plane to take off
  - Newton's third law of motion → a downward push on the air produces an upward force
  - ❶ _____ → a wing elevates due to low pressure above it
- Weight
  - ❷ _____, forcing a plane down → requires very strong wings
- Thrust
  - ❸ _____ → keeps the plane in the air by making air flowing over and under the wings
- Drag
  - slows down a plane due to the ❹ _____ → requires thin wings to ensure speed

Time Limit: 3 min. 40 sec.

Furniture in Colonial America

02-07

1 ➡ Arriving in the New World during the 1600s, early American settlers had few resources for or interest in elaborate furniture. They were satisfied with a few benches, a table, and some mattresses on the floor. After they overcame some basic survival problems, such as growing food and dealing with hostile Indians at times, they turned their attention to making their homes more comfortable. Living in the midst of uncut forests of maple, cherry, walnut, and oak, the colonists were able to use the best quality wood for their furniture. Indeed, the use of that prime wood is what makes furniture from the colonial period so desirable to antique collectors today.

Maple, for example, is strong and long lasting and can be worked without being damaged. And because it is hard, maple wood can be brought to a highly polished finish. Cherry is not as hard as maple, but it has a fine grain and a smooth feel and is also easy to work with.

3 ➡ Early American furniture was often handmade by the settlers themselves. Those settlers who did their own work excelled at carving. One of the most popular forms of carving was the maple-leaf theme. Soon, skilled cabinetmakers came from Europe, and they copied the English custom of using heavy pieces with straight lines and little ornamentation. Designs were kept simple out of necessity since colonial homes were small with low ceilings and tiny windows. Stools were more practical than chairs. Tabletops were solid timber boards with square legs made from logs.

Colonial home life was centered around the fireplace, which provided the only source of warmth in bitterly cold winters. Furniture took shapes such as high-backed chairs and baby cradles with hoods that would serve as shields against the cold. The leading stylistic influence during the 1700s was the work of Thomas Chippendale, an English furniture maker. Chippendale published a book in 1754 that introduced his highly original work to America. He invented many new designs, including bookcases with doors, high chests of drawers, kettle stands, and drop-leaf tables. American designers such as William Savery in Philadelphia adopted the Chippendale style and used it to make the Chippendale highboy, a chest of drawers with richly decorated trim.

The craftsmanship of American furniture makers is considered to be superior to that of European artisans of the time, another factor making these pieces high in demand as antiques. But the demand exceeds supply, making early American furniture expensive and hard to find. To satisfy some of the demand, manufacturers make reproductions using the same wood and techniques as the originals. Early American furniture remains a popular choice with homeowners in the twenty-first century.

📖 Words & Phrases

elaborate adj fancy; decorated
hostile adj unfriendly; aggressive
antique n old furniture
polished adj glossy; refined
excel v to perform at a high level
ornamentation n a decoration

shield n protection; a guard
original adj creative
adopt v to use; to employ
decorate v to adorn; to ornament
superior adj better
exceed v to surpass; to outdo

1 According to paragraph 1, why is colonial furniture popular today?

   Ⓐ It is very comfortable.

   Ⓑ It is inexpensive.

   Ⓒ It has unusual designs.

   Ⓓ It is made of the best wood.

2 According to paragraph 3, furniture designs in colonial America were simple because

   Ⓐ the heavy wood was difficult to work with

   Ⓑ homes that people lived in tended to be small

   Ⓒ American furniture makers lacked the skill for more complicated designs

   Ⓓ Chippendale favored plain designs

Mastering the Question Type

3 The word "it" in the passage refers to

   Ⓐ cherry   Ⓑ maple

   Ⓒ a fine grain   Ⓓ a smooth feel

4 The word "that" in the passage refers to

   Ⓐ the craftsmanship of American furniture makers

   Ⓑ the time

   Ⓒ another factor

   Ⓓ the demand

📝 Summary Note   **Fill in the blanks with the appropriate words.**

Furniture in Colonial America

- Early Americans did not need fancy furniture
  - just had simple furnishings
  - needed to focus on ❶ _____
- Kinds of wood
  - maple → strong and ❷ _____
  - cherry → smooth and easy to work with
- Most settlers made their own furniture
- Some cabinetmakers came from England
- ❸ _____
  - English furniture maker
  - published book on work in America
  - had many new designs
- American furniture workers developed good reputation
  - considered better than ❹ _____
  - are popular items today

Exercise 3 Read the following passage and answer the questions.

Time Limit: 3 min. 40 sec.

Economic Bubbles

02-08

At times, a certain asset may suddenly increase in value. It might rise to an incredible height while attracting numerous investors. However, at some point, the asset's value declines both swiftly and tremendously, resulting in people losing enormous amounts of money in what is known as an economic bubble.

2 ➜ Throughout history, there have been numerous economic bubbles covering a wide range of assets. For instance, from 1634 to 1637, something known as Tulip Mania happened in the Netherlands. People became so infatuated with tulips, particularly those streaked with various colors, that the prices for tulip bulbs became absurdly high. At times, one or two tulip bulbs were sufficient to purchase a luxury home in a highly desired part in Amsterdam, a city in the Netherlands. However, at some point, people became more rational, and the prices of tulip bulbs declined to more reasonable levels.

3 ➜ In more recent times, there have been other economic bubbles. In the 1990s, when the World Wide Web was still in its infancy, the stock prices of Internet-related companies rose to tremendous heights and created millionaires overnight. Yet many of them subsequently went bankrupt in a matter of days when the Dot-Com Bubble burst. Countless companies went out of business while others lost millions of dollars in their market caps. In Japan in the 1980s, there was another economic bubble created both by real estate and the stock market. It took decades for the Japanese economy to recover when that bubble burst. In the United States in 2007 and 2008, the housing market rapidly increased in value when interest rates were low and people desired homes. Many individuals purchased houses for the express purpose of reselling them rather than for living in them. However, when interest rates began to rise, people started defaulting on their mortgages, causing the Housing Bubble to burst.

Most economic bubbles follow a similar pattern that is easily recognizable. What first happens is something called displacement, which is when people notice a new product or type of technology. During the boom period, the price of that particular asset begins rising, resulting in more investors getting involved and purchasing it. The next stage is euphoria, which happens when investors stop being cautious and go all-in on the asset. This results in the price of the asset going to astronomical heights. At this point, smart investors start to take profits by selling the asset even if it is still increasing in value. Finally, panic sets in as the price of the asset declines. When many investors decide to get out of the market, the price may go into freefall, causing people to lose fortunes and to go bankrupt.

📖 Words & Phrases

asset (n) something that has value
tremendously (adv) greatly; very much
infatuated (adj) filled with foolish love for something
absurdly (adv) ridiculously
rational (adj) logical
reasonable (adj) not extreme; normal; not too much
infancy (n) a beginning period

millionaire (n) a person with a million dollars or more
go bankrupt (phr) to lose all of one's money
default (v) to be unable to pay back a loan or borrowed money
euphoria (n) a feeling of elation
panic (n) extreme fear

1 In paragraph 2, the author uses "Tulip Mania" as an example of

(A) the first time in history that an asset lost a lot of value

(B) a type of economic bubble that did not follow the regular pattern

(C) an economic bubble that burst and made people lose money

(D) a situation in which an economic bubble happened but did not burst

2 According to paragraph 3, which of the following is true of the economic bubble in Japan?

(A) It took place because of the Internet.

(B) It was related to the stock market.

(C) It happened when interest rates rose.

(D) It caused people to lose money overnight.

Mastering the Question Type

3 The word "It" in the passage refers to

(A) A certain asset (B) Value

(C) An incredible height (D) Some point

4 The word "them" in the passage refers to

(A) the stock prices (B) Internet-related companies

(C) tremendous heights (D) millionaires

Summary Note Fill in the blanks with the appropriate words.

Economic Bubbles

- Asset rises in value and then declines greatly
  – people lose money
- ❶ _____ in Netherlands
  – value of tulips rose to high levels and then declined
- Dot-Com Bubble
  – Internet-related companies
    → ❷ _____ went bankrupt
  → companies lost millions in stock prices
- Japan in the 1980s
  – bubble due to real estate and stock market
- U.S. Housing Bubble in ❸ _____
- Economic bubbles follow pattern
  – displacement
  – boom period → investors get involved
  – ❹ _____ → prices go to great heights
  – profit-taking → some investors get out
  – panic → prices decline rapidly

Exercise 4 Read the following passage and answer the questions.

Time Limit: 3 min. 40 sec.

Hydrogen Technology

02-09

An economy dependent on fossil fuel for energy has an uncertain future as oil, coal, and natural gas supplies are not replaceable once consumed. The burning of fossil fuels produces emissions that pollute the air all over the world, not just where the fuel is burned.

2 → One solution is the accelerated development of hydrogen technology, which avoids some of the problems accompanying fossil fuels. First, hydrogen reduces pollution. Hydrogen combined with oxygen in a fuel cell produces electric energy, which can be used to power engines and produce heat to warm buildings. The key benefit of hydrogen and oxygen combinations is that no greenhouse gases or other pollutants are produced. The only byproducts are heat and water. A second advantage of hydrogen-based energy is that it can be produced locally as opposed to having to be imported from other countries, and it can be acquired from multiple sources, such as methane, gasoline, biomass, coal, or water. All but water, however, cause their own forms of pollution.

Third, when the hydrogen source is water, the result is a sustainable production system. Water can be separated into hydrogen and oxygen by the process of electrolysis, in which an electric current is passed through water. That electric current can be produced from renewable energy sources like wind, solar, and tidal energy, sources which are not dependent on oil and are nonpolluting. A disadvantage of those sources, however, is that they are not always available. Wind may die down, the sun may be obscured by clouds, and tidal power has not yet been fully developed. Hydrogen energy offers an answer in that, once hydrogen is produced through electrolysis, it can be stored in a fuel cell to produce enough electricity to supply power during periods when renewable sources are not producing.

4 → Besides electrolysis, hydrogen production can also be achieved by a chemical reaction in aluminum waste. That process yields hydrogen and alumina, which can be recycled to make aluminum. A Canadian company holds the patent on that process. Critics of hydrogen technology warn of the dangers inherent in hydrogen, which is a highly combustible gas. New and costly technologies must be invented in order to ensure the safe handling of hydrogen during its production. Hydrogen-powered cars will be unaffordable to most people for many years. In 2022, hydrogen-powered cars cost around 60,000 dollars.

In 2003, the U.S. government announced a 1.2-billion-dollar hydrogen fuel initiative to reverse American's dependence on foreign oil by investing in hydrogen-powered fuel cells. Those cells would replace internal combustion engines in cars and trucks. Congress appropriated funds to pay for this initiative.

📖 Words & Phrases

emission n a release; a discharge
accelerated adj speeded up; quickened
accompany v to come with; to follow
as opposed to phr rather than
acquire v to obtain
sustainable adj supportable; endurable
obscure v to conceal; to hide

yield v to produce
recycle v to reuse; to use again
inherent adj intrinsic; natural
combustible adj flammable
ensure v to make certain; to confirm
appropriate v to approve; to assign

1   According to paragraph 2, one advantage of hydrogen technology is that

　Ⓐ it is inexpensive

　Ⓑ it can be used to power airplanes

　Ⓒ it does not have to be imported

　Ⓓ it is not combustible

2   According to paragraph 4, a disadvantage of hydrogen technology is that

　Ⓐ an important patent on it is held by Canada

　Ⓑ it will be too expensive for many years

　Ⓒ it cannot be stored in fuel cells

　Ⓓ it causes almost as much pollution as fossil fuels

Mastering the Question Type

3   The word "All" in the passage refers to

　Ⓐ Byproducts

　Ⓑ Other countries

　Ⓒ Multiple sources

　Ⓓ Their own forms of pollution

4   The word "it" in the passage refers to

　Ⓐ an answer

　Ⓑ hydrogen

　Ⓒ electrolysis

　Ⓓ a fuel cell

📝 Summary Note　　Fill in the blanks with the appropriate words.

Hydrogen Technology

- Is different from fossil fuels
  - reduces pollution
  - does not produce ❶ .... or other pollutants
- Can be produced ❷ ....
  - does not need to import from other countries
  - comes from many different sources → methane, gasoline, biomass, coal, and water
- Can be ❸ ....
  - wind, solar, and tidal energy
- Is somewhat dangerous
  - highly ❹ ....
  - very expensive

Read the following passage and answer the questions.

Time Limit: 3 min. 40 sec.

The Rise of the Roman Empire

02-10

1 → According to legend, Rome was founded in 753 B.C. In 509 B.C. the Roman Republic was constituted after the citizens of Rome overthrew the ruling Etruscans. Throughout the next 200 years, Rome expanded over most of the Italian peninsula, offering citizenship to the cities it conquered and demanding in exchange that the cities supply Rome with more soldiers for its army. By 275 B.C., Rome dominated the Italian peninsula.

Rome's crusade toward becoming an empire occurred during the first and second centuries B.C. Rome's principal competitor was Carthage, a sea power on the northern coast of Africa against whom Rome battled in a series of three wars called the Punic Wars. Rome ultimately prevailed over it, gaining control of the coasts of Africa and Spain and mastery of the shipping and trade routes of the Mediterranean Sea. Rome also expanded toward the east, acquiring Greece, Macedonia, and Turkey by 133 B.C. Two reasons explain Rome's success in overcoming its enemies. Rome's alliances with cities in Italy provided a source of manpower with which it could maintain its military might, and Rome established efficient governmental institutions that permitted it to govern effectively, allowing Romans to develop pride and certainty in their expansionist goals.

3 → The Republic began to falter from within as victories abroad were not matched by successes supporting its own citizens at home. Rich Romans called patricians profited while the poor and commoners, called plebians, shared in none of the newly found wealth. Conflicts at home and abroad led to internal military conflicts, resulting in a series of dictators who attempted to quell the chaos, including Julius Caesar, who defeated Gaul in 51 B.C. and declared himself sole Roman leader in 45 B.C. A group favoring the restoration of the Republic assassinated Caesar in 44 B.C. After years of internal battles for the control of the Rome, in 27 B.C., Caesar's adopted son Octavian became the first Roman emperor, taking the name Augustus, which means exalted in Latin. His assumption of power ushered in 200 years of peace known as the Pax Romana.

Augustus fortified defenses along the borders of the Roman Empire and maintained control of the foreign provinces, facilitated by a strong civil service that was staffed by administrators who governed effectively. During his reign, called by historians the Augustan Age, art and literature flourished. He ruled until 14 A.D. and was succeeded by a series of capable emperors who presided over the height of the empire's power. Beginning around 160, however, Rome was under continual attack by Germanic tribes from the north and Parthians from the east. The enormous size of the empire made it increasingly difficult to defend, setting the stage for its eventual collapse in 476.

📖 Words & Phrases

constitute Ⓥ to create; to establish
overthrow Ⓥ to topple; to overturn
dominate Ⓥ to rule; to govern; to control
prevail Ⓥ to win; to triumph
alliance Ⓝ an agreement; a partnership
falter Ⓥ to fail; to stumble
quell Ⓥ to subdue; to suppress

assassinate Ⓥ to kill
exalt Ⓥ to praise; to acclaim
internal adj domestic
fortify Ⓥ to strengthen; to reinforce
facilitate Ⓥ to help; to aid
flourish Ⓥ to prosper; to thrive
preside Ⓥ to direct; to rule

1   According to paragraph 1, Rome's army grew because

     Ⓐ it overthrew the Etruscans

     Ⓑ it dominated the Italian peninsula

     Ⓒ it demanded soldiers in return for citizenship

     Ⓓ it needed to fight against many invaders

2   According to paragraph 3, the Roman Republic failed because

     Ⓐ it could not support its own citizens

     Ⓑ it could not defend itself against Carthage

     Ⓒ Julius Caesar could not defeat Gaul

     Ⓓ it expanded too fast

| Mastering the Question Type |

3   The word "it" in the passage refers to

     Ⓐ an empire

     Ⓑ Carthage

     Ⓒ the northern coast of Africa

     Ⓓ Rome

4   The word "that" in the passage refers to

     Ⓐ the Roman Empire

     Ⓑ foreign provinces

     Ⓒ a strong civil service

     Ⓓ administrators

📝 **Summary Note**   **Fill in the blanks with the appropriate words.**

The Rise of the Roman Empire

- Rome founded in 753 B.C.
  - became ❶ _____
  - began to dominate the Italian peninsula
- Rival was Carthage
  - fought ❷ _____ against it
  - finally defeated the Carthaginians
- Republic began to falter
  - did not support its own citizens → rich people succeeded, but poor did not
- Caesar was assassinated in ❸ _____
- Octavian became Emperor Augustus
- Roman Empire was successful but ultimately fell in ❹ _____ .

Time Limit: 3 min. 40 sec.

John Maynard Keynes

02-11

1 ➡ Before the Great Depression in the 1930s, classical economics preached the theory of laissez faire. That theory stated that the government should take no role in the economy. It predicted that unregulated market forces would steer the economy in the direction of full employment, high wages, and low inflation. But the crash that began in 1929 demonstrated the inadequacy of such a hands-off approach. It was British economist John Maynard Keynes who overturned classical theories on how the economic world works. His innovation was to stress the role of governmental control of the economy. That perspective led to a new field called macroeconomics, which looks at the total performance of a nation's economy.

Before Keynes, economic performance was measured on a local level, focusing on the behavior of individual consumers and companies. Keynes showed how such a narrow focus ignores the often more influential role of total spending, investment, and government regulations.

In his 1936 masterpiece *General Theory of Employment, Interest, and Money*, Keynes analyzed the causes of depressions. He concluded that governments should take an active role to avoid them. His premise was that the rate of economic growth depends on aggregate demand for goods, which is measured by the total spending by consumers, businesses, and government. When consumers save more and spend less, business income declines, prompting companies to reduce their own spending and investment. This reduction in total spending can sink an economy into a depression. An increase in spending is needed to trigger a recovery.

4 ➡ To prevent depressions, Keynes suggested that governments should spend more money and lower interest rates. Businesses and consumers would find it easier to borrow money, which, in turn, would allow them to spend more. The resulting heightened demand for consumer goods would encourage investment and increase employment. Another governmental policy to stimulate demand and increase employment, Keynes suggested, was for the government to hire people to work on public-works projects. That idea is considered to be a philosophical source of President Franklin Roosevelt's New Deal. A key element of that program was the federally funded construction and cultural programs that put depression-scarred Americans back to work.

Keynesian economics remains the governing policy of modern-day economics. But some of Keynes's assumptions have proved to be wrong. He assumed that labor productivity decreases as employment expands. But empirical findings show that the opposite relationship is true. He also wrongly predicted that real wages decrease as employment increases. And he thought that inflation would occur only near full employment. But history has seen that inflation sometimes can rise even in times of high unemployment, a condition known as stagflation.

📖 Words & Phrases

preach v to teach; to promote
inadequacy n insufficiency
overturn v to cancel; to invalidate
premise n an assumption
aggregate n a total

trigger v to cause; to prompt
sink v to submerge; to lower
stimulate v to provoke; to activate
empirical adj experiential; observed

1   According to paragraph 1, the event that exposed the weakness of the laissez faire theory was

    Ⓐ the invention of macroeconomics

    Ⓑ the work of John Maynard Keynes

    Ⓒ the prosperity of the 1920s

    Ⓓ the Great Depression

2   According to paragraph 4, Keynes believed that depressions could be avoided by

    Ⓐ increasing government spending

    Ⓑ raising interest rates

    Ⓒ lowering taxes

    Ⓓ decreasing government regulation

3   The word "It" in the passage refers to

    Ⓐ The Great Depression

    Ⓑ The theory of laissez-faire

    Ⓒ The government

    Ⓓ The economy

4   The word "which" in the passage refers to

    Ⓐ an active role

    Ⓑ his premise

    Ⓒ the rate of economic growth

    Ⓓ aggregate demand for goods

📝 Summary Note   Fill in the blanks with the appropriate words.

John Maynard Keynes

- Changed the way people looked at economics
  - introduced ❶ _____ → looks at nation's overall economy

- Wrote *General Theory of Employment, Interest, and Money*
  - looked at causes of depressions
  - thought governments should be involved in economy
    - → spend ❷ _____
    - → lower interest rates
    - → hire people on ❸ _____

- Keynesian economics
  - many governments use today → President Roosevelt's ❹ _____
  - has some wrong ideas

Building Summary Skills

The following summaries are based on the passages you worked on earlier. Complete each of them by filling in the blanks with suitable words or phrases.

Exercise 1   The Mechanics of Flight

moves the plane forward	take off and stay in the air	four forces
slows the plane down	keep the plane in flight	

_____ combine to make airplane flight possible. Lift enables a plane
to _____. Weight offsets lift and must be overcome by lift in order to
_____. Thrust _____. Drag is air resistance that
_____. The pilot must precisely manage each force in order to take off, change direction
and speed, or land.

Exercise 2   Furniture in Colonial America

the small colonial houses	Thomas Chippendale	early American settlers
expensive and in great demand	the finest quality wood	

_____ had to focus on survival, leaving them no time for furniture design. As they
prospered, they turned to making plainly designed furniture that was suited to their small homes. Colonial furniture is
valued today because it was made from _____. It was handmade with simple designs
that would fit in _____. Many artisans were influenced by the work of English furniture
maker _____. Today, colonial furniture is _____, creating a
market in reproductions.

Exercise 3   Economic Bubbles

follow certain patterns	very swiftly	Internet-related companies
prices of tulip bulbs	suddenly rise	

Economic bubbles may happen when assets _____ in value, often to great heights.
However, they also decline in value _____, making people lose money. Tulip Mania
in the Netherlands from 1634 to 1637 was a bubble that saw the _____ rise
incredibly high and then decline. The Dot-Com Bubble in the 1990s was an economic bubble connected to
_____. Most economic bubbles _____ that people are able
to detect.

Exercise 4 | Hydrogen Technology

fuel cells	hydrogen-poweveld fuel cells	fossil fuels
hydrogen technology	less pollution	

Hydrogen technology may be a good replacement for _____ as a source
of energy. It causes _____, can be produced locally, and can be stored in
_____. Sources of hydrogen include water, methane, gasoline, coal, and wind and solar
energy, but _____ is expensive and will not be affordable for many years. In 2003, the
U.S. government announced a plan to invest in _____.

Exercise 5 | The Rise of the Roman Empire

476 A.D.	the Mediterranean Sea	an efficient system of government
27 B.C.	the Roman Republic	

_____ was established in 509 B.C. It extended its control over the Italian peninsula
and, eventually, the major powers bordering _____. Its initial success was due to its
ability to use the cities it conquered as a source of manpower for its armies. And it held onto power by establishing
_____. But it declined when it was unable to govern its own citizens. The unrest led to
the start of the Roman Empire in _____. with Augustus as the first emperor. The empire
lasted until _____.

Exercise 6 | John Maynard Keynes

the Great Depression	Franklin Roosevelt	take more active roles
lower unemployment	lowering interest rates	

John Maynard Keynes proposed that governments should _____ in
the economy. He believed that governments could avoid depressions by increasing spending and
_____. He also favored public-works projects to _____.
President _____ used that strategy to help the United States out of
_____. Keynes's belief that inflation occurs only in times of high employment has been
proved incorrect.

Newspapers in the American Colonies

02-12

The first newspaper in the American colonies was published in Boston in 1690. It was called *Publick Occurrences, Both Foreign and Domestick*. But it was closed down by the British after just one issue. Fourteen years passed before the second newspaper, a weekly paper called the *Boston News-Letter*, appeared.

Early newspapers contained little more than items taken from other papers, especially those from London. As a result, most of the news was many months old since editors had to wait for ship captains to bring papers from Europe. Those captains also were occasional sources of news as they could provide eyewitness accounts of natural disasters as well as secondhand descriptions of faraway events. Some news was also received from letter writers around the colonies, who would describe events occurring in their regions.

³→ James Franklin was the first editor to see the newspaper as a means of expressing social and political commentary. Franklin, who was the older brother of Benjamin Franklin, published the *New England Courant*. He and his friends wrote humorous and satirical essays about current events and local society, angering many but turning newspapers into entertainment.

But editors in the early eighteenth century did not yet enjoy freedom of the press. For example, when James Franklin printed an editorial criticizing the British government, he was put in prison. When he was released, he was banned from publishing any more newspapers. But his thirteen-year-old brother, Benjamin, took over production and delivery of the paper and soon became the editor in his brother's place. Franklin left to run his own newspaper in Philadelphia, *The Pennsylvania Gazette*, which Franklin bought in 1729. Franklin used the paper as an outlet for his wit and satire, creating fictitious characters offering their funny and sometimes cutting observations about daily life.

⁵→ In colonial times, a newspaper office usually consisted of just two people: the owner and an apprentice. The apprentice would live and work with the owner in order to learn the trade. The apprenticeship usually lasted from ages twelve to twenty-one. Owners often considered their apprentices to be their personal property and treated them cruelly. Newspapers of the time were filled with ads offering rewards for runaway apprentices. When an apprentice turned twenty-one, and if he had saved enough money, he would open his own newspaper office. No females were allowed to be apprentices.

Printing presses had not improved much since their invention by Gutenberg in 1440. Newspapers in the colonies were printed on wood presses with a lever-operated screw to lower the platen to the bed of the press. An apprentice would apply ink to the wooden type with a wool ball on a stick. Each lowering of the platen had to be performed manually, with a top speed of about 200 impressions per hour.

⁷→ By the middle of the 1750s, newspapers were starting to play an important role in giving voice to the growing antagonism toward British rule and in stirring up the drive toward independence. Opinions that formerly were distributed in pamphlets began to find a home in newspapers. The Declaration of

Independence, signed on July 4, 1776, appeared two days later in the *Philadelphia Evening Post*. Some of the leaders of the Constitutional Convention in 1789, James Madison, Alexander Hamilton, and John Jay, attempted to win public support for their views by publishing the *Federalist Papers* in two newspapers.

1   The word "accounts" in the passage is closest in meaning to

   Ⓐ performances

   Ⓑ records

   Ⓒ explanations

   Ⓓ occurrences

2   The word "who" in the passage refers to

   Ⓐ editors

   Ⓑ ship captains

   Ⓒ those captains

   Ⓓ letter writers

3   According to paragraph 3, the *New England Courant* was important because

   Ⓐ it was the first newspaper to include political and social commentary

   Ⓑ it was edited by Benjamin Franklin's older brother

   Ⓒ it contained news from London

   Ⓓ it included letters from other colonies

4   The word "them" in the passage refers to

   Ⓐ owners

   Ⓑ their apprentices

   Ⓒ newspapers

   Ⓓ ads

5 According to paragraph 5, which of the following is NOT true of apprentices?

    Ⓐ They were male.

    Ⓑ They sometimes ran away.

    Ⓒ They became apprentices at the age of ten.

    Ⓓ They were apprentices until they turned twenty-one.

6 Which of the following best expresses the essential information in the highlighted sentence? *Incorrect* answer choices change the meaning in important ways or leave out essential information.

    Ⓐ Newspapers were a driving force in winning support for the Constitution.

    Ⓑ Newspapers played an important role in expressing the colonists' desire for independence.

    Ⓒ The Declaration of Independence was announced in many colonial newspapers.

    Ⓓ The British did not permit freedom of the press.

7 The author mentions "the *Federalist Papers*" in paragraph 7 in order to

    Ⓐ give an example of how newspapers influenced public opinion

    Ⓑ show where the Declaration of Independence was published

    Ⓒ describe some articles published in the *Philadelphia Evening Post*

    Ⓓ note a pamphlet that appeared in one issue of a newspaper

8 **Directions:** An introductory sentence for a brief summary of the passage is provided below. Complete the summary by selecting the THREE answer choices that express the most important ideas in the passage. Some answer choices do not belong in the summary because they express ideas that are not in the passage or are minor ideas in the passage.

Newspapers in colonial America grew slowly but became very influential in society.

-
-
-

Answer Choices

① The second newspaper appeared fourteen years after the first one.	④ The newspaper industry was sustained by an apprentice system.
② Newspapers received letters from people living around the colonies.	⑤ Wood printing presses could make 200 impressions per hour.
③ Newspapers became popular when they began to print social and political commentary.	⑥ Newspapers were crucial in supporting the move toward independence from Britain.

02-13

The Pottery of Ancient Indians in Arizona

Arizona Anasazi pottery shards

1 ➡ The American Indians of what today is the state of Arizona first arrived in North America around 25,000 B.C. They came from Asia by crossing the Bering Strait in Alaska and by gradually moving down the coast to land occupied by modern-day California, Arizona, and Mexico. The tribes were nomadic until about 2,000 years ago, when they began to utilize agriculture. Once they settled in one place, they developed the skill of making pottery. Pottery remnants provide important clues to the ages and lifestyles of ancient Indians because they are often the only artifacts still intact. Fired clay does not deteriorate over time.

2 ➡ Nobody knows for sure how or why Indians discovered how to make pottery. **1** The most accepted theory is that the discovery was an accident. **2** Indians covered their woven baskets with mud clay. **3** They would put the baskets over the fire to dry the corn and other grains that were inside. **4** The heating process caused the clay to harden. Thus, the Indians realized that they could mold clay into shapes and make them permanent by heating them over fire and then cooling them. Support for this theory can be found in the texture marks on many ancient pots, indicating that they may have been molded around cloth baskets.

The earliest pottery was used for chores with no attempts being made to transform them into works of art. The rise of agriculture created a need for vessels to store seeds and grains and to carry food. They also were used as cooking pots as they could not be destroyed by exposure to fire. These early pieces were plain and unsymmetrical. Eventually, however, the ancient Indians of Arizona began to decorate their pottery with symbols and artwork. The meanings of the decorative designs are not always clear to modern scholars, and Indians were not willing to explain them to outsiders. However, archaeologists know that the artwork reflected Indian traditions, history, rituals, and legends. Common subjects include birds, deer, buffalo, humans, and gods, and pottery was commonly used during religious ceremonies and burials.

4 ➡ Though the Indians had discovered the benefits of the wheel, which they used for transportation and tools, they did not create the potter's wheel. They crafted their pots by the painstaking method of coiling and pinching. One theory is that they intentionally did not use a wheel because they preferred the experience of doing the work by hand, a process more in tune with nature.

5→ The Arizona Indians obtained their clay from secret ancestral sources. Completed pots were smoothed and then painted with pigments made from boiled plants or finely ground rocks. Brushes were made from the chewed ends of twigs. One of the first Arizona tribes to embrace pottery-making was the Hohokam, beginning in about 200 A.D. Their work is known by its red and buff coloring, geometric shapes, and abstract pictures of snakes, fish, and ceremonial dancing. Another tribe, the Anasazi, used black-and-white designs. Their style is recognized by their symmetry, distinctive forms, and mathematical repetition of features. The Anasazi pottery tradition lasted from 400 to 1500.

Around 950, the Mimbres Indians adopted an unusual, less realistic style, representing a significant change in the artistic methods of the Arizona tribes. The Mimbres would combine human and animal figures into one in order to describe their myths, legends, and history, often resulting in humorous scenes that scholars still cannot decipher.

9   The word "nomadic" in the passage is closest in meaning to
  Ⓐ primitive
  Ⓑ searching
  Ⓒ industrious
  Ⓓ wandering

10 The word "they" in the passage refers to
  Ⓐ pottery remnants
  Ⓑ important clues
  Ⓒ ancient Indians
  Ⓓ the only artifacts

11 According to paragraph 1, pottery provides information about the lives of ancient Indians because
  Ⓐ it displays pictures of Indians' homes
  Ⓑ the Indians left no written history
  Ⓒ it was used to carry agricultural products
  Ⓓ it does not decay over time

12 Why does the author mention "cloth baskets" in paragraph 2?

    Ⓐ To show that Indians had discovered weaving

    Ⓑ To explain how they were used to carry mud

    Ⓒ To explain how Indians discovered pottery

    Ⓓ To note how Indians cooked corn in them

13 The word "them" in the passage refers to

    Ⓐ the meanings of the decorative designs

    Ⓑ modern scholars

    Ⓒ Indians

    Ⓓ outsiders

14 According to paragraphs 4 and 5, which of the following is NOT true of the ancient Indians of Arizona?

    Ⓐ They derived paint from plants and rocks.

    Ⓑ They used the potter's wheel.

    Ⓒ They used geometric shapes on some pottery.

    Ⓓ The Anasazi tribe used black-and-white designs.

15 Look at the four squares [■] that indicate where the following sentence could be added to the passage.

Scholars have proposed many explanations.

Where would the sentence best fit?

16 **Directions:** Complete the table below by matching FIVE of the seven answers below that describe functions of pottery. TWO of the answer choices will NOT be used.

Answer Choices

① Pots were used to store seeds.

② Some subjects were animals.

③ Pottery was discovered when clay was heated.

④ Religious ceremonies were shown.

⑤ People carried food in pottery containers.

⑥ Indians used the coiling and pinching method.

⑦ Some works displayed history and traditions.

Pottery as Art

-
-
-

Pottery as Tools

-
-

Vocabulary Check-Up

A **Choose the words with the closest meanings to the highlighted words.**

1 The play begins precisely at 8:00.

- (A) approximately
- (B) usually
- (C) exactly
- (D) hopefully

2 You should wear a hat to shield yourself from the sun.

- (A) protect
- (B) distract
- (C) uncover
- (D) distance

3 There was a feeling of panic when the war began.

- (A) fear
- (B) anger
- (C) concern
- (D) nervousness

4 The moon was obscured by the clouds.

- (A) revealed
- (B) outlined
- (C) hidden
- (D) submerged

5 Hydrogen is a highly combustible gas.

- (A) reactive
- (B) fluid
- (C) motionless
- (D) flammable

6 Research into hydrogen technology was facilitated by money from Congress.

- (A) aided
- (B) terminated
- (C) followed
- (D) preceded

7 After starting out in the lead, he began to falter near the finish line.

- (A) sicken
- (B) slow down
- (C) celebrate
- (D) accelerate

8 He had his own inadequacy to blame for being fired.

- (A) poverty
- (B) personality
- (C) appearance
- (D) insufficiency

9 We collected an aggregate amount of 200 dollars for a retirement gift.

- (A) insufficient
- (B) unexpected
- (C) total
- (D) ample

10 Many people went bankrupt during the economic crisis.

- (A) profited
- (B) spent money
- (C) lost money
- (D) bought assets

B Match the words with the correct definitions.

1 negate • • Ⓐ fancy; decorated

2 alliance • • Ⓑ to subdue; to suppress

3 elaborate • • Ⓒ a person with a million dollars or more

4 coordinate • • Ⓓ an assumption

5 infancy • • Ⓔ to harmonize

6 millionaire • • Ⓕ speeded up; quickened

7 antique • • Ⓖ an agreement; a partnership

8 quell • • Ⓗ a beginning period

9 premise • • Ⓘ old furniture

10 accelerated • • Ⓙ to nullify; to cancel

03 Factual Information

◣ Overview

Introduction

Factual Information questions ask you to identify facts, details, or other information that is explicitly mentioned in the passage. The information is found in just one or two paragraphs in the passage. So you can find the correct answer without even reading the whole passage. You just need to quickly find the right spot in the passage that has the information about which the question asks. This is one of the most frequent question types on the TOEFL iBT.

Question Types

▶ According to the passage, which of the following is true of X?

▶ According to paragraph X, who [when, where, what, how, why] . . . ?

▶ According to the passage, X did Y because

▶ The author's description of X mentions which of the following?

▶ Select the TWO answer choices from paragraph 1 that identify X. *To receive credit, you must select TWO answers.*

Useful Tips

• Read the questions first to know what exactly is being asked.

• Scan the passage to find out where the relevant information in the passage is.

• Remove the choices that are not relevant to the passage.

• Do not choose an answer just because it is mentioned in the passage.

Q According to the passage, the English upper class began using wallpaper because

- (A) it was cheaper than tapestries
- (B) they started using wood walls
- (C) tapestries were no longer fashionable
- (D) tapestries could no longer be imported

The History of Wallpaper

03-01

In the Middle Ages, the wealthy covered their walls with large tapestries, which not only provided color but also insulated the cold stone walls. But only the very rich could afford them, and they were often unavailable during times of war, when international trade was difficult. In England, tapestries had to be imported from France, but after Henry III was thrown out of the Catholic Church in 1645, trade with Europe dried up. The upper classes began using wallpaper instead. By the eighteenth century, England was the leading manufacturer in Europe. When the steam-powered printing press was invented in 1813, British manufacturers were able to mass-produce wallpaper, causing its price to fall. Suddenly, it was affordable to the working classes as well. In the twentieth century, wallpaper was accepted as a cheap and effective way of brightening the dark rooms of working-class homes.

☑ Correct Answer

Choice ⓓ is the correct answer. The third and fourth sentences of the passage show that the upper classes in England had to use wallpaper because imported French tapestries were no longer available after Henry III's excommunication from the Catholic Church.

Basic Drill

Read the passages and answer the questions.

Drill 1

John Smith and the Jamestown Colony

03-02

In 1606, King James I of England sent a group of three ships to colonize Virginia. There were two purposes: to search for treasure and to spread Christianity among the Native American Indians. When the ships arrived in Virginia in 1607, the settlers chose Jamestown as their colony, and John Smith was named by the king to be one of its leaders. The Jamestown colony struggled for survival because it was located on swampy ground with impure water. About two-thirds of the 105 settlers died of malaria, malnutrition, and dysentery. Smith's strong leadership held the colony together for a time. But the colonists were at continuous warfare with the Indians, and in 1609, Smith was injured in a battle and forced to return to England. The colonists survived throughout the 1600s by learning to produce their own food and by discovering tobacco as a cash crop.

1   According to the passage, why did Jamestown find it difficult to survive?

   Ⓐ John Smith was an ineffective leader.
   Ⓑ It was located by a swamp with dirty water.
   Ⓒ John Smith was injured and returned to England.
   Ⓓ Tobacco could not be grown there.

2   According to the passage, the colony survived because

   Ⓐ the colonists learned how to grow their own crops
   Ⓑ the weaker settlers died of malaria and other diseases
   Ⓒ the settlers found a source of clean water
   Ⓓ the Indians taught the settlers how to farm crops

Drill 2

Progressive Taxation

03-03

Taxes on income can be either progressive or flat. A flat tax is proportional to the amount one earns, so the tax rate is the same for all levels of income. With a progressive tax, however, the rate increases with income. The justification for the higher rate is to avoid the inequity of a flat tax. This occurs because when everyone pays the same rate, the wealthy pay a smaller percentage of their income than do lower income earners. That happens because the less well-off have to use a greater share of their income for necessities such as food, housing, and clothing. Once the richer taxpayers pay for the same necessities, they have a larger portion of their income left over for savings, luxuries, and leisure. The theory behind a progressive income tax is that it places a greater burden on those better able to afford it.

1   According to the passage, the problem with a flat tax is that

   Ⓐ it takes too much from high-income people
   Ⓑ it decreases as income goes down
   Ⓒ the rich pay a smaller share than the poor
   Ⓓ the poor cannot afford luxuries

2   The author's description of the progressive tax mentions which of the following?

   Ⓐ Why the rate increases for some people
   Ⓑ Which countries make use of it
   Ⓒ How most people feel about it
   Ⓓ What rate most people have to pay

Ancient Egyptian Painting

03-04

Egyptian painting began about 5,000 years ago as it arose out of the advanced civilization centered in the fertile Nile Valley. Because of the extremely dry climate, many ancient Egyptian paintings survive today. Paintings were intended to provide company for the dead in the afterlife, so they were placed in tombs in which the dead were buried. Artists tried accurately to portray the time in which the person lived so that the deceased would always feel the comfort of seeing the people and places they knew. Subjects also included journeys through the afterworld and the gods to be found there. Because Egyptian society was very religious, many paintings depict gods and goddesses as well as pharaohs, supreme rulers who were also treated as gods. The artistic style was to use clear and simple lines and shapes in order to achieve a sense of order.

1   According to the passage, the purpose of Egyptian paintings was to

    (A) entertain the ruling class

    (B) decorate pharaohs' homes

    (C) give offerings to the gods

    (D) comfort the dead

2   Select the TWO answer choices from the passage that identify subjects of ancient Egyptian paintings. *To receive credit, you must select TWO answers.*

    (A) Egyptian rulers   (B) Gods

    (C) Priests   (D) Pyramids

Australia and the Theory of Continental Drift

03-05

Two hundred million years ago, virtually all of the land on the Earth was joined as a single mass called Pangaea. Studies of geology show that about 180 to 160 million years ago, the Earth's crust broke into separate plates that moved in different directions. This process of dividing the Earth into continents is called continental drift. About sixty-five million years ago, Australia started to separate from the southern half of the land mass along with Antarctica, South America, and Africa. Over the next 100 million years, Australia stayed connected to the other two continents. But about forty-five million years ago, it broke off from the others. Australia's isolation from other land masses accounts for its unique animal and plant life. Its varied land features—dry plains and mountains—also resulted from its upheaval during its drift. Australia continues to move today as it is drifting north at a rate of about ten millimeters per year.

1   According to the passage, continental drift was the cause of

    (A) Australia's unusual animals

    (B) Australia's waterfalls

    (C) Antarctica's connection to Australia

    (D) Africa's dry plains

2   According to the passage, what happened about sixty-five million years ago?

    (A) Australia separated from the other continents.

    (B) The Earth's crust broke into moving plates.

    (C) Australia began to move away from the southern land mass.

    (D) Australia began drifting north.

Exercises with Long Passages

Read the following passage and answer the questions.

Time Limit: 3 min. 40 sec.

Dadaism

03-06

Dadaism was a cultural protest movement that began in Zurich, Switzerland, in 1916. It was conceived as a rebellion against traditional social values, especially reason and logic, which the Dadaists saw as being morally bankrupt and which had led the world into the destructiveness of World War I. Their answer was to embrace anarchy and the irrational. By seeking the destruction of a flawed value system, they believed they could build a new one guided by a more humane outlook.

2 → The movement began in 1916 when Hugo Ball recited the first Dadaist manifesto at the Café Voltaire in Zurich. They declared that they had lost confidence in culture and vowed to destroy the existing order and reconstruct it. The Dadaists embarked on their crusade by trying to shock the public by constructing offensive or outrageous works of art and literature. They expressed themselves with creations that were anti-art, meaning that they ignored aesthetics, had no underlying meaning, and sought to offend.

In the peak years of the movement, 1916 to 1920, Dadaism spread throughout Europe, inspiring many periodicals that served as outlets for Dadaist views. The most influential Dadaist artist was French sculptor Marcel Duchamp. He exhibited what he called ready-mades, or common objects that he would submit as works of art, such as bicycle wheels or a birdcage. His intent was to ridicule the idea that art had to convey some profound message. Duchamp's most famous work was *Fountain*, a urinal. It was rejected by the art community when Duchamp first showed it in 1917. But it later became celebrated as a brilliant reflection of the Dadaist movement. In 2004, it won a British prize as "the most influential work of modern art."

4 → New York hosted many Dadaists after World War I, including Duchamp, who joined a group that included American artist Man Ray. Much of their work was photographed by the famous New York photographer Alfred Stieglitz. The New York branch of the movement, unlike the more serious European branch, used humor and irony to express its rejection of traditional values. By the mid-1920s, the Dadaist movement had lost its uniqueness and was absorbed by other cultural strains, including surrealism and socialist realism. During World War II, many European Dadaists moved to the United States. Others were killed in Hitler's concentration camps. Hitler condemned their work as "degenerate art."

The word Dada has an uncertain origin. Some say it is simply a nonsense word. Others say it was borrowed from the Romanian words *da, da*, meaning "yes, yes." And another view is that the founders chose it from a French dictionary: *Dada* is the French word for hobby-horse, a child's riding toy.

📖 Words & Phrases

conceive v to think; to believe

embrace v to accept

anarchy n chaos; disorder

irrational adj unreasonable

manifesto n a public declaration; a policy statement

aesthetics n the study of the idea of beauty

exhibit v to display

submit v to present; to put forward

profound adj deep; esoteric

uniqueness n singularity; remarkableness

absorb v to assimilate; to incorporate

condemn v to criticize; to blame

degenerate adj corrupt; immoral; low

1 In paragraph 2, why does the author mention "Hugo Ball"?

    Ⓐ To state that he owned the Café Voltaire

    Ⓑ To describe his importance to the Dada movement

    Ⓒ To point out some of the work he created

    Ⓓ To claim that he coined the name "Dada"

2 The word "it" in the passage refers to

    Ⓐ the word Dada

    Ⓑ an uncertain origin

    Ⓒ a nonsense word

    Ⓓ a French dictionary

3 According to paragraph 2, the Dadaists expressed their views with artwork that

    Ⓐ was conservative

    Ⓑ aimed to offend

    Ⓒ strove for beauty

    Ⓓ was abstract

4 According to paragraph 4, when Dadaism lost its influence, its ideas were expressed in

    Ⓐ socialist realism

    Ⓑ degeneration

    Ⓒ communism

    Ⓓ anarchism

📝 **Summary Note** **Fill in the blanks with the appropriate words.**

Dadaism

- Began in Zurich, Switzerland, in 1916
- Was a cultural protest movement
  - rebelled against traditional social values
  - against ❶ _____
- Hugo Ball initiates movement
  - wanted to show loss of faith in society
  - wanted to destroy society and start over
- Peaked from ❷ _____
- ❸ _____ was most influential Dadaist
- Movement went to United States later
- Became absorbed by other genres such as ❹ _____ and socialist realism

Exercise 2 Read the following passage and answer the questions.

Time Limit: 3 min. 40 sec.

Geysers

03-07

1 → A geyser is a special kind of hot underground spring that periodically ejects streams of hot water and steam into the air. Geysers are very rare because they require a unique combination of geology that exists only in a few places on the Earth. Approximately 1,000 can be found today, with half of them in Yellowstone National Park in the United States.

Hot springs are formed when surface water seeps down through the ground until it reaches rock heated by magma, which is melted volcanic rock. The hot water rises up to the surface through spaces between the underground rock layer. The water becomes part of a geyser if the rising water is constricted into a narrow passageway that connects the underground water to the surface. The water cools as it escapes to the surface, causing it to exert downward pressure on the hotter water below. The hot water has no place to go, being blocked by the solid layer of underground rock. As a result, the pressure and the heat rise on the water, superheating it to temperatures around 95.6 degrees Celsius.

The boiling water surges through the vent leading to the surface. This escape reduces the pressure on the water below, causing the superheated water to burst out the vent into the air and resulting in a spray that is seen as the end product of the geyser. The spray may continue for several minutes. Eventually, this release in pressure causes the remaining water to cool below the boiling point, and the eruption ends with the groundwater again seeping back into the ground. The cycle repeats itself at predictable intervals.

There are two types of geysers. Fountain geysers erupt from pools of water, usually in a series of violent bursts, whereas cone geysers emanate from mounds of mineral deposits known as geyserite. They form steady sprays lasting from a few seconds to several minutes. The most famous geyser is the cone geyser at Yellowstone National Park known as Old Faithful. It derives its name from its regularity as it erupts about every seventy-four minutes on average. Each eruption lasts between 1.5 and five minutes, and the heights of the eruptions vary between 100 and 180 feet.

5 → The rarity of geysers is attributable to the unusual conditions necessary to produce them. The volcanic rock must be dissolvable in hot water to form mineral deposits that line and strengthen the walls of the passageway leading to the surface. Any interference with the vent can destroy the geyser. For example, many geysers have died from litter and debris thrown into them by people while others have succumbed when nearby power plants have diverted water away from them.

📖 Words & Phrases

eject v to throw out; to expel
seep v to leak; to permeate
exert v to use; to apply
surge v to flow; to gush
emanate v to arise; to originate
derive v to get; to gain; to obtain
erupt v to explode; to blow up; to burst out

be attributable to phr to be caused by
dissolvable adj decomposable; perishable
vent n an opening; an outlet
debris n waste; remains
succumb v to fail; to break down
divert v to redirect; to switch

1   The word "constricted" in the passage is closest in meaning to

    (A) heated

    (B) lowered

    (C) compressed

    (D) accelerated

2   The word "them" in the passage refers to

    (A) many geysers

    (B) litter and debris

    (C) people

    (D) nearby power plants

Mastering the Question Type

3   According to paragraph 1, which of the following is true of geysers?

    (A) They are common in the United States.

    (B) They are underground springs.

    (C) There are about 1,000 in Yellowstone National Park.

    (D) They are parts of volcanoes.

4   In paragraph 5, the author's description of geysers mentions which of the following?

    (A) Where they are commonly found

    (B) What can create them

    (C) How they may be destroyed

    (D) Why power plants are built near them

📝 Summary Note   Fill in the blanks with the appropriate words.

Geysers

- A hot ❶ _____ that shoots hot water into the air

- Are only 1,000 in the world

- Hot springs
  - form by surface water going down to ❷ _____
  - water then rises to the surface because of pressure
  - becomes very hot and shoots up into the air

- Two types of geysers
  - fountain geysers
  - ❸ _____

- Old Faithful
  - most famous geyser
  - found in Yellowstone National Park
  - erupts every ❹ _____

Exercise 3 Read the following passage and answer the questions.

Time Limit: 3 min. 40 sec.

The Works Projects Administration

03-08

During the Great Depression in the United States in the 1930s, factories were forced to close, putting millions out of work. The unemployed had to depend on public relief money. In 1935, President Franklin D. Roosevelt established the Works Progress Administration, which was designed to provide government-funded jobs for those on relief. The agency, later renamed the Works Projects Administration (WPA), was the largest agency in Roosevelt's New Deal, his program for economic recovery.

2 ➜ The first head of the agency was Harry L. Hopkins. He estimated that 3.5 million people would be eligible to work in the WPA and that he would need 1,200 dollars per year for each worker. Congress approved four billion dollars to begin. Wages were set at different levels according to the region of the country, the local market wage, and the skill required. In order to maximize the number of workers, each person was limited to no more than thirty hours a week. Reflecting the culture of the era, the WPA did not permit both a husband and his wife to work. It was assumed that the head of a household was a man and that if a woman worked, she would be taking a job away from a man. The women who did work were usually assigned to sewing projects and made clothing and supplies for hospitals and orphanages.

The bulk of WPA jobs were on public works projects, such as government buildings, airports, bridges, national parks, highways, dams, sewers, libraries, and recreational facilities, but it also funded cultural pursuits through its Federal Art Project, Federal Writers' Project, and Federal Theater Project. Many out-of-work actors and playwrights suddenly had an outlet for their talents. Artists were put to work painting murals on public buildings, and writers were employed to create a series of state and regional guidebooks. Among the authors participating in the Federal Writers' Project was Saul Bellow, a later winner of the Nobel Prize.

Blacks especially benefited from the WPA, where employment discrimination was less than what they faced from private employers. In particular, the agency gave blacks their first entry into white-collar occupations. The WPA attracted criticism from political conservatives, who complained that the program wasted taxpayers' money on unneeded and frivolous work, such as raking leaves in parks. And many of its better educated workers had left-wing or communist sympathies. Critics also alleged that the allocation of projects and funds was often influenced by politics; those Congressional leaders who supported President Roosevelt, they charged, were more likely to have WPA projects assigned to their areas of the country.

5 ➜ The influence of the WPA began to wane by 1940. America's entry into World War II in 1941 boosted factory employment and rendered the agency less necessary. It was terminated in 1943.

📖 Words & Phrases

design v to intend; to plan
relief n aid; help; assistance
estimate v to calculate roughly; to guess
reflect v to mirror; to express
assume v to suppose; to presume
assign v to allocate; to distribute

pursuit n an activity; an endeavor
discrimination n bias; prejudice
frivolous adj trivial; unimportant
allege v to claim; to assert
boost v to foster; to promote
terminate v to end; to finish; to stop

1 The word "eligible" in the passage is closest in meaning to

Ⓐ qualified

Ⓑ eager

Ⓒ applying

Ⓓ asked

2 The word "they" in the passage refers to

Ⓐ critics

Ⓑ projects and funds

Ⓒ politics

Ⓓ those Congressional leaders who supported President Roosevelt

Mastering the Question Type

3 Select the TWO answer choices that are mentioned in paragraph 2 as being factors that were used to set WPA wages. *To receive credit, you must select TWO answers.*

Ⓐ Workers' geographic locations

Ⓑ Workers' skills

Ⓒ Workers' political parties

Ⓓ Workers' ages

4 According to paragraph 5, the WPA's influence decreased because

Ⓐ its workers had communist sympathies

Ⓑ President Roosevelt died

Ⓒ employment rose when America entered World War II

Ⓓ it ran out of money

✎ Summary Note   Fill in the blanks with the appropriate words.

The Works Project Administration

- Established by President Franklin D. Roosevelt during the ❶ _____
  – began in 1935
  – provided government jobs for people

- Funding
  – 3.5 million workers at $1,200 per year
  – could work ❷ _____ hours a week

- WPA jobs
  – were on ❸ _____ → airports, bridges, parks, highways, dams, and other buildings
  – employed many different people → actors could act, artists could paint, and writers could write

- Criticism
  – conservatives disliked
  – thought that projects were a ❹ _____

Time Limit: 3 min. 40 sec.

Fresco Painting

03-09

1 → Fresco is a technique in which pigments are painted directly onto a wet plaster wall. The word *fresco* comes from the Italian *affresco*, meaning "fresh." Fresco painting can be either buon fresco, done on wet plaster, or a secco, done on dry plaster. A secco fresco is usually used to apply finishing touches or to correct mistakes on a dried buon fresco painting.

The artist prepares for a fresco painting by drawing an outline of the composition onto a rough underlayer of dried plaster called the *ariccio*. This sketch is often made with a red pigment called *sinopia*. Then, the artist applies a second layer of wet plaster called the *intonaco*. He then smooths this top layer to prepare it for painting.

3 → The artist next takes a paper on which he has drawn a cartoon or a full-scale drawing of what he intends to paint. He traces the cartoon onto the wet *intonaco* and begins painting while using the cartoon as a guide. The paint consists of powdered pigments ground up into lime water. The wet plaster absorbs the pigment, which dries along with the plaster. No binder is needed as the chemical composition of the plaster binds the plaster to the pigment. The shine of smooth lime plaster creates a rich texture that highlights the colors.

Buon fresco painting is challenging because of the need to time the painting to finish before the plaster dries, as a layer of wet plaster dries in approximately ten to twelve hours. The artist typically begins painting after one hour and continues until about two hours before the surface is completely dry. The artist must therefore plan the project in advance and then split it into sections and choose which section to work on at a time. The area that he can cover in a day is called the *giornata*, which translates as "a day's work." A wall may have many *giornate*, which blend together as one and hence are not visible at first. But after hundreds of years, these separate areas may become distinguishable.

Once the *giornata* has dried, no changes are possible unless the dried plaster is removed with a sharp tool and another wet layer is applied. Minor repairs can be made with the secco technique, which requires a binder, such as egg, to hold the pigment to the wall. Sometimes a *secco* fresco is used to cover the borders between *giornate* as the borders disappear with age.

Frescoes first appeared in Egyptian tomb paintings, which used the secco method while the Romans created buon frescos. Fresco painting achieved its greatest expression during the Italian Renaissance, the premier example of which is the ceiling of the Sistine Chapel that was done by Michelangelo.

📖 Words & Phrases

trace Ⅴ to copy; to outline; to sketch

pigment Ⓝ a colored powder

absorb Ⅴ to soak up; to incorporate

composition Ⓝ a work

rough adj uneven

texture Ⓝ feel; touch

in advance phr beforehand

split Ⅴ to separate; to divide

blend Ⅴ to intermingle; to merge

border Ⓝ a boundary

premier adj best; primary

1 The word "distinguishable" in the passage is closest in meaning to
- Ⓐ invisible
- Ⓑ noticeable
- Ⓒ faded
- Ⓓ darkened

2 The word "which" in the passage refers to
- Ⓐ fresco painting
- Ⓑ its greatest expression
- Ⓒ the Italian Renaissance
- Ⓓ the premier example

Mastering the Question Type

3 According to paragraph 1, a secco fresco is used to
- Ⓐ cover up mistakes
- Ⓑ apply wet plaster
- Ⓒ dry a buon fresco painting
- Ⓓ remove old plaster

4 According to paragraph 3, what is the purpose of a cartoon?
- Ⓐ To amuse the artist
- Ⓑ To absorb pigments
- Ⓒ To provide a guide for the artist
- Ⓓ To highlight various colors

📝 Summary Note Fill in the blanks with the appropriate words.

Fresco Painting

- Put paint directly onto plaster wall
  - ❶ _____ → uses wet plaster
  - Secco → uses dry plaster
- Steps to making fresco
  - artist draws outline on dry plaster
  - uses ❷ _____ and applies wet plaster
  - traces drawing onto wet plaster and starts painting
  - wet plaster absorbs pigments
- Must plan the fresco properly because of drying plaster
- Can make repairs by using ❸ _____ method
- Frescoes in different cultures
  - Egyptian tomb paintings
  - Romans
  - ❹ _____ in the Italian Renaissance

Exercise 5 Read the following passage and answer the questions.

Time Limit: 3 min. 40 sec.

The Great Basin

03-10

The Great Basin is a 200,000-square-mile desert region in the western United States. It forms a high plateau between mountain ranges that covers much of the states of Utah and Nevada in addition to parts of surrounding states. It is called a basin, which is a sloping container for holding water, because it has no outlet to the nearest sea, the Pacific Ocean.

2 → The geologic name for the area encompassing the Great Basin is the Basin and Range Province. That province has a history of underground faults that has created an efficient water drainage system. During the last ice age, the province was dotted with large lakes that are now dried up, leaving extensive flat lands such as the Bonneville Salt Flats, where automobile races are held. Rain and melting snow quickly evaporate in the dry desert climate. The precipitation that remains seeps into the ground or gathers into temporary lakes that gradually dry up. Water flow is also blocked by the mountains surrounding the province. So none of the water that enters the region ever escapes by way of streams or rivers leading to the ocean. It is this internal drainage that maintains the Great Basin in its dry condition.

Geologists claim that the Great Basin is in the process of cracking and expanding, causing the topmost layer to become thinner over time. They predict that these forces eventually may split the Great Basin along one of its valleys, thereby opening a waterway to the ocean. Wildlife found in the Great Basin include jackrabbits, coyotes, squirrels, packrats, and mountain lions. Nonnative animals such as wild horses and burros have also been successfully imported. Because most of the land is open range with vegetation, cattle and sheep raising are common occupations.

Humans first populated the Great Basin about 12,000 years ago. When the Europeans discovered the New World, the region was peopled with Native American Indian tribes such as the Shoshone and the Ute. Spanish explorers reached the area in the late 1700s, after which it was settled by fur trappers.

5 → The United States acquired the territory through two treaties. With the 1846 Oregon Treaty, Great Britain gave up its claims to part of the Great Basin. With the 1848 Treaty of Guadalupe Hidalgo, the Mexican War ended, giving the United States land that had been part of Mexico. The Mormons were the first to found a large settlement when they established Salt Lake City in the late 1840s. After gold was discovered in California in 1848, waves of pioneers traveled across the Great Basin as they went on their way to seek their fortunes, opening much of the land to development. The area ultimately was divided into the several states that constitute the Great Basin today.

📖 Words & Phrases

plateau n an elevated land
outlet n a channel; an exit
encompass v to contain
fault n a large crack in the Earth's surface
extensive adj vast; wide
seep v to flow; to leak
precipitation n rain, snow, or hail
temporary adj short-lived; brief; momentary

internal adj interior; inner; inside
vegetation n plants; flora
acquire v to gain; to obtain
treaty n a pact; an agreement
wave n an unending group
pioneer n a discoverer
ultimately adv finally; in the end
constitute v to make up; to comprise

1 The word "evaporate" in the passage is closest in meaning to

    (A) fall

    (B) accumulate

    (C) erode

    (D) disappear

2 The word "they" in the passage refers to

    (A) two treaties

    (B) the Mormons

    (C) pioneers

    (D) their fortunes

Mastering the Question Type

3 According to paragraph 2, which of the following is true of water that enters the Great Basin?

    (A) It flows underground into the Pacific Ocean.

    (B) It is collected in wells for human consumption.

    (C) It is never carried away by rivers or streams.

    (D) It irrigates desert farmland.

4 According to paragraph 5, the Mexican portion of the Great Basin became part of the United States when

    (A) the Treaty of Guadalupe Hidalgo was signed

    (B) the Oregon Treaty was signed

    (C) the Mormons founded Salt Lake City

    (D) gold was discovered in Mexico

Summary Note   Fill in the blanks with the appropriate words.

The Great Basin

- Desert region in the United States
  - ❶ _____ between mountain ranges
  - in Utah, Nevada, and surrounding states
- Geography
  - once had lakes but have disappeared
  - now has flat areas like the ❷ _____
  - sometimes has ❸ _____ when it rains
- Wildlife
  - native animals like jackrabbits, coyotes, squirrels, packrats, and mountain lions
  - nonnative animals like wild horses and burros
- Humans have been there since ❹ _____
- Land has belonged to the United States since the 1840s

Time Limit: 3 min. 40 sec.

Nationalism

03-11

Until about 1800, people in most of the world were loyal to the places where they and their families lived. Most did not see themselves as part of a larger state or nation. But the rise of industry and the need to raise armies prompted rulers to try to inspire a sense of national identity and common cause. This drive toward lifting the interests of the nation above those of individuals or groups became known as nationalism. World history over the past 200 years can be explained as one of redrawing the political map with new nation-states.

2 ➝ Many historians date modern nationalism from the French Revolution in the late 1700s. The French monarchy was replaced by a republic in which the citizens no longer were expected to see themselves as subjects of the king. Rather, they found their identity in the abstract concept of France as their mother country. The process was repeated throughout Europe during the next century. With the breakup of the Austro-Hungarian and Ottoman empires at the end of World War II, Europe became a continent of independent nations. Ethnic and language traditions, however, continued to be honored by groups within the nation.

The philosophical basis of nationalism is that the nation is the most important unit of social and economic life to which all other human activities and desires must yield. Helping to secure national pride are flags, foods, sports, traditions, histories, folk tales, music, literature, and culture. There may even be a national religion.

4 ➝ Nationalists point to criteria that distinguish nations from one another, such as a common language, culture, and values. These traits are often represented by a single ethnic group to which almost all citizens of a nation belong. Many nations, however, host different ethnic groups side by side, sometimes with violent or politically disruptive results. Former nations such as Yugoslavia and the Soviet Union have been torn apart by clashes of ethnic groups. Iraq has recently been ravaged by ancient religious conflicts. Additionally, the long-simmering Arab-Israeli conflict is fueled by claims that the other side is not a real nation entitled to its own territory.

Some ethnic groups refuse to recognize their nation and instead seek to secede to rule themselves. Separatist movements in Quebec, Canada, and in the Basque region of Spain have been active for many years but have not yet succeeded. Requiring that all speak the same language has been an important means of enforcing national identity. New nations often attempt to outlaw minority languages. The national language tends to be the one spoken by the upper classes, resulting in the high-status language replacing the low-status ones.

📖 Words & Phrases

loyal adj faithful; devoted
prompt v to cause; to inspire
abstract adj theoretical; ideal
ethnic adj racial; cultural
secure v to obtain; to acquire; to gain
criteria n factors; traits
disruptive adj upsetting; causing disorder

clash n a collision; a confrontation
simmer v to rage; to be angry
ravage v to destroy; to devastate
fuel v to stimulate
secede v to separate; to become independent
enforce v to impose; to insist on
outlaw v to ban; to forbid; to prohibit

1 The word "they" in the passage refers to

- (A) most historians
- (B) the citizens
- (C) subjects of the king
- (D) the Austro-Hungarian and Ottoman empires

2 The word "yield" in the passage is closest in meaning to

- (A) suppress
- (B) overcome
- (C) surrender
- (D) tolerate

Mastering the Question Type

3 In paragraph 2, the author's description of the beginnings of nationalism mentions which of the following?

- (A) The fall of the Roman Empire
- (B) The French Revolution
- (C) World War II
- (D) American independence

4 According to paragraph 4, the Arab-Israeli conflict is caused in part by

- (A) one ethnic group seeking to secede from a nation
- (B) a single nation splitting apart
- (C) two ethnic groups seeking to unite as one nation
- (D) each side's refusal to admit that the other is a nation

Summary Note Fill in the blanks with the appropriate words.

Nationalism

- Is new concept
  - did not exist before the ❶ _____
  - people once associated selves with local area
  - with nationalism, associated selves with state
- ❷ _____ in the late 1700s
  - was beginning of nationalism
  - people did not have allegiance to king
  - had concept of "mother country"
- Distinguishing characteristics
  - common language, culture, and values
  - single ❸ _____
  - common flag, food, sports, tradition, history, and literature
- Can cause problems with different ethnic groups in same country
  - ❹ _____ torn apart
  - Iraq has had problems
  - Quebec is trying to separate from Canada

Building Summary Skills

The following summaries are based on the passages you worked on earlier. Complete each of them by filling in the blanks with suitable words or phrases.

Exercise 1 Dadaism

a more humane	the current fashion	common objects
other cultural movements	the end of World War I	

Dadaism was a cultural movement that arose at _____ as a protest against reason and logic. Dadaists felt that _____ world could be created once the traditional system was dismantled. The movement was joined by artists who condemned art that fit _____ or conveyed meaning or beauty. They created artworks out of _____ that had no serious artistic message. By the 1920s, Dadaism was absorbed into _____.

Exercise 2 Geysers

volcanic rocks	predictable intervals	in the form of spray
the water cools	a hot underground spring	

A geyser is _____ that ejects streams of water and steam. It is formed when water is heated by _____ and is subjected to pressure from the cooler water above it. The water boils and escapes through passageways in the ground. It erupts into the air _____. The eruption ends when _____. The cycle repeats itself at _____.

Exercise 3 The Works Projects Administration

Franklin D. Roosevelt	government-funded jobs	cultural projects
the Great Depression	bridges, highways, libraries, and dams	

The Works Projects Administration (WPA) helped put Americans back to work during _____. It was created by President _____ and was the largest agency of the New Deal, his economic recovery program. It provided _____ for those receiving relief payments. Most WPA jobs were on public-works projects, such as _____. But it also funded _____, giving work to writers, actors, and artists.

Exercise 4 Fresco Painting

the artist begins painting	planned and timed	lime water
a fresh layer of wet plaster	on dry plaster	

In buon fresco painting, the artist applies paint directly onto wet plaster. The work is done in four stages: An outline is drawn _____ (*ariccio*); a layer of wet plaster is applied (*intonaco*); the final version is drawn on paper and traced onto a cartoon (*intonaco*); and _____ with the cartoon as a guide. The paint consists of powdered pigments mixed with _____, which is easily absorbed by wet plaster. Frescos must be carefully _____ so that the work is finished before the plaster dries. Once it dries, no changes can be made until the dried plaster is removed and _____ applied.

Exercise 5 The Great Basin

Native American Indian tribes	escaping to the Pacific Ocean	the last ice age
the mountains of Utah and Nevada	the mid-nineteenth century	

The Great Basin is a desert plateau mostly in _____. It was formed during _____. Humans first populated it 12,000 years ago, and Spanish explorers found _____ there in the 1700s. Its underground drainage system and hot, dry climate prevent water from _____. The region was populated in _____ after the Mormons founded Salt Lake City and gold was discovered in California.

Exercise 6 Nationalism

political conflict or violence	the French Revolution	ethnic or religious
a tribe or region	a common language, culture, and values	

A sense of national pride, or nationalism, arose around the time of _____.
Industrialization and the need to raise armies led to people identifying themselves as being from a country as opposed to from _____. Nations are often united by _____. When a nation includes different _____ groups however, _____ can result.

The Know-Nothing Party

03-12

In the 1840s, some native-born Americans decided that the two leading parties, the Democrats and the Whigs, were not doing enough to limit the number of immigrants, especially in larger cities. These nativists feared that their way of life was being threatened by the new arrivals, many of whom were Irish Catholic. They spread rumors of a conspiracy by Pope Pius IX to seize control of America by appointing priests and bishops who were loyal to him. In turn, the priests would demand obedience from their Catholic followers.

2 → Newly arriving immigrants tended to join the Democratic Party in cities like New York. As they grew in numbers, their political influence expanded, causing the nativists to fear that they would blindly obey the pope's commands instead of acting in Americans' best interest. The nativist movement organized a political party in New York in 1843, called the American Republican Party. As its influence spread around the country, it changed its name to the Native American Party in 1845.

Dissatisfied with the Democratic Party, which eagerly courted immigrants, the nativists began to form secret societies. On election day, the members would quietly throw their support behind candidates who shared their views. When they were asked about these secret organizations, the members would reply, "I know nothing." They therefore became known as the Know-Nothings.

4 → The group favored specific laws designed to lessen the influence of the newly arrived foreigners. They sought to limit the numbers of annual immigrants, especially from Catholic countries. They urged that immigrants be barred from running for public office. ■ They advocated a twenty-one-year wait before immigrants could become citizens. ■ They favored a ban on Sunday liquor sales. ■ And their plan for the public schools was that only Protestant teachers be hired and that the Protestant version of the Bible be read in schools. ■

5 → Crucial to the rise of the Know-Nothings as a political force was the breakdown of the two-party system, as the Whig party had gradually lost strength. The failure of the Whigs supplied the Know-Nothings with a pool of potential converts. And the timing was right for a party that could provide an outlet for nativist feelings. The Know-Nothings finally achieved national political power in the election of 1854. Adopting platforms of fighting crime, closing bars on Sundays, and appointing only native-born individuals to office, they elected mayors in several cities, won control of some state legislatures, and elected some men to Congress. In 1855, they adopted a new name, the American Party. They seemed ready to join the Democrats as one of the two major parties.

The movement peaked in the 1856 presidential election. Its candidate, former President Millard Fillmore, won twenty-two percent of the popular vote, finishing third behind the Democrat and the Republican. But the party soon split over the slavery issue. Those who were pro-slavery joined the Democrats, and the anti-slavery faction switched to the Republicans, who were led by Abraham Lincoln. By the 1860 election, the American Party was no longer a national political force. The Know-Nothing movement teaches two lessons about American politics, which have been repeated throughout history. First, ethnic and religious prejudice often influences politics, and second, political discontent arises when existing political parties fail to give voice to those frustrated by social upheavals.

1 The word "conspiracy" in the passage is closest in meaning to

    Ⓐ plot

    Ⓑ desire

    Ⓒ statement

    Ⓓ discussion

2 According to paragraph 2, the first nativist political party was

    Ⓐ the Democratic Party

    Ⓑ the American Republican Party

    Ⓒ the Know-Nothing Party

    Ⓓ the Native American Party

3 According to paragraph 2, which of the following can be inferred about the American Republican Party?

    Ⓐ Most of its members had been Whigs.

    Ⓑ It welcomed new immigrants.

    Ⓒ It was active until 1860.

    Ⓓ Its members did not like Catholics.

4 According to paragraph 4, which of the following is NOT true of the Know-Nothings' beliefs?

    Ⓐ They supported limits on the number of immigrants.

    Ⓑ The believed public schools should hire only Protestant teachers.

    Ⓒ They wanted Catholic children banned from public schools.

    Ⓓ They desired a twenty-one-year wait for citizenship for immigrants.

5 Why does the author mention "the Whigs" in paragraph 5?

    Ⓐ To name another party that disliked immigrants

    Ⓑ To identify a source of Know-Nothing members

    Ⓒ To note the dominant party in the United States in the early 1850s

    Ⓓ To show that the Whigs got members from the Know-Nothings

6   The word "they" in the passage refers to

       Ⓐ the Know-Nothings

       Ⓑ native-born individuals

       Ⓒ mayors in several cities

       Ⓓ some men

7   The word "faction" in the passage is closest in meaning to

       Ⓐ leadership

       Ⓑ owners

       Ⓒ group

       Ⓓ party

8   Look at the four squares [■] that indicate where the following sentence could be added to the passage.

    Most of their proposed laws were defeated, however.

    Where would the sentence best fit?

Human Migration across the Bering Strait

Map of the Bering Strait

03-13

Modern humans first lived on the Earth 40,000 years ago in Africa. How they arrived in the Americas is a subject of debate among anthropologists. The most accepted explanation today is the Bering Strait land bridge theory. Recent evidence, however, supports the view that migration occurred by other routes as well.

2 → The Bering Strait is a narrow passage between Siberia in Russia and Alaska to the west of Canada. In 1856, Samuel Haven proposed that about 20,000 years ago during the last ice age, the sea level dropped when the water became locked up in glaciers. The level was about sixty meters lower than it is today. This exposed the land beneath the strait, allowing humans and animals to walk from Siberia to Alaska. Evidence for this land bridge is confirmed by soil cores taken from the waters of the strait, showing that the land during that era was dry plains. Remains of large mammals have also been found, suggesting that Asian tribes were hunters who followed the animals into North America about 12,000 years ago. Mammals native to Africa and Asia, such as lions and cheetahs, later evolved in North America into species that no longer exist today. In addition, the North American camelid, which became extinct in North America, evolved into camels in Asia.

3 → The archaeological record shows that the migration went from west to east. The land bridge was about 2,000 kilometers wide. From Alaska, these nomadic hunters moved down into North America by following ice-free routes along the Pacific coastline. Some groups then made their way eastward past the Rocky Mountains and all the way to the Atlantic coast. Other tribes continued south into Central and South America. The people who crossed the Bering Strait are called the Clovis people after the town of Clovis, New Mexico, where their spear points were found in 1932. Clovis points have a distinctive shape. Similar points have been found as far east as the east coast of the United States and as far south as Chile. Some scientists theorize that the Clovis people who crossed the Bering Strait continued to all parts of North and South America.

But evidence has also been found that some humans arrived at least 1,000 years before the Clovis people. These findings have caused some to believe that the Americas also may have been populated by a route other than the Bering Strait, perhaps by boats crossing the South Pacific. Archaeologists have found indications that boats were used in Australia and Japan as far back as 25,000 to 40,000 years ago. They speculate that some could have sailed to the coast of the Americas and then down the Pacific coast. Unfortunately, many potential coastal sites are now under water, making it difficult to search for signs left by ancient sailors.

5 → Measurements of human skeletons also point to multiple sources of migration. Native Americans have broad faces and prominent cheekbones that match those of Asian people. But other skeletons have been found with narrow skulls and flattened faces, consistent with Polynesians and Europeans. Recent studies in molecular genetics confirm that American Indians share an Asian origin. But a newly discovered DNA line has shown a non-Asian influence as well. DNA research has also revealed that Americans may have diverged genetically from Siberians 20,000 years ago, much earlier than the archaeological evidence indicates.

9 The word "extinct" in the passage is closest in meaning to

   Ⓐ prosperous

   Ⓑ rare

   Ⓒ threatening

   Ⓓ vanished

10 According to paragraph 2, why were humans able to walk across the Bering Strait?

   Ⓐ They were hunting animals.

   Ⓑ The strait froze solid.

   Ⓒ The sea level dropped.

   Ⓓ Volcanoes caused the ground level to rise.

11 The author discusses "Clovis points" in paragraph 3 in order to

   Ⓐ show that Clovis people migrated to South America

   Ⓑ claim that Clovis people were hunters

   Ⓒ explain how Clovis people made primitive weapons

   Ⓓ argue that Clovis people originally came from Asia

12 According to paragraph 3, people crossing the Bering Strait migrated to all of the following places EXCEPT:

   Ⓐ Africa

   Ⓑ New Mexico

   Ⓒ the Atlantic coast

   Ⓓ Chile

13 Which of the following best expresses the essential information in the highlighted sentence? *Incorrect* answer choices change the meaning in important ways or leave out essential information.

(A) Some evidence suggests that humans may have come to the Americas by a route other than the Bering Strait.

(B) Some scientists believe that the first Americans arrived by boat, not by land.

(C) It has been proved that primitive boats could have crossed the Pacific in the past.

(D) The Bering Strait was the most likely point of entry to the Americas by Asians.

14 The word "prominent" in the passage is closest in meaning to

(A) inconspicuous

(B) noticeable

(C) flattened

(D) disfigured

15 According to paragraph 5, which of the following can be inferred about the fact that migration went from west to east?

(A) Asia had a worse climate than North America.

(B) Asian people followed animals across the land bridge.

(C) People lived in Asia before they lived in North America.

(D) Many North American animals later became extinct in Asia.

16 **Directions:** An introductory sentence for a brief summary of the passage is provided below. Complete the summary by selecting the THREE answer choices that express the most important ideas in the passage. Some answer choices do not belong in the summary because they express ideas that are not in the passage or are minor ideas in the passage.

This passage discusses migration across the Bering Strait.

-
-
-

Answer Choices

1. In 1856, Samuel Haven proposed his theory that the ice age occurred about 20,000 years ago.

2. During the last ice age, the low sea level in the Bering Strait exposed a land bridge across the Bering Strait.

3. Humans walked across a land bridge from Asia into North America.

4. The North American camelid disappeared in North America but became the camel in Asia.

5. Boats were used in Japan at least 25,000 years ago.

6. Humans migrated to all parts of the Americas.

Vocabulary Check-Up

A Choose the words with the closest meanings to the highlighted words.

1 The student exhibited her paintings in the museum gallery.

- (A) finished
- (B) framed
- (C) advertised
- (D) displayed

2 During a flood, the water surges into the basement.

- (A) flows
- (B) drips
- (C) sprinkles
- (D) evaporates

3 After fighting a fever for five days, she finally succumbed.

- (A) succeeded
- (B) recovered
- (C) died
- (D) stabilized

4 Reflecting the desires of the people in her state, the senator voted against the bill.

- (A) Expressing
- (B) Rejecting
- (C) Examining
- (D) Soliciting

5 He was frustrated because his boss assigned him some frivolous work.

- (A) fruitful
- (B) boring
- (C) difficult
- (D) unimportant

6 The heart surgeon applied the latest research to remove the blockage.

- (A) instruments
- (B) innovations
- (C) studies
- (D) protections

7 Without a passport, you will have trouble crossing the borders of countries.

- (A) customs
- (B) boundaries
- (C) passages
- (D) distances

8 Drops of water quickly evaporate in a heated pan.

- (A) boil
- (B) flow
- (C) disappear
- (D) change

9 It took brave pioneers to go where no men had ever been before.

- (A) Indians
- (B) soldiers
- (C) cowboys
- (D) discoverers

10 The hurricane ravaged the low-lying areas of the city.

- (A) devastated
- (B) abandoned
- (C) touched
- (D) spared

B Match the words with the correct definitions.

1 plateau   •   • Ⓐ deep; esoteric

2 manifesto   •   • Ⓑ an opening; an outlet

3 profound   •   • Ⓒ an indicator

4 disruptive   •   • Ⓓ factors; traits

5 vent   •   • Ⓔ singularity; remarkableness

6 discrimination   •   • Ⓕ to contain

7 criteria   •   • Ⓖ an elevated land

8 uniqueness   •   • Ⓗ upsetting; causing disorder

9 encompass   •   • Ⓘ bias; prejudice

10 guide   •   • Ⓙ a public declaration; a policy statement

04 Negative Factual Information

◼ Overview

Introduction

Negative Factual Information questions ask you to find wrong information that is not mentioned in the passage. You should decide which of the answer choices is not discussed in the passage or does not agree with one or more statements in the passage. Like Factual Information questions, scanning is the key skill for this question type. However, you need to scan more of the passage to make sure that your answer is correct.

Question Types

- ◈ According to the passage, which of the following is NOT true of X?
- ◈ The author's description of X mentions all of the following EXCEPT:
- ◈ In paragraph 2, all of the following questions are answered EXCEPT:

Useful Tips

- Make use of the key words in the question and the answer choices to spot relevant information in the passage.
- Do not forget that the necessary information may be spread out over one or two paragraphs.
- Make sure that your answer is NOT mentioned in the passage and does not contradict the passage.

Q According to the passage, which of the following is NOT true of gravity?

- Ⓐ It is responsible for the creation of black holes.
- Ⓑ It contributes to the spread of cosmic radiation.
- Ⓒ It can cause some red giants to form.
- Ⓓ It may cause the collapse of molecular clouds.

Stellar Evolution

04-01

    Stars are born from giant molecular clouds, which contain diffuse particles of matter. When a cloud collides with another or with other galactic material, gravity causes it to collapse into a star. Young stars remain unstable for billions of years until they become hot enough to generate nuclear reactions that prevent them from collapsing. They enter a mature stage in which the fusion of hydrogen into helium causes nuclear fusion to stop. Gravity then collapses the star inward, raising its temperature so high that it expands rapidly, becoming a red giant for another few million years. When all their nuclear fuel is burned out, smaller stars become white dwarfs, which eventually cool to black dwarfs. Larger stars explode as supernovas and become neutron stars. If a star is big enough, it collapses into a black hole, whose matter is so dense that gravity prevents any light from escaping.

☑ Correct Answer

In order to answer this question, you just need to scan for the word gravity in the passage. Gravity involves the collapse of molecular clouds, the formation of red giants, and the creation of black holes. Choice Ⓑ is the correct answer because cosmic radiation is not mentioned in the passage.

Basic Drill

Read the passages and answer the questions.

Drill 1

The Culture of Cotton in the United States

Before 1800, most Americans wore clothing made of wool or linen. Cotton was expensive and labor intensive because the seeds had to be removed before cotton could be spun into thread. Planters had to limit their cotton crops to the amount they could clean, but in 1793, Eli Whitney invented the cotton gin, a machine with wire teeth that separated seeds from cotton fiber. Suddenly, one worker could clean fifty pounds of cotton per day, twice the amount possible before the cotton gin. Cotton production soared, as southern farmers turned their land, formerly used for tobacco and rice, into cotton plantations. At the peak of the plantation system in the 1850s, seventy-five percent of all slaves in the southern states, approximately 1.8 million people, were working in cotton production. The 1850s were known as the decade of King Cotton, but the Civil War in 1860 brought an end to prosperity for southern planters.

04-02

1 According to the passage, which of the following is NOT true of cotton?

- (A) It was expensive and required many workers.
- (B) The cotton gin made it easier for people to remove the seeds.
- (C) Cotton production decreased in the south before the Civil War.
- (D) Many cotton farmers formerly grew tobacco and rice.

2 The author's description of cotton production mentions all of the following EXCEPT:

- (A) The effect that the end of slavery had on cotton production
- (B) The time when cotton production in the south peaked
- (C) The reason that cotton planters' prosperous times ended
- (D) The manner in which the cotton gin separated seeds

Drill 2

Planetary Moons

The solar system has more than 290 moons, or natural satellites, that circumnavigate the planets and asteroids. The largest moons are Jupiter's and Saturn's, followed by Earth's moon. Moons were formed at virtually the same times as the larger bodies that they orbit. Some were spun off from their planet during its birth. Others originally were asteroids captured by the planet's gravitational pull, and still others, like Earth's moon, may have been blasted into orbit by a gigantic collision with another celestial object. Most moons, like Earth's, do not rotate but are tidally locked, meaning that one side always faces its partner. When moons are large enough, they exert their own gravitational force on their planet, just as Earth's moon pulls on the planet's oceans, causing the tides. Moons, unlike stars, do not generate their own light, and appear to shine at night only because they are reflecting the sun's light.

04-03

1 According to the passage, which of the following is NOT true of how moons are formed?

- (A) They were propelled into orbit by a collision.
- (B) They spun off when their planet was born.
- (C) They were asteroids that were captured by a planet's gravity.
- (D) They were stars that used up all their fuel.

2 According to the passage, which of the following is NOT true of moons?

- (A) One side usually faces the body it orbits.
- (B) Moons shine by burning their own fuel.
- (C) Large moons pull on other bodies with gravity.
- (D) Jupiter and Saturn have the largest moons.

Biochemistry

04-04

The study of the chemical processes inside living things is called biochemistry. An organism grows and functions through the activity in its cells. Biochemistry focuses on the parts of the cell: proteins, carbohydrates, lipids, and nucleic acids. Proteins are chains of amino acids that bind to other molecules and aid in cell growth and repair. Cells are regulated by special kinds of protein called enzymes. Carbohydrates store energy and provide structure for the cells while lipids include compounds such as waxes, fat, and steroids. Nucleic acids are best known as DNA—deoxyribonucleic acid—and RNA—ribonucleic acid—the substances that carry genetic data. Recent technology has improved biochemistry, permitting scientists to detect with greater clarity the structure and functions of the cell. These new techniques include electron microscopy, chromatography, and radioisotope labeling. Cancer research depends on the clues provided by biochemistry.

1 In the passage, all of the following questions are answered EXCEPT:

   Ⓐ Why do some people get involved in biochemistry?
   Ⓑ How has technology led to the improvement of biochemistry?
   Ⓒ What are some of the different parts of a cell?
   Ⓓ What is the function of enzymes in cells?

2 In the passage, the author's description of new technology mentions all of the following EXCEPT:

   Ⓐ Radioisotope labeling   Ⓑ Electron microscopy
   Ⓒ Radiation therapy   Ⓓ Chromatography

The Culture of the Hopi Indians

04-05

Agriculture is a key element of Hopi culture. Farming is not just a subsistence tool; it is a part of Hopi mythology. The Hopi believe that their time on the Earth is the "fourth way of life," which they entered when people were offered ears of corn by Maasaw, a Hopi god. Other tribes pushed ahead and took the largest ears, leaving the smallest ears for the Hopi. They see this as a symbol of Hopi life: They have had to overcome the hardships of living in the dry southwest region of the United States. Corn represents humility, cooperation, respect, and reverence for the land. Hopi culture has changed as technology has intruded on the Hopi's farm-based lifestyle. Electricity, cars, and consumer goods have diverted them from their spiritual ties to the land and toward consumerism. But they continue to hold on to their traditional values through making and selling Kachina dolls and pottery.

1 According to the passage, which of the following is NOT true of the ways technology has affected Hopi culture?

   Ⓐ It has interfered with their agricultural lifestyle.
   Ⓑ It has made them desire consumer goods.
   Ⓒ It has caused them to abandon making dolls.
   Ⓓ It has weakened their spiritual ties.

2 In the passage, the author's description of the role of corn in Hopi life mentions all of the following EXCEPT:

   Ⓐ An example of hardships   Ⓑ Maasaw
   Ⓒ A symbol of reverence for the land   Ⓓ Kachina dolls

Exercise 1 Read the following passage and answer the questions.

Time Limit: 3 min. 40 sec.

Native American Indian Languages

Before the arrival of the Europeans in North America, Native American Indians spoke over a thousand languages. Most of them were mutually unintelligible. Three Indians from different tribes living within a hundred miles of one another were unlikely to be able to communicate except by sign language. Contrary to the popular stereotype, Indian languages were neither primitive nor simple. Many had complex grammar and phonological structures.

2 ➜ Despite the hundreds of languages in what is now the United States, linguists have grouped them into several large families and many smaller ones. A language family is a collection of languages having a common origin but which have evolved over time into separate languages. For example, just as English, Dutch, and Russian grew out of the Indo-European language family, Apache and Navajo originated in the Athabaskan family of Native American languages. Other large families include Algonquin, Iroquois, Sioux, Muskogean, and Eskimo-Aleut.

3 ➜ A result of the European conquest was the gradual extinction of most indigenous languages. As the Indian population fell from about twenty million to two million today, languages disappeared as well. Many are spoken only by the oldest members of a tribe. When they die, their languages will die with them. Only eight languages remain with more than a few thousand speakers in the United States and Canada. The largest is Navajo with about 148,000 speakers. Others are Cree (60,000), Ojibwa (51,000), Cherokee (22,500), Dakota (20,000), Apache (15,000), Blackfoot (10,000), and Choctaw (9,200).

Native American languages are linguistically diverse. But many share common features that distinguish them from Indo-European languages. The glottal stop is common. It is the sound made by briefly closing the vocal chords, as in the middle of the English sound "uh-oh." Many of the languages use nasal vowels. And like Chinese, some use changes in tone or pitch to form different words.

5 ➜ One well-known trait of Native American languages is polysynthesis, which is the expressing of complex ideas with a single word consisting of several elements tacked on to a root word. Thus, a verb might have an attached subject or object, usually as a prefix. And the verb tense might be indicated by a word ending. Plurals might be shown by simple repetition of the word instead of an ending like "-s." Thus, the plural of rabbit—*ma*—in one Indian language would be *ma ma*.

As with all languages, Native American languages borrowed from nearby language groups, and English borrowed Indian vocabulary as well. English has many common words of Indian origin, such as moccasin, toboggan, chocolate, and tobacco. Many states and cities derived their names from Indian words and names of tribes. These places include Chicago, Manhattan, Wisconsin, Delaware, Iowa, and Arizona.

📖 **Words & Phrases**

unintelligible adj incomprehensible

primitive adj crude; rudimentary

complex adj complicated; intricate

phonological adj relating to speech sounds

origin n a root; a source

originate v to begin; to arise

gradual adj steady; slow

extinction n a disappearance; an extermination

diverse adj different

distinguish v to differentiate

be tacked on to phr to be added to; to be attached to

derive v to borrow; to take

1 The word "Many" in the passage refers to

(A) The Europeans

(B) Native American Indians

(C) Different tribes

(D) Indian languages

2 The word "indigenous" in the passage is closest in meaning to

(A) intelligible

(B) native

(C) primitive

(D) disappearing

3 According to paragraphs 2 and 3, which of the following is NOT true of Native American languages?

(A) Some languages can be grouped together into various families.

(B) The arrival of Europeans caused most of the languages to disappear.

(C) The largest remaining Native American language is Navajo.

(D) Early Indians communicated only with sign language.

4 According to paragraph 5, which of the following is NOT true of polysynthesis?

(A) Verb tense can be shown by a word ending.

(B) It involves a plural indicated by repetition.

(C) A meaning may be changed by tone or pitch.

(D) A subject can be attached to verb as a prefix.

Summary Note Fill in the blanks with the appropriate words.

Native American Indian Languages

- Over ❶ _____ languages in the Americas
  – most Indians could not understand one another
  – had to communicate with ❷ _____
  – used complicated grammar and structures
- Have divided languages into various groups
- Some languages related to one another
- Many Native American languages disappearing today
  – only ❸ _____ with thousands of speakers
- Features of languages
  – use a glottal stop
  – use tone or pitch changes to make new words
  – use ❹ _____

Mars and Earth

04- 07

1 ➜ Earth and Mars were formed at around the same time. About 4.6 billion years ago, they both condensed from a giant cloud of hot gas that shrouded the recently formed sun. They settled next to each other in order from the sun. Earth is about ninety-three million miles from the sun, and Mars is about 142 million miles. They both have hard crusts and dense cores, and they are made from the same chemical elements, albeit in different proportions.

But despite their similar origins and composition, the planets display critical differences that make life possible on just one. One key contrast is size. Mars is only a tenth of the mass of Earth, which means that its gravitational pull is much weaker—about thirty-eight percent of Earth's gravity. As a result, Mars has lost much of its atmosphere and surface water and has cooled more quickly. This rapid cooling explains why Mars has much less volcanic activity than Earth, which is still very hot at its core.

Because of Earth's hotter center, its surface is constantly altered by plate tectonics. As the plates under the crust scrape against one another, new crust rises to the surface, and old crust is swallowed up into Earth's interior. While Mars was shaped by plate tectonics in its first 500 million years, those forces stopped when its interior cooled. As a result, 400-million-year-old rocks are common on Mars but rare on Earth, which is continually squeezing new rocks to the surface and burying older ones. Earthly rocks are eroded by wind whereas the thinner Martian atmosphere generates little wind, preserving the surface in its ancient state.

4 ➜ Half of the surface of Mars is scarred by impact craters. That the craters have been undisturbed for billions of years tells planetary scientists that underground geologic movements ceased before the craters were made. They deduce the same conclusion from the presence of immense volcanoes. Their size and height suggest that they arose billions of years ago and then ceased erupting. Volcanoes on Earth, on the other hand, are still reshaping the planetary landscape today. Water played a role in molding the Martian surface. But it disappeared about 3.8 billion years ago for reasons unknown. Dried riverbeds and paths of glaciers can still be seen. Earth, in contrast, is still covered by water over two-thirds of its surface, a fraction that is increasing in recent decades.

Mars lacks the kind of magnetic field that protects Earth from the electrically charged particles, or solar wind, that bombard it from the sun. The Martian atmosphere is therefore inhospitable to life, consisting of ninety-five percent carbon dioxide. Earth's atmosphere is mostly composed of a life-sustaining seventy-eight percent nitrogen and twenty-one percent oxygen.

📖 Words & Phrases

condense v to compact; to compress
crust n the upper level of the Earth
dense adj compact; condensed
proportion n a ratio; a measure
composition n make-up
critical adj crucial; very important
constantly adv continuously; incessantly
alter v to change

erode v to wear away
generate v to produce; to create
scrape v to grate; to scratch
scar v to mark
immense adj enormous; huge
deduce v to infer
bombard v to attack
inhospitable adj unwelcoming; hostile

1 The word "shrouded" in the passage is closest in meaning to

Ⓐ formed

Ⓑ emerged from

Ⓒ obscured

Ⓓ burned up

2 The word "They" in the passage refers to

Ⓐ Billions of years

Ⓑ Planetary scientists

Ⓒ Underground geologic movements

Ⓓ The craters

Mastering the Question Type

3 According to paragraph 1, which of the following is NOT true of Earth and Mars?

Ⓐ They are approximately the same size.

Ⓑ They contain many of the same chemical elements.

Ⓒ They were created at the same time.

Ⓓ They both have hard outer crusts.

4 In paragraph 4, the author's description of features of Mars mentions all of the following EXCEPT:

Ⓐ Craters

Ⓑ Glacier markings

Ⓒ Volcanoes

Ⓓ Oceans

📝 Summary Note Fill in the blanks with the appropriate words.

Mars and Earth

- Similarities
  - formed ❶_____ years ago
  - next to each other in solar system
  - have hard crusts and dense cores
  - made from same elements
- Differences
  - Mars has smaller mass and less gravity
  - Mars has little atmosphere and ❷_____
  - Earth has very hot core → gives Earth plate ❸_____
  - Mars has many impact craters
  - Earth volcanoes more active and change the planet
  - much of Earth covered by water
  - no ❹_____ on Mars

Time Limit: 3 min. 40 sec.

The Chemistry of Pottery

04-08

The process of firing clay involves two stages: dehydration and vitrification. After the clay is molded into the desired shape, the excess water molecules—called chemical water—seep to the surface. They are propelled by capillary action, the process by which water rises through narrow passages in soil or clay. Once it reaches the surface, the moisture evaporates as the clay is heated.

2 ➡ The chemical dynamics of this process are as follows. Clay's chemical composition is two molecules of water to two molecules of silica (silicon dioxide) and one molecule of alumina (aluminum oxide). During the dehydration stage, the molecules of water evaporate, accounting for about fourteen percent of the clay mixture. The temperature must reach 350 degrees Celsius for evaporation to begin. Dehydration is complete when the temperature reaches about 500 degrees Celsius.

As the temperature becomes even hotter, the molecules of silica and alumina begin to bond tightly. They partially fill the spaces left by the escaped water. This bonding gives the clay object its strength and hardness. At this stage, the clay can no longer absorb water and can never return to its soft, malleable state.

Next is the vitrification stage, during which the surface acquires a glass-like smoothness. As the temperature rises above 500 degrees Celsius, the clay's impurities, such as iron oxide, melt away. Those impurities combine to form a glassy substance that flows around the alumina molecules and glues them together, forming a hard bond. A further increase in temperature causes alumina silicate to grow and interweave with the glassy substance. This interweaving creates a very rigid and crystalline structure in the clay object. That chemical structure is what gives stoneware and porcelain its characteristic ring when struck.

5 ➡ Because of finished clay's chemical bonds, the clay is unable to expand. In addition, if a clay pot is heated over an open fire, the section over the flame will heat faster than other areas, causing uneven heating. The resulting internal stresses may make the pot shatter. Potters in Africa avoid this problem by firing at lower temperatures to avoid the combining of the silica and alumina. This lower-heat firing allows African pottery to withstand uneven heating over an open flame. It also makes the pottery more porous; heat can gradually escape through the pot, permitting the contents to cool.

Chemical analysis is used by archaeologists to pinpoint the source and age of a pottery artifact. The advantage of chemical analysis over cutting away sections is that results can be obtained from very small samples without damaging the piece. One common technique of chemical testing is to dissolve a sample into acid. This process emits atoms that can be analyzed with a spectrograph, which identifies the elements contained in the pottery.

📖 **Words & Phrases**

dehydration n the act of drying up; desiccation
vitrification n the process of changing into glass
excess adj extra; surplus; additional
propel v to push; to thrust
evaporate v to dry up; to vaporize

dynamic n a movement; an operation
account for phr to represent; to explain
absorb v to soak up
rigid adj hard; inflexible
shatter v to break into small pieces

withstand v to tolerate; to survive
porous adj permeable; penetrable
pinpoint v to identify; to determine
dissolve v to melt
emit v to send out; to give off

1   The word "malleable" in the passage is closest in meaning to

Ⓐ fluid

Ⓑ moldable

Ⓒ evaporated

Ⓓ fragile

2   The word "It" in the passage refers to

Ⓐ This lower-heat firing

Ⓑ African pottery

Ⓒ Uneven heating

Ⓓ An open flame

3   According to paragraph 2, which of the following is NOT true of the dehydration stage?

Ⓐ The surface becomes glassy.

Ⓑ Water evaporates.

Ⓒ The temperature reaches 500 degrees.

Ⓓ Fourteen percent of the clay mixture is water.

4   In paragraph 5, all of the following questions can be answered EXCEPT:

Ⓐ How do potters in Africa fire their pots?

Ⓑ What happens when a clay pot is heated over an open fire?

Ⓒ Why is African pottery more porous?

Ⓓ What kinds of pots do African potters usually make?

Summary Note   Fill in the blanks with the appropriate words.

The Chemistry of Pottery

- Two stages to firing clay
  - dehydration & vitrification

- Dehydration stage
  - ❶ _____ evaporate in heat
  - temperature goes from ❷ _____ degrees Celsius
  - heating makes elements bond so strengthens and hardens clay

- Vitrification stage
  - gives surface glass-like smoothness
  - ❸ _____ in clay come out
  - forms ❹ _____ outside the clay
  - changes chemical structure of stoneware

Read the following passage and answer the questions.

The Culture of the Alaskan Eskimo

04-09

1 → The indigenous peoples of Alaska are divided into four main groups: Eskimo (54,761), Tlingit-Haida (22,365), Athabascan (18,838), and Aleut (16,978). The largest group, the Eskimo, is a broad term referring to all tribes that live above the timber line in the Arctic area of Alaska. It includes the Inuit and the Yupik. The word Eskimo means "eaters of raw meat." The Eskimo are nomadic, moving with the seasons to follow caribou and sea animals. A taboo among the Eskimo is to mix sea animals with land animals as they are kept separate in Eskimo kitchens.

The harsh environment compelled the Eskimo to develop advanced tools. They invented the kayak for transportation and the igloo, a house made of blocks of frozen snow. Most Eskimo live in small villages and hunt and fish for their food. Unemployment is high, yet oil development since the 1960s has offered careers to some. At the same time, however, it has threatened the traditional Eskimo lifestyle.

The Eskimo resemble East Asians more than they do the Native Americans of the United States. The reason is that they arrived in Alaska much later than the original migrants who walked across the Bering land bridge. As the land bridge had been submerged before the Eskimo came from Asia, they must have arrived by boat.

Traditional Eskimo were hunters and fishermen who hunted whales, seals, and walruses from covered seal-skin boats called *qajait*, named kayaks by Europeans. When the waterways froze in winter, the Eskimo would cut holes in the ice and wait for seals and walruses to come to the surface for air. On land, the Eskimo traveled with dog sleds led by a team of huskies.

5 → The Eskimo relied on animals to sustain their lifestyle. Not only did the animals provide food, but they were also sources of clothes and tools. Eskimo women would sew clothing and footwear from animal hides using needles made from animal bones and thread from the intestines. The heavy outer garment was the parka. Women made the hood of the parka extra large so as to fit a baby carried in a sling on the mother's back. Boots were fashioned from caribou or seal skins. Work was strictly divided by gender as men were hunters and fishermen while women cared for children, made clothing and tools, and cooked food. Marriages were not always monogamous as some men practiced polygamy.

One myth in American popular culture is that the Eskimo left their old and infirm relatives out on the ice to die. But the truth is that this method of dying was sometimes voluntarily chosen by those who could no longer work and contribute to the community welfare.

📖 Words & Phrases

indigenous [adj] native
nomadic [adj] wandering; traveling; migrant
taboo [n] a forbidden practice
harsh [adj] severe; brutal
compel [v] to force; to coerce
resemble [v] to look like; to be similar to
sustain [v] to support; to maintain

hide [n] a skin; a pelt
garment [n] clothes
fashion [v] to make; to design
polygamy [n] the state of having more than one spouse
myth [n] a fallacy; a misunderstanding
voluntarily [adv] willingly; by choice
infirm [adj] sick; feeble

1 The word "it" in the passage refers to

Ⓐ frozen snow

Ⓑ their food

Ⓒ unemployment

Ⓓ oil development

2 The word "submerged" in the passage is closest in meaning to

Ⓐ created

Ⓑ underwater

Ⓒ existing

Ⓓ used

Mastering the Question Type

3 According to paragraph 1, which of the following is NOT true of the Eskimo?

Ⓐ They live nomadic lives that require them to travel.

Ⓑ They do not mix sea animals and land animals.

Ⓒ They are the largest indigenous group in Alaska.

Ⓓ They include the Athabascan people.

4 In paragraph 5, the author's description of the Eskimo division of labor mentions all of the following EXCEPT:

Ⓐ Who built igloos

Ⓑ Who cared for children

Ⓒ Who went hunting and fishing

Ⓓ Who made clothing

Summary Note   Fill in the blanks with the appropriate words.

The Culture of the Alaskan Eskimo

- People who live in the Arctic area of Alaska
  - are **❶** ....
  - hunt caribou and seals
- Development of tools
  - invented **❷** .... for transportation
  - made igloo for home
- Traditional lifestyle
  - were hunters and fishermen → caught **❸** ....
  - used animals for **❹** ....
  - men hunted and fished
  - woman took care of children and made clothes and tools

Exercise 5 Read the following passage and answer the questions.

Time Limit: 3 min. 40 sec.

Galactic Coordinates

1 ➡ Places on the Earth can be fixed by their coordinates of latitude and longitude. In the same way, the Milky Way Galaxy can be plotted by a galactic coordinate system. It was created by the International Astronomical Union in 1958. It is an altitude-azimuth coordinate system that is similar to the better-known coordinate system on the Earth. Simple equations can convert from one system to the other.

The galactic equator traces the zero-degree latitude line. That line is parallel to the general orientation of the plane of the Milky Way. Thus, bodies with a galactic latitude near zero degrees are located in the Milky Way's arms. Objects with a positive galactic latitude lie above the arms in the northern galactic hemisphere. And those with a negative latitude fall below the arms in the southern galactic hemisphere.

Galactic longitude is arbitrarily defined as being in the direction pointing to the center of the galaxy. Longitude moves from zero to 360 degrees. Lines of longitude move counterclockwise as viewed from the top of the galactic sphere. The Earth's sun is at the center of the sphere at the point where zero degrees latitude bisects ninety degrees longitude. The North Galactic Pole is at ninety degrees latitude. The South Galactic Pole is at minus ninety degrees latitude.

4 ➡ With these coordinates superimposed on the imaginary sphere that defines the boundaries of the galaxy, astronomers can find celestial objects on the grid of their latitude and longitude. For example, the brightest star in Earth's sky is Sirius, which is located at 227 degrees longitude and minus 8.4 degrees latitude. The mapping aids them in conducting star surveys and in tracking the movements of objects through the galactic field. It can also help answer questions about how the density of stars varies with distance from the galactic equator or how much the disk of the Milky Way is flattened at its edges.

5 ➡ Galactic coordinates are useful for marking the locations of objects far outside the solar system. The Earth's distance from stars beyond our sun is so great that the planet's orbiting of the sun has little effect on human perception of distant objects' positions. But that same orbital movements would make measurements of bodies inside the solar system inaccurate under the galactic coordinate system.

Objects beyond the Milky Way do not rotate along with it. Thus, they are perceived by people as changing positions to a substantial degree. But they do so in a predictable way relative to the galactic coordinates. As measured with respect to the rotating Milky Way, other galaxies revolve around Earth every 220 million years.

📖 Words & Phrases

plot v to locate; to map
coordinate n a point marking a location
convert v to change
hemisphere n one half of the globe
trace v to track
arbitrarily adv without any specific reason; randomly

bisect v to divide into two parts
superimpose v to place over something else
conduct v to do; to carry out
vary v to differ
perception n an observation
substantial adj significant; considerable

1 The word "celestial" in the passage is closest in meaning to

    Ⓐ nearby

    Ⓑ speeding

    Ⓒ heavenly

    Ⓓ mapped

2 The word "them" in the passage refers to

    Ⓐ these coordinates

    Ⓑ the boundaries of the galaxy

    Ⓒ astronomers

    Ⓓ celestial objects

3 According to paragraph 1, which of the following is NOT true of the galactic coordinate system?

    Ⓐ Locations can be plotted in the Milky Way Galaxy.

    Ⓑ It was created several decades ago.

    Ⓒ It is based on altitude and azimuth.

    Ⓓ It can locate places on the Earth.

4 According to paragraphs 4 and 5, which of the following is NOT true of the uses of galactic coordinates?

    Ⓐ They can be used to measure the flattening of the Milky Way at its edges.

    Ⓑ They can be used to estimate the distance between Earth and the sun.

    Ⓒ They can be used to locate objects outside the solar system.

    Ⓓ They can be used to conduct star surveys.

📝 Summary Note **Fill in the blanks with the appropriate words.**

Galactic Coordinates

- Can plot ❶ _____ on galactic coordinate system
  - created by International Astronomical Union in ❷ _____
  - is ❸ _____ coordinate system
- Works like latitude and longitude
- Can find celestial objects with it
- Can mark objects far outside ❹ _____

The Electrolytic Detector

04-11

In the late 1800s, the only means of long-distance communication besides the mail service were the telegraph and the telephone. But both required wires to carry their signals. The possibility of wireless transmissions seemed like a fantasy of science fiction. But by the early 1900s, radio broadcasts had become a reality.

2 → The principles making radio possible were developed throughout the nineteenth century. The first breakthrough was made by British physicist Michael Faraday in 1831. He discovered that when an electric current passes through one wire, it produces a current in another wire even though the wires do not touch each other. In 1864, James Maxwell showed that this current—composed of electromagnetic waves—travels at the speed of light. Heinrich Hertz proved that the waves pass through solid objects. With these discoveries in place, the race was on to develop a system of wireless radio.

3 → Among the contenders was Reginald Fessenden, a Canadian inventor. Fessenden began experimenting with radio detectors in order to explore the possibility of voice transmission. In 1900, he was the first person to transmit his voice, but the sound was unrecognizable because the waves were not continuous. He invented a barretter detector, taking its name from the French word *échangeur*, to receive AM (amplitude modulated) signals, but it was not sensitive enough. One day in 1901, he accidentally left a filament of wire in acid for too long until only a tip of the wire was in contact with the acid. Fessenden noticed that, with the wire in the acid, the barretter was very sensitive to nearby continuous radio waves.

4 → Fessenden called his invention a liquid barretter, but it became known as an electrolytic detector. The detector consisted of several connected parts forming an electric circuit. A silver-coated platinum wire was dipped into a small platinum cup filled with nitric or sulfuric acid and connected to the ground. A battery was connected between the wire and the acid, prompting a current to flow in the detector. Someone wearing headphones that were hooked up to the detector could hear a hissing noise, which could be adjusted by turning a dial until the hissing noise stopped. At that point, the detector was highly sensitive to incoming radio waves.

5 → This wet form of the device was known as a bare-point electrolytic detector, after the bare wire that was immersed in the acid. A better design was the sealed-point electrolytic detector, which was more stable because it was sealed in glass. Thus, the acid could not spill or evaporate. Fessenden patented his detector in 1903. The device was used in early radio receivers. It set the standard for sensitivity in radio receivers until it was supplanted by the vacuum tube in 1915.

📖 Words & Phrases

breakthrough n a discovery
contender n a competitor; a contestant
explore v to examine; to research
sensitive adj responsive; easily affected
filament n a threadlike object
dip v to dunk; to immerse

prompt v to cause
hook up phr to connect
adjust v to attune; to adapt
immerse v to dip; to sink; to submerge
supplant v to replace

1 The word "transmission" in the passage is closest in meaning to

   (A) detection   (B) transcription

   (C) conveyance   (D) interpretation

2 The word "it" in the passage refers to

   (A) his voice

   (B) the sound

   (C) a barretter detector

   (D) the French word *échangeur*

3 In paragraphs 2 and 3, the author's description of the discovery of electromagnetic waves mentions all of the following people EXCEPT:

   (A) Heinrich Hertz

   (B) James Maxwell

   (C) Reginald Fessenden

   (D) Michael Faraday

4 According to paragraphs 4 and 5, which of the following is NOT true of the electrolytic detector?

   (A) It worked without a battery.

   (B) A wire touched acid.

   (C) It formed an electric circuit.

   (D) It made a hissing noise.

Summary Note   **Fill in the blanks with the appropriate words.**

The Electrolytic Detector

- Many advances in radio technology
  - Michael Faraday → made discovery of currents through wires
  - James Maxwell → showed currents travel at **❶** ....
  - Heinrich Hertz → proved waves go through **❷** ....
- Race to create wireless radio
  - Reginald Fessenden → Canadian inventor
  - worked on **❸** ....
  - invented barretter to receive AM signals
- Liquid barretter
  - later called **❹** ....
  - formed an electric circuit
  - could hear noise through it
  - used in early radio receivers

Building Summary Skills

The following summaries are based on the passages you worked on earlier. Complete each of them by filling in the blanks with suitable words or phrases.

Exercise 1 Native American Indian Languages

endings or prefixes	eight languages	polysynthesis
tobacco and chocolate	Native Indian languages	

Native American Indians spoke over a thousand languages. But the European conquest of America began the slow extinction of most _____. Today, just _____ remain with more than a thousand speakers. The largest are Navajo, Cree, Ojibwa, and Cherokee. The languages are characterized by _____, in which a single word can express many ideas with _____ added to a root word. Many common English words, such as _____, were borrowed from Indian languages.

Exercise 2 Mars and Earth

a weaker force of gravity	origins and compositions	tectonic movements
a lack of water	the same chemical elements	

Earth and Mars share similar _____. They both condensed from a cloud of gas around the sun and are made of _____. But Mars is much smaller, resulting in _____, a thinner atmosphere, and _____. While volcanic activity continues to shape Earth today, the Martian surface is no longer changed by _____. Without the kind of magnetic field that protects Earth, Mars is bombarded by electrically charged particles from the sun.

Exercise 3 The Chemistry of Pottery

the age and the source	500 degrees Celsius	high temperatures
expansion	its glassy surface	

Pottery is made by exposing clay to _____. The process involves two stages. In the dehydration stage, clay is heated to between 350 and 500 degrees Celsius. As the clay heats, it dehydrates and hardens. In the vitrification stage, clay is heated above _____, which removes the impurities and gives clay _____. Pottery may shatter during heating as its chemical bonds hinder _____. Heating at a lower temperature can avoid this problem. Chemical analysis can detect _____ of a pottery shard.

Exercise 4 | The Culture of the Alaskan Eskimo

dog sleds	parkas	Alaskan Indians
inventing kayaks	caribou and sea animals	

The Eskimo are the largest group of _____. They are nomadic, moving with the seasons to follow their food supply of _____. They have adapted to the harsh environment by _____ for water travel, _____ for land travel, and igloos for shelter. Men do the hunting and the fishing while women do the domestic chores and childcare. Animals provide not only food but also clothing and tools. Women sew outer garments called _____, which are made from animal hides. Some men marry more than one wife.

Exercise 5 | Galactic Coordinates

the galactic coordinate system	the galactic coordinates	astronomers
the galaxy	the Milky Way	

Celestial objects in the Milky Way Galaxy can be mapped with _____, which was invented by the International Astronomical Union in 1958. Lines of latitude and longitude are imposed on an imaginary grid over _____. Using these lines, _____ can assign locations to stars and track their movements through _____. The system also permits the mapping of objects outside the Milky Way as they move in predictable ways relative to _____.

Exercise 6 | The Electrolytic Detector

incoming radio waves	Reginald Fessenden	1915
an electric circuit	the electrolytic detector	

Radio transmission was made possible by _____, which was invented by _____ in 1901. The detector formed _____ when a platinum wire was dipped in acid. The circuit could detect _____. A person wearing headphones connected to the detector could hear the hissing sound of the radio waves. The device was used in early radio receivers until _____.

Theories of Life on Mars

In the mid-1700s, astronomers observed polar ice caps on Mars. William Herschel saw that the ice caps changed in size with the seasons. The presence of water and seasons, features present on the Earth, prompted speculation that life might exist on Mars.

2 → Improved telescopes in the nineteenth century further fueled these speculations. They allowed Mars's surface features to be identified. In 1877, Italian astronomer Giovanni Schiaparelli used a twenty-two-centimeter telescope to draw the first map of Mars. His map depicted long lines that he called *canali*, the Italian word for channels. But his term was mistakenly translated into English as canals. Because channels are usually natural and canals are manmade, the mistake gave birth to imaginative theories of life on Mars over the next 100 years.

3 → The leading proponent of the view that the canals were built by intelligent beings was an American astronomer, Percival Lowell. At the Lowell Observatory in the high altitude and clear air of Flagstaff, Arizona, Lowell studied Mars extensively and made detailed drawings of its surface features. He published books about his Mars studies, including *Mars and Its Canals* in 1906 and *Mars As the Abode of Life* in 1908. Lowell proposed that the canals had been constructed by a long-extinct civilization as an elaborate irrigation system. The canals conveyed water from the polar regions to the dry population centers of the planet. Lowell's ideas were embraced by popular culture. British novelist H.G. Wells wrote the most famous novel describing life on Mars, *War of the Worlds*. He imagined that Martians invaded the Earth in order to flee the death of their own planet. Bigger and better telescope lenses in the twentieth century failed to confirm that the features Lowell observed really were canals. In fact, they ultimately were shown to be optical illusions.

4 → Life on Mars was dealt a further blow beginning in 1965. The United States launched the *Mariner* spacecrafts to fly close to the surface to take photographs and to test the atmosphere. Those probes showed that Mars has a thin atmosphere made mostly of carbon dioxide and that the polar ice caps are frozen carbon dioxide, not water. The photos revealed that Mars had no rivers, oceans, or any other visible signs of life. Scientists concluded that Mars's thin atmosphere and lack of a magnetic field made it vulnerable to harmful cosmic radiation. Biological and soil experiments were conducted by the *Viking* project in 1976. To the scientists' surprise, the tests showed that Mars's surface has no organic matter at all. Thus, the present view is that Mars is a dead planet, yet there may have been life early in its history that later became extinct.

5 → Beginning in 1996, the United States launched a highly successful series of landings on Mars. While they have not found life, they have expanded humans' knowledge of Martian geology and chemistry. A robotic exploration vehicle in 2001 sent back to Earth spectacular images of Mars's terrain. Other missions have detected hydrogen and methane. In 2004, Martian vehicles provided conclusive evidence that water existed in the distant past. Additional American missions are currently ongoing. The European Space Agency wants to land humans on Mars by 2035. And in 2004, the American president declared a national goal of sending astronauts to land on and explore Mars.

1 The word "They" in the passage refers to

    (A) Improved telescopes

    (B) These speculations

    (C) Mars's surface features

    (D) Long lines

2 According to paragraph 2, the first map of Mars showed which of the following surface features?

    (A) Mountains

    (B) Craters

    (C) Deserts

    (D) Canals

3 The word "conveyed" in the passage is closest in meaning to

    (A) evaporated

    (B) collected

    (C) transported

    (D) condensed

4 In paragraph 3, why does the author mention "*War of the Worlds*"?

    (A) To show that another astronomer agreed with Lowell

    (B) To give an example of how Lowell's view was adopted by popular culture

    (C) To identify a famous novel written in the early 1900s

    (D) To prove that there were actually canals on Mars

5 In paragraph 4, what does the author imply about water on Mars?

    (A) It never existed because Mars has no oxygen.

    (B) It disappeared because of Mars's thin atmosphere and cosmic radiation.

    (C) It was carried by artificial canals.

    (D) It was used to irrigate the deserts.

6   According to paragraph 4, which of the following is NOT true of Mars?

    Ⓐ It has frozen carbon dioxide.

    Ⓑ It lacks all signs of life.

    Ⓒ It has a thick atmosphere.

    Ⓓ Its surface has no organic matter.

7   Which of the following can be inferred from paragraph 5 about Earth?

    Ⓐ Its atmosphere is made mostly of carbon dioxide and water.

    Ⓑ Its atmosphere is thinner than Mars's.

    Ⓒ Its oceans were once frozen carbon dioxide.

    Ⓓ Its magnetic field protects life forms from cosmic radiation.

8   **Directions:** An introductory sentence for a brief summary of the passage is provided below. Complete the summary by selecting the THREE answer choices that express the most important ideas in the passage. Some answer choices do not belong in the summary because they express ideas that are not in the passage or are minor ideas in the passage.

This passage discusses the history of theories of life on Mars.

-
-
-

Answer Choices

1 H.G. Wells wrote *War of the Worlds*.

2 The Italian word for channels is *canali*.

3 Observations of polar ice caps and canals suggested that life existed on Mars.

4 Recent space probes have proved that life is lacking on Mars.

5 Improved telescopes showed that there are no canals on Mars.

6 The *Viking* project conducted soil surveys on Mars.

Landscape Architecture in the United States

The United States Capitol in Washington, D.C.

Landscape architecture is the design and development of land for human use and enjoyment. Before the middle of the nineteenth century, landscape architecture was practiced as an art but not as a profession. Since ancient times, the art had been employed only by the wealthy. Romans had their courtyards, Persians their gardens, Italians their city plazas, and the French their palace grounds. The upper classes in the American colonies adopted the landscape style of the British, especially their elaborate gardens. As most landscape projects included gardens, the designers were called landscape gardeners.

2 → The inventor of the term landscape architecture was a British scholar, Gilbert Laing Meason, who used it in a book in 1828. He was the first to draw attention to the connection between the natural landscape and the principles of building design. In the United States, the label was adopted by Frederick Law Olmstead, the first person to claim that title as his profession.

Olmstead revolutionized the field when he and architect Calvert Vaux entered a competition for the design of New York's proposed Central Park. With New York's rise in population in the early 1800s, the city's leaders realized the need to set aside open spaces for a public park. The New York legislature approved money for a large rectangular space in the middle of the city. In 1858, Olmstead and Vaux's design was selected, and it was built over the next fifteen years.

4 → Olmstead's concept was to make the park a symbol of democracy and egalitarian ideals. He saw it as a place that welcomed all classes of people and encouraged them to contemplate and recreate away from the pressures of everyday life. His novel design idea was to create what he called "separate circulation systems" for different classes of users—pedestrians, horseback riders, and horse-drawn carriages. Traffic moving through the park was concealed in sunken roadways hidden by shrubs to preserve the appearance of an unspoiled landscape. Today, the park includes running tracks, ice skating rinks, a wildlife sanctuary, baseball fields, playgrounds, and a world-famous restaurant, Tavern on the Green.

Olmstead also designed the grounds of the United States Capitol in Washington, D.C. He installed the marble terraces that project from the sides of the building. Some visitors to the Capitol complained that they had no place to water their horses. In response, Olmstead designed an open-air brick building, the Summer House, which had a fountain from which horses could drink.

Landscape architects founded their own organization in 1899, the American Society of Landscape Architects. It is now a profession equal to that of doctors and lawyers and requires an advanced degree plus a license to practice. The field is multidisciplinary as a landscape architect must be familiar with mathematics, science, engineering, art, and technology. The architect must also understand the social context of the work and be adept at dealing with politicians, public interest groups, and government agencies.

7 ➡ The profession has become increasingly specialized. Landscape designers and technicians or engineers plan and build the project. Landscape managers are concerned with the long-term care of the landscape. They might work in forestry, nature conservation, or estate management. Landscape scientists work with the architects on technical problems in areas such as soil, hydrology, or botany. Public policy and planning strategies are developed with the aid of landscape planners. Garden designers work on private gardens as well as historic-garden preservation.

9   The word "elaborate" in the passage is closest in meaning to

    Ⓐ unique   Ⓑ formal

    Ⓒ intricate   Ⓓ traditional

10   According to paragraph 2, the term landscape architecture was first used by

    Ⓐ Gilbert Laing Meason

    Ⓑ the Romans

    Ⓒ Frederick Law Olmstead

    Ⓓ the American Society of Landscape Architects

11   The word "it" in the passage refers to

    Ⓐ a public park

    Ⓑ a large rectangular space

    Ⓒ the city

    Ⓓ 1858

12   According to paragraph 4, Olmstead's goal in designing Central Park was to

    Ⓐ establish landscape architecture as a profession

    Ⓑ create a restful place for all people

    Ⓒ provide a recreational area for the wealthy

    Ⓓ plant trees to conceal traffic

13 According to paragraph 4, which of the following is NOT part of the current Central Park?

Ⓐ Tavern on the Green

Ⓑ Running tracks

Ⓒ A wildlife sanctuary

Ⓓ Horse-drawn carriages

14 The word "adept" in the passage is closest in meaning to

Ⓐ enthusiastic

Ⓑ reluctant

Ⓒ skilled

Ⓓ professional

15 In paragraph 7, why does the author mention "Landscape scientists"?

Ⓐ To give an example of a specialized field of landscape architecture

Ⓑ To list one of the professions requiring an advanced degree

Ⓒ To name the professionals who solve hydrology problems

Ⓓ To show that landscape architects must understand social problems

16 **Directions:** An introductory sentence for a brief summary of the passage is provided below. Complete the summary by selecting the THREE answer choices that express the most important ideas in the passage. Some answer choices do not belong in the summary because they express ideas that are not in the passage or are minor ideas in the passage.

This passage discusses the development of landscape architecture in the United States.

-
-
-

Answer Choices

☐1 Landscape architecture became a separate profession in the middle of the nineteenth century.

☐2 Landscape managers are concerned with the long-term care of landscapes.

☐3 Landscape architecture requires an advanced degree and knowledge of many disciplines.

☐4 Olmstead added the Summer House to the Capitol as a drinking fountain for horses.

☐5 Central Park was built over fifteen years.

☐6 Olmstead, the designer of New York's Central Park, was the first great American landscape architect.

Vocabulary **Check-Up**

A **Choose the words with the closest meanings to the highlighted words.**

1 The international fair served diverse foods.

- Ⓐ different
- Ⓑ multiple
- Ⓒ plentiful
- Ⓓ popular

2 The freezing process quickly condensed the fluid into solid ice.

- Ⓐ consolidated
- Ⓑ created
- Ⓒ compressed
- Ⓓ dissolved

3 The rebels bombarded the palace with gunfire.

- Ⓐ entered
- Ⓑ surrounded
- Ⓒ captured
- Ⓓ attacked

4 The doctor applied a rigid cast to immobilize the patient's broken wrist.

- Ⓐ flexible
- Ⓑ plaster
- Ⓒ hard
- Ⓓ removable

5 The witness was unable to pinpoint the exact date of his injury.

- Ⓐ identify
- Ⓑ write
- Ⓒ approximate
- Ⓓ summarize

6 The harsh climate doomed the expedition.

- Ⓐ wet
- Ⓑ hostile
- Ⓒ changeable
- Ⓓ unexpected

7 As she is elderly and infirm, my grandmother cannot travel.

- Ⓐ miserable
- Ⓑ lonely
- Ⓒ sickly
- Ⓓ unpleasant

8 The cloudy night impaired his perception of the passing comet.

- Ⓐ observation
- Ⓑ understanding
- Ⓒ recording
- Ⓓ prediction

9 Two construction companies were contenders for the government contract to build the bridge.

- Ⓐ builders
- Ⓑ participants
- Ⓒ writers
- Ⓓ competitors

10 Millions of dollars were missing, prompting an investigation.

- Ⓐ causing
- Ⓑ suggesting
- Ⓒ terminating
- Ⓓ rejecting

B **Match the words with the correct definitions.**

1 tacked on •   • (A) to place over something else

2 filament •   • (B) without any specific reason

3 proportion •   • (C) a forbidden practice

4 porous •   • (D) added; attached

5 stereotype •   • (E) a ratio; a measure

6 superimpose •   • (F) the state of having more than one spouse

7 polygamy •   • (G) to push; to thrust

8 arbitrarily •   • (H) a threadlike object

9 propel •   • (I) permeable; penetrable

10 taboo •   • (J) commonly accepted wisdom about the nature of a person or thing

05 Sentence Simplification

◣ Overview

Introduction

Sentence Simplification questions ask you to choose a sentence that best paraphrases the original sentence in the passage. The correct answer uses different vocabulary and different grammar to restate the essential meaning of the original sentence in a simpler way. This type of question does not appear in every reading passage. There is also never more than one Sentence Simplification question in a passage.

Question Types

▶ Which of the following best expresses the essential information in the highlighted sentence? *Incorrect* answer choices change the meaning in important ways or leave out essential information.

Useful Tips

- Figure out what essential information is in the original sentence.
- Do not focus on minor information such as details and examples.
- Keep in mind that incorrect answers contradict something in the original sentence or leave out important information from the original sentence.
- Make sure that your answer agrees with the main argument of the paragraph or the passage as a whole.

Q Which of the following best expresses the essential information in the highlighted sentence? *Incorrect* answer choices change the meaning in important ways or leave out essential information.

Ⓐ Any time a plate pushes upward, it forms a volcano on the Earth's surface.

Ⓑ Volcanoes are formed when the rise of tectonic plates makes a gap in the Earth's surface.

Ⓒ Volcanoes are always formed when gaps in the Earth's crust appear.

Ⓓ A mountain can be changed into a volcano when a plate pushing upward opens a gap in the Earth's crust.

Volcanoes

05-01

When people think of volcanoes, they typically imagine large cone-shaped mountains that erupt with hot lava. In fact, there are many different kinds of volcanoes, and they are commonly found on flat ground or under the ocean. They are created when two or more tectonic plates either come together or pull apart. Tectonic plates are large pieces of the Earth's crust that are constantly, yet very slowly, moving. When tectonic plates come together, they create mountain ridges. Some of the mountains are volcanoes, which are formed when the plates that push upward create gaps in the Earth's crust. Likewise, when tectonic plates pull apart, they often leave similar gaps in the Earth's crust, which create volcanoes. Most of the time, however, volcanoes that are formed by tectonic plates pulling apart are flat volcanoes. In the ocean, there are both flat and mountainous volcanoes.

☑ **Correct Answer**

The essential information in the original sentence is that the rise of plate tectonics creates a volcano by making a gap in the Earth's crust. So the correct answer is Ⓑ.

Basic Drill

Read the passages and answer the questions.

Drill 1

Sea Level and Land

05-02

Sea level refers to the average height of the ocean as compared to land. Measuring the height of the ocean is difficult as it can be as much as two meters higher in one part of the world than in another. In addition, the sea level can rise because of tides, which are caused by the position of the moon. High tide refers to the time when the sea level is high compared to land, the result of which is there is little beach near the ocean while low tide is the time when the sea is low compared to land, so the size of the beach expands. Melting icebergs are another cause of rising sea levels. Icebergs are enormous chunks of ice which float in the world's coldest oceans. They may melt during warm weather or when they drift southward and thus cause the world's average sea level to rise. As a result of icebergs melting, some islands are in danger of being swallowed by the sea.

Q Which of the following best expresses the essential information in the highlighted sentence? *Incorrect* answer choices change the meaning in important ways or leave out essential information.

    Ⓐ The moon's location affects tides, causing sea levels to rise.

    Ⓑ Sea levels always rise because they are affected by the moon.

    Ⓒ High tide is a result of the position of the moon.

    Ⓓ The moon's position is caused by the tides making sea levels rise.

Drill 2

Migratory Birds

Every fall and winter, birds set out on their annual migrations to southern lands. They take these long journeys for many different reasons; for example, they may need to go where there is more food, where they can live comfortably, or where they can breed in peace. Migratory birds often remain in northern places during the summer and migrate south when the temperature starts to dip. Birds spend their winters in warm, southern regions and then return north when it starts to become too hot. The advantages of migration are that birds have more hours to feed their young during the long, northern summers, and there is lots of food like insects for them to eat. When the temperature starts to become cold, they can return to warmer regions, where there is not much difference in the lengths of the days and the food supply. The disadvantage is that migration can be a dangerous trek and requires vast stores of energy.

Q Which of the following best expresses the essential information in the highlighted sentence? *Incorrect* answer choices change the meaning in important ways or leave out essential information.

    Ⓐ Birds live in the north in summer but fly south for the winter.

    Ⓑ Migratory birds leave their northern habitat to move to the south when it becomes colder.

    Ⓒ When temperatures become colder, migratory birds fly north to avoid the cold.

    Ⓓ Migrating south for winter is one way that birds avoid dipping temperatures in the north in winter.

Weather Changes in the Desert

05-04

The weather can change drastically in the desert over the course of a mere day. For example, the temperature can be 40°C at two PM, yet on that same day, it may potentially drop to -15°C by three AM. The sand reflects sunlight during the day, making both the sand and the air temperature extremely hot. The principle behind this is the same as when one walks along a beach on a hot day and feels the burning hot sand under one's feet. It is the same principle in the desert. At nighttime, because the sand does not absorb any of the sun's heat during the day, the temperature becomes very cold. In forests and grasslands, the sun's heat is absorbed by trees and grass during the day, so the temperature is not as cold as during the night, but in deserts, there are almost no trees and little grass. Thus, heat is not absorbed, and the results are extremely hot days followed by frigid nights.

Q Which of the following best expresses the essential information in the highlighted sentence? *Incorrect* answer choices change the meaning in important ways or leave out essential information.

Ⓐ The sand in deserts becomes cold at night since it does not absorb the sun's energy.
Ⓑ Temperatures in sandy places can be cold since sand cannot absorb any of the sun's heat.
Ⓒ Deserts become cold at night because the sand fails to retain the daytime solar heat.
Ⓓ Sand only absorbs small amounts of energy from the sun, resulting in cold desert nights.

Plant Defenses Against Plant-Eating Animals

05-05

There are many ways that plants can defend themselves against animals that consume them. Their various defenses allow them to survive in areas where there are many herbivores. Plant defenses include protections on the surface of plants, like thorns on roses, materials in the plants that make them difficult for animals to digest, and poisons that kill or make herbivores very sick. Plants also have other amazing ways of protecting themselves by attracting animals called carnivores that hunt and eat herbivores. For example, plants create smells that predators of herbivores like, or plants provide them food or shelter. Defenses can always exist in plants, or they can develop after the plant has been damaged by herbivores. Plant species often have many ways to defend itself from herbivores, which is why many are millions of years old.

Q Which of the following best expresses the essential information in the highlighted sentence? *Incorrect* answer choices change the meaning in important ways or leave out essential information.

Ⓐ Plants are always protected by various defenses like poisons or thorns because herbivores always eat them.
Ⓑ Plants protect themselves from herbivores by developing various defense mechanisms.
Ⓒ Some herbivores become sick or die when eating plants, which helps protect these plants from animals.
Ⓓ Thorns, poison, and hard-to-digest leaves are ideal protection for many plants.

Exercises with Long Passages

Exercise 1 Read the following passage and answer the questions.

Time Limit: 3 min. 30 sec.

Eye Variation Among Different Species

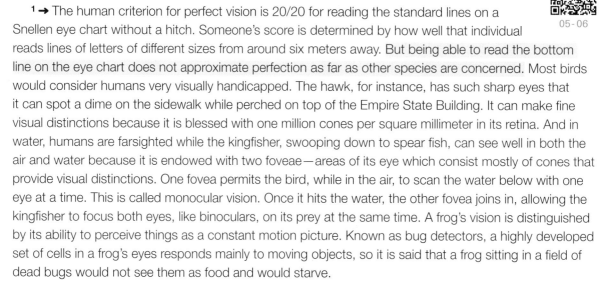

05-06

1 ➤ The human criterion for perfect vision is 20/20 for reading the standard lines on a Snellen eye chart without a hitch. Someone's score is determined by how well that individual reads lines of letters of different sizes from around six meters away. But being able to read the bottom line on the eye chart does not approximate perfection as far as other species are concerned. Most birds would consider humans very visually handicapped. The hawk, for instance, has such sharp eyes that it can spot a dime on the sidewalk while perched on top of the Empire State Building. It can make fine visual distinctions because it is blessed with one million cones per square millimeter in its retina. And in water, humans are farsighted while the kingfisher, swooping down to spear fish, can see well in both the air and water because it is endowed with two foveae—areas of its eye which consist mostly of cones that provide visual distinctions. One fovea permits the bird, while in the air, to scan the water below with one eye at a time. This is called monocular vision. Once it hits the water, the other fovea joins in, allowing the kingfisher to focus both eyes, like binoculars, on its prey at the same time. A frog's vision is distinguished by its ability to perceive things as a constant motion picture. Known as bug detectors, a highly developed set of cells in a frog's eyes responds mainly to moving objects, so it is said that a frog sitting in a field of dead bugs would not see them as food and would starve.

The bee has a compound eye, which is used for navigation. It has 15,000 facets that divide what it sees into a pattern of dots, or mosaic. With this kind of vision, the bee sees the sun only as a single dot, a constant point of reference. Thus, the eye is a superb navigational instrument that constantly measures the angle of its line of flight in relation to the sun. A bee's eye also gauges flight speed. And if that is not enough to leave our 20/20 perfect vision paling in comparison, the bee is capable of seeing something humans cannot: ultraviolet light. Therefore, what humans consider perfect vision is in fact rather limited when examining other species. However, there is still much to be said for the human eye. Of all the mammals, only humans and some primates enjoy the pleasures of color vision.

📖 Words & Phrases

criterion n a standard; a basis
hitch n a problem
approximate v to come close to; to approach
handicapped adj limited; restricted
perch v to alight; to sit down
retina n the area at the back of an eye
swoop v to fly down suddenly
be endowed with phr to be blessed with
monocular adj involving a single eye
prey n a victim

perceive v to see; to notice
constant adj continuous; incessant; perpetual
respond to phr to react to
starve v to die of hunger
navigation n the act of finding directions
facet n an aspect; an angle; a phase; a side
gauge v to measure; to check
pale v to diminish; to recede; to fade
superb adj excellent; exceptional

1 According to paragraph 1, what kind of vision does a kingfisher have?

    Ⓐ It has the ability to see a coin from very high up.

    Ⓑ It can use just one eye to look at something.

    Ⓒ It can detect things according to how they move.

    Ⓓ It has a compound eye that it uses for navigation.

2 According to the passage, how does human eyesight compare with most animals?

    Ⓐ Most animals have worse eyesight than humans.

    Ⓑ All animals can see in ultraviolet light, unlike humans.

    Ⓒ Humans typically have poorer eyesight than animals.

    Ⓓ Humans and animals have comparable eyesight.

3 Which of the following best expresses the essential information in the first highlighted sentence? *Incorrect* answer choices change the meaning in important ways or leave out essential information.

    Ⓐ Other species might not consider perfect human eyesight to be ideal for them.

    Ⓑ Some other animals can also read the eye chart, which means they have perfect eyesight.

    Ⓒ Other species are not particularly concerned about being able to read the bottom of an eye chart.

    Ⓓ Different species have different methods of determining what perfect eyesight is.

4 Which of the following best expresses the essential information in the second highlighted sentence? *Incorrect* answer choices change the meaning in important ways or leave out essential information.

    Ⓐ One type of vision the bee has is the ability to see the sun as a mere dot.

    Ⓑ The bee constantly refers to the sun's position even though it only appears as a small dot.

    Ⓒ A small dot is all that bees need to determine their reference point.

    Ⓓ The bee uses the sun as a reference point, which appears as a dot in its vision.

📝 Summary Note **Fill in the blanks with the appropriate words.**

Eye Variation Among Different Species

- Hawks
  - very sharp eyes → can make fine distinctions from ❶ ....

- Kingfishers
  - can see in water and air
  - have ❷ .... → give it monocular vision

- Frogs
  - perceive objects ❸ ....

- Bees
  - have ❹ ....
  - see patterns of dots
  - use sun as point of reference

Time Limit: 3 min. 30 sec.

The White Ant

White ants are more commonly known as termites. They were given the name white ants because they look a little like ants; however, their diets and lifestyles are completely different. Termites mostly feed on dead plants and trees, and they are considered pests in parts of the world where people use wood to build houses. They can also cause a lot of damage to farmers' crops. On the other hand, they are very useful animals in that they recycle a lot of dead trees and plants back into the ecosystem. Because they eat dead trees and plants, they often nourish living parts of forests with their mineral-rich feces.

2 ➜ Termites are similar in size and social habits to regular ants, but that is where the similarities end. They are softer, whiter, shorter legged, fatter, and much slower than ants. Surprisingly, they belong to the same species as praying mantises and cockroaches. Termites use parts of their mouths to bite into dead wood, so their teeth are quite strong. They usually live inside dark nests and tunnels, and they only leave their homes to make new tunnels or nests to live in or to find food.

White ants are highly social in that they live in colonies of several hundred to several million individuals. They cooperate with one another to find and gather the food not only that they need but that the colony as a whole requires. They are also highly organized according to what job or task each one must perform for the colony. Most termites are workers; however, there are also soldiers, male ants that are responsible just for reproduction, and queens that lay eggs.

4 ➜ In some parts of the world, white ants create enormous nests that eventually become mounds which can tower into the sky. In many African countries, the landscape is scattered with these gigantic piles which are sometimes as high as six meters. Termites tend to build straight upward rather than horizontally. Some scientists believe they do this to create better air circulation inside their big nests. With improved air circulation, the temperature inside stays almost the same all day long regardless of the outside temperature. This is important because if the temperature changed a lot, then many of the termite eggs could die before they hatched. There are also complex tunnels inside the mounds that allow termites to do their work more easily and in more organized ways. Most tunnels are used for a specific job, and termites always seem to know which tunnel to use and which way to go when they have a specific job to do. In some ways, white ants seem smarter than people.

📖 Words & Phrases

mostly adv mainly; chiefly
pest n a harmful insect; a nuisance
nourish v to enrich
feces n waste; manure
social adj enjoying the company of others
colony n a group
cooperate v to work together
as a whole phr in general

task n a job; a duty
reproduction n procreation; generation
enormous adj huge; gigantic
circulation n a flow; a movement
regardless of phr irrespective of; nonetheless
hatch v to come out; to break open
mound n a large pile

1 According to paragraph 2, which of the following are true of termites when compared to ants? *To receive credit, you must select TWO answers.*

(A) They can move faster.   (B) Their bodies are softer.

(C) They show more sociability.   (D) They have shorter legs.

2 According to paragraph 4, why do termites build nests straight up?

(A) They are unable to build nests horizontally.

(B) They can build larger nests this way.

(C) It helps them improve the air quality in their nests.

(D) Scientists are not sure why they do it.

Mastering the Question Type

3 Which of the following best expresses the essential information in the first highlighted sentence? *Incorrect* answer choices change the meaning in important ways or leave out essential information.

(A) Termites have strong teeth for biting into dead wood.

(B) Termites' teeth have evolved to be strong over the years.

(C) Termites' teeth become stronger when they bite into dead wood.

(D) Termites that bite dead wood have stronger teeth than those which do not.

4 Which of the following best expresses the essential information in the second highlighted sentence? *Incorrect* answer choices change the meaning in important ways or leave out essential information.

(A) Six-meter-high termite nests are found in every country in Africa.

(B) Gigantic piles of termites that are six meters high may be seen in Africa.

(C) It is possible to see high termite nests in many African countries.

(D) African termites build very high nests in all the countries there.

Summary Note   Fill in the blanks with the appropriate words.

The White Ant

• Commonly called ❶ ....
  – look like ants but are very different

• Characteristics
  – eat dead plants and trees
  – damage homes and farmers' crops
  – help ❷ ....

• Different from ants
  – softer, whiter, ❸ ...., fatter, and slower
  – belong to the praying mantis and cockroach family
  – have very strong teeth

• Types of white ants
  – workers, soldiers, males for ❹ ...., and queens

Read the following passage and answer the questions.

Time Limit: 3 min. 30 sec.

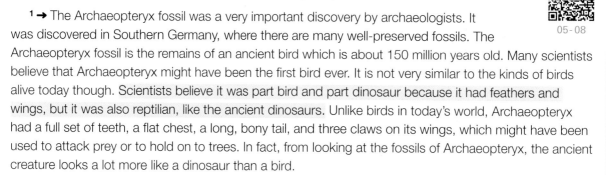

The Archaeopteryx Fossil

[1] ➡ The Archaeopteryx fossil was a very important discovery by archaeologists. It was discovered in Southern Germany, where there are many well-preserved fossils. The Archaeopteryx fossil is the remains of an ancient bird which is about 150 million years old. Many scientists believe that Archaeopteryx might have been the first bird ever. It is not very similar to the kinds of birds alive today though. Scientists believe it was part bird and part dinosaur because it had feathers and wings, but it was also reptilian, like the ancient dinosaurs. Unlike birds in today's world, Archaeopteryx had a full set of teeth, a flat chest, a long, bony tail, and three claws on its wings, which might have been used to attack prey or to hold on to trees. In fact, from looking at the fossils of Archaeopteryx, the ancient creature looks a lot more like a dinosaur than a bird.

A big debate amongst scientists is what Archaeopteryx used its feathers for. Some scientists suggest they were used to control their body temperature while others believe that they were used for flight. This is a very important question for scientists because they want to know how animals first started to fly. There are two theories about the origin of flight and about what Archaeopteryx used its feathers for. The first argument is called trees-down; this is the theory that ancient birds used their feathers to glide down to the ground from trees much like how flying squirrels do today. The other argument is called ground-up; this is the theory that ancient birds lived on the ground and used their feathers to help them make long leaps into trees whenever they needed to. For example, if they needed to get away from predators, then they could jump into the trees from a great distance and hold on to them with their claws.

[3] ➡ Scientists are curious as to why ancient birds stroked their wings like modern birds. They believe it might be related to the way that some kinds of dinosaurs used their strong forearms to grab downward and to hold on to their prey. If Archaeopteryx did this, then it might have learned that it could also use its strong forearms to flap its wings and to stay in the air for longer periods of time. Over millions of years, animals that were related to Archaeopteryx might have been able to stay in the air for longer and longer until they could finally fly like modern birds.

📖 Words & Phrases

fossil [n] the preserved remains of an animal
archaeologist [n] a scholar who studies the societies and people of the past
ancient [adj] very old
reptilian [adj] relating to reptiles, such as snakes and lizards
debate [n] a discussion; a controversy
origin [n] the beginning
argument [n] reason; argumentation
glide [v] to fly or move in a smooth way
get away [phr] to run away
curious [adj] inquisitive
leap [n] a long jump
flap [v] to flutter; to beat wings

1 According to paragraph 1, Archaeopteryx used the claws on its wings for

    Ⓐ flying   Ⓑ grabbing things

    Ⓒ defensive purposes   Ⓓ fishing

2 According to paragraph 3, why do scientists want to know why ancient birds stroked their wings?

    Ⓐ They will be able to find out about the birds' mating habits.

    Ⓑ They might be able to understand more about evolution.

    Ⓒ They will be able to learn when animals first learned how to fly.

    Ⓓ They will learn the secret to how Archaeopteryx could fly for so long.

3 Which of the following best expresses the essential information in the first highlighted sentence? *Incorrect* answer choices change the meaning in important ways or leave out essential information.

    Ⓐ Scientists think Archaeopteryx was created when a bird and a dinosaur mated with each other, giving it characteristics of both.

    Ⓑ Since Archaeopteryx had feathers but was reptilian, scientists think it was a cross between a bird and a dinosaur.

    Ⓒ Archaeopteryx had feathers like a bird and was also reptilian, so this makes scientists believe it was an ancient dinosaur.

    Ⓓ Many scientists believe that the ancient dinosaurs were both part bird and part dinosaur.

4 Which of the following best expresses the essential information in the second highlighted sentence? *Incorrect* answer choices change the meaning in important ways or leave out essential information.

    Ⓐ Archaeopteryx's first flight and the purpose of its feathers can be explained in two ways.

    Ⓑ Two theories perfectly describe the uses of Archaeopteryx's feathers and flight origins.

    Ⓒ Scientists are not sure how Archaeopteryx learned to fly or how it used its feathers.

    Ⓓ The great mysteries of Archaeopteryx are the use of its feathers and how it learned to fly.

Summary Note   **Fill in the blanks with the appropriate words.**

The Archaeopteryx Fossil

- Remains of ancient bird found in ❶ _____

- Characteristics
  - about ❷ _____ years old
  - maybe first bird ever
  - was part bird and part dinosaur

- Don't know the use of feathers
  - some think to control ❸ _____
  - others think to fly

- Theories on flight origins
  - trees-down → used feathers to ❹ _____ from trees
  - ground-up → used feathers to leap into trees

Exercise 4 Read the following passage and answer the questions.

Time Limit: 3 min. 40 sec.

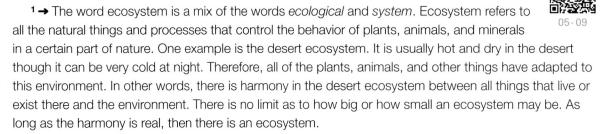

Ecosystems

1 ➜ The word ecosystem is a mix of the words *ecological* and *system*. Ecosystem refers to all the natural things and processes that control the behavior of plants, animals, and minerals in a certain part of nature. One example is the desert ecosystem. It is usually hot and dry in the desert though it can be very cold at night. Therefore, all of the plants, animals, and other things have adapted to this environment. In other words, there is harmony in the desert ecosystem between all things that live or exist there and the environment. There is no limit as to how big or how small an ecosystem may be. As long as the harmony is real, then there is an ecosystem.

Ecosystems have become an important issue in modern politics and amongst environmental groups because many of the world's ecosystems are being destroyed. In recent years, representatives from 175 countries—almost every country in the world—signed an international agreement called the Convention on Biological Diversity. This convention states that nations and individuals should protect ecosystems and natural living areas and try to maintain the populations of plants and animals that exist in all ecosystems. This convention mentions that all parts of an ecosystem work together in harmony and as a whole, so an ecosystem is like a unit or one body. If a part of a body is cut off or killed, then there is a good chance that the entire body will die or stop working properly. When any part of an ecosystem is destroyed, it is likely that the ecosystem will be destroyed or will stop working properly.

3 ➜ It is important to learn about how the harmony or balance is maintained in an ecosystem. The balance is maintained through many different interactions between the various parts of an ecosystem. For example, when there are too many mosquitoes in a forest, then frogs eat plenty of them. Because frogs eat a lot, they tend to be healthier, and thus they have more babies. But then there are too many frogs, so other animals start to eat more frogs. The cycle repeats itself over and over until there is harmony in the ecosystem. There are some plants and animals that help one another survive more easily. Insects like termites break down dead trees and return nutrients to the soil. This makes the soil richer, and plants can grow more easily in the soil. There are millions of things that happen to maintain the balance or harmony in an ecosystem. But when one part of the ecosystem dies because of what humans do to the environment, then there may be terrible consequences for the ecosystem.

📖 Words & Phrases

adapt to `phr` to get used to; to get accustomed to

limit `n` a boundary; a constraint

representative `n` a delegate

convention `n` an agreement; a pact

diversity `n` variety

maintain `v` to keep constant or steady

state `v` to declare; to write; to say

destroy `v` to kill; to eliminate

properly `adv` correctly; appropriately

interaction `n` a communication

various `adj` different; diverse

break down `phr` to decompose; to disintegrate

nutrient `n` a substance that helps life to grow

soil `n` the top layers of the ground

consequence `n` a result; an aftereffect

1   According to paragraph 1, which of the following is true of the desert?

    Ⓐ It is always hot in the desert.

    Ⓑ Not every plant has adapted to life in the desert.

    Ⓒ Plants and animals live in harmony with the desert.

    Ⓓ Ecosystems are often limited by their size.

2   According to paragraph 3, how is balance in an ecosystem maintained?

    Ⓐ Animals must work within their species to maintain balance.

    Ⓑ Humans must lend a helping hand to affect an ecosystem positively.

    Ⓒ The birth and death cycles must repeat several times before harmony is achieved.

    Ⓓ Various animals and plants must interact with one another.

Mastering the Question Type

3   Which of the following best expresses the essential information in the first highlighted sentence? *Incorrect* answer choices change the meaning in important ways or leave out essential information.

    Ⓐ Politicians are combining with environmental groups to help save the world's ecosystems.

    Ⓑ Since the world's ecosystems are being destroyed, environmental groups are gaining more importance in modern politics.

    Ⓒ Both politicians and environmental groups are concerned with ecosystems since many are being ruined.

    Ⓓ The issue of the destruction of ecosystems is often debated by environmental groups in the political arena.

4   Which of the following best expresses the essential information in the second highlighted sentence? *Incorrect* answer choices change the meaning in important ways or leave out essential information.

    Ⓐ Without plants and animals, ecosystems could not survive.

    Ⓑ Some plants and animals work together to ensure their survival.

    Ⓒ The presence of plants and animals makes survival easier.

    Ⓓ Plants and animals always try to help one another survive more easily.

Summary Note   **Fill in the blanks with the appropriate words.**

Ecosystems

- All things and processes that control behavior of ❶ _____ in one area
  - everything adapts to ecosystem
  - must live ❷ _____ with others

- Are important to environment
  - many ecosystems being ❸ _____
  - countries and environmental groups trying to protect them

- Must learn how to maintain harmony
  - plants and animals help each other survive
  - many things happen to ❹ _____

Exercise 5 Read the following passage and answer the questions.

Time Limit: 3 min. 40 sec.

Dolphin Intelligence

05-10

Many scientists believe dolphins are highly intelligent creatures because dolphins have large brains, show intelligent behavior, and are creative. All of these factors make dolphins very compelling animals for scientists to study. Some scientists believe that by studying dolphins, they can learn how humans became such intelligent animals.

Dolphins' brains are quite large compared to other animals. In fact, their brains are bigger than humans' once their weight is taken into consideration. However, when one looks at the weight of the brain compared to the overall body size, then humans have slightly larger brains. Compared to chimpanzees, which are also considered intelligent animals and which many people believe are related to humans, a bottle-nosed dolphin's brain is four times as large. One part of the brain, the cerebral cortex, is forty percent larger in dolphins than in humans. This is an area of the brain where many scientists believe that much complex thinking occurs.

3 ➡ The complex behavior of dolphins shows that they are very intelligent. For example, they usually swim in small groups of six to twelve individuals. Researchers believe that dolphins can recognize one another in their groups. Some scientists in Scotland have shown that two or three dolphins often make strong bonds with one another, which is similar to humans making close friendships. In addition, dolphins work together as a unit to help one another survive and live well. When a shark approaches, dolphins move together at the exact same time to avoid the threat. Some scientists even believe they make clicking sounds to warn one another of danger. They appear to work well together and are always aware of their surroundings, which is not true of most humans.

4 ➡ Dolphins are also exceptional because of their creativity. An American scientist named Karen Pryor performed an experiment on captive dolphins to learn how creative they are. The dolphins had been taught tricks, but Pryor wanted to see if she could make them act creatively. For instance, if they performed their tricks in an original way, they were rewarded with extra fish. When the dolphins performed the same trick that they had done before, they were not rewarded. The dolphins learned after a while that they would be rewarded for doing original tricks, so they started doing more and more original and creative ones. Pryor measured the amount of time it took the dolphins to learn what was wanted of them. Afterward, she conducted an experiment in which people were taught simple tricks and then were rewarded for doing the tricks originally. Interestingly, it took the humans about the same amount of time as it took the dolphins to learn what was wanted of them.

📖 **Words & Phrases**

overall adj total; complete

complex adj complicated; intricate

creative adj original; imaginative; inventive

cerebral cortex n a part of the brain

recognize v to know; to identify

bond n a connection; a tie

threat n a danger; a risk

be aware of phr to notice; to know about

exceptional adj extraordinary; special; unusual

captive adj confined; caged

reward v to recompense

extra adj additional; more

measure v to assess; to quantify

surroundings n an environment; a location

1   According to paragraph 3, what do dolphins do when a shark approaches?

     (A) They attack the shark in conjunction.

     (B) They flee in separate directions.

     (C) They move simultaneously to avoid it.

     (D) They act differently on each occasion.

2   According to paragraph 4, what did Karen Pryor do?

     (A) She conducted experiments on dolphin creativity.

     (B) She wrote a book about how humans and dolphins learn creativity.

     (C) She studied dolphins in the wild.

     (D) She created a number of new tricks for dolphins to perform.

Mastering the Question Type

3   Which of the following best expresses the essential information in the first highlighted sentence?
Incorrect answer choices change the meaning in important ways or leave out essential information.

     (A) A dolphin's cerebral cortex comprises forty percent of its brain.

     (B) Humans have larger cerebral cortexes but smaller brains than dolphins.

     (C) Forty percent of dolphins have larger cerebral cortexes than humans.

     (D) A dolphin's cerebral cortex is almost one and a half times as large as a human's.

4   Which of the following best expresses the essential information in the second highlighted sentence?
Incorrect answer choices change the meaning in important ways or leave out essential information.

     (A) Humans learned in about the same amount of time what the dolphins wanted them to do.

     (B) It is interesting that both humans and dolphins spent a similar amount of time learning certain tasks.

     (C) Dolphins were, interestingly enough, somewhat quicker than humans at learning what they were supposed to do.

     (D) Humans took the same amount of time to accomplish the tasks as dolphins did.

Summary Note   Fill in the blanks with the appropriate words.

Dolphin Intelligence

- Very intelligent creatures
  - have ❶ _____
  - can learn about humans by studying dolphins

- Brains → weigh more than humans'
  - ❷ _____ is forty percent larger than in humans

- Exhibit complex behavior
  - ❸ _____ for protection
  - develop friendships with other dolphins
  - make clicking sounds as warnings
  - engage in ❹ _____ → can create new tricks on their own; take same amount of time as humans

Silicon

05-11

¹ ➜ Silicon is a very important element similar to carbon and is found almost everywhere on the planet. The Earth's crust is more than one-quarter silicon, which makes it the second most abundant element in the world. Silicon does not exist alone. It is contained inside minerals like clay, sand, and rocks. When silicon is taken from rocks, sand, and other minerals, it has a dark gray color and looks metallic. It is similar to glass in that it can be broken or chipped easily. Significantly, it can conduct electricity and other forms of energy very easily, which is why it is used in the production of semiconductors.

² ➜ Silicon is important because it is used to make computers and various computer parts like semiconductors. It is not merely used to make semiconductors, however. It is used in many different ways. In fact, a lot more silicon is used to make aluminum than computer products. Actually, the silicon made for the aluminum in car parts represents about fifty-five percent of the world's use of the element. The second largest use is to make silicones, which are durable substances that are similar to plastic or rubber. The third largest use is to make semiconductors. In addition, there are hundreds of other products silicon is used in, making it one of the most used substances on the planet.

Silicon is taken from minerals by placing rocks, sand, clay, or other minerals into very hot furnaces. The furnaces are heated to more than 1,900°C, which causes the mineral that contains the silicon to burn away, leaving only liquefied silicon with small traces of carbon in it. The element collects at the bottom of the furnace and is then drained and cooled. When it is cool, the silicon turns solid. This form of silicon is ninety-eight percent pure with the remaining part carbon. This kind of silicon is fine for making car parts. But for making high-quality semiconductors, technicians must use nearly one-hundred-percent pure silicon. Therefore, the silicon used in computer parts must be purified.

The purification of silicon is a complex process. Scientists and technicians nowadays use a chemical process to purify silicon for use in computer parts. In one method, called the Siemens process, impure silicon is exposed to special gases by using high temperatures. In this process, the silicon molecules become much larger, making the carbon molecules tiny in comparison. The silicon subsequently becomes almost completely pure.

📖 Words & Phrases

element ⓝ a substance
abundant ⓐⁿⁿ plentiful; ample
contain ⓥ to include; to have
chip ⓥ to break off; to fragment
significantly ⓐⁿⁿ importantly
conduct ⓥ to carry; to transmit; to convey
represent ⓥ to account for; to equal
durable ⓐⁿⁿ strong; sturdy

furnace ⓝ an oven that can achieve very high temperatures
liquefy ⓥ to make or become liquid
trace ⓝ a small amount
drain ⓥ to flow out
purify ⓥ to make pure; to refine
expose ⓥ to uncover; to display
tiny ⓐⁿⁿ extremely small

1 According to paragraph 1, how much of the Earth's crust is silicon?

    Ⓐ Around ten percent   Ⓑ Around twenty-five percent

    Ⓒ Around fifty percent   Ⓓ Around seventy-five percent

2 According to paragraph 2, what is the primary commercial use of silicon?

    Ⓐ Making silicones

    Ⓑ Making semiconductors

    Ⓒ Building computers

    Ⓓ Making aluminum in car parts

Mastering the Question Type

3 Which of the following best expresses the essential information in the first highlighted sentence? *Incorrect* answer choices change the meaning in important ways or leave out essential information.

    Ⓐ Silicon can conduct electricity well, so it is sometimes found in semiconductors.

    Ⓑ People use silicon to make semiconductors because it is good at conducting energy, including electricity.

    Ⓒ Because silicon produces semiconductors, it is able to conduct electricity and other forms of energy.

    Ⓓ It is significant that the conduction of electricity enables silicon to produce semiconductors.

4 Which of the following best expresses the essential information in the second highlighted sentence? *Incorrect* answer choices change the meaning in important ways or leave out essential information.

    Ⓐ It takes almost pure silicon to make semiconductors of high quality.

    Ⓑ Technicians make high-quality semiconductors entirely from pure silicon.

    Ⓒ Without pure silicon, technicians cannot make high-quality semiconductors.

    Ⓓ The manufacture of silicon results in high-quality semiconductors.

📝 Summary Note   Fill in the blanks with the appropriate words.

Silicon

- Very important element
  - similar to ❶ ....
  - second most abundant element
  - is contained in many minerals
  - can ❷ .... easily

- Has many uses
  - used for computers and computer parts like semiconductors
  - makes ❸ .... for car parts
  - makes silicones

- Processing method
  - must be heated to ❹ .... Celsius
  - becomes liquid and collects in pools
  - when turns solid, can be used

Building Summary Skills

The following summaries are based on the passages you worked on earlier. Complete each of them by filling in the blanks with suitable words or phrases.

Exercise 1 Eye Variation Among Different Species

when they move	20/20 eyesight	compound eyes
monocular vision	hawks	

While humans consider _____ to be perfect, this is not true for members of the animal kingdom, which see in different ways. _____ can see extremely small objects from distances high in the sky. The kingfisher has _____, where it uses just one eye to see above and under the water. Frogs see things only _____. And bees have _____ that see everything as a mosaic of dots.

Exercise 2 The White Ant

six meters high	eat wood	social insects
termites	the mantis and cockroach family	

_____ are sometimes called white ants, but they are very different from ants. They are considered pests because they _____, which can bother humans. They do not resemble ants at all but are members of _____. They are _____ that live in communities of up to several million insects. They have enormous nests that can be up to _____.

Exercise 3 The Archaeopteryx Fossil

its feathers	a full set of teeth	Germany
three claws	150 million years ago	

An Archaeopteryx fossil was first found in _____. It was a bird that lived over _____. It did not resemble modern birds, having _____, a flat chest, a long, bony tail, and _____ on its wings. There are a couple of theories that attempt to explain how Archaeopteryx used _____. Scientists want to know about this so that they can learn how birds first learned to fly.

Exercise 4 | Ecosystems

environmentalists	caring about ecosystems	achieve harmony
plants, animals, and minerals	the Convention of Biological Diversity	

The ecosystem refers to all natural things and processes that control the behavior of
_____ in a certain part of nature. All living things must _____
to survive in their own ecosystem. _____ and countries are becoming more involved
in _____. Many countries signed _____ recently. It is
important to know about the ecosystem in order to keep it functioning properly.

Exercise 5 | Dolphin Intelligence

humans and chimpanzees	Karen Pryor	their large brains
at about the same rate as humans	predators attack	

Scientists believe dolphins are intelligent because of _____ and ability to be creative.
In fact, dolphins have larger brains than _____. They form bonds like friendship, and
this helps when _____. _____, a scientist, experimented
with them and discovered that they have the ability to engage in creative behavior. Dolphins can also learn tricks
_____.

Exercise 6 | Silicon

extreme temperatures	like semiconductors	to conduct electricity
aluminum parts	highly abundant and extremely common	

Silicon is a _____ element that can be found almost everywhere on the Earth. It has
many qualities, particularly its ability _____, which makes it ideal for manufacturing.
It has many different uses, including computers, computer parts _____, and
_____ in cars. It must be purified by heating it to _____.
After it hardens, it can be used to manufacture various items.

Biological Pest Control

05-12

Marigold flowers and cabbages

1 ➡ Many agriculturists have moved from chemical pesticides to biological pest control to control pests and diseases in their gardens and farms. Biological pest control is a method in which predatory animals and insects are introduced into an area so that they will hunt, kill, and eat parasitic pests that damage crops. Another form of biological pest control is to include various plants in gardens or fields that can naturally deter parasitic pests known to bring disease and destruction.

This style of pest and disease control takes into consideration the principles of organic gardening. Organic gardeners seek to minimize or eliminate the use of chemicals in their agricultural practices. Conventional practices which use chemicals are known to kill both harmful and useful garden life forms indiscriminately. But by using a holistic approach, gardeners are able to take advantage of the webs of interaction between different plants and animals in gardens.

3 ➡ It is believed that these practices increase the level of biodiversity in gardens, which furthers health altogether. This belief comes from the principle that increased biodiversity creates a sustainable ecosystem in which pests and diseases are not eliminated but are instead reduced to manageable levels. The goal of biological pest control in this respect is to create a system of checks and balances by which an agriculturist's ecosystem will operate in a self-sustaining manner, allowing it to thrive. This self-sustaining state can be described as equilibrium.

A good example of the damage that is caused to an ecosystem by chemical pesticides is when an area is sprayed to kill mosquitoes. When this is done, the pesticides also kill dragonflies. These insects are important biocontrol agents which capture and eat mosquitoes and their larvae. This kind of spraying often increases mosquito populations on a long-term basis since the dragonflies are not around to consume the incubating mosquito larvae.

5 ➡ An excellent biological control insect is the ladybug and its larvae. These insects hunt, kill, and consume many crop-destroying insect pests such as aphids, greenflies, mites, and caterpillars. Many agriculturists introduce these helpful insects to their gardens to protect their plants. They even plant rows of bushes called beetle banks where ladybugs can live and breed to create larger populations. These useful insects can be purchased at most gardening shops.

6 → Some plants can also be used to protect gardens and crops. These special biological pest control plants can be helpful in several different ways. Regulatory plants can mask crop plants from pests by being planted nearby or mixed with crop plants. This confuses pests and draws them away from the important crop plants. The plants can also produce olfactory inhibitors, which change the smells that draw pests, sending them signals through their olfactory glands that drive them away from important plant crops. These plants might also serve as breeding areas for helpful insects.

Some such biocontrol plants are basil, which drives away flies and mosquitoes, catnip, which repels flea beetles, and garlic, which deters the Japanese beetle. One of the most useful of these plants is marigold, which drives away Mexican beetles, slugs, and other harmful pests. When these plants are used, they work together in conjunction with helpful predatory insects to create a state of stasis in which the levels of harmful pest damage are minimized without the use of any chemicals. Biological pest control has proven itself to be very successful economically. As tests have been done over the years, a benefit-to-cost ratio of 32:1 has been attributed to biological pest control while the average chemical pesticide program returned a benefit-to-cost ratio of 13:1.

1   The word "deter" in the passage is closest in meaning to
    Ⓐ encourage
    Ⓑ prevent
    Ⓒ kill
    Ⓓ weaken

2   According to paragraph 1, what is biological pest control?
    Ⓐ A method of killing insects based on organic gardening
    Ⓑ Using biological weapons in order to kill pests
    Ⓒ Destroying pest populations in their larval stages
    Ⓓ A way that swiftly eliminates all pests from gardens

3   The word "it" in the passage refers to
    Ⓐ biological pest control
    Ⓑ a system of checks and balances
    Ⓒ an agriculturalist's ecosystem
    Ⓓ a self-sustaining manner

4 Why does the author mention "equilibrium" in paragraph 3?

   Ⓐ To explain why most gardens have some pests

   Ⓑ To detail the methods needed to attain this state

   Ⓒ To argue in favor of using biological pest control methods

   Ⓓ To describe the ideal state of a garden

5 According to paragraph 5, which of the following is NOT a pest that the ladybug eliminates?

   Ⓐ Caterpillars

   Ⓑ Larvae

   Ⓒ Aphids

   Ⓓ Mites

6 The word "mask" in the passage is closest in meaning to

   Ⓐ separate

   Ⓑ distinguish

   Ⓒ disguise

   Ⓓ prevent

7 According to paragraph 6, which of the following is NOT true of the ways pest control plants protect crop plants from harmful insects?

   Ⓐ They mislead pests about the location of crop plants.

   Ⓑ They emit certain smells to confuse pests.

   Ⓒ They help useful insects to increase in number.

   Ⓓ They paralyze pests' olfactory glands.

8 Which of the following best expresses the essential information in the highlighted sentence? *Incorrect* answer choices change the meaning in important ways or leave out essential information.

   Ⓐ The most valuable plant for driving away pests is the marigold.

   Ⓑ Marigolds are useful for getting rid of various pests.

   Ⓒ If marigolds are planted somewhere, Mexican beetles and other pests will not live there.

   Ⓓ Mexican beetles, slugs, and other pests will be killed when marigolds are planted.

05-13

Tundra Vegetation

Winter landscape in the Brooks Range in Alaska's tundra

¹ ➜ Tundra is classified as an area where layers of soil beneath the surface are permanently frozen. While the surface thaws in the short summer season, the subsoil remains in a state of permafrost. These soil and temperature conditions determine the type of vegetation which is able to grow on the tundra.

Strong winds sweep over the tundra, and rainfall is rare. Most precipitation occurs in the form of snow. Tundra regions experience comparable levels of precipitation to desert climates. During summer, the permafrost thaws enough so that some plants are able to grow and reproduce. But the subsoil under the surface stays frozen, and water cannot sink below it. The trapped water creates lakes and marshes in the summer months.

During the summer months in tundra regions, the temperature becomes high enough to melt snow on the surface but not ice underground. Due to the low temperatures and the short growing season, trees rarely grow there. The separation between tundra and forested regions is defined by the natural barrier of trees called the timberline. The most common types of vegetation in tundra regions are grasses, mosses, and lichens. These forms of plant life are capable of surviving the long winter months of frigid temperatures and growing quickly during the short summer growing season.

One definitive characteristic of tundra is a very low level of biodiversity. No more than 1,700 species of flora and forty-eight kinds of land mammals can be found in these regions. Only in the summer months, when the upper layers of permafrost thaw just enough to create marshlands, do thousands of insect species populate the tundra.

⁵ ➜ Tundra exists in various areas around the world. Most of it is found in the extreme northern and southern polar regions as well as in areas at a high elevation. These regions can be divided into Arctic, Antarctic, and alpine types, and each has its own distinct characteristics.

Arctic tundra is a large area of stark landscape north of the taiga belt in the far Northern Hemisphere. It stays completely frozen for most of the year. It includes northern Lapland in addition to vast portions of northern Russia and Canada. It is impossible for trees to grow there. The land is often bare and rocky. **1** Lichens and moss grow on these rocks while small tufts of grass spring up sporadically in between the boulders and stones. **2** Only a few hearty mammal species are able to maintain heavy populations. **3** Some of these are caribou, arctic foxes, polar bears, lemmings, and musk oxen. **4**

7 → The Antarctic tundra occurs on the opposite side of the Earth as the Arctic tundra. It can be found on this icy continent as well as on several Antarctic and sub-Antarctic islands. The rocky soil of the Antarctic Peninsula is one of the only regions on the continent that is capable of sustaining life. Several hundred species of lichens, mosses, and liverworts can be found there. Many terrestrial and aquatic algae species are also able to thrive. There are only two species of flowering plants to be found, the Antarctic hair grass and Antarctic pearlwort. This inhospitable tundra region also supports mammals such as seals as well as penguins.

Alpine tundra can be found at high elevations on mountains around the world. This type of tundra cannot support tree growth. Some lower regions of Alpine tundra do not retain permafrost as snow and ice drain away down mountain slopes. Animals like the Kea parrot, marmot, mountain goats, chinchilla, and pika can be found in Alpine tundra areas. But different species of animals and vegetation are found in the many Alpine tundra regions around the planet.

9   According to paragraph 1, tundra is considered
   Ⓐ the area immediately under the earth
   Ⓑ land with frozen areas directly under the soil
   Ⓒ a place with extremely cold winters and summers
   Ⓓ an area where no vegetation grows

10   The word "it" in the passage refers to
   Ⓐ the permafrost
   Ⓑ the subsoil
   Ⓒ the surface
   Ⓓ water

11   The word "frigid" in the passage is closest in meaning to
   Ⓐ moderate
   Ⓑ chilly
   Ⓒ freezing
   Ⓓ temperate

12 Which of the following best expresses the essential information in the highlighted sentence? *Incorrect* answer choices change the meaning in important ways or leave out essential information.

Ⓐ During summer, the entire permafrost thaws to make swampy areas, thereby attracting thousands of insects.

Ⓑ Countless insects go to the tundra in summer to live on the permafrost.

Ⓒ Various insects live in the tundra in summer after marshlands are created by melting permafrost.

Ⓓ The permafrost thaws to create marshlands in months other than summer, which attracts insects.

13 According to paragraph 5, which of the following is NOT a type of tundra?

Ⓐ Polar

Ⓑ Antarctic

Ⓒ Arctic

Ⓓ Alpine

14 The word "sustaining" in the passage is closest in meaning to

Ⓐ engendering

Ⓑ creating

Ⓒ supporting

Ⓓ developing

15 According to paragraph 7, why is the Antarctic Peninsula unique?

Ⓐ It is one of the few places in Antarctica where life exists.

Ⓑ Many rare mosses live in that part of Antarctica.

Ⓒ Seals and penguins make their summer homes in the region.

Ⓓ It is the only tundra in the world that supports a large amount of plant life.

16 Look at the four squares [■] that indicate where the following sentence could be added to the passage.

There is almost nothing for animals to eat there.

Where would the sentence best fit?

Vocabulary Check-Up

A Choose the words with the closest meanings to the highlighted words.

1 The furnace in the factory was turned up as high as possible.

   (A) temperature

   (B) oven

   (C) assembly line

   (D) kiln

2 A various number of animals live in Africa.

   (A) unique

   (B) exceptional

   (C) small

   (D) diverse

3 The cat prepared to leap onto the table.

   (A) run

   (B) crawl

   (C) jump

   (D) climb

4 There was a hitch in the program, which caused a two-hour delay.

   (A) bug

   (B) problem

   (C) issue

   (D) setback

5 Mr. Baker had a huge mound of files sitting on his desk for him to read through.

   (A) folder

   (B) hill

   (C) assortment

   (D) pile

6 Today, many countries are trying to develop sustainable energy sources.

   (A) renewable

   (B) winnable

   (C) terrible

   (D) damaging

7 Some animals can actually help nourish the soil with various nutrients.

   (A) enrich

   (B) enroll

   (C) enliven

   (D) encroach

8 The soldier suddenly perceived the enemy troops approaching from the rear.

   (A) contacted

   (B) shot

   (C) noticed

   (D) destroyed

9 The paleontologists discovered the ancient fossils while they were out digging.

   (A) individual

   (B) old

   (C) strange

   (D) worn-out

10 The company managed to retain its best workers and kept its rival from stealing then.

   (A) hire

   (B) promote

   (C) refrain

   (D) keep

B Match the words with the correct definitions.

1 cerebral cortex •   • Ⓐ the ossified remains of an animal

2 criterion •   • Ⓑ to die from not eating food

3 fossil •   • Ⓒ an area; a location

4 reptilian •   • Ⓓ waste; manure

5 starve •   • Ⓔ to turn into a flowing substance like water

6 handicapped •   • Ⓕ a part of the brain

7 surroundings •   • Ⓖ having the characteristics of animals like snakes and lizards

8 liquefy •   • Ⓗ extraordinary; special; unusual

9 feces •   • Ⓘ unable to do something as well as most people or things can

10 exceptional •   • Ⓙ a standard or basis for something

PART II

Making Inferences

In this part, the reading comprehension questions include rhetorical purpose, inference, and insert text. The learning objectives of these comprehension questions are to understand the rhetorical function of a statement or paragraph, the logic of the passage, and the strongly implied ideas in the text.

06 Rhetorical Purpose

◤ Overview

Introduction

Rhetorical Purpose questions ask you to understand why and how the author uses a particular piece of information in a passage. This information can be used to argue, define, explain, or compare ideas. Because this type of question usually focuses on the logical development of the passage, you need to figure out how a word, a phrase, or information relates to the rest of the passage.

Question Types

➤ The author discusses "X" in paragraph in order to
➤ Why does the author mention "X"?
➤ The author uses "X" as an example of

Useful Tips

• Read the question first and then recognize the author's purpose immediately by scanning the specific phrases or paragraphs.
• Focus on the logical links between sentences and paragraphs, not on the overall organization of the passage.
• Familiarize yourself with words or phrases with rhetorical functions like *to illustrate, to criticize, to explain, to contrast, to compare,* and *to note.*

Q In the passage, why does the author mention "elongated toes"?

  Ⓐ To point out why condors are able to swim

  Ⓑ To explain the uses of the toes for hunting

  Ⓒ To differentiate the condor from most vultures

  Ⓓ To show how they help condors fly

The California Condor

06-01

    The California condor is a large American bird that is related to vultures and is the largest bird in North America that flies over land. There are very few of these condors left in the world. In fact, nowadays, they can only be found in the western coastal mountains of the United States. Like vultures, condors are scavengers, which means that they eat animals that are already dead and not animals that they kill themselves. California condors have a wingspan of as much as 9.2 feet and can weigh up to thirty-one pounds, making them one of the largest birds in North America. Adult California condors are black all over except under the wings. An unusual aspect of these birds is that they have elongated toes, which help them walk. Most vultures do not have such toes.

☑ **Correct Answer**

The author mentions that condors have elongated toes and then adds that most vultures do not have them. So the correct answer is Ⓒ.

Basic Drill

Read the passages and answer the questions.

Drill 1

Social Grooming in Monkey Packs

06-02

Monkeys are highly social animals. A good example of this is the fact that they groom one another. Social grooming is a way in which animals that live close to each other can make bonds with other individuals. This is similar to the way that people make friendships. Social grooming can also be used as a way of apologizing to other monkeys or a way to avoid fighting. On top of that, it is a method that these animals use to maintain good hygiene. Because monkeys have thick fur, they often get a lot of insects, leaves, dirt, and twigs stuck on them. When other individuals groom them, they take out the dirt, insects, and other objects while making an important bond with that individual they have just groomed. These bonds are important in social life, just like friendships are important for people.

1 The author discusses "Social grooming" in order to

- Ⓐ illustrate that monkeys prefer to be clean
- Ⓑ demonstrate that monkeys do not like to fight
- Ⓒ show that monkeys can bond with others
- Ⓓ emphasize a disadvantage of thick fur

2 Why does the author mention "good hygiene" in the passage?

- Ⓐ To show one advantage of social grooming
- Ⓑ To compare it with social grooming
- Ⓒ To show that friendship is important to monkeys
- Ⓓ To explain why monkeys are often dirty

Drill 2

The Definition and Types of Social Groups

06-03

In sociology, a group is a collection of people or animals that are similar in some ways, that interact, that accept certain social responsibilities, and that have a common identity. According to this definition, human civilization could be considered a social group. In sociology, there are three kinds of social groups: primary, secondary and reference. Primary groups are small groups with very close relationships. Close friends and family are members of a primary group. Secondary groups are large groups whose relationships are formal or based upon certain social circumstances, such as those between schoolmates or work colleagues. Sometimes primary groups can be formed from secondary groups, like when schoolmates become friends. Reference groups are groups that have no real members but which individuals themselves think they belong to. For example, some people wear dark clothing and makeup and consider themselves to be "Goths" even though no such social group formally exists.

1 The author discusses "a group" in the passage in order to

- Ⓐ deduce that human civilization is one kind of social group
- Ⓑ describe how people rely on a common identity
- Ⓒ show that there are three kinds of social groups
- Ⓓ prove that certain groups do not need to be formally recognized

2 In the passage, the author uses "Goths" as an example of

- Ⓐ a primary group
- Ⓑ a secondary group
- Ⓒ a reference group
- Ⓓ a formal social group

Literary Criticism

06-04

Literary criticism is the study, discussion, and interpretation of literature. Nowadays, most literary critics use some form of literary theory to appraise novels, poems, and plays. Literary theory is based on certain philosophical ideas that critics utilize when they discuss certain books or poems. These philosophical ideas might include Marxism, feminism, or realism. Most professional literary critics are university professors or reporters who write for literary magazines. An example of a Marxist literary critic might be a university professor who examines *The Little Prince* based upon social theories created by the economist and philosopher Karl Marx. Therefore, he would argue that all of the characters that the Little Prince meets in his travels act greedily because humans are basically all greedy. This is a simplified concept of Karl Marx.

1 In the passage, why does the author mention "Marxism, feminism, or realism"?

   Ⓐ To argue that philosophical perspectives must be considered in literary criticism

   Ⓑ To name a few perspectives on which literary theory can be based

   Ⓒ To show what philosophical ideas professional critics study

   Ⓓ To prove that literary critics cannot discuss literature without philosophy

2 The author discusses "*The Little Prince*" in the passage in order to

   Ⓐ show how it can be interpreted from a Marxist perspective

   Ⓑ argue that it was written based on Marxist social theories

   Ⓒ describe how it was criticized by a Marxist professor

   Ⓓ explain Marxist philosophy in a simple way

Seanchai: Irish Storytellers

06-05

In ancient Ireland, before there were any books, there was a group of people called *seanchai*. *Seanchai* means "storyteller" in Irish Gaelic. These people earned money by traveling from village to village while telling stories. They often spoke about ancient Irish legends. Sometimes they just told stories that they had heard in the last village. Later, when the British occupied Ireland and made the Irish people speak English instead of Irish Gaelic, the *seanchai* continued to travel from town to town telling their stories in their native language. After a while, just speaking their language became more important than the stories themselves because it was a way of keeping the Irish language alive. Today, there are not many native Irish Gaelic speakers, but there are some in certain areas of the country. Gaelic is also taught in schools. The *seanchai* played a large part in the survival of the language.

1 In the passage, why does the author mention "ancient Irish legends"?

   Ⓐ To discuss when people started writing them down

   Ⓑ To focus on the language in which they were written

   Ⓒ To explain what some Irish storytellers told people

   Ⓓ To name some of the most popular ones

2 The author discusses "the British" in the passage in order to

   Ⓐ complain about the manner in which they treated the Irish

   Ⓑ describe how their actions made the *seanchai* important

   Ⓒ prove that they were responsible for preserving Irish Gaelic

   Ⓓ note the history between the British and the Irish

Exercises with Long Passages

Exercise 1 Read the following passage and answer the questions.

Time Limit: 3 min. 30 sec.

Prairie Dogs

06-06

   Prairie dogs are small rodents that live in the prairies of North America. They are highly social animals that live in families which typically consist of one male and two to four females. The prairies are large, flat lands with wild grass that grows everywhere. There, prairie dogs dig underground holes and tunnels in which they live. Small holes and tunnels are perfect for these rodents because they are long, skinny animals that grow, on average, twelve to sixteen inches long and are only about four inches tall. The tunnels that they build connect with one another, and prairie dogs often use the same tunnel system for twenty or thirty years.

   2 → Their tunnel systems are expansive. Within the shared tunnel complex, there are separate rooms for sleeping, eating, and babysitting. They can span a large distance and can go as deep as thirty-three feet beneath the ground. The tunnels also help protect prairie dogs from predators. Around the holes of their tunnels, prairie dogs often pull out the grass and weeds so that they can see if any predators are coming. If they see one approaching, they make a high-pitched call to warn the other members of their family. In fact, some scientists believe that they use specific calls for each kind of predator that they encounter. After the call, all members of the family that are above ground immediately dive into their tunnels, where they are safe from danger.

   Farmers regard prairie dogs as pests and try to kill as many of them as they can to prevent farm-related problems. This is particularly true with farm machinery and cattle. Prairie dog tunnels weaken the ground, so the heavy tractors used to plough it are often damaged, and cattle, which are prone to stepping into prairie dogs' holes, are likely to suffer broken legs.

   4 → Nevertheless, experts believe that prairie dogs are vital to the prairie ecosystem. They are an important prey species for the many eagles, hawks, and foxes that hunt prairie dogs as their main source of food. Wild animals like bison and deer prefer to graze on the prairies where prairie dogs live because the wild grasses tend to be both healthier and lusher, and the prairie dogs' tunnel systems soften the ground after it becomes compact as a result of cows' grazing. Furthermore, the tunnel systems allow rainwater to channel deep into the ground. This channeling is important because it helps prevent floods and erosion of the prairie soil.

📖 Words & Phrases

rodent [n] a small mammal which has sharp front teeth, such as a rat, a mouse, and a squirrel

social [adj] living in groups

skinny [adj] very thin; lean

expansive [adj] spreading over a large area

separate [adj] divided; unconnected

span [v] to spread out

predator [n] an animal that preys on others

weed [n] a wild plant; an unwanted plant

warn [v] to alert; to caution

specific [adj] particular; special

encounter [v] to come across; to meet

regard [v] to consider

plough [v] to turn up the soil

be prone to-V [phr] be apt to-V; be liable to-V

nevertheless [adv] however; nonetheless; in spite of that

expert [n] a specialist; a professional; an authority

vital [adj] essential; necessary

graze [v] to browse; to eat grass

lush [adj] green; verdant

compact [adj] dense; compressed

erosion [n] the process of wearing away

1 According to the passage, which of the following is NOT true of the tunnel systems of the prairie dog?

(A) They can be more than thirty feet deep in the ground.

(B) They provide protection from enemies.

(C) They are used for more than twenty years.

(D) They consist of separate tunnels.

2 According to paragraph 4, farmers try to get rid of prairie dogs because

(A) they destroy crops   (B) they spread disease

(C) they undermine the ground   (D) they cause soil erosion

Mastering the Question Type

3 In paragraph 2, why does the author mention "separate rooms for sleeping, eating, and babysitting"?

(A) To show the complex nature of prairie dog tunnel systems

(B) To define the social nature of prairie dogs

(C) To emphasize that prairie dogs are assigned tasks

(D) To illustrate prairie dogs' family lives

4 In paragraph 4, the author uses "bison and deer" as examples of

(A) animals that destroy prairie dogs' tunnel systems

(B) animals that benefit from prairie dogs

(C) animals that compete with prairie dogs for food

(D) animals that prey on prairie dogs

Summary Note   Fill in the blanks with the appropriate words.

Prairie Dogs

- Characteristics
  - ❶ _____ living in North America
  - live in families of one male and two to four females
  - live on ❷ _____
  - homes are series of tunnels
- Prairie dog tunnels
  - very large system
  - protect prairie dogs from predators
  - can help warn others about coming predators
- Can damage ❸ _____ and injure cattle
- Importance to ecosystem
  - are food for many predators
  - tunnels ❹ _____ so grass grows better
  - tunnels let water into ground easier

Urbanization in Los Angeles

06-07

Urbanization is the increase in population over time or the increase in area of towns and cities. Critics argue that urbanization has created many problems and has dramatically decreased people's quality of life in the cities. In the United States, urbanization has had a largely negative impact on the economies, societies, and ecosystems surrounding towns and cities. In particular, the city of Los Angeles in California has had a lot of problems with urbanization. It has led to a degradation of the city and an increase in ghettos.

2 ➡ The city of Los Angeles is the largest city in the United States in terms of the area that it occupies. There, the negative effects of urbanization include urban sprawl. Urban sprawl is the unplanned, uncontrolled spreading of development in and around a large city. Critics of Los Angeles point out that urban sprawl is responsible for many ugly and unsafe buildings and neighborhoods that have resulted in heavy amounts of pollution and violent crime. Los Angeles city planners were in such a hurry to increase the size of the city that they quickly and cheaply constructed its buildings and neighborhoods, thereby creating a series of unattractive neighborhoods and environments. As a consequence, the attitudes of the residents have become largely negative as a reflection of their unattractive environments. Negative attitudes lead to negative behavior, such as the forming of violent gangs and the increased use of drugs and alcohol. Furthermore, as the number of people living within each neighborhood increases, so do the pollution and the unsanitary living conditions that characterize those city neighborhoods.

3 ➡ Economically, the process of urbanization was intended to create economic opportunities for all people who move to the cities. In the United States, urban planners felt that citizens would have access to better jobs, education, and markets. To a large extent, many American citizens have enjoyed these opportunities. But in cities like Los Angeles, space and houses became limited, which made certain communities very expensive to live in. Poor people could therefore not afford to live in nice communities, and many moved to areas known as ghettos. Usually, the people who live in ghettos do not have access to better education because they cannot afford it, and thus cannot get better jobs later in life. For people who live in ghettos, it is very hard to make better lives for themselves and to leave the area. This is perhaps the most negative aspect of urbanization.

📖 Words & Phrases

critic (n) an opponent; a dissenter; an objector
negative (adj) undesirable; harmful; damaging
impact (n) an effect
degradation (n) deterioration; decline
in terms of (phr) with respect to
occupy (v) to take up
sprawl (n) an extension
construct (v) to build; to put up
as a consequence (phr) as a result

resident (n) an inhabitant; a dweller
reflection (n) an echo; a mirror image
furthermore (adv) moreover; in addition
unsanitary (adj) unhygienic; unhealthy
have access to (phr) to approach
cannot afford (phr) not to be able to pay for
to a large extent (phr) to a large degree
aspect (n) a side; a facet

1 The word "dramatically" in the passage is closest in meaning to

    Ⓐ excitingly   Ⓑ vividly

    Ⓒ greatly   Ⓓ theatrically

2 According to paragraph 3, which of the following is NOT true of urbanization?

    Ⓐ It improved the living conditions of many Americans.

    Ⓑ It caused ghettos to form in the city of Los Angeles.

    Ⓒ It was supposed to create more opportunities to make money.

    Ⓓ It helped people in Los Angeles get better jobs and education.

3 The author discusses "The city of Los Angeles" in paragraph 2 in order to

    Ⓐ identify the city as a major source of pollution

    Ⓑ illustrate an example of random urbanization

    Ⓒ describe what urbanization is like

    Ⓓ show the reason why people are attracted to big cities

4 In paragraph 2, the author uses "violent gangs" as an example of

    Ⓐ a negative aspect of urbanization

    Ⓑ something that only affects Los Angeles

    Ⓒ the leading cause of murders in big cities

    Ⓓ groups that are being arrested by police

📝 Summary Note   **Fill in the blanks with the appropriate words.**

Urbanization in Los Angeles

- Characteristics
  - increase in population of city
  - has ❶ _____ on economy, society, and ecosystem of area

- Los Angeles
  - many negative effects from ❷ _____
  - ugly and unsafe buildings
  - pollution and violent crime
  - increase of gangs and use of drugs and alcohol
  - ❸ _____

- Economic effects
  - some have enjoyed better jobs and educations
  - many cities have created ghettoes
  - people cannot get ❹ _____
  - people cannot get good jobs
  - people cannot improve their lives

Read the following passage and answer the questions.

Time Limit: 3 min. 20 sec.

Neoclassical Theater

06-08

1 → Neoclassical theater was the most important form of theater from the sixteenth to the eighteenth century in Western Europe, especially in France. Elaborate scenery and costumes were very important in neoclassical theater, as were overacting and maintaining common themes and methods of acting. In neoclassical theater, the plots were similar and repetitive just like modern-day soap operas. They also tended to use a lot of farce and tragedy.

2 → Neoclassical theater developed in France during the sixteenth century, and it changed the way playwrights wrote their plays. It also changed methods of production and the way sets were designed. French neoclassical theater was based largely on unities; there were unity of time, unity of action, unity of place, and several others. In other words, French neoclassical dramatists wanted the time, place, and action of the play to be unified and to be more like real life. Therefore, according to the neoclassicists, there could not be a change of day in the play without a sunset and then a sunrise, just like in real life. Additionally, when the action in the play changed from one place to another, the background scenery had to be changed. Another important aspect of neoclassical theater was the use of farce, which is a way of making important situations or people seem ridiculous. The opposite of farce, tragedy, was also commonly used in neoclassical theater. Tragedy is a dramatic method in which people make sad situations seem even sadder.

3 → The three most popular neoclassical playwrights were Pierre Corneille, Jean Racine, and Molière. They all had different styles of writing and lived and worked in Paris at the same time. Parisian audiences loved watching the different styles of the playwrights and comparing the three. Corneille was the first to begin writing, and the content of his plays created a lot of controversy. His most famous play, *Le Cid*, written in 1637, was popular and controversial simply because it did not follow the established unities of neoclassical theater. To this day, critics argue about whether it should be classified as a neoclassical play. Unlike Corneille, Jean Racine tried to stick to the rules of neoclassical theater as much as possible. His most famous tragedy, *Andromache*, written in 1664, is perhaps the best example of neoclassical theater. Meanwhile, Molière was the king of farce and the most influential neoclassical playwright. His characters were used to depict real people, and he was interested in showing the reality of human weakness as much as possible.

📖 Words & Phrases

elaborate `adj` complicated; complex; detailed
maintain `v` to continue; to keep up
costume `n` an outfit; clothes
theme `n` a subject; a category
plot `n` a plan; an action
repetitive `adj` recurrent; happening again and again
soap opera `n` a popular television drama series; a serial
tend to-V `phr` be apt to-V
farce `n` a humorous play
tragedy `n` a serious and sad drama

unity `n` sameness; oneness; integrity
unify `v` to unite; to combine
ridiculous `adj` absurd
opposite `n` reverse; contrary
controversial `adj` disputed; debatable
established `adj` conventional; traditional
classify `v` to categorize; to sort
stick to `v` to stay with; to follow
influential `adj` powerful; important; significant

1 According to paragraph 2, which of the following is NOT true of neoclassical theater?

(A) It unified the time, place, and action of the play.

(B) It made use of both farce and tragedy as part of its repertoire.

(C) It caused playwrights to change their way of writing.

(D) It insisted that a play be performed within a day.

2 The word "depict" in the passage is closest in meaning to

(A) ridicule

(B) amuse

(C) describe

(D) imitate

Mastering the Question Type

3 Why does the author mention "modern-day soap operas" in paragraph 1?

(A) To help readers understand the plots of neoclassical theater

(B) To show that farce and tragedy were essential components of neoclassical theater

(C) To indicate that soap operas have similar themes to neoclassical theater

(D) To contrast neoclassical theater with present-day dramas

4 In paragraph 3, the author discusses "Pierre Corneille, Jean Racine, and Molière" in order to

(A) show that neoclassical theater embraced various styles of writing

(B) argue that good plays should cause a great amount of controversy

(C) give good examples of neoclassical theater

(D) explain why they succeeded at attracting audiences

Summary Note   Fill in the blanks with the appropriate words.

Neoclassical Theater

- Western European theater in ❶ _____
  - used elaborate scenery and costumes → overacting
  - ❷ _____ plots

- Development
  - began in sixteenth-century France
  - was based on unities → unities of ❸ _____, and others
  - utilized farce → making important situations seem ridiculous
  - utilized tragedy → made sad situations sadder

- Popular playwrights
  - Pierre Corneille, Jean Racine, and Molière
  - had different styles but lived in Paris at same time
  - ❹ _____ was most famous and most influential

Read the following passage and answer the questions.

Gerontology

06-09

Gerontology is the study of old people and the process of aging. Gerontological investigations include social, biological, and psychological studies. These studies include examinations of physical, mental, and social changes in people as they get older and the effects of an aging population on society. Gerontologists apply what they learn to government policies and programs that support the elderly.

2 ➡ Many gerontologists come from a variety of educational backgrounds. For example, gerontologists might have university degrees in sociology, medicine, psychology, or even business management. Furthermore, they work in hospitals, universities, and government institutions. On an administrative level, gerontologists develop programs and coordinate services that will benefit older people.

All of these experts conduct their research in an effort to understand and improve the lives of elderly people. They work and communicate directly with the elderly, who are seen as individuals, with their families, or in groups with other elderly people who are approximately the same age. The information gained from research and conversations with old people is considered when old age homes and recreational activities are designed to improve the lives of the elderly. In addition, gerontologists write articles for magazines and publish books that allow other experts to understand more about the special concerns of the elderly and their families.

4 ➡ Within the field of gerontology, there are also subfields called biogerontology and biomedical gerontology. They are concerned with the possibilities of slowing down or controlling the aging process with medical treatment. Here, gerontological experts have specific medical backgrounds and goals. They are known as biogerontologists and biomedical gerontologists. Biogerontologists study the biological process of aging that results in senility. Senility is when elderly people cannot think accurately anymore and sometimes act as if they were children once again. It seems to be some kind of degenerative process of the mind. On the other hand, biomedical gerontologists are scientists who work to control, prevent, or reverse the aging process in people and animals. Both types of experts work in the anti-aging field, which has become a very popular occupation in modern days.

Today, there is a high demand for people who might be able to control or reverse the aging process. Breakthroughs in the field can result in large earnings for such medical specialists. Perhaps there will never be a cure for aging, but biogerontologists and biomedical gerontologists are certain that they can slow down the aging process. This will allow people to live longer and more fulfilling lives until a great age.

📖 Words & Phrases

biological adj related to the study of living organisms
psychological adj concerned with a person's mind and thoughts
a variety of phr various; many kinds of
administrative adj managerial; supervisory
coordinate v to organize; to harmonize
benefit v to help; to aid

expert n a specialist; a professional; an authority
conduct v to do; to perform
accurately adv precisely; correctly
degenerative adj getting worse as time progresses
reverse v to change; to rearrange
breakthrough n an innovation; an advance; a discovery
cure n a remedy

1 The word "They" in the passage refers to

Ⓐ The possibilities of slowing down or controlling the aging process

Ⓑ Gerontological experts

Ⓒ Specific medical backgrounds

Ⓓ Goals

2 According to paragraph 4, which of the following is true of senility?

Ⓐ It damages old people's thinking abilities.

Ⓑ It is an unavoidable biological phase of aging.

Ⓒ It tends to improve over the course of time.

Ⓓ It can be healed by controlling the aging process.

Mastering the Question Type

3 In paragraph 2, why does the author mention "sociology, medicine, psychology, or even business management"?

Ⓐ To show that gerontologists come from various backgrounds

Ⓑ To demonstrate that gerontologists must have many degrees

Ⓒ To state how different gerontologists work together

Ⓓ To illustrate what fields gerontologists work in

4 In paragraph 4, the author uses "senility" as an example of

Ⓐ the biggest problem suffered by adults

Ⓑ a problem studied by biogerontologists

Ⓒ an illness that kills many elderly people

Ⓓ an illness whose symptoms doctors do not understand

📝 Summary Note   Fill in the blanks with the appropriate words.

Gerontology

- Study of ❶ _____ and aging
  - can be social, biological, and psychological studies
  - examine physical, mental, and social changes
- Try to understand and improve lives of elderly
  - do research
  - have ❷ _____ with elderly
  - write articles and publish books
- ❸ _____ and biomedical gerontology
  - tries to ❹ _____ aging process
  - examines issues like senility

Time Limit: 4 min

Rattlesnakes in Arizona

06-10

1 ➡ Rattlesnakes are venomous snakes found all over North and South America. Unlike many other reptiles, they bear their babies live rather than in eggs. These young rattlesnakes emerge fully loaded with deadly venom. After shedding their skin several times, the snakes develop rattles. The rattle is a formation of dead skin at the end of the snake's tail. Rattlesnakes shake their rattles when they perceive a threat. They also use their rattles to communicate with other rattlesnakes in a process called caudal luring.

2 ➡ Rattlesnakes have sophisticated skin membranes between their eyes and nostrils called pits. These organs can detect motion, vibrations, or changes in temperature at a great distance. Rattlesnakes do not have ears but use their pits to register sound, and they can use their tongues to detect predators by picking up air molecules.

The fangs of rattlesnakes work like the hypodermic needles used in a doctor's office. They are a defensive measure that can inject venom into the body of a would-be attacker. This venom acts to paralyze and sometimes kill victims, and its potency varies according to the type of rattlesnake that produces it. People who have survived a venomous rattlesnake bite often suffer a loss of motor skills and tissue damage even after they have recovered from the initial bite.

Seventeen types of rattlesnakes can be found in Arizona with the most common variety being the western diamondback. These snakes have camouflage patterns on them and can be very difficult to see since they blend in with their surroundings. This makes western diamondbacks especially dangerous to hikers and other people walking around in areas that they inhabit. Many people are bitten after unwittingly stepping on these snakes.

5 ➡ The Mohave, also known as the three-stepper or greenback snake, is the most venomous rattlesnake in North America. Its venom has twenty times the toxicity level of other common rattlesnakes such as the western diamondback, and most human deaths by rattlesnake bite in North America are caused by bites by Mohave snakes. The nickname "three-stepper" refers to how many steps a person usually takes before collapsing and dying after getting bitten.

Only one kind of rattlesnake has blue eyes. It is the Arizona speckled rattlesnake. Its eyes have been known to take on coloring from white to gray to blue, and they can even change to red when the snake is surrounded by red rocks. Although this snake is not as deadly as the Mohave, it is twice as venomous as the western diamondback, and is known to eat bats for sustenance.

Generally, however, snakes are not known to initiate attacks on humans and almost always flee if given the opportunity. As a matter of fact, some specialists believe that rattlesnakes can sense the intentions of people in their proximity and react accordingly. For example, one controlled study demonstrated that rattlesnakes in an enclosed space will react more defensively to ranchers who are prone to kill them but will react more passively to herpetologists who like and do not threaten them.

📖 **Words & Phrases**

venomous adj having venom
emerge v to appear
loaded adj filled
shed v to get rid of; to remove
sophisticated adj delicate; complex

inject v to give a shot
paralyze v to harden; to become inflexible
hypodermic adj beneath the skin
camouflage n a disguise

unwittingly adv without knowing
sustenance n food
proximity n nearness; closeness
herpetologist n a scientist who studies reptiles and amphibians

1 Select the TWO answer choices from paragraph 2 that identify what rattlesnakes use their pits to detect. *To receive credit, you must select TWO answers*.

(A) Predators

(B) Sound

(C) Distance

(D) Temperature changes

2 According to paragraph 5, which of the following is true of the Mohave?

(A) It can change the color of its eyes according to its surroundings.

(B) It is called three-stepper because it bites humans before they take three steps.

(C) It is the most venomous of all the rattlesnakes in Arizona.

(D) It is considered dangerous to hikers in particular.

Mastering the Question Type

3 In paragraph 1, why does the author mention "caudal luring"?

(A) To point out a habit that only rattlesnakes have

(B) To explain why rattlesnakes warn potential victims

(C) To give the scientific name of a rattlesnake's rattle

(D) To name a form of rattlesnake communication

4 In paragraph 5, why does the author mention "the western diamondback"?

(A) To point out why it bites so many people in the wild

(B) To compare the potency of its venom with that of another snake

(C) To claim that it is the most lethal snake in North America

(D) To explain how it got the nickname "three-stepper"

Summary Note Fill in the blanks with the appropriate words.

Rattlesnakes in Arizona

- Characteristics
  - are venomous snakes in North and South America
  - babies are ❶ _____, not in eggs
  - shed skin and develop rattles
  - have pits to detect motion, vibrations, ❷ _____, and sound
- Venom
  - used for ❸ _____ purposes
  - paralyzes and kills victims
- Arizona rattlesnakes
  - are seventeen types
  - ❹ _____ is most common
  - Mohave is most poisonous → called three-stepper

Exercise 6 Read the following passage and answer the questions.

Time Limit: 3 min. 20 sec.

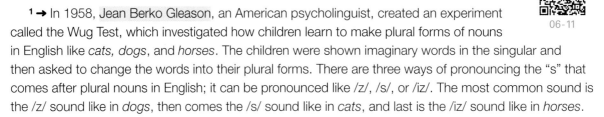

Jean Berko Gleason's Wug Test

1 → In 1958, Jean Berko Gleason, an American psycholinguist, created an experiment called the Wug Test, which investigated how children learn to make plural forms of nouns in English like *cats, dogs,* and *horses*. The children were shown imaginary words in the singular and then asked to change the words into their plural forms. There are three ways of pronouncing the "s" that comes after plural nouns in English; it can be pronounced like /z/, /s/, or /iz/. The most common sound is the /z/ sound like in *dogs*, then comes the /s/ sound like in *cats*, and last is the /iz/ sound like in *horses*.

2 → In the experiment, children were presented with a picture of some kind of pretend creature. They were then told that the creature was a wug. The experimenter said, "This is a wug." Another card was pulled out with another wug, and the experimenter said, "Now there are two of them. These are two . . . ?" Children who understood the proper use of the plural form for nouns ending with a "g" would say, "They are two wugs," with a /z/ sound. Very young children were often confused by this and said, "Two wug." Generally, children who were four years of age or older answered the question correctly. The researchers also carried out several other experiments to generate plural forms ending with the /s/ sound and with the /iz/ sound and discovered that children usually learned these rules later in their lives because they are not as common as the /z/-sound plurals.

The Wug Test additionally included questions that explored a child's understanding of the proper use of verbs and the using of the possessive, such as "This is Rob's bike." Possessives are parts of grammar that show ownership. The children were further prompted to use the -er suffix of a noun to demonstrate a person's job, such as someone who drives is a driver. Again, the children were given a nonsense word, this time zib. The researcher asked the children, "A man who zibs is a . . . ?" Some young children replied, "Zibber," but many young children replied, "Zibman."

4 → The Wug Test demonstrated that even very young children have established grammatical systems which allow them to make plurals, possessives, and other forms of words they have never heard before. This test was the first of its kind to prove that children learn their language skills naturally without needing to be taught grammar rules.

📖 Words & Phrases

psycholinguist Ⓝ a person who studies the mental faculties involved in the development, use, and interpretation of language

experiment Ⓝ a scientific test; research

investigate Ⓥ to examine; to look into

plural ⓐⓓⓙ more than one

imaginary ⓐⓓⓙ not real; make-believe

singular ⓐⓓⓙ single; sole; one

pronounce Ⓥ to say; to articulate

present Ⓥ to show

proper ⓐⓓⓙ correct; precise

carry out ⓟⓗⓡ to do; to perform

generate Ⓥ to produce

include Ⓥ to contain; to cover

explore Ⓥ to research; to investigate; to examine

ownership Ⓝ possession

prompt Ⓥ to cause

suffix Ⓝ a word ending

demonstrate Ⓥ to show; to prove

reply Ⓥ to answer

establish Ⓥ to set up; to create

1   The word "pretend" in the passage is closest in meaning to

   (A) artificial

   (B) deceptive

   (C) domestic

   (D) incorrect

2   According to paragraph 2, which of the following is true of the Wug Test?

   (A) It was an experiment to show that children must be taught the rules of language.

   (B) It investigated whether children could use English verbs to show ownership.

   (C) It examined how children learn to produce plural forms of English nouns.

   (D) It proved that children acquire /z/-sound possessives before /s/-sound ones.

3   The author discusses "Jean Berko Gleason" in paragraph 1 in order to

   (A) call him the world's foremost psycholinguist

   (B) cast doubt upon some of the research he did

   (C) describe a test that he conducted with children

   (D) suggest that he created a new language for children

4   In paragraph 4, why does the author mention "grammatical systems"?

   (A) To prove that Gleason created one of his own

   (B) To compare those used in two different languages

   (C) To show that children cannot understand them

   (D) To describe one of the results of the Wug Test

Summary Note   **Fill in the blanks with the appropriate words.**

Jean Berko Gleason's Wug Test

- Tested how children make ❶ _____ of nouns

- Method
  – showed children ❷ _____
  – asked children to make words plural

- Objectives of test
  – see if children could create plurals properly
  – checked children's understanding of use of ❸ _____
  – showed children established ❹ _____ for unknown words

Building Summary Skills

The following summaries are based on the passages you worked on earlier. Complete each of them by filling in the blanks with suitable words or phrases.

Exercise 1 Prairie Dogs

grazer-tamped ground soft	machinery and cattle	the ecosystem
social animals	erosion to the soil	

Prairie dogs are small, slender _____ that burrow complex tunnels in the large flatlands of North America. Many farmers consider prairie dogs to be pests because their tunnels can cause damage to _____. But scientists recognize that prairie dogs are important to _____. For example, prairie dogs are the food source for some predator species, and their intricate tunnels create the conditions needed to grow preferred grasses for cattle and keep _____. Furthermore, the tunnels help channel rainwater that could cause _____.

Exercise 2 Urbanization in Los Angeles

cheaply and quickly	better education and jobs	the spread of cities
unsanitary conditions	the uncontrolled and unplanned development	

Urbanization is _____ accompanied by the increase in population in those areas. The city of Los Angeles in the United States is a good example of urban sprawl. Urban sprawl is _____ that takes place in city areas. In Los Angeles, many neighborhoods were constructed _____. As a result, unattractive, unsafe, and crowded neighborhoods, called ghettos, gave rise to _____ and violent crime among the poor. There, opportunities for _____ are seldom seen.

Exercise 3 Neoclassical Theater

methods of farce	Molière	French neoclassical dramatists
time, place, and action	the sixteenth to the eighteenth century	

Neoclassical theater was the most important form of theater from _____ in Western Europe, especially in France. _____ wanted the _____ of the play to be unified and to be more like real life. Playwrights used costumes and scenery to evoke a sense of real time and place in their productions, and they employed _____ to make important situations seem ridiculous or methods of tragedy to make sad situations even sadder. The most influential neoclassical playwright was _____, who used farce to highlight human weaknesses.

Exercise 4   Gerontology

| related health information | issues of the elderly | the aging process |
| control, prevent, or even reverse | old age homes and recreational activities |

Gerontologists are scientists who are concerned with _____. They come from various backgrounds. Many gerontologists research, study, and plan the day-to-day conditions and needs of the elderly, which include the development of _____ as well as administrative services and the publication of _____. Two particular types of gerontologists are biogerontologists and biomedical gerontologists. Biogerontologists study _____ while biomedical gerontologists try to find ways to _____ the process of aging.

Exercise 5   Rattlesnakes in Arizona

| a defense mechanism | naturally aggressive | seventeen types |
| an ability to bear live young | North and South America |

Rattlesnakes can be found all over _____. Their unique physical characteristics such as pits and _____ set them apart from other snakes and help them to adapt to their environments. _____ of rattlesnakes have been identified in Arizona alone. Among them are the western diamondback, the Mohave, and the Arizona speckled rattlesnake. Although rattlesnake venom is often fatal to humans, studies have shown that rattlesnakes are not _____. In fact, rattlesnakes only seem to attack humans as _____.

Exercise 6   Jean Berko Gleason's Wug Test

| appropriate use of plurals | change verb forms | learn language naturally |
| an American psycholinguist | how children learn language |

In 1958, Jean Berko Gleason, _____, conducted experiments to find out _____. One experiment was the Wug Test. In order to examine children's _____, each child was shown a toy creature called a wug and then prompted to finish the sentence, "These are two . . . ?" In a separate experiment, each child was asked to _____ of words to noun forms as related to occupations. For example, a person who drives is a driver. The results of the experiment proved that children _____ without being taught grammar rules.

Max Weber

06-12

1 ➜ Max Weber is considered one of the founders of modern sociology, but he also made major contributions to modern political science and economics. Weber began his career researching the sociology of religion. He argued that religion was one of the major reasons for the difference in cultures between Western and Eastern countries. Furthermore, he believed that religion and culture are the main things that create political systems in countries. He also stressed the importance of qualities that are common to people who belong to certain religions. For example, Weber felt that many Western Europeans had a strong work ethic. Interestingly, Weber defined whole races through generalizations and specifically dubbed the work ethic of Western Europeans "the Protestant Ethic." The essential thesis of Weber's work was his belief that capitalism was formed in the West as a result of Western people's religion and by the same token, that capitalism could never be successful in the East because of people's religions.

2 ➜ Weber's work on the sociology of religion started with what was to be his most famous essay, *The Protestant Ethic and the Spirit of Capitalism*. After its publication, he wrote other essays about all of the major world religions. In them, he described three main themes. They were the effect of religious ideas on economic activities, the relation between social status and religious ideas, and the characteristics of Western civilization that made it different than Eastern civilization. The purpose of his work was to find the reasons why the cultures of the East and the West developed differently. It is important to note that he did not consider one civilization to be better than the other, like many of his colleagues did. His ideas were simply based on observation. In his work, Weber argued that Protestant religious ideas shaped the development of the economic system of Western Europe and the United States. There were other phenomena that shaped the Western economic system. They included scientific and mathematical discoveries, the creation of a legal system, the organization of governments, and the founding of small businesses. Weber believed that through social organization, religion, and the development of a modern economic system, Western people were outgrowing their primitive, superstitious beliefs.

In contrast, Weber found that Eastern religions were fundamentally different than Western ones, and this is the reason why capitalism did not develop in China. Weber believed that while Western religions overcame primitive superstitions, Eastern religions like Confucianism, Taoism, and Hinduism systematized these beliefs. They then became important parts of their religions. Moreover, in Confucianism and Taoism, "superior" men should not try to become rich. They should only serve society as best as they can. For Weber, this meant that capitalism could not develop in many Eastern countries. He also felt that the social world was divided into the educated and the uneducated in Eastern countries. The educated continuously tried to behave like prophets while the uneducated were preoccupied simply with living and believed in magic. Therefore, he believed that a viable economy could not be created.

1   In paragraph 1, why does the author mention "modern political science and economics"?

     Ⓐ To show that Weber earned respect in several academic fields

     Ⓑ To prove that Weber considered sociology the more important discipline

     Ⓒ To claim that Weber was a politico-economist rather than a sociologist

     Ⓓ To point out that Weber studied sociology based on political science and economics

2   The phrase "by the same token" in the passage is closest in meaning to

     Ⓐ for the same reason

     Ⓑ for the same price

     Ⓒ for a small cost

     Ⓓ at the same time

3   According to paragraph 1, which of the following is true of the Protestant Ethic?

     Ⓐ It implies that differences in cultures result in different religious ethics.

     Ⓑ It shows how Weber generalized the characteristics of Western people.

     Ⓒ It reflects Weber's belief that capitalism could not be successful without religion.

     Ⓓ It indicates that Weber was ignorant of non-Protestant religions.

4   The word "phenomena" in the passage is closest in meaning to

     Ⓐ reasons

     Ⓑ developments

     Ⓒ components

     Ⓓ occurrences

5   According to paragraph 2, what did Weber use to formulate his ideas?

     Ⓐ Religious studies

     Ⓑ Essays

     Ⓒ Observations

     Ⓓ His colleagues

6   According to paragraph 2, which of the following is NOT true of the influences on the economic systems of Western Europe and the United States?

(A) The founding of small businesses

(B) Scientific and mathematical discoveries

(C) Religious monopolies

(D) The organization of governments

7   Which of the following best expresses the essential information in the highlighted sentence? *Incorrect* answer choices change the meaning in important ways or leave out essential information.

(A) China could not develop capitalism because Eastern and Western religions were incompatible.

(B) Eastern religions should have followed Western ones to develop capitalism in China.

(C) Religions and capitalism in the East developed very differently from those of the West.

(D) Unlike in the West, religions prevented capitalism from developing in China.

8   The word "viable" in the passage is closest in meaning to

(A) extensive

(B) successful

(C) advanced

(D) standardized

Children's Language Acquisition

06-13

Language acquisition refers to the way in which people learn languages, whether it is their first language or a subsequent one. Nowadays, a hotly debated issue amongst linguists is whether children are born with a natural ability to learn languages or whether they learn how to understand languages from their environment. This debate is known as the nativist vs. the non-nativist debate.

2 → Linguists that support the nativist theory believe that children learn through their natural ability to organize the laws of language. However, they cannot use this ability if there are no other people to talk to. According to the nativist theory, children do not need any kind of training in language learning because their brains are ready to learn languages from the time they are born. A newborn child, the nativists argue, is able to understand languages because he has a basic understanding of grammar which is natural or native to him. As the child grows, he uses an innate grammar knowledge to make sense of the world and to express and decode ideas in complex ways. If this theory is true, then people must have some basic knowledge in their genes that helps them simply to understand language from the time they are babies.

3 → On the other hand, there are many different non-nativist theories. They include the most popular one, called social interactionism. Social interactionists believe that adults play an important part in children's language acquisition. These linguists believe that parents, especially mothers, talk to their children in a manner similar to formal language lessons. And although children seem to learn language easily, their progress is the result of getting language lessons almost all of the time. Social-interactionists also believe that children have an ability to learn much more quickly than teenagers or adults. However, this theory is being challenged because there are many societies in the world where mothers do not speak to their children very much, yet their children are nonetheless able to become fluent quickly.

4 → Another important theory of children's language acquisition is the Critical Period Hypothesis. Linguists who support this theory argue that a child's innate ability to learn a language deeply and with a proficiency that is normally associated with first language acquisition will typically end at around the age of twelve. After that, these scholars believe that it is impossible for anyone to learn any language profoundly. People who support this theory use the example of a girl known as Genie, also called the Wild Child.

5 → Genie was raised in isolation. ▇1 Her father was a disturbed man who decided to keep her away from all contact with other people and never talked to her or allowed her to learn anything. ▇2 She was thirteen when she was discovered and taken away from her father. ▇3 Although her circumstances were very tragic, linguists were excited at the opportunity to teach this girl some language skills because through her example they could test the Critical Period Hypothesis and the nativist or non-nativist theories. ▇4 Genie was able to learn some language. However, she would never reach the level that a normal teenager would. Linguists believe that Genie's case proves the Critical Period Hypothesis, but they still debate whether or not it supports the nativist or non-nativist arguments.

9 The word "subsequent" in the passage is closest in meaning to

ⓐ previous

ⓑ later

ⓒ foreign

ⓓ resultant

10 According to paragraph 2, which of the following is NOT true of the nativist theory of language acquisition?

ⓐ Children are capable of organizing language rules without training.

ⓑ Language input from others is needed to activate children's ability to learn language.

ⓒ Children are born with innate grammar knowledge.

ⓓ Children are not genetically predisposed to learn language naturally from birth.

11 The author uses "social interactionism" in paragraph 3 as an example of

ⓐ the theory that children have an inborn ability to learn their first languages

ⓑ the theory that adults contribute to children's language acquisition

ⓒ the fact that children need formal language lessons to learn language

ⓓ the theory that children below a certain age tend to learn language more easily

12 The word "innate" in the passage is closest in meaning to

ⓐ inherent

ⓑ essential

ⓒ extraordinary

ⓓ creative

13 According to paragraph 4, which of the following can be inferred of the Critical Period Hypothesis?

ⓐ It totally rejects the nativist position.

ⓑ It strongly supports the non-nativist position.

ⓒ It basically agrees with the nativist position.

ⓓ It provides a neutral stance on children's language acquisition.

14 According to paragraph 5, which of the following best describes Genie's language progress?

ⓐ She never learned language skills.

ⓑ She learned many language skills.

ⓒ She learned some language skills.

ⓓ She proved the nativist theory.

15 Look at the four squares [■] that indicate where the following sentence could be added to the passage.

As a matter of fact, Genie was confined to a room with very little light and tied to a potty chair most of the time.

Where would the sentence best fit?

16 **Directions:** Complete the table below by indicating which of the answer choices describe characteristics of Social Interactionism and which describe characteristics of the Critical Period Hypothesis. TWO of the answer choices will NOT be used.

Answer Choices

1. Young children receive informal language lessons from their mothers.

2. Children lose their ability to learn languages around the time of puberty.

3. Young children do not have the ability to learn languages more easily than teenagers and adults.

4. Adults play an important role in their children's language acquisition.

5. The discovery of Genie allowed scientists to test this theory.

6. A newborn baby never understands languages.

7. Ironically, some mothers do not speak to their children as much as others, yet their children's language is not affected.

Social Interactionism
-
-
-

Critical Period Hypothesis
-
-

Vocabulary Check-Up

A Choose the words with the closest meanings to the highlighted words.

1 The airplane will be landing in approximately ten minutes.

  (A) closely
  (B) nearly
  (C) falsely
  (D) appropriately

2 The extent of the damage forced them to abandon the project.

  (A) loss
  (B) aftermath
  (C) degree
  (D) cause

3 People perceive that some movies are like fairy tales.

  (A) know
  (B) change
  (C) open
  (D) relate

4 The queen knew that she had unwittingly offended the princess.

  (A) accidentally
  (B) magnificently
  (C) individually
  (D) extremely

5 Always try to stick with the plan.

  (A) customize
  (B) follow
  (C) remember
  (D) forget

6 This student will apply knowledge from many of her life experiences at her job.

  (A) refer
  (B) send
  (C) use
  (D) discount

7 To prevent the spread of germs, it is recommended that you often wash your hands.

  (A) nourish
  (B) view
  (C) help
  (D) stop

8 The loaded truck was too heavy for the bridge.

  (A) dangerous
  (B) rusty
  (C) filled
  (D) long

9 The elderly man collapsed on the floor.

  (A) fell down
  (B) danced
  (C) slipped
  (D) slept

10 The children replied in unison to the teacher's questions.

  (A) answered
  (B) shouted
  (C) stood
  (D) opened

B Match the words with the correct definitions.

1 coordinate ●   ● Ⓐ perspective

2 plough ●   ● Ⓑ not real; make-believe

3 attitude ●   ● Ⓒ a debate

4 elaborate ●   ● Ⓓ words that make no sense; an absurd situation

5 camouflage ●   ● Ⓔ to turn up the soil

6 social ●   ● Ⓕ complicated; complex; detailed

7 imaginary ●   ● Ⓖ research; study

8 controversy ●   ● Ⓗ to balance; to organize

9 investigation ●   ● Ⓘ living in communities; needing companionship

10 nonsense ●   ● Ⓙ a disguise to hide or blend into the surroundings

◤ Overview

Introduction

Inference questions ask you to understand an argument or an idea that is strongly suggested but not clearly mentioned in the passage. So you should use logical thinking in order to make an inference based on some information in the passage. You need to figure out the logical implications of the author's words as well as the surface meaning of those words.

Question Types

❯ Which of the following can be inferred about X?
❯ Which of the following can be inferred from paragraph about X?
❯ The author of the passage implies that X

Useful Tips

• Think logically to draw a reasonable conclusion from what is implied in the passage.
• Remember that the correct answer does not contradict the main idea of the passage.
• Do not choose an answer just because it is mentioned in the passage.

07-01

Q The author of the passage implies that operant conditioning

- Ⓐ is more likely to be used on animals than on humans
- Ⓑ makes use of negative reinforcement more often than positive
- Ⓒ is widely used for behavior modification in the classroom
- Ⓓ uses rewards and punishments as neutral stimuli to elicit wanted behavior

Behaviorism

Common methods of behavioral modification are based on behaviorism. Behaviorism is the belief that observable experiences can be measured, and it emphasizes the relationship between actions and consequences. Two well-known methods of behavioral modification are classical conditioning and operant conditioning. In classical conditioning, a neutral object or event is used to get a response from a different object or event. For example, in his famous dog experiment, Ivan Pavlov introduced the neutral ringing bell stimuli along with the meaningful food stimuli until the sound of the bell alone made the dog salivate by association.

Unlike classical conditioning, operant conditioning is based on a system of rewards and punishments. It is a principal method of classroom management. A reward or punishment follows an action. If an action is desirable, a reward will be given to positively reinforce it. On the other hand, if a teacher stops withholding a privilege when unwanted behavior stops, negative reinforcement has been issued. Negative reinforcement is defined as the removal of a punishment or negative consequence when an undesirable action stops.

☑ Correct Answer

According to the passage, behaviorism is commonly used to change someone's behavior, and operant conditioning is a principal method of classroom management. Therefore, choice Ⓒ is the correct answer.

Read the passages and answer the questions.

Siberia

Environmentalists have turned their attention to Siberia's harsh landscape because they are concerned with the causes and effects of global warming. Known for its frigid temperatures, ice, and snow, Siberia makes up more than one half of Russia. It encompasses all but the upper northeastern tip of Asia. Siberia, together with Canada, Scandinavia, and small patches of Alaska, forms the Arctic tundra. There, even in the absence of trees, vegetation and animal life have supported traditional livelihoods for thousands of years. These livelihoods include reindeer herding, hunting, and fishing. But today, that environment is changing. The Arctic landscape has become home to large-scale industrial sites and their surrounding towns that add to the rising pollutants from the Earth's middle latitudes. While this increase gravely impacts the delicate ecosystem of the Arctic tundra, it also poses a major global threat.

07-02

1   The author of the passage implies that Siberia's harsh landscape

   Ⓐ prevented people from living there until industrial sites were created

   Ⓑ is too dangerous for environmentalists to study

   Ⓒ accelerates global warming

   Ⓓ is suffering damage due to pollution

2   Which of the following can be inferred from the passage about the Arctic tundra?

   Ⓐ It occupies most of Russia.

   Ⓑ It is located only in Siberia.

   Ⓒ It has a variety of plant and animal life.

   Ⓓ It is a good place to build new towns.

Jacob Levy Moreno

Jacob Levy Moreno is the father of sociometrics, psychodrama, and group psychotherapy. Born in Romania in 1889 but raised in Vienna, he moved to the United States in 1925. Moreno studied and expanded on the tenets of Carl Jung but discounted the theories of Sigmund Freud, who believed in confining therapy to the private fancies of individual patients.

07-03

Unlike Freud, Moreno focused on public or social therapy. He viewed learning and living as socially constructed experiences. He reasoned that if patients could learn to work out distantly represented problems within nonjudgmental and safe group settings, they would be better equipped to work out the real problems that occur in day-to-day situations. If real problems could be easily worked out, then the lives of the patients would be happier.

1   According to paragraph 1, what can be inferred about Jacob Levy Moreno?

   Ⓐ He advanced the beliefs of Carl Jung and Sigmund Freud.

   Ⓑ He was satisfied with the work of traditional psychology.

   Ⓒ He was more likely to agree with Carl Jung than Sigmund Freud.

   Ⓓ He paid attention to the subconscious of individual patients.

2   In paragraph 2, the author implies that Jacob Levy Moreno

   Ⓐ wanted his patients to learn problem-solving strategies

   Ⓑ did not understand the value of cooperative groups

   Ⓒ put more weight on individuality than on collectivity

   Ⓓ solved all of the problems that his patients had

The Rosetta Stone

07-04

The Rosetta Stone was discovered near the Egyptian port city of Rosetta in 1799. It was a valuable find for academics because it provided the critical key needed to decipher ancient texts. Dated to 196 B.C., the pinkish-gray stone was scribed by priests as a celebratory tribute to the Egyptian Pharaoh Ptolemy V.

To ensure that it could be read by all, the priests transcribed their homage into Egyptian and Greek by using the three prevailing scripts of the day: hieroglyphs, Greek, and demotic. Hieroglyphs catered to religious rules and represented important concepts with stylized pictures, Greek was the language of the ruling class, and demotic was the form used by the masses for everyday speech and writing. Although Greek and demotic flourished, hieroglyphs became a forgotten form, and the meanings behind Egyptian artifacts became a mystery.

In 1822, however, Jean-François Champollion, a young history lecturer who could speak several languages, including Greek, endeavored to compare the scripted equivalents, and he broke the elusive hieroglyphic code.

1. According to paragraph 2, which of the following can be inferred about the languages of ancient Egypt?
   - (A) Hieroglyphs could only be read by the elite of the society.
   - (B) The languages were reflections of the classes that used them.
   - (C) The Greek language derived from the ancient Egyptian language.
   - (D) Common Egyptians spoke demotic and wrote hieroglyphs.

2. According to paragraph 3, which of the following can be inferred about the Rosetta Stone?
   - (A) It provided new information about Ptolemy V.
   - (B) It provided the means to translate ancient hieroglyphs.
   - (C) It represented ancient Egyptian art.
   - (D) It highlighted religious rites in ancient Egypt.

The Appalachian Mountains

07-05

The Appalachian Mountains form the oldest mountain chain on the North American continent. They cross from Canada in the north to the United States in the south and are about 19,884 miles long. The entire mountain system can be divided into three main sections. The northern section includes the mountains that stretch from Newfoundland in Canada to the Hudson Valley. The central section includes those from the Hudson Valley to the New River Valley in Virginia and West Virginia. The southern section includes the mountains that pick up from the New River Valley and continue to the end of the mountain chain in central Alabama. Because the Appalachian Mountains run parallel to the Atlantic Coast, they form a natural dividing line between the eastern seaboard of the United States and the Midwest area of the country.

1. The author of the passage implies that the Appalachian Mountains
   - (A) range from Canada to part of the United States
   - (B) are the longest mountain chain in North America
   - (C) end where Canada meets the United States
   - (D) extend all the way to the west coast of North America

2. According to the passage, what can be inferred about the Midwest area of the United States?
   - (A) It is protected from cold sea winds by the Appalachian Mountains.
   - (B) It is divided into three parts by the Appalachian Mountains.
   - (C) It is linked to the east coast of the United States by the Appalachian Mountains.
   - (D) It is separated from the Atlantic Ocean by the Appalachian Mountains.

Exercises with Long Passages

Exercise 1 Exercise 1 Read the following passage and answer the questions.

Time Limit: 3 min. 50 sec.

Jean Piaget's Stages of Cognitive Development

07-06

Swiss psychologist Jean Piaget classified four stages of cognitive development: sensorimotor, pre-operational, concrete operational, and formal operational. The stages unfold chronologically and are roughly age related. The characteristics of several stages may overlap within the same time frame. But the ages for each reflect an approximate understanding of reality during that period.

The sensorimotor stage occurs during infancy when the construction of knowledge is restricted to sensory input and motor action experiences. It is marked by two chief accomplishments. The first is differentiation between self and other. The second is object permanence. This is the realization that objects and events exist irrespective of being seen, touched, or heard.

3 → Between two and seven years of age, the pre-operational stage takes place. It weights symbolic representations of reality with language development and is comprised of two successive substages. They are the symbolic thought substage and the intuitive thought substage. The symbolic thought substage occurs between ages two and four. It is characterized by naming and pretend play that are limited by egocentrism and animism. Egocentrism inhibits perception from another's viewpoint, and animism is the belief that human-like feelings and actions are attributes of inanimate objects. Between the ages of four and seven, intuitive thought initiates a form of metacognition. It allows a child to know. But it does not provide an understanding of how that knowledge was derived. This phenomenon results from concentration on one facet or idea to the exclusion of all others. It is marked by a child's inability mentally to conserve an object's inherent properties when that object's appearance is changed.

4 → The concrete operational stage takes place from ages seven to eleven. At that time, concrete operational thinkers begin to interpret information logically. They can categorize objects according to shared or connected properties. They can also reverse the processes of seriation and transitivity. Seriation is the process of ordering stimuli along a quantitative continuum. Transitivity is the problem-solving strategy exercised in concretely represented if-then scenarios.

5 → The formal operation stage might be reached by ages eleven to fifteen. It is characterized by abstract and ideological reasoning as well as adolescent egocentrism, a heightened self-consciousness that prompts self-assessment and judgment of others. With a propensity for speculation and hypothesis testing, individuals in this stage can devise and execute a broad range of systematic algorithms to reach logical conclusions. This ability allows adolescents to explore greater possibilities than concrete operational thinkers who hold more rigidly to preconceived notions.

Since its introduction in the 1950s, Piaget's theory about the stages of cognitive development has been criticized for its narrow estimates of children's competencies at different developmental levels. Other criticisms are for its failure to factor social discourse, culture, and education into the rate and degree of progression from one stage to another. Furthermore, recent studies show that several stages are apt to co-occur according to the domain of knowledge elicited. Nevertheless, Piaget's stages continue to profoundly influence pedagogical trends.

📖 Words & Phrases

cognitive adj relating to thought processes

permanence n continuity; constancy

inanimate adj lifeless

intuitive adj instinctive; spontaneous

exclusion n the act of keeping someone or something out

propensity n a tendency

preconceived adj presumed; presupposed

competency n ability

elicit v to draw out; to stimulate

pedagogical adj related to teaching

1 According to paragraph 4, which of the following is true of transitivity?

    Ⓐ It demands great physical changes.

    Ⓑ It moves a child from one stage to another.

    Ⓒ It operates on the cause-and-effect basis.

    Ⓓ It helps interpret information intuitively.

2 According to paragraph 5, which of the following is true of individuals between the ages of eleven and fifteen?

    Ⓐ Logical thinking based on abstraction becomes prominent.

    Ⓑ Objects start to be categorized according to their characteristics.

    Ⓒ Egocentrism hinders assessing and judging others' viewpoints.

    Ⓓ Metacognition begins to allow an understanding of knowledge sources.

3 In paragraph 3, the author implies that the pre-operational stage

    Ⓐ is divided into two co-occurring substages

    Ⓑ is marked by the use of words to represent reality

    Ⓒ allows children to see things from another's point of view

    Ⓓ differentiates between living and nonliving things

4 What can be inferred about Piaget's stages of cognitive development?

    Ⓐ They occur in sequential order.

    Ⓑ They provide a conclusive analysis of children's abilities.

    Ⓒ They are rarely associated with age.

    Ⓓ They are apt to co-occur.

📝 Summary Note Fill in the blanks with the appropriate words.

Jean Piaget's Stages of Cognitive Development

- **❶** _____ stage
  - occurs during infancy
  - builds knowledge through senses and motor action experiences

- Pre-operational stage
  - occurs during ages two to seven
  - relies on **❷** _____ and intuitive thought

- Concrete operational stage
  - occurs during ages **❸** _____
  - can interpret information logically

- Formal operational stage
  - occurs during ages eleven to fifteen or older
  - uses **❹** _____ reasoning

Exercise 2 Read the following passage and answer the questions.

Time Limit: 5 min.

Numeric Symbols

07-07

A number is a concept. It is abstract. It cannot be seen, heard, felt, tasted, or smelled. A numeral is a symbol that is created to represent a number, and a number can be represented in many ways. Among the classifications of numbers are ordinal and cardinal numbers. An ordinal number acts as a determiner and answers the question "which one?" It also indicates order while a cardinal number tells how many.

Numerals are symbols that represent numbers, and a numeration system is a method of putting symbols to numbers. There are three kinds of numeration systems: simple, multiplicative, and positional. Simple systems apply the same power of a base and add each value in the numeral. For example, a series of lines would be added together to tally a sum. Multiplicative systems use multipliers to avoid grouping symbols more than once after a base and its symbols have been defined. Generally, numerals appear in pairs with one multiplier followed by a grouping symbol. Each time the base is reached, a new symbol is used. If the base is four, dashes or lines would represent 1, 2, 3, and 4, but 5 would be represented with a new symbol and so forth. Any arrangement of the symbols is added together for tallying. The positional systems refine the multiplicative systems because it incorporates value positions. With value positions, symbols can be reused but represent different numbers based on the position or order that they take in a symbol grouping.

3 → Each of the numeric systems has been used throughout history where different cultures have marked numbers with their own symbols and base numbers. For example, early Egyptian civilization used a simple grouping numeration system based on ten. In order to decode Egyptian numerals, long stretches of symbol groupings had to be sorted out and added together. On the other hand, the Chinese-Japanese system used a multiplicative system. Like the Egyptian system, it was based on ten; however, instead of using one symbol as a multiplier, the system used nine different symbols that were written vertically, not left to right like the Egyptian system.

The Babylonians had a modified positional numeration system based on 60. They had two symbols for multipliers—a ten symbol and a one symbol—and only wrote them in value positions. They did not have a symbol to represent zero. The Babylonian system was weak because each grouping was open to many interpretations. The Mayan's modified positional numeration system was based on twenty. It contained a zero and was written vertically. The bottom numerals represented the one's place, and the ascending order gave way to greater values. However, the third place shifted from a 20×20 representation to 20×18 and altered the course of the successive place values.

5 → The Hindu-Arabic is the most highly developed numeration system. It is a positional numeration system based on ten. It uses ten multipliers, and each multiplier is called a digit. The ten digits are 0, 1, 2, 3, 4, 5, 6, 7, 8, and 9. Each digit can be expressed by a single symbol and is different from the others. When a digit holds a particular position, it indicates how many of that place value are represented. So the Hindu-Arabic system is not only more sophisticated but is also much simpler to use. Furthermore, any positional numeral in a given base can be translated into the Hindu-Arabic system. For instance, the Hindu-Arabic system has supplied the format for the binary system that is used to program today's computers.

📖 Words & Phrases

abstract adj existing as a quality rather than something real
represent v to symbolize; to stand for
tally v to count

refine v to improve; to polish
incorporate v to include; to combine
decode v to interpret; to make out
ascending adj rising

give way phr to yield; to give in
sophisticated adj advanced; having a refined knowledge
binary adj based on two

1   According to paragraph 3, which of the following is true of the Chinese-Japanese numeration system?

    (A) It is a positional system.

    (B) It is a simple grouping system.

    (C) It is a multiplicative system.

    (D) It is a system that altered the course of successive place values.

2   According to paragraph 5, which of the following is the most efficient numeration system?

    (A) A positional system based on ten

    (B) A multiplicative system based on twenty

    (C) A modified positional system based on sixty

    (D) A simple grouping system based on ten

3   In paragraph 3, the author implies that numeration systems

    (A) are important to every culture

    (B) were the most highly developed in Egypt

    (C) were introduced by ancient Egyptians

    (D) are all decoded in a fast and simple way

4   Which of the following can be inferred from paragraph 5 about the Hindu-Arabic system?

    (A) It was based on twenty at first.

    (B) Many people have trouble learning it.

    (C) It was developed before all other systems.

    (D) It can adapt to other bases.

📝 **Summary Note**   **Fill in the blanks with the appropriate words.**

Numeric Symbols

- Numbers
  - are just ❶ _____
- Numerals
  - are ❷ _____ that represent numbers
- Numeration system → method of putting symbols to numbers
- Historical numerical systems
  - Egyptian system based on 10
  - Chinese-Japanese system was ❸ _____
  - Babylonians had system based on 60
  - Mayans had system based on 20
  - ❹ _____ was most developed system
    - → positional system based on ten
    - → was much simpler than other systems

Exercise 3 Read the following passage and answer the questions.

Time Limit: 3 min. 30 sec.

Lake Superior

1 → Lake Superior is the world's largest freshwater lake and is located in North America. It forms a natural boundary between the United States and Canada. Together with Lakes Huron, Ontario, Michigan, and Erie, it forms the Great Lakes. It is bordered by Ontario, Canada, to the north and east, by Michigan and Wisconsin to the south, and by Minnesota to the west. Of the Great Lakes, Lake Superior sits the highest north and the farthest west. It is very remote, densely forested, and sparsely populated.

Lake Superior is so large that it could fill all of the other Great Lakes—Huron, Ontario, Michigan, and Erie—plus three more lakes the size of Lake Erie. It contains about 2,900 cubic miles of water—or 12.11 quadrillion liters. Lake Superior is 350 miles long and 160 miles wide, and it reaches a maximum depth of nearly 1,333 feet. Its surface elevation is 600 feet. Fed by more than 300 streams and rivers, it empties into Lake Huron.

3 → Because of its vast size and depth, Lake Superior is also the coldest of the Great Lakes and remains at a constant forty degrees Fahrenheit. The temperature of the lake regulates the climate of the surrounding area and keeps it cooler in the summer and warmer in the winter. It also causes the greatest lake effect snows on the Earth. They sometimes reach twenty to thirty miles inland and produce snowfalls with depths of 16.5 feet in some places.

4 → Lake Superior is the largest freshwater lake by area and the third largest by volume. Its surface area is roughly 32,000 square miles. While twenty percent of the Earth's freshwater supply comes from the Great Lakes, a full ten percent comes from Lake Superior. This is significant since only three percent of the Earth's water is fresh water, and two-thirds of that is frozen in glaciers and frozen ice caps. Freshwater is important because other grades of water contain salts that are harmful to people, and many species, including humans, need fresh water to survive.

5 → The water from Lake Superior is the drinking water for the more than forty million people who reside in its adjacent states, and, more recently, it is being bottled and shipped abroad. To maintain its level of purity, a pact was made between the United States and Canada in 1972 to eliminate unwanted pollutants and to improve the water supply. Currently, water levels are monitored and controlled by the International Lake Superior Board of Control.

📖 Words & Phrases

remote adj isolated

densely adv thickly; compactly

sparsely adv lightly; sporadically

populate v to furnish with inhabitants or members

empty into phr to flow into

vast adj huge; boundless; immense

constant adj steady; unchanging

regulate v to control

volume n amount; quantity

roughly adv approximately

significant adj important

glacier n an extremely large mass of ice; an ice floe

reside v to live; to dwell

adjacent adj neighboring; bordering; adjoining

eliminate v to remove; to get rid of

pollutant n a contaminant

pact n a formal agreement

1   According to paragraph 1, which of the following is true of Lake Superior?

    Ⓐ It is surrounded by many towns and villages.

    Ⓑ It divides the United States and Canada.

    Ⓒ It has many rivers that flow from it.

    Ⓓ Its main feature is a frozen glacial cap.

2   According to paragraph 4, which of the following is true of the Earth's fresh water?

    Ⓐ Ten percent of it is not suitable for human drinking due to its salinity.

    Ⓑ Twenty percent of its supply comes from Lake Superior.

    Ⓒ Around sixty percent of it exists in frozen form.

    Ⓓ Three percent of it is used as drinking water for animal species.

Mastering the Question Type

3   Which of the following can be inferred from paragraph 3 about Lake Superior?

    Ⓐ It is easily affected by the weather changes of the surrounding area.

    Ⓑ Its water remains at a low temperature all year round.

    Ⓒ It causes heavy snow to fall far inland every winter.

    Ⓓ It is large enough to change weather systems throughout North America.

4   In paragraph 5, the author implies that Lake Superior is an important resource because

    Ⓐ it has become a top commodity for U.S. exporters

    Ⓑ it contains natural mineral salts

    Ⓒ it can be controlled by humans

    Ⓓ it provides people with fresh water to drink

📝 Summary Note   **Fill in the blanks with the appropriate words.**

Lake Superior

- Geography
  - located in North America between the United States and Canada
  - world's largest ❶ _____
  - remote, heavily forested, and has few people
- Extremely large lake
  - could fill all other ❷ _____ easily
- Is very cold and has constant ❸ _____ of 40 degrees Fahrenheit
- Supplies ❹ _____ of world's freshwater supply
- Provides drinking water for forty million people

Exercise 4 Read the following passage and answer the questions.

Time Limit: 3 min. 50 sec.

Memory Theories

Theories about memory are important because they offer explanations about how individuals learn. Learning is a relatively permanent influence on behavior, knowledge, and thinking skills that results from when information is derived through experience. Such experience is the physical contact with or the observation of facts or events, and then memory is retained information from that experience.

Memory formation involves three main processes. They are encoding, storage, and retrieval. Encoding is the process of taking information in as it is experienced. Storage is the mental process of storing or representing that information in the mind. And retrieval is the process of recalling that information as it is needed for specific and related tasks.

3 ➔ Encoding relies on learning and attention. While learning involves how the senses interpret an experience, attention is concentrating and focusing mental resources on a specific task. Attention includes being able to shift from one activity to another and to use different skills to accomplish a relevant goal. For example, in order to attend to writing a sentence, an individual must focus on the purpose of the letter as well as how to write the letters and spell the words correctly on paper. Proper capitalization, grammar, and punctuation must be implemented for the task to be successfully completed. Attending to something relevant takes effort.

4 ➔ Storage is the potentially progressive manner in which experiences are categorized as memories for later retrieval. The three types of memory storage are sensory memory, short-term memory, and long-term memory. Sensory memory lasts only an instant and is the actual introduction to information in its original form. For example, touching a hot pot or hearing a crack of thunder will imprint a sensory memory. Because the experience is instantaneous, attention to relevant information is vital to its retention.

5 ➔ Short-term memory normally lasts for up to thirty seconds. It is limited by the amount of information that individuals can hold at any one time. In order to retain information longer, it must be repeated and learned by rote or sparked by orchestrated cues. Long-term memory is relatively permanent information that has been worked and attached to various schemas. Schemas are concepts or frameworks of knowledge that exist in an individual's mind. They organize and interpret information. When a set of information is inducted into long-term memory, it forms attachments to vast and intricate networks of ideas that exercise it and strengthen its placement there.

Retrieval is the process of searching for relevant information. Like encoding, it can be automatic or require the effort and attention of the individual. The storage of the information impacts the ease or likelihood of retrieval since not all experiences are retained.

According to theorists, memories can be actively constructed by individuals. Understanding how the memory processes function is important to educators and students. It aids in the formulation of new teaching and learning strategies that support the acquisition and retrieval of base knowledge that is needed to understand new concepts.

📖 Words & Phrases

permanent adj long-lasting; enduring
derive v to obtain
retain v to keep
involve v to include; to entail
relevant adj related; pertinent
implement v to carry out; to plan

progressive adj ongoing; advancing
imprint v to impress; to mark
instantaneous adj immediate; instant
vital adj essential; indispensable
by rote phr by habitual repetition

orchestrated adj organized; arranged
induct v to admit; to let in
intricate adj complicated; complex
acquisition n a possession; a gain
formulation n preparation; a design

1   According to paragraph 4, which of the following is true of sensory memory?

    Ⓐ It interferes with the working ability of the senses.

    Ⓑ It disappears in a very short time without attention.

    Ⓒ It processes information into a more concrete memory.

    Ⓓ It changes one experience to another.

2   The word "cues" in the passage is closest in meaning to

    Ⓐ observations

    Ⓑ appearances

    Ⓒ comments

    Ⓓ prompts

Mastering the Question Type

3   According to paragraph 3, which of the following can be inferred about encoding?

    Ⓐ It is necessary for the retention of long-term memories.

    Ⓑ It requires deliberate attention.

    Ⓒ It is not central to learning.

    Ⓓ It takes place after information is stored.

4   In paragraphs 4 and 5, the author implies that short-term memory

    Ⓐ cannot be transformed into long-term memory

    Ⓑ is formed by things affected people's senses

    Ⓒ lasts longer than sensory memory does

    Ⓓ is more important than long-term memory

📝 Summary Note   Fill in the blanks with the appropriate words.

Memory Theories

- Provide explanations for how people learn

- Involve three processes
  - encoding, storage, and ❶ _____

- Encoding
  - relies on learning and ❷ _____
  - sees how senses interpret experience and focus mental resources on task

- Storage
  - way in which memories are categorized for later use
  - has ❸ _____, short-term memory, and long-term memory

- Retrieval
  - act of searching for relevant information
  - can be ❹ _____ or require effort

Exercise 5 Read the following passage and answer the questions.

Time Limit: 3 min. 30 sec.

Clipper Ships

07 - 10

1 → Clipper ships saw their heyday in the early to mid-1800s. Spurred on by the dissolution of the East India Trading Company and the advent of the California Gold Rush, clipper ships answered the call for fast and efficient transportation of perishable cargo.

2 → Merchants from the east wanted to rush their goods west to California and take advantage of prices that had inflated to unbelievable heights. A barrel of flour that cost four dollars in New York sold for forty dollars in San Francisco, and a four-month-old newspaper from Philadelphia cost a dollar. One of the most pressing of the commodities was tea from China. Tea was a popular item that tasted better when it was fresh. The slow trips that started at ports in China stopped at the port of New York, circled around Cape Horn, and ended on the western side of the United States, resulting in spoiled tea that was not fit for human consumption. Americans loved tea and were willing to pay for it. So ship owners were confident that any money invested in new ship designs would be recouped in their profits and be well worth the trouble.

Nat Palmer, Edward Collins, Donald McKay, and John Willis Griffiths are credited by many historians as the innovators of the new type of ship. Nat Palmer, an experienced seaman and captain, was the first to envision a sailing vessel with a flat bottom instead of the V-shaped form that prevailed at that time. Edward Collins, a financier of the project, owned a shipping company and was willing to take a risk on the novel structure. Donald McKay, a talented craftsman and shipyard owner, was hired to build the ships hands-on, and John Willis Griffiths, a noted genius, laid the plans based on principles of science and higher math on paper.

4 → Aptly named for its ability to clip time, the clipper had a knifelike bow to slice easily through the water, a narrow hull so that the ship would move smoothly, and tall masts to collect every bit of wind that might hurry the ship along. Griffiths even removed everything from the deck to lessen wind resistance that normally slowed ships down. The final result was the spectacular and streamlined *Rainbow*. The *Rainbow* was the first true clipper ship. It provided the template for a new generation of ships that amazed the world with their swiftness and inspired poets to romanticize the movements of their graceful lines.

📖 Words & Phrases

heyday n a period of greatest success; a prime

spur v to stimulate; to prompt

dissolution n a breakup; a termination

advent n an arrival; a beginning

perishable adj decomposable; quickly decaying

inflate v to increase rapidly

pressing adj urgent; necessary

commodities n goods; products

fit adj suitable; appropriate

consumption n the act of eating or drinking; the act of using something

recoup v to regain; to recover

credit v to acknowledge; to recognize

envision v to conceive; to see

prevail v to be widespread

novel adj new

financier n an investor; a sponsor

hands-on adj practical; direct

aptly adv suitably; properly; appropriately

clip v to shorten; to curtail

bow n the front part of a ship

hull n the main body of a ship

mast n a tall, upright pole that supports a sail

deck n the floor of a ship

lessen v to decrease; to diminish; to lower

resistance n a hindrance; an obstruction

spectacular adj impressive; amazing

template n a model; a prototype

swiftness n rapidity; fastness; speed

graceful adj elegant; beautiful; charming

1 According to paragraph 1, which of the following is true of clipper ships?

(A) They were needed to transport goods more efficiently.

(B) They were sold for high profits.

(C) They were popular in the eighteenth century.

(D) They were quickly replaced by faster ships.

2 According to paragraph 4, which of the following was NOT a characteristic of the clipper ship?

(A) It had a streamlined front part with a sharp edge.

(B) It had a strong main body made of steel.

(C) It had tall masts to support its sails.

(D) It had a lightweight deck.

3 In paragraph 2, the author implies that clipper ships

(A) replaced traditional ships completely once they were invented

(B) were used to deliver newspapers from Philadelphia to New York

(C) were expensive to make but returned small profits to ship owners

(D) provided an efficient means to transport tea to California

4 According to paragraph 4, which of the following can be inferred about the *Rainbow*?

(A) It inspired authors to write novels about the sea.

(B) It had a unique design that other clipper ships could not imitate.

(C) It was renowned for its appearance and speed.

(D) It was the first commercial clipper ship to be used in Asia.

📝 Summary Note **Fill in the blanks with the appropriate words.**

Clipper Ships

• Provided fast and efficient transportation in ❶ _____

• Reason for existence
  – needed fast ships to transport from American east coast to California
  – goods could not survive long boat trips

• Clipper ship inventors
  – Nat Palmer, Edward Collins, ❷ _____, and John Willis Griffiths
  – created fast ship that sailed smoothly
    → had tall masts
    → had nothing on deck to reduce ❸ _____
    → ❹ _____ (first true clipper ship)

Read the following passage and answer the questions.

Time Limit: 3 min. 30 sec.

The Northwest Coast of the United States

07-11

1 ➤ The northwest coast of the United States is uniquely characterized by the formidable Cascade Mountain Range. This chain of high active volcanoes, also known as the High Cascades, runs from British Columbia in Canada through the regional states of Washington and Oregon. It crosses the international boundary between Canada and the United States and makes up the northernmost third of the subdivided Pacific Mountain System. As the mountain system enters the United States from Canada, where it is known as the Coast Mountains, it follows the bent of the Pacific Coast about 150 to 200 miles inland. Traveling southward into California, it joins with the Sierra Nevada Mountains. The Sierra Nevadas link with the Basin Range to complete the mountain chain.

The Cascade Mountain Range is best known for its enormous and volatile snow-capped volcanoes. They include Mount Baker, Mount Rainier, Mount Adams, Mount St. Helens, and Mount Hood. Mounts Baker, Rainier, Adams, and St. Helens are located in the state of Washington. Mount Hood is located in Oregon. These huge natural formations generally rise in isolation and are separated by great intervening plateaus. Deep cuts mark them in a jagged line and are indicative of the glaciers that sculpted them.

3 ➤ Besides the volcanic giants, there are many non-volcanic mountains. Most notable among them are the 150-mile stretch of highlands that are located just south of Canada in the North Cascades of Washington. Although these rocky pinnacles are judged to be smaller than their volcanic counterparts, they are comprised of hundreds of summits with height differentials that often exceed those of the peaks of the Sierra Nevadas.

4 ➤ The remarkable geography of the northwest coast is further distinguished by the ongoing climatic battle that takes place around the coastal mountain range. While the Cascade Mountains are beset with extensive glaciers and heavy snowfalls, they are also notoriously prone to low clouds and heavy warm weather rains. Such conditions are conducive to temperate rainforests.

5 ➤ Thick rainforests cover the deep narrow valleys surrounding the mountains, particularly from the west, and run from Alaska through Canada and into Northern California. Furthermore, they are included among the Pacific temperate rainforests of North America which make up the largest temperate rainforest zone on the planet. Inherent to west-facing coastal mountains, these rainforests typically foster the tallest species of trees in the world and are part of the Nearctic ecozone that encompasses the greater portion of North America.

📖 Words & Phrases

uniquely adv incomparably; solely

characterize v to typify; to distinguish

formidable adj very impressive; awesome

regional adj local; provincial

boundary n a border; a frontier

bent n grassland

volatile adj unstable; changeable; unsettled

in isolation phr alone

intervening adj in-between

jagged adj uneven; rough

notable adj unusual; remarkable

pinnacle n a peak; a summit; a zenith

counterpart n an equivalent

be comprised of phr to be made up of; to consist of

exceed v to go above; to surpass

remarkable adj extraordinary; notable; significant

be prone to phr be liable to; be subject to

beset v to trouble; to plague

extensive adj widespread; wide-ranging; far-reaching

conducive adj helpful; enabling

inherent adj intrinsic

foster v to promote; to nourish

encompass v to include; to cover

1 According to paragraph 1, which of the following is true of the Cascade Mountains?

Ⓐ They extend from North to South America.

Ⓑ They include the Pacific Mountain System.

Ⓒ They are known as the Coast Mountains in Canada.

Ⓓ They are coastal mountains near the Pacific Ocean.

2 According to paragraph 4, which of the following are the Cascade Mountains easily affected by? *To receive credit, you must select TWO answers.*

Ⓐ Temperate rainforests

Ⓑ Sudden climatic changes

Ⓒ Plenty of warm weather rains

Ⓓ Low-altitude clouds

3 Which of the following can be inferred from paragraph 3 about the Cascade Mountain Range?

Ⓐ It consists of high volcanic mountains and lower non-volcanic mountains.

Ⓑ It is famous for rock-capped volcanoes.

Ⓒ It ends in the state of Washington.

Ⓓ It has higher peaks than the Sierra Nevadas.

4 According to paragraph 5, what can be inferred about the rainforests of the Cascade Mountains?

Ⓐ They have plants similar to those of tropical rainforests.

Ⓑ They are the largest tropical rainforests in the world.

Ⓒ They are a very good place for tall trees to grow.

Ⓓ They take up most of the Nearctic region.

Summary Note Fill in the blanks with the appropriate words.

The Northwest Coast of the United States

- Cascade Mountain Range is there
  - has many ❶ _____
    → many famous ones, including ❷ _____
  - goes from Canada down to California
  - has many non-volcanic mountains

- Geography
  - has many ❸ _____ and heavy snowfalls
  - also has ❹ _____
  - tallest trees in the world grow there

Building Summary Skills

The following summaries are based on the passages you worked on earlier. Complete each of them by filling in the blanks with suitable words or phrases.

Exercise 1 Jean Piaget's Stages of Cognitive Development

chronological order	the formal operational	children's competencies
social and cultural influences	four stages of cognitive development	

Swiss psychologist Jean Piaget introduced a theory about the _____. They are the sensorimotor stage, the pre-operational stage, the concrete operational stage, and _____ stage. Each of the stages is roughly age related and occurs in _____.
Although Piaget's theory gained wide acceptance in the 1950s, today it is criticized for its narrow view of _____ and its failure to address _____ on learning as well as the possibility that stages are apt to co-occur.

Exercise 2 Numeric Symbols

abstract concepts	numerals	the positional Hindu-Arabic system
distinct symbols and systems	simple, multiplicative, and positional	

Because numbers are _____, different cultures have used _____ to represent them. The symbols that are used to represent the numbers are called _____, and they are typically arranged in one of three kinds of numeration systems: _____. Of these, _____ is the most advanced. It is the simplest to use and can be adapted to any base.

Exercise 3 Lake Superior

the remnants of glaciers	the Earth's freshwater supply	to protect the lake
the largest freshwater lake	the United States and Canada	

North America's Lake Superior, a natural boundary between _____, is _____ in the world. It was formed from _____ and provides a significant portion of _____. Fresh water that is free of salts and other unhealthy pollutants is needed by humans and many other species for survival. For that reason, the United States and Canada work together _____ from pollutants and to monitor and improve its water supply.

Exercise 4 Memory Theories

controlled by the learner	sensory memory	past experiences
encoded, stored, and retrieved	teaching and learning strategies	

Memory theories focus on how experiences are _____. There are three types of memory storage: _____, short-term memory, and long-term memory. Since the encoding and retrieval processes that surround memory storage can be _____, understanding memory processes is influential in the development of _____. Such strategies seek to engage learners so that new learning finds stable connections to _____.

Exercise 5 Clipper Ships

perishable items like tea	merchant vessels	transport commodities
the California Gold Rush	scientific and mathematical principles	

As a result of the breaking up of the East India Trading Company and _____, merchants sought a quick and efficient means to _____ to the west coast of the United States. This was particularly true for merchants who wanted to ensure that _____ reached the coast in a timely fashion. In answer to this unprecedented need, American innovators applied _____ to create the first true clipper ship, the *Rainbow*. The *Rainbow* became a prototype for the new swift and streamlined _____.

Exercise 6 The Northwest Coast of the United States

glaciers and heavy snowfalls	temperate rainforests	the Northwest coast
the Pacific Mountain System	heavy warm weather rains	

The Cascade Mountain Range runs along _____ of the United States and into Canada. It makes up the northernmost third of _____ and is comprised of volcanic and non-volcanic mountains. Although the Cascade Mountain Range is best known for its _____, it also houses _____ that grow under the low clouds and _____ that are common in the mountain region.

Abraham Maslow's Hierarchy of Needs

07-12

Maslow's hierarchy of needs

Abraham Maslow was born in Brooklyn in 1908. The firstborn son of Jewish immigrants, he possessed an uncanny intelligence that put him in company with the greatest social thinkers of the day. The Freudians touted the impact of the personal subconsciousness on behavior. The behaviorists emphasized external punishments and rewards as factors that influenced action. And the gestalt theorists tried to see how the whole was comprised of many factors. Moved by a steady discourse of eagerly anticipated discussions, Maslow resolved to combine these disparate and often warring schools of thought and to refine a new conception of human motivation.

2 ➜ Maslow's perspective was humanistic. He stressed that individuals have an innate capacity for personal growth, the freedom to choose and act toward their own destiny, and other positive attributes that affect their quality of life. In 1948, Maslow published two papers that addressed the inner needs of people and how they are satisfied. They were entitled "Cognition of the Particular and of the Generic" and "Some Political Consequences of Basic-Need Gratification." In them, Maslow argued that there are greater needs than the physiological ones posited by the predominant Freudian thinkers and behaviorists. He also pulled the seemingly oppositional schools of thought together, along with the gestalt perspective, to clarify the unacknowledged attributes of fulfilled individuals. He observed that individuals whose basic needs had been gratified performed differently than other people.

3 ➜ At the core of Maslow's tenets is his hierarchy of needs. It is based on observations meant to discern the values by which people guide their lives. Maslow sought to prove that individuals are not born with distinct capacities to achieve through political birthrights. Instead, they are given or not given the tools that are needed to achieve greatness—or at least success. Unlike the Freudians and neo-Freudians, who had developed a portrait of what people are like when they are thwarted or frustrated in their lower needs, Maslow was determined to look at the end results when people have their needs met and to see how they got there. He insisted that the study of mental health should include the healthy, not just the diseased.

4 ➜ Maslow argued that each individual has a set of basic needs. They include the physical well-being associated with hunger, thirst, and sleep, safety from harm, belongingness or love within a social realm, and a positive and empowering self-esteem. He also maintained that these needs are arranged in a particular sequence or hierarchy. First, the need for food and sleep must be met, and they are

then followed by the need for safety and love. The final stage of the hierarchy is self-actualization. Self-actualization encompasses the motivation to develop one's full potential as a human being, and it is only possible after all of the lower needs have been satisfied. According to Maslow, most people never reach the point of self-actualization because they stop maturing once they develop a high sense of self-esteem. In fact, Maslow proposed that once the lower needs are fulfilled, motivation to assert oneself to move up the hierarchy lessens. He reasoned that the lower needs were stronger and more fiercely animal related while the needs higher up were weaker and more distinctly human.

1   The word "uncanny" in the passage is closest in meaning to
   Ⓐ unusual
   Ⓑ reliable
   Ⓒ competitive
   Ⓓ hidden

2   The word "gratified" in the passage is closest in meaning to
   Ⓐ frustrated
   Ⓑ identified
   Ⓒ fulfilled
   Ⓓ reduced

3   According to paragraph 2, which of the following is true of Abraham Maslow?
   Ⓐ He emphasized meeting physiological needs more than anything else.
   Ⓑ He was severely criticized by Freudians and behaviorists.
   Ⓒ He claimed that gestalt psychology could contribute to enhancing cognition.
   Ⓓ He integrated different schools of psychology to develop his own theory.

4   The word "they" in the passage refers to
   Ⓐ their lives
   Ⓑ individuals
   Ⓒ distinct capacities
   Ⓓ political birthrights

5 In paragraph 3, the author implies that Maslow

(A) was critical of Freudians and neo-Freudians

(B) believed that success in life depended on obvious inborn capacities

(C) was not interested in mentally unhealthy minds

(D) tended to focus on how to satisfy basic needs

6 In paragraph 4, the author's description of an individual's set of basic needs mentions all of the following EXCEPT:

(A) Love

(B) Protection from harm

(C) Self-respect

(D) Self-fulfillment

7 According to paragraph 4, self-actualization is unlikely to occur because

(A) people stop maturing once they develop a high sense of self-esteem

(B) needs are arranged in a particular order or hierarchy

(C) self-actualization and self-esteem are the same

(D) motivation is not necessary for the satisfaction of basic needs

8 **Directions:** Complete the table below by matching FIVE of the seven answer choices with the psychological theory that they exemplify. TWO of the answer choices will NOT be used.

Answer Choices

1. Human behavior is governed by the subconscious.

2. Individuals are born with potential capacities for personal growth.

3. Once basic needs are met, self-actualization results.

4. Man tends to perceive things as a whole.

5. Human needs are arranged in a particular order.

6. Punishments and rewards are required to change action.

7. It is essential to focus on what people are like when their basic needs are not met.

Behaviorism

-

Freudianism

-
-

Humanistic Psychology

-
-

07-13

Shipping and Shipbuilding in the British Colonies
in North America

1 ➡ Early shipbuilding practices in the British colonies of North America were crude and tedious. All planking was sawn by hand, and the bulkier components were shaped and fitted by use of the adze, the broadaxe, and the plane. As a part of the cumbersome process, a pit was dug, and a platform, or staging, was set up across it. A log was placed upon the platform, and a pair of men would work together to operate a two-man saw in a push-pull fashion. With one man in the pit and the other on the platform, they would haul the saw blade across the log until the log ripped into a plank. So much skill was required to master this feat that the work of the sawyer became a recognized trade.

2 ➡ In the early settlements of the 1600s, English shipwrights were imported to train apprentices. The second man was the shipwright's helper, and together they were a gang. A third man had the job of turning the log away from the staging when the saw cut loomed too near it or when it was time to start a new cut. Although shipbuilding led to other industries, such as the making of sails, rope, nails, anchors, and chains, the cost of converting timber to usable planks was so great that the timber industry itself did not develop for a while. Shipbuilders also used a good deal of green lumber in their ship construction.

3 ➡ **1** By the mid-1650s, most of the colonies did not lay down a ship more than once every three years. **2** Builders would send out and sell a vessel as well as its fully loaded cargo to English or foreign owners after it reached its destination. **3** These slow-moving ships closely followed the 400-year-old traditional lines of the popular English and Danish styles. **4** They bore three masts and square-rigging on a broad base, but they were usually much smaller. Nevertheless, by the late 1600s, colonial shipbuilders were strong competitors in the shipbuilding and shipping trades and helped propel heavy trans-Atlantic commerce.

4 ➡ Colonial Boston became the jewel in the crown of Britain's commercial exploits. Under Puritanical management, its harbor and plentiful resources ensured a robust trade economy that would be a matter of course for the young American colonies. The coastal and continental resources that provided for fur trapping, iron making, and the production of textiles paled in comparison to the rich supplies of timber and fish that seemed to be inexhaustible exports for the young colony. Although none of the trades, not even the fisheries, provided constant employment, these resources laid the underpinnings for a secure economic boon that anchored the shipping and shipbuilding industries.

5 ➡ By the early 1700s, Boston Harbor was the number-one seaport in America and the third largest port in the British Atlantic realm. A lucrative salt-cod trade resulted in strong collaborative ties among shipbuilders, fishermen, and merchants. It also led to shipping innovations that bolstered the path for the infamous Triangle Trade Route and made Boston America's largest, wealthiest, and most influential city through the 1760s.

9   The word "cumbersome" in the passage is closest in meaning to

      Ⓐ inconvenient

      Ⓑ bulky

      Ⓒ delicate

      Ⓓ unskilled

10   Select the TWO answer choices from paragraph 1 that identify tools used to build ships. *To receive credit, you must select TWO answers.*

      Ⓐ A plane

      Ⓑ A handsaw

      Ⓒ A pit

      Ⓓ An axe

11   According to paragraph 2, which of the following is true of shipbuilders in the 1600s?

      Ⓐ They only used undried lumber to build ships quickly.

      Ⓑ They all came from Britain to teach people how to build ships.

      Ⓒ They usually worked in teams of three.

      Ⓓ They became rich through shipbuilding in colonial America.

12   The word "propel" in the passage is closest in meaning to

      Ⓐ stay afloat

      Ⓑ change direction

      Ⓒ decrease weight

      Ⓓ send forth

13   In paragraph 3, the author implies that colonial ships

      Ⓐ would be sold along with the cargo they carried

      Ⓑ only set sail once every three years

      Ⓒ were paired with older ships on journeys

      Ⓓ had to compete with traditional styles

14   The author discusses "Colonial Boston" in paragraph 4 in order to

      Ⓐ name some influential people who lived there

      Ⓑ compare it with other cities in the American colonies

      Ⓒ explain its importance to the colonial economy

      Ⓓ note that it was the largest city in the American colonies

15 In paragraph 5, all of the following questions are answered EXCEPT:

Ⓐ What was Boston like in the 1760s?

Ⓑ Where did the Triangle Trade Route go?

Ⓒ How large was Boston Harbor in the 1700s?

Ⓓ What was one result of the salt-cod trade?

16 Look at the four squares [■] that indicate where the following sentence could be added to the passage.

The manufacturing of ships was slow, but it continued at a steady and profitable pace.

Where would the sentence best fit?

Vocabulary Check-Up

A Choose the words with the closest meanings to the highlighted words.

1 The young boy would wear a cape and pretend that he could fly.

   Ⓐ insist

   Ⓑ find out

   Ⓒ make believe

   Ⓓ hope

2 Spoiled children are apt to have tantrums when they do not get their way.

   Ⓐ likely

   Ⓑ sure

   Ⓒ forbidden

   Ⓓ quick

3 The constant drip from the tap left her no choice but to call a plumber.

   Ⓐ steady

   Ⓑ loud

   Ⓒ broken

   Ⓓ wasteful

4 The friends made a pact to meet again in one year.

   Ⓐ bet

   Ⓑ agreement

   Ⓒ race

   Ⓓ plan

5 The student body will induct the new members at their next meeting.

   Ⓐ introduce

   Ⓑ applaud

   Ⓒ admit

   Ⓓ listen to

6 Her greatest acquisition was a signed autograph from the singer.

   Ⓐ possession

   Ⓑ achievement

   Ⓒ desire

   Ⓓ fear

7 The cashier sorts out the receipts from the pile.

   Ⓐ receives

   Ⓑ combine

   Ⓒ creates

   Ⓓ selects

8 Her formidable talent won her a part in the show.

   Ⓐ impressive

   Ⓑ natural

   Ⓒ raw

   Ⓓ single

9 The steady breeze was conducive for kite flying.

   Ⓐ harmful

   Ⓑ helpful

   Ⓒ difficult

   Ⓓ needed

10 The water supply to the city and several adjacent areas remains affected by the earthquake.

   Ⓐ remote

   Ⓑ surrounding

   Ⓒ suburban

   Ⓓ neighboring

B Match the words with the correct definitions.

1   advent   •   • (A) to live; to dwell

2   reside   •   • (B) related to teaching

3   algorithm   •   • (C) a creator

4   volatile   •   • (D) by habitual repetition

5   inflate   •   • (E) a trait; an attribute

6   innovator   •   • (F) rising

7   by rote   •   • (G) likely to change abruptly; dangerously unpredictable

8   pedagogical   •   • (H) a beginning

9   ascending   •   • (I) to increase rapidly

10 characteristic   •   • (J) a determined procedure for solving a problem

◤ Overview

Introduction

Insert Text questions ask you to determine where the best place for a given sentence would be in the passage. In this type of question, you will see four black squares appearing in one paragraph. You need to understand the logical stream of the passage and focus on any grammatical connections between sentences, such as conjunctions, pronouns, demonstratives, and repeated words or phrases.

Question Types

◈ Look at the four squares [■] that indicate where the following sentence could be added to the passage.

[a sentence to be inserted into the passage]

Where would the sentence best fit?

Click on a square [■] to add the sentence to the passage.

Useful Tips

- Put the sentence in each place next to the squares.
- Try to pay attention to the logical connection between sentences.
- Be familiar with the connecting words, such as *on the other hand, for example, on the contrary, similarly, in contrast, furthermore, therefore, in other words, as a result,* and *finally.*

Q Look at the four squares [■] that indicate where the following sentence could be added to the passage.

Initially, they were disregarded.

Where would the sentence best fit?

Impressionism

08-01

The term Impressionism comes from a painting by Claude Monet entitled *Impression, Sunrise*. **1** Ironically, it was attributed to the nineteenth-century art movement, of which Monet was a member, by the art critic Louis Leroy. **2** This movement had its beginnings in Paris and included a loosely associated group of Parisian artists who broke the conventions of academic painting at that time. **3** Many of the original Impressionists, such as Monet, Pierre August Renoir, Paul Cezanne, and Edouard Manet, were rejected from an important juried art show at the Salon of Paris. **4** In reaction to this, they organized their own show in which the public would be allowed to judge. They called it "Salon of the Refused." The characteristics of their radical paintings were visible brushstrokes, the use of light colors, and open composition. There was also an emphasis on light and its changing qualities, ordinary subject matter, unusual visual angles, and the accentuation of the effects of the passage of time.

☑ Correct Answer

The new sentence is best inserted at square **3**. The pronoun *they* in the given sentence refers to "Parisian artists" in the third sentence of the passage, and the verb *disregarded* is semantically related to "rejected" in the fourth sentence of the passage.

Basic Drill

Read the passages and answer the questions.

Drill 1

The Bauhaus Movement

08-02

The Bauhaus movement is named after a German art school called Staatliches Bauhaus that was responsible for one of the strongest influences in Modernist architecture and interior design. **1** Ironically, this school only operated for a relatively short period of time between the First and Second World Wars from the years 1919 to 1933 and very briefly in the United States from 1937 to 1938. **2** Constant leadership changes and power struggles at the school resulted in a constant shift of the school's focus, technique, instructors, and politics. **3** The catalyst for the utilitarian style of this movement was a text published by the critic Adolf Loos in 1908. **4** It was entitled *Ornament and Crime* and claimed that surface decoration was primitive. The school's original founder, architect Walter Gropius, proclaimed in his opening manifesto that the school's goal was, "to create a new guild of craftsmen, without the class distinctions which raise an arrogant barrier between craftsmen and artist."

Q   Look at the four squares [■] that indicate where the following sentence could be added to the passage.

Its philosophy centered on the belief that things must be useful to be valuable.

Where would the sentence best fit?

Drill 2

Market Regulation

08-03

Market regulation takes place when a government seeks to control some or all aspects of a particular market through the application of laws. **1** The government does this to achieve various purposes, such as the creation of a centrally planned market or in the hope of remedying a market failure. **2** Market regulation is also enacted by a corrupt government for the purpose of benefiting well-connected companies or politicians. **3** One type of market that is commonly regulated is that of public services. **4** This takes place in order to balance the opposing interests of maximizing profits and serving the best interests of the people who use the public services. Some good examples of this are government regulations placed on alcohol and prescription drug markets. Most countries seek to control these markets. Then, they can ensure that the products are safe and only sold to the appropriate customers.

Q   Look at the four squares [■] that indicate where the following sentence could be added to the passage.

However, such actions are not always in the best interests of the private sector.

Where would the sentence best fit?

Cognitive Science

08-04

Cognition is defined as the process by which the mind or intelligence functions or thinks. **1** Cognitive science is an interdisciplinary field of research that employs psychology, neuroscience, linguistics, philosophy, computer science, anthropology, and biology to understand this process. **2** Cognitive science may be distinguished between the studies of human and animal brains. **3** There are three major approaches to the study of cognitive science: symbolic, connectionist, and dynamical systems. **4** The symbolic approach is one that attempts to explain cognition through the use of operations performed on symbols. These operations run parallel to the workings of a digital computer and are expressed by means of explicit computational theories and modes of mental processes. These mental processes are not considered on the physical brain level. The connectionist approach looks at cognition through models of artificial neural networks that exist on the level of physical brain properties. The third approach is that of dynamical systems. It contends that cognition is best explained in the form of a continuous dynamical system in which all the elements are interrelated.

Q Look at the four squares [■] that indicate where the following sentence could be added to the passage.

It includes aspects of awareness, perception, reasoning, and judgments.

Where would the sentence best fit?

Hypatia of Alexandria

08-05

Hypatia of Alexandria was a philosopher, mathematician, and astronomer in Egypt. She is thought to have been born in the year 370 A.D. None of Hypatia's writings has survived. **1** So historians know of her only by letters written to her by a pupil as well as from several descriptions in personal histories recorded by other authors. **2** From these, historians have learned that Hypatia was a highly respected scholar and member of the intellectual community in Alexandria. **3** Hypatia was a follower of the Platonic school of philosophy and is reputed to have invented the astrolabe, which was used to map the positions of stars, and the hydrometer, which is still used to determine the specific gravity of liquids. **4** By 415, Hypatia, who was a pagan, had run afoul of the rising Christian movement and was murdered by a vicious mob of them.

Q Look at the four squares [■] that indicate where the following sentence could be added to the passage.

Her interests resulted in many new inventions.

Where would the sentence best fit?

Exercise 1 Read the following passage and answer the questions.

Time Limit: 3 min. 50 sec.

The 1973 Oil Crisis

08-06

¹→ The 1973 oil crisis began because of the Yom Kippur War being fought between Israel and Syria and Egypt at that time. Syria and Egypt, which were members of the OPEC (Organization of Petroleum Exporting Countries), convinced the Arab members of this organization to cut the supply of petroleum to nations that supported Israel. This embargo immediately affected the United States, Canada, and many of their allies in Western Europe.

While reducing the much-needed supply of petroleum to the Western world, the Arab oil powers also increased the price of oil all over the world. This sharp increase had dramatic inflationary effects on economies everywhere. The United States and the Netherlands, both staunch supporters of Israel, were especially targeted by this embargo and experienced immediate economic effects.

The most immediate effect of the embargo was that the price of oil by the barrel quadrupled. The Arab politicians and other elites that controlled the oil instantly became very wealthy. Many of these suddenly rich oil countries invested their newfound wealth in weapons that increased tensions in the Middle East even more. **A1** As the retail price of gasoline by the gallon skyrocketed, shares on the New York Stock Exchange lost ninety-seven billion dollars in value in the course of six weeks. **A2** The supply of Arab oil into the U.S. dropped from 1.2 million barrels a day to just 19,000 barrels a day. **A3** The United States suffered its worst fuel shortage since the Second World War. **A4**

In order to control the long lines for gasoline at gas stations and the price gouging that resulted, the U.S. government initiated a number of measures. One was to limit the price of "old oil," which was already discovered, while leaving the pricing of "new oil" open in order to encourage exploration. Another measure was that drivers of vehicles with odd-numbered license plates were only allowed to purchase gas for their cars on odd-numbered days of the month. In turn, drivers of cars with even-numbered license plates were only allowed to purchase gas on even-numbered days.

The U.S. government also began to encourage its citizens to reduce their usage of gasoline and generally to conserve energy whenever possible. In order to implement this, the national speed limit was dropped to fifty-five miles per hour. Daylight savings time was also mandated to decrease the need for lighting. **B1** One popular conservation campaign used the slogan "Don't Be Fuelish." to encourage people to cut down on their use of energy. **B2** By March of 1974, the Yom Kippur War was over, and all of the Arab OPEC countries, with the exception of Libya, abandoned their embargo against the United States. **B3** The supply of oil rose, and prices leveled off, but a series of recessions had already been triggered and plagued many Western countries throughout the 1980s. **B4**

📖 Words & Phrases

convince (v) to persuade
embargo (n) a prohibition
ally (n) a supporter; a collaborator
staunch (adj) committed
tension (n) strain
skyrocket (v) to increase very rapidly

price gouge (phr) the act of overcharging; a rip-off
initiate (v) to begin
conserve (v) to preserve
implement (v) to carry out; to execute
impose (v) to force

level off (phr) to stabilize
recession (n) a temporary economic decline
trigger (v) to cause; to prompt
plague (v) to bother

1 According to paragraph 1, the oil crisis in the United States was caused by

   Ⓐ the adoption of daylight savings time

   Ⓑ a decrease in the supply of oil

   Ⓒ price gouging by gas stations

   Ⓓ Israel's embargo of the Arab nations

2 The word "abandoned" in the passage is closest in meaning to

   Ⓐ participated in

   Ⓑ resumed

   Ⓒ considered

   Ⓓ ended

Mastering the Question Type

3 Look at the four squares [■] that indicate where the following sentence could be added to the passage.

This oil shock resulted in chaos in Western societies.

Where would the sentence best fit?

4 Look at the four squares [■] that indicate where the following sentence could be added to the passage.

Nevertheless, the impact of the oil crisis set in motion far-reaching effects.

Where would the sentence best fit?

📝 Summary Note   Fill in the blanks with the appropriate words.

The 1973 Oil Crisis

- Began because of ❶ _____
  - fought between Israel, Syria, and Egypt
  - Arab OPEC members stop supplying oil to Israel's supporters → U.S., Canada, and Western European countries

- Effects of oil embargo
  - reduced supply of oil to West
  - increased ❷ _____ worldwide
  - caused inflation

- Effects in the United States
  - ❸ _____ loses value
  - long lines for gas
  - made a national ❹ _____
  - mandated daylight savings time

- Embargo ended in 1974

Time Limit: 3 min. 50 sec.

Bird Migration

08-07

1 ➤ Many birds are known to migrate long distances. It is common for a number of species to spend the summer months in the mild climates of the Northern Hemisphere. There, they breed and fatten themselves on abundant food sources. When the winter months approach, these migratory birds fly south to spend the winter months in warm tropical and Southern Hemisphere regions.

This migratory behavior is most commonly found in land-dwelling birds. Various species are known to migrate the greatest distances. They migrate in search of food as the fall and winter months in the Northern Hemisphere provide little in the way of food. These birds are genetically predisposed to take on the risks that migration carries in order to satisfy a sense of migratory restlessness. This feeling is expressed by the German word *Zugunruhe*.

Zugunruhe has been found to exist even in caged birds that are closed off from the environmental cues that could spark the urge to migrate. This instinctual urge is exhibited in the direction that these captive birds prefer to fly. **A1** That is the same direction in which wild members of their species migrate. **A2** They even exhibit this preferred flight direction at the same time of year that the same species of birds in the wild perform their annual migration. **A3** This direction changes at times when the wild birds change their flight course. **A4** Based on these observations, scientists, who do not fully understand bird migration, believe that the birds' ability repeatedly to follow the same migratory route every year is based on a combination of circannual endogenic programming within the birds' genes. They also believe that cognitive ability in the birds' minds forms crude mental maps based on memories of landmarks and habitats.

4 ➤ These migratory paths are programmed into the genetic structures of these birds. But they have been known to alter their routes for various reasons. Some of these reasons are to increase aerodynamic efficiency, to respond to changes in weather conditions, and to avoid the risk of predation. One bird, the Eleonora's falcon, is known to have adapted its migration pattern by having a very late breeding season. As a result, it can hunt migrating passerines as they fly by on their way south for the winter.

B1 One type of bird that does not migrate long distances is broad-winged birds such as vultures, eagles, buzzards, and storks. **B2** These large birds are only able to soar by way of thermal columns of rising hot air. **B3** This necessity inhibits them from flying over vast oceans since thermal columns only occur over land. **B4** This inability to cross the larger bodies of water results in these large birds crossing the narrowest of landmasses during their migratory cycle. One example is the massive numbers of raptors and storks which can be seen crossing the Mediterranean Sea at its narrowest points, such as Gibraltar and the Bosporus, on their way south from Europe to Africa for the winter months.

📖 Words & Phrases

hemisphere n one half of the Earth

abundant adj plentiful; ample; copious

be predisposed to-V phr to be inclined to-V

urge n a strong desire

circannual adj occurring every year

endogenic adj caused by factors inside the organism

cognitive adj relating to the mental process of knowing

crude adj unrefined

alter v to change

predation n the act of one organism eating another

soar v to fly high

thermal adj related to heat

inhibit v to restrain; to hold back

1   According to paragraph 1, many birds spend the summer months

      Ⓐ living in the Southern Hemisphere

      Ⓑ resting for their migration

      Ⓒ staying in the Northern Hemisphere

      Ⓓ searching for scarce food

2   According paragraph 4, why did the Eleonora's falcon change its migration pattern?

      Ⓐ To improve its flying efficiency

      Ⓑ To hunt other migrating birds

      Ⓒ To avoid being attacked by larger birds

      Ⓓ To choose the warmest climate

Mastering the Question Type

3   Look at the four squares [■] that indicate where the following sentence could be added to the passage.

Observable data is collected through band recoveries, netting records, and personal observations that help determine migration routes.

Where would the sentence best fit?

4   Look at the four squares [■] that indicate where the following sentence could be added to the passage.

Of course, scientists have also investigated the migratory habits of species that travel shorter distances.

Where would the sentence best fit?

📝 Summary Note   **Fill in the blanks with the appropriate words.**

Bird Migration

- Characteristics
  - birds fly long distances
  - fly south in winter and north in summer
  - are ❶ .... to migrate
- *Zugunruhe*
  - describes ❷ .... that induces migration
  - has been found even in ❸ ....
- Understanding bird migration
  - scientists do not fully understand it
  - think it is a combination of ❹ .... to follow same path
  - can sometimes alter their routes for various reasons

Exercise 3 Read the following passage and answer the questions.

Time Limit: 5 min.

Georgia O'Keeffe

08-08

Georgia O'Keeffe was one of the most influential American artists of the twentieth century. Today, she is famous for paintings that use images of natural objects such as flowers, rocks, shells, landscapes, and animal bones in order to create abstraction and representation. In 1928, a set of six calla lily paintings by O'Keeffe sold for 25,000 dollars. At the time, that was the largest amount of money ever paid for a group of paintings by an American artist who was still alive.

2 ➡ O'Keeffe was born in Wisconsin in 1887 as the second of seven children. **A1** Her parents, who were dairy farmers, recognized her artistic abilities when she was young and made sure she received art instruction very early on. **A2** Her first instructor was a local watercolorist named Sarah Mann. **A3** After graduating from high school, O'Keeffe attended the Art Institute of Chicago and later the Art Students League in New York City. **A4** It was in New York that she attended an exhibition of Rodin's watercolors at a gallery named 291. It was owned by Alfred Stieglitz, who was to become her husband some years later.

For the next few years, O'Keeffe struggled with illness and financial troubles. In 1908, believing that she could not support herself through painting, she stopped it altogether. **B1** Then, in 1912, her creative spark was rekindled when she attended an art class at the University of Virginia Summer School. **B2** There, her instructor Alon Bement introduced her to new ideas about design through the harmonious interactions of lines, shapes, and colors. **B3** These ideas greatly influenced and altered O'Keeffe's ideas about the creative artistic process. **B4**

Eventually, Alfred Stieglitz found his way back into O'Keeffe's life by helping along her career as a painter. He arranged for an apartment for her to live in New York City. There, they fell deeply in love, and Stieglitz divorced his wife so that they could marry. Shortly after they married, Stieglitz began taking photographs of O'Keeffe, including some nudes. These were exhibited in a retrospective exhibition of his work and swiftly created a public fervor.

In the following years, O'Keeffe became part of the early American modernist art circles. Around this time, O'Keeffe shifted away from her past work in watercolors and began using oils to paint. She soon developed a new style of painting on a very large scale by depicting natural forms in a very close-up manner, as if they were under a magnifying lens. Her husband, Stieglitz, began exhibiting her work at his gallery. O'Keeffe's artistic career blossomed, leading to her great commercial success, such as the sale of her calla lily paintings in 1928.

6 ➡ Then, in the summer of 1929, O'Keeffe visited New Mexico with a friend and discovered the area's unique architectural and landscape forms. From 1929 to 1949, O'Keeffe spent a portion of every year working in New Mexico. There, she drew inspiration from the animal bones she collected and painted during her second summer in the state. The images of cow skulls, expansive blue skies, and jagged red rock hills were to become some of the most memorable images to find their way into her work. Eventually, she discovered a piece of property north of Abiquiu, which she named Ghost Ranch. The colorful surrounding desert landscape and sweeping cliffs and hills of this area were to offer her inspiration for the rest of her career.

📖 **Words & Phrases**

abstraction n the use of shapes and patterns in art
rekindle v to reawaken

retrospective adj looking back
fervor n passion; enthusiasm; eagerness

magnify v to enlarge
expansive adj spread-out; vast; wide

1   According to paragraph 2, which of the following is true of Georgia O'Keeffe's parents?

   (A) They never realized how talented she was.

   (B) They taught her how to paint.

   (C) They recognized and encouraged her talent.

   (D) They were well-known painters.

2   In paragraph 6, why does the author mention "New Mexico"?

   (A) To claim it was the place where O'Keeffe died

   (B) To focus on its importance to O'Keeffe's art career

   (C) To argue that it has the best natural scenery in the country

   (D) To explain why O'Keeffe enjoyed visiting it from time to time

3   Look at the four squares [■] that indicate where the following sentence could be added to the passage.

   As a matter of fact, by the age of eight, O'Keeffe was determined to be an artist.

   Where would the sentence best fit?

4   Look at the four squares [■] that indicate where the following sentence could be added to the passage.

   Instead, she accepted a teaching position in Amarillo, Texas.

   Where would the sentence best fit?

Summary Note   Fill in the blanks with the appropriate words.

Georgia O'Keeffe

- Was an influential American artist
  - painted ❶ _____
  - sold paintings for very high prices

- Early life
  - was born in ❷ _____
  - parents recognized her talent and helped her nurture it
  - attended various art institutes

- Married ❸ _____
  - helped her resume painting
  - took nude photographs of her

- Changed style
  - had used watercolors
  - started using oils
  - painted on a large scale
  - moved to ❹ _____ to paint images there

Read the following passage and answer the questions.

Gold Rushes in the Nineteenth Century

08-09

1 ➜ In North America in the 1800s, many vast fortunes were made by gold and silver prospectors. The nineteenth century was a time when several mineral deposits or lodes rich with gold and silver were discovered. As soon as one of these discoveries was made public, a fevered migration called a rush would ensue. A rush was a situation in which thousands of prospectors would travel to areas near the site of the discovery. There, they would attempt to make their own discoveries and fortunes. This process accelerated the settlement of whites in frontier areas such as California, Nevada, Alaska, and the Yukon Territories in Northern Canada. It also helped displace native peoples and their cultures at an even faster pace than was already happening.

These prospectors ranged from the most uneducated lower-class laborers to well-heeled entrepreneurs. At the heart of every quest was a deep desire to become rich. Many prospectors were able to amass great fortunes. But many more did not, and a great many died in their search. All prospectors, both the rich and poor and young and old, were required to endure great hardships during their search. Food and water were scarce, and desert temperatures were hot enough to make horses and mules drop dead. Winters were always even worse as prospectors suffered endless cases of frostbite in which their limbs had to be amputated.

The first major gold rush in American history was the California Gold Rush, which began when gold was found at Sutter's Mill, California, in 1848. Those early prospectors who arrived in 1848 were called forty-eighters. Many of them came from nearby areas such as Oregon or other regions in California. These lucky prospectors found it very easy to remove thousands of dollars' worth of easily accessible gold from streams every day. **A1** But for those who arrived in 1949, called forty-niners, it was more difficult as so much of the more reachable gold had already been taken. **A2** By 1855, some 300,000 prospectors had come to California from all over the United States and abroad. **A3** The prospectors traveled to California by wagon train and ship, and many used very simple means to retrieve gold flakes from beneath running water in stream beds. **A4** This simple method was called panning.

Another major North American Gold Rush occurred in 1896. That was when a Native American named Skookum Jim Maon and his group discovered rich placer gold deposits in the Klondike River in the northern Yukon Territories of Canada. At this time, the Yukon Territories were scarcely populated with whites due to the harsh winters that kept this region covered in frigid snow for most of the year. Once again, as soon as the news of this discovery got out, there was a stampede of prospectors. They raced into this area while looking to make their fortunes by panning for gold.

5 ➜ **B1** By 1898, the population along the Klondike had swollen from a few thousand to 40,000 people. **B2** That was an upsurge that brought with it the threat of famine and typhoid fever from polluted water supplies. **B3** Once again, as is captured in the Klondike Gold Rush literature of Jack London such as *White Fang*, *Call of the Wild*, and his most famous short story, *To Build a Fire*, many fortunes were made. **B4** But because of the terribly harsh conditions, for every fortune that was made, a hundred other people suffered misfortune.

📖 Words & Phrases

lode n a deposit of ore
ensue v to follow
accelerate v to speed up
well-heeled adj wealthy

entrepreneur n a risk-taking businessperson
amass v to collect; to accumulate
amputate v to sever; to cut off

accessible adj available; reachable
retrieve v to get; to gain; to obtain
frigid adj very cold; freezing
upsurge n a sudden, large increase

1 According to paragraph 1, the Yukon Territories are found in

    Ⓐ northern Canada

    Ⓑ Alaska

    Ⓒ the northern United States

    Ⓓ California and Nevada

2 According to paragraph 5, Jack London is well known as

    Ⓐ a miner

    Ⓑ an explorer

    Ⓒ a doctor

    Ⓓ a writer

Mastering the Question Type

3 Look at the four squares [■] that indicate where the following sentence could be added to the passage.

This placer gold was released naturally from primary veins as a result of weathering.

Where would the sentence best fit?

4 Look at the four squares [■] that indicate where the following sentence could be added to the passage.

This time, however, the Northwest Mounted Police monitored the activities of the prospectors to ensure safety and order.

Where would the sentence best fit?

📝 Summary Note   Fill in the blanks with the appropriate words.

Gold Rushes in the Nineteenth Century

- Many gold and silver lodes discovered in nineteenth century in America
  - sparked ❶ ....
  - many people became rich

- Gold rush
  - occurs when many people go to area to find gold
  - happened in California, Nevada, Alaska, and ❷ ....

- Prospectors
  - were both rich and poor people
  - endured great hardships
  - some even died

- ❸ ....
  - began in 1848 when gold discovered at Sutter's Mill
  - thousands went to California

- North American Gold Rush
  - up in Canada and Alaska
  - ❹ .... wrote about it in his literature

Exercise 5 Read the following passage and answer the questions.

Time Limit: 3 min. 40 sec.

Nuclear Reactors

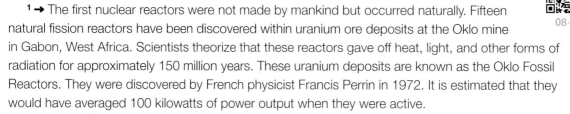

08-10

1 ➤ The first nuclear reactors were not made by mankind but occurred naturally. Fifteen natural fission reactors have been discovered within uranium ore deposits at the Oklo mine in Gabon, West Africa. Scientists theorize that these reactors gave off heat, light, and other forms of radiation for approximately 150 million years. These uranium deposits are known as the Oklo Fossil Reactors. They were discovered by French physicist Francis Perrin in 1972. It is estimated that they would have averaged 100 kilowatts of power output when they were active.

A1 Modern nuclear reactors are devices in which nuclear chain reactions are harnessed for their useful power output. **A2** This is done by initiating, controlling, and sustaining nuclear fission at a steady rate. **A3** The main use for nuclear reactors is to generate electrical power. **A4** But they are also used to do research with beamline experiments to produce weapons-grade plutonium and radioisotopes. They can even propel nuclear-powered submarines and ships.

Nuclear fission is the only reaction process that is currently used commercially since it is considered to be a safe and pollution-free power source. **B1** Conversely, nuclear fusion is currently an experimental technology. **B2** It is looked down upon by many scientists because of the potential health and safety risks it creates. **B3** Other methods for creating controlled nuclear reactions are radioisotope thermoelectric generators and atomic batteries. **B4** Both of these generate heat and power through passive radioactive decay.

There are several different nuclear reactor technologies used to create commercial fission-powered electricity. They can be divided into two classes, fast and slow reactors. They are based on the energy of the neutrons used to sustain the fission chain reaction.

Slow reactors are also known as thermal reactors. They utilize slow neutrons. These neutrons are moderated by materials that slow them until they approach the average kinetic energy of the surrounding particles. This process is called thermalization. This is the most common type of reactor for generating power. The first commercial plutonium reactors were of this variety and used graphite as the moderator.

Fast reactors utilize fast neutrons to create and sustain the necessary fission chain reaction and lack the moderating material required by slow reactors. This type of reactor requires highly enriched fuel, such as weapons-grade plutonium. This ensures that the amount of U-238 is reduced to as little as possible in order to avoid radioactive contamination. Some of the early Russian ship and submarine propulsion units as well as some early power stations used fast reactors. However, the fast reactor has not achieved the success that slow reactors have in any application even though the construction of this kind of reactor continues.

📖 Words & Phrases

fission n the splitting of an atom, which produces a release of energy
ore n rock or earth from which metal can be obtained
give off phr to emit; to send out
harness v to control; to use
sustain v to continue; to maintain

generate v to produce
propel v to push forward
conversely adv in contrast
fusion n the melting together of more than two things
potential adj possible; likely

thermal adj relating to heat
utilize v to use; to take advantage of
moderate v to check; to curb; to restrain
kinetic adj related to motion
contamination n pollution

1   According to paragraph 1, which of the following is true about the Oklo Fossil Reactors?
    (A) They were discovered in France in 1972.
    (B) They send out radiation by the process of nuclear fission.
    (C) They have been active since 1972.
    (D) They had uranium deposits that have been used up.

2   The word "these" in the passage refers to
    (A) the potential health and safety risks
    (B) other methods
    (C) nuclear reactions
    (D) radioisotope thermoelectric generators and atomic batteries

Mastering the Question Type

3   Look at the four squares [■] that indicate where the following sentence could be added to the passage.
    As a power source, nuclear fission promises many potential applications.
    Where would the sentence best fit?

4   Look at the four squares [■] that indicate where the following sentence could be added to the passage.
    For this reason, scientists opt for more stable means of generating power.
    Where would the sentence best fit?

Summary Note   Fill in the blanks with the appropriate words.

Nuclear Reactors

- First ones occurred naturally
  – in uranium ore deposits in ❶ _____ in Gabon, Africa
  – gave off heat, light, and radiation for 150 million years
- Modern reactors
  – harness nuclear chain reactions to make energy
  – initiate, control, and sustain ❷ _____
- Nuclear fission
  – safe and pollution free
- Nuclear fusion
  – experimental and possibly ❸ _____
- Different kinds of reactors
  – slow reactors
    → use slow neutrons
    → create energy through ❹ _____
  – fast reactors
    → use fast neutrons
    → need highly enriched uranium

Exercise 6 Read the following passage and answer the questions.

Time Limit: 3 min. 50 sec.

The Great Portrait Painters of Colonial America

08-11

Two of the most renowned portrait painters of the American Colonial Period were John Singleton Copley and Gilbert Stuart. During this time, before the advent of cameras and photography, realistic portrait painters were important since they served to create the only visual historical record of important people and places.

John Singleton Copley was a Boston-born artist who was known for his innovative style. Most of his portraits were of important figures in colonial New England as well as the men and women of the middle class. They commonly portrayed their subjects in poses with objects that indicated the details of their lives, such as a carpenter with a saw or a teacher with a book. Some of Copley's most famous paintings are of Revolutionary War heroes Samuel Adams and Paul Revere. But at the start of the revolution, around the year 1774, Copley himself moved to Europe to avoid the fighting and to continue perfecting his painting skills.

Another important painter of this time was Gilbert Stuart. His painting career did not develop as smoothly as that of Copley, who was a major influence on Stuart. But ultimately, Stuart's paintings are held in even higher esteem than those of Copley's. After training under the Scottish painter Cosmo Alexander, Stuart followed Copley's example and moved to Europe to avoid the Revolutionary War and to continue painting. But Stuart's early efforts to establish himself were unsuccessful.

4 → After suffering several early failures, Stuart became the protégé of Benjamin West in London. By 1777, Stuart was able to exhibit his work at the Royal Academy and finally began to meet with success and acclaim. The prices of Stuart's paintings soon rose dramatically, but despite this success, he habitually mismanaged his money. Due to his neglectfulness towards his finances, Stuart was forced to flee to Ireland in 1787 to escape going to debtors' prison.

Upon returning to the United States in 1793, Stuart opened a studio in Philadelphia. Here he established his lasting fame painting portraits of important Americans. **A1** Perhaps the most famous of his works is a series of iconic portraits of George Washington. **A2** This new fame kept Stuart busy and well paid for years. **A3** The best known of his George Washington likenesses is known as the Athenaeum Head and is currently featured on the U.S. one-dollar bill. **A4** Stuart's most acclaimed portrait of Washington is a large painting that hangs in the East Room of the White House. This portrait was saved from destruction by the First Lady of the time, Dolley Madison, during the War of 1812 when British soldiers burned down the presidential mansion.

B1 By the end of his career, Stuart had painted more than one thousand American political figures. **B2** His style was praised for its vitality and naturalness. **B3** The great American founding father and president John Adams was heard to remark that sitting for a portrait painter was usually a terribly uncomfortable experience but that sitting for Stuart was a pleasure because of his loose manner and amusing conversation. **B4** Stuart was also known not to work from sketches but just to begin painting directly on the canvas.

📖 Words & Phrases

advent n an appearance
esteem n respect; admiration; regard
protégé n a pupil; a student; an apprentice

acclaim n public praise
neglectfulness n carelessness; indifference
flee v to run away; to take flight; to escape

iconic adj symbolic; important; impressive
vitality n vigor; liveliness; energy

1 The word "They" in the passage refers to

Ⓐ His portraits

Ⓑ Important figures

Ⓒ The men and women of the middle class

Ⓓ Their subjects

2 According to paragraph 4, Stuart fled to Ireland in order to

Ⓐ paint prominent politicians

Ⓑ avoid being imprisoned

Ⓒ sell his paintings

Ⓓ open a studio

3 Look at the four squares [■] that indicate where the following sentence could be added to the passage.

However, he painted many subjects from the Old World as well.

Where would the sentence best fit?

4 Look at the four squares [■] that indicate where the following sentence could be added to the passage.

Indeed, Stuart's easy demeanor won him a devoted following.

Where would the sentence best fit?

Summary Note Fill in the blanks with the appropriate words.

The Great Portrait Painters of Colonial America

- Were two major painters
  - John Singleton Copley and Gilbert Stuart

- John Singleton Copley
  - had an innovative style
  - painted important people and members of ❶ _____
  - created visual record of various events
  - painted ❷ _____ and Paul Revere

- Gilbert Stuart
  - was influenced greatly by Copley
  - became protégé of ❸ _____
  - moved to America to open studio in Philadelphia
  - made famous paintings of ❹ _____
  - painted over 1,000 American political figures

Building Summary Skills

The following summaries are based on the passages you worked on earlier. Complete each of them by filling in the blanks with suitable words or phrases.

Exercise 1   The 1973 Oil Crisis

a series of recessions	withhold petroleum	Syria and Egypt
the purchase of weapons	the U.S. government	

In 1973, during the Yom Kippur War, _____ tried to stifle support for Israel. They convinced the Arab members of the OPEC to _____ from the United States, Canada, and many of their allies in Western Europe. _____ took many steps to ease the effects of the shortage while elite Arabs grew rich from their increased profits and invested much of their newfound wealth in _____. Meanwhile, although the Yom Kippur War ended in 1974, the ramifications of the oil crisis included _____ in many Western countries throughout the 1980s.

Exercise 2   Bird Migration

Zugunruhe	food and other basic needs	genetic programming
migratory patterns	thermal columns of air	

Many land-dwelling bird species have _____. According to scientists, these patterns are the result of _____ as well as environmental factors. Both short and long-distance migration patterns have been studied. Although both types are generally associated with birds that take flight to warmer climates for _____ during cold weather months, short-distance migrators, like buzzards and vultures, which are typically broad-winged, must rely on _____ to travel. Migration is instinctual; the urge to migrate—known by the German word _____—has been found even in birds raised in cages.

Exercise 3   Georgia O'Keeffe

photographer	New Mexico	painting natural scenes close up
a set of six calla lily paintings	natural objects and landscapes	

Georgia O'Keeffe is one of the best-known painters of the twentieth century. Her works include _____. She adopted a unique style of _____ as if they were magnified. Her career was aided by her husband, _____ Alfred Stieglitz, for whom she posed nude. Recognized as a great talent during her own lifetime, O'Keeffe reportedly garnered the highest compensation of that time for _____ that earned her 25,000 dollars. Later, inspired by the colorful images of _____, she moved to reside there and reflected those images in her work.

Exercise 4 Gold Rush in the Nineteenth Century

Jack London	frostbite, famine, and plague	discoveries of gold ore
great rushes of whites	the insurmountable odds	

During the mid-1800s century, _____ sparked the imaginations of thousands of prospectors. These greedy, courageous, and starry-eyed adventurers rapidly migrated to California and the Yukon Territories of North Canada. Suffering great hardships to overcome _____ of striking it rich, _____ infiltrated sparsely populated areas and brought with them the threat of _____. Author _____ captured this period in his famous works that include *White Fang*, *Call of the Wild*, and *To Build a Fire*.

Exercise 5 Nuclear Reactors

thermal reactors	the energy of neutrons	nuclear reactors
uranium deposits	a safe and pollution-free source of power	

Nuclear reactors can be natural or manmade. Natural reactors have been found in _____ in West Africa. In order to generate electrical power, scientists have designed _____ that initiate, control, and sustain nuclear fission at a steady rate. Unlike nuclear fusion, nuclear fission is considered to be _____, and it is used commercially. Nuclear reactors are classified as fast or slow. This classification is based on _____ employed in the reaction process. Although slow _____ are the most common and successful, the construction of fast reactors still continues.

Exercise 6 The Great Portrait Painters of Colonial America

Samuel Adams and Paul Revere	the American Revolution	fine work
the American Colonial Period	George Washington and John Adams	

John Singleton Copley and Gilbert Stuart are recognized as the most outstanding portrait painters of _____. Although both men fled to Europe to avoid the trials of _____, each became renowned for his masterful portraits of the politically elite. Copley's subjects included _____. Stuart's included _____. Although they were contemporaries and Copley was a major influence on Stuart, the painters never met. Ironically, Stuart's reputation for _____ eventually surpassed Copley's.

The Development of Pottery

08-12

The advent of pottery in primitive human cultures around the world signified a milestone in human history. Sometimes referred to as the container revolution, pottery enabled primitive people to boil and steam food, which, in turn, allowed them to gain sustenance from new and more varied sources. Durable and watertight pottery containers also allowed them to capture and store freshwater from rainfall or clean rivers and lakes.

2 → The earliest pottery has been traced back to a few civilizations that appear to have developed this advancement independent of one another. The oldest pottery known to historians comes from the Jomon people of Japan from around the year 10,500 B.C. Evidence of the independent development of pottery has also come from North Africa around 10,000 B.C. and from South America around 7,000 B.C.

Collecting pottery shards has proven to be one of the best ways for archaeologists to identify the developmental levels of ancient cultures, especially ones that were pre-literate and therefore unable to leave behind a recorded history. By digging up different shards from different stratum layers, archaeologists can easily date the stages of a culture's development. They are able to do this by looking at the style and decoration of the pottery fragments. Furthermore, trace element analysis enables these researchers accurately to identify the source of the clay used to make the pottery.

4 → The early pottery was formed with a technique called handwork. Handworked pieces are constructed from clay rolled into long strands by hand and then coiled to form the body of the vessel. Each of these early pieces of pottery would have been one of a kind due to the irregularity that is a characteristic of handwork. After these primitive pieces of pottery were shaped by hand, they would be fired in a primitive kiln, which would have resembled more of a wood fire.

5 → The next major development in pottery came about with the invention of the pottery wheel in Mesopotamia sometime between 6,000 and 2,400 B.C. This device revolutionized the production of pottery since it enabled potters to mass produce their work to meet the growing needs of the world's first cities. The pottery wheel is a spinning turntable powered by a foot pedal that spins clay very quickly, allowing potters to shape pottery with rotational symmetry. This resulted in a much more regular piece of pottery than handwork.

■ By 800 A.D., Muslim potters in Samarra and Baghdad began employing lead-based glazes further to finish their pottery. ■ This process of glazing came from the Romans, who had spread it around the Mediterranean and North Africa. ■ These potters also discovered new forms of glazing as they attempted to imitate the Chinese white ceramics popular at that time. ■ Although they were able closely to imitate the work of the Chinese, their experimentation also resulted in new methods of glazing that used tin oxide instead of lead.

In order to harden pottery, it must be fired in a kiln which holds heat at very high temperatures. The Chinese developed an efficient wood-fired kiln very early in the history of pottery, called the anagama. This useful device was capable of sustaining the necessary temperatures without the use of coal and was soon adopted by the Koreans and Japanese as well.

The modern era of pottery factories capable of truly large-scale mass production came about in 1785 with the English city of Stoke-on-Trent. This was one of the first industrial cities to make pottery manufacturing its primary industry. The city was known to have more than 200 pottery manufacturers that employed upward of 20,000 workers. This city is so famous for pottery that its nickname is "The Potteries."

1 The word "sustenance" in the passage is closest in meaning to

Ⓐ inspiration

Ⓑ nourishment

Ⓒ support

Ⓓ instruction

2 According paragraph 2, evidence of the oldest pottery was found in

Ⓐ Mesopotamia

Ⓑ China

Ⓒ North Africa

Ⓓ Japan

3 Which of the following best expresses the information in the highlighted sentence? *Incorrect* answer choices change the meaning in important ways or leave out essential information.

Ⓐ Pottery shards provide information about the cultures of prehistoric people.

Ⓑ Early people recorded their history on pottery shards.

Ⓒ Archaeologists study ancient cultures.

Ⓓ Pre-literate people tried to hide their pottery in underground strata.

4 The author discusses "handwork" in paragraph 4 in order to

Ⓐ show the regular patterns of early pottery

Ⓑ distinguish it from later advances in pottery making

Ⓒ explain that it was the best method for pottery making

Ⓓ discuss the types of decorations used in early pottery

5 According to paragraph 5, the significance of the invention of the pottery wheel was that

     Ⓐ it allowed each piece to be unique

     Ⓑ it encouraged artists to paint scenes on pottery

     Ⓒ it enabled potters to mass-produce their works

     Ⓓ it inspired many more people to become potters

6 The word "imitate" in the passage is closest in meaning to

     Ⓐ use

     Ⓑ make

     Ⓒ copy

     Ⓓ shape

7 Look at the four squares [■] that indicate where the following sentence could be added to the passage.

The introduction of glazes contributed to the quality of the vessels.

Where would the sentence best fit?

8 **Directions:** Complete the table below by matching FIVE of the seven answer choices that describe early advances in pottery manufacturing. TWO of the answer choices will NOT be used.

Answer Choices

1. It led to the mass production of pottery.

2. It was invented by the Chinese.

3. It originated in the Roman Empire.

4. It hardened the pottery.

5. It did not use coal.

6. It used tin oxide to finish the pottery.

7. It helped shape the pottery evenly.

Pottery Wheel
-
-

Wood-fired Kiln
-
-
-

Frederick Winslow Taylor

08-13

Frederick Winslow Taylor thought there was always "one best way" to fix a problem. He was a man who developed the theory of scientific management. His thoughts and studies on efficiency changed the managing practices and the workplace environments for managers and workers all over the world. He was an American engineer who spearheaded the Efficiency Movement at the beginning of the twentieth century. This movement led to the rise of industrialism in the strongest nations around the world.

2 → Taylor's path toward efficiency in engineering began when he was unable to attend Harvard University because of his poor eyesight. As an alternative career, he became an apprentice machinist in 1874. During this time, he learned firsthand about the kinds of conditions that exist in factories. Despite his life as a factory worker, he was able to get a degree in mechanical engineering. He studied through a correspondence course from the Stevens Institute of Technology and graduated in 1883.

At the core of Taylor's beliefs about efficiency was the idea that the "one best way" to do any kind of work could be discovered through careful scientific analysis. Based on this principle, he created his best-known experiment, called the time and motion study. This consisted of breaking a job down to its basic component parts and measuring each operation to the second.

■ The most famous of such studies done by Taylor was with shovels. ■ It started when he saw that workers were using the same shovels for many different materials. ■ After closely analyzing their movements, he figured out that the most effective load was around ten kilograms. ■ Then, he designed shovels for each material that could lift exactly that amount. Ironically, however, Taylor was usually not successful when he tried to apply his concepts to actual factories. His recognition came in later years when his ideas were implemented by followers of his teachings.

Due to his failures at applying his principles, Taylor was fired from the large steel firm where he worked and began to write books on his management beliefs. He felt strongly that the common management styles of the time were amateurish. He also strongly believed that management should be studied as a discipline and that if management was done properly, workers would cooperate with their managers, thus eliminating the need for trade unions.

6 → By 1900, Taylor became a professor at the Tuck School of Business at Dartmouth College. There, he published his major work, *The Principles of Scientific Management*. In this book, he developed four major principles of scientific management. His management principles were to replace the rule-of-thumb work methods with methods that were created by the scientific study of tasks; to hire, train, and develop each worker scientifically rather than allowing them to train themselves; to cooperate with workers to make sure that scientifically developed methods were being followed; and to divide work equally between managers and workers so that managers could use scientific management principles in their planning strategies while workers used the same principles in the tasks they performed.

7 → By 1908, Harvard began teaching business management at the graduate degree level with a

curriculum based on Taylor's ideas as well as his four principles of scientific management. Along with the concepts of mass production introduced by Henry Ford, Taylor's ideas became highly influential around the world, including in countries such as Switzerland, France, and especially the Soviet Union. Managers around the world who implemented Taylor's thoughts referred to them as Taylor's Principles and sometimes disparagingly as Taylorism.

9 The word "spearheaded" in the passage is closest in meaning to

- (A) led
- (B) controlled
- (C) stopped
- (D) advertised

10 In paragraph 2, why does the author mention "Harvard University"?

- (A) To describe its influence on Taylor's life
- (B) To claim that Taylor graduated from it
- (C) To note that Taylor's first factory was there
- (D) To state that Taylor taught some classes there

11 According to paragraph 2, which of the following is true of Frederick Winslow Taylor?

- (A) He failed the Harvard admissions test.
- (B) He earned a degree in electrical engineering.
- (C) He worked in a factory as an assistant.
- (D) He learned about scientific management from an MIT correspondence course.

12 In the passage, the word "This" refers to

- (A) Any kind of work
- (B) Careful scientific analysis
- (C) This principle
- (D) The time and motion study

13 Which of the following best expresses the essential information in the highlighted sentence? *Incorrect* answer choices change the meaning in important ways or leave out essential information.

     Ⓐ Taylor was fired from a steel firm for writing books about his management beliefs.

     Ⓑ Taylor's books described his experiences at a steel firm.

     Ⓒ The steel firm prevented Taylor from applying his principles.

     Ⓓ Taylor wrote his own management books after losing his job because of his failed principles.

14 According to paragraph 6, which of the following is NOT true of Taylor's principles of management?

     Ⓐ Work should be divided equally between workers and managers.

     Ⓑ Scientifically created work methods should be adopted.

     Ⓒ Management should be taught as a separate discipline.

     Ⓓ Management must cooperate with workers in implementing scientific methods.

15 According to paragraph 7, what can be inferred about Taylor's Principles?

     Ⓐ They came into existence with the help of Henry Ford.

     Ⓑ They were not welcomed by every manager.

     Ⓒ They were put into practice first in Western Europe.

     Ⓓ They were only recognized as an academic theory.

16 Look at the four squares [■] that indicate where a sentence could be added to the passage.

Nevertheless, at the time, it did not win him any fame.

Where would the sentence best fit?

Vocabulary Check-Up

A Choose the words with the closest meanings to the highlighted words.

1 The staunch members of the ladies' group would not give up their fight.

- (A) elder
- (B) new
- (C) committed
- (D) angry

2 Many people are thankful for their abundant blessings.

- (A) plentiful
- (B) moderate
- (C) adequate
- (D) timely

3 The scarcity of food during that long winter left many families in despair.

- (A) availability
- (B) shortage
- (C) variety
- (D) packaging

4 The United States imposed a shipping embargo on Cuba.

- (A) prohibition
- (B) requirement
- (C) suspension
- (D) surveillance

5 Contestants ranged from babies in strollers to old men shaking their canes.

- (A) sprang
- (B) fled
- (C) extended
- (D) grew

6 A dictator imposes his will on his people.

- (A) forces
- (B) fosters
- (C) announces
- (D) legislates

7 Cave dwellers depicted their lives by drawing on cave walls.

- (A) honored
- (B) shortened
- (C) pictured
- (D) remembered

8 After days of rising, the price of the stock leveled off.

- (A) plunged
- (B) receded
- (C) spiked
- (D) stabilized

9 The great chef is renowned for his blueberry pancakes.

- (A) sought after
- (B) watched
- (C) remembered
- (D) famous

10 His big brother always took the largest portion of dessert.

- (A) fraction
- (B) share
- (C) ingredient
- (D) container

B Match the words with the correct definitions.

1 recession •   • (A) a show; a display

2 crude •   • (B) public praise

3 amass •   • (C) to carry out; to execute

4 implement •   • (D) related to motion

5 esteem •   • (E) to collect; to accumulate

6 exhibition •   • (F) to get; to obtain

7 retrieve •   • (G) looking back

8 retrospective •   • (H) a temporary economic decline

9 kinetic •   • (I) respect; admiration; regard

10 acclaim •   • (J) unrefined

PART Ⅲ

Reading to Learn

In this part, the reading comprehension questions include prose summary and fill in a table. The learning objectives of these comprehension questions are to recognize the major ideas and the relative importance of information in a passage and to organize the main ideas and other important information in the appropriate categories.

UNIT

09 Prose Summary

Overview

Introduction

In Prose Summary questions, you will be asked to complete a summary chart by choosing the three most important ideas from six choices. In order to solve Prose Summary questions, you should understand the overall theme of the passage and distinguish important ideas from minor ones in the passage.

Question Types

❯ **Directions**: An introductory sentence for a brief summary of the passage is provided below. Complete the summary by selecting the THREE answer choices that express important ideas in the passage. Some sentences do not belong in the summary because they express ideas that are not presented in the passage or are minor ideas in the passage. *This question is worth 2 points.*

> Drag your answer choices to the spaces where they belong.
> To remove an answer choice, click on it. To review the passage, click on **View Text**.

[An introductory sentence]

-
-
-

Answer Choices

1. X X X X X X X X X X X X X X X X X X X X
2. X X X X X X X X X X X X X X X X X X X X
3. X X X X X X X X X X X X X X X X X X X X
4. X X X X X X X X X X X X X X X X X X X X
5. X X X X X X X X X X X X X X X X X X X X
6. X X X X X X X X X X X X X X X X X X X X

Useful Tips

- Try to understand the overall structure of the passage.
- Write down the main idea of each paragraph on your scratch paper.
- Distinguish major points from minor details in the passage.
- Incorrect answer choices usually deal with minor points of the passage or are not mentioned in the passage.

Dmitri Mendeleev and the Periodic Table

09-01

Dmitri Mendeleev was a Russian chemist born in 1834. As a young man, Mendeleev was spellbound by glass, and this interest would later cause him to study liquids and the properties of light. Mendeleev was also interested in all of the chemical elements. A chemical element is a substance that cannot be broken down further. The smallest part of each element is called an atom, which contains electrons, protons, and neutrons. Several chemists before Mendeleev worked on creating a table of elements, usually based upon atomic weight, but it was Dmitri whose table was most successful as he mapped the elements based upon their atomic mass. His periodic table of elements is also arranged to show that elements with similar chemical properties also have atomic weights which increase in regular increments. Mendeleev's periodic table of elements is still used today.

Q **Directions:** An introductory sentence for a brief summary of the passage is provided below. Complete the summary by selecting the THREE answer choices that express important ideas in the passage. Some sentences do not belong in the summary because they express ideas that are not presented in the passage or are minor ideas in the passage. *This question is worth 2 points.*

The periodic table of elements is credited to Dmitri Mendeleev.

-
-
-

Answer Choices

1. Before Mendeleev, chemists unsuccessfully attempted to arrange the elements according to their atomic weight.

2. An atom is composed of protons, neutrons, and electrons.

3. The periodic table of elements organizes chemical elements according to their atomic masses.

4. Mendeleev's interest in glass caused him to investigate the properties of liquids and light.

5. Chemical elements are the smallest units of a substance.

6. The periodic table of elements groups together elements with similar properties.

☑ Correct Answer

Answer Choices ①, ③, and ⑥ are correct answers because they directly deal with Mendeleev's periodic table of elements. Choices ②, ④, and ⑤ are only minor ideas in the passage.

Basic Drill

Read the passages and answer the questions.

Drill 1

Types of Seismic Waves

09-02

Seismic waves are waves that travel through the Earth as a consequence of an earthquake. There are two types of seismic waves. One is the body wave, which travels internally through the Earth, and the other is the surface wave, which travels just under the Earth's exterior.

The initial tremors experienced during an earthquake can be attributed to body waves, which are comprised of both P waves and S waves. The paths these two waves journey are dependent on both the composition and density of the Earth. P waves elicit alternate compressions and dilations of the ground whereas S waves are busy displacing the Earth in a transverse fashion.

Surface waves move with a low frequency, a long duration, and a large amplitude and are culpable for an earthquake's corresponding destructiveness. There are two types of surface waves; Rayleigh waves cause the ground to roll like ripples of water, and Love waves cause the horizontal sheering of the ground.

Q **Directions:** An introductory sentence for a brief summary of the passage is provided below. Complete the summary by selecting the THREE answer choices that express important ideas in the passage. Some sentences do not belong in the summary because they express ideas that are not presented in the passage or are minor ideas in the passage.

Earthquakes result in seismic waves.

-
-
-

Answer Choices

[1] Surface waves are comprised of Rayleigh waves and Love waves that cause surface displacement.

[2] Seismic waves can be either body waves or surface waves.

[3] P waves and S waves compress and dilate the ground repeatedly to cause tremors.

[4] An earthquake's first tremors are caused by two types of body waves: P waves and S waves.

[5] There are four major types of seismic waves.

[6] Fault lines mark areas that are predisposed to earthquake activity.

Drill 2

Asteroid 1989 FC

09-03

An asteroid is an astronomical object that drifts in the solar system and orbits the sun. One type of asteroid is known as NEAs, or near-Earth asteroids, because their orbits are very close to Earth's orbit around the sun. Some NEAs have intersecting orbits with Earth, thereby posing a risk of collision.

One such NEA did pose a significant risk to Earth on March 23, 1994. The Apollo asteroid 4581 Asclepius, later to be known as 1989 FC, missed colliding with Earth by 400,163 miles. While that may not seem like a near-miss situation, to put it in perspective, Asteroid 1989 FC moved into the same position in space that Earth had occupied only six hours previously. Had the asteroid struck Earth, it would have created the largest explosion known to man. The impact would have been equivalent to one large atomic bomb detonating every second for fifty days in a row.

Q **Directions:** An introductory sentence for a brief summary of the passage is provided below. Complete the summary by selecting the THREE answer choices that express important ideas in the passage. Some sentences do not belong in the summary because they express ideas that are not presented in the passage or are minor ideas in the passage.

Asteroids create a risk of colliding with Earth.

-
-
-

Answer Choices

1 Meteorologists are investigating ways to track asteroids.

2 NEAs can possibly enter Earth's orbit and pose the threat of hitting Earth.

3 There is an ongoing debate over whether the public should be informed about asteroids that threaten Earth.

4 If Asteroid 1989 FC had hit Earth, the explosion would have been the largest ever recorded.

5 In 1994, Asteroid 1989 FC almost collided with Earth.

6 NEA is an abbreviation for near-Earth asteroid.

Foods and Carbohydrates

09-04

In order to survive, a person must eat a variety of foods. Every type of food people eat can be broken down into three main types of nutrients: protein, fat, and carbohydrate. Each plays an important role in maintaining the body, but it is carbohydrates that are human's main sources of energy.

A carbohydrate is a biological molecule that helps with the storage and transportation of energy within the body. A carbohydrate is also known as a sugar, or saccharide. The basic unit of a carbohydrate is a monosaccharide. Monosaccharides can be linked together in limitless ways to form other carbohydrates, such as disaccharides and glucose.

When talking about food, nutritionists divide carbohydrates into two categories: foods that contain complex carbohydrates and foods that contain simple carbohydrates. A complex carbohydrate is one that takes longer to break down in the body than a simple carbohydrate. Examples of foods that are high in carbohydrates are rice, potatoes, breads, and cereals.

Q **Directions:** An introductory sentence for a brief summary of the passage is provided below. Complete the summary by selecting the THREE answer choices that express important ideas in the passage. Some sentences do not belong in the summary because they express ideas that are not presented in the passage or are minor ideas in the passage.

Carbohydrates are essential to a healthy diet.

-
-
-

Answer Choices

1. Although fats, proteins, and carbohydrates are necessary components of a healthy diet, carbohydrates provide the bulk of energy.

2. Rice, potatoes, breads, and cereals are rich sources of carbohydrates.

3. Nutritionists may suggest a low carbohydrate diet as a way to lose weight.

4. There are two types of carbohydrates, complex and simple, according to the length of time it takes the body to break them down.

5. Disaccharides and glucose are formed from carbohydrate molecules that are known as monosaccharides.

6. The biological molecules of carbohydrates are saccharides that can be linked together in a variety of forms.

Metamorphic Rocks

09-05

Metamorphic rocks are created when a different form of rock, for example, igneous rock or sedimentary rock, changes in makeup due to extreme heat and pressure. This process is known as metamorphism, and the pre-existing rock, before the heat and the pressure are applied, is known as the protolith. For instance, perhaps there is an island that is made up of mostly sedimentary rock, and it suddenly undergoes a volcanic eruption. During the eruption, the heat and the pressure applied to the sedimentary rock— the protolith—cause it to change. Now, the sedimentary rock is known as metamorphic rock.

Scientists can learn a lot about the makeup of the Earth's crust by studying metamorphic rock as it reveals valuable information about the Earth's inner temperatures and pressures and how the Earth has changed over geologic time. Two examples of metamorphic rock are slate and marble.

Q **Directions:** An introductory sentence for a brief summary of the passage is provided below. Complete the summary by selecting the THREE answer choices that express important ideas in the passage. Some sentences do not belong in the summary because they express ideas that are not presented in the passage or are minor ideas in the passage.

Metamorphic rock is the result of changes inside the Earth.

-
-
-

Answer Choices

1 Metamorphic rock is formed when other rocks are exposed to extreme heat and pressure in a process called metamorphism.

2 Metamorphic rocks reveal information about the Earth's temperatures, pressures, and geological changes.

3 Slate and marble are two examples of metamorphic rock.

4 The rock that changes into metamorphic rock is called the protolith.

5 Islands are made mostly of igneous rock but may sometimes change to metamorphic rock.

6 When sedimentary rock is subjected to a volcanic eruption, it changes into metamorphic rock.

Exercises with Long Passages

Exercise 1 Read the following passage and answer the questions.

Time Limit: 3 min. 40 sec.

How to Measure Geologic Time

09-06

The geologic time scale is the time scale used by scientists to describe the time and the relationship between events that happened during the history of the Earth. Because the Earth is over 4.57 billion years old, the time scale that humans use to mark their own time—days, years, and centuries—is in too small of increments to be of use when measuring Earth time. The geologic time scale is broken down into units according to particular events that occurred in various periods. Generally, the periods of time on the geologic time scale are delineated by major geological events, such as the extinction of the dinosaurs or the rise of man.

The time scale is also divided into three main components: eons, eras, and periods. An eon is the largest unit of time. Eons are then divided in eras, which, in turn, are divided into different periods. The periods are generally classified as upper, middle, and lower. The terms *late* and *early* may also be substituted for the terms *upper* or *lower*. For instance, suppose an archaeologist and a geologist found a dinosaur fossil that was embedded in a particular kind of rock. The archaeologist would research the makeup of the dinosaur bone in a lab and then use the geologic time scale to try to classify the eon, the era, and the period from which the bone evolved. He might say to the geologist, "This dinosaur bone is a fossil from the Early Jurassic Period of the Mesozoic Era, which falls under the Phanerozoic Eon." The geologist might find that the rock was upper Jurassic sandstone of the same period, era, and eon as the bone.

[3] → The geologic time scale was first conceived in the late seventeenth century by Danish geologist Nicholas Steno. Steno concluded that rock layers found on the Earth were laid down over certain periods of time and that by studying the formation and the composition of rock, a time scale of the Earth could be created. Steno also pointed out that any given layer of rock is probably older than the one above it and younger than the one below it. Many scientists after Steno provided valuable research and input into the creation of the geologic time scale. British geologists dominated the process, and their influence can be evidenced in the naming of some of the periods. Cambrian and Siluria were British tribes while the term Devonian originates in the English county Devonshire.

In conclusion, scientists from all over the world created the geologic time scale based upon the relationship between the different rock layers and fossils. This time scale has allowed scientists to make precise hypotheses about the history of the Earth.

📖 Words & Phrases

measure (v) to gauge; to assess; to calculate
various (adj) different
delineate (v) to describe; to outline
extinction (n) a disappearance
component (n) a constituent; an element; a factor
classify (v) to organize
substitute (v) to take the place of; to replace
suppose (v) to imagine; to pretend
embed (v) to ingrain

evolve (v) to change; to develop; to advance
composition (n) a makeup
conceive (v) to envision
valuable (adj) helpful; useful
dominate (v) to control; to lead
precise (adj) exact
originate (v) to begin
hypothesis (n) an assumption; a theory

1 The word "increments" in the passage is closest in meaning to

    (A) increases   (B) tools

    (C) fragments   (D) intervals

2 According paragraph 3, which of the following is true of Nicholas Steno?

    (A) He conceived the geologic time scale.

    (B) He lived during the Cambrian Period.

    (C) He was a British geologist.

    (D) He found a dinosaur bone embedded in rock.

Mastering the Question Type

3 **Directions:** An introductory sentence for a brief summary of the passage is provided below. Complete the summary by selecting the THREE answer choices that express important ideas in the passage. Some sentences do not belong in the summary because they express ideas that are not presented in the passage or are minor ideas in the passage.

The geologic time scale allows scientists to place historic events within relevant timeframes.

-
-
-

Answer Choices

1. Dinosaur bones are from the Jurassic Period.

2. Nicholas Steno invented the geologic time scale.

3. Nicholas Steno's key insight was that layers of rock form over long periods and that each layer is younger that the one below it.

4. British geologists named the time periods after English tribes and regions.

5. Periods are classified into three parts: upper, middle, and lower.

6. Periods on the time scale are defined by major geologic events.

Summary Note   Fill in the blanks with the appropriate words.

How to Measure Geologic Time

- Geologic time scale
  - scientists measure time and relationship between events on the Earth
  - need ❶ ....
  - can be broken down into various units
- Three main time components
  - ❷ ....
  - can further divide into upper, middle, and lower
- First thought of in late seventeenth century by geologist ❸ ....
  - looked at ❹ .... and discovered they came from different time periods
  - has enabled scientists to make good hypotheses about the Earth

Read the following passage and answer the questions.

The Pleiades

09-07

The Pleiades is a type of open star cluster, a group of a few thousand stars that were formed out of the same interstellar cloud and are still loosely bound to one another due to gravity. The Pleiades in particular refers to the open cluster that is found in the constellation Taurus. The Pleiades is also known as M45 or the Seven Sisters.

2 ➡ The stars that comprise the Pleiades are relatively young in astronomical terms, having formed within the last one hundred million years. These stars in particular are of a type called blue-white stars, which means that they are some of the hottest and strongest stars in the galaxy. Because they are so powerful, it is speculated that the Pleiades will only live for a short time because they will burn themselves out very quickly. It is thought that the group of stars will survive for another two hundred and fifty million years before it disperses due to other gravitational forces within the galaxy. In terms of distance, the Pleiades is known to lie 440 light years away from Earth and spans twelve light years in total diameter.

3 ➡ Not just made up of stars, the Pleiades also contain what are called reflection nebulae, clouds of dust that reflect light from nearby stars. The reflection nebulas also contribute to the overall brightness of the Pleiades. While it was once thought that the dust particles surrounding the Pleiades were part of the original interstellar cloud that bore the Pleiades, it is now thought that the Pleiades is simply passing through a particularly dusty part of the galaxy.

The Pleiades has been important to many cultures over the course of history. The ancient Greeks considered the Pleiades to be a constellation, and it was even mentioned in Homer's classics the *Iliad* and the *Odyssey*. The Pleiades is noted three different times in the Bible, and it received the name Seven Sisters thanks to Greek mythology and the title Seven Mothers thanks to Hindu mythology. The ancient Aztecs based their calendar upon the Pleiades, and the Native Americans measured the sharpness of one another's vision based upon how many stars one could see in the Pleiades. The vast amount of mythology surrounding the Pleiades shows just how much prominence and brilliance this group of stars holds in the night sky.

📖 Words & Phrases

cluster n a group

interstellar adj between stars

gravity n a pull

constellation n a group of stars that appear to make a picture in the sky

comprise v to make up; to consist of

galaxy n a system of stars, gas, and dust held together by gravitational forces

speculate v to guess

disperse v to scatter; to spread out

in terms of phr in relation to; concerning

diameter n the measurement across the center of a circle

reflect v to return; to throw back

contribute to phr to help; to lead to; to be instrumental in

particle n a very small piece of matter

mythology n a set of widely held fictitious stories or beliefs

indigenous adj native

vast adj huge; great

prominence n importance

1   According to paragraph 2, blue-white stars

   Ⓐ are prone to burn themselves out rapidly

   Ⓑ are among the oldest stars

   Ⓒ burn slower than most stars

   Ⓓ are found only in Earth's galaxy

2   According to paragraph 3, the dust particles surrounding the Pleiades come from

   Ⓐ the original interstellar cloud   Ⓑ reflected light

   Ⓒ a dusty region of the galaxy   Ⓓ nearby stars

Mastering the Question Type

3   **Directions:** An introductory sentence for a brief summary of the passage is provided below. Complete the summary by selecting the THREE answer choices that express important ideas in the passage. Some sentences do not belong in the summary because they express ideas that are not presented in the passage or are minor ideas in the passage.

   The Pleiades is a well-known star cluster.

   •

   •

   •

Answer Choices

1. The Pleiades has been celebrated in the history and mythology of many cultures.

2. The Pleiades is mentioned in ancient Greek, Aztec, Hindu, and Native American texts.

3. The brightness of the Pleiades is enhanced by reflection nebulae.

4. Native Americans used the Pleiades to determine how good people's eyesight was.

5. The Pleiades is also known as M45 and the Seven Sisters.

6. The Pleiades consists of a relatively young group of blue-white stars that will burn out quickly.

Summary Note   Fill in the blanks with the appropriate words.

The Pleiades

• Is an ❶ _____ cluster
  – formed of several thousand stars → still bound to one another
  – called the Seven Sisters

• Characteristics of Pleiades
  – are blue-white stars
  – are very hot and strong → will burn out quickly
  – ❷ _____ from Earth

• ❸ _____ → are contained in Pleiades, making them brighter

• Historical importance
  – mentioned by ancient Greeks and in Hindu mythology
  – Bible mentions three times
  – had importance to ❹ _____ and Native Americans

Exercise 3 Read the following passage and answer the questions.

Time Limit: 3 min. 50 sec.

The Daguerreotype

09-08

The daguerreotype is an early type of photograph that involved a very complex and exhausting process to create. A photograph is formed when an image is directly exposed onto a polished surface of silver. The main drawback to this photographic process is that there is no negative, which means that an exact image cannot be reproduced.

The daguerreotype was named after one of its inventors, a French chemist named Louis Daguerre. He was also an artist who was interested in the different properties of light. In 1839, after years of working with another French inventor Joseph Nicephore Nièpce, Daguerre discovered that a mixture of silver and chalk would darken when exposed to light.

3 ➜ The daguerreotype process begins when silver halide particles are sprinkled onto a polished piece of silver. Then, an image is focused through a lens onto the silver plate. The image is captured when the silver plate is placed over a heated cup of mercury. The heat produces mercury vapors that condense onto those places on the plate where the exposure to light was the strongest. The picture is developed when the mercury attaches itself to the silver. The last step in the daguerreotype process is to fix the image to the plate by dipping it into a solution called soda. Treating the plate with gold chlorine also helps strengthen the image. Still, since the image is delicate and the photograph cannot be recreated, Daguerre and those after him made certain to cover the image with a piece of glass.

The daguerreotype process of photography quickly spread around the world. One of the reasons that it became so popular was that, compared to earlier methods in photography, the daguerreotype was a much faster process. By the mid-nineteenth century, traveling photographers using the daguerreotype moved from town to town and took portraitures for people. It was the first time in history that a person could own an exact image of his likeness that was not first filtered through the eyes of an artist.

Unfortunately, however, the passing of time meant that newer forms of photography were invented, and the daguerreotype fell out of use because the process proved too exhausting for the photographer and too expensive for the average person. In addition, because the daguerreotype image could not be copied, new forms of photography that provided a negative became much more desirable. One of the later types of photography that did provide a negative worked by fixing an image to a piece of glass by using silver salt.

📖 Words & Phrases

involve v to include; to require
complex adj intricate; complicated
expose v to display
drawback n a disadvantage; a flaw
property n a characteristic; a trait
sprinkle v to scatter
polished adj shining
capture v to represent

vapor n a gaseous substance
condense v to concentrate
dip v to dunk
solution n a liquid; a mix
delicate adj fragile; weak
portraiture n the act of portrait making
filter v to screen

1 According to paragraph 3, which of the following is used in the daguerreotype process of photography?

    Ⓐ Iron fillings   Ⓑ Silver halide particles

    Ⓒ Long wooden handles   Ⓓ Safety glasses

2 The word "it" in the passage refers to

    Ⓐ the mercury   Ⓑ the silver

    Ⓒ the image   Ⓓ the plate

3 **Directions:** An introductory sentence for a brief summary of the passage is provided below. Complete the summary by selecting the THREE answer choices that express important ideas in the passage. Some sentences do not belong in the summary because they express ideas that are not presented in the passage or are minor ideas in the passage.

The daguerreotype process of photography took the place of artists in fashioning realistic images of people.

-
-
-

Answer Choices

[1] One later type of photography fixed images to glass with silver salt.

[2] A lens focused an image onto a surface of silver sprinkled with silver halide particles.

[3] French chemist Louis Daguerre discovered how properties of a silver and chalk mixture would react to light.

[4] The drawback to the daguerreotype process was that it did not provide a negative.

[5] The daguerreotype became popular because it was much faster than earlier methods of photography.

[6] Photographs created by the daguerreotype were protected between sheets of glass.

📝 Summary Note   **Fill in the blanks with the appropriate words.**

The Daguerreotype

- Early type of photograph → complex and exhausting to complete
  - had no ❶ _____ so could not reproduce images
- ❷ _____ → invented daguerreotype
  - interested in properties of light
  - used mixture of silver and chalk
- Daguerreotype process
  - uses ❸ _____ particles
  - captures image
  - heat produces ❹ _____
  - mercury attaches to silver and produces image
- Development
  - spread quickly around world
  - eventually fell out of use

Exercise 4 Read the following passage and answer the questions.

Time Limit: 3 min. 40 sec.

Sand Dunes

09-09

A sand dune is a geological feature that is simply a mound of sand that has formed due to wind erosion called the Eolian process. The shape and the size of a sand dune are entirely dependent on the wind and can differ in look from other adjoining sand dunes. Although they can differ, there are some standard descriptive terms that apply to all types of sand dunes; the slack is the valley between two adjoining sand dunes while a dune field refers to a landscape filled with dunes. If a dune field is particularly large, it is referred to as an erg. The side of a dune is known as a slipface.

The two most common places that sand dunes are found are along coastal regions and inland in large, dry regions such as deserts. Along coasts, sand dunes protect the land against stormy seas and subsequent erosion. Although the conditions sound harsh, many kinds of seaweed and seabirds find coastal dunes to be an ideal habitat while various species of cacti, snakes, and spiders find the conditions of desert dunes to be ideal.

3 → There are a variety of dune shapes, each caused in part by the vigor and the direction of the wind as well as the landscape that surrounds it. The most common dune shape is the crescent dune. This type of dune is generally wider than it is long and is formed when the wind blows continuously from one direction. Star-shaped dunes are very symmetrical with three or more sides that radiate down from a high peak. This kind of dune is common in deserts, such as the Grand Erg Oriental in the Sahara, due to winds shifting in various directions. This dune grows upward as opposed to laterally. Reversing dunes are those that come in varying shapes and sizes due to periodic reversals of wind direction.

No matter what the dune shape, each type can occur in three forms: simple, compound, or complex. A simple dune is one that has the minimum number of sides, or slipfaces, that form a geometric shape. A compound dune is a larger dune that contains many smaller dunes of the same shape as itself, and a complex dune is a combination of two or more dune types.

Sand dunes are an essential part of certain habitats, especially in coastal regions, where they prevent the erosion of coastal land and also foster environments for certain kinds of wildlife. On the other hand, sand dunes can also contribute to a problem known as desertification. Desertification happens when there is a degradation of land due to climatic changes. The same winds that create sand dunes often help them encroach on human habitats in the form of sandstorms or sand avalanches, which can cause major damage to buildings and crops. Every year, in places like Africa and the Middle East, sand fences are put up to try to stop sand from migrating into inhabited areas.

📖 Words & Phrases

mound (n) a hill
erosion (n) the process of being worn away
descriptive (adj) explanatory
subsequent (adj) following; ensuing
vigor (n) strength; energy; power
crescent (n) the shape of the waxing or waning moon

symmetrical (adj) balanced; in proportion
radiate (v) to emit; to give off
laterally (adv) from side to side
degradation (n) worsening; deterioration; a decline
encroach (v) to intrude

1 The word "adjoining" in the passage is closest in meaning to

    (A) eroded   (B) neighboring

    (C) distant   (D) increasing

2 According to paragraph 3, which of the following is true of the shapes of dunes?

    (A) They are caused by the wind.

    (B) They are symmetrical.

    (C) They are altered by human activity.

    (D) The most common shape is the star-shaped dune.

Mastering the Question Type

3 **Directions:** An introductory sentence for a brief summary of the passage is provided below. Complete the summary by selecting the THREE answer choices that express important ideas in the passage. Some sentences do not belong in the summary because they express ideas that are not presented in the passage or are minor ideas in the passage.

Sand dunes are unique features of the environment.

-
-
-

Answer Choices

1. All sand dunes, no matter what their size and shape, are formed by wind erosion.

2. The slack is the valley between two adjoining sand dunes.

3. A large dune field is known as an erg.

4. Every year, sand fences are put up to stop sand from encroaching on human habitats and crops.

5. Sand dunes protect against erosion and provide habitats for wildlife.

6. Sand dunes can occur in three forms: simple, compound, and complex.

Summary Note   Fill in the blanks with the appropriate words.

Sand Dunes

- Geological feature → large mounds of sand
  - shapes depend upon ❶ _____

- Are usually in coastal regions and deserts

- Have many different shapes
  - ❷ _____ is most common
  - can be star shaped

- Different types
  - simple → has minimum number of sides
  - compound → larger dune with ❸ _____ with same shape
  - complex → combination of two or more dune types

- Effects
  - help prevent erosion and create environment for animals to live in
  - contribute to ❹ _____

The Development of Advanced Radio Telescopes

09-10

A radio telescope is a radio receiver that "sees" radio waves. Unlike a normal telescope, which sees light, a radio telescope is used primarily in the area of astronomy because it can detect radio waves that are emitted by celestial objects. Such objects in space, also called radio objects, can be things such as hot gas, electrons, and wavelengths given off by different atoms and molecules.

2 → The first radio telescope was invented by Grote Reber in 1937. He was an American who graduated with a degree in engineering. He went on to work as an amateur radio operator. Later, he decided to try to build his own radio telescope in his backyard. Reber's first two radio receivers failed to pick up any signals from outer space, but in 1938, his third radio telescope successfully picked up radio waves from space.

A radio telescope consists of a large parabolic-shaped dish antenna or a combination of two or more. The significance of the parabolic shape allows incoming radio waves to be concentrated on one focal point. This permits signals to be picked up as strongly as possible. A larger dish means that more signals can be received and focalized.

4 → In the late 1950s and the early 1960s, the largest radio telescope of the time was invented. It was a seventy-six-meter telescope; however, larger telescopes have been made since then. The largest current radio telescope in the world is the RATAN-600 in Russia, whose diameter is 576 meters. It has provided valuable feedback on the sun's radio wavelengths and atmosphere. The largest radio telescope in Europe is a 100-meter diameter telescope in Germany, and the largest radio telescope in the United States is the Big Ear in the state of Ohio. The largest array of telescopes is the Giant Metrewave Radio Telescope in India.

Radio telescopes have provided scientists with valuable information about the universe. One of the most important functions of radio telescopes is their ability to allow scientists to track different space probes, the unmanned space missions in outer space. Radio telescopes allow for the travel of space probes into places like the surface of Mars that are too dangerous for men to explore. Without radio wave technology, scientists would not know much of what inhabits the universe nor would they be able to see it. Radio waves are humans' eyes and ears in outer space.

📖 Words & Phrases

primarily adv mainly; chiefly
astronomy n the scientific study of the universe
detect v to pick up
emit v to give off
celestial adj heavenly
significance n importance
parabolic adj bent like an arc

concentrate on phr to focus on; to converge on
focalize v to limit; to concentrate
atmosphere n the air
current adj present; contemporary
array n a range; a display
track v to trace
inhabit v to live in; to dwell in

1 According to paragraph 2, which of the following is NOT true of Grote Reber?

   (A) He was an amateur radio operator.   (B) He was an astronomer.

   (C) He was an engineer.   (D) He was an inventor.

2 According to paragraph 4, the largest radio telescope in the world is

   (A) the Big Ear   (B) the Giant Metrewave

   (C) the RATAN-600   (D) a 100-meter diameter telescope

Mastering the Question Type

3 **Directions:** An introductory sentence for a brief summary of the passage is provided below. Complete the summary by selecting the THREE answer choices that express important ideas in the passage. Some sentences do not belong in the summary because they express ideas that are not presented in the passage or are minor ideas in the passage.

A radio telescope allows for advances in astronomy.

-
-
-

Answer Choices

1 A radio telescope is capable of detecting celestial objects.

2 The largest radio telescope in the United States is the Big Ear in the state of Ohio.

3 A radio telescope is made up of one or more parabolic dishes that concentrate radio waves into one focal point.

4 Astronauts are trained to be able to read radio telescopes.

5 Space probes are unmanned missions in outer space.

6 Radio telescopes enable space probes to travel into areas too dangerous to explore.

Summary Note   Fill in the blanks with the appropriate words.

The Development of Advanced Radio Telescopes

- Radio receivers that see radio waves
  - can detect ❶ _____ emitted by celestial objects
  - can be hot gas, electrons, and wavelengths
- ❷ _____ → invented first radio telescope in 1937
- Shape
  - large parabolic-shaped dish antenna → enables incoming radio waves to be focused on one point
- Development
  - large 76-meter one built
  - Russians have one 576 meters in diameter
  - 100-meter telescope in Germany
  - ❸ _____ is largest in United States
- Uses
  - provide information about universe
  - can track different space probes → all for ❹ _____ space travel

Exercise 6 Read the following passage and answer the questions.

Time Limit: 3 min. 30 sec.

The Ionization of an Atom

09-11

The process of ionization involves converting an atom into a charged ion by changing the difference between the number of protons and the number of electrons attached to an atom. An atom can become either positive or negative in charge. It depends on whether one or more electrons are removed or added. If an electron is removed, then an extra proton exists, and thus the atom is now a positive ion. If a free-floating electron is added, then the atom is now a negative ion. Depending on which one the atom becomes, either a positive or negative ion, the ionization process is slightly different for each.

In 1913, a Danish physicist, Neils Bohr, postulated that during the process of ionization, the energy required by an atom either to join with another atom or to remove itself never exceeds the potential energy required to break that barrier. As an example, according to Bohr's theory, if a person wants to jump over a bar that is two feet tall, that person must at least jump two feet in the air. According to this theory, when an electron attaches itself to or removes itself from an atom, the energy required by the atom is never lower than the potential energy of the barrier.

Water is a good example that shows the process of ionization. Water is made up of two hydrogen ions that each have a positive charge (H+) and one oxygen ion that has a charge of negative two (2O-). When two hydrogen atoms and one oxygen atom come in close contact with each other, the positive charge of the hydrogen (due to two missing electrons) attaches to the two extra electrons of the oxygen atom. This happens because an atom strives to be in its most balanced state. Thus, H_2O stays tightly bound and is only itself ionized if it comes into contact with another molecule whose energy potential has a stronger pull.

Practically speaking, the process of atom ionization is what allows scientists to create and manipulate molecules for such things as making new products like plastics or chemical agents. Ionization has also become very popular, environmentally speaking. Companies today make air purifiers, which are nothing more than ionizers. Purifiers work by attracting free radical ions out of the air and by rebalancing their charges with electrons.

5 ➜ The ionization process outlined above and based upon Neils Bohr's model is known as classical ionization. There are also more complex ionization processes such as tunnel ionization and non-sequential ionization. However, these processes are less common and are often carried out in laboratories.

📖 Words & Phrases

convert v to change
charged adj electric
attached to phr added to; linked with
remove v to get rid of
extra adj additional; superfluous
exceed v to surpass
potential adj possible; likely
barrier n a blockade

come in contact with phr to get in touch with
strive v to try with great effort
molecule n a group of atoms
manipulate v to operate; to process; to handle
agent n a means; an instrument
complex adj intricate; complicated
sequential adj successive; consecutive; serial
carry out phr to do; to perform

1 The word "postulated" in the passage is closest in meaning to

(A) confirmed   (B) published

(C) suggested   (D) explained

2 According to paragraph 5, which of the following can be inferred about ionization?

(A) It always takes place in a laboratory.   (B) A water molecule is a negative ion.

(C) There are several methods of it.   (D) Atoms require negative charges.

Mastering the Question Type

3 **Directions:** An introductory sentence for a brief summary of the passage is provided below. Complete the summary by selecting the THREE answer choices that express important ideas in the passage. Some sentences do not belong in the summary because they express ideas that are not presented in the passage or are minor ideas in the passage.

Ionization is the process of changing an atom into a charged ion.

-
-
-

Answer Choices

1. Tunnel ionization and non-sequential ionization are complex ionization processes.

2. The process of ionization makes it possible to create and manipulate molecules.

3. Neils Bohr developed the classical model of ionization, the most common ionization process.

4. Ionization has become popular with companies that produce air purifiers.

5. Neils Bohr's theory works with breaking barriers and water charges.

6. Bohr's key insight was that the energy used by an electron in leaving or joining an atom must be at least as high as the energy potential of the force keeping the electron in place.

Summary Note   **Fill in the blanks with the appropriate words.**

The Ionization of an Atom

- Converts an atom into a charged ion
  - changes number of ❶ .... in atom → can make it positive or negative in charge
- ❷ ....
  - postulated on ionization of atoms
  - made postulation based on energy needed
- Water can show ionization process
- Uses
  - lets scientists create and manipulate ❸ .... for new products
    → used for plastics and chemical agents
  - popular for air purifiers
- Types of ionization
  - classical ionization, ❹ ...., and non-sequential ionization

Building Summary Skills

The following summaries are based on the passages you worked on earlier. Complete each of them by filling in the blanks with suitable words or phrases.

Exercise 1 How to Measure Geologic Time

the time scale	major geological events	the geologic time scale
eons, eras, and periods	historic artifacts and fossils	

Nicholas Steno devised _____ in the late seventeenth century. The time scale calibrates the history of the Earth according to _____. The scale is divided into _____. These smaller increments allow scientists to categorize and reference _____ within certain timeframes and to piece together a map of the Earth's history. Since its inception, many scientists have contributed to _____.

Exercise 2 The Pleiades

advancements of many cultures	about 440 light years	gravitational forces
the constellation Taurus	reflection nebulae	

The Pleiades is found in _____. It is formed of the hottest and brightest stars in the galaxy as well as _____ that further enhance its overall shine. Estimated to be _____ away from Earth and spanning twelve light years in diameter, scientists predict that it will burn itself out before _____ can pull it apart. Meanwhile, its intense power and brilliance have won it a prominent role in the mythologies and _____.

Exercise 3 The Daguerreotype

Louis Daguerre	exact images of people	less cumbersome
take portraitures	the introduction of the negative	

The daguerreotype was invented by French chemist _____ in 1839 when he discovered that a mixture of silver and chalk would darken an image exposed to light. This discovery made it possible to create _____. Furthermore, although early methods of photography had been attempted, the daguerreotype process was _____ than its predecessors and meant that early photographers could travel from town to town to _____ of their subjects. Unfortunately, the daguerreotype lacked the means to produce copies, and with _____, the daguerreotype soon lost favor.

Exercise 4 Sand Dunes

ideal habitats	wind erosion	the type of sand dune
buildings and crops	coastal areas or in desert regions	

A sand dune is a mound of sand formed from _____. Generally, dunes are created along _____. The ferocity and the direction of the wind determines _____ that is formed. Although sand dunes provide _____ for various plants and animals as well as prevent subsequent erosion, they also encroach on human habitats through a process called desertification. In desertification, sand storms and sand avalanches cause major damage to _____.

Exercise 5 The Development of Advanced Radio Telescopes

Grote Reber	576 meters	concentration
a parabolic shape	information from space	

Radio telescopes are important to scientists because they are able to see and track _____. First developed by American _____ in 1937, radio telescopes are designed with _____ that concentrates signals into a strong focal point that can more easily be detected. A larger dish size determines a greater degree of _____. Since then, the early 1960s saw the invention of a radio telescope with a 76-meter diameter, but today the largest radio telescopes exceed 100 meters in diameter with the largest having a diameter of _____. Furthermore, radio telescopes can be found around the world.

Exercise 6 The Ionization of an Atom

classical ionization	attract free radical ions	Neils Bohr
changing the charge of an atom	environmentally friendly	

Ionization is the process of _____. It allows scientists to manipulate atoms into new products. Possibly because it is _____, the process of ionization has become particularly profitable for companies that market air purifiers. Ionization enables the purifiers to _____ and to rebalance their charges with electrons. This type of ionization is called _____ and was first theorized by _____ in 1931. Although other types of ionization processes have been developed, they are less commonly used.

The Atmosphere of Venus

09-12

1 → Venus, also called the morning star and the evening star, is the second-closest planet to the sun and the brightest object in the night sky. The planet orbits the sun every two hundred and twenty-four Earth days. It is sometimes referred to as Earth's sister planet because the two share both a similar size and bulk. What is not similar, however, is Venus's atmosphere in comparison to Earth's.

The atmosphere on Venus is much heavier and has a higher density than that of Earth's. Venus's atmosphere also expands significantly higher than Earth's. However, a thick cloud cover makes the surface of Venus nearly impossible to see unless observed through radar mapping.

3 → The pressure and the temperature of Venus's upper atmosphere are comparable to those of Earth. But the heat and the pressure of the lower atmosphere are not unlike a furnace. Venus's atmosphere is very thick and consists mainly of carbon dioxide and a small amount of nitrogen. If man could survive the extreme heat of Venus's surface (400 degrees Celsius), then he would have to contend with a surface pressure that is more than ninety times that of Earth's. Venus's extremely high temperature is thanks to the greenhouse effect caused by such a large amount of carbon dioxide. The greenhouse effect is a process by which the sun's infrared radiation is more readily absorbed by the atmosphere. Just like in a real greenhouse used to grow plants year round, the proliferation of carbon dioxide traps radiation and warms Venus's atmosphere. Due to this phenomenon, Venus boasts a higher atmospheric temperature than Mercury even though Venus is twice the distance from the sun.

4 → However, scientists postulate that Venus's atmosphere was not always so hot. **1** Studies show that large bodies of water were once on Venus's surface but that the eventual evaporation of all the water caused the runaway greenhouse effect which regulates the planet today. **2** Thus Venus has become a critical study for today's scientists as human beings are only beginning to struggle with the early stages of the greenhouse effect. **3** Earth's problems do not stem from evaporated water supplies but from a propagation of carbon dioxide and other greenhouse gases due to industrial and automobile emissions. **4**

Another interesting characteristic to note regarding Venus's atmosphere is that its daytime temperatures and nighttime temperatures are not far removed from each other. This is due to thermal inertia, the ability of a substance to store heat despite changing temperatures, and the transfer of heat by Venus's strong winds. Winds on the surface of Venus move slowly in comparison with Earth's winds. Yet Venus's air is so dense that a slow-moving wind there can move large obstructions and even skip stones along the planet's surface.

In 1966, humankind made its first attempt at sending a recording instrument into Venus's atmosphere. The *Venera 3* probe did collide with Venus's surface. However, the abrupt impact caused its communication system to fail, and it was unable to send any feedback. In 1967, *Venera 4* successfully entered Venus's atmosphere and was able to take many readings, one of which recorded that Venus's atmosphere was between ninety and ninety-five percent carbon dioxide. Subsequent *Venera* probes were sent into Venus's atmosphere, but most of them succumbed to the crushing air pressure.

1   According to paragraph 1, Venus is named the morning star and the evening star because
     (A) it is very bright
     (B) it is close to the sun
     (C) it can be seen from evening until morning
     (D) it is used to find the direction by sailors

2   The word "that" in the passage refers to
     (A) the atmosphere
     (B) a higher density
     (C) a thick cloud cover
     (D) the surface of Venus

3   Which of the following best expresses the essential information in the highlighted sentence?
     Incorrect answer choices change the meaning in important ways or leave out essential
     information.
     (A) Earth experiences greater surface pressure than Venus.
     (B) If a man could survive Venus's surface temperature, he could also survive its surface
         pressure.
     (C) The surface pressure and the heat of Venus are much greater than those on Earth.
     (D) Venus's surface temperature and pressure make it uninhabitable by humans.

4   According to paragraph 3, the greenhouse effect on Venus is owed to
     (A) the small amounts of nitrogen
     (B) the rapidly increasing amounts of carbon dioxide
     (C) growing plants
     (D) the high atmospheric temperatures

5   The word "propagation" in the passage is closest in meaning to
     (A) generation
     (B) elimination
     (C) evaporation
     (D) desecration

6   In paragraph 4, the author implies that Earth

Ⓐ might suffer the same greenhouse effect as Venus

Ⓑ once had an atmosphere similar to Venus's

Ⓒ has bodies of water similar to those on Venus today

Ⓓ is experiencing a reduction of carbon dioxide emissions

7   Look at the four squares [■] that indicate where the following sentence could be added to the passage.

Although the causes are different, the ramifications are the same.

Where would the sentence best fit?

8   **Directions:** An introductory sentence for a brief summary of the passage is provided below. Complete the summary by selecting the THREE answer choices that express important ideas in the passage.

Scientists look at Venus to predict Earth's future.

-
-
-

Answer Choices

① Venus once had large bodies of water that evaporated and caused a rapid increase in carbon dioxide.

② Earth's wind has a greater velocity than Venus's because the air movement on Venus is denser.

③ Spaceship landings on Venus have revealed much about its carbon dioxide-filled atmosphere.

④ If a man could survive the hot temperature of Venus, then he would have to contend with the great surface pressure.

⑤ The first space probe of Venus was sent in 1966.

⑥ Scientists are concerned that conditions on Earth that propagate significant quantities of carbon dioxide will produce a greenhouse effect similar to Venus's.

Aquifers

1 ➔ An aquifer is an underground layer of rock and other unfused materials that allow water to pass through them and from which groundwater can be removed by using a water well. Aquifers can be either unconfined or confined. An unconfined aquifer is one that does not have a restrictive layer between it and the surface. A confined aquifer is one that has an aquitard as its upper boundary and oftentimes another unconfined aquifer above that. An aquitard is a region of the Earth that restricts the flow of groundwater from one aquifer to another. If an aquifer is completely impenetrable, it is called either an aquiclude or an aquifuge. Aquitard layers are made up of materials with low hydraulic conductivity, such as clay or other nonporous rock.

2 ➔ Nearly everywhere under the Earth's shallow surface, groundwater can be found. The Earth's crust is itself divided into two regions: saturated and unsaturated. In saturated areas, all possible spaces are filled with water. This is where aquifers can be found. In unsaturated areas, air still fills some spaces that groundwater has not yet reached. In saturated areas, the pressure in aquifers is greater than the atmospheric pressure. At the water table, the pressure on the water is equal to that of the atmosphere. On the other hand, in unsaturated areas, the water is under negative pressure, which causes the water to suction upward and adhere to the upper boundary of whatever is above it.

3 ➔ In areas without mountains, aquifers are typically made up of alluvium, a sediment that has been deposited by a river or other running water. Alluvium is typically made up of small particles such as silt or clay and also some larger particles like sand and gravel. Rivers are continuously picking up and dropping fine particles. When a river is moving quickly, it is picking up and dropping more particles than when it is moving slowly. As one would guess, because larger particles in a river require more energy to move them, bigger rocks and pieces of gravel are often found closer to water sources whereas aquifers located a long way from water sources are usually found to be made up of finer materials.

Aquifers are essential to human life because they allow people to withdraw water from the Earth despite where they live. **1** Obviously, the closer one is to a large open body of water, the less one is required to dig in depth to locate a viable aquifer. **2** Those who live in drier areas or regions of higher elevation would need to dig further to find an aquifer. **3** Some aquifers are also bigger than others. **4** If the water well being dug is purely for the purpose of enabling one residence to have drinking water, then the aquifer could be small. If, however, the aquifer is going to be used for farming irrigation or mining, then a larger aquifer would be required. It is important that human beings not exploit the use of aquifers as, like most natural resources, supplies are limited. Freshwater aquifers in particular should not be overused since the replenishing of readily drinkable water is limited. Some aquifers, however, have little threat of being depleted anytime soon. For example, the Great Artisan Basin in Australia is one of the biggest groundwater aquifers in the world. It is responsible for providing water to even the most remote portions of Australia and lies underneath twenty-three percent of the continent.

9   The word "unfused" in the passage is closest in meaning to

   (A) fixed

   (B) scattered

   (C) unattached

   (D) unrelated

10   In paragraph 1, the author uses "an aquiclude" as an example of

   (A) a completely impenetrable aquifer

   (B) an aquitard

   (C) an unconfined aquifer

   (D) a nonporous rock

11   According to paragraph 2, aquifers can be found in which of the following places?

   (A) Unsaturated regions of the Earth's crust

   (B) Saturated regions of the Earth's crust

   (C) Places above the water table

   (D) Spaces not filled with groundwater

12   Which of the following best expresses the essential information in the highlighted sentence? *Incorrect* answer choices change the meaning in important ways or leave out essential information.

   (A) Aquifers have no large rocks, which are too heavy to be carried away from water sources.

   (B) A rapidly flowing river deposits fine particles in shallow areas and large rocks in deeper areas.

   (C) Large rocks sink to the bottoms of aquifers while small materials float to the surface.

   (D) Aquifers form close to rivers' sources and thus are filled with large rocks.

13   According to paragraph 3, which of the following is NOT true of alluvium?

   (A) It is sediment made of silt, clay, sand, or gravel.

   (B) It requires more energy to move it than to move large rocks.

   (C) It is the main component of aquifers in non-mountainous areas.

   (D) It is deposited by running water.

14   The word "depleted" in the passage is closest in meaning to

   (A) reinforced

   (B) polluted

   (C) emptied

   (D) conserved

15 Look at the four squares [■] that indicate where the following sentence could be added to the passage.

How much water is needed must be considered when planning to dig down to an aquifer.

Where would the sentence best fit?

16 **Directions:** An introductory sentence for a brief summary of the passage is provided below. Complete the summary by selecting the THREE answer choices that express important ideas in the passage.

Aquifers are underground repositories of groundwater.

-
-
-

Answer Choices

1. An aquitard is a region of the Earth that limits the flow of groundwater from one aquifer to another.

2. Aquifers should not be overused as their water supplies are limited.

3. Alluvium is made up of small particles deposited by running water such as rivers.

4. Aquifers are found in the saturated areas of the Earth's crust.

5. Some aquifers are impenetrable because their upper boundaries are made up of non-porous rock.

6. The water from aquifers can be accessed by manmade wells.

Vocabulary Check-Up

A **Choose the words with the closest meanings to the highlighted words.**

1 The worker manipulated the machine with dexterity.

- (A) started
- (B) replaced
- (C) repaired
- (D) operated

2 Archaeologists have often speculated about the whereabouts of Atlantis.

- (A) guessed
- (B) talked
- (C) dreamt
- (D) wrote

3 Many indigenous plants had medicinal value for early civilizations.

- (A) evergreen
- (B) leafy
- (C) native
- (D) rare

4 Astronomers classify stars according to their size and age.

- (A) count
- (B) track
- (C) categorize
- (D) study

5 The baker sprinkled colored sugar over the holiday cookies.

- (A) scattered
- (B) spread
- (C) mixed
- (D) heated

6 Many publishers condense novels to make them easier and faster for people to read.

- (A) lengthen
- (B) rewrite
- (C) discontinue
- (D) shorten

7 After twenty-five years of marriage, she could not conceive of being married to anyone else.

- (A) stand
- (B) imagine
- (C) admit
- (D) avoid

8 The focal point of the gossip was the new girlfriend of the man who lived across the street.

- (A) sharp
- (B) undeniable
- (C) main
- (D) dull

9 Many alchemists tried their hand at converting common elements into gold.

- (A) changing
- (B) turning
- (C) stirring
- (D) breaking

10 A passionate artist strives to create great works of art.

- (A) practices
- (B) attempts
- (C) learns
- (D) hopes

B **Match the words with the correct definitions.**

1 molecule   •

2 celestial   •

3 crescent   •

4 barrier   •

5 galaxy   •

6 erosion   •

7 vapor   •

8 increment   •

9 embed   •

10 space   •

• Ⓐ related to the sky or heaven

• Ⓑ to set firmly and deeply in a surrounding mass

• Ⓒ a blockade

• Ⓓ a gaseous substance

• Ⓔ an increase on a fixed scale

• Ⓕ the physical universe beyond Earth's atmosphere

• Ⓖ a group of atoms

• Ⓗ the process of being worn away

• Ⓘ the shape of the waxing or waning moon

• Ⓙ a system of stars, gas, and dust held together by gravitational forces

10 Fill in a Table

◣ Overview

Introduction

Fill in a Table questions ask you to identify and organize major ideas and important supporting information from across the passage. Then, you should classify them into the appropriate categories. Passages used for this type of question usually have particular types of organization such as compare/contrast, cause/effect, or problem/solution. A five-answer table is worth 3 points, and a seven-answer table is worth 4 points.

Question Types

❯ **Directions**: Complete the table below to summarize the information about X discussed in the passage. Match the appropriate statements to the categories with which they are associated. TWO of the answer choices will NOT be used. *This question is worth 3 points*

> Drag your answer choices to the spaces where they belong.
> To remove an answer choice, click on it. To review the passage, click on **View Text**.

Answer Choices

1. X X X X X X X X X X X X X X X X X X X
2. X X X X X X X X X X X X X X X X X X X
3. X X X X X X X X X X X X X X X X X X X
4. X X X X X X X X X X X X X X X X X X X
5. X X X X X X X X X X X X X X X X X X X
6. X X X X X X X X X X X X X X X X X X X
7. X X X X X X X X X X X X X X X X X X X

Category 1
- •
- •
- •

Category 2
- •
- •

Useful Tips

- Look at the categories of information in the table first.
- Using your scratch paper, make an outline of the passage according to these categories.
- Distinguish between major and minor information in the passage.
- Wrong answers usually include information that is not mentioned in the passage or that is not directly relevant to the categories in the table.

Emergence

The concept of emergence describes the way in which a complex pattern arises. This is a constantly changing process that may occur over a long period of time. The evolution of the human body is a good example. Its form emerged over thousands of generations. The human body is very complex, but it is formed by millions of tiny cells, which are not. Emergence also occurs on disparate-sized scales. An example is between neurons and the human brain. Interactions between many neurons produce a human brain which is capable of thought, but none of the neurons that made it is capable of thought. The brain is much bigger than any of the single neuron parts that created it.

A common way of looking at emergence in nature is through structures, which can come from organic or inorganic sources. A good example of a living structure is a flock of birds. The flock takes a shape and has behavioral characteristics, but these properties are not exhibited by individual birds. Another example of an organic emergent structure is an ant colony. The ant colony is emergent because no single ant, including the queen, could organize such an effective colony of workers, yet collectively, a colony structure arises. An example of an inorganic emergent structure is a hurricane. This storm system forms as a result of various factors such as pressure, temperature, and humidity, which combine to form a violent storm. But any single factor would not form the same storm.

Emergence also occurs in human culture. One place this kind of emergence has occurred on a large scale is in the stock market. As a system, it regulates the prices of companies around the world; however, there is no single leader that controls the entire market. Agents only know about a limited number of companies and must follow strict rules of the market. Through these interactions, the complexity of the market as a whole emerges. Another type of this emergence is with the World Wide Web. In this case, there is no central website, yet links between major and minor websites create the complex whole that is known as the World Wide Web.

Q **Directions:** Complete the table below to summarize the information about structural and cultural emergence discussed in the passage. Match the appropriate statements to the categories with which they are associated. TWO of the answer choices will NOT be used. *This question is worth 3 points.*

Answer Choices

1. The queen bee is fed by workers many times a day.

2. A flock of birds exhibits a shape and certain behavior.

3. The stock market forms a complex pattern.

4. The human brain is composed of numerous thinking neurons.

5. A hurricane is the result of various climatic factors.

6. Small and large websites are linked to create the World Wide Web.

7. Ants build an effective colony collectively.

Structural Emergence
-
-
-

Cultural Emergence
-
-

☑ Correct Answer

Choices 2, 5, and 7 are associated with structural emergence, and choices 3 and 6 are associated with cultural emergence. Choice 1 is not relevant to the passage, and choice 4 includes incorrect information.

Read the passages and answer the questions.

Drill 1

The Fruit Tree Leaf Roller

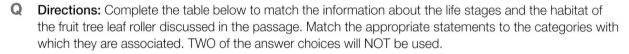
10-02

The fruit tree leaf roller (*Archips argyrospilus*) is a caterpillar that damages trees throughout California. This pest defoliates ornamental trees such as deciduous and live oaks. It also damages the fruits of cherry, apple, apricot, and plum trees, among others. These caterpillars can even drop to the ground and defoliate grass and plants growing beneath trees. This insect goes through four stages of development, beginning as an egg that is one of many deposited on a tree twig or branch. After emerging from the cement mass, the newly hatched larvae begin to eat away at their host tree as they mature and develop into full-grown caterpillars. After it feeds long enough, the larva rolls itself in a leaf wrapped and lined in silk webbing called a pupa. Eight to eleven days later, an adult moth emerges from the pupa. The adult then migrates to a new location to mate and to lay eggs for the next life cycle.

Q **Directions:** Complete the table below to match the information about the life stages and the habitat of the fruit tree leaf roller discussed in the passage. Match the appropriate statements to the categories with which they are associated. TWO of the answer choices will NOT be used.

Answer Choices

① The larva rolls itself into a pupa.

② A silk lined leaf is called a pupa.

③ The egg is deposited on a twig or branch.

④ Deciduous trees are safe nesting places.

⑤ An adult moth emerges.

⑥ The caterpillars are found in California.

⑦ The caterpillar is harmful to fruit trees and low-lying plants.

Life Stages of the Fruit Tree Leaf Roller

-
-
-

Habitat of the Fruit Tree Leaf Roller

-
-

Neolithic Culture

10-03

The Neolithic Age took place between the Paleolithic, or Old Stone Age, and the Bronze Age. The Neolithic Age is not defined by the time at which it occurred but by the behavioral and cultural characteristics that accompanied the time. One such characteristic is the cultivation of wild and domestic crops. This culture of farming signaled an end to the nomadic lifestyle for early humans as they created agricultural bases where they lived and worked for their entire lifetimes. Another characteristic is the domestication of animals. The advent of animal husbandry led to advancements in every aspect of human development from science to psychology. One of the first cultures in which the Neolithic Age has been identified through fossil evidence was in Southwest Asia and the Middle East. There, in southeastern Anatolia and northern Mesopotamia, development occurred soon after 10,000 B.C. and spread east and westward.

Q **Directions:** Complete the table below by indicating which of the answer choices describe Neolithic humans and which describe Pre-Neolithic humans. TWO of the answer choices will NOT be used.

Answer Choices

1 They moved from place to place.

2 Agriculture formed the basis of their livelihoods.

3 The Paleolithic Age preceded the Bronze Age.

4 They made advancements in animal husbandry.

5 Farming allowed them to settle in one place.

6 They did not use agriculture.

7 Fossil evidence has been found for both ages of people.

Neolithic Humans
-
-
-

Pre-Neolithic Humans
-
-

Mangrove Stands

10-04

Mangrove stands are found in saltwater areas where trees and bushes are able to grow. There are about 110 species of bushes and trees that grow in saltwater mangrove stands around the world. These swamplands occupy rivers and coastal environments with lots of fine sediment that is easy for mangrove roots to grow in. Mangroves also thrive in areas with high organic content for nourishment. These areas must also be somewhat protected from the action of strong waves. The plants in these stands have successfully adapted to several problems, such as anoxia, salinity, and frequent flooding by tides. The underwater roots of mangroves are havens for saltwater creatures like oysters, sponges, and even crabs. Aside from being havens for these creatures, mangrove stands serve an important purpose as barriers against storms and other natural forces that would otherwise batter the coast. These stands also impede erosion and provide natural barriers against unusually large waves.

Q **Directions:** Complete the table below to summarize the information about the characteristics and benefits of mangroves discussed in the passage. Match the appropriate statements to the categories with which they are associated. TWO of the answer choices will NOT be used.

Answer Choices

1. Mangroves have adapted to salty water.

2. Crabs and oysters live in salt water.

3. Mangroves provide protection from storms.

4. Mangroves grow best where there is protection from strong waves.

5. Many saltwater creatures can find homes in mangroves' root systems.

6. Anoxia and salinity hamper the growth of many plants.

7. The erosion of coastlines is prevented by mangrove stands.

Characteristics

-
-

Benefits

-
-
-

The Effects of Television on Families in the U.S.

The effects of television on members of families in the United States have been closely studied. Some scholars feel that daily exposure to television programming heavily affects the communication patterns within families. Others believe that children's thinking capacity is improved. One study concerned with the effects of television on the family used parent-child groups called dyads to fill out comparative surveys. It showed that parents that let their children watch television are able to control their children more effectively. However, their communication was less effective. Exposure to different types of television shows can make it more difficult for parents and children to communicate. The reason is that they have differing perspectives. Violence on television has proven to lead to a less advanced perspective. This, in turn, leads to less advanced moral reasoning in the mind of a child, especially when the parents do not explain the lack of realism in such violent shows.

10-05

Q **Directions:** Complete the table below about the positive and negative effects of television viewing on families discussed in the passage. Match the appropriate statements to the types of effects with which they are associated. TWO of the answer choices will NOT be used.

Answer Choices

1. Children are unable to understand the viewpoints of their parents.

2. Television may improve children's cognitive abilities.

3. The moral reasoning of children may be impaired by violence.

4. Parents have less effective communication with their children.

5. Parent-child groups are called dyads.

6. Parents do not like to watch violence on television.

7. Parents are able to control their children more effectively.

Positive Effects
-
-

Negative Effects
-
-
-

Exercises with Long Passages

Exercise 1 Read the following passage and answer the questions.

Time Limit: 4 min.

Possible Solutions to Overfishing

10-06

Overfishing is a problem that occurs when commercial fishing activities lower fish stocks to a point at which the fish cannot naturally reproduce in great enough numbers or fast enough to bring the level back up. The life cycle equilibrium that fills oceans with fish for humans to eat is locked in an unsustainable cycle because of fishermen's desire to profit.

2 → When a stock collapses, it is defined as declining to a point in which fewer than ten percent of a previously observed maximum abundance level exists. A major international scientific study printed in the journal *Science* concluded that one-third of all worldwide fishing stocks have collapsed. If this current trend is allowed to continue, all worldwide fishing stocks will have collapsed within the next fifty years.

An example of overfishing was seen in the 1970s. That was when the stocks of anchovy fisheries off the coast of Peru crashed. At the same time, scientists claimed that the stocks of natural anchovies in Peruvian waters had been driven away by the El Nino effect. Between the years 1971 and 1972, Peruvian fishermen were able to harvest sixty percent fewer anchovies than they had in previous years. This collapse represented a major loss to Peru's economy.

Scientists concerned with this problem have come up with a set of overfishing principles of precautionary approach to tackle this emerging problem. They have introduced harvest control rule management principles to fisheries around the world. A system called the Traffic Light Color Convention has been designed to introduce rules to combat overfishing, depletion, and the collapse of fishing stocks. This is a simple convention that attempts to classify fishing waters. A green light means open fishing while a yellow light stands for highly regulated fishing that is cautious of stock levels. A red light means an area should not be fished in until the fish stocks have returned to a safe and sustainable level.

In addition to the Traffic Light Color Convention, the United Nations Convention on the Law of the Sea Treaty has several articles concerned with the problem of overfishing. The first article to address this problem is number 61. It states that all coastal states should maintain the living resources in their fishing zones by making sure that they are not endangered by overexploitation. This article also calls for the maintenance and restoration of populations that are seriously threatened. The next article about this matter is number 62. It states that all coastal states are bound to promote the best possible use of commercial living resources in their economic zones. Finally, article 65 provides general rights for coastal states to control the exploitation of marine mammals for commercial gain.

6 → Another possible solution to the problem of overfishing is gene splicing. It can accelerate the reproduction of fish many times. This method was invented by Aqua Bounty Farms, a company in Newfoundland. It is hoped that once further developed, this program will allow fish farmers to use enclosed tank systems to meet worldwide fish demands while natural stocks are left alone and allowed to repopulate.

📖 Words & Phrases

equilibrium n a balance
unsustainable adj insupportable
collapse v to break down
crash v to fail

precautionary adj preventive
tackle v to deal with; to address
depletion n exhaustion
exploitation n abuse

marine adj maritime; nautical; relating to the sea
accelerate v to speed up; to quicken

1 According to paragraph 2, which of the following will occur if current trends in overfishing continue?

(A) The numbers of fish will decline to below ten percent of current levels.

(B) Large fisheries will be forced to close.

(C) Advancements in science will be needed to increase the supply.

(D) One-third of all of the fish in the world will disappear.

2 According to paragraph 6, which of the following solutions to overfishing was developed by Aqua Bounty Farms?

(A) Enclosed tank systems

(B) The regulating of the exploitation of fisheries

(C) Color-coded fishing zones

(D) Gene splicing

Mastering the Question Type

3 **Directions:** Complete the table below. Select the appropriate statements from the answer choices and match them to the type of remedy for overfishing practices to which they relate. TWO of the answer choices will NOT be used.

Answer Choices

1 Calls for the restoration of endangered fish populations

2 Divides fishing areas into open, closed, and monitored fishing areas

3 Introduces rules to fight against the decline and collapse of fishing stocks

4 Requires licenses to fish in regulated areas

5 Uses traffic lights to regulate fishing zones

6 Provides general rights for coastal states to control exploitation

7 Calls for the maintenance of fish populations in coastal waters

The Law of the Sea Treaty
-
-
-

The Traffic Light Color Convention
-
-

Summary Note Fill in the blanks with the appropriate words.

Possible Solutions to Overfishing

- Occurs when fish stocks drop to levels that cannot be replaced
  - drops to fewer than ❶ _____ of previously observed maximum abundance level
  - most fishing stocks will collapse in next ❷ _____
- Scientists have ways to prevent collapse
  - ❸ _____ → classifies fishing waters by color
  - United Nations Convention on the Law of the Sea Treaty → coastal states should maintain fishing stocks
- ❹ _____ of fish → done by Aqua Bounty Farms
  - try to accelerate fish reproduction

The Communication and Learning of Honeybees

10 - 07

Honeybees are a highly advanced species of bees capable of learning and communication, which they use to locate food sources. They also use these skills to deploy worker bees to harvest these food resources.

2 ➡ The process of learning is important for honeybees since they create an efficient and successful foraging system for an individual hive. As forager bees leave the hives in the morning, they search for plants and flowers that offer rewards of pollen and nectar. If the plants or flowers do not provide much food, the forager bees quickly learn not to make repeat visits. If they do provide a lot of food, then the bees learn to visit repeatedly. This type of conditioning is called associative learning and is usually only found in vertebrates.

Scientists studied the honeybees' ability to learn in an experiment that used a simple Y-shaped maze. The forager bees were trained to enter a maze, which was marked with a certain color, to receive a reward. These bees were then presented with a choice of directions. One was marked with the same color that was at the entrance while the other was marked with a different color. The bees quickly learned that the reward was located in the direction that was marked with the same color.

The scientists administering this test also reversed the color and extended the length of the path to see if the bees could relearn new conditions, which they did. By lengthening the distance that the bees had to travel before identifying the correct color marker, scientists were able to prove that bees could retain the information of the color markers for up to five seconds. This proved that honeybees have a short-term memory comparable to that of many birds.

After locating the most rewarding plants and flowers, the forager bees return to the hive and communicate their findings to worker bees. They do this to recruit the worker bees to forage for pollen and nectar in the same area. There are two competing theories about how forager bees recruit workers. These two theories are the dance language theory and the odor plume theory.

Since the time of Aristotle in ancient Greece, it has been known that honeybees perform dances after successfully foraging for pollen and nectar and returning to the hive. The two dances they do are the round dance and the waggle dance. The round dance consists of a bee flying in small circles while the waggle dance takes on a zigzag pattern. These dances are meant to communicate the presence and the location of rewarding plants and flowers so as to gather a group of recruits to go out to forage for more nectar and pollen. According to the dance language theory, this behavior serves to communicate the location of good nectar sources to honeybee recruits.

The odor plume theory claims that honeybee dance language is used only to attract attention while honeybees are recruited to forage for nectar and pollen by the existence of an odor plume given off by the nectar. To prove this, scientists have done studies in which odorless sugar sources have shown that forager bees were unable to recruit other honeybees to fly to those sources.

📖 Words & Phrases

deploy v to send out
forage v to search
pollen n a fine powder produced by flowers

nectar n a sweet liquid produced by flowers
associative adj linking separate ideas and thoughts to one another

vertebrate n an animal that has a backbone
recruit v to choose a new member
odor plume n the diffusion of smell

1 The word "they" in the passage refers to

    Ⓐ rewards of pollen or nectar

    Ⓑ the plants or flowers

    Ⓒ the forager bees

    Ⓓ repeat visits

2 According to paragraph 2, which of the following is NOT true of associative learning?

    Ⓐ Only vertebrates are capable of it.

    Ⓑ Bees leave their hives only at night.

    Ⓒ Bees search for food.

    Ⓓ Bees do not return if no food is found.

Mastering the Question Type

3 **Directions:** Complete the table below. Select the appropriate phrases from the answer choices and match them to the type of theory to which they relate. TWO of the answer choices will NOT be used.

Answer Choices

① Scientists proved it by using odorless sugar sources.

② Bees fly in circles.

③ Bees' sense of smell is stimulated.

④ Other bees are informed of the presence of nectar and pollen.

⑤ It explains why bees search for pollen.

⑥ Bees communicate in a zigzag motion.

⑦ It was discovered with the use of time-lapsed photography.

Dance Language Theory
-
-
-

Odor Plume Theory
-
-

Summary Note Fill in the blanks with the appropriate words.

The Communication and Learning of Honeybees

- Use learning and communication to locate ❶ _____
  - creates efficient and successful foraging system
  - can learn where good food sources are so will return
- Scientists conducted tests on honeybees
  - can learn where food sources are ❷ _____
  - show have short-term memory like birds
- Honeybee communication
  - Dance language theory
    - → perform dances when find food and return to hive
    - → round dance and ❸ _____
    - → communicate presence and location of food
  - ❹ _____ → dancing just attracts attention to get foragers

Time Limit: 3 min. 40 sec.

Cultural Diffusion

10 - 08

Cultural diffusion is the term used to describe the spread of ideas, behaviors, and material objects between different cultures. This term is used especially when this movement occurs without being linked to a population movement or mass exodus of people.

2 ➜ Theories that involve the concept of cultural diffusion often stir up controversy in anthropological circles. This happens because they often contradict theories on mass migration. This opposition between cultural diffusion and mass migration can be found in theories regarding similar human burial sites involving the skulls of cave bears around the Arctic Circle on the continents of North America, Europe, and Asia. Nevertheless, many anthropologists prefer to consider theories based on cultural diffusion, or the borrowing of traits between cultures, as they commonly describe it.

Throughout human and prehuman history, cultures have never been or remained completely isolated from one another. Even in the isolationist culture of feudal Japan, the religious philosophy of Buddhism was able to spread from India and China, where it originated from traveling monks. This is an example of how cultural diffusion can take place on a grand scale. This type of cultural diffusion happens today. When considering cultural diffusion, there are three major forms: direct, forced, and indirect diffusion.

Direct diffusion takes place when two cultures are located geographically close to each other. This results in intermarriage between citizens, economic trade, and physical combat. An example of direct diffusion would be a marriage between two people from bordering countries, such as a Mexican and an American, or members of two bordering countries, such as the United States and Canada, engaging in the same sport, such as hockey or baseball, together.

Forced diffusion happens when a stronger culture conquers or enslaves a weaker one and forces its own customs on the subjugated people. An example of this would be when African slaves were brought to the United States and forced to become Christian. Another good example would be the way England once colonized India, forcing many Indians to learn to speak English.

Indirect diffusion is the most common form that occurs these days. This type of diffusion occurs when cultural traits are passed between cultures through an intermediary or middleman without the sending and receiving cultures ever being in direct contact. This happens when a European visits the United States and discovers the Japanese dish called sushi. Another example would be when an African receives a Mickey Mouse T-shirt from a visitor and wears it even though he has never been to Disneyland.

These forms of cultural diffusion have risen and fallen in trends of frequency throughout history. In ancient times, direct diffusion was very common since groups of humans lived in adjoining settlements. But today, because of mass media and the invention of the Internet, indirect diffusion is the most common form.

📖 Words & Phrases

diffusion n spread
exodus n a departure; a migration
controversy n a debate, an argument
contradict v to deny; to rebut; to challenge
regarding prep about; concerning
originate v to start; to begin

subjugate v to defeat; to overpower; to conquer
middleman n a go-between
frequency n the number of times that something happens during a period of time
adjoining adj neighboring; adjacent

1   According to paragraph 2, it is difficult to define theories about cultural diffusion because

    Ⓐ cultural diffusion theories conflict with migration theories

    Ⓑ cultural diffusion is still taking place throughout the world

    Ⓒ cultural diffusion only occurs indirectly

    Ⓓ trends in cultural diffusion theories are always changing

2   The word "it" in the passage refers to

    Ⓐ the isolationist culture   Ⓑ Buddhism

    Ⓒ India   Ⓓ China

Mastering the Question Type

3   **Directions:** Complete the table below by matching FIVE of the seven answer choices comparing the three forms of cultural diffusion. TWO of the answer choices will NOT be used.

Answer Choices

   1 A native African many spend a holiday in Disneyland.

   2 Indians were compelled to adopt the English language.

   3 Skulls of cave bears were found near the Arctic Circle.

   4 This occurs when cultures are situated close enough to interact.

   5 This occurred when Americans enslaved Africans.

   6 Culture is passed through an intermediary.

   7 Two cultures are interested in the same sport.

Direct
-
-

Forced
-
-

Indirect
-

Summary Note   Fill in the blanks with the appropriate words.

Cultural Diffusion

- Spread of ❶ _____ between cultures

- Three major forms of diffusion
  - direct diffusion
    - → two cultures ❷ _____ geographically
    - → caused by cultural, economic, and physical interaction
  - ❸ _____
    - → stronger culture conquers weaker one
    - → African slaves brought to America and become Christian
  - indirect diffusion
    - → most common form today
    - → caused by ❹ _____

- Different forms occur at different times in history

Exercise 4 Read the following passage and answer the questions.

Time Limit: 3 min. 50 sec.

The Nesting Habits of Rodents

10 - 09

Rodents are an order of mammals that include between 2,000 and 3,000 species and comprise more than forty percent of all mammals. The success of their order is due to their small size, short breeding cycle, and overall ability to survive by consuming a wide variety of foods.

While most rodents are rather small, they vary greatly in weight and physical characteristics. A clear example of this variation can be seen in the differences between the African pygmy mouse, a rodent that usually weighs about seven grams, compared to the largest rodent still alive today, the capybara, which can weigh up to forty-five kilograms.

Common differences between rodent species are clearly evident when looking at the patterns of nests built by different rodents. For example, the North American beaver is a rodent that builds its nest by gnawing on and felling trees. The beaver uses these trees as well as various branches to construct a dam across a river or stream that will eventually create an artificial pond. Within this pond, the beaver builds a semi-aquatic home called a lodge.

4 ➡ A rodent nest that is much different from that of the beaver is the one built by a squirrel. The squirrel is known to build its nest, called a drey, amongst the branches of a tree. The squirrel is also known to build storage areas in or around its nests, where it hoards acorns and other kinds of nuts to provide itself with nourishment during the winter season. Scientists have discovered that squirrels possess extremely short memories, so they must store their nuts in places where landmarks will remind them that they hid nuts nearby. For example, squirrels may store their nuts on the north sides of trees in order to help themselves remember the locations of their food stores.

Another rodent whose nest building patterns are vastly different is the prairie dog. Prairie dogs are famous for creating highly organized colonies or towns in which large groups of prairie dog families live. A family usually consists of one male and two to four females. These towns are actually expansive tunnel systems that prairie dogs have burrowed through the ground. These tunnel systems are constructed to maximize fresh air ventilation and to control the flow of rainwater. They even have different rooms for sleeping, eating, and babysitting. These burrows additionally contain several routes for escape in the event they are infiltrated by predators.

Yet another species of rodent, the mouse, is known to build its nest above ground. Most mice construct nests of grass, fibers, and shredded materials in a small area. This is the place where they sleep, mate, and raise their young. While most mice ensconce their nests in small, cozy protected aboveground areas, some mice have been observed to dig shallow burrows. Other types of mice have been seen making nests in the walls of old homes, in tree stumps, and even in the exhaust pipes of abandoned cars.

📖 Words & Phrases

rodent n a general class of animals that includes rats, mice, and squirrels

order n a division of plants or animals classified by similarity

vary v to differ

evident adj obvious; clear

gnaw v to chew; to bite

fell v to cut down

artificial adj not natural; synthetic

hoard v to store; to amass

ventilation n freely circulating or moving air

infiltrate v to sneak in; to penetrate

ensconce v to establish in a safe, comfortable place

observe v to watch; to monitor

1 The word "comprise" in the passage is closest in meaning to

(A) consider   (B) resemble

(C) look at   (D) make up

2 According to paragraph 4, what must squirrels rely on to find their food caches?

(A) Their instincts   (B) Their sense of smell

(C) Landmarks   (D) The locations of beaver nests

Mastering the Question Type

3 **Directions:** Complete the table below by matching FIVE of the seven answer choices with the appropriate rodent. TWO of the answer choices will NOT be used.

Answer Choices

1 Its nest is called a drey.

2 It constructs its nests in small, cozy areas.

3 Its home is semi-aquatic.

4 It sometimes digs shallow burrows.

5 It stores food for the winter.

6 It lives in highly organized towns or colonies.

7 It uses fallen trees for its home.

Squirrel
-
-

Mouse
-
-

Prairie Dog
-

Summary Note   Fill in the blanks with the appropriate words.

The Nesting Habits of Rodents

- Rodents are forty percent of all mammals
  - about ❶_____ species
  - are small and have short breeding cycles
  - can vary in physical characteristics
- Rodent nests are all different
  - beaver
    - → cuts down trees and uses to dam river
    - → has ❷_____ home
  - squirrel
    - → builds nest in tree branches
    - → hoards acorns and other food near nest
  - prairie dog
    - → has highly organized colony
    - → lives in groups of one male and ❸_____ females
    - → lives underground in tunnels
  - mouse
    - → builds nest ❹_____
    - → makes nest of many different materials

Time Limit: 3 min. 40 sec.

The Intelligence of Capuchin Monkeys

10 - 10

Capuchin monkeys are considered the most intelligent of New World monkey species. They can be found in Central and South America. They live in forests and spend most of their days searching for food. At night, they sleep together in trees, having tucked themselves in between the branches. They remain there at night to avoid their natural predators, such as large falcons, snakes, and cats.

2 ➜ Capuchins are omnivorous creatures that consume fruits, nuts, seeds, and buds as well as insects, spiders, bird eggs, and small rodents. They have also been observed using stones to crack open the shells of crabs, which they then eat. The tufted capuchin is noted as being especially intelligent and has been observed to use tools on a long-term basis. This is one of the few examples of primate tool use other than with apes. These capuchins have been seen to imitate the fruit-cracking behavior of macaws when eating palm nuts.

Capuchins select the ripest fruit, bite off the tip, and drink the juice. They then toss the fruit aside, appearing to have discarded it. But once these discarded fruits harden, capuchins gather them and place them on a large, flat boulder, where they use previously gathered river stones to crack open the fruits to get the nuts inside. The river stones used by the capuchins are considered long-term tools since they use the same stones that they have gathered and used during previous fruit-cracking sessions. Young capuchins observe older ones complete this task and eventually learn from them.

Another example of capuchin intelligence and tool use happens during the mosquito season. Around this time, older capuchins gather millipedes and crush them. They then rub the crushed millipede paste on one another's backs. This paste they make acts as a natural insect repellent.

One study on capuchin monkeys used a mirror test to examine the self-awareness of these animals. When a capuchin was confronted with a mirror reflection, it was observed to react in a way that indicated a state of self-awareness that was between seeing the mirror as another individual and recognizing the image as itself. This experiment showed that capuchin monkeys are much more self-aware than many other species of primates.

For hundreds of years, these monkeys have used their intelligence to serve humans. They are easily recognized as the organ grinder monkeys that traveled with musicians of the past. They have also served as entertainers with traveling circuses and carnivals. These days, capuchin monkeys serve paraplegics and people with spinal cord injuries as service animals. Around the houses of these injured people, the monkeys help by completing simple tasks such as microwaving food, washing their human's face, and opening drink bottles.

📖 Words & Phrases

tuck v to fold
omnivorous adj eating all kinds of food
consume v to eat; to use up
crack v to break
note v to mention; to remark

discard v to throw away; to abandon
eventually v in the end; finally
confront v to face; to encounter
paraplegic n someone who cannot move the lower half of his body

1   According to paragraph 2, which of the following do capuchin monkeys feed on? *To receive credit, you must select TWO answers.*

Ⓐ Spiders   Ⓑ Snakes

Ⓒ Small birds   Ⓓ Palm nuts

2   According to the passage, which of the following is NOT true of capuchin monkeys?

Ⓐ They populate tropical forests in South America.

Ⓑ They are trained to do domestic tasks for humans.

Ⓒ They hunt small animals at night.

Ⓓ They are cleverer than any other American monkey species.

3   **Directions:** Complete the table below to summarize the information about the abilities of capuchin monkeys discussed in the passage. Match the appropriate statement to the ability with which they are associated. TWO of the answer choices will NOT be used.

Answer Choices

1 They can learn sign language.

2 They use stones to open crabs.

3 They find their homes with their sense of smell.

4 They open bottles for their human companions.

5 They drink the juice of fruits and eat the insides later.

6 They can cook food for humans.

7 They can wash the faces of humans.

Food Acquisition Skills

•

•

Service Skills

•

•

•

📝 **Summary Note**   **Fill in the blanks with the appropriate words.**

The Intelligence of Capuchin Monkeys

• Most intelligent New World monkey species

• Characteristics
  – sleep together in trees to avoid predators
  – are ❶ _____
  – can use tools on long-term basis

• Tool use
  – use stones to crack open nuts from fruit
  – crush millipedes to rub on bodies as ❷ _____

• Intelligence
  – when look in mirror, are ❸ _____
  – are organ grinder monkeys people use
  – can serve ❹ _____ people
  – can learn to do simple tasks

Time Limit: 3 min. 50 sec.

The Puebloan Culture

10 - 11

People of the Anasazi culture populated the southwestern region of the United States from around the year 1200 B.C. until 1300 A.D., when they mysteriously disappeared. The largest concentration of architectural ruins left behind by this extinct culture can be found in the Four Corners area, which includes parts of Utah, Arizona, New Mexico, and Colorado.

2 → The modern-day descendants of the Anasazi people would prefer to be called Puebloans, as they are members of the Pueblo culture. The reason is that the word Anasazi came from another tribe called the Navajo, who spoke a different language. In their language, the term Anasazi means "enemy ancestors." Early on, this word was used to describe the extinct culture whose remains had existed in this region, so it is still used today, but many people would like for it to be removed from usage.

The ancient Pueblo culture is best known for its dwellings built into the sides of cliffs that were made from types of stone and clay, such as jacal, adobe, and sandstone. Many of these ancient cliff dwelling ruins can be viewed in national historical parks such as Chaco Culture National Historical Park, Mesa Verde National Park, and Bandelier National Monument. Some of these dwellings are only accessible by rope or rock climbing.

4 → The earliest Puebloan homes were not in the sides of cliffs, however. They were based on pit house designs that were common to many ancient cultures in a period called Basketmaker. These early homes were organized in small villages. They featured simple construction and were organized in L-shapes, semicircles, or rectangles. As time passed, they became more elaborate and sturdier. By the great Pueblo period of 1150 A.D., construction methods had evolved to the point that these dwellings were built into the sides of cliffs. These ancient Puebloans were also known for their extraordinarily unique style of pottery as well as the many artistic drawings they made in the form of petroglyphs and pictographs.

Archaeologists and anthropologists are not certain why the ancient Puebloans left their established cliff dwellings in the twelfth and thirteenth centuries. Many possible factors have been suggested. Some are prolonged periods of drought, topsoil erosion, environmental damage, religious or cultural change, and even hostility from newly arrived groups of people.

The current scientific opinion about the ancient Puebloans' mysterious disappearance contends that it was caused by a combination of a climate change that was disastrous to their agriculture and also the arrival of new tribes who drove them out. This opinion is disputed by many modern Puebloan people, who think that their ancient ancestors did not disappear. Rather, they believe they simply migrated to areas in the Southwest that offered more dependable rainfall and better streams. They also claim that the ancient Puebloans merged with various other peoples, such as native Mexicans and various other Southwestern tribes.

📖 Words & Phrases

concentration [n] a close gathering
extinct [adj] vanished; gone
dwelling [n] a house
accessible [adj] approachable; reachable; available

elaborate [adj] detailed
sturdy [adj] robust; durable; well-built
prolonged [adj] lengthy
erosion [n] a gradual destruction

hostility [n] hatred; enmity; animosity
contend [v] to argue; to assert; to maintain
merge [v] to mix; to combine; to mingle

1 According to paragraph 2, today's Anasazi descendants prefer to be called Puebloans because

    Ⓐ they live in villages called pueblos

    Ⓑ the term Anasazi did not originate from their language

    Ⓒ the name is too outdated to be used today

    Ⓓ the name confuses their culture with that of the Navajo

2 According to paragraph 4, which of the following is true of the earliest dwellings of the Puebloans?

    Ⓐ They were built before the Basketmaker period.

    Ⓑ They were grouped together in small villages.

    Ⓒ They were adorned with exquisite artistry.

    Ⓓ They were complex structures set in several geometric designs.

3 **Directions:** Complete the table below by matching FIVE of the seven answer choices with the appropriate theory about the disappearance of the Puebloans. TWO of the answer choices will NOT be used.

Answer Choices

1 The Puebloans were driven out by other tribes.

2 They migrated to areas with better water sources.

3 They followed the animals that they hunted.

4 Cultural changes led to their disappearance.

5 They were seeking to relieve their excessive population.

6 The Puebloans merged with other tribes.

7 The villages suffered long periods of drought.

Academic Theories
-
-
-

Current Puebloan People's Theories
-
-

📝 Summary Note   Fill in the blanks with the appropriate words.

The Puebloan Culture

- Members of the Anasazi culture
  - lived in ❶ _____ from 1200 B.C. to 1300 A.D. → suddenly disappeared

- Modern-day descendants
  - prefer to be called ❷ _____ → "Anasazi" is word from another culture

- Dwellings → lived in sides of cliffs
  - ruins still exist in some national parks
  - earliest homes were ❸ _____
  - → were simple at first but became more elaborate and sturdier

- Puebloans departure
  - are many theories
    - → drought or other environmental damage
    - → religious or cultural change
    - → ❹ _____ from other groups
    - → modern-day Puebloans think migrated to other areas

Building Summary Skills

The following summaries are based on the passages you worked on earlier. Complete each of them by filling in the blanks with suitable words or phrases.

Exercise 1   Possible Solutions to Overfishing

issues of exploitation	accelerating fish reproduction	regulate fishing
safe and sustainable levels	the decline and collapse of fish stocks	

The problem of overfishing has led to _____. Several steps are needed to combat the problem. Fishing rules have been implemented to _____ in depleted areas until their fish stocks return to _____. The United Nations Convention on the Law of the Sea Treaty issued several articles that address related _____, and methods of _____ have been introduced.

Exercise 2   The Communication and Learning of Honeybees

the odor plume theory	a short-term memory	the memory capacity
the whereabouts	the round dance and the waggle dance	

Scientists are interested in how bees learn and communicate. They have investigated _____ of honeybees and determined that honeybees have _____ similar to that of birds. Scientists have also studied the ways and purposes that bees communicate through dances, particularly _____. The study has led to debate on _____ because while some scientists argue that the dance is merely used to attract the attention of worker bees, which are cued to the existence of rewarding plants through their aromas, other scientists argue that the dance itself communicates _____ of the desired plants.

Exercise 3   Cultural Diffusion

geographically close	indirect diffusion	forced diffusion
direct, indirect, and forced	exposure brought through a middleman	

Although anthropologists do not agree on all aspects of cultural diffusion, they have identified three main forms: _____. Direct diffusion occurs when populations are _____ enough to allow for interaction through activities that include trade or marriage. Indirect diffusion can occur from _____ such as a traveling merchant who carries wares and stories from one culture to another. _____ is the imposition of one culture's values and customs on another through subjugation. Today, with the widespread use of mass media and the Internet, _____ is the most prevalent form.

Exercise 4 | The Nesting Habits of Rodents

forty percent of all mammal species	the type of nest	short breeding cycles
away from predators	the 2,000 to 3,000 rodent species	

Rodents are a varied and hardy kind of mammal that make up more than _____.
Included among _____ are beavers, squirrels, prairie dogs, and mice. Although each is
distinguished by _____ that it builds, rodents are usually characterized as relatively small
animals that have _____ and the ability to eat many kinds of food for survival. Their high
survival rate is owed to nests that are built in safety _____. Beavers build nests by felling
trees, squirrels build them between tree branches, mice construct nests above ground, and prairie dogs dig tunnels.

Exercise 5 | The Intelligence of Capuchin Monkeys

household and personal tasks	river stones	a high level of intelligence
sociable	make a salve from millipedes	

Scientists have taken an interest in the capuchin monkeys because they are _____
and demonstrate _____. For example, they sleep together at night, and during
the day, they look for and process food with _____. They have even learned to
_____ to protect themselves from insect bites. In the past, capuchin monkeys were well
known for their adeptness at entertaining, but today, scientists are more interested in training the monkeys to perform
_____ for paraplegics and victims of spinal cord injuries.

Exercise 6 | The Puebloan Culture

the Anasazi cliff dwelling people	Puebloans	environmental changes
about 1300 A.D.	the emergence of a hostile tribe	

Known for their strong homes and exquisite artistry, _____ of southwestern North
America mysteriously disappeared _____. Anthropologists and archaeologists, as well
as the descendants of that culture, who prefer to be called _____, speculate about the
disappearance. Some of their explanations involve _____ that would have devastated an
agricultural lifestyle while others suggest that the Anasazi people merged with other cultures. Still another explanation
is that _____ drove them from their territory.

Desertification

10-12

Desertification is the process by which once fertile lands in subhumid, arid, and semiarid areas become infertile desert. These changes can be caused by climatic variations and by human activities. Much modern desertification is the result of heavy demands by increasing populations for land on which crops can be raised and cattle can graze.

The biggest problems of desertification are the loss of biodiversity and productive capacity. These effects can be seen in the American Southwest, where many once-dominant bunchgrasses have been wiped out and replaced by creosote bushes since the early 1900s. Another place these changes are evident is on the central highland plateau of Madagascar, where ten percent of the entire country has undergone the desertification process. This terrible loss of vegetation and farmland is due to the slash-and-burn agricultural practices used by the indigenous people.

3 ➡ One of the major modern causes of the desertification process is the grazing of livestock beyond the sustainable limit for a piece of land. For example, cows and sheep pound the soil with their hooves, which causes the substrate to become compacted and decreases its ability to absorb moisture. The weight and the constant stomping by the livestock also grind the soil into finer particles. All of these activities make the soil more vulnerable to erosion by wind and water. The grazing activity of the livestock as well as the collection of wood for fires additionally reduce and eliminate plants that bind the soil.

4 ➡ Another cause of desertification is the over-farming of land. As fertile soil is used to plant crops, the crops are harvested, and the land is reused. Eventually, it is stripped of its minerals and moisture. As farmers break up the land to plant new crops, the soil is left exposed to the forces of erosion. These poor farming practices contributed to the desertification of the midwestern United States in the 1930s. This economic disaster that drove a large portion of the population away from their homes as they attempted to abandon unproductive lands was termed the Dust Bowl. Desertification is also occurring rapidly over large portions of China. Because the populations of rural areas have increased since the middle of the twentieth century and species of livestock which require higher food intakes have been introduced, desertification is on the rise.

5 ➡ As desertification has been recognized as a major threat to biodiversity, some countries have developed biodiversity action plans to reverse the ill effects. These plans have been designed to limit the damaging factors and to protect the endangered flora and fauna as well. One method to counter desertification that is being used is the planting of leguminous plants. These plants are known to extract nitrogen from the air and then pump it into the soil. This process has proven to restore fertility in lands that have begun the process of desertification. Another method is to stack stones around the bases of trees in order to create a larger surface area for morning dew to collect on and retain soil moisture.

6 ➡ Another method to repair land is the digging of artificial grooves into the ground, which retain rainfall and trap wind-blown seeds. These grooves protect the land against desertification. This method shows that land can be protected through simple efforts. Environmental scientists in Iran have begun

a new process of spraying petroleum over semiarid land where crops are planted. This process coats seedlings to prevent the loss of moisture and stops the wind from blowing them away.

7 ➜ Some very simple yet successful methods to limit desertification are the erection of sand fences to prevent sand from moving into areas as well as windbreaks to keep the wind from eroding the soil. Another important restriction that combats desertification is the restriction of areas where land-damaging off-road vehicles can be driven.

1 The word "vulnerable" in the passage is closest in meaning to

Ⓐ susceptible

Ⓑ critical

Ⓒ accessible

Ⓓ favorable

2 According to paragraph 3, soil gets more affected by erosion because of

Ⓐ dominant bunchgrasses

Ⓑ free-roaming animals

Ⓒ the stomping of hooves by livestock

Ⓓ the planting of leguminous plants

3 Which of the following can be inferred from paragraph 4 about desertification in the Midwest in the 1930s?

Ⓐ Those who abandoned their homes moved back when the land improved.

Ⓑ Better farming practices could have prevented the Dust Bowl.

Ⓒ The land was polluted by toxic minerals.

Ⓓ The Dust Bowl gave rise to economic prosperity.

4 The word "counter" in the passage is closest in meaning to

Ⓐ neutralize

Ⓑ accelerate

Ⓒ eliminate

Ⓓ offset

5   The word "which" in the passage refers to

    (A) another method

    (B) land

    (C) artificial grooves

    (D) the ground

6   According to paragraphs 5 and 6, which of the following is NOT a way to prevent desertification?

    (A) Stacking stones around trees

    (B) Introducing livestock

    (C) Making furrows in the ground

    (D) Spraying petroleum over semiarid land

7   In paragraph 7, why does the author mention "the restriction of areas"?

    (A) To show how land developers comply with scientists

    (B) To note that simple measures can lessen environmental damage

    (C) To highlight the dangers of modern technology

    (D) To encourage people to avoid hiking in certain regions

8   **Directions:** Complete the table below by indicating which of the answer choices describe the causes of desertification and which describe the methods to decrease desertification. TWO of the answer choices will NOT be used.

Answer Choices

1. Rural populations have declined in China.

2. Sheep and cows compact the soil.

3. Farmers break up mineral-depleted soil.

4. Creosote bushes became common in the early 1900s.

5. Sand fences and windbreaks are set up.

6. Livestock grind soil into fine particles.

7. Large stones are placed around trees.

Causes
-
-
-

Methods
-
-

Varieties of Tropism

A tropism is considered by scientists to be a phenomenon of the biological variation in which a living organism turns or grows in response to stimulus from its environment. The direction the organism grows or turns in is dependent on the direction of the stimulus. The opposite of tropism is nastic movement, in which the response to stimulus is considered nondirectional.

2 → Tropisms are named for the stimulus which generates them. The word *tropism* comes from the Greek word *trope*, which means "to turn" or "to change." Some of the varieties of tropism are chemotropism, geotropism, hydrotropism, heliotropism, phototropism, and thigmotropism. Tropisms are usually associated with plants or other fixed organisms. If an organism is capable of physically moving by its own will or motility, its activity or movement in response to stimulus is not considered to be a tropism but rather a taxis, which is a directional response, or a kinesis, which is a nondirectional response.

3 → Chemotropism occurs as a result of chemical stimulus, usually in plants or bacteria. A good example of this type of movement is evident during the growth of a pollen tube. It can be witnessed when lipids are present at the surface of the stigma, thereby stimulating accelerated growth in the pollen tubes. These tubes can also be stimulated to grow even faster by the presence of more than one grain of pollen in the stigma of a flower.

4 → Charles Darwin was the first to document the presence of geotropism, or gravitropism, which is the turning or growth movement of a plant or fungi in response to the Earth's gravity. This is visible in the downward growth of the roots of plants and also in jungle vines which grow downward from the tops of trees. It can also be seen by taking a close look at the growth directions of lichens and mosses on rocks.

Hydrotropism is the directional growth in response to the stimulus of water and its direction of movement. It is very difficult to observe in the roots of plants even though it is present since the action of water is not visible as it constantly courses through the soil and would require the disturbance of the subject in order to observe it. But this process is easy to imagine, as the water thirsty roots of plants reach out and grow in the direction that will give them the best access to moisture.

Heliotropism is also referred to as the diurnal motion of plants. This term describes plants' movements in direct response to the movement of the sun across the sky. Flowers may assume a random orientation at night, but when the sun rises in the east, they turn toward it and follow it across the sky as it sets in the west. This motion is accomplished by motor cells within the flexible segments of the stem just below the flower. They do this by pumping potassium ions into their tissue, which changes the pressure, resulting in motion.

7 → Phototropism is different than heliotropism in that it describes the motion of plants in response to light stimulus, but not just that of the sun. The growth of plants toward a light source is termed positive phototropism while growth away from a light source is termed negative phototropism. Most plants experience positive phototropism while their roots exhibit negative phototropic tendencies as they grow deeper into the soil. Many mosses and lichens are phototropic and can be found growing on the parts of rocks that are exposed to the sun while mold and mildew grow in areas that receive no sunlight. Some climbing plants such as vines exhibit thigmotropic reactions to the stimulus of touch or contact. Plants that react in this way contain cells that produce auxin, which causes them to move as they grow around surfaces such as walls, pots, and poles.

9 The word "associated" in the passage is closest in meaning to

Ⓐ compared

Ⓑ separated

Ⓒ linked

Ⓓ handled

10 According to paragraph 2, tropisms are named for

Ⓐ the variety of affected plants

Ⓑ the stimulus that affects plants

Ⓒ the static movement of plants

Ⓓ the rate and direction of plant growth

11 According to paragraph 2, which of the following is true of a taxis?

Ⓐ It is a kind of tropism.

Ⓑ It is a directed response to stimulus.

Ⓒ It is more responsive than a kinesis.

Ⓓ It impairs motility.

12 Which of the following can be inferred from paragraph 3 about chemotropism?

Ⓐ Adding pollen to a flower creates a chemical stimulus.

Ⓑ The action of water is always visible in plants.

Ⓒ Lipids are a part of a plant.

Ⓓ Pollen is a natural inhibitor of plant growth.

13 According to paragraph 4, which of the following is a sign of geotropism?

Ⓐ Vines climbing a tree trunk

Ⓑ Fungi growing on another plant

Ⓒ Downward lichen growth on a rock

Ⓓ Roots appearing above ground

14 The word "it" in the passage refers to

   (A) hydrotropism

   (B) the stimulus of water

   (C) its direction of movement

   (D) the action of water

15 According to paragraph 7, which of the following is NOT true of climbing vines?

   (A) They exhibit thigmotropic reactions.

   (B) They contain auxin.

   (C) They are affected by touch.

   (D) They harbor mold and mildew.

16 **Directions:** Complete the table below to summarize the information about some types of tropism discussed in the passage. Match the appropriate statements to the types of tropism with which they are associated. TWO of the answer choices will NOT be used.

Answer Choices

1. It describes the motion of plants in response to the sun.

2. It is present in plants that pump potassium ions into their tissue.

3. Its negative category affects the downward growth of roots.

4. It causes moss to grow on rocks exposed to sunlight.

5. It explains why some plants grow around surfaces like walls and poles.

6. It involves a directional response to water.

7. It stimulates growth in the pollen tubes with lipids.

Phototropism
-
-

Heliotropism
-
-

Hydrotropism
-

Vocabulary Check-Up

A Choose the words with the closest meanings to the highlighted words.

1 Illness can result when bodily systems are not in equilibrium.

- (A) balance
- (B) operation
- (C) entropy
- (D) disharmony

2 The general was reluctant to deploy his troops into the enemy-controlled town.

- (A) accelerate
- (B) retreat
- (C) send
- (D) withdraw

3 Using the cover of darkness, the soldiers infiltrated the enemy's defenses.

- (A) examined
- (B) discovered
- (C) extended
- (D) penetrated

4 The concept of evolution did not originate with Darwin.

- (A) elaborate
- (B) begin
- (C) blossom
- (D) terminate

5 A small controversy erupted among the women about who had the best recipe.

- (A) contest
- (B) decision
- (C) debate
- (D) fight

6 The famous miser Ebenezer Scrooge would hoard his money and never spend it.

- (A) save
- (B) give
- (C) invest
- (D) count

7 The young boy tucked the coin into his pocket.

- (A) dropped
- (B) grabbed
- (C) opened
- (D) placed

8 He set off the security alarm with his artificial hip implants.

- (A) manmade
- (B) flexible
- (C) recent
- (D) inserted

9 Dinosaurs became extinct after their food sources were depleted.

- (A) ridiculous
- (B) extreme
- (C) nonexistent
- (D) nomadic

10 The key was ensconced under the welcome mat.

- (A) uncovered
- (B) concealed
- (C) dropped
- (D) extracted

B **Match the words with the correct definitions.**

1 merge •   • Ⓐ a rate of occurrence

2 ventilation •   • Ⓑ to bite persistently

3 plume •   • Ⓒ to mix; to mingle

4 frequency •   • Ⓓ the process of being gradually worn away or destroyed

5 recruit •   • Ⓔ someone who is incapable of moving his legs or lower body

6 gnaw •   • Ⓕ a powdery substance that contains the fertilizing agent from male

7 accelerate •   • Ⓖ freely circulating or moving air

8 pollen •   • Ⓗ a member enlisted to help

9 erosion •   • Ⓘ to speed up; to quicken

10 paraplegic •   • Ⓙ a spreading cloud of smoke or vapor

Actual Test

Actual Test

01

CONTINUE

Reading Section Directions

This section measures your ability to understand academic passages in English. You will have **35 minutes** to read and answer questions about **2 passages**. A clock at the top of the screen will show you how much time is remaining.

Most questions are worth 1 point but the last question for each passage is worth more than 1 point. The directions for the last question indicate how many points you may receive.

Some passages include a word or phrase that is <u>underlined</u> in blue. Click on the word or phrase to see a definition or an explanation.

When you want to move to the next question, click on **Next**. You may skip questions and go back to them later. If you want to return to previous questions, click on **Back**. You can click on **Review** at any time, and the review screen will show you which questions you have answered and which you have not answered. From this review screen, you may go directly to any question you have already seen in the Reading section.

Click on **Continue** to go on.

11 - 01

The Terrestrial and Jovian Planets

The planets in Earth's solar system are arrayed on nearly the same flat plane with their orbits forming roughly concentric ellipses around the sun. But the ones closest to the sun have very different characteristics from the outer planets. The former are called the terrestrial planets, which include—in order from the sun—Mercury, Venus, Earth, and Mars. The latter are the Jovian planets, consisting of Jupiter, Saturn, Uranus, and Neptune. Compared with the terrestrial worlds, the Jovian planets are larger, rotate faster, and have stronger magnetic fields. In addition, the Jovian planets all have ring systems and many moons orbiting them. The term Jovian is derived from the Roman god Jupiter, or *Jovis* in Latin. The planet that traditionally was considered to be the ninth and outermost planet—Pluto—fits into neither category as it displays some traits of both groups. In 2006, scientists removed Pluto from the list of planets.

The principal distinction between the two categories of planets is their composition. The terrestrial planets primarily consist of rocks and have metallic iron cores and silicate surfaces. Because Earth has those components, the four planets that are similarly composed are called terrestrial, after the Latin word for Earth—*terra*. As a consequence of their rocky surfaces, the terrestrial planets are dotted with mountains, canyons, craters, and volcanoes. Their solid cores make them subject to tectonic shifts, causing their surfaces to move over time, as can be seen with continental drift on Earth. Because of these solid surfaces, spaceships can land on terrestrial planets.

In contrast, the Jovian planets are called gas giants because they are largely composed of a gaseous mixture of hydrogen and helium with traces of methane, water, and ammonia. The gas giants have liquid cores of rock or metal. But the cores are not solid masses, they are more like concentrations of heavy elements such as iron and silicon. And their inner cores are **dwarfed** by the gaseous compounds that constitute most of the Jovian planets' masses. The gases are under immense pressure, so there is no clear boundary between the cores of the planets and their atmospheres; thus it would not be possible to land a spaceship on these planets.

While the first two Jovian planets, Jupiter and Saturn, are classic gas giants, Uranus and Neptune are members of a subgroup called ice giants because they consist largely of ice and have lesser proportions of water, methane, and ammonia. Ice predominates on those Jovian planets because of their greater distance from the sun. Because the Jovian planets are much larger than the terrestrial ones, they exert much stronger magnetic fields, which, in turn, account for their denser atmospheres. Whereas the surfaces of the Earthlike planets are visible to telescopes and space probes, the cores of the Jovian planets remain obscured by thick layers of gaseous atmosphere.

The terrestrial planets are much cooler internally. Surface temperatures on Earth render it the only one of the planets **hospitable** to humans. The surface temperatures of the other terrestrial planets range from Mercury's 510 degrees Celsius to Mars's negative 80 degrees Celsius. Being much farther from the sun, the Jovian planets are cooler, ranging from minus 148 degrees Celsius on Jupiter to minus 214 degrees Celsius on

Neptune.

Rotating rapidly, the Jovian planets experience wind patterns that cause bands or stripes across their outer layer of gas. The bands are high- and low-pressure regions that, unlike Earth's localized sites of low or high pressure, circle the planets completely, which is a result of their high-velocity rotations. In addition, all four planets have systems of rings and moons with Saturn's rings being the most prominent as seen from Earth. The rings are composed of particles of ice crystals. The origins of the rings are not well understood. The most likely origin is that the rings formed when the moons of Saturn drifted too close to the planet. The tidal forces from Saturn could have torn the moons into tiny fragments. These fragments are the current ring system. None of the terrestrial planets has rings, and they have just three moons: one for Earth and two for Mars. Saturn alone has 146 moons while Jupiter has ninety-five, Uranus has twenty-eight, and Neptune has fourteen.

📖 *Glossary*
dwarf: to make something appear smaller or inferior
hospitable: providing a pleasant environment

1 According to paragraph 1, which of the following is NOT true of the Jovian planets?

(A) They have rings around them.

(B) They lack magnetic fields.

(C) They rotate faster than the terrestrial planets.

(D) They are larger than the terrestrial planets.

2 The word "subject" in the passage is closest in meaning to

(A) resistant

(B) impenetrable

(C) susceptible

(D) changeable

3 According to paragraph 2, the four planets closest to the sun are called the terrestrial planets because

(A) they were named for the Roman god of Earth

(B) they are made of mixtures of gases

(C) they have no volcanic action

(D) they are all composed of rocks

The Terrestrial and Jovian Planets

1 → The planets in Earth's solar system are arrayed on nearly the same flat plane with their orbits forming roughly concentric ellipses around the sun. But the ones closest to the sun have very different characteristics from the outer planets. The former are called the terrestrial planets, which include— in order from the sun—Mercury, Venus, Earth, and Mars. The latter are the Jovian planets, consisting of Jupiter, Saturn, Uranus, and Neptune. Compared with the terrestrial worlds, the Jovian planets are larger, rotate faster, and have stronger magnetic fields. In addition, the Jovian planets all have ring systems and many moons orbiting them. The term Jovian is derived from the Roman god Jupiter, or *Jovis* in Latin. The planet that traditionally was considered to be the ninth and outermost planet— Pluto—fits into neither category as it displays some traits of both groups. In 2006, scientists removed Pluto from the list of planets.

2 → The principal distinction between the two categories of planets is their composition. The terrestrial planets primarily consist of rocks and have metallic iron cores and silicate surfaces. Because Earth has those components, the four planets that are similarly composed are called terrestrial, after the Latin word for Earth—*terra*. As a consequence of their rocky surfaces, the terrestrial planets are dotted with mountains, canyons, craters, and volcanoes. Their solid cores make them subject to tectonic shifts, causing their surfaces to move over time, as can be seen with continental drift on Earth. Because of these solid surfaces, spaceships can land on terrestrial planets.

4 Which of the following best expresses the essential information in the highlighted sentence? *Incorrect* answer choices change the meaning in important ways or leave out essential information.

(A) A spaceship can easily penetrate the atmosphere of a Jovian planet.

(B) Because it is composed of high-pressure gases, a Jovian planet's core and atmosphere are indistinguishable.

(C) The Jovian planet's rapid rotation exerts great pressure on the planet's gaseous atmosphere.

(D) The solid surface of a Jovian planet is exposed to intense pressure from the gases in the atmosphere.

5 Select the TWO answer choices that are mentioned in paragraph 3 as being the most common gases that make up the Jovian planet. *To receive credit, you must select TWO answers.*

(A) Oxygen

(B) Ammonia

(C) Hydrogen

(D) Helium

³➡ In contrast, the Jovian planets are called gas giants because they are largely composed of a gaseous mixture of hydrogen and helium with traces of methane, water, and ammonia. The gas giants have liquid cores of rock or metal. But the cores are not solid masses, they are more like concentrations of heavy elements such as iron and silicon. And their inner cores are **dwarfed** by the gaseous compounds that constitute most of the Jovian planets' masses. The gases are under immense pressure, so there is no clear boundary between the cores of the planets and their atmospheres; thus it would not be possible to land a spaceship on these planets.

📖 *Glossary*

dwarf: to make something appear smaller or inferior

6 The author discusses "much stronger magnetic fields" in paragraph 4 in order to

(A) explain why the Jovian planets rotate faster than the terrestrial planets

(B) explain how the ring systems of the Jovian planets formed

(C) explain why the Jovian planets have dense atmospheres

(D) explain why the Jovian planets are cooler than the terrestrial planets

7 According to paragraph 5, which of the following can be inferred about Neptune?

(A) It has no rings around it.

(B) It is smaller than Venus.

(C) It is colder than Mars.

(D) It has a solid surface.

4 ➡ While the first two Jovian planets, Jupiter and Saturn, are classic gas giants, Uranus and Neptune are members of a subgroup called ice giants because they consist largely of ice and have lesser proportions of water, methane, and ammonia. Ice predominates on those Jovian planets because of their greater distance from the sun. Because the Jovian planets are much larger than the terrestrial ones, they exert much stronger magnetic fields, which, in turn, account for their denser atmospheres. Whereas the surfaces of the Earthlike planets are visible to telescopes and space probes, the cores of the Jovian planets remain obscured by thick layers of gaseous atmosphere.

5 ➡ The terrestrial planets are much cooler internally. Surface temperatures on Earth render it the only one of the planets hospitable to humans. The surface temperatures of the other terrestrial planets range from Mercury's 510 degrees Celsius to Mars's negative 80 degrees Celsius. Being much farther from the sun, the Jovian planets are cooler, ranging from minus 148 degrees Celsius on Jupiter to minus 214 degrees Celsius on Neptune.

📖 *Glossary*

hospitable: providing a pleasant environment

8 According to paragraph 6, Saturn's rings were formed by

(A) some of the planet's moons being torn into fragments

(B) the planet's gravity attracting passing particles

(C) volcanic ash being propelled beyond the planet's atmosphere

(D) the planet's rapid rotation dispersing gases into space

9 Look at the four squares [■] that indicate where the following sentence could be added to the passage.

It is likely that these numbers will rise as more are discovered orbiting these distant planets in the future.

Where would the sentence best fit?

Click on a square [■] to add the sentence to the passage.

---

6 ➔ Rotating rapidly, the Jovian planets experience wind patterns that cause bands or stripes across their outer layer of gas. The bands are high- and low-pressure regions that, unlike Earth's localized sites of low or high pressure, circle the planets completely, which is a result of their high-velocity rotations. In addition, all four planets have systems of rings and moons with Saturn's rings being the most prominent as seen from Earth. The rings are composed of particles of ice crystals. The origins of the rings are not well understood. The most likely origin is that the rings formed when the moons of Saturn drifted too close to the planet. The tidal forces from Saturn could have torn the moons into tiny fragments. **1** These fragments are the current ring system. **2** None of the terrestrial planets has rings, and they have just three moons: one for Earth and two for Mars. **3** Saturn alone has 146 moons while Jupiter has ninety-five, Uranus has twenty-eight, and Neptune has fourteen. **4**

10 **Directions:** An introductory sentence for a brief summary of the passage is provided below. Complete the summary by selecting the THREE answer choices that express the most important ideas in the passage. Some answer choices do not belong in the summary because they express ideas that are not in the passage or are minor ideas in the passage. *This question is worth 2 points.*

> Drag your answer choices to the spaces where they belong.
> To remove an answer choice, click on it. To review the passage, click on **View Text**.

The Jovian and terrestrial planets have many differences, making them distinct from one another.

-
-
-

Answer Choices

1. The terrestrial planets consist mainly of rocks while the Jovian planets are largely gaseous.

2. Pluto was taken off the list of planets because it is too small and has no moons.

3. The Jovian planets have traces of methane, water, and ammonia.

4. The Jovian planets have thicker atmospheres that prevent people from seeing their cores.

5. The terrestrial planets lack the rings that characterize the Jovian planets.

6. The Jovian planets have more moons than the terrestrial planets.

11-02

Right-hand Dominance

Humans are disproportionately right-handed. Scientists have not been able to agree over the exact percentages of right versus left-handers because there is no accepted standard for identifying which hand is dominant. For example, some people who write or throw with their right hands may perform other tasks with their left hands or may kick a ball with their left foot. Absent an objective measure, therefore, the range of estimates is wide. Right-handers are said to make up between eighty-five and ninety-five percent of all people and left-handers around five to fifteen percent while a tiny percentage are ambidextrous, so they can use both hands with equal ability.

Perhaps the most unusual fact about right-hand dominance is how little is known about its causes. Several theories have been proposed. Some evidence exists that the phenomenon is genetic, but geneticists cannot agree on the process by which handedness may be passed on by inheritance. Social and cultural forces can cause a preference for one hand, such as when teachers or parents force a naturally left-handed child to use the right hand. It has also been observed by anthropologists that left-handedness tends to be less common in restrictive societies and more common in permissive ones, yet no consensus has been reached on how that could occur.

The most **credible** explanations center on functions inside the brain. It has been shown that the brain's two **hemispheres** control the opposite side of the body. It has been suggested that the nerves in the brain cross over at neck level to the other side of the body so that the right half of the brain governs the left side of the body while the left half governs the right side. Scientists believe that the left half of the brain evolved in such a way as to predominate over the right half. As a result, the right side of the body is controlled by the more influential left hemisphere, causing the right side to be more adept at physical tasks. But when a person is born with a dominant right hemisphere, that person will be left-handed. Some researchers have argued that some left-handedness may have a pathological origin, having been caused by brain trauma during birth.

A theory grounded in evolution is the Warrior and Shield Theory. It explains that right-handedness evolved over time to be dominant because a right-handed warrior would hold his shield in his left hand to protect his heart and to leave his right hand free to hold a weapon. A left-handed warrior, in contrast, would hold his weapon in his left hand and his shield in his right, thereby leaving his heart exposed. A right-handed warrior, with his heart protected against enemy attacks, was therefore more likely to survive. By the process of natural selection, the trait for right-handedness became favored over that for left-handedness.

Another theory focuses on the naturally asymmetrical arrangement of the human body. Such asymmetry is evidenced by the observable facts that the right side of the face is slightly different from the left, that one leg is stronger or longer that the other, and that one foot is larger than the other one. Right-handedness, the theory proposes, is just another example of this natural asymmetry.

A consequence of right-hand dominance is that most common consumer products are geared to right-handers only, leaving left-handers to struggle to adapt to designs not made with them in mind. Some of these include scissors, doorknobs, locks, screwdrivers, automobile fixtures, refrigerators, can openers, clothes buttons and fasteners, and musical instruments. The result of this design bias can be more than mere inconvenience. Some left-handed soldiers shooting rifles designed for right-handers have sustained eye and head injuries from ejected shell casings.

Hand dominance does not seem to occur in nonhuman animal species. While some individual animals can be seen developing a preference for one hand or the other, there is no evidence that this preference is common to the species as a whole as it is in humans. Some scientists claim to have observed such dominance in animals but only in controlled settings, such as a zoo or laboratory, and only when the animals are performing manual tasks that do not mirror how they use their hands in the wild.

📖 *Glossary*

credible: believable

hemisphere: one half of a spherical or roughly round body

11 The word "Absent" in the passage is closest in meaning to

- (A) Using
- (B) Resisting
- (C) Lacking
- (D) Substituting

12 In paragraph 2, all of the following questions are answered EXCEPT:

- (A) What have anthropologists noticed about restrictive societies?
- (B) Why is there a problem with the genetic theory on handedness?
- (C) Which countries have the greatest percentage of left-handed people?
- (D) How can social forces determine a person's handedness?

Right-hand Dominance

Humans are disproportionately right-handed. Scientists have not been able to agree over the exact percentages of right versus left-handers because there is no accepted standard for identifying which hand is dominant. For example, some people who write or throw with their right hands may perform other tasks with their left hands or may kick a ball with their left foot. Absent an objective measure, therefore, the range of estimates is wide. Right-handers are said to make up between eighty-five and ninety-five percent of all people and left-handers around five to fifteen percent while a tiny percentage are ambidextrous, so they can use both hands with equal ability.

2 → Perhaps the most unusual fact about right-hand dominance is how little is known about its causes. Several theories have been proposed. Some evidence exists that the phenomenon is genetic, but geneticists cannot agree on the process by which handedness may be passed on by inheritance. Social and cultural forces can cause a preference for one hand, such as when teachers or parents force a naturally left-handed child to use the right hand. It has also been observed by anthropologists that left-handedness tends to be less common in restrictive societies and more common in permissive ones, yet no consensus has been reached on how that could occur.

13 Which of the following can be inferred from paragraph 3 about a boy who throws with his right hand?

- (A) His brain's left hemisphere is dominant.
- (B) His brain suffered trauma at birth.
- (C) His brain's right hemisphere is dominant.
- (D) His brain's nerves did not fully develop before birth.

14 The word "that" in the passage refers to

- (A) natural selection
- (B) the trait
- (C) right-handedness
- (D) left-handedness

15 The word "asymmetrical" in the passage is closest in meaning to

- (A) deformed
- (B) imbalanced
- (C) geometrical
- (D) variable

📖 *Glossary*
credible: believable
hemisphere: one half of a spherical or roughly round body

³→ The most <u>credible</u> explanations center on functions inside the brain. It has been shown that the brain's two <u>hemispheres</u> control the opposite side of the body. It has been suggested that the nerves in the brain cross over at neck level to the other side of the body so that the right half of the brain governs the left side of the body while the left half governs the right side. Scientists believe that the left half of the brain evolved in such a way as to predominate over the right half. As a result, the right side of the body is controlled by the more influential left hemisphere, causing the right side to be more adept at physical tasks. But when a person is born with a dominant right hemisphere, that person will be left-handed. Some researchers have argued that some left-handedness may have a pathological origin, having been caused by brain trauma during birth.

A theory grounded in evolution is the Warrior and Shield Theory. It explains that right-handedness evolved over time to be dominant because a right-handed warrior would hold his shield in his left hand to protect his heart and to leave his right hand free to hold a weapon. A left-handed warrior, in contrast, would hold his weapon in his left hand and his shield in his right, thereby leaving his heart exposed. A right-handed warrior, with his heart protected against enemy attacks, was therefore more likely to survive. By the process of natural selection, the trait for right-handedness became favored over that for left-handedness.

Another theory focuses on the naturally asymmetrical arrangement of the human body. Such asymmetry is evidenced by the observable facts that the right side of the face is slightly different from the left, that one leg is stronger or longer that the other, and that one foot is larger than the other one. Right-handedness, the theory proposes, is just another example of this natural asymmetry.

16 In paragraph 6, the author uses "eye and head injuries" as examples of

Ⓐ the Warrior and Shield Theory

Ⓑ problems faced by left-handers

Ⓒ the lack of training soldiers receive

Ⓓ problems with rifle designs

17 In paragraph 6, the author's description of items that left-handers have trouble using mentions all of the following EXCEPT:

Ⓐ Refrigerators

Ⓑ Violins

Ⓒ Pencils

Ⓓ Shirt buttons

18 According to paragraph 7, which of the following is true of hand dominance in animals?

Ⓐ It is the same as in humans.

Ⓑ It is observed only in the wild.

Ⓒ Animals in controlled settings adopt the hand-dominance of their handlers.

Ⓓ It has been observed only with manual tasks.

19 Look at the four squares [■] that indicate where the following sentence could be added to the passage.

Left-handers often search for custom-made versions of these products.

Where would the sentence best fit?

Click on a square [■] to add the sentence to the passage.

⁶➡**1** A consequence of right-hand dominance is that most common consumer products are geared to right-handers only, leaving left-handers to struggle to adapt to designs not made with them in mind. **2** Some of these include scissors, doorknobs, locks, screwdrivers, automobile fixtures, refrigerators, can openers, clothes buttons and fasteners, and musical instruments. **3** The result of this design bias can be more than mere inconvenience. **4** Some left-handed soldiers shooting rifles designed for right-handers have sustained eye and head injuries from ejected shell casings.

⁷➡Hand dominance does not seem to occur in nonhuman animal species. While some individual animals can be seen developing a preference for one hand or the other, there is no evidence that this preference is common to the species as a whole as it is in humans. Some scientists claim to have observed such dominance in animals but only in controlled settings, such as a zoo or laboratory, and only when the animals are performing manual tasks that do not mirror how they use their hands in the wild.

20 Directions: Complete the table below to summarize characteristics of each kind of handedness. Match the appropriate statement to either right- or left-handedness. TWO of the answer choices will NOT be used. *This question is worth 3 points.*

Drag your answer choices to the spaces where they belong.
To remove an answer choice, click on it. To review the passage, click on **View Text**.

Answer Choices

1. It includes the vast majority of people.

2. One cause may be brain trauma at birth.

3. The Warrior and Shield Theory may explain this trait.

4. This trait can be changed by electrical stimulation.

5. The natural asymmetry of the body may cause this trait.

6. A specially designed pair of scissors is needed by this group.

7. Most animals are in this category.

Right-handedness
-
-
-

Left-handedness
-
-

Actual Test

02

Reading Section Directions

This section measures your ability to understand academic passages in English. You will have **35 minutes** to read and answer questions about **2 passages**. A clock at the top of the screen will show you how much time is remaining.

Most questions are worth 1 point but the last question for each passage is worth more than 1 point. The directions for the last question indicate how many points you may receive.

Some passages include a word or phrase that is <u>underlined</u> in blue. Click on the word or phrase to see a definition or an explanation.

When you want to move to the next question, click on **Next**. You may skip questions and go back to them later. If you want to return to previous questions, click on **Back**. You can click on **Review** at any time, and the review screen will show you which questions you have answered and which you have not answered. From this review screen, you may go directly to any question you have already seen in the Reading section.

Click on **Continue** to go on.

Water in the Desert

11 - 03

A temporary lake formed in a desert

Deserts are regions that receive fewer than twenty-five centimeters of annual precipitation. Although deserts are usually thought of as being hot, they also are found in cold climates, such as Antarctica. Deserts are classified according to the amount of rainfall they receive. The driest deserts are called hyper-arid, where rain is absent for at least twelve consecutive months. Arid deserts experience some rainfall but receive fewer than 250 millimeters per year. Finally, semiarid deserts see between 250 and 500 millimeters of rain.

Despite the long-term lack of rain, deserts are occasionally drenched by violent storms. During such downpours, dried stream channels, called arroyos, rapidly fill and spill over, sometimes causing dangerous flash floods. As the water rushes down mountains and erodes the land, it carries gravel, rock, and sand, which are deposited on the bottom of the arroyos, creating fan-shaped formations called alluvial fans. Some deserts are also traversed by their own permanent rivers, known as exotic rivers, which are fed by water from outside the desert. Some well-known exotic rivers are the Nile River in Egypt, the Yellow River in China, and the Colorado River in Arizona. Other sources of water include underground springs or reservoirs, which provide life-sustaining moisture to desert vegetation. Deserts abound with plant species that have adapted to the dry environment by extending taproots deep into the ground to absorb the water below.

Temporary lakes may form when rainfall is sufficient. These lakes occur in basins offering no outlets. When the lakebeds dry up, they leave a flat plain **encrusted** with salt, an area known as a playa. Over a hundred playas dot the landscape of North American deserts, including Great Salt Lake in Utah. A scarcity of rain does not always create a desert. There must also be a high rate of evaporation relative to precipitation—a measure known as potential evapotranspiration. That gauge totals the water lost through both normal evaporation and the evaporation that occurs from plant life. Potential evapotranspiration is the amount of water that could evaporate in any area. When this potential exceeds actual precipitation, desert-like conditions will arise.

Thus deserts can be either very hot or very cold so long as the potential evaporation is greater than the precipitation. Icy deserts like Antarctica collect rain in frozen snow that never seeps into the ground. And hot deserts like the Sahara receive little rain—so little that the amount is less than the potential evaporation.

Water is responsible for the concentration of mineral deposits under the desert surface. Rainfall passes through mineral layers and redeposits the minerals near the water table, where they can be easily extracted in mining operations. Mineral deposits also are enriched by the evaporation of water in the playas, which yield minerals such as gypsum and salt compounds such as sodium nitrate and sodium chloride. An example of such evaporation is shown by the Great Basin Desert in the western United States, which contains boron, an essential ingredient in the manufacture of drugs, **water softeners**, glass, and various agricultural chemicals.

The role of water in creating deserts is illustrated by the Atacama Desert in northern Chile in South America. That desert spans the area between the Pacific Ocean to the west and the Andes Mountains to the east. High atmospheric pressure over the Andes causes dry, cold air to descend to the surface. This air lacks water vapor and is easily heated by the sun, raising the ground temperatures and lowering the humidity, which are perfect conditions for a desert. Rain is sparse in the Atacama because of a phenomenon called rain shadow. Warm, humid air from the Amazon Rainforest is blocked from reaching the Atacama by the Andes. That air is cooled by the cold mountain air and condenses into rain or snow in the mountains. As the air descends the west side of the mountains, it warms up, and the clouds break up, so rain therefore does not fall to the ground. Hence the Andes Mountains have the unusual effect of causing extreme moisture in the Amazon River basin at the same time that they cause extreme dryness on the other side of the mountains. Interestingly, the driest and wettest places on the Earth are nearly adjacent to each other.

📖 *Glossary*

encrusted: covered with a hard layer or coating
water softener: a device or substance that removes certain minerals from water

1 The word "consecutive" in the passage is closest in meaning to

  Ⓐ alternate
  Ⓑ annual
  Ⓒ successive
  Ⓓ proximate

2 According to paragraph 1, which of the following deserts receives the least amount of rainfall?

  Ⓐ Arid deserts
  Ⓑ Hyper-arid deserts
  Ⓒ Semiarid deserts
  Ⓓ Cold deserts

3 In paragraph 2, the author uses "exotic rivers" as examples of

  Ⓐ some of the world's longest rivers
  Ⓑ rivers that flow through some deserts
  Ⓒ rivers that flow both above and below the ground
  Ⓓ temporary desert rivers formed by rainfall

4 According to paragraph 2, some desert plants survive by

  Ⓐ living at the bottoms of reservoirs
  Ⓑ extracting moisture from humid air
  Ⓒ sending taproots far underground
  Ⓓ floating on the surfaces of exotic rivers

5 According to paragraph 2, which of the following can be sources of water in deserts?

  Ⓐ Underground springs
  Ⓑ Playas
  Ⓒ Manmade wells
  Ⓓ Arroyos

Water in the Desert

1 → Deserts are regions that receive fewer than twenty-five centimeters of annual precipitation. Although deserts are usually thought of as being hot, they also are found in cold climates, such as Antarctica. Deserts are classified according to the amount of rainfall they receive. The driest deserts are called hyper-arid, where rain is absent for at least twelve consecutive months. Arid deserts experience some rainfall but receive fewer than 250 millimeters per year. Finally, semiarid deserts see between 250 and 500 millimeters of rain.

2 → Despite the long-term lack of rain, deserts are occasionally drenched by violent storms. During such downpours, dried stream channels, called arroyos, rapidly fill and spill over, sometimes causing dangerous flash floods. As the water rushes down mountains and erodes the land, it carries gravel, rock, and sand, which are deposited on the bottom of the arroyos, creating fan-shaped formations called alluvial fans. Some deserts are also traversed by their own permanent rivers, known as exotic rivers, which are fed by water from outside the desert. Some well-known exotic rivers are the Nile River in Egypt, the Yellow River in China, and the Colorado River in Arizona. Other sources of water include underground springs or reservoirs, which provide life-sustaining moisture to desert vegetation. Deserts abound with plant species that have adapted to the dry environment by extending taproots deep into the ground to absorb the water below.

6 In paragraph 3, why does the author mention "potential evapotranspiration"?

Ⓐ To explain how salt forms in dried lakebeds

Ⓑ To note the most important condition for creating a desert

Ⓒ To show how plants aid in causing evaporation

Ⓓ To contrast it with normal evaporation

3 → Temporary lakes may form when rainfall is sufficient. These lakes occur in basins offering no outlets. When the lakebeds dry up, they leave a flat plain **encrusted** with salt, an area known as a playa. Over a hundred playas dot the landscape of North American deserts, including Great Salt Lake in Utah. A scarcity of rain does not always create a desert. There must also be a high rate of evaporation relative to precipitation—a measure known as potential evapotranspiration. That gauge totals the water lost through both normal evaporation and the evaporation that occurs from plant life. Potential evapotranspiration is the amount of water that could evaporate in any area. When this potential exceeds actual precipitation, desert-like conditions will arise.

Thus deserts can be either very hot or very cold so long as the potential evaporation is greater than the precipitation. Icy deserts like Antarctica collect rain in frozen snow that never seeps into the ground. And hot deserts like the Sahara receive little rain—so little that the amount is less than the potential evaporation. Water is responsible for the concentration of mineral deposits under the desert surface. Rainfall passes through mineral layers and redeposits the minerals near the water table, where they can be easily extracted in mining operations. Mineral deposits also are enriched by the evaporation of water in the playas, which yield minerals such as gypsum and salt compounds such as sodium nitrate and sodium chloride. An example of such evaporation is shown by the Great Basin Desert in the western United States, which contains boron, an essential ingredient in the manufacture of drugs, **water softeners**, glass, and various agricultural chemicals.

📖 *Glossary*

encrusted: covered with a hard layer or coating

water softener: a device or substance that removes certain minerals from water

7 The word "sparse" in the passage is closest in meaning to

Ⓐ light

Ⓑ scanty

Ⓒ dense

Ⓓ sufficient

8 In paragraph 5, the author's description of the Atacama Desert mentions all of the following EXCEPT:

Ⓐ Its specific location

Ⓑ The lack of water vapor in the air

Ⓒ The effects of rain shadow on it

Ⓓ The occurrence of some violent storms

⁵➡ The role of water in creating deserts is illustrated by the Atacama Desert in northern Chile in South America. That desert spans the area between the Pacific Ocean to the west and the Andes Mountains to the east. High atmospheric pressure over the Andes causes dry, cold air to descend to the surface. This air lacks water vapor and is easily heated by the sun, raising the ground temperatures and lowering the humidity, which are perfect conditions for a desert. Rain is sparse in the Atacama because of a phenomenon called rain shadow. Warm, humid air from the Amazon Rainforest is blocked from reaching the Atacama by the Andes. That air is cooled by the cold mountain air and condenses into rain or snow in the mountains. As the air descends the west side of the mountains, it warms up, and the clouds break up, so rain therefore does not fall to the ground. Hence the Andes Mountains have the unusual effect of causing extreme moisture in the Amazon River basin at the same time that they cause extreme dryness on the other side of the mountains. Interestingly, the driest and wettest places on the Earth are nearly adjacent to each other.

9   Look at the four squares [■] that indicate where the following sentence could be added to the passage.

A comparison of two of the largest deserts illustrates this phenomenon.

Where would the sentence best fit?

Click on a square [■] to add the sentence to the passage.

■ Thus deserts can be either very hot or very cold so long as the potential evaporation is greater than the precipitation. ■ Icy deserts like Antarctica collect rain in frozen snow that never seeps into the ground. ■ And hot deserts like the Sahara receive little rain—so little that the amount is less than the potential evaporation. ■ Water is responsible for the concentration of mineral deposits under the desert surface. Rainfall passes through mineral layers and redeposits the minerals near the water table, where they can be easily extracted in mining operations. Mineral deposits also are enriched by the evaporation of water in the playas, which yield minerals such as gypsum and salt compounds such as sodium nitrate and sodium chloride. An example of such evaporation is shown by the Great Basin Desert in the western United States, which contains boron, an essential ingredient in the manufacture of drugs, <u>water softeners</u>, glass, and various agricultural chemicals.

📖 *Glossary*

water softener: a device or substance that removes certain minerals from water

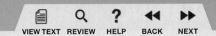
10 Directions: An introductory sentence for a brief summary of the passage is provided below. Complete the summary by selecting the THREE answer choices that express the most important ideas in the passage. Some answer choices do not belong in the summary because they express ideas that are not in the passage or are minor ideas in the passage. *This question is worth 2 points.*

> Drag your answer choices to the spaces where they belong.
> To remove an answer choice, click on it. To review the passage, click on **View Text**.

Water conditions are crucial to the formation of deserts.

-
-
-

Answer Choices

1. Fewer than 250 millimeters of rain per year falls in arid deserts.

2. Despite their extreme dryness, deserts have several sources of water.

3. The Colorado River is located in the American state of Arizona.

4. The key factor in creating a desert is the rate of potential evapotranspiration.

5. The Atacama Desert demonstrates the forces that combine to make a desert.

6. Sudden violent rainstorms in the desert are called arroyos.

11-04

Urban Heat Islands

Cities are usually warmer than their surrounding suburban and rural areas, often by as much as ten degrees Fahrenheit. Scientists attribute this to the urban heat island effect, by which several characteristics of urban areas combine to elevate artificially the ambient temperature.

The main cause of urban heat islands is architectural; the high buildings in city centers expose numerous surfaces that reflect and absorb sunlight. The reflected light hits other buildings and cannot escape into the surrounding air. The absorbed light, mostly by the dark materials covering the outside of buildings, heats up the buildings themselves. These materials, such as concrete and asphalt, have greater thermal conductivity and reflective ability than do materials used in rural or suburban construction. This tendency of heat to be trapped between and near buildings is called the canyon effect. Another impact of tall buildings is that they block the wind, which normally blows hot air away and cools the remaining air.

Another contributing factor to heat retention is the absence of evapotranspiration, the loss of water by evaporation from the ground and from the leaves of plants. This phenomenon is blunted in urban locales due to the paucity of vegetation and standing water, both of which have cooling effects. People also play a role in creating urban heat islands. The population density in cities translates into more human heat-generating processes and technology, such as automobiles, buses, and trains, air conditioning units, and factory production. All of these activities result in air pollution, which leads to the greenhouse effect, in which hot air on the ground cannot escape through the air above it because of polluting particles in the atmosphere.

The influence of the heat island effect seems to be greater at night. The ground and other surfaces lose heat at night by a process of radiation into the air above. But in cities, this upward radiation is blocked by tall buildings, which tend to hold the heat at the level where people live and where temperatures are measured. Because almost half of the world's population lives in urban areas, the urban heat island effect can influence the lives of more than three billion people. Thus, it is closely studied by **demographers** and meteorologists. Thousands die in heat waves every year, and urban heat islands increase the severity and duration of those waves. Nighttime in affected areas provides no relief since urban nights do not enjoy the same cool-down effect that occurs in areas outside the cities.

Another adverse consequence of urban heat islands is that more energy is needed to power air conditioning and refrigeration. One study concluded that the heat island effect costs the city of Los Angeles more than 100 million dollars per year in increased energy consumption. Local weather conditions can also be affected, for example, by altered wind patterns, more clouds and fog, greater pollution, more lightning, and more rain. One strategy for mitigating the impact of heat island effects is to use construction materials in houses, **pavements**, and highways that reflect, not absorb, the sunlight. Another method is to cultivate more vegetation like many city dwellers do on the roofs of their apartment buildings and offices.

Some controversy exists over whether urban heat islands contribute to global warming. One school of thought stresses that no evidence has been found that the effect is any more than a local one as the long-term upward trend in temperatures is about the same in both urban and non-urban areas. This view gained support from a 2004 study comparing a city's temperatures on calm nights with those on windy nights. No difference was found in temperatures even though the urban-heat island theory would predict that windy nights should be cooler because the wind should blow the hot air away from the city. The conclusion of the study was that global temperatures have risen as much on windy nights as on calm nights, showing that overall global warming is not caused by urban development. Those with a dissenting view tend to be individuals skeptical of global warming. They contend that urban heat islands account for nearly all of the warming recorded by land-based instruments. But there have been no scientific studies substantiating this minority view.

📖 *Glossary*

demographer: a person who studies human populations
pavement: a paved surface such as a road or sidewalk

11 The word "ambient" in the passage is closest in meaning to

(A) surrounding

(B) indoor

(C) measurable

(D) daytime

12 Which of the following best expresses the essential information in the highlighted sentence? *Incorrect* answer choices change the meaning in important ways or leave out essential information.

(A) Heat causes concrete and asphalt to expand, raising the ambient temperature.

(B) Materials used to build cities retain more heat than materials used in non-urban areas.

(C) Rural and suburban areas are hotter than cities because there are no tall buildings to block the sunlight.

(D) Urban buildings are made of light-colored materials that reflect the sunlight up into the atmosphere.

13 According to paragraph 2, which of the following is NOT true of the effects of tall buildings in urban areas?

(A) They are responsible for the canyon effect.

(B) They may block the blowing of the wind.

(C) They can absorb large amounts of sunlight.

(D) They may help cool the surrounding air.

Urban Heat Islands

Cities are usually warmer than their surrounding suburban and rural areas, often by as much as ten degrees Fahrenheit. Scientists attribute this to the urban heat island effect, by which several characteristics of urban areas combine to elevate artificially the ambient temperature.

² → The main cause of urban heat islands is architectural; the high buildings in city centers expose numerous surfaces that reflect and absorb sunlight. The reflected light hits other buildings and cannot escape into the surrounding air. The absorbed light, mostly by the dark materials covering the outside of buildings, heats up the buildings themselves. These materials, such as concrete and asphalt, have greater thermal conductivity and reflective ability than do materials used in rural or suburban construction. This tendency of heat to be trapped between and near buildings is called the canyon effect. Another impact of tall buildings is that they block the wind, which normally blows hot air away and cools the remaining air.

14 The word "it" in the passage refers to

   Ⓐ the greenhouse effect

   Ⓑ hot air on the ground

   Ⓒ the air

   Ⓓ the atmosphere

15 According to paragraph 3, evaporation is less in urban areas because of

   Ⓐ the absence of vegetation

   Ⓑ the presence of standing water

   Ⓒ the numerous tall buildings

   Ⓓ asphalt and concrete

16 According to paragraph 4, the urban heat island effect is greater at night because

   Ⓐ fewer cars are on the roads

   Ⓑ upward radiating heat is blocked by buildings

   Ⓒ energy consumption is lower

   Ⓓ heat moves more slowly without sunlight

³ ➜ Another contributing factor to heat retention is the absence of evapotranspiration, the loss of water by evaporation from the ground and from the leaves of plants. This phenomenon is blunted in urban locales due to the paucity of vegetation and standing water, both of which have cooling effects. People also play a role in creating urban heat islands. The population density in cities translates into more human heat-generating processes and technology, such as automobiles, buses, and trains, air conditioning units, and factory production. All of these activities result in air pollution, which leads to the greenhouse effect, in which hot air on the ground cannot escape through the air above it because of polluting particles in the atmosphere.

⁴ ➜ The influence of the heat island effect seems to be greater at night. The ground and other surfaces lose heat at night by a process of radiation into the air above. But in cities, this upward radiation is blocked by tall buildings, which tend to hold the heat at the level where people live and where temperatures are measured. Because almost half of the world's population lives in urban areas, the urban heat island effect can influence the lives of more than three billion people. Thus, it is closely studied by **demographers** and meteorologists. Thousands die in heat waves every year, and urban heat islands increase the severity and duration of those waves. Nighttime in affected areas provides no relief since urban nights do not enjoy the same cool-down effect that occurs in areas outside the cities.

📖 *Glossary*

demographer: a person who studies human populations

17 The author discusses "vegetation" in paragraph 5 in order to

- (A) illustrate how city dwellers use the roofs of their apartments
- (B) report on vegetable consumption by city residents
- (C) note one strategy for lessening the urban heat island effect
- (D) contrast the rate of growth of urban and rural vegetation

18 The word "dissenting" in the passage is closest in meaning to

- (A) approving
- (B) opposing
- (C) prevailing
- (D) agreeing

19 Look at the four squares [■] that indicate where the following sentence could be added to the passage.

They also argue that there are problems with temperature record-keeping in urban areas.

Where would the sentence best fit?

> Click on a square [■] to add the sentence to the passage.

📖 *Glossary*

pavement: a paved surface such as a road or sidewalk

⁵ ➤ Another adverse consequence of urban heat islands is that more energy is needed to power air conditioning and refrigeration. One study concluded that the heat island effect costs the city of Los Angeles more than 100 million dollars per year in increased energy consumption. Local weather conditions can also be affected, for example, by altered wind patterns, more clouds and fog, greater pollution, more lightning, and more rain. One strategy for mitigating the impact of heat island effects is to use construction materials in houses, pavements, and highways that reflect, not absorb, the sunlight. Another method is to cultivate more vegetation like many city dwellers do on the roofs of their apartment buildings and offices.

Some controversy exists over whether urban heat islands contribute to global warming. One school of thought stresses that no evidence has been found that the effect is any more than a local one as the long-term upward trend in temperatures is about the same in both urban and non-urban areas. This view gained support from a 2004 study comparing a city's temperatures on calm nights with those on windy nights. No difference was found in temperatures even though the urban-heat island theory would predict that windy nights should be cooler because the wind should blow the hot air away from the city. **1** The conclusion of the study was that global temperatures have risen as much on windy nights as on calm nights, showing that overall global warming is not caused by urban development. **2** Those with a dissenting view tend to be those individuals of global warming. **3** They contend that urban heat islands account for nearly all of the warming recorded by land-based instruments. **4** But there have been no scientific studies substantiating this minority view.

20 **Directions:** An introductory sentence for a brief summary of the passage is provided below. Complete the summary by selecting the THREE answer choices that express the most important ideas in the passage. Some answer choices do not belong in the summary because they express ideas that are not in the passage or are minor ideas in the passage. *This question is worth 2 points.*

Drag your answer choices to the spaces where they belong.
To remove an answer choice, click on it. To review the passage, click on **View Text**.

This passage discusses the causes and characteristics of urban heat islands.

-
-
-

Answer Choices

1 The architecture of a city, with its tall buildings and heat-retaining materials, prevents daytime heat from escaping.

2 Los Angeles spends about 100 million dollars every year to pay for the increase in energy consumption caused by the urban heat island effect.

3 The urban heat island effect decreases at night, when hotter daytime air radiates up into the atmosphere.

4 The urban heat island effect occurs due to low evaporation levels and the heat-producing technology needed to meet city dwellers' energy needs.

5 The impact of urban heat islands on global warming has not yet been established though a recent study suggests no significant effect.

6 Concrete and asphalt cover the ground, reducing potential evaporation and holding the heat at ground level.

Actual Test

03

CONTINUE

Reading Section Directions

This section measures your ability to understand academic passages in English. You will have **35 minutes** to read and answer questions about **2 passages**. A clock at the top of the screen will show you how much time is remaining.

Most questions are worth 1 point but the last question for each passage is worth more than 1 point. The directions for the last question indicate how many points you may receive.

Some passages include a word or phrase that is underlined in blue. Click on the word or phrase to see a definition or an explanation.

When you want to move to the next question, click on **Next**. You may skip questions and go back to them later. If you want to return to previous questions, click on **Back**. You can click on **Review** at any time, and the review screen will show you which questions you have answered and which you have not answered. From this review screen, you may go directly to any question you have already seen in the Reading section.

Click on **Continue** to go on.

Limestone Caves

11-05

The interior of a limestone cave in Puerto Rico

A cave, which is an empty, underground chamber, is primarily formed by one of three methods. Sea caves result from the action of water, wind, and sand grinding against the rocks on a shoreline. Lava tube caves are created from volcanic eruptions as lava solidifies. Limestone caves, the most numerous of all caves, are produced by the dissolving of limestone rock by rainwater and melting snow. Occurring in all parts of the world, limestone caves are also the deepest and largest caves ever found. The longest is the Mammoth-Flint Ridge cave system in Kentucky, which is more than 420 miles long. The process by which such caves are formed extends over millions of years.

Limestone is rock that is created in shallow seas from the gradual accumulation of dead marine animals such as coral. After millions of years of deposits on the ocean floor, the material grows into large, solid blocks of limestone that eventually rise above the water level. Rainwater and melting snow seep through cracks and passages through the top layer of soil, absorbing carbon dioxide, which is a product of decaying organic matter. The mixture of the water and carbon dioxide creates carbonic acid, which acts as a **solvent** of limestone. This acidic water seeks out any weaknesses in the limestone, such as cracks or holes, and it slowly dissolves the limestone around those weakened areas. The resulting solution is calcium carbonate, which in mineral form is called calcite, the mineral that resides in limestone.

The calcium carbonate then descends to the water table, which is the upper limit at which the Earth is saturated with water. As the calcium carbonate repeats this process over thousands of years, it erodes the surrounding limestone, ultimately forming channels. The dissolving process produces a distinctive land mass known as **karst**. Connections from the cave to the surface may be forged in two ways. The rock above the cave may collapse, forming a vertical passage called a sinkhole, or a stream may cut into the side of a cave, creating a horizontal entrance.

As the channels continue to widen and lengthen, they are able to hold even more water, which, in turn, dissolves even more limestone. The result is that the channel gets bigger and bigger until it reaches the size of a cave or becomes large enough to accommodate humans. The cave may become dry in two ways: The water table may drop, leaving the cave exposed to the air, or the cave may be elevated by an earthquake or other tectonic shift. When either of those events occurs, the water evaporates or drains out, allowing air to fill the cave and subsequently drying it. The cave may continue to enlarge if a surface stream passes through it, dissolving more of the limestone. And the calcium carbonate may continue to drip slowly through the ceiling of the cave, forming dried deposits of calcium carbonate called speleothems. The best-known speleothems are stalactites and stalagmites. The former are icicle-like formations that hang from the cave's ceiling, and the latter are pillars that rise from the floor.

Though natural light never penetrates the interior of a cave, cave explorers called spelunkers have carried artificial light into many caves, sometimes revealing spectacular formations of speleothems. In addition to stalactites and stalagmites, other kinds of speleothems include drapery, thin sheets of rock that hang from the ceiling, flowstone, thin sheets of dried mineral water covering walls and floors, gypsum flowers, spiral crystals that sprout from porous rock, and helictites, twisted cylinders growing out of the rock. Some of the most elaborately decorated caves have become popular tourist attractions equipped with walkways, railings, and electric lights. Two of the most interesting are Carlsbad Caverns in New Mexico and Luray Caverns in Virginia.

Caves have provided homes and shelter to humans and animals. Prehistoric people, such as Neanderthals and Cro-Magnons, were cave dwellers. The earliest known artwork has been found on the walls of caves. Today, caves provide homes to many species of animals, including birds, bats, crickets, lizards, and rats. Bears often hibernate in caves, and bats sleep in caves during the day and exit at night to hunt for insects. Bat droppings, known as guano, provide food for the myriad of insects that inhabit caves.

📖 *Glossary*

solvent: something able to dissolve or break down other substances
karst: a type of landform that often has sinkholes, caves, and underground streams and rivers

1 In paragraph 1, why does the author mention "Lava tube caves"?

　Ⓐ To name one of the ways that caves are formed

　Ⓑ To note one result of some volcanic eruptions

　Ⓒ To name one kind of common limestone cave

　Ⓓ To show that caves occur in all parts of the world

2 According to paragraph 1, which of the following is the most common cave?

　Ⓐ Limestone caves

　Ⓑ Lava tube caves

　Ⓒ Sea caves

　Ⓓ Glacier caves

3 The word "accumulation" in the passage is closest in meaning to

　Ⓐ deterioration

　Ⓑ exposure

　Ⓒ motion

　Ⓓ collection

📖 *Glossary*

solvent: something able to dissolve or break down other substances

Limestone Caves

1 ➡ A cave, which is an empty, underground chamber, is primarily formed by one of three methods. Sea caves result from the action of water, wind, and sand grinding against the rocks on a shoreline. Lava tube caves are created from volcanic eruptions as lava solidifies. Limestone caves, the most numerous of all caves, are produced by the dissolving of limestone rock by rainwater and melting snow. Occurring in all parts of the world, limestone caves are also the deepest and largest caves ever found. The longest is the Mammoth-Flint Ridge cave system in Kentucky, which is more than 420 miles long. The process by which such caves are formed extends over millions of years.

Limestone is rock that is created in shallow seas from the gradual accumulation of dead marine animals such as coral. After millions of years of deposits on the ocean floor, the material grows into large, solid blocks of limestone that eventually rise above the water level. Rainwater and melting snow seep through cracks and passages through the top layer of soil, absorbing carbon dioxide, which is a product of decaying organic matter. The mixture of the water and carbon dioxide creates carbonic acid, which acts as a solvent of limestone. This acidic water seeks out any weaknesses in the limestone, such as cracks or holes, and it slowly dissolves the limestone around those weakened areas. The resulting solution is calcium carbonate, which in mineral form is called calcite, the mineral that resides in limestone.

4 According to paragraph 3, which of the following can connect a cave to the surface?

    Ⓐ Calcium carbonate

    Ⓑ Sinkholes

    Ⓒ The water table

    Ⓓ Karst

5 The word "saturated" in the passage is closest in meaning to

    Ⓐ overflowing

    Ⓑ purified

    Ⓒ soaked

    Ⓓ compatible

6 According to paragraph 4, in which of the following ways can a cave dry out? *To receive credit, you must select TWO answers.*

    Ⓐ Limestone in the cave dissolves.

    Ⓑ Wind passes through the cave.

    Ⓒ The water table drops.

    Ⓓ An earthquake raises the cave.

3 ➜ The calcium carbonate then descends to the water table, which is the upper limit at which the Earth is saturated with water. As the calcium carbonate repeats this process over thousands of years, it erodes the surrounding limestone, ultimately forming channels. The dissolving process produces a distinctive land mass known as karst. Connections from the cave to the surface may be forged in two ways. The rock above the cave may collapse, forming a vertical passage called a sinkhole, or a stream may cut into the side of a cave, creating a horizontal entrance.

4 ➜ As the channels continue to widen and lengthen, they are able to hold even more water, which, in turn, dissolves even more limestone. The result is that the channel gets bigger and bigger until it reaches the size of a cave or becomes large enough to accommodate humans. The cave may become dry in two ways: The water table may drop, leaving the cave exposed to the air, or the cave may be elevated by an earthquake or other tectonic shift. When either of those events occurs, the water evaporates or drains out, allowing air to fill the cave and subsequently drying it. The cave may continue to enlarge if a surface stream passes through it, dissolving more of the limestone. And the calcium carbonate may continue to drip slowly through the ceiling of the cave, forming dried deposits of calcium carbonate called speleothems. The best-known speleothems are stalactites and stalagmites. The former are icicle-like formations that hang from the cave's ceiling, and the latter are pillars that rise from the floor.

📖 *Glossary*

karst: a type of landform that often has sinkholes, caves, and underground streams and rivers

7 Which of the following best expresses the essential information in the highlighted sentence? *Incorrect* answer choices change the meaning in important ways or leave out essential information.

   Ⓐ Speleothems can be seen only when illuminated by artificial light carried by spelunkers.

   Ⓑ Speleothems are formed when sunlight dries out the carbonic acid on the limestone walls of caves.

   Ⓒ Spelunkers are guided by the natural light shining through cracks in the ceilings of caves.

   Ⓓ Artificial light encourages the growth of spectacular formations of speleothems.

8 According to paragraph 6, which of the following is NOT found inside caves?

   Ⓐ Bat droppings

   Ⓑ Prehistoric artwork

   Ⓒ Cave dwellers

   Ⓓ Reptiles

Though natural light never penetrates the interior of a cave, cave explorers called spelunkers have carried artificial light into many caves, sometimes revealing spectacular formations of speleothems. In addition to stalactites and stalagmites, other kinds of speleothems include drapery, thin sheets of rock that hang from the ceiling, flowstone, thin sheets of dried mineral water covering walls and floors, gypsum flowers, spiral crystals that sprout from porous rock, and helictites, twisted cylinders growing out of the rock. Some of the most elaborately decorated caves have become popular tourist attractions equipped with walkways, railings, and electric lights. Two of the most interesting are Carlsbad Caverns in New Mexico and Luray Caverns in Virginia.

⁶ ➔ Caves have provided homes and shelter to humans and animals. Prehistoric people, such as Neanderthals and Cro-Magnons, were cave dwellers. The earliest known artwork has been found on the walls of caves. Today, caves provide homes to many species of animals, including birds, bats, crickets, lizards, and rats. Bears often hibernate in caves, and bats sleep in caves during the day and exit at night to hunt for insects. Bat droppings, known as guano, provide food for the myriad of insects that inhabit caves.

9 Look at the four squares [■] that indicate where the following sentence could be added to the passage.

The newly formed cave then undergoes a drying process.

Where would the sentence best fit?

Click on a square [■] to add the sentence to the passage.

As the channels continue to widen and lengthen, they are able to hold even more water, which, in turn, dissolves even more limestone. **1** The result is that the channel gets bigger and bigger until it reaches the size of a cave or becomes large enough to accommodate humans. **2** The cave may become dry in two ways: The water table may drop, leaving the cave exposed to the air, or the cave may be elevated by an earthquake or other tectonic shift. **3** When either of those events occurs, the water evaporates or drains out, allowing air to fill the cave and subsequently drying it. **4** The cave may continue to enlarge if a surface stream passes through it, dissolving more of the limestone. And the calcium carbonate may continue to drip slowly through the ceiling of the cave, forming dried deposits of calcium carbonate called speleothems. The best-known speleothems are stalactites and stalagmites. The former are icicle-like formations that hang from the cave's ceiling, and the latter are pillars that rise from the floor.

10 Directions: An introductory sentence for a brief summary of the passage is provided below. Complete the summary by selecting the THREE answer choices that express the most important ideas in the passage. Some answer choices do not belong in the summary because they express ideas that are not in the passage or are minor ideas in the passage. *This question is worth 2 points.*

Drag your answer choices to the spaces where they belong.
To remove an answer choice, click on it. To review the passage, click on **View Text**.

Limestone caves are formed through an intricate process that can take millions of years.

-
-
-

Answer Choices

1. Limestone rock forms on the sea floor from the accumulated remains of dead animals.

2. The longest limestone cave is the Mammoth-Flint Ridge cave system in Kentucky.

3. Gypsum flowers are types of speleothems that project from porous limestone rock.

4. Water seeping through limestone creates carbonic acid, which dissolves the limestone.

5. The process during which limestone dissolves produces a land mass called karst.

6. Over thousands of years, limestone dissolves, opening large channels that become caves.

11-06

How Birds Navigate While Migrating

Bird migration is one of the most interesting yet least understood natural phenomena. Every fall, birds from northern latitudes fly in groups to the warmer southern latitudes and then return north in the spring. Scientists agree on the main reasons for migration: to follow the food supply and to avoid harsh climate conditions. For example, insects disappear during the cold months, prompting insect-dependent birds to fly south to warm areas where insects breed. No similar consensus has emerged, however, about how birds are able to navigate. Despite many recent experiments, bird experts still do not know how birds arrive at the same destination every year and then find their way back home in the spring.

Some have suggested that birds find their way by following landmarks, such as rivers and mountain ranges. Experiments have confirmed that some species do follow such topographic features. But that method cannot explain how some birds travel at night. Other studies show that some nocturnal birds navigate by the stars. But that explanation cannot explain daytime migration or travel when the skies are cloudy. The most popular explanation currently is that birds are guided by the Earth's magnetic poles. The mechanism by which that works has not yet been proved. One theory points to the fact that some birds' brains contain magnetite, a naturally occurring magnetic compound consisting of iron oxide. Magnetite has been found in many animals, including birds. With magnets embedded in their brains, birds would be able to sense the magnetic fields of the North and South poles.

A recent experiment with homing pigeons provided some evidence that magnetite does play a crucial role in migration. Homing pigeons are known to have the ability to return to their homes after being taken hundreds of miles away. Researchers found that they could train homing pigeons to recognize changes in a magnetic field. When a surrounding magnetic field was normal, the birds would gather at one end of a cage. But when the field's polarity was altered, they hopped to the other end, suggesting that they were detecting and responding to changes in the magnetic field.

Another theory has been offered to explain this sensitivity to magnetic poles, a theory that draws upon quantum mechanics, which is the study of how particles move inside an atom. It relies on the fact that electrons come in pairs that orbit the nucleus of an atom. The two electrons spin in opposite directions, creating two magnets that neutralize each other. But when molecules split and react with other molecules to form compounds, the electron pairs may no longer spin in opposite directions. Instead, they may repel each other, as when two north ends of magnets are pressed together. The electrons struggle to change direction in order to achieve a stable state in which the two electrons again neutralize each other, giving off no magnetic field. The theory is that these disturbed electron pairs are created in birds when they are exposed to changes in light. The birds can sense the efforts of the electrons in trying to reach a condition of stability because of the slight changes in the pull of the North and South poles. In this way, the birds can detect the direction of the poles while they are in flight.

In one experiment to confirm this effect, a group of European robins were tricked by artificial light to believe that it was time for spring migration. The birds became eager to fly north. The changes in light triggered the electron-pair movement described above, exposing the robins to the magnetic field accompanying the electron pairs. The birds became disoriented and flew in all directions. The simulated magnetic fields were much too weak to be detected by the birds' natural magnetite, suggesting to the experimenters that the electron pairs, not the magnetite, were responsible for the birds' confused flying. The current view, therefore, is that light plays an important role in guiding bird migration. This may be why birds turn their heads from side to side before flying off. Their eyes are collecting the surrounding light, which then allows them to process and analyze the existing magnetic fields and to keep themselves pointed in the right direction.

📖 *Glossary*
topographic: relating to the art of showing the elevations of natural features on maps
polarity: the attraction toward an object or in a specific direction

11 The word "phenomena" in the passage is closest in meaning to

   (A) events

   (B) trends

   (C) discoveries

   (D) theories

12 According to paragraph 1, which of the following is true of the influence of insects on bird migration?

   (A) Insects generate a magnetic field that birds can detect.

   (B) Insects provide a food supply that exists only in warm climates.

   (C) Birds follow the paths taken by flying insects.

   (D) Birds know when to migrate by a sudden increase in the insect population.

13 According to paragraph 2, birds can detect the magnetic fields of the North and South poles because

   (A) they can sense the motions of electron pairs

   (B) they can locate the poles by following landmarks

   (C) they ingest metal particles that are attracted by the poles

   (D) they have magnetite in their brains

📖 *Glossary*

topographic: relating to the art of showing the elevations of natural features on maps

How Birds Navigate While Migrating

1 ➡ Bird migration is one of the most interesting yet least understood natural phenomena. Every fall, birds from northern latitudes fly in groups to the warmer southern latitudes and then return north in the spring. Scientists agree on the main reasons for migration: to follow the food supply and to avoid harsh climate conditions. For example, insects disappear during the cold months, prompting insect-dependent birds to fly south to warm areas where insects breed. No similar consensus has emerged, however, about how birds are able to navigate. Despite many recent experiments, bird experts still do not know how birds arrive at the same destination every year and then find their way back home in the spring.

2 ➡ Some have suggested that birds find their way by following landmarks, such as rivers and mountain ranges. Experiments have confirmed that some species do follow such topographic features. But that method cannot explain how some birds travel at night. Other studies show that some nocturnal birds navigate by the stars. But that explanation cannot explain daytime migration or travel when the skies are cloudy. The most popular explanation currently is that birds are guided by the Earth's magnetic poles. The mechanism by which that works has not yet been proved. One theory points to the fact that some birds' brains contain magnetite, a naturally occurring magnetic compound consisting of iron oxide. Magnetite has been found in many animals, including birds. With magnets embedded in their brains, birds would be able to sense the magnetic fields of the North and South poles.

14 The author discusses "Homing pigeons" in paragraph 3 in order to

   (A) provide an example of how humans can train birds

   (B) describe an experiment showing the importance of magnetite

   (C) show that homing pigeons return home by following landmarks

   (D) report homing pigeons' behavior inside a cage

15 According to paragraph 4, which of the following can be inferred about an electron pair in two north ends of magnets?

   (A) The two electrons spin in opposite directions.

   (B) One electron will move to the south end.

   (C) One electron will be captured by the nucleus.

   (D) The two electrons spin in the same direction.

16 According to paragraph 4, which of the following is NOT true of electrons?

   (A) Changes in light cause electron pairs to change the direction of their spin.

   (B) Magnetite contains electrons that repel each other.

   (C) Electrons that spin in opposite directions neutralize each other.

   (D) The nucleus of an atom is orbited by electron pairs.

📖 *Glossary*

polarity: the attraction toward an object or in a specific direction

---

3 ➡ A recent experiment with homing pigeons provided some evidence that magnetite does play a crucial role in migration. Homing pigeons are known to have the ability to return to their homes after being taken hundreds of miles away. Researchers found that they could train homing pigeons to recognize changes in a magnetic field. When a surrounding magnetic field was normal, the birds would gather at one end of a cage. But when the field's polarity was altered, they hopped to the other end, suggesting that they were detecting and responding to changes in the magnetic field.

4 ➡ Another theory has been offered to explain this sensitivity to magnetic poles, a theory that draws upon quantum mechanics, which is the study of how particles move inside an atom. It relies on the fact that electrons come in pairs that orbit the nucleus of an atom. The two electrons spin in opposite directions, creating two magnets that neutralize each other. But when molecules split and react with other molecules to form compounds, the electron pairs may no longer spin in opposite directions. Instead, they may repel each other, as when two north ends of magnets are pressed together. The electrons struggle to change direction in order to achieve a stable state in which the two electrons again neutralize each other, giving off no magnetic field. The theory is that these disturbed electron pairs are created in birds when they are exposed to changes in light. The birds can sense the efforts of the electrons in trying to reach a condition of stability because of the slight changes in the pull of the North and South poles. In this way, the birds can detect the direction of the poles while they are in flight.

17 Which of the following best expresses the essential information in the highlighted sentence? *Incorrect* answer choices change the meaning in important ways or leave out essential information.

(A) The bird's failure to detect the magnetic fields led researchers to conclude that the electron pairs caused the birds' confusion.

(B) The birds' failure to detect the electron pairs showed that magnetite was the cause of their disorientation.

(C) Experimenters found that the electron pairs were stronger than the birds' magnetite and helped them find their destinations.

(D) Magnetic fields that are triggered by artificial light are detected by the birds' magnetite, causing them to fly in the right direction.

18 The word "them" in the passage refers to

(A) birds

(B) their heads

(C) their eyes

(D) the existing magnetic fields

In one experiment to confirm this effect, a group of European robins were tricked by artificial light to believe that it was time for spring migration. The birds became eager to fly north. The changes in light triggered the electron-pair movement described above, exposing the robins to the magnetic field accompanying the electron pairs. The birds became disoriented and flew in all directions. The simulated magnetic fields were much too weak to be detected by the birds' natural magnetite, suggesting to the experimenters that the electron pairs, not the magnetite, were responsible for the birds' confused flying. The current view, therefore, is that light plays an important role in guiding bird migration. This may be why birds turn their heads from side to side before flying off. Their eyes are collecting the surrounding light, which then allows them to process and analyze the existing magnetic fields and to keep themselves pointed in the right direction.

19 Look at the four squares [■] that indicate where the following sentence could be added to the passage.

However, researchers believe they will understand it soon.

Where would the sentence best fit?

Click on a square [■] to add the sentence to the passage.

Some have suggested that birds find their way by following landmarks, such as rivers and mountain ranges. Experiments have confirmed that some species do follow such topographic features. But that method cannot explain how some birds travel at night. Other studies show that some nocturnal birds navigate by the stars. But that explanation cannot explain daytime migration or travel when the skies are cloudy. **1** The most popular explanation currently is that birds are guided by the Earth's magnetic poles. **2** The mechanism by which that works has not yet been proved. **3** One theory points to the fact that some birds' brains contain magnetite, a naturally occurring magnetic compound consisting of iron oxide. **4** Magnetite has been found in many animals, including birds. With magnets embedded in their brains, birds would be able to sense the magnetic fields of the North and South poles.

20 Directions: Complete the table below to summarize the information about the two experiments with birds discussed in the passage. Match the appropriate statements to the type of bird. TWO of the answer choices will NOT be used. *This question is worth 3 points.*

Drag your answer choices to the spaces where they belong.
To remove an answer choice, click on it. To review the passage, click on **View Text**.

Answer Choices

① They could be trained to detect changes in magnetic fields.

② They were tricked by artificial light.

③ They became confused by artificial light.

④ They wanted to fly south.

⑤ They followed landmarks like rivers and mountains.

⑥ They were studied in cages.

⑦ They responded to electron pairs.

Pigeons

•

•

Robins

•

•

•

Appendix

Mastering Word List

This part provides lists of important vocabulary words in each unit. They are essential words for understanding any academic texts. Many of the words are listed with their derivative forms so that students can expand their vocabulary in an effective way. These lists can be used as homework assignments.

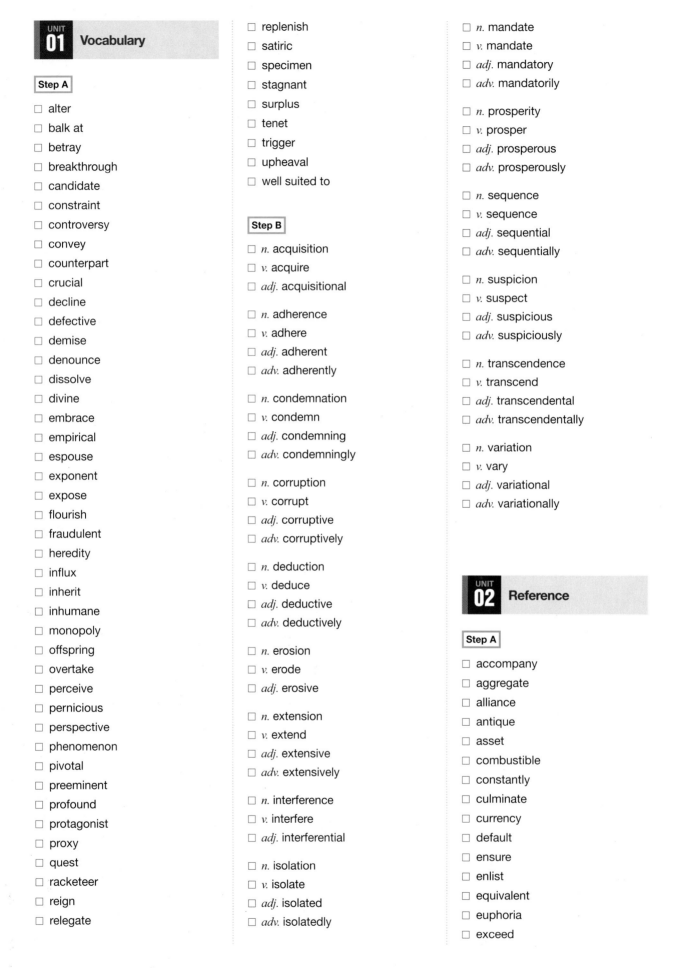

UNIT 01 Vocabulary

Step A

- [ ] alter
- [ ] balk at
- [ ] betray
- [ ] breakthrough
- [ ] candidate
- [ ] constraint
- [ ] controversy
- [ ] convey
- [ ] counterpart
- [ ] crucial
- [ ] decline
- [ ] defective
- [ ] demise
- [ ] denounce
- [ ] dissolve
- [ ] divine
- [ ] embrace
- [ ] empirical
- [ ] espouse
- [ ] exponent
- [ ] expose
- [ ] flourish
- [ ] fraudulent
- [ ] heredity
- [ ] influx
- [ ] inherit
- [ ] inhumane
- [ ] monopoly
- [ ] offspring
- [ ] overtake
- [ ] perceive
- [ ] pernicious
- [ ] perspective
- [ ] phenomenon
- [ ] pivotal
- [ ] preeminent
- [ ] profound
- [ ] protagonist
- [ ] proxy
- [ ] quest
- [ ] racketeer
- [ ] reign
- [ ] relegate

- [ ] replenish
- [ ] satiric
- [ ] specimen
- [ ] stagnant
- [ ] surplus
- [ ] tenet
- [ ] trigger
- [ ] upheaval
- [ ] well suited to

Step B

- [ ] *n.* acquisition
- [ ] *v.* acquire
- [ ] *adj.* acquisitional

- [ ] *n.* adherence
- [ ] *v.* adhere
- [ ] *adj.* adherent
- [ ] *adv.* adherently

- [ ] *n.* condemnation
- [ ] *v.* condemn
- [ ] *adj.* condemning
- [ ] *adv.* condemningly

- [ ] *n.* corruption
- [ ] *v.* corrupt
- [ ] *adj.* corruptive
- [ ] *adv.* corruptively

- [ ] *n.* deduction
- [ ] *v.* deduce
- [ ] *adj.* deductive
- [ ] *adv.* deductively

- [ ] *n.* erosion
- [ ] *v.* erode
- [ ] *adj.* erosive

- [ ] *n.* extension
- [ ] *v.* extend
- [ ] *adj.* extensive
- [ ] *adv.* extensively

- [ ] *n.* interference
- [ ] *v.* interfere
- [ ] *adj.* interferential

- [ ] *n.* isolation
- [ ] *v.* isolate
- [ ] *adj.* isolated
- [ ] *adv.* isolatedly

- [ ] *n.* mandate
- [ ] *v.* mandate
- [ ] *adj.* mandatory
- [ ] *adv.* mandatorily

- [ ] *n.* prosperity
- [ ] *v.* prosper
- [ ] *adj.* prosperous
- [ ] *adv.* prosperously

- [ ] *n.* sequence
- [ ] *v.* sequence
- [ ] *adj.* sequential
- [ ] *adv.* sequentially

- [ ] *n.* suspicion
- [ ] *v.* suspect
- [ ] *adj.* suspicious
- [ ] *adv.* suspiciously

- [ ] *n.* transcendence
- [ ] *v.* transcend
- [ ] *adj.* transcendental
- [ ] *adv.* transcendentally

- [ ] *n.* variation
- [ ] *v.* vary
- [ ] *adj.* variational
- [ ] *adv.* variationally

UNIT 02 Reference

Step A

- [ ] accompany
- [ ] aggregate
- [ ] alliance
- [ ] antique
- [ ] asset
- [ ] combustible
- [ ] constantly
- [ ] culminate
- [ ] currency
- [ ] default
- [ ] ensure
- [ ] enlist
- [ ] equivalent
- [ ] euphoria
- [ ] exceed

- □ falter
- □ hostile
- □ inadequacy
- □ inherent
- □ institution
- □ internal
- □ monetary
- □ nurture
- □ obscure
- □ offset
- □ ornamentation
- □ overthrow
- □ overturn
- □ plummet
- □ polished
- □ preach
- □ premise
- □ preside
- □ prompt
- □ quell
- □ traverse

Step B

- □ <i>n.</i> attainment
- □ <i>v.</i> attain
- □ <i>adj.</i> attainable
- □ <i>adv.</i> attainably

- □ <i>n.</i> constitution
- □ <i>v.</i> constitute
- □ <i>adj.</i> constitutional
- □ <i>adv.</i> constitutionally

- □ <i>n.</i> counteraction
- □ <i>v.</i> counteract
- □ <i>adj.</i> counteractive
- □ <i>adv.</i> counteractively

- □ <i>n.</i> domination
- □ <i>v.</i> dominate
- □ <i>adj.</i> dominant
- □ <i>adv.</i> dominantly

- □ <i>n.</i> elaboration
- □ <i>v.</i> elaborate
- □ <i>adj.</i> elaborate
- □ <i>adv.</i> elaborately

- □ <i>n.</i> emission
- □ <i>v.</i> emit

- □ <i>adj.</i> emissive

- □ <i>n.</i> exaltation
- □ <i>v.</i> exalt
- □ <i>adj.</i> exalted
- □ <i>adv.</i> exaltedly

- □ <i>n.</i> facilitation
- □ <i>v.</i> facilitate
- □ <i>adj.</i> facilitative

- □ <i>n.</i> fortification
- □ <i>v.</i> fortify
- □ <i>adj.</i> fortifying

- □ <i>n.</i> infatuation
- □ <i>v.</i> infatuate
- □ <i>adj.</i> infatuated
- □ <i>adv.</i> infatuatedly

- □ <i>n.</i> manipulation
- □ <i>v.</i> manipulate
- □ <i>adj.</i> manipulative
- □ <i>adv.</i> manipulatively

- □ <i>n.</i> negotiation
- □ <i>v.</i> negotiate
- □ <i>adj.</i> negotiatory

- □ <i>n.</i> prevalence
- □ <i>v.</i> prevail
- □ <i>adj.</i> prevalent
- □ <i>adv.</i> prevalently

- □ <i>n.</i> reason
- □ <i>v.</i> reason
- □ <i>adj.</i> reasonable
- □ <i>adv.</i> reasonably

- □ <i>n.</i> reconciliation
- □ <i>v.</i> reconcile
- □ <i>adj.</i> reconcilable
- □ <i>adv.</i> reconcilably

- □ <i>n.</i> reduction
- □ <i>v.</i> reduce
- □ <i>adj.</i> reducible
- □ <i>adv.</i> reducibly

- □ <i>n.</i> retraction
- □ <i>v.</i> retract
- □ <i>adj.</i> retractable
- □ <i>adv.</i> retractably

- □ <i>n.</i> sustainability

- □ <i>v.</i> sustain
- □ <i>adj.</i> sustainable
- □ <i>adv.</i> sustainedly

- □ <i>n.</i> stimulation
- □ <i>v.</i> stimulate
- □ <i>adj.</i> stimulative
- □ <i>adv.</i> stimulatively

UNIT 03 Factual Information

Step A

- □ aesthetics
- □ anarchy
- □ attributable
- □ boost
- □ clash
- □ criterion
- □ crust
- □ depict
- □ debris
- □ dissolvable
- □ divert
- □ encompass
- □ ethnic
- □ extensive
- □ fertile
- □ frivolous
- □ inequity
- □ irrational
- □ outlaw
- □ pigment
- □ plateau
- □ precipitation
- □ premier
- □ proportional
- □ portray
- □ pursuit
- □ ravage
- □ secede
- □ secure
- □ seep
- □ simmer
- □ split
- □ surge

- ☐ succumb
- ☐ temporary
- ☐ texture
- ☐ treaty
- ☐ ultimately
- ☐ vegetation
- ☐ vent

Step B

- ☐ *n.* absorption
- ☐ *v.* absorb
- ☐ *adj.* absorptive
- ☐ *adv.* absorptively

- ☐ *n.* abstraction
- ☐ *v.* abstract
- ☐ *adj.* abstract
- ☐ *adv.* abstractly

- ☐ *v.* allege
- ☐ *adj.* alleged
- ☐ *adv.* allegedly

- ☐ *n.* assignment
- ☐ *v.* assign
- ☐ *adj.* assignable
- ☐ *adv.* assignably

- ☐ *n.* assumption
- ☐ *v.* assume
- ☐ *adj.* assumptive
- ☐ *adv.* assumptively

- ☐ *n.* conception
- ☐ *v.* conceive
- ☐ *adj.* conceptional / conceptive
- ☐ *adv.* conceptionally

- ☐ *n.* degenerateness
- ☐ *v.* degenerate
- ☐ *adj.* degenerate
- ☐ *adv.* degenerately

- ☐ *n.* derivation
- ☐ *v.* derive
- ☐ *adj.* derivative
- ☐ *adv.* derivatively

- ☐ *n.* disruption
- ☐ *v.* disrupt
- ☐ *adj.* disruptive
- ☐ *adv.* disruptively

- ☐ *n.* ejection
- ☐ *v.* eject
- ☐ *adj.* ejective
- ☐ *adv.* ejectively

- ☐ *n.* emanation
- ☐ *v.* emanate
- ☐ *adj.* emanative
- ☐ *adv.* emanatively

- ☐ *n.* enforcement
- ☐ *v.* enforce
- ☐ *adj.* enforceable
- ☐ *adv.* enforcedly

- ☐ *n.* eruption
- ☐ *v.* erupt
- ☐ *adj.* eruptive
- ☐ *adv.* eruptively

- ☐ *n.* estimation
- ☐ *v.* estimate
- ☐ *adj.* estimative

- ☐ *n.* exhibition
- ☐ *v.* exhibit
- ☐ *adj.* exhibitive
- ☐ *adv.* exhibitively

- ☐ *n.* relief
- ☐ *v.* relieve
- ☐ *adj.* relievable
- ☐ *adv.* relievedly

- ☐ *n.* submission
- ☐ *v.* submit
- ☐ *adj.* submissive
- ☐ *adv.* submissively

- ☐ *n.* termination
- ☐ *v.* terminate
- ☐ *adj.* terminative
- ☐ *adv.* terminatively

UNIT 04 Negative Factual Information

Step A

- ☐ arbitrarily
- ☐ asteroid
- ☐ bisect

- ☐ blast
- ☐ bombard
- ☐ celestial
- ☐ circumnavigate
- ☐ clarity
- ☐ complex
- ☐ coordinate
- ☐ critical
- ☐ dehydration
- ☐ dense
- ☐ diverse
- ☐ garment
- ☐ gigantic
- ☐ gradual
- ☐ gravitational
- ☐ harsh
- ☐ humility
- ☐ immense
- ☐ indigenous
- ☐ infirm
- ☐ inhospitable
- ☐ nomadic
- ☐ phonological
- ☐ pinpoint
- ☐ plot
- ☐ polygamy
- ☐ porous
- ☐ primitive
- ☐ prompt
- ☐ propel
- ☐ proportion
- ☐ rigid
- ☐ scar
- ☐ shatter
- ☐ substantial
- ☐ superimpose
- ☐ supplant
- ☐ tacked on to
- ☐ unintelligible
- ☐ vitrification
- ☐ withstand

Step B

- ☐ *n.* adjustment
- ☐ *v.* adjust
- ☐ *adj.* adjustable / adjusted
- ☐ *adv.* adjustably

- □ *n.* collision
- □ *v.* collide
- □ *adj.* collisional
- □ *adv.* collisionally

- □ *n.* compulsion
- □ *v.* compel
- □ *adj.* compelling
- □ *adv.* compellingly

- □ *n.* condensation
- □ *v.* condense
- □ *adj.* condense

- □ *n.* conduction
- □ *v.* conduct
- □ *adj.* conductive
- □ *adv.* conductively

- □ *n.* conversion
- □ *v.* convert
- □ *adj.* convertible
- □ *adv.* convertibly

- □ *n.* exploration
- □ *v.* explore
- □ *adj.* exploratory / explorative
- □ *adv.* exploratively

- □ *n.* evaporation
- □ *v.* evaporate
- □ *adj.* evaporative
- □ *adv.* evaporatively

- □ *n.* generation
- □ *v.* generate
- □ *adj.* generative
- □ *adv.* generatively

- □ *n.* immersion
- □ *v.* immerse
- □ *adj.* immersible

- □ *n.* intrusion
- □ *v.* intrude
- □ *adj.* intrusive
- □ *adv.* intrusively

- □ *n.* origination
- □ *v.* originate
- □ *adj.* originative
- □ *adv.* originatively

- □ *n.* resemblance
- □ *v.* resemble

- □ *adj.* resemblant
- □ *adv.* resemblingly

- □ *n.* reverence
- □ *v.* revere
- □ *adj.* reverent
- □ *adv.* reverently

- □ *n.* rotation
- □ *v.* rotate
- □ *adj.* rotational
- □ *adv.* rotationally

- □ *n.* subsistence
- □ *v.* subsist
- □ *adj.* subsistent
- □ *adv.* subsistingly

- □ *n.* volunteer
- □ *v.* volunteer
- □ *adj.* voluntary
- □ *adv.* voluntarily

UNIT 05 Sentence Simplification

Step A

- □ ancient
- □ archaeologist
- □ be aware of
- □ be endowed with
- □ carnivore
- □ consequence
- □ convention
- □ debate
- □ diversity
- □ drain
- □ drastically
- □ durable
- □ enormous
- □ exceptional
- □ facet
- □ feces
- □ flap
- □ fossil
- □ frigid
- □ furnace
- □ gauge

- □ herbivore
- □ hitch
- □ measure
- □ migratory
- □ monocular
- □ mound
- □ nutrient
- □ overall
- □ perch
- □ pest
- □ properly
- □ regardless of
- □ reptilian
- □ retina
- □ significantly
- □ soil
- □ superb
- □ surroundings
- □ swoop

Step B

- □ *n.* abundance
- □ *v.* abound
- □ *adj.* abundant
- □ *adv.* abundantly

- □ *n.* approximation
- □ *v.* approximate
- □ *adj.* approximate
- □ *adv.* approximately

- □ *n.* argument
- □ *v.* argue
- □ *adj.* argumentative
- □ *adv.* argumentatively

- □ *n.* captivity
- □ *v.* captivate
- □ *adj.* captive

- □ *n.* circulation
- □ *v.* circulate
- □ *adj.* circulatory

- □ *n.* colony
- □ *v.* colonize
- □ *adj.* colonial
- □ *adv.* colonially

- □ *n.* cooperation
- □ *v.* cooperate

☐ *adj.* cooperative
☐ *adv.* cooperatively

☐ *n.* destruction
☐ *v.* destroy
☐ *adj.* destructive
☐ *adv.* destructively

☐ *n.* exposure
☐ *v.* expose
☐ *adj.* exposed

☐ *n.* interaction
☐ *v.* interact
☐ *adj.* interactive
☐ *adv.* interactively

☐ *n.* liquefaction
☐ *v.* liquefy
☐ *adj.* liquefying

☐ *n.* maintenance
☐ *v.* maintain
☐ *adj.* maintainable

☐ *n.* navigation
☐ *v.* navigate
☐ *adj.* navigational
☐ *adv.* navigationally

☐ *n.* nourishment
☐ *v.* nourish
☐ *adj.* nourishing

☐ *n.* purification
☐ *v.* purify
☐ *adj.* purifying / purified

☐ *n.* representative
☐ *v.* represent
☐ *adj.* representative
☐ *adv.* representatively

☐ *n.* reproduction
☐ *v.* reproduce
☐ *adj.* reproductive
☐ *adv.* reproductively

☐ *n.* threat
☐ *v.* threaten
☐ *adj.* threatening
☐ *adv.* threateningly

UNIT 06 Rhetorical Purpose

Step A

☐ accurately
☐ appraise
☐ aspect
☐ be prone to
☐ camouflage
☐ collapse
☐ compact
☐ costume
☐ cure
☐ deadly
☐ degenerative
☐ enclosed
☐ encounter
☐ farce
☐ furthermore
☐ graze
☐ have access to
☐ herpetologist
☐ hygiene
☐ hypodermic
☐ impact
☐ lush
☐ nevertheless
☐ opposite
☐ plough
☐ predator
☐ proximity
☐ psycholinguist
☐ regard
☐ rodent
☐ shed
☐ sophisticated
☐ span
☐ sprawl
☐ suffix
☐ sustenance
☐ unity
☐ unsanitary
☐ unwittingly
☐ venomous

Step B

☐ *n.* administration

☐ *v.* administer
☐ *adj.* administrative
☐ *adv.* administratively

☐ *n.* classification
☐ *v.* classify
☐ *adj.* classifiable
☐ *adv.* classifiably

☐ *n.* controversy
☐ *v.* controvert
☐ *adj.* controversial
☐ *adv.* controversially

☐ *n.* coordination
☐ *v.* coordinate
☐ *adj.* coordinate
☐ *adv.* coordinately

☐ *n.* criticism / critic
☐ *v.* criticize
☐ *adj.* critical
☐ *adv.* critically

☐ *n.* degradation
☐ *v.* degrade
☐ *adj.* degradative

☐ *n.* emergence
☐ *v.* emerge
☐ *adj.* emergent
☐ *adv.* emergently

☐ *n.* expansion
☐ *v.* expand
☐ *adj.* expansive
☐ *adv.* expansively

☐ *n.* inhabitance
☐ *v.* inhabit
☐ *adj.* inhabitable

☐ *n.* injection
☐ *v.* inject
☐ *adj.* injectable

☐ *n.* paralysis
☐ *v.* paralyze
☐ *adj.* paralyzing
☐ *adv.* paralyzingly

☐ *n.* reflection
☐ *v.* reflect
☐ *adj.* reflective
☐ *adv.* reflectively

□ *n.* reversal
□ *v.* reverse
□ *adj.* reverse
□ *adv.* reversely

□ *n.* separation
□ *v.* separate
□ *adj.* separate
□ *adv.* separately

□ *n.* specification
□ *v.* specify
□ *adj.* specific
□ *adv.* specifically

□ *n.* tragedy
□ *v.* tragedize
□ *adj.* tragic
□ *adv.* tragically

□ *n.* unification
□ *v.* unify
□ *adj.* unifiable

□ *n.* vitality
□ *v.* vitalize
□ *adj.* vital
□ *adv.* vitally

UNIT 07 Inference

Step A

□ adjacent
□ advent
□ apt
□ artifact
□ attribute
□ beset
□ binary
□ cater
□ chronologically
□ clip
□ cognitive
□ commodities
□ competency
□ decipher
□ decode
□ elicit

□ envision
□ formidable
□ formulation
□ foster
□ heyday
□ hieroglyphic
□ homage
□ implement
□ imprint
□ inanimate
□ instantaneous
□ intricate
□ intuitive
□ lessen
□ levy
□ notable
□ pact
□ pedagogical
□ pinnacle
□ preconceived
□ propensity
□ recall
□ recoup
□ relevant
□ retain
□ sparsely
□ spectacular
□ spur
□ swiftness
□ tally
□ template
□ volatile

Step B

□ *n.* ascension
□ *v.* ascend
□ *adj.* ascendant

□ *n.* characteristic
□ *v.* characterize
□ *adj.* characteristic
□ *adv.* characteristically

□ *n.* consumption
□ *v.* consume
□ *adj.* consuming
□ *adv.* consumingly

□ *n.* elimination

□ *v.* eliminate
□ *adj.* eliminative

□ *n.* elusion
□ *v.* elude
□ *adj.* elusive
□ *adv.* elusively

□ *n.* exclusion
□ *v.* exclude
□ *adj.* exclusive
□ *adv.* exclusively

□ *n.* indication
□ *v.* indicate
□ *adj.* indicative
□ *adv.* indicatively

□ *n.* induction
□ *v.* induct
□ *adj.* inductive
□ *adv.* inductively

□ *n.* inflation
□ *v.* inflate
□ *adj.* inflationary

□ *n.* inhibition
□ *v.* inhibit
□ *adj.* inhibitive

□ *n.* intervention
□ *v.* intervene
□ *adj.* intervening

□ *n.* modification
□ *v.* modify
□ *adj.* modifying

□ *n.* observation
□ *v.* observe
□ *adj.* observational
□ *adv.* observationally

□ *n.* orchestration
□ *v.* orchestrate
□ *adj.* orchestrated

□ *n.* remark
□ *v.* remark
□ *adj.* remarkable
□ *adv.* remarkably

□ *n.* restriction
□ *v.* restrict

☐ *adj.* restrictive
☐ *adv.* restrictively

UNIT 08 Insert Text

Step A

☐ ally
☐ amass
☐ catalyst
☐ circannual
☐ contend
☐ conversely
☐ crude
☐ displace
☐ embargo
☐ endogenic
☐ ensue
☐ entitle
☐ entrepreneur
☐ esteem
☐ explicit
☐ fervor
☐ financial
☐ fission
☐ flee
☐ fusion
☐ give off
☐ harness
☐ hemisphere
☐ iconic
☐ judge
☐ kinetic
☐ level off
☐ lode
☐ neglectfulness
☐ neural
☐ ore
☐ plague
☐ predation
☐ price gouge
☐ protégé
☐ rekindle
☐ renowned
☐ retrospective

☐ skyrocket
☐ soar
☐ staunch
☐ swell
☐ tension
☐ thermal
☐ upsurge
☐ utilitarian
☐ vicious
☐ well-heeled

Step B

☐ *n.* access
☐ *v.* access
☐ *adj.* accessible
☐ *adv.* accessibly

☐ *n.* amputation
☐ *v.* amputate
☐ *adj.* amputating / amputated

☐ *n.* conservation
☐ *v.* conserve
☐ *adj.* conservational

☐ *n.* contamination
☐ *v.* contaminate
☐ *adj.* contaminative

☐ *n.* conviction
☐ *v.* convince
☐ *adj.* convincing / convinced
☐ *adv.* convincingly

☐ *n.* enactment
☐ *v.* enact
☐ *adj.* enacting / enacted

☐ *n.* imposition
☐ *v.* impose
☐ *adj.* imposing / imposed

☐ *n.* initiation
☐ *v.* initiate
☐ *adj.* initiative

☐ *n.* magnification
☐ *v.* magnify
☐ *adj.* magnifying / magnified

☐ *n.* recess
☐ *v.* recede
☐ *adj.* recessive

☐ *adv.* recessively

☐ *n.* retrieval
☐ *v.* retrieve
☐ *adj.* retrieving / retrieved

☐ *n.* urge
☐ *v.* urge
☐ *adj.* urgent
☐ *adv.* urgently

☐ *n.* utilization
☐ *v.* utilize
☐ *adj.* utilizing / utilized

☐ *n.* moderation
☐ *v.* moderate
☐ *adj.* moderate
☐ *adv.* moderately

☐ *n.* acclamation
☐ *v.* acclaim
☐ *adj.* acclaimed

UNIT 09 Prose Summary

Step A

☐ amplitude
☐ array
☐ astronomy
☐ atmosphere
☐ capture
☐ carry out
☐ celestial
☐ cluster
☐ component
☐ comprise
☐ conceive
☐ constellation
☐ crescent
☐ culpable
☐ current
☐ delicate
☐ diameter
☐ dip
☐ drawback
☐ embed
☐ emit

- encroach
- exterior
- filter
- galaxy
- gravity
- hypothesis
- igneous
- increment
- interstellar
- laterally
- mythology
- parabolic
- particle
- polished
- portraiture
- precise
- prominence
- property
- sedimentary
- seismic
- significance
- solution
- sprinkle
- strive
- subsequent
- symmetrical
- transverse
- tremor
- valuable
- vapor
- vigor

Step B

- *n.* alternation
- *v.* alternate
- *adj.* alternate
- *adv.* alternately

- *n.* attachment
- *v.* attach
- *adj.* attached / attachable

- *n.* concentration
- *v.* concentrate
- *adj.* concentrative
- *adv.* concentratively

- *n.* contribution
- *v.* contribute

- *adj.* contributory

- *n.* delineation
- *v.* delineate
- *adj.* delineating

- *n.* description
- *v.* describe
- *adj.* descriptive
- *adv.* descriptively

- *n.* detonation
- *v.* detonate
- *adj.* detonative / detonatable

- *n.* dilation
- *v.* dilate
- *adj.* dilatable
- *adv.* dilatably

- *n.* dispersion
- *v.* disperse
- *adj.* dispersed
- *adv.* dispersedly

- *n.* evolution
- *v.* evolve
- *adj.* evolutionary
- *adv.* evolutionarily

- *n.* focalization
- *v.* focalize
- *adj.* focalizing / focalized

- *n.* radiation
- *v.* radiate
- *adj.* radiative / radiational

- *n.* speculation
- *v.* speculate
- *adj.* speculative
- *adv.* speculatively

- *n.* substitution
- *v.* substitute
- *adj.* substitutional
- *adv.* substitutionally

- *n.* supposition
- *v.* suppose
- *adj.* supposing / supposed
- *adv.* supposedly

UNIT 10 Fill in a Table

Step A

- accessible
- adjoining
- affect
- anoxia
- artificial
- batter
- caterpillar
- consume
- crack
- crash
- deciduous
- deploy
- discard
- dwelling
- elaborate
- ensconce
- equilibrium
- eventually
- evident
- exodus
- extinct
- fell
- forage
- frequency
- gnaw
- harvest
- hoard
- hostility
- impede
- larva
- marine
- mature
- merge
- middleman
- nectar
- Neolithic
- note
- observe
- odor plume
- omnivorous
- Paleolithic
- paraplegic
- pollen

- ☐ precautionary
- ☐ prolonged
- ☐ recruit
- ☐ regarding
- ☐ salinity
- ☐ sturdy
- ☐ subjugate
- ☐ tackle
- ☐ tuck
- ☐ unsustainable
- ☐ vertebrate

- ☐ *n.* ventilation
- ☐ *v.* ventilate
- ☐ *adj.* ventilative

Step B

- ☐ *n.* association
- ☐ *v.* associate
- ☐ *adj.* associative
- ☐ *adv.* associatively

- ☐ *n.* confrontation
- ☐ *v.* confront
- ☐ *adj.* confronting

- ☐ *n.* contention
- ☐ *v.* contend
- ☐ *adj.* contending
- ☐ *adv.* contendingly

- ☐ *n.* contradiction
- ☐ *v.* contradict
- ☐ *adj.* contradictory
- ☐ *adv.* contradictorily

- ☐ *n.* defoliation
- ☐ *v.* defoliate
- ☐ *adj.* defoliating

- ☐ *n.* depletion
- ☐ *v.* deplete
- ☐ *adj.* depletive

- ☐ *n.* diffusion
- ☐ *v.* diffuse
- ☐ *adj.* diffusional

- ☐ *n.* exploitation
- ☐ *v.* exploit
- ☐ *adj.* exploitative
- ☐ *adv.* exploitatively

- ☐ *n.* infiltration
- ☐ *v.* infiltrate
- ☐ *adj.* infiltrative

How to
Master Skills for the
TOEFL® iBT
READING

| Answers and Translations

Advanced

 DARAKWON

How to
Master Skills for the

Second Edition

TOEFL® iBT

READING Advanced

❙ Answers and Translations

DARAKWON

UNIT 01 Vocabulary

Basic Drill p.14

Drill 1 1 Ⓐ 2 Ⓑ

해석

로절린드 프랭클린

1962년에 DNA 분자의 구조를 발견한 공로로 세 명의 남자가 노벨상을 받았다. 하지만 그러한 발견이 가능했던 것은 로절린드 프랭클린이라는 여자 때문이었다. 프랭클린은 모리스 윌킨스와의 연구에서 X선 결정학으로 알려진 기술을 사용해 DNA가 나사선 형태, 즉 나선형을 띠고 있음을 밝혀냈다. 그러한 결과로 제임스 왓슨과 프랜시스 크릭은 결정적인 통찰력을 얻게 되어 1953년에 DNA 분자가 이중 나선 구조로 되어 있다는 결론을 내릴 수 있었다. 이러한 획기적인 발견 덕분에 과학자들은 유전자가 어떻게 유전되는지를 유추해 낼 수 있었다. 1950년대 초반에는 여성 과학자들이 종종 남성 과학자들의 그늘에 가려서 일을 했기 때문에 프랭클린의 중추적인 업적은 과학사의 가장자리로 밀려났다.

Drill 2 1 Ⓓ 2 Ⓐ

해석

차터 스쿨

미국의 차터 스쿨 운동은 1990년대에, 특히 도심지의 공립 학교들이 실패했다고 인식되면서, 그에 대한 반응으로 시작되었다. 이 개념은 일반적으로 공립 학교에 주는 돈을 사립 학교에 줌으로써 사립 학교들이 건물을 짓고, 교사를 고용하고, 그리고 자체적인 커리큘럼을 세울 수 있도록 하는 것이다. 차터 스쿨은 공립 학교의 통제를 받지 않고 운영되며, 보다 나은 학업적 결과를 나타낼 것으로 기대된다. 차터라는 명칭은 학교가 충족시켜야 할, 법적으로 규정된 학력 향상 계약을 가리킨다. 많은 차터 스쿨들이 성공적이었던 반면에 기대했던 향상 효과를 거두지 못한 학교들도 많았다. 따라서 이러한 혁신 학교의 타당성 및 효과에 관한 논쟁은 아직도 계속되고 있다.

Drill 3 1 Ⓐ 2 Ⓒ

해석

필립 로스

평론가들에 의해 지난 50년간 미국 최고의 소설가로 종종 꼽히는 필립 로스는 미국에서 유대인으로서 살았던 경험에 대한 개인적인 생각뿐만 아니라 역사에 대한 풍자적인 시선을 글로 나타내고 있다. 그의 첫 번째 저서 *굿바이, 콜럼버스*는 1960년에 전미 도서상을 수상했으며, 이후에는 영향력 있는 영화로 만들어졌다. 그가 1969년에 쓴 소설인 *포트노이의 불평*은 비평가들의 찬사를 받으면서도 청소년기에 대한 일부 묘사로 인해 막대한 논란을 불러일으키기도 했다. 일부 도시에서는 수년 동안 이러한 책의 판매가 금지되었다. 로스는 종종 한 명의 등장 인물을 자신의 분신으로 삼아서 이러한 인물을 여러 소설에 재등장시킨다. 예를 들어 네이선 주커만은 1979년부터 1986년 사이 다섯 편의 소설에서 주인공이었는데, 1997년과 2000년 사이의 세 편의 소설에서 다시 등장을 한다.

Drill 4 1 Ⓒ 2 Ⓐ

해석

맬서스 재앙

1798년 영국의 경제학자인 토머스 맬서스는 인구가 식량 생산량보다 더 빨리 증가하는 경향이 있다는 이론을 제시했다. 그는 잉여 인구의 다수가 전쟁 및 질병으로 사망할 것으로 예측했다. 그 후 남은 사람들은 재앙, 즉 기아와 불행의 시기를 겪게 될 것이었다. 맬서스 재앙은 자원을 보충할 수단이 없었던 고립된 문화권에서 이미 발생한 바 있었다. 예를 들어 이스터 섬의 원주민들은 섬 전체를 벌목한 후에 소멸했다. 벌목으로 인해 토양이 침식되었고 그들이 식량으로 삼았던 동식물들이 사라졌다. 일부 과학자들은 현재 보다 광범위한 맬서스 재앙이 시작될 수도 있다는 점을 나타내는 징후들을 목격하고 있다. 이들은 아이티, 르완다, 그리고 이디오피아에서 최근에 발생한 비극적 상황들을 언급한다.

Exercises with Long Passages

Exercise 1 1 Ⓒ 2 Ⓑ 3 Ⓐ 4 Ⓒ   p.16

해석

다윈과 월러스

찰스 다윈은 흔히 진화론의 창시자로 여겨지며, 그는 1859년 *종의 기원*에서 처음으로 진화론을 설명했다. 종들이 오랜 시간에 걸쳐 진화할 수 있다는 개념은 이미 19세기 초반에 존재하고 있었다. 하지만 다윈의 위대한 통찰력은 진화 과정을 일으키는 메커니즘, 즉 자연 선택을 설명한 것에 있었다. 자연 선택의 과정은 동물 및 식물이 바람직한 형질을 후손에게 물려 줌으로써 환경에 적합한 종의 발달을 유인하는 경향을 일컫는다. 이와 동시에 우성 형질을 물려받지 못한 생물은 번성하지 못하는 경향을 보인다. 이러한 방식으로 유리한 형질들은 자연적으로 선택된다고 말해진다.

다윈은 동식물 학자에게 필요한 교육을 받지 못했다. 실제로 그의 교육은 *H.M.S. 비글호*를 타고 5년 간 항해를 하면서 얻은 실무적인 것이었는데, 이 기간 동안 그는 동식물의 화석과 표본을 수집해서 자신이 관찰한 생물들 간의 차이점을 자세히 기록했다. 다윈은 자신의 이론을 1844년에 완성했지만 발표는 몇 년 후에 했는데, 그 이유는 이로 인하여 종교계에 파장이 생길 것을 두려워했기 때문이었다. 인간이 영장류에서 진화했다는 아이디어는, 인간의 창조에 있어서 신이 주도적인 역할을 담당했다고 주장하는, 전통적인 종교 교리와 충돌하는 것이었다.

따라서 다윈은 자신의 아이디어에 대해 침묵하는 것으로 만족했다. 하지만 1858년, 연락을 하고 지내던 젊은 동식물 학자인 알프레드 러셀 월러스로부터 한 통의 편지와 논문 초고를 받고서 화가 났다. 그는 월러스가 자연 선택의 우위성을 포함하여 다윈의 핵심적인 아이디어를 그대로 반영한 진화론을 발표할 준비를 하고 있다는 것을 알고 경악했다. 그는 진퇴양난에 처했다. 만약 자신이 서둘러 논문을 발표한다면 다른 사람의 업적을 가로챈 것으로 여겨질 것이었다. 하지만 월러스가 먼저 발표를 하도록 내버려둔다면 발표에 대한 두려움 때문에 자신의 평생 업적을 남에게 빼앗길 판이었다.

해답은 타협에 있었다. 그는 두 명의 동료 과학자들과 이 문제를 의논했는데, 그들은 두 사람의 논문 모두를 1858년 런던 과학 협회의 학회에 제출할 것을 제안했다. 처음에는 두 논문 모두 관심을 끌지 못했다. 하지만 이듬해 다윈의 책이 큰 반응을 얻자 진화론은 월러스보다 다윈과 더 큰 연관성을 갖게 되었다. 이는 부분적으로 월러스의 선한 성품 때문이었다. 그는 기꺼이 대부분의 공로를 다윈에게 넘겼고, 심지어 이 이론을 다윈설이라고 부르기도 했다. 한편 월러스는 인생 후반기에 심령론과 외계 생명체와 같은 비과학적인 주제에 심취하면서 자신의 명성에 타격을 입었다.

Exercise 2 1 ⓒ 2 ⓑ 3 ⓓ 4 ⓐ   p.18

해석

경제학의 시카고 학파

지난 세기 동안 미국의 경제 사상은 대부분 시카고 대학의 경제학과에서 비롯되었다. 그 영향력이 너무 광범위했기 때문에, 그곳의 이론적 접근법들은 학계에서 시카고 학파로 알려지게 되었다. 이는 시카고 대학의 경제학과뿐만 아니라 보다 넓은 경제학적 세계관도 가리킨다. 전 세계적으로 많은 대학과 정부 기관에서 시카고 학파의 추종자들을 찾아볼 수 있다.

시카고 학파는 몇 차례의 역사적 단계를 거쳐 왔다. 각 단계에 따라 고유한 관점이 존재한다. 시카고 학파는 1920년대에 프랭크 H. 나이트와 제이콥 바이너로부터 시작되었다. 이들은 당시 유행하고 있던 경험주의적인 경제학 접근법, 즉 경제 지표들의 성과에 관한 자료를 분석하여 결론을 이끌어 내는 방식을 거부했다. 나이트와 바이너는 모든 사회적 현상을 경제적으로 설명할 수 있다는 경제 제국주의를 비난했다. 또한 이들은 자유 방임적 접근법에 있어서도 회의적이었다. 대신 불황을 피하기 위한 적극적인 정부 정책을 옹호했다. 하지만 그들은 경제의 모든 단계에서 정부의 역할을 인정하는 전면적인 케인즈주의 정책은 반대했다. 오히려 자신의 이익을 극대화하기 위한 개인 및 그룹의 선택을 강조하면서, 신고전주의적인 패러다임으로 모든 경제 문제를 해결할 수 있을 것으로 확신했다.

시카고 학파가 두 번째로 꽃을 피운 시기는 1960년대로, 이때 조지 J. 스티글러와 밀턴 프리드만이 있었다. 두 번째 시카고 학파는 신고전주의 경제학을 고수했으며 정부 규제를 찬양하는 케인즈주의를 반대했다. 거시경제학적 측면에서는 통화주의를 강조한 것으로 가장 잘 알려져 있다. 통화주의는 시카고 학파와 가장 밀접한 관계를 맺게 된 밀턴 프리드만에 의해 발전했다. 19세기 화폐 수량설의 영향을 받은 프리드만의 견해에 따르면 물가는 유통 중인 통화량과 직접적으로 관련되어 있다. 케인즈주의와 달리 통화주의는 과세 및 지출에 의한 정부의 직접적인 통제를 기피하고 화폐의 공급에 제한을 두는 것을 선호한다. 프리드만은 연방 준비 제도의 지배적인 역할을 지지했다. 연방 준비 제도는 인플레이션을 억제하거나 침체된 경제를 부양하기 위해 필요에 따라 이자율을 올리거나 낮출 수 있다. 또 다른 도구는 미 재무부가 발행한 장기 채권의 판매이다. 정부는 이를 이용하여 시민들에게 확정 이율로 채권을 판매함으로써 자금을 마련할 수 있다.

미시경제학적인 측면에서는 조지 스티글러가 시카고 학파를 이끌었다. 그는 신고전주의적인 패러다임을 유지하면서 가능할 때마다 이를 새로운 분야로 확대시켜야 한다고 주장했다. 그 결과 미시경제학에서는 검색 이론, 인적 자본 이론, 그리고 재산권 및 거래 비용 이론 등이 등장했다. 시카고 학파는 지속적으로 신고전주의를 수용함으로써, 모든 사회적 및 정치적 현상들을 경제적인 측면에서 바라보는, 제국주의적인 견해를 조장한다는 비판을 받고 있다.

Exercise 3 1 ⓑ 2 ⓒ 3 ⓐ 4 ⓓ   p.20

해석

초월주의

초월주의는 1800년대 중반 미국 문화의 르네상스의 핵심을 이루었던 철학이었다. 뉴잉글랜드를 중심으로 한 초월주의 운동은 1836년 랄프 왈도 에머슨이 쓴 *자연*이라는 수필집에 의해 시작되었는데, 그는 여기에서 새로운 철학의 수사적 구호가 된 "우리는 우리 발로 스스로 걷고, 우리 손으로 스스로 일하고, 우리의 마음을 거침없이 표현할 것이다... 모든 인간에게 영감을 주는 신성한 영혼으로부터 각자가 영감을 받았음을 믿기 때문에 인류의 국가가 처음으로 존재하게 될 것이다."라는 구절을 썼다.

또한 1836년에는 에머슨과 기타 초월주의자들이 매사추세츠 케임브리지에서 초월주의 클럽을 결성함으로써 아이디어를 나눌 수 있는 토론의 장이 마련되었다. 1840년 이 그룹은 자신들의 철학을 *더 다이얼*이라는 잡지에 발표하기 시작했다. 초월주의라는 용어는 독일의 철학자 임마누엘 칸트의 개념에서 유래되었는데, 그는 지식이 실재가 아니라 실재를 아는 방식에 관심을 가질 때 "초월적"인 것이 된다고 주장했다. 명상 및 일이나 예술을 통한 자연과의 교감을 통해, 사람들은 감각을 뛰어넘어 진실과 아름다움을 이해할 수 있다. 이 사상은 감각과 경험에 의존해서 지식을 얻을 수 있다는 아이디어를 반대한다. 오히려 사물의 실체에 도달할 수 있도록 인도해 주는 내면의 영적인 본질을 바라보아야 한다고 주장한다.

초월주의자들은 진리에 이르는 길이 자신의 내면에 있다고 믿었다. 사회는 인간에게 유용한 상품과 물리적 생존 수단을 제공해 주는 필요악이었다. 올바른 삶을 살기 위해서는 관습과 사회적 인습을 무시하고 자신의 이성에 의지해야 한다. 그들은 조직화된 종교가, 사람들과 신과의 개인적인 관계를 방해하기 때문에, 그러한 과정에서 장애가 된다고 믿었다. 초월주의는 미국의 문학과 정신사에 지대한 영향을 끼쳤다. 에머슨은 *자립*과 같은 수필을 통해 이러한 운동의 주창자가 되었다. 헨리 데이빗 소로의 *월든 연못에서*는 사회라는 제약이 없어도 인류가 생존하고 번성할 수 있다고 주장했다. 시인 월트 휘트먼과 에밀리 디킨슨은 자연을 연구함으로써 발견할 수 있는 보편적인 진리를 보여 주었다.

에머슨은 진정한 초월적 삶이란 도달할 수 없는 것임을 인정했다. 그럼에도 불구하고 이 운동은 보스턴 근처의 브룩팜과 같은 유토피아적인 공동체를 만들어 냈다. 1841년 조지 리플리에 의해 설립된 브룩팜은 조르주 푸리에의 사회주의적 관점에서 영감을 받은 것이었는데, 그는 비슷한 신념을 가진 사람들이 자신의 물품을 공유하고 모두를 위한 식량을 재배함으로써 조화롭게 살 수 있다고 믿었다. 하지만 이 농장은 농사에 부적절한 척박한 토양 위에 자리잡고 있었다. 보다 성공적이었던 것은 브룩팜의 학교들로, 이 학교들이 공동체에 유일한 수익을 가져다 주었다. 이러한 실험은 학교 본관에 화재가 발생함으로써 결국 1847년에 실패로 끝났다.

Summary Note

❶ Immanuel Kant
❷ commune with nature
❸ Ralph Waldo Emerson
❹ Brook Farm

Summary Note

❶ suburban areas
❷ blockbusting
❸ the racial composition
❹ the busing of students

Exercise 4 1 ⓒ 2 ⓐ 3 ⓒ 4 ⓐ   p.22

Exercise 5 1 ⓒ 2 ⓑ 3 ⓓ 4 ⓐ   p.24

해석

백인들의 이동

미국의 대도시들은 백인들에 의해 만들어졌고 백인들로 채워졌다. 남북 전쟁이 끝난 후, 공장의 일자리를 얻기 위해 흑인들이 북부의 도시들로 유입되기 시작했다. 이러한 흑인들의 유입은 2차 대전 당시 군수 산업에서 일자리를 찾으려는 흑인들이 몰려들면서 증가되었다. 이로 인해 주택 부족 현상이 일어났고, 민권 운동이 시작됨에 따라 백인들이 지배하던 도시에서는 인종간의 긴장감이 고조되었다. 재산을 가지고 있던 백인들은 이러한 사회적인 문제를 피해 인근의 교외 지역으로 빠져나가기 시작했는데, 이 현상을 백인들의 이동이라고 한다.

미국인들은 전통적으로 도시 아니면 농장에서 살았다. 하지만 2차 세계 대전 이후 주택 수요가 폭증하자 교외 지역이 형성되었는데, 이는 예전 농지 위에 세워진 주거 단지로, 이곳 사람들은 차를 타고 시내의 직장에 다녔다. 일부 백인들에게 교외 지역은, 도시의 가난한 흑인들이 일으키는 소동과 시내 학교의 질적 저하가 걱정되지 않는, 평안한 안식처로 여겨졌다.

부동산 중개업자들은 종종 흑인에 대한 백인들의 반감을 이용함으로써 백인들의 이동을 조장하는데 커다란 역할을 했다. 부동산 중개인들이 사용했던 가장 악랄한 방법은 블록버스팅이었다. 부동산 중개업자들은 주택을 직접 매입하거나 백인 대리인을 이용해 매입한 다음 이를 흑인 가정에게 되파는 수법으로 백인 동네에서 몰래 집을 팔았다. 백인 집주인들은 흑인 가정이 이사해 오는 것을 보고 이웃에 흑인들이 넘쳐나면 자신들의 집값이 떨어질 것이라고 생각해서 공황 상태에 빠졌다. 이러한 두려움은 자기 충족적이어서 더 많은 주택이 시장에 나오는 순간 주택 가격이 내려갔다. 종종 구매를 희망하는 사람은 부동산 중개업자뿐이었는데, 이들은 주택을 매입해서 새로운 흑인 가족에게 더욱 비싼 가격으로 이를 되팔았다. 이런 식으로 부동산 중개인들은 중개 수수료를 챙겼을 뿐만 아니라 잠시 소유했던 주택을 매도함으로써 이윤을 남기기도 했다.

백인들의 이동은 도시의 인종 구성에 변화를 가져왔을 뿐만 아니라 공공 교육에도 커다란 영향을 미쳤다. 1954년 미 대법원이 공립 학교에서의 인종 차별을 금지시킴으로써 더 이상 대부분 흑인으로만 구성된, 혹은 백인으로만 구성된 학교는 존재하지 않게 되었다. 이러한 결정으로, 특히 흑인 학교를 따로 요구하는 오랜 전통을 지닌 남부에서, 사회적 격변이 일어났다. 이러한 저항을 무력화시키기 위해 이후 법원은 학생들의 강제 버스 통학을 명령했는데, 이에 따라 흑인들은 수 마일 떨어진 이전의 백인 학교까지, 그리고 백인 학생들은 수 마일 떨어진 이전의 흑인 학교까지 버스로 통학을 할 수도 있었다. 백인 학부모들은 인근 학교보다도 좋지 못한 학교까지 버스를 타고 통학하느라 자녀들이 시간을 낭비하는 것을 못마땅해 했다. 그들의 해결책은 자녀들을 사립 학교에 등록시키는 것이었는데, 사립 학교는 조세 혜택을 받지 않아서 인종 할당제를 지키지 않고서도 운영될 수 있었다.

해석

토머스 헌트 모건

20세기 초 과학자들은 유전의 물리적인 기초를 알아내기 위해 애쓰고 있었다. 형질이 유전된다는 것은 알고 있었지만, 형질이 후대로 전해지는 메커니즘은 알지 못했다. 한 가지 가능성은 1888년에 발견된, 세포의 핵 안에 들어 있고 실과 같은 구조를 지닌 염색체에 있었다. 하지만 유전적인 정보를 전달하는데 있어서 염색체의 정확한 역할을 입증해 줄 실험은 어느 누구도 하지 못했다.

콜롬비아 대학의 유전학자인 토머스 헌트 모건이 염색체를 이해하기 위한 실험에서 자그마한 파리를 실험 대상으로 삼았다. 정식 명칭이 *노랑초파리*인 초파리가 모건의 실험에서 이상적인 대상이었는데, 그 이유는 이들을 키우고 먹이는 데 비용이 많이 들지 않았고, 좁은 공간에서도 다량으로 번식이 가능했으며, 다 자라기까지 열흘 밖에 걸리지 않았고, 그리고 염색체가 네 개뿐이어서 연구하기가 쉬웠기 때문이었다.

파리 실험실이라는 적절한 이름이 붙여진 콜롬비아 대학의 작은 연구실에서 실험을 진행한 모건과 그의 팀은 초파리를 수백만 단위로 번식시키기 시작했다. 이 과정은 수고스러운 것으로서, 유전된 형질에 어떠한 변화가 있는지를 살펴보기 위해서는 각각 파리를 핀셋으로 집어 이를 확대경으로 관찰해야 했다. 모건은 초파리를 방사선에 노출시키고, 밝은 곳이나 완전히 어두운 곳에서 키우고, 원심 분리기에 넣어 돌리고, 오븐에 굽는 과정을 통해 돌연변이라고도 불리는 변종을 만들어 내려고 했다. 모건은 6년 동안 열심히 실험을 했지만, 자신이 번식시키고자 했던 돌연변이는 파리의 자손에서 찾아내지 못했다.

1910년 실험을 포기하려던 순간 그는 일반적인 붉은 눈 대신 하얀색 눈을 가진 파리 한 마리를 발견했다. 이 돌연변이는 이후 세대에서도 다시 나타났는데, 이는 돌연변이가 유전에 의해 전해진다는 점을 암시했다. 모건은 세대간의 형질을 추적하는 법을 알게 되었고, 이로써 특정 형질이 어떻게 특정 염색체와 연결되는지도 알 수 있었다. 이런 식으로 그는 마침내 염색체가 유전 인자의 전달자라는 점을 밝혀냈다. 이후 이러한 인자들은 유전자, 즉 사슬 형태를 지닌 핵산 입자인 것으로 확인되었다.

모건의 연구 결과로 인해 일부 형질이 남성 또는 여성에만 유전되는 반성 유전을 설명할 수 있게 되었다. 또한 그는 유전자가 염색체에서 특정한 자리를 차지하고 고정된 선형 순서로 염색체에 배열되어 있다는 점도 밝혀냈다. 그의 통찰력 덕분에 최근의 인간 게놈 프로젝트도 성공할 수 있었는데, 이로써 모든 인간 유전자의 서열과 위치가 성공적으로 밝혀졌다. 과학자들은 이러한 지식을 활용하여 현재 특정 질환을 일으키는 유전자를 찾아낼 수 있으며, 결함이 있는 유전자를 제거하고 그 자리에 건강한 유전자를 집어넣을 수도 있다.

Summary Note

❶ fruit flies
❷ ten days
❸ four chromosomes
❹ mutation in eye color

해석

추문 폭로자

1800년대 후반과 1900년대 초반, 잡지 및 신문 기자들이 정재계의 부정과 비리를 폭로하는 기사를 쓰기 시작했다. 아동 노동, 식품 가공 공장의 비위생적인 공정, 제약 회사의 기만적인 주장, 매춘, 노동력 착취, 그리고 비인간적 수감 시설 등이 이들의 공격 대상이었다.

이러한 개혁가 중에서 가장 유명했던 사람은 소설가인 업튼 싱클레어로, 그는 *정글*에서 정육업계의 비위생적인 환경을 극적으로 표현했다. 또 다른 사람으로 신문 기자이자 사진 작가였던 제이콥 리스를 들 수 있다. 그는 뉴욕시 빈민가의 참담한 현실을 폭로했다. 이러한 기사들에 대중들이 열광하기 시작한 것은 대체적으로 1903년 *매클루어스*지에 실린 연재물 때문이었다. 이 잡지는 링컨 스테펀스 시 정부의 비리와 아이다 M. 타벨의 스탠더드 오일사에 대한 탐사 보도를 게재했다.

사회적인 의식을 가지고 있었던 이러한 종류의 언론은 시어도어 루즈벨트 대통령에 의해 처음 받아들여졌다. 그는 의회를 설득해 순수식품의약품법과 식육 검사법과 같은 개혁 법안을 통과시켰다. 하지만 1906년에 데이빗 그레이엄 필립스가 *코스모폴리탄*지에 루즈벨트의 일부 측근들의 정치적 비리를 보도하는 연재 기사를 썼다. 루즈벨트 대통령은 반격했다. 그는 연설에서 일부 기자들을 존 번연의 *천로역정* 중 퇴비용 쇠스랑을 들고 일하는 등장 인물에 비유했다. 이 인물은 항상 퇴비, 즉 동물의 분뇨를 찾기 위해 아래쪽만 보고 다니며, 주변 세상은 결코 올려다 보지 않았다. 그는 부정을 바로잡는 것에 대한 진정한 관심을 나타낸 기자들을 칭찬했다. 하지만 부정을 들춰내서 자신들이 찾아낸 부정을 이슈화시키는 것에만 관심을 가진 기자들은 비난했다. 그는 이들을 추문 폭로자라고 불렀다.

책임감 있는 탐사 보도 기자들은 루즈벨트가 붙인 불쾌한 호칭에 배신감을 느꼈다. 루즈벨트가 존경했던 개혁가 중 한 명이었던 링컨 스테펀스는 연설에 격노했다. 그 다음 날, 그는 루즈벨트에게 "음, 각하께서는 각하를 만들었던 이 모든 탐사 보도에 종말을 고하셨습니다."라고 말했다. 실제로 루즈벨트의 비난으로 인해 대체로 긍정적인 것으로 받아들여지면서 여러 사회적인 병폐에 대한 관심을 고조시키고 이를 고쳤던 운동은 끝이 났다. 그럼에도 불구하고 이 운동이 번성했던 시기, 특히 1900년과 1915년 사이에는 추문 폭로 운동이 중요한 성과를 거두었다. 일례로 기업의 독점이 사라졌고, 아동 노동이 없어졌으며, 노동자 보상법이 도입되었고, 그리고 식품 가공의 안정성이 증진될 수 있었다.

이후 20세기가 되자 추문 폭로자라는 용어는 정치인들이 맞서기를 꺼려하는 공공의 위험에 초점을 맞추는 작가나 영화 제작자에게 사용되었다. 최근의 추문 폭로자로는 안전하지 못한 자동차에 관한 폭로 기사를 쓴 랄프 네이더, 워터게이트 스캔들의 사건을 기록한 밥 우드워드와 칼 번스타인, 그리고 패스트푸드 산업에 관한 영화를 제작한 모건 스펄럭를 들 수 있다.

📝 Summary Note

❶ the 1900s
❷ *McClure's Magazine*
❸ food processing
❹ *Pilgrim's Progress*

Building Summary Skills　p.28

Exercise 1　Darwin and Wallace

Charles Darwin is known as the discoverer of the theory of evolution. He formulated his theory while on a voyage around the world, during which he observed differences among animal species. His key insight was that species evolve through the process of natural selection. He delayed publishing the theory for fear of religious controversy. Alfred Russel Wallace discovered the theory later and told Darwin about it. That prompted Darwin to publish his book *On the Origin of Species*.

Exercise 2　The Chicago School of Economics

The University of Chicago has become the leading center of economic thought in the United States. Its views have become known as the Chicago School. In the 1960s, it was led by Milton Friedman, who favored a monetarist approach. He believed in controlling the economy by regulating the money supply. He advocated a strong role for the Federal Reserve in setting interest rates and selling treasury bonds.

Exercise 3　Transcendentalism

Transcendentalism was a philosophy that arose in New England in the mid-1800s. It was first expressed in Ralph Waldo Emerson's essay *Nature*. Transcendentalists believed in looking within oneself for an understanding of nature, not in society's creations such as organized religion. They preached meditation and self-reliance in order to rise above, or transcend, their physical senses. Transcendentalists attempted to design towns, such as Brook Farm, where they could practice their beliefs. However, all these experiments failed.

Exercise 4　White Flight

After World War II, blacks began moving north in greater numbers while looking for jobs. Whites began to move out to avoid the poverty and the decline in school systems that they felt were caused by this black influx. Real estate agents cooperated in this white flight by secretly selling homes to blacks in formerly white communities. Once this blockbusting occurred, whites would put their houses up for sale, allowing real estate agents to earn more commissions. White flight caused racial disparity in the public schools. Court decisions have tried to equalize these differences by ordering the busing of school children.

Exercise 5　Thomas Hunt Morgan

Thomas Hunt Morgan wanted to find out how the body passed traits to later generations. He designed experiments with fruit flies. When one fly was born with an uncommon eye color—a mutation—Morgan was able to reproduce it in the fly's offspring. This led him to conclude that eye color was passed by chromosomes, thread-like structures in a cell's nucleus. He determined that each trait was linked to a gene, or a chain of molecules inside a cell.

Exercise 6 Muckrakers

The muckrakers were reporters and novelists who exposed some of the abuses in politics and business in the early 1900s. President Theodore Roosevelt approved of these reformers and endorsed several reform laws. But when a series of articles alleged political corruption by Roosevelt's friends, Roosevelt spoke out against them by calling them muckrakers. His criticism ended the movement. But the term continues to be applied in a positive way to those who reveal public corruption or business misbehavior.

Mini TOEFL iBT Practice Test p.30

1 Ⓓ 2 Ⓓ 3 Ⓑ 4 Ⓓ 5 Ⓐ
6 Ⓐ 7 Ⓒ 8 Precambrian Period: ①, ③
Cambrian Period: ②, ④, ⑤

9 Ⓐ 10 Ⓑ 11 Ⓑ 12 Ⓓ 13 Ⓑ
14 Ⓒ 15 Ⓒ 16 ②, ④, ⑤

해석

[1-8]

캄브리아 폭발

오늘날 지구에서 발견되는 모든 동물종은 약 5억 7천만 년에서 5억 3천만 년 전에 처음 등장한 생물에서 그 기원을 찾을 수 있다. 비교적 짧았던 이 기간 동안 생물의 다양성이 이례적으로 증가했는데, 이는 화석 기록에서 찾아볼 수 있다. 이처럼 급격한 진화는 지질학적 시간으로 캄브리아기에 일어났기 때문에 캄브리아 폭발이라고 알려져 있다. 약 6억 년 전인 선캄브리아기에는 진화에 의해 나타난 생물들이 거의 없었고 그 구조도 단순했다. 하지만 캄브리아 폭발 동안 복잡성 및 다양성이 갑작스럽게 증가했다. 이에 대한 증거는 화석, 유해, 혹은 암석이나 토양 속에 보존된 생물들의 흔적에 들어 있다. 그처럼 빠른 속도로 진화가 이루어진 이유는 현재의 과학자들도 잘 모르고 있다.

캄브리아 폭발은 찰스 다윈에게 특별한 문제를 가져다 주었는데, 그는 1859년에 생물의 진화 과정에 대한 자신의 이론을 발표했다. 다윈의 이론은 매우 오랜 시간이 지난 후 현재와 같은 다양한 생물 종들이 등장했다고 주장한다. 자연 선택에 따른 미미한 변화로 현재의 종이 나타나기까지 오랜 시간이 필요했다. 이러한 아이디어에서는 진화란 점진적으로 일어나는 것이며 이 점진적인 변화는 화석에 기록되어 있어야 했다. 하지만 실제 기록상으로 캄브리아 폭발 당시에 생겨난 종은 선캄브리아기에 존재하지 않았다. 다윈 스스로도 이러한 화석 기록의 부재가 자신의 이론의 타당성을 반박하는 주장이 될 수 있다는 점을 인정했다. 실제로 그러한 주장은, 생명체가 신성한 존재에 의해 한 번의 시기에 창조되었다는 입장을 지닌, 창조론 혹은 지적설계론을 믿는 사람들에 의해 제기되고 있다.

다윈은 선캄브리아기에도 진화가 일어났지만 화석 기록에서 찾아볼 수 없을 뿐이라고 주장함으로써 그러한 반박을 피했다. 다시 말해서 폭발이 전혀 일어나지 않았을 수도 있다. 선캄브리아기의 진화 단계에 있던 생물들이 너무 연약해서 화석으로 보존될 수 없었다는 사실로 그러한 현상이 설명될 수도 있다. 모든 생

물이 화석이 되는 것은 아니다. 두 가지 조건이 충족되어야 한다. 첫째, 죽는 곳인 암석이나 토양에 흔적을 남길 만큼 단단한 부분을 생물이 가지고 있어야 한다. 선캄브리아기의 생물들은 캄브리아기에 등장한 갑각류와 달리 단단한 부분을 가지고 있지 않았을 수도 있다. 둘째, 신체 일부가 용해되거나 부패되지 않는 비적대적인 환경에 유해가 묻혀야 한다. 따라서 선캄브리아기의 많은 표본들이 사라져 버렸을 수도 있다.

그럼에도 불구하고 대다수 과학자들은 이전에 비해서 캄브리아기에 보다 크고 빠른 변화가 일어났다는 점에 동의한다. 그들은 진화 과정의 속도가 그처럼 빨랐던 이유를 설명하는데, 일부는 외부에서, 일부는 생명체 내부에서 그 원인을 찾고 있다. 한 가지 이론은 캄브리아기 직전에 지구 대기의 산소량이 증가했다는 점을 지적한다. 산소량이 적으면 생명체가 다양해지고 복잡해지기가 어렵다. 또 다른 외부적 요인으로는 지각의 급격한 이동을 들 수 있는데, 이로 인해 생물 개체군이 서로 분리되어 각기 다른 종으로 진화할 수 있었다. 내부적 요인에 의한 설명은 유전자 발달과 관련이 있다. 동물은 유전자가 최소한의 복잡성을 갖추기 전까지 다른 종으로 진화할 수 없다. 보다 다양한 형태를 생성하기 위해서는 충분한 유전자 도구 상자가 필요하다. 아마도 캄브리아기에 이르러서야 이러한 도구 상자가 효과를 발휘하게 되었을 것이다.

[9-16]

비트 운동

비트 세대는 1950년대 뉴욕시에서 시작된 비순응적 사회 운동에 붙여진 이름이다. 비트 세대의 메시지는 의식의 흐름 기법을 사용하여 당시 주류적인 가치를 거부했던 사람들의 통찰력과 열망을 표현했던 작가들에 의해 전파되었다. 비트 세대 작가들의 작품들이 오랫동안 인기를 얻은 경우는 거의 없었지만, 그들의 견해는 1960년대 및 그 이후의 록 음악 아티스트들과 사회 운동에 영감을 주었다.

비트라는 용어는 1946년 허버트 헝크에 의해 처음 만들어졌다. 그는 이 단어를 피곤 또는 기진맥진과 같은 의미로 만들었다. 1948년 이 단어는 잭 케루악의 비트 세대라는 표현에서 사용되었는데, 그는 그 의미를 명랑 또는 행복감으로 바꾸어 놓았다. 이러한 표현은 뉴욕T/임즈에 실린 "이것이 비트 세대이다."라는 존 클레론 홈즈의 기사를 통해 1952년 마침내 대중의 의식 속에 자리잡게 되었다. 최초의 비트족은 1940년대 중반에 모인 뉴욕 출신의 친구들이었다. 여기에는 잭 케루악, 알렌 긴스버그, 닐 캐서디, 그리고 윌리엄 S. 버로우즈가 포함되어 있었다. 이 핵심 그룹은 샌프란시스코로 자리를 옮겼고, 그곳에서 시인인 로렌스 펄링게티 및 다른 많은 사람들이 이들과 합류하게 되었다.

가장 먼저 인기를 얻은 비트 문학 작품은 알렌 긴스버그의 장시인 울부짖음이었다. 긴스버그는 1955년 샌프란시스코의 한 갤러리에서 이 시를 큰 소리로 낭독했는데, 그 내용 때문에 논란이 일었다. 그 명성은 자신의 서점에서 시집을 판매했던 로렌스 펄링게티에 대한 음란물 재판에 의해 더 커졌다. 하지만 판사가 "결점을 보충하는 사회적 중요성"이 있기 때문에 이 작품은 음란물이 아니라는 판결을 내림으로써 펄링게티는 무죄를 선고받았다.

가장 성공적인 비트 소설가는 잭 케루악이었다. 케루악은 1957년에 발표한 자신의 최고의 소설인 길 위에서를 통해 자신을 기초로 만든 등장 인물인 샐 파라다이스와 케루악의 친구 닐 캐서디를 기초로 만든 딘 모리아티가 자동차로 미국을 여행하는 과정을 묘사했다. 이 소설로 인해 캐서디는 무책임한 생활 방식, 여성 편력, 무도덕성, 그리고 삶에 대한 욕정으로 유명한 문화 아이콘이 되었다. 길 위에서는 그 내용만큼이나 케루악의 집필 방식으로도 유명해졌다. 케루악은 작품을 쓰는 동안 마약에 취해 있었고, 종이를 바꾸느라 사고의 흐름이 끊기지 않도록 긴 두루마리 종이 위에 타이핑을 한 것으로 알려졌다. 그는 "최초의 생각이 최선의 생각"이라는 믿음을 가지고 자신이 쓴 글은 결코 고치지 않는다고 주장한 것으로 말해진다. 비록 자신이 3주 만에 그 책을 썼다고 주장했지만, 실제로 그는 여러 해에 걸쳐 소설을 계획했고 여러 차례 초고를 작성했다.

또한 윌리엄 S. 버로우즈가 쓴 소설인 *벌거벗은 점심*도 영향력이 있었는데, 이 역시 음란물 재판에서 살아남았다. 그 자신이 마약 중독자였던 버로우즈는 작품에서 마약으로 인한 환상과 마약 중독자 및 범죄자들 간의 여행 이야기를 들려준다. 1960년대에는 비트 철학의 추종자들이 히피족 또는 이피족으로 알려지게 되었다. 그들의 문화는 샌프란시스코를 중심으로 시작되었으며, 이곳은 록 음악, 마약 문화, 그리고 베트남전 반대 시위의 중심지가 되었다. 비트 세대가 문학에 지속적으로 기여한 바는, 인간의 본성과 사회의 불편한 측면을 보여 주는 주제를 포함하여, 보다 개인적인 주제에 관한 글쓰기를 장려했다는 점이다. 비트 세대로 인해 구어체의 대화식 표현도 인정을 받게 되었으며, 저속한 표현 역시 인간 감정을 표현하는 수단으로서 용인되었다.

Vocabulary Check-Up
p.36

A
| 1 | B | 2 | C | 3 | A | 4 | D | 5 | B |
| 6 | D | 7 | A | 8 | B | 9 | D | 10 | C |

B
| 1 | E | 2 | J | 3 | A | 4 | H | 5 | B |
| 6 | I | 7 | F | 8 | G | 9 | D | 10 | C |

UNIT 02 Reference

Basic Drill
p.40

Drill 1 1 B 2 D

해석

프렌치 인디언 전쟁

1700년대 중반 13개 식민지의 서쪽에 있던 오하이오 카운티는 영국과 프랑스 간의 분쟁 지역으로, 양국은 각각 그곳에 교역소와 기지를 건설함으로써 해당 지역의 일부를 점령한 상태였다. 양국 모두 그곳에 처음부터 살고 있던 미 원주민들, 즉 인디언의 영토권은 무시했다. 1753년 영국은 당시 스물 한 살의 소령이던 조지 워싱턴을 보내 프랑스인들과 협상을 하도록 했으나, 프랑스인들은 영토권을 포기하라는 워싱턴의 요구를 거절했다. 1754년 영국은 프랑스에 대한 공격을 감행했고, 이것이 프렌치 인디언 전쟁의 첫 번째 전투가 되었다. 양국 모두 인디언 부족들의 도움을 받았는데, 인디언들은 해당 지역에 대한 자신들의 권리를 보전하고자 했다. 전쟁은 1763년 강화 조약이 체결됨으로써 끝이 났으며, 조약에 따라 영국은 캐나다 전체를 얻게 되었고, 스페인은 루이지애나를 차지했으며, 프랑스는 카리브해 및 뉴펀들랜드 인근의 일부 섬에 대해서만 그 권리를 인정받게 되었다.

Drill 2 1 B 2 A

해석

개발 경제학

개발 경제학이란 경제학의 한 분야로서 빈곤한 개발 도상국들이 직면하는 특수한 경제 문제에 초점을 맞춘다. 고전 경제학과 달리 개발 경제학은 경제 성장에 영향을 미치는 사회적 및 정치적 요인들을 연구한다. 개발 도상국들의 부채 문제와 엄격한 상환 조건으로 부채를 유지시키는데 일조하는 세계 은행 및 국제 통화 기금의 역할도 다룬다. 이 분야의 학자들은 장기적인 최선의 해결책이 부채의 상당 부분을 탕감해 주는 것이라고 주장했다. 또한 채무국들은 안정적인 정부와 자립 경제를 마련할 수 있도록 도움을 받아야만 한다. 목표는 이러한 국가들을 채권국의 무역 파트너로 만드는 것이다. 그러한 목적을 달성하기 위한 한 가지 중요한 방법은 탄탄한 중산층을 양산하는 것이다. 이를 위한 방법에는 모든 사람들에게 교육을 보장하고, 자유 무역을 허용하며, 그리고 의료 서비스를 제공하는 것이 포함된다. 정부는 선거를 통한 대표 선출과 독립적인 사법 시스템을 받아들여야 한다.

Drill 3 1 C 2 C

해석

1873년의 공황

미국의 남북 전쟁이 끝난 이듬해부터 철도 건설이 호황을 맞이했다. 하지만 투기꾼들의 과도한 투자와 철도 회사의 지나친 공사로 무질서한, 그리고 통제가 불가능한 성장이 이루어졌다. 당시 연방 정부에게는 민간 철도업체들의 횡포를 규제할 힘이 부족했다. 또한 그랜트 대통령의 통화 공급 제한 조치 때문에 투자자들이 경제 성장에 필요한 자금을 대출 받기가 더욱 어려워졌다. 이러한 위기는 1873년의 공황에서 최고조에 달했는데, 이때 선도적인 투자 은행 회사들이 파산을 선언했다. 이로써 도미노 효과가 발생해서 철도가 폐쇄되고 실업률이 급증했으며, 뉴욕 증시가 폭락하면서 6년에 걸친 불황이 시작되었다. 1877년 무렵에는 임금 삭감과 열악한 근로 환경 때문에 노동자들이 파업에 돌입했다. 철도 파업으로 기차가 운행을 중단하자 헤이스 대통령은 파업을 끝내기 위해 연방군을 파견했다.

Drill 4 1 A 2 C

해석

레프 비고츠키의 근접 발달 영역 이론

아동이 어떻게 발달하는지를 설명하기 위한 두 가지 경쟁적인 이론이 발전해 왔다. 한 가지 이론은 아동이 선천적인 특성, 즉 본성의 산물이라고 주장한다. 다른 이론은 아동이 환경에 의해, 즉 양육으로 규정된다고 주장한다. 러시아의 심리학자인 레프 비고츠키는 근접 발달 영역(ZPD) 이론을 제안함으로써 이들 방법을 통합시켰다. ZPD는 아동의 현재의 실제 능력과 잠재 능력 사이의 격차를 나타낸다. ZPD의 기준선은 아동이 도움을 받지 않고 문제를 해결하거나 임무를 수행할 수 있는 능력이다. ZPD의 상한선은 아동이 교사 및 성인의 도움을 받아 도달할 수 있는 수준이다. 비고츠키는 아동이 비계 설정, 즉 멘토가 단계적으로 적절한 가르침을 주는 과정에 의해 근접 발달 영역이 좁아지게 된다고 주장했다. 이런 식으로, 아동의 독립적인 능력이 향상되고 잠재적인 능력이 증가함에 따라, 아동의 ZPD는 끊임없이 바뀌게 된다.

Exercise 1　1 Ⓓ　2 Ⓐ　3 Ⓑ　4 Ⓑ　　　　　p.42

해석

비행의 메커니즘

비행기는 양력, 중력, 추진력, 그리고 항력의 네 가지 힘을 조절하는 능력 때문에 날 수 있다. 첫 번째 힘이자 비행기가 이륙하고 비행 상태를 유지하게 만드는 힘은 양력이다. 양력은 뉴턴의 세 번째 운동 법칙으로 설명된다. 모든 작용은 크기가 동일하고 방향은 반대인 반작용을 만들어 낸다. 비행기 날개가 공기를 가를 때 날개가 각도를 조절하면 스쳐 지나가는 공기를 누를 수 있다. 뉴턴의 법칙에 따라 그렇게 아래로 누르는 힘은 동일한 크기의 위로 밀어 올리는 힘, 즉 양력을 만들어 내서 비행기가 위로 올라가게 된다.

양력은 또한 공기와 같이 빠르게 움직이는 유체는 느리게 움직이는 유체에 비해 더 낮은 압력을 받는다는 베르누이의 원리를 이용함으로써 이해될 수 있다. 비행기 날개의 위쪽은 곡면으로 되어 있기 때문에 공기가, 날개의 평평한 아래 부분을 통과하는 공기보다 더 먼 거리를 이동하지만, 양쪽 공기는 날개의 끝 부분에 동시에 도달하는데, 이는 위쪽을 지나는 공기가 평평한 아래쪽을 통과하는 공기보다 더 빨리 이동함으로써 날개 위쪽의 압력이 낮아져 날개가 위로 올라간다는 점을 의미한다.

비행기에 작용하는 두 번째 힘은 중력이다. 중력은 양력을 상쇄시켜 비행기가 반대 방향으로 이동하도록 만든다. 중력이 양력보다 큰 경우에는 비행기가 날 수 없다. 비행기 설계자들의 어려움은 비행기를 뜨게 만들 정도로 튼튼하면서도 고속으로 장거리를 비행할 수 있을 정도로 효율적인 날개를 만드는 것이다. 또 다른 힘은 비행기를 앞쪽으로 밀어내는 추진력인데, 이는 프로펠러나 제트 엔진으로 얻을 수 있다. 추진력이 충분하지 않으면 공기가 비행기 날개의 상하 부분을 지나가지 못하게 되어 양력의 효과가 없어져서 비행기가 추락하게 된다.

마지막으로, 비행기는 항력을 극복해야 한다. 비행기는 공기 중에서 비행할 때 진행 방향의 공기를 밀어내는데, 이때 금속이 공기와 접촉하면서 마찰력이 발생한다. 이 마찰력이 항력이 되어 비행기의 속도를 떨어뜨린다. 항력에 대처하기 위해, 고속 비행 및 미사일의 경우 날개가 얇아야 항력이 최소화되지만, 농약 살포 비행기와 같은 저속 비행기의 경우에는 양력이 항력보다 더 중요하기 때문에 날개가 두꺼울 수 있다.

비행하는 동안에는 네 가지 힘 모두를 정확하게 조절해야 한다. 조종사는 이륙, 방향 및 속도 조정, 혹은 착륙을 하고자 할 때마다 조종 장치를 조작한다. 추진력이 항력보다 크면 비행기의 속도가 증가하고 양력이 중력보다 크면 비행기는 상승한다. 조종사가 착륙 기어를 내리거나 부익을 올림으로써 추진력이 감소되고 항력이 증가하는 경우에는 비행기의 속도가 느려진다. 착륙 기어와 부익을 원위치 시키면 조종사는 비행기를 상승시키거나 비행 속도를 높일 수 있다.

📝 Summary Note

❶ Bernoulli's Principle

❷ offsets lift

❸ propels a plane forward

❹ friction between air and metal

Exercise 2　1 Ⓓ　2 Ⓑ　3 Ⓐ　4 Ⓐ　　　　　p.44

해석

식민지 시대의 미국 가구

1600년대 신세계에 도착한 초기의 미국 정착민들에게는 정교한 가구를 만들 수 있는 자원이나 그에 대한 관심이 거의 없었다. 그들은 몇 개의 벤치, 테이블, 그리고 바닥에 까는 매트리스에 만족해 했다. 식량을 기르고 때때로 적대적인 인디언을 상대하는 것과 같은 기본적인 생존 문제가 해결된 후에야 집을 보다 편안한 곳으로 만드는 일에 관심을 갖게 되었다. 단풍나무, 벚나무, 호두나무, 그리고 참나무로 이루어진 천연의 숲 한 가운데에 살았던 식민지 개척자들은 최상품 나무를 이용해 가구를 만들 수 있었다. 실제로 그처럼 우수한 목재가 사용되었기 때문에 식민지 시대에 만들어진 가구들은 오늘날 골동품 수집가들에게 매우 인기가 높다.

예를 들어 단풍나무는 튼튼하고 내구성이 뛰어나며 손상 없이 작업이 가능하다. 또한 단단하기 때문에 마무리 작업으로 단풍나무 목재에 광택을 낼 수도 있다. 벚나무는 단풍나무만큼 단단하지는 않지만, 결이 곱고 감촉이 좋으며 작업하기도 쉽다.

초기의 미국 가구들은 종종 정착자민들의 손으로 만들어졌다. 직접 작업을 했던 정착민들은 조각 기술이 뛰어났다. 가장 인기 있었던 조각 형태 중 하나는 단풍나무의 잎 문양이었다. 얼마 지나지 않아 숙련된 고급 가구 제작자들이 유럽에서 건너왔는데, 이들은 직선 형태이면서 장식은 거의 없는, 무거운 가구를 사용하는 영국의 관습을 그대로 따랐다. 식민지 시대의 주택은 크기가 작고 천장도 낮았으며 창문도 상당히 작았기 때문에 디자인은 필요에 의해서 단순한 형태를 유지했다. 등받이가 있는 의자보다 등받이가 없는 의자가 더 실용적이었다. 테이블은 단단한 목판으로 만들어졌고 통나무로 만들어진 네모난 다리를 가지고 있었다.

식민지 시대의 가정 생활은 벽난로를 중심으로 이루어졌으며, 벽난로는 혹독하게 추운 겨울에 온기를 공급해 주는 유일한 존재였다. 등받이가 높은 의자나 추위를 막는 역할을 할 수 있는, 덮개가 달린 아기 요람과 같은 형태의 가구들이 만들어졌다. 1700년대 가구 양식에 커다란 영향을 끼친 것은 영국의 가구 제작자인 토머스 치펜데일의 작품이었다. 치펜데일은 1754년에 출간한 책에서 매우 창의적인 자신의 작품을 미국에 소개했다. 그는 문이 달린 책장, 높이가 높은 서랍장, 주전자 스탠드, 그리고 현수판식 테이블과 같은 여러 가지 새로운 디자인들을 고안했다. 필라델피아의 윌리엄 세이브리와 같은 미국 디자이너들은 치펜데일의 스타일을 채택해서 가장자리 장식이 화려하고 다리가 긴 치펜데일 장롱을 제작했다.

미국 가구 제작자들의 솜씨는 당시의 유럽 가구 제작자들보다 우수하다고 여겨지며, 이는 골동품으로서 미국의 가구에 대한 수요가 많은 또 다른 요인이 되고 있다. 하지만 수요가 공급보다 많기 때문에 초기 미국 가구는 가격도 비싸고 찾기도 어렵다. 이러한 수요를 충족시키기 위해 제작자들이 원래 제품과 동일한 목재와 기술을 사용해서 복제품을 생산하고 있다. 초기의 미국 가구는 21세기의 주택 소유들들 사이에서 여전히 인기를 끌고 있다.

📝 Summary Note

❶ surviving

❷ long lasting

❸ Thomas Chippendale

❹ Europeans

Exercise 3　1 Ⓒ　2 Ⓑ　3 Ⓐ　4 Ⓓ　　　　　p.46

거품 경제

때때로 특정 자산의 가치가 급격히 높아질 수 있다. 많은 투자자들을 매료시키면서 엄청난 수준까지 증가할 수도 있다. 하지만 어떤 경우에는 자산 가치가 빠르게 큰 폭으로 하락함으로써 사람들이 막대한 돈을 잃을 수도 있는데, 이러한 상황은 거품 경제라고 알려져 있다.

역사상 다양한 자산과 관련해서 여러 차례의 거품 경제가 발생했다. 예를 들어 1634년부터 1637년까지 네덜란드에서는 튤립 파동으로 알려진 사건이 벌어졌다. 사람들은, 특히 다양한 색의 줄무늬가 있는 튤립에 열광을 했고 튤립 구근의 가격이 말도 안 되게 높아졌다. 한두 개의 튤립 구근으로 네덜란드의 도시인 암스테르담에서 인기 있는 지역의 호화 주택을 구입할 수 있는 경우도 있었다. 하지만 어느 순간 사람들은 보다 이성적이 되었고 튤립 구근의 가격은 보다 합리적인 수준으로 떨어졌다.

보다 최근에 또 다른 거품 경제가 일어났다. 1990년대 월드 와이드 웹이 초창기 상태였을 때, 인터넷 관련 기업들의 주가가 막대한 수준으로 증가했고, 하룻밤 사이에 백만장자가 등장했다. 하지만 이들 중 다수는 닷컴 버블이 터지면서 며칠 만에 파산하게 되었다. 수많은 기업들이 파산을 했으며, 시가 총액 손실액이 수백만 달러에 이르렀다. 1980년대 일본에서는 부동산과 주식 시장에서 동시에 거품 경제가 발생했다. 그러한 거품이 터지고 일본 경제가 회복을 하기까지 수십 년이 걸렸다. 미국에서는 2007년과 2008년에 이자율이 낮고 사람들이 주택을 원하면서 주택 시장의 가치가 빠르게 증가했다. 많은 개인들이 그곳에서 살기보다는 특히 되팔려는 목적으로 주택을 구입했다. 하지만 이자율이 상승하자 사람들은 주택 담보 대출금을 상환하지 못하기 시작했고, 이로 인해 주택 거품이 터지게 되었다.

대부분의 거품 경제는 쉽게 알아차릴 수 있는 유사한 패턴을 따른다. 제일 먼저 전이라는 일이 발생하는데, 이는 사람들이 새로운 제품이나 새로운 유형의 기술을 목격할 때 일어난다. 호황기에는 그러한 특정 자산의 가격이 상승하기 시작해서 그 결과 보다 많은 투자자들이 유입되어 이를 구입하게 된다. 그 다음 단계는 유포리아라고 불리는 것으로, 이는 투자자들이 주의를 기울이지 않고 그러한 자산에 모든 것을 걸 때 일어난다. 이로써 해당 자산의 가격이 천문학적인 수준으로 증가한다. 이 시점에서 현명한 투자자들은, 가치가 여전히 상승하는 중이라도, 자산을 매각함으로써 이익을 얻기 시작한다. 마지막으로 해당 자산의 가격이 하락하면 패닉 상태가 시작된다. 많은 투자자들이 시장에서 빠져나가기로 결심해서 가격이 급락하면 그로 인해 사람들이 재산을 잃고 파산하게 된다.

📝 Summary Note

❶ Tulip Mania

❷ millionaires

❸ 2007 and 2008

❹ euphoria

Exercise 4 1 ⓒ 2 Ⓑ 3 ⓒ 4 Ⓑ p.48

수소 기술

석유, 석탄, 그리고 천연 가스는 한 번 사용하면 다시 사용할 수 없기 때문에 화석 연료에 에너지를 의존하는 경제는 미래가 불확실하다. 화석 연료를 태우면, 연료가 연소되는 장소뿐만 아니라, 전 세계의 공기를 오염시키는 배기 가스가 배출된다.

한 가지 해결책은 화석 연료와 관련된 몇 가지 문제들을 피할 수 있는 수소 기술의 개발을 촉진하는 것이다. 첫째, 수소는 오염을 감소시킨다. 수소는 연료 전지에서 산소와 결합하여 전기 에너지를 만들어 내며, 이러한 에너지는 엔진을 작동시키고 건물에 난방을 제공하는데 사용될 수 있다. 수소와 산소의 결합으로 얻을 수 있는 주요한 이점은 온실 가스나 기타 오염 물질이 생기지 않는다는 점이다. 유일한 부산물은 열과 물이다. 수소를 기반으로 하는 에너지의 두 번째 장점은 다른 나라에서 수입할 필요 없이 해당 지역에서 생산이 가능하다는 점으로, 이는 메탄, 휘발유, 바이오매스, 석탄, 또는 물과 같은 여러 에너지원으로부터 얻을 수 있다. 하지만 물을 제외하고는 각각 오염 물질을 배출한다.

셋째, 물에서 수소를 얻는 경우, 그 결과 지속 가능한 생산 시스템이 만들어진다. 물은 물에 전류를 통과시키는 전기 분해 과정에 의해 산소와 수소로 분리될 수 있다. 이러한 전류는 풍력, 태양력, 그리고 조력과 같은 재생 가능한 에너지원으로부터 얻을 수 있는데, 이들은 석유에 의존하지 않는데다 오염 물질을 배출하지도 않는다. 하지만 이들 에너지원의 단점은 항상 사용할 수 있는 것이 아니라는 점이다. 바람이 그칠 수도 있고, 태양이 구름에 가려질 수도 있으며, 조력 발전은 아직 완전히 개발되지 못했다. 이러한 점에 있어서 수소는 해답이 되는데, 일단 전기 분해로 수소가 생성되면 이를 연료 전지에 저장함으로써 재생 가능한 에너지원이 전력을 생산하지 못하는 기간에도 충분한 전력을 공급받을 수 있다.

전기분해뿐만 아니라 알루미늄 폐기물의 화학 반응에 의해서도 수소가 생산될 수 있다. 이 과정에서 수소와 알루미나가 생성되는데, 알루미나를 재활용하면 알루미늄을 생산할 수 있다. 캐나다의 한 기업이 그러한 과정과 관련된 특허를 보유하고 있다. 수소 기술을 비판하는 사람들은 가소성이 매우 높은 기체인 수소에 내재된 위험성을 경고한다. 생산 과정에서 수소를 안전하게 취급하기 위해서는 새롭고 값비싼 기술이 개발되어야 할 것이다. 여러 해 동안은 대부분의 사람들이 가격 때문에 수소 자동차를 구입하기가 힘들 것이다. 2022년 수소 자동차의 가격은 약 60,000달러이다.

2003년 미국 정부는 수소 연료 전지에 투자함으로써 미국의 해외 석유 의존도를 역전시키기 위한 12억 달러의 수소 연료 계획을 발표했다. 이러한 전지는 승용차 및 트럭의 내연 기관을 대체하게 될 것이다. 의회도 이러한 계획에 필요한 예산을 승인했다.

📝 Summary Note

❶ greenhouse gases

❷ locally

❸ sustainable

❹ combustible

Exercise 5 1 ⓒ 2 Ⓐ 3 Ⓑ 4 ⓒ p.50

로마 제국의 탄생

전설에 의하면 로마는 기원전 753년에 세워졌다. 기원전 509년에는 로마 시민들이 에트루리아 정부를 전복시킨 후 로마 공화정이 설립되었다. 그 후 200년 동안 로마는 이탈리아 반도의 대부분으로 세력을 확장하면서 정복한 도시에 시민권을 부여하고 그에 대한 대가로 도시들에게 로마에 더 많은 병력을 제공할 것을 요구했다. 기원전 275년 무렵, 로마는 이탈리아 반도 전체를 지배하게 되었다.

제국이 되기 위한 로마의 행동은 기원전 1세기와 2세기에 이루어졌다. 로마의 주된 경쟁 상대는 아프리카 북부 해안에 위치해 있던 해상 세력인 카르타고였는데, 로마는 카르타고를 상대로 세 차례의 포니에 전쟁을 치렀다. 결국 로마가 승리를 거두어 아프리카와 스페인 해안에 대한 지배권과 지중해의 수송로 및 무역로를 장악하게 되었다. 또한 로마는 동쪽으로도 세력을 뻗쳐 기원전 133년경 예는 그리스, 마케도니아, 그리고 터키를 손에 넣었다. 로마가 적을 굴복시킬 수 있었던 것은 두 가지 요인 때문이었다. 로마는 이탈리아의 도시들과의 동맹을 맺어 병력을 제공받음으로써 군사력을 유지할 수 있었고, 효율적인 통치를 가능하게 만든 효율적인 정부 체제를 갖추고 있었는데, 이로 인하여 로마인들은 팽창주의적인 목표에 대해 자부심과 확신을 가질 수 있었다.

로마 공화국은 해외에서 거둔 성공만큼 로마 시민들을 뒷받침하지 못함으로써 내부적으로 흔들리기 시작했다. 귀족이라고 불렸던 부유한 로마인들은 번영을 누렸지만, 빈민층 및 평민이라고 불렸던 보통 사람들은 새롭게 얻은 부에서 아무것도 얻지 못했다. 로마 안팎의 갈등으로 내부적인 무력 충돌이 일어났고, 결국 기원전 45년에 스스로를 로마의 유일한 지도자로 선포한 줄리어스 시저를 포함하여, 혼란을 진압하고자 했던 일련의 독재자들이 등장하게 되었다. 기원전 44년에는 공화정의 부흥을 원했던 사람들이 시저를 암살했다. 로마를 장악하기 위한 수년 간의 내전이 벌어진 후 기원전 27년에 시저의 양아들인 옥타비아누스가 로마 초대 황제가 되어 아우구스투스라는 칭호를 받았는데, 이는 라틴어로 '고귀하다'라는 뜻이다. 그가 권력을 차지하면서 팍스 로마나라고 알려진 200년 간의 평화 시대가 시작되었다.

아우구스투스는 로마 제국의 국경 방어를 강화하고 국외 지역에 대한 통치를 계속했는데, 이러한 일은 효율적인 통치를 하는 집정관들을 파견하여 강력한 행정 서비스를 제공함으로써 가능했다. 역사가들이 아우구스투스 황제 시대라고 부르는 그의 통치 기간 동안 예술과 문학이 발전했다. 그는 기원후 14년까지 통치했고, 그 뒤를 이어받은 유능한 황제들이 로마 제국의 전성기를 이끌었다. 하지만 약 160년부터 로마는 북쪽의 게르만족과 동쪽의 파르티아인들로부터 끊임없는 공격을 받기 시작했다. 제국의 거대한 크기 때문에 방어가 점점 더 어려워져서 마침내 476년 로마 제국은 붕괴했다.

📝 Summary Note

❶ a republic

❷ three wars

❸ 44 B.C.

❹ 476 A.D.

Exercise 6   1 ⓓ   2 ⓐ   3 ⓑ   4 ⓓ   p.52

해석

존 메이너드 케인즈

1930년대 대공황이 일어나기 전 고전주의 경제학은 자유방임주의를 설파했다. 이 이론에 따르면 경제에서 정부는 어떠한 역할도 맡아서는 안 되었다. 이는 규제가 없는 시장으로 인해 경제가 완전 고용, 고임금, 그리고 낮은 인플레이션을 향해 나아갈 것이라고 예측했다. 하지만 1929년에 시작된 공황으로 그러한 비개입주의의 오류가 입증되었다. 경제의 작동 방식에 관한 고전주의의 이론을 뒤엎은 것은 영국의 경제학자인 존 메이너드 케인즈였다. 그가 획기적이었던 것은 경제를 통제하는 정부의 역할을 강조했기 때문이었다. 이러한 관점은 일국 경제의 전체 성과를 살피는 거시 경제학이라는 새로운 분야를 탄생시켰다.

케인즈 이전의 경제적 성과는 지역 단위로 측정되었고, 개별 소비자 및 기업의 행동에 초점이 맞추어져 있었다. 케인즈는 그처럼 편협한 시각 때문에 보다 영향력이 큰, 총소비, 투자, 그리고 정부 규제의 역할이 어떻게 무시되는지를 보여 주었다.

1936년에 나온 그의 역작 고용, 이자 및 화폐의 일반 이론에서 케인즈는 불황의 원인을 분석했다. 그는 불황을 피하기 위해서는 정부가 적극적인 역할을 맡아야 한다고 결론지었다. 그의 전제는 경제 성장률이, 소비자, 기업, 그리고 정부의 총소비로 측정되는, 상품에 대한 총수요에 따라 결정된다는 것이었다. 소비자가

저축을 늘리고 소비를 줄이면 기업의 수입이 감소해서 기업은 소비와 투자를 줄이게 된다. 이러한 총소비의 감소로 경제가 불황에 빠질 수 있다. 경제를 회복시키기 위해서는 소비가 증가해야 한다.

케인즈는 경제 불황을 막기 위해 정부가 지출을 늘리고 이자율을 낮추어야 한다고 주장했다. 그러면 기업과 소비자들이 대출을 받기가 쉬워지는데, 이는 또다시 소비를 증가시킬 수 있다. 그 결과 소비재에 대한 수요가 늘어나서 투자가 이루어지고 고용률이 증가할 것이다. 케인즈의 주장에 따르면, 수요를 자극하고 고용률을 증가시킬 수 있는 또 다른 정부 정책은 정부가 사람들을 고용해서 공공사업에 투입시키는 것이었다. 이러한 아이디어는 프랭클린 루즈벨트 대통령의 뉴딜 정책의 철학적 배경이 되었던 것으로 생각된다. 이 프로그램의 핵심은 연방 정부가 지원하는 건설 공사와, 불황으로 피해를 입은 미국인들을 다시 일할 수 있게 만든 문화 프로그램이었다.

케인즈주의 경제학은 현대 경제학의 관리 방침으로 남아 있다. 하지만 케인즈의 가정 중 일부는 잘못된 것으로 밝혀졌다. 그는 고용이 확대되면 노동 생산성이 감소한다고 가정했다. 하지만 경험적 연구에 따르면 그와 반대되는 관계가 나타난다. 또한 고용이 증가하면 실질 임금이 감소할 것이라고 예상했는데, 이것도 잘못되었다. 그리고 그는 인플레이션이 완전 고용에 근접한 상황에서만 발생한다고 생각했다. 하지만 역사적으로 볼 때 인플레이션은 스태그플레이션이라고 알려진 실업률이 높은 상황에서도 발생할 수 있다.

📝 Summary Note

❶ macroeconomics

❷ more money

❸ public-works projects

❹ New Deal

Building Summary Skills   p.54

Exercise 1   The Mechanics of Flight

Four forces combine to make airplane flight possible. Lift enables a plane to take off and stay in the air. Weight offsets lift and must be overcome by lift in order to keep the plane in flight. Thrust moves the plane forward. Drag is air resistance that slows the plane down. The pilot must precisely manage each force in order to take off, change direction and speed, or land.

Exercise 2   Furniture in Colonial America

Early American settlers had to focus on survival, leaving them no time for furniture design. As they prospered, they turned to making plainly designed furniture that was suited to their small homes. Colonial furniture is valued today because it was made from the finest quality wood. It was handmade with simple designs that would fit in the small colonial houses. Many artisans were influenced by the work of English furniture maker Thomas Chippendale. Today, colonial furniture is expensive and in great demand, creating a market in reproductions.

Exercise 3 Economic Bubbles

Economic bubbles may happen when assets suddenly rise in value, often to great heights. However, they also decline in value very swiftly, making people lose money. Tulip Mania in the Netherlands from 1634 to 1637 was a bubble that saw the prices of tulip bulbs rise incredibly high and then decline. The Dot-Com Bubble in the 1990s was an economic bubble connected to Internet-related companies. Most economic bubbles follow certain patterns that people are able to detect.

Exercise 4 Hydrogen Technology

Hydrogen technology may be a good replacement for fossil fuels as a source of energy. It causes less pollution, can be produced locally, and can be stored in fuel cells. Sources of hydrogen include water, methane, gasoline, coal, and wind and solar energy, but hydrogen technology is expensive and will not be affordable for many years. In 2003, the U.S. government announced a plan to invest in hydrogen-powered fuel cells.

Exercise 5 The Rise of the Roman Empire

The Roman Republic was established in 509 B.C. It extended its control over the Italian peninsula and, eventually, the major powers bordering the Mediterranean Sea. Its initial success was due to its ability to use the cities it conquered as a source of manpower for its armies. And it held onto power by establishing an efficient system of government. But it declined when it was unable to govern its own citizens. The unrest led to the start of the Roman Empire in 27 B.C. with Augustus as the first emperor. The empire lasted until 476 A.D.

Exercise 6 John Maymard Keynes

John Maynard Keynes proposed that governments should take more active roles in the economy. He believed that governments could avoid depressions by increasing spending and lowering interest rates. He also favored public-works projects to lower unemployment. President Franklin Roosevelt used that strategy to help the United States out of the Great Depression. Keynes's belief that inflation occurs only in times of high employment has been proved incorrect.

Mini TOEFL iBT Practice Test
p.56

1 C 2 D 3 A 4 B 5 C

6 B 7 A 8 3, 4, 6

9 D 10 A 11 D 12 C 13 A

14 B 15 **1** 16 Pottery as Art: 2, 4, 7

Pottery as Tools: 1, 5

해석

[1-8]

미국 식민지 시대의 신문

미국 식민지 시대의 최초의 신문은 1690년 보스턴에서 발행되었다. *퍼블릭 어커런시스: 국제 및 국내 소식*이라는 신문이었다. 그러나 이 신문은 단 한 번만 발행된 후 영국에 의해 폐간되었다. 14년이 지난 뒤 두 번째 신문이 등장했는데, 이는 *보스턴 뉴스레터*라는 이름의 주간지였다.

초기 신문에는 다른 신문들, 특히 런던에서 발행된 신문에서 가져온 기사 외에는 실린 내용이 거의 없었다. 그 결과 편집자들은 선장들이 유럽에서 신문을 가져다 줄 때까지 기다려야 했기 때문에 대부분의 뉴스가 수 개월 전의 것들이었다. 이러한 선장들은 직접 목격한 자연 재해를 설명해 주고 멀리서 일어난 사건들을 전해 듣고서 이를 알려 주기도 했기 때문에 때때로 뉴스 정보원이 되기도 했다. 일부 뉴스는 식민지 전역에 있는 서신 기자들로부터 입수되었는데, 이들은 자신의 지역에서 발생하는 사건을 전해 주었다.

제임스 프랭클린은 신문을 사회적 및 정치적 논평의 수단으로 바라본 최초의 편집자였다. 벤자민 프랭클린의 형이기도 했던 제임스 프랭클린은 *뉴잉글랜드 커런트*를 발행했다. 그와 그의 친구들은 시사 문제 및 지역 사회에 관한 해학과 풍자가 넘치는 기사를 썼는데, 이로써 많은 사람들의 분노를 사기도 했지만 신문이 오락적인 매체가 될 수 있었다.

하지만 18세기 초의 편집자들은 언론의 자유를 누리지 못했다. 예를 들면 제임스 프랭클린은 영국 정부를 비판하는 사설을 써서 감옥에 수감되었다. 석방된 후에는 신문을 발행하는 일이 금지되었다. 하지만 13살이었던 그의 남동생 벤자민이 신문 발행과 배달 업무를 맡았고, 얼마 후 형을 대신해 편집장이 되었다. 프랭클린은 1729년에 인수한 신문인 *펜실베이니아 가제트*를 발행하기 위해 펜실베이니아로 떠났다. 프랭클린은 이 신문에 자신의 재치와 풍자를 담아 냈고, 일상 생활에 대한 재미있고 때로는 날카로운 통찰력을 보여 주는 가상의 인물들을 만들어 냈다.

식민지 시대에는 신문사 사무실에 보통 사주와 견습생 두 사람밖에 없었다. 견습생은 신문을 만드는 일을 배우기 위해 사주와 함께 살면서 일을 했다. 견습 기간은 보통 12살에서 21살까지였다. 사주는 견습생을 개인 소유물로 생각해서 이들을 가혹하게 대하는 경우가 많았다. 당시 신문에는 달아난 견습생을 알려 주면 보상을 하겠다는 광고들이 빼곡했다. 견습생이 21살이 되고 충분한 돈을 모아둔 경우에는 자신의 신문사를 차릴 수 있었다. 여성은 견습생이 될 자격이 없었다.

1440년 구텐베르크가 금속 활자를 발명한 후 인쇄기는 그다지 발전하지 못했다. 식민지 시대의 신문들은 지레로 작동되는 나사로 인쇄기 반대에 압반을 내리는 방식의 목판 인쇄기에서 인쇄되었다. 견습생이 나무 막대 끝에 있는 공 모양의 양모로 목판 활자에 잉크를 발랐다. 압반을 내리는 작업은 매번 손으로 해야 했는데, 가장 빠른 경우 한 시간에 200번 정도 찍어 내는 작업을 할 수 있었다.

1750년대 중반 신문들은 영국의 지배에 대한 커져가는 적개심을 표출하며 독립에 대한 열망을 자극하는데 있어서 중요한 역할을 담당하기 시작했다. 예전에는 팜플렛으로 배포되었던 의견들이 신문에서 자리를 찾기 시작했다. 1776

년 7월 4일 서명된 독립 선언서는 이틀 뒤 *필라델피아 이브닝 포스트*에 실렸다. 1789년 제헌 의회의 몇몇 지도자들, 즉 제임스 매디슨, 알렉산더 해밀턴, 그리고 존 제이는 두 신문에 *연방주의자 기고 모음집*을 발표흠으로써 자신들의 견해에 대한 대중들의 지지를 얻고자 했다.

[9-16]
애리조나의 고대 인디언들의 도기

오늘날 애리조나주에 해당하는 지역의 아메리카 인디언은 기원전 약 25,000년에 처음 북아메리카에 도착했다. 이들은 아시아에서 알래스카의 베링 해협을 건너 해안가를 따라 현재의 캘리포니아, 애리조나, 그리고 멕시코에 해당되는 곳까지 내려왔다. 이 부족들은 약 2천 년 전까지 유목 생활을 하다가 이후 농사를 짓기 시작했다. 한 곳에 정착한 후에는 도기를 만드는 기술을 익혔다. 도기 유물은 고대 인디언들의 시대 및 생활 방식에 대한 중요한 실마리를 제공해 주는데, 그 이유는 이들이 손상되지 않고 남아 있는 유일한 유물인 경우가 많기 때문이다. 불에 구운 점토는 시간이 지나도 상태가 나빠지지 않는다.

인디언들이 어떻게 그리고 왜 도기 만드는 법을 알게 되었는지는 아무도 모른다. [학자들은 여러 가지 설명을 내놓고 있다.] 그러한 발견이 우연에 의한 것이었다는 이론이 가장 널리 인정받고 있다. 인디언들은 자신이 엮은 바구니에 진흙을 발랐다. 그들은 바구니를 불 위에 두고 그 안에 들어 있는 옥수수나 다른 곡식을 말렸다. 열을 가하는 과정에서 점토가 단단해졌다. 그래서 인디언들은 점토로 형태를 만들고 이를 불 위에서 구운 다음 식히면 영구적인 형태가 만들어진다는 점을 알게 되었다. 이 이론에 대한 근거는 고대의 여러 도자기에서 찾아볼 수 있는 천 자국인데, 이는 천으로 만들어진 바구니를 가운데 두고 도자기의 형태를 잡았을 것이라는 점을 암시한다.

최초의 도기들은 집안일에 사용되었고, 이를 예술 작품으로 만들려는 시도는 전혀 없었다. 농사가 시작되면서 씨앗과 곡식을 저장하고 음식을 담을 그릇이 필요했다. 또한 도기는 불에 닿아도 부서지지 않았기 때문에 요리용 냄비로도 사용되었다. 이러한 초기의 도기들은 문양을 가지고 있지 않았고 비대칭적이었다. 하지만 애리조나의 고대 인디언들은 결국 상징과 삽화로 도기를 장식하기 시작했다. 장식의 의미가 항상 현대 학자들에게 분명한 것은 아니며, 인디언들은 그 의미를 외부인들에게 설명하는 것을 꺼렸다. 하지만 고고학자들은 삽화들이 인디언의 전통, 역사, 의식, 그리고 전설을 반영했다는 점을 알고 있다. 일반적인 주제로는 새, 사슴, 물소, 인간, 그리고 신을 들 수 있으며, 도기는 보통 종교적인 행사 및 장례식에서 사용되었다.

인디언들은 바퀴의 이점을 알고서 이를 운송 수단 및 도구로 사용했지만, 돌림판을 만들지는 않았다. 그들은 감아 올리면서 빚는 방식의 수고스러운 방법으로 도기를 제작했다. 한 가지 이론에 따르면, 그들은 손으로 직접 작업하는 방식, 즉 보다 자연과 조화를 이루는 방식을 선호했기 때문에 의도적으로 돌림판을 사용하지 않았다고 한다.

애리조나 인디언들은 조상들이 물려 준 비밀 장소에서 점토를 채취했다. 도기가 만들어지면 표면을 매끄럽게 한 후 식물을 물에 끓이거나 암석을 곱게 갈아서 만든 염료로 채색을 했다. 붓은 잔가지 끝을 이빨로 씹어서 만들었다. 도기를 제작한 애리조나 최초의 부족 중 하나는 호호캄족으로, 이들은 기원후 약 200년경부터 존재했다. 이들의 도기는 붉고 누런 빛깔, 기하학적 무늬, 그리고 추상적으로 표현된 뱀, 물고기, 그리고 제식 무용 그림으로 식별할 수 있다. 또 다른 부족인 아나사지 인디언들은 흑백 디자인을 사용했다. 이들의 도기에서는 대칭적이고 독특한 형태, 그리고 수학적으로 반복되는 문양들이 특징이다. 아나사지인들의 도기의 전통은 400년부터 1500년까지 이어졌다.

950년경 밈브레스 인디언들이 특이하고 덜 사실적인 양식을 채택함으로써 애리조나 부족들의 예술 방식에 커다란 변화가 나타났다. 밈브레스 인디언들은 자신들의 신화, 전설, 그리고 역사를 나타내기 위해 인간과 동물의 모습을 하나

로 통합했는데, 이로써 종종 학자들도 해독할 수 없는 재미있는 장면들이 그려졌다.

UNIT 03 Factual Information

Basic Drill   p.66

Drill 1 1 ⓑ   2 ⓐ

해석

존 스미스와 제임스타운 식민지

1606년 영국의 제임스 1세는 버지니아를 식민지로 만들기 위해 세 척의 배를 보냈다. 여기에는 두 가지 목적이 있었다. 보물을 발견하는 것과 아메리카 인디언들에게 기독교를 전파하는 것이었다. 1607년에 배가 버지니아에 도착하자 개척자들은 제임스타운을 식민지로 선택했고, 존 스미스가 국왕에 의해 그곳 지도자 중 한 명으로 임명되었다. 제임스타운은 물이 깨끗하지 않은 늪지대에 위치해 있었기 때문에 제임스타운 식민지는 생존을 위한 사투를 벌여야 했다. 105명의 정착민 중 약 3분의 2가 말라리아, 영양 실조, 그리고 이질로 사망했다. 스미스의 강력한 지도력 덕분에 식민지는 한동안 단합이 되었다. 하지만 식민지 주민들은 인디언들과 끊임 없는 전쟁을 치러야 했고, 1609년에는 스미스가 전투에서 부상을 당해 영국으로 돌아가야만 했다. 식민지 주민들은 스스로 식량을 생산하는 법을 배우고 환금 작물인 담배를 발견함으로써 1600년대에 살아남을 수 있었다.

Drill 2 1 ⓒ   2 ⓐ

해석

누진세

소득세는 누진세이거나 단일세이다. 단일세는 개인이 버는 금액에 비례하기 때문에 소득 수준에 상관 없이 세율이 일정하다. 하지만 누진세의 경우, 세율은 소득에 따라 증가한다. 더 높은 세율이 정당화되는 이유는 단일세의 불평등을 피할 수 있기 때문이다. 이러한 불평등은 모든 사람들이 동일한 세율로 세금을 내면 부유한 사람이 저소득자보다 더 적은 퍼센트의 세금을 내기 때문에 발생한다. 소득이 적은 사람일수록 소득의 더 많은 부분을 의식주와 같은 필수품에 사용하기 때문에 그러한 일이 일어나는 것이다. 부유한 납세자들의 경우 동일한 필수품에 대한 비용을 지불한 후에도 남아 있는 소득이 더 많기 때문에 이를 저축, 사치

품 구입, 그리고 여가 생활에 쓸 수 있다. 누진세에 숨겨져 있는 원칙은 세금을 더 많이 낼 능력이 있는 사람들에게 더 큰 부담을 지운다는 것이다.

Drill 3 1 ⓓ 2 ⓐ, ⓑ

해석

고대 이집트의 회화

이집트 회화는 약 5천 년 전 비옥한 나일 계곡을 중심으로 발달한 문명에서 시작되었다. 극도로 건조했던 기후 덕분에 많은 고대 이집트 회화가 오늘날까지 보존될 수 있었다. 회화는 사후 세계에서 죽은 사람과 같이 있기 위해 만들어졌기 때문에 죽은 사람이 매장된 무덤에 그려졌다. 화가는 망자가 잘 아는 사람들과 장소를 보고 편안함을 느낄 수 있도록 그 사람이 살았던 시대를 정확히 묘사하려고 노력했다. 또한 내세로 가는 여정과 그곳에서 만나게 될 신들도 주제에 포함되었다. 이집트 사회는 매우 종교적이어서 많은 회화들이 신과 여신뿐만 아니라 신으로도 여겨졌던 최고 통치자, 즉 파라오들도 묘사했다. 회화 양식에 있어서는 정돈된 느낌을 나타나기 위해 명확하고 단순한 선과 형태가 사용되었다.

Drill 4 1 ⓐ 2 ⓒ

해석

호주와 대륙 이동설

2백만 년 전 사실상 지구의 모든 육지는 판게아라고 불리는 하나의 땅 덩어리로 이루어져 있었다. 지질학적 연구에 따르면 약 1억 8천만 년에서 1억 6천만 년 전에 지구의 지각은 여러 개의 판으로 쪼개져 서로 다른 방향으로 이동을 했다. 이처럼 지구가 대륙으로 나뉘어진 과정을 대륙 이동이라고 부른다. 약 6천 5백만 년 전 호주는, 남극, 남아메리카, 그리고 아프리카와 함께, 땅 덩어리의 남반구에서 떨어져 나오기 시작했다. 그 후 1억 년 동안 호주는 나머지 두 대륙과 붙어있었다. 그러나 약 4천 5백만 년 전에 이들과 떨어졌다. 호주가 다른 대륙들과 떨어져 있었다는 점은 호주의 동식물들이 특이하다는 점을 설명해 준다. 건조한 평원 및 산과 같은 호주의 다양한 지리적 특성들 또한 대륙 이동 시에 생긴 대변동의 결과이다. 호주는 오늘날에도 해마다 약 10밀리미터의 속도로 북쪽으로 이동하고 있다.

Exercises with Long Passages

Exercise 1 1 ⓑ 2 ⓐ 3 ⓑ 4 ⓐ   p.68

해석

다다이즘

다다이즘은 1916년 스위스 취리히에서 시작된 문화 저항 운동이었다. 이는 전통적인 사회 가치, 특히 이성과 논리에 대한 반항으로 간주되었는데, 다다이스트들은 그러한 가치들이 도덕적으로 파산했다고 생각했으며, 그로 인해 세계는 파괴적인 1차 세계 대전을 겪게 되었다. 그들의 해답은 무정부주의와 비이성을 수용하는 것이었다. 이들은 결함 있는 가치 체계를 파괴함으로써 보다 인간적인 세계관으로 인도되는 새로운 체계를 만들 수 있다고 믿었다.

이 운동은 1916년 휴고 발이 취리히에 있는 카페 볼테르에서 최초의 다다이즘 선언문을 낭독하면서 시작되었다. 이들은 문화에 대한 확신이 없어졌다고 선언하고 기존 질서를 파괴해서 재건할 것을 맹세했다. 다다이스트들은 공격적이거나 충격적인 예술 및 문학 작품을 만들어서 대중에게 충격을 가하는 것으로 자신들의 운동을 시작했다. 이들은 반예술 작품들로 자신들을 표현했는데, 이는 그들이 미학을 무시하고, 아무런 내재적 의미를 갖고 있지 않으며, 그리고 반칙을

조장하려 한다는 점을 의미했다.

운동이 절정기에 달했던 1916년에서 1920년 사이, 다다이즘은 유럽 전역에 퍼져서 다다이즘적인 견해를 표출하는 창구 역할을 하던 다수의 간행물에 영향을 끼쳤다. 가장 영향력이 컸던 다다이스트는 프랑스 조각가인 마르셀 뒤샹이었다. 그는 자신이 기성품이라고 불렀던, 즉 자전거 바퀴나 새장과 같은 일상용품들을 예술 작품으로서 전시했다. 예술은 어떤 심오한 메시지를 전달해야 한다는 사고를 조롱하겠다는 것이 그의 의도였다. 뒤샹의 가장 유명한 작품은 소변기인 *샘*이었다. 1917년 뒤샹이 이 작품을 처음 선보였을 때 예술계는 이를 거부했다. 하지만 나중에 이 작품은 다다이즘 운동을 탁월하게 나타낸 작품으로 유명해졌다. 2004년에는 "현대 미술 작품 중 가장 영향력이 큰 작품"으로 선정되어 영국에서 상을 받았다.

1차 세계 대전 후 뒤샹을 비롯한 많은 다다이스트들이 뉴욕에서 활동했는데, 뒤샹은 미국인 예술가인 맨 레이가 포함된 무리에 합류하게 되었다. 이들의 작품 중 대부분은 뉴욕의 유명 사진작가인 알프레드 스티글리츠에 의해 촬영되었다. 보다 진지했던 유럽의 다다이즘과 달리, 뉴욕의 다다이즘은 유머와 아이러니를 이용하여 전통적인 가치에 대한 거부감을 표현했다. 1920년대 중반 다다이즘 운동은 독창성을 잃어버리고 초현실주의 및 사회주의 리얼리즘을 비롯한 다른 문화적 흐름에 흡수되었다. 2차 세계 대전 당시에는 유럽의 많은 다다이스트들이 미국으로 건너갔다. 히틀러의 강제 수용소에서 죽음을 맞이한 이들도 있었다. 히틀러는 그들의 작품을 "타락한 예술"이라고 비난했다.

다다라는 단어의 기원은 불분명하다. 어떤 이들은 이것이 아무런 의미가 없는 말이라고 말한다. 루마니아어로 "맞아, 맞아"를 뜻하는 *다, 다*에서 유래했다고 말하는 사람들도 있다. 또 다른 견해는 다다이즘의 창시자들이 이 용어를 불어 사전에서 골랐다고 한다. *다다*라는 단어는 불어에서 아이들이 타고 노는 장난감 목마를 뜻한다.

📝 Summary Note

❶ reason and logic
❷ 1916 to 1920
❸ Marcel Duchamp
❹ surrealism

Exercise 2 1 ⓒ 2 ⓐ 3 ⓑ 4 ⓒ   p.70

해석

간헐천

간헐천은 특이한 종류의 뜨거운 지하 온천으로서 주기적으로 뜨거운 물과 증기를 공중으로 내뿜는다. 간헐천은 매우 드문 편인데, 그 이유는 지구의 극소수 지역에서만 존재하는 독특한 지질학적 조건이 요구되기 때문이다. 오늘날 발견되는 간헐천은 1,000개 정도로, 그 가운데 절반이 미국의 옐로스톤 국립 공원에 존재한다.

표층수가 지하로 흘러 들어가서 마그마, 즉 화산의 용융암에 의해 데워진 암석에 닿으면 온천이 만들어진다. 뜨거운 물이 지하 암석층 사이의 틈을 뚫고 지표면으로 올라온다. 올라오는 물이 지하수와 지표면을 연결하는 좁은 통로 안으로 들어가면 이 물은 간헐천의 일부가 된다. 물은 지표면으로 나오면서 식는데, 이로써 아래쪽의 더 뜨거운 물에 하방 압력이 가해지게 된다. 뜨거운 물은 지하의 단단한 암석층에 막혀서 빠져나갈 곳이 없다. 그 결과, 물에 압력과 열기가 더해져 물이 가열됨으로써 물 온도가 약 95.6도까지 올라간다.

끓는 물은 지표면으로 이어진 분출구를 통해 밖으로 나온다. 이렇게 물이 빠져나가면 아래쪽 물에 가해지는 압력이 낮아져서 과열된 물이 분출구 밖으로 빠

져나오게 되는데, 이로써 간헐천의 최종 산출물로 여겨지는 물줄기가 나타난다. 물줄기는 몇 분 동안에 걸쳐 나타날 수도 있다. 마침내 이처럼 압력이 방출되면 남아 있는 물이 식어서 그 온도가 끓는점 아래로 내려가고, 지하수가 다시 지하로 스며들면서 분출은 끝이 난다. 이러한 사이클은 예측이 가능한 간격을 두고 계속 반복된다.

간헐천은 두 종류가 있다. 분수형 간헐천은 물웅덩이에서 분출하는 간헐천으로 이때는 보통 연속적으로 격렬하게 물이 터져 나오지만, 원추형 간헐천의 경우 간헐석이라고 하는 광물 퇴적 더미에서 물이 분출된다. 이때는 몇 초에서부터 몇 분까지 꾸준하게 물이 분출된다. 가장 유명한 간헐천은 옐로스톤 국립 공원에 있는 원추형 간헐천으로, 이는 올드 페이스풀이라고 알려져 있다. 이 간헐천은 평균적으로 약 74분마다 물을 분출하는데, 이러한 규칙성 때문에 그와 같은 이름이 붙여졌다. 분출은 1.5분에서 5분사이에 이루어지며, 분출 시 물기둥의 높이는 100피트에서 180피트 사이이다.

간헐천이 희소한 이유는 간헐천 형성에 필요한 조건들이 특이하다는 점에 있다. 간헐천을 지표면으로 이끄는 통로의 벽을 만들고 이를 강화시키는 광물 퇴적층이 형성되기 위해서는 화산암이 뜨거운 물에 용해되어야 한다. 분출구에 어떠한 방해물이라도 있으면 간헐천이 사라질 수도 있다. 예를 들어 사람들이 버린 쓰레기와 잔해 때문에 많은 간헐천이 사라진 경우도 있고, 인근 발전소들이 간헐천의 물을 다른 곳으로 흘려 보냄으로써 사라진 간헐천도 있다.

📝 Summary Note

❶ underground spring
❷ heated rock
❸ cone geysers
❹ 74 minutes

Exercise 3 1 Ⓐ 2 Ⓐ 3 Ⓐ, Ⓑ 4 Ⓒ p.72

해석

공공 사업 촉진국

1930년대 미국의 대공황 기간 동안 많은 공장들이 문을 닫아야 했고 이로 인해 수백만 명이 일자리를 잃었다. 실업자들은 공적 구조 기금에 의존해야 했다. 1935년 프랭클린 D. 루즈벨트 대통령은 구조 기금을 받는 사람들에게 정부가 지원하는 일자리를 제공하기 위한 공공 사업 진흥국을 설립했다. 이후 공공 사업 촉진국(WPA)으로 이름이 바뀐 이 기관은 루즈벨트의 경제 부흥 계획인 뉴딜 정책에서 가장 규모가 큰 기관이었다.

이 기관의 초대 국장은 해리 L. 홉킨즈였다. 그는 WPA로 3백 5십만 명의 사람들이 일자리를 얻을 것이며, 노동자 한 명당 연간 1200달러가 필요할 것으로 추산했다. 의회는 우선 40억 달러의 예산을 승인했다. 임금은 지역, 현지 임금 수준, 그리고 요구되는 기술 등에 따라 각기 다르게 책정되었다. 노동자 수를 최대한 늘리기 위해 노동 시간은 한 명당 주 30시간 이하로 제한되었다. 당시의 문화를 반영하여 WPA는 아내와 남편이 동시에 일하지 못하도록 했다. 가장은 남성이며, 여성이 일을 하면 남성의 일자리를 빼앗는 꼴이 될 것이라고 생각되었다. 일을 했던 여성들은 보통 바느질 일을 맡아서 병원이나 고아원에서 쓸 옷이나 물건들을 만들었다.

WPA가 제공했던 일자리들은 대부분 정부 건물, 공항, 다리, 국립 공원, 고속도로, 댐, 하수도, 도서관, 그리고 레크리에이션 시설과 같은 공공 시설의 건설과 관련된 것이었지만, WPA는 또한 연방 예술 프로젝트, 연방 작가 프로젝트, 그리고 연방 연극 프로젝트를 통해 문화 산업에도 지원을 했다. 일자리를 잃었던 많은 배우들과 작가들이 갑자기 자신의 재능을 발휘할 수 있는 기회를 얻게 되었다. 화가들은 공공 건물의 벽화를 그리는 일을 맡았고, 작가들은 주와 지역의 안

내 책자를 만드는 일자리를 얻을 수 있었다. 연방 작가 프로젝트에 참가했던 작가에는 이후 노벨상을 수상한 솔 벨로우도 포함되어 있었다.

흑인들이 특히 WPA의 혜택을 많이 받았으며, 여기에서는 고용 차별이, 개인 고용주에게서 받는 경우보다 심하지 않았다. WPA는 특별히 화이트칼라의 자리에 흑인들을 우선적으로 채용했다. WPA는 보수주의 정치인들로부터 비판을 받았는데, 이들은 이 프로그램으로 인해 공원에서 나뭇잎을 긁어 모으는 것과 같은 불필요하고 하찮은 일에 납세자들의 돈이 낭비되고 있다고 불평했다. 그리고 보다 교육 수준이 높았던 노동자들 중 다수는 좌파적인 혹은 공산주의적인 성향을 가지고 있었다. 비판가들은 또한 프로젝트 및 기금의 배정에 종종 정치권의 영향이 미친다고 주장했다. 그들의 주장에 따르면, 루즈벨트 대통령을 지지하는 의회 지도자들은 자신들의 지역에 더 많은 WPA 일자리를 배정받을 가능성이 컸다.

WPA의 영향력은 1940년 무렵에 감소하기 시작했다. 1941년 미국이 2차 세계 대전에 참전하면서 공장의 고용률이 증가했고, 이 기관의 필요성이 줄어들었다. WPA는 1943년에 폐쇄되었다.

📝 Summary Note

❶ Great Depression
❷ 30
❸ public-works projects
❹ waste of tax money

Exercise 4 1 Ⓑ 2 Ⓑ 3 Ⓐ 4 Ⓒ p.74

해석

프레스코화

프레스코는 마르지 않은 회벽에 직접 안료를 칠하는 기법이다. 프레스코라는 말은 "신선하다"라는 뜻을 가진 이탈리아어인 아프레스코에서 유래된 것이다. 프레스코화는 마르지 않은 회반죽에 그린 부온 프레스코화일 수도 있고, 마른 회반죽에 그린 세코 프레스코화일 수도 있다. 세코 프레스코는 일반적으로 마무리 손질을 하거나 마른 부온 프레스코화의 잘못된 부분을 수정하기 위해 사용된다.

화가는 아리치오라고 불리는 마른 회반죽으로 된 거친 바탕에 구성물의 윤곽을 그려서 프레스코화를 그릴 준비를 한다. 이러한 스케치는 종종 시노피아라는 붉은 염료로 이루어진다. 그런 다음 인토나코라고 불리는, 마르지 않은 두 번째 회반죽 층을 바른다. 그 후에는 이 맨 위 층을 매끄럽게 만들어 채색할 준비를 마친다.

그 다음에는 화가가 종이를 꺼내서 그 위에 밑그림을 그리거나 본인이 그리려고 하는 대상을 실물 크기로 드로잉한다. 마르지 않은 인토나코에 밑그림을 대고 밑그림을 가이드 삼아 색칠을 하기 시작한다. 물감은 석회수에 갈아 넣은 분말 염료로 만들어진다. 마르지 않은 회반죽이 염료를 흡수하면 염료는 회반죽과 함께 건조된다. 회반죽의 화학 성분이 회반죽과 염료를 결합시키기 때문에 아무런 접합제도 필요하지 않다. 매끄러운 석회의 광택은 색채를 돋보이게 만드는 풍부한 질감을 만들어 낸다.

부온 프레스코화는 회반죽이 마르기 전에 작업을 끝낼 수 있도록 작업 시간을 계산해야 하기 때문에 어려운데, 젖은 회반죽은 약 10시간에서 12시간이 지나면 건조된다. 일반적으로 화가는 한 시간 후에 작업을 시작해서 회반죽이 완전히 건조되기 약 2시간 전까지 작업을 계속한다. 그렇기 때문에 화가는 미리 작업 계획을 세워서 그림을 부분으로 나누고 한 번에 어떤 부분을 작업할 것인지 결정해야 한다. 화가가 하루에 작업할 수 있는 면적을 조르나타라고 부르는데, 이는 "일일 작업량"을 뜻한다. 벽 하나가 여러 개의 조르나타로 이루어질 수도 있으며, 이들은 섞여서 하나로 보이기 때문에 처음에 보면 눈에 잘 띄지 않는다. 하지만 수

백 년이 지나면 각각의 부분들이 서로 구분되어 보일 수도 있다.

*조르나타*가 마르면, 날카로운 도구를 사용해 마른 회반죽을 제거하거나 젖은 회반죽을 또 다시 바르지 않는 이상, 수정은 불가능하다. 사소한 수정은 세코 기법으로 가능한데, 이 경우 염료를 벽에 접착시키기 위해 달걀과 같은 접합제가 필요하다. 때때로 *조르나타* 사이의 경계를 덮어 버리기 위해 *세코* 프레스코 기법을 쓰기도 하며, 이러한 경계는 시간이 지나면 사라진다.

프레스코는 이집트 무덤 벽화에서 처음으로 발견되었고, 여기에서는 세코 기법이 사용되었던 반면에 로마인들은 부온 프레스코 기법을 사용했다. 프레스코화의 표현력은 이탈리아 르네상스 시대에 가장 뛰어났으며, 최고의 사례는 미켈란젤로가 시스티나 성당 천장에 그린 프레스코화이다.

📝 **Summary Note**

❶ Buon fresco
❷ red pigment
❸ the secco
❹ Michelangelo

Exercise 5   1 Ⓓ   2 Ⓒ   3 Ⓒ   4 Ⓐ   p.76

해석

그레이트 베이슨 제곱

그레이트 베이슨은 미국 서부에 있는 200,000제곱마일의 사막 지역이다. 이곳은 고원 지대로서 유타 및 네바다주의 상당 부분과 이웃 주들의 일부 지역에 걸쳐 있는 산맥 사이에 위치해 있다. 가장 가까운 바다인 태평양으로 이어지는 출구가 없기 때문에 베이슨, 즉 물을 담고 있는 경사진 분지라고 불린다.

그레이트 베이슨을 둘러싸고 있는 지역의 지질학적 명칭은 베이슨 앤드 레인지 프로빈스이다. 이 지역에는 역사적으로 효율적인 배수 시스템 역할을 해 온 지하 단층이 있다. 마지막 빙하기 당시 이 지역에는 거대한 호수들이 곳곳에 있었지만, 현재는 호수들이 말라 버려서 본빌 솔트 플랫과 같은 광활한 평지가 나타났는데, 여기에서는 자동차 경주가 열리고 있다. 비와 눈은 건조한 사막 기후에서 빠르게 증발한다. 증발하지 않은 강우는 지하로 스며들거나, 서서히 말라 버리는, 일시적으로 생기는 호수에 모인다. 물의 흐름 또한 이 지역을 둘러싸고 있는 산맥에 의해 차단된다. 따라서 이 지역으로 유입된 물은 바다로 연결되는 강이나 시내를 따라서 빠져나갈 수가 없다. 이런 내부적인 배수 시스템 때문에 그레이트 베이슨에서 건조한 기후가 유지되는 것이다.

지질학자들은 그레이트 베이슨에서 균열과 팽창의 과정이 나타나고 있으며, 이로 인해 시간이 지남에 따라 최상층이 점점 얇아지고 있다고 주장한다. 그들은 이러한 힘들로 인해 결국에는 그레이트 베이슨이 계곡 중 하나를 따라 쪼개져서 해양으로 이어지는 수로가 열릴 것으로 예상한다. 그레이트 베이슨에서 찾아볼 수 있는 야생 동물로는 산토끼, 코요테, 다람쥐, 산림쥐, 그리고 퓨마를 들 수 있다. 야생마나 당나귀와 같은 외래 동물들도 성공적으로 유입되었다. 대부분의 땅이 초목으로 우거진 방목지이기 때문에, 소떼와 양떼를 기르는 직업이 일반적이다.

약 12,000년 전에 처음으로 사람들이 그레이트 베이슨에 거주하기 시작했다. 유럽인들이 신세계를 발견했을 당시 이 지역에는 쇼숀족 및 유트족과 같은 아메리카 인디언 부족들이 살고 있었다. 1700년대 말에는 스페인 탐험가들이 도착했고, 그 후에는 모피 사냥꾼들이 이곳에 정착했다.

미국은 두 개의 조약을 통해 이곳 영토를 획득했다. 1846년 오리곤 조약으로 영국은 그레이트 베이슨의 일부 지역에 대한 영토권을 포기했다. 1848년 과달루프 이달고 조약으로 멕시코 전쟁이 끝남으로써 멕시코의 일부였던 땅이 미국

으로 넘어갔다. 처음으로 대규모 정착촌을 건설했던 사람은 몰몬교도들이었는데, 이들이 1840년대 말 솔트 레이크 시티를 세웠다. 1848년 캘리포니아에서 금이 발견된 후 거금을 벌기 위해 수많은 개척자들이 그레이트 베이슨을 거쳐가면서 이 지역의 상당 부분이 개발되기 시작했다. 결국 이 지역은 오늘날 그레이트 베이슨을 형성하고 있는 여러 개의 주로 나뉘었다.

📝 **Summary Note**

❶ high plateau
❷ Bonneville Salt Flats
❸ temporary lakes
❹ 12,000 years ago

Exercise 6   1 Ⓑ   2 Ⓒ   3 Ⓑ   4 Ⓓ   p.78

해석

민족주의

약 1800년까지 전 세계 대다수 지역의 사람들은 자신과 자신의 가족들이 사는 지역에 충성했다. 대부분은 자신들이 보다 큰 주나 국가의 일부라고 생각하지 않았다. 하지만 산업이 발전하고 군대를 양성할 필요성이 생기자 통치자들은 국가 정체성 및 공동의 대의 명분을 확립시키려고 했다. 개인이나 그룹보다 국가의 이익을 우선시하는 이러한 운동은 민족주의라고 알려지게 되었다. 지난 200년 간의 세계사는 새로운 민족 국가로 정치 지도를 다시 그리는 역사였다고 설명할 수 있다.

많은 역사가들은 현대 민족주의의 기원을 1700년대 말 프랑스 혁명에서 찾고 있다. 프랑스 군주제는 공화제로 바뀌었는데, 공화제에서는 시민들이 더 이상 자신을 왕의 백성으로 생각하지 않았다. 오히려 모국인 프랑스라는 추상적인 개념에서 자신의 정체성을 찾았다. 이러한 과정은 그 다음 세기에 유럽 전역에서 되풀이되었다. 2차 세계 대전이 끝나고 오스트리아-헝가리 제국과 오토만 제국이 분열되자 유럽은 독립 국가들의 대륙이 되었다. 그러나 각 민족들의 전통과 언어는 국가 내에서 계속 존중되었다.

민족주의의 철학적 기반은 사회 및 경제 활동에 있어서 국가가 가장 중요한 존재이며, 국가는 기타 인간의 모든 활동과 욕구보다 우선시되어야 한다는 것이다. 국기, 음식, 스포츠, 전통, 역사, 민간 설화, 음악, 문학, 그리고 문화는 국가에 대한 자부심을 높여 준다. 심지어 국교가 있을 수도 있다.

민족주의자들은 공통된 언어, 문화, 그리고 가치관같이 한 국가를 다른 국가와 구분시키는 기준을 언급한다. 이러한 특징들은, 종종 한 국가의 거의 모든 국민들이 속해 있는, 단일 민족에 의해 나타난다. 하지만 많은 국가에서 다양한 민족들이 함께 살고 있는데, 이러한 경우 때때로 폭력적이거나 정치적인 분열을 가져오는 결과가 나타나기도 한다. 유고슬라비아나 소련과 같은 예전 국가들은 민족들의 충돌로 와해되었다. 최근에는 이라크가 오래된 종교 분쟁으로 황폐해지고 있다. 또한 아랍 국가들과 이스라엘 간의 오랜 분쟁도 상대방이 고유한 영토를 가질 수 있는 진정한 국가가 아니라는 주장에서 시작되었다.

일부 민족들은 자신의 국가를 인정하지 않고 대신 분리 독립을 통해 스스로 통치하고자 한다. 캐나다의 퀘벡과 스페인의 바스크 지역의 분리 독립 운동이 여러 해 동안 활발히 이루어졌지만, 아직까지 성공을 거두지는 못했다. 모든 사람이 동일한 언어를 사용하도록 강요하는 것은 국가 정체성을 강화시키는 중요한 수단이었다. 신생국들은 종종 소수 집단의 언어를 법으로 금지하기도 한다. 국가의 언어는 상류층이 사용하는 언어인 경우가 많기 때문에 상류층의 언어가 하류층의 언어를 대체하는 결과가 나타난다.

Building Summary Skills p.80

Exercise 1 Dadaism

Dadaism was a cultural movement that arose at the end of World War I as a protest against reason and logic. Dadaists felt that a more humane world could be created once the traditional system was dismantled. The movement was joined by artists who condemned art that fit the current fashion or conveyed meaning or beauty. They created artworks out of common objects that had no serious artistic message. By the 1920s, Dadaism was absorbed into other cultural movements.

Exercise 2 Geysers

A geyser is a hot underground spring that ejects streams of water and steam. It is formed when water is heated by volcanic rocks and is subjected to pressure from the cooler water above it. The water boils and escapes through passageways in the ground. It erupts into the air in the form of spray. The eruption ends when the water cools. The cycle repeats itself at predictable intervals.

Exercise 3 The Works Projects Administration

The Works Projects Administration (WPA) helped put Americans back to work during the Great Depression. It was created by President Franklin D. Roosevelt and was the largest agency of the New Deal, his economic recovery program. It provided government-funded jobs for those receiving relief payments. Most WPA jobs were on public-works projects, such as bridges, highways, libraries, and dams. But it also funded cultural projects, giving work to writers, actors, and artists.

Exercise 4 Fresco Painting

In buon fresco painting, the artist applies paint directly onto wet plaster. The work is done in four stages: An outline is drawn on dry plaster (*ariccio*); a layer of wet plaster is applied (*intonaco*); the final version is drawn on paper and traced onto a cartoon (*intonaco*); and the artist begins painting with the cartoon as a guide. The paint consists of powdered pigments mixed with lime water, which is easily absorbed by wet plaster. Frescos must be carefully planned and timed so that the work is finished before the plaster dries. Once it dries, no changes can be made until the dried plaster is removed and a fresh layer of wet plaster applied.

Exercise 5 The Great Basin

The Great Basin is a desert plateau mostly in the mountains of Utah and Nevada. It was formed during the last ice age. Humans first populated it 12,000 years ago, and Spanish explorers found Native American Indian tribes there in the 1700s. Its underground drainage system and hot, dry climate prevent water from escaping to the Pacific Ocean. The region was populated in the mid-nineteenth century after the Mormons founded Salt Lake City and gold was discovered in California.

Exercise 6 Nationalism

A sense of national pride, or nationalism, arose around the time of the French Revolution. Industrialization and the need to raise armies led to people identifying themselves as being from a country as opposed to from a tribe or region. Nations are often united by a common language, culture, and values. When a nation includes different ethnic or religious groups, however, political conflict or violence can result.

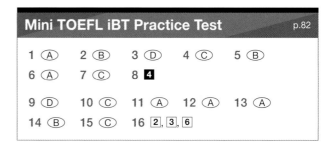

Mini TOEFL iBT Practice Test p.82

1 Ⓐ   2 Ⓑ   3 Ⓓ   4 Ⓒ   5 Ⓑ
6 Ⓐ   7 Ⓒ   8 **4**
9 Ⓓ   10 Ⓒ   11 Ⓐ   12 Ⓐ   13 Ⓐ
14 Ⓑ   15 Ⓒ   16 ②, ③, ⑥

해석

[1-8]

무지당

　1840년대, 미국에서 태어난 일부 미국인들은 두 개의 주요 정당인 민주당과 휘그당이 특히 대도시에서 이민자들의 수를 충분히 제한하지 못하고 있다고 생각했다. 이러한 이민 배척주의자들은 주로 아일랜드 가톨릭 신자였던 이민자들에 의해 자신의 삶이 위협받고 있다고 느꼈다. 이들은 교황 비오 9세가 자신에게 충성하는 사제와 주교들을 임명함으로써 미국을 장악할 것이라는 음모설을 퍼뜨렸다. 그렇게 되면 사제들이 카톨릭 신자들에게 복종을 요구할 것이었다.

　미국에 새로 도착한 이민자들은 뉴욕과 같은 도시에서 민주당을 지지하는 경향이 있었다. 그 수가 늘어나면서 이들의 정치적인 영향력이 커짐에 따라 이민 배척주의자들은 이들이 미국의 최선의 이익을 위해 행동하지 않고 맹목적으로 교황의 명령에 복종할 것이라고 두려워했다. 이민 배척주의 운동으로 인해 1843년 뉴욕에서는 미국 공화당이라고 하는 정당이 창당되었다. 그 영향력이 전국으로 확대되자 1845년에는 당명이 미국 원주민당으로 바뀌었다.

　적극적으로 이민자들의 환심을 사려고 했던 민주당에 불만을 가진 이민 배척주의자들은 비밀 결사를 조직하기 시작했다. 선거일에 이 단체의 회원들은 자신과 견해가 같은 후보자들에게 조용히 지지표를 던졌다. 자신의 비밀 조직에 관한 질문을 받으면 회원들은 "아무것도 몰라요."라고 대답하곤 했다. 그래서 이들은 무지당 당원으로 알려지게 되었다.

이러한 무리는 신규 이민자들의 영향력을 감소시키기 위한 특별법에 찬성했다. 그들은 연간 이민자 수, 특히 카톨릭 국가에서 오는 이민자들의 수를 제한하려고 했다. 이민자들은 공직 선거에 출마해서는 안 된다고 주장했다. 이민자들이 시민권을 얻기 위해서는 21년을 기다려야 한다는 입장에 찬성했다. 일요일에는 주류 판매가 금지되기를 원했다. 그리고 공립 학교의 경우, 개신교 교사들만 고용되어야 하며 교내에서는 개신교판 성경이 읽혀져야 한다고 주장했다. [그러나 그들이 제안한 대부분의 법안은 묵살되었다.]

휘그당의 점진적인 세력 약화에 따른 양당 체제의 붕괴는 무지당이 하나의 정치 세력으로서 부상하게 된 결정적인 원인이 되었다. 휘그당의 몰락으로 무지당에 잠재적 전향자들이 유입되었다. 그리고 이민 배척주의의 분출구가 될 수 있는 당이 필요한 상황이었다. 무지당은 1854년 선거에서 마침내 정치 권력을 획득했다. 범죄와 싸우고, 휴일에 술집 영업을 금지시키고, 그리고 미국에서 태어난 사람들에게만 공직의 기회를 주겠다는 공약을 채택한 이들은 여러 도시에서 시장을 당선시켰고, 일부 주 입법부에 영향력을 행사했으며, 그리고 일부 당원들을 의회에 진출시켰다. 1855년에는 미국당이라는 새로운 당명을 채택했다. 이들은 양당 중 하나였던 민주당과 손을 잡을 것처럼 보였다.

이 운동은 1856년 미 대통령 선거에서 정점에 도달했다. 대통령 후보였던 전직 대통령 밀러드 필모어가 국민 투표에서 22%의 득표율을 얻어 민주당과 공화당에 이어 3위를 차지했다. 그러나 이 당은 얼마 후 노예 문제를 둘러싸고 분열하기 시작했다. 노예제를 찬성하는 사람들은 민주당에 합류했고, 노예제에 반대하는 사람들은 아브라함 링컨이 이끄는 공화당에 합류했다. 1860년 선거에서 미국당은 더 이상 전국적인 정치 세력이 아니었다. 무지 운동은 미국 정치에 관한 두 가지 교훈을 알려 주는데, 이는 역사를 통해 되풀이되어 왔다. 첫째, 민족과 종교에 대한 편견이 종종 정치에 영향을 미친다는 점과, 둘째, 기존 정당들이 사회 격변으로 좌절감을 느낀 사람들에게 발언권을 주지 못하면 정치적 불만이 생긴다는 점이다.

[9-16]
인류의 베링 해협 횡단

현대 인류는 4만 년 전 아프리카에서 처음 살기 시작했다. 이들이 어떻게 아메리카 대륙에 도착했는지는 인류학자들 사이에서 논쟁 거리이다. 오늘날 가장 많이 인정받는 설명은 베링 해협 육교설이다. 하지만 최근에 발견된 증거에 따르면 다른 경로를 통한 이동도 있었을 것으로 생각된다.

베링 해협은 러시아의 시베리아와 캐나다 서쪽 알래스카 사이에 위치한 좁은 통로이다. 1856년 사무엘 헤이븐은 약 2만 년 전 빙하기 당시 물이 빙하에 갇혀 있었을 때에는 해수면이 낮았다는 주장을 내놓았다. 오늘날보다 60미터 가량 해수면이 낮았다. 이로 인해 베링 해협 밑의 땅이 드러났고, 인간과 동물들이 시베리아에서 걸어서 알래스카로 이동할 수 있었다. 이러한 육교의 증거는 해협의 수역에서 채취한 토심으로 확인되었고, 이는 해당 시기에 이 지역이 건조한 평원이었다는 점을 보여 주었다. 또한 크기가 큰 포유류의 잔해가 발견되었는데, 이로써 아시아 부족들은 약 12,000년 전 이 동물들을 쫓아 북아메리카에 들어온 사냥꾼들이었음을 알 수 있다. 사자 및 치타와 같이 아프리카와 아시아가 원산지인 포유 동물들은 이후 북아메리카에서 진화를 해서 오늘날에는 존재하지 않는 종이 되었다. 또한 북아메리카에서 멸종된 북아메리카 케멀리드는 아시아에서 낙타로 진화했다.

고고학적 기록에 따르면 이동은 서쪽에서 동쪽으로 진행되었다. 육교의 폭은 2,000킬로미터 정도였다. 유목 생활을 했던 이들 사냥꾼은 태평양 해안선에 있는 얼음이 없는 길을 따라 알래스카에서 북아메리카로 넘어갔다. 그 후 몇몇 무리들이 동쪽으로 이동해서 로키 산맥을 지나 대서양 해안까지 갔다. 남쪽으로 가서 중앙아메리카와 남아메리카에 도달한 무리들도 있었다. 베링 해협을 건

너간 사람들은 뉴멕시코의 클로비스라는 마을의 이름을 따서 클로비스족이라고 불리는데, 1932년에 이곳에서 그들이 쓰던 창끝이 발견되었다. 클로비스 창끝은 독특한 모양을 하고 있다. 비슷한 모양의 창끝이 미국의 동부 해안과 칠레의 남부 지역에서도 발견되었다. 일부 학자들은 베링 해협을 건넌 클로비스족이 계속해서 북아메리카와 남아메리카의 각지로 이동했다는 이론을 제시한다.

하지만 클로비스족보다 최소한 1,000년 먼저 도착한 사람들이 있었다는 증거들이 발견되고 있다. 이러한 발견으로 인해 몇몇 사람들은 베링 해협 이외의 경로로, 아마도 배를 타고 남태평양을 건너서, 인간이 아메리카 대륙에 거주하게 되었을 것이라고 믿는다. 고고학자들은 25,000년에서 40,000년 전 호주와 일본에서 배가 사용되었다는 증거를 찾아냈다. 이들은 몇몇 사람들이 아메리카 대륙의 해안가까지 항해를 했고, 그 후 아래로 내려가 태평양 해안에 도달했을 수도 있다고 생각한다. 안타깝게도 해안 유적지가 될 수도 있는 곳들이 현재 물속에 잠겨 있기 때문에 고대 항해사들이 남긴 흔적을 찾는 일은 쉽지가 않다.

또한 인간의 뼈를 측정해 보면 다수의 이동 경로가 존재했음을 알 수 있다. 아메리카 원주민들이 경우 아시아인들과 같이 이마가 넓고 광대뼈가 튀어나와 있다. 하지만 폭이 좁은 두개골과 평평한 얼굴 형태를 지닌 뼈들도 발견되었는데, 이는 폴리네시아인이과 유럽인들과 일치하는 부분이다. 분자 유전학 분야에서의 최근 연구에 따르면 아메리카 인디언과 아시아인들의 조상이 동일하다는 점이 확인되었다. 하지만 새로 발견된 DNA 계열에서는 아시아의 영향을 찾아볼 수 없다. 또한 DNA 조사로 아메리카인들은, 고고학적 증거를 통해 알려진 것보다 훨씬 빠른 20,000년 전에, 유전학적으로 시베리아인으로부터 갈라져 나왔다는 점이 밝혀졌다.

Vocabulary Check-Up
p.88

A 1 ⓓ 2 ⓐ 3 ⓒ 4 ⓐ 5 ⓓ
   6 ⓒ 7 ⓑ 8 ⓒ 9 ⓓ 10 ⓐ

B 1 ⓖ 2 ⓙ 3 ⓐ 4 ⓗ 5 ⓑ
   6 ⓘ 7 ⓓ 8 ⓔ 9 ⓕ 10 ⓒ

UNIT 04 Negative Factual Information

Basic Drill
p.92

Drill 1 1 ⓒ 2 ⓐ

해석
미국의 목화 재배

1800년 전 대부분의 미국인들은 모직물이나 리넨으로 만들어진 옷을 입었다. 목화로 실을 만들려면 목화씨를 제거해야 했기 때문에 면직물은 값도 비싸고 노동력도 많이 필요했다. 농장주들은 씨를 제거할 수 있을 만큼의 목화만 생산해야 했지만, 1793년에 엘리 휘트니가 조면기, 즉 목화 섬유로부터 씨를 분리해 내

는 톱니가 달린 기계를 발명했다. 갑자기 한 명의 노동자가 하루에 50파운드의 목화에서 씨를 제거할 수 있게 되었는데, 이는 조면기가 발명되기 전보다 두 배나 많은 양이었다. 이전에는 담배 및 쌀 농사를 지었던 농장들이 목화 농장으로 바뀌면서 목화 생산량은 급증했다. 농장 시스템이 전성기를 맞이한 1850년대에는 남부 주 전체 노예의 75%에 해당되는 약 180만 명의 사람들이 목화 농장에서 일을 하고 있었다. 1850년대는 목화 왕의 10년이라고 알려졌지만, 1860년에 남북 전쟁이 일어나면서 남부 농장주들의 번영은 끝이 났다.

Drill 2   1 ⓓ   2 ⓑ

해석

행성의 위성

태양계에는 행성과 소행성 주위를 도는 290개 이상의 달, 즉 천연 위성들이 존재한다. 가장 큰 위성은 목성과 토성의 위성이며, 그 다음으로는 지구의 달이 가장 크다. 위성들은 자신이 궤도를 그리며 도는 더 큰 천체와 거의 동시에 만들어졌다. 일부 위성들은 탄생 중인 행성으로부터 떨어져 나왔다. 처음에는 소행성이었지만 행성의 인력에 끌려 온 위성들도 있으며, 지구의 달과 같이 다른 천체와 크게 충돌한 후 폭파되어 궤도로 들어오게 된 위성도 있을 수 있다. 지구의 달과 같은 대부분의 위성들은 자전을 하지 않고 조석 고정 상태에 있는데, 이는 한쪽 면이 항상 파트너 행성을 바라보고 있다는 의미이다. 위성이 충분히 크면, 지구의 달이 지구의 해양을 끌어당겨 조수를 일으키는 것과 같이, 위성의 중력이 행성에 영향을 끼친다. 위성은 항성과 달리 스스로 빛을 내지 못하며, 태양빛을 반사시키기 때문에 밤에만 빛나는 것처럼 보인다.

Drill 3   1 ⓐ   2 ⓒ

해석

생화학

생물체 내부의 화학 과정을 연구하는 학문을 생화학이라고 부른다. 유기체는 세포에서 이루어지는 활동을 통해 성장하고 기능한다. 생화학은 단백질, 탄수화물, 지방질, 그리고 핵산과 같은 세포 성분에 초점을 맞춘다. 단백질은 다른 입자와 연결된 일련의 아미노산으로 세포의 성장과 복구를 돕는다. 세포는 효소라고 불리는 특수한 단백질에 의해 통제된다. 탄수화물은 에너지를 저장하고 세포의 구조를 만드는 반면, 지방질에는 왁스, 지방, 그리고 스테로이드와 같은 화합물이 포함되어 있다. 핵산은 유전 정보를 지니고 있는 DNA, 즉 디옥시리보핵산과 RNA, 즉 리보핵산으로 가장 잘 알려져 있다. 최근의 기술 발달로 생화학 분야가 발전함에 따라 과학자들은 세포의 구조와 기능을 보다 명확하게 알아낼 수 있다. 이러한 새로운 기술에는 현미경 관찰법, 색층 분석법, 그리고 방사성 동위원소 표지법이 포함된다. 암 연구는 생화학에서 얻은 단서에 의존한다.

Drill 4   1 ⓒ   2 ⓓ

해석

호피 인디언들의 문화

농업은 호피 문화의 핵심 요소이다. 농사는 생계 수단일 뿐만 아니라 호피 신화의 일부이기도 하다. 호피족은 지구에서 자신들의 시대가 "생명의 네 번째 길"이라고 믿는데, 호피족의 신인 마소가 사람들에게 옥수수를 주었을 때 자신들이 이 길에 들어섰다고 믿는다. 다른 부족들이 앞서서 가장 큰 옥수수들을 가져 갔기 때문에 호피족에게는 가장 작은 옥수수만이 남아 있었다. 그들은 이를 호피족 삶의 상징으로 여긴다. 즉 그들은 미국의 건조한 남서부 지역에서 삶의 역경을 이겨내야 했다. 옥수수는 겸손, 협동, 존경, 그리고 땅에 대한 경외심을 나타낸다. 농사에 기반을 둔 호피족의 삶에 기술이 침투해 들어오면서 호피족의 문화도 변화를 겪고 있다. 전기, 자동차, 그리고 소비재들이 그들과 땅 사이의 영적 결속력

을 약화시키고 그들의 주의를 소비주의로 돌려 놓았다. 하지만 그들은 아직도 카치나 인형과 도기를 만들어 판매하면서 자신의 전통적인 가치들을 계속 지켜나가고 있다.

Exercises with Long Passages

Exercise 1   1 ⓓ   2 ⓑ   3 ⓓ   4 ⓒ   p.94

해석

아메리카 인디언들의 언어

유럽인들이 북아메리카에 도착하기 전, 아메리카 인디언들은 천 개가 넘는 언어를 사용했다. 이들 대부분은 서로 뜻이 통하지 않았다. 100마일 이내의 거리에서 함께 살고 있더라도 부족이 다른 세 명의 인디언에게는 수화 이외의 의사소통 수단이 없을 가능성이 높았다. 일반적인 고정 관념과는 반대로 인디언 언어는 원시적이지도 않고 단순하지도 않았다. 많은 언어의 문법과 음운 구조들이 복잡했다.

현재 미국에 해당되는 지역에 수백 개의 언어가 존재했지만, 언어학자들은 이들을 몇 개의 대어족과 여러 개의 소어족으로 나눈다. 어족이란 기원은 같지만 오랜 시간에 걸쳐 다른 언어로 발달한 언어들을 통칭하는 것이다. 예를 들어 영어와 네덜란드어, 그리고 러시아어가 인도유럽 어족에서 나온 것과 마찬가지로 아파치어와 나바호어는 아타바스칸 어족의 아메리카 인디언어에서 유래되었다. 다른 어족으로는 알곤퀸, 이러쿼이, 수, 무스코기, 그리고 에스키모-알류트 어족을 들 수 있다.

유럽인들의 정복으로 인해 대부분의 토착 언어들은 서서히 사라져 갔다. 인디언 인구가 약 2천만 명에서 2백만 명으로 줄어들면서 언어들 역시 사라졌다. 많은 언어들이 부족의 최고령층에서만 사용되고 있다. 그들이 죽으면 언어도 함께 사멸할 것이다. 사용자가 수천 명 이상인 언어는 미국과 캐나다에 여덟 개만 남아 있다. 가장 사용자 수가 많은 것은 사용자 수가 148,000명인 나바호어이다. 나머지는 크리어(60,000명), 오지브와어(51,000명), 체로키어(22,500명), 다코타어(20,000명), 아파치어(15,000명), 블랙풋어(10,000명), 그리고 촉토어(9,200명)이다.

아메리카 인디언들의 언어는 언어학적으로 다양하다. 하지만 많은 언어들이 인도유럽 어족과는 구별되는 공통된 특징을 나타낸다. 바로 성문 폐쇄음이 흔하다는 점이다. 이는 영어의 "어-오" 소리의 가운데 부분처럼 성대를 잠깐 닫아 내는 소리이다. 다수의 인디언 언어들은 비모음을 사용한다. 그리고 중국어와 마찬가지로 일부 언어에서는 어조나 음조를 사용해 다른 단어를 만들어 낸다.

아메리카 인디언 언어의 특징 중 잘 알려진 것은 포합으로, 이는 어근에 여러 가지 요소를 결합시킨 한 단어로 복잡한 아이디어를 표현하는 것이다. 그렇기 때문에 동사에, 보통 접두사의 형태로, 주어나 목적어가 붙을 수도 있다. 그리고 동사의 시제는 단어의 어미로 나타낼 수 있다. 복수는 "-s"와 같은 어미 대신 단어를 반복함으로써 나타낼 수 있다. 그래서 한 인디언 언어의 경우 토끼를 뜻하는 *ma*의 복수형은 *ma ma*가 된다.

아메리카 인디언들의 언어는 다른 모든 언어와 마찬가지로 근처 언어군의 단어들을 차용했으며, 영어 역시 인디언 어휘들을 차용했다. 영어에는 모카신, 터보건, 초콜릿, 그리고 타바코와 같이 인디언어에 기원을 둔 상용어들이 많이 있다. 여러 주와 도시들도 인디언 언어의 단어와 인디언 부족 이름에서 그 이름을 가져 왔다. 이러한 지역에는 시카고, 맨하탄, 위스콘신, 델라웨어, 아이오와, 그리고 애리조나가 포함된다.

📝 Summary Note

❶ 1,000
❷ sign language
❸ eight languages
❹ polysynthesis

📝 Summary Note

❶ 4.6 billion
❷ surface water
❸ tectonic movement
❹ magnetic field

Exercise 2   1 ⓒ   2 Ⓑ   3 Ⓐ   4 Ⓓ   p.96

해석

화성과 지구

지구와 화성은 거의 같은 시기에 생성되었다. 약 46억 년 전 두 행성은, 생성된지 얼마 되지 않은 태양을 덮고 있던, 뜨거운 기체로 이루어진 거대한 구름에서 만들어졌다. 두 행성은 태양과의 거리에 있어서 이웃하는 순서로 자리잡았다. 지구는 태양으로부터 약 9천 2백만 마일의 거리에, 화성은 약 1억 4천 2백만 마일의 거리에 위치해 있다. 두 행성 모두 단단한 지각과 밀도가 높은 핵을 지니고 있으며, 비율이 다르기는 하지만, 동일한 화학적 성분으로 만들어졌다.

기원과 구성이 비슷하기는 하지만 이들 행성은 결정적인 차이를 나타내기 때문에 한 행성에서만 생명이 존재할 수 있다. 중요한 한 가지 차이점은 크기이다. 화성은 지구 질량의 10분의 1에 불과한데, 이는 화성의 중력이 지구 중력의 약 30%으로, 지구 중력보다 훨씬 더 약하다는 점을 의미한다. 그 결과 화성은 대기 및 표층수의 상당 부분을 잃어버려서 보다 빨리 냉각되었다. 이러한 급속한 냉각 때문에 여전히 뜨거운 핵을 가지고 있는 지구에 비해서 화성의 화산 활동은 훨씬 적은 편이다.

지구는 중심 부분이 뜨겁기 때문에 지구의 지표면은 판구조에 의해 끊임없이 변화한다. 지각 아래의 판들이 서로 부딪치면서 새로운 지각이 지표면으로 올라오고 기존의 지각은 지구의 내부로 빨려 들어간다. 화성은 처음 5억 동안 판구조에 의해 형성되었지만, 그러한 힘은 화성의 내부가 냉각될 때 작동이 멈춰 버렸다. 그 결과 4억년 된 암석은 화성에서 흔히 볼 수 있는 반면 지구에서는 거의 볼 수가 없는데, 지구에서는 끊임없이 새로운 암석이 지표로 올라오고 오래된 암석은 땅속에 묻히기 때문이다. 대기층이 얇은 화성에서는 바람이 거의 불지 않아 표면이 태고의 상태를 유지하고 있는 반면, 지구의 암석들은 바람에 의해 침식되고 있다.

화성 표면의 절반에는 충돌 분화구의 흔적이 존재한다. 이 분화구들이 수십억 년 동안 그대로 남아 있다는 점에서 행성학자들은 분화구가 형성되기 전에 지질 운동이 멈추었다는 사실을 알 수 있다. 그들은 거대한 화산의 존재에 대해서도 동일한 결론을 내리고 있다. 화산의 크기나 높이를 볼 때 이 화산들은 수십억 년 전에 만들어진 후 분출을 멈추었다는 점을 알 수 있다. 반면에 지구의 화산들은 오늘날에도 여전히 지구의 지형을 바꾸고 있다. 물은 화성의 표면 형성에 일정한 역할을 했다. 하지만 물은 밝혀지지 않은 이유로 약 38억 년 전에 없어졌다. 말라 버린 강 바닥과 빙하의 흔적을 지금도 찾아볼 수 있다. 이와 대조적으로 지구 표면의 3분의 2이상은 물로 덮여 있으며, 최근 몇 십년 동안 그 비율이 증가하고 있다.

화성의 경우, 전기를 띤 입자, 즉 태양에서 쏟아져 내리는 태양풍으로부터 지구를 보호해 주는 것과 같은 자기장이 존재하지 않는다. 그렇기 때문에 95%의 이산화탄소로 이루어진 화성의 대기는 생명체가 살기에 적합하지 않다. 지구의 대기는 대부분 생명체가 살기에 적당한 78%의 질소와 21%의 산소로 이루어져 있다.

Exercise 3   1 Ⓑ   2 Ⓐ   3 Ⓐ   4 Ⓓ   p.98

해석

도기의 화학

점토를 굽는 과정은 탈수와 유리화의 두 단계로 이루어진다. 점토를 원하는 형태로 만든 후에는 화학수라고 불리는 여분의 물 분자가 표면으로 스며 나온다. 이들은, 흙이나 점토 내의 좁은 통로를 통해 물이 올라오는 과정인, 모세관 현상에 의해 나온다. 수분이 표면에 도달한 후 점토에 열이 가해지면 수분은 증발하게 된다.

이러한 과정의 화학적 역학은 다음과 같다. 점토의 화학 성분은 두 개의 규소 분자와 결합한 두 개의 물 분자와 한 개의 알루미나(산화알루미늄) 분자이다. 탈수 단계에서 점토 혼합물의 약 14%에 해당되는 물 분자가 증발한다. 탈수가 시작되기 위해서는 온도가 350℃에 도달해야 한다. 온도가 약 500℃에 도달하면 탈수는 끝이 난다.

그보다 더 높은 온도에서는 규소와 알루미나 분자가 단단하게 결합하기 시작한다. 수분이 빠져 나간 공간 중 일부를 이들이 채운다. 이러한 결합으로 인해 점토로 만들어진 물체가 강도와 경도를 갖게 된다. 이 단계에서 점토는 더 이상 수분을 흡수하지 못하며, 부드럽고 변형이 가능했던 상태로 되돌아갈 수 없다.

그 다음은 유리화 단계로, 이때 표면이 유리처럼 매끄럽게 된다. 온도가 500℃를 넘으면 산화철과 같은 점토의 불순물들이 녹아 버린다. 이러한 불순물들은 결합해서 유리질 물질을 만들어 내는데, 이 물질이 알루미나 분자 주변을 흐르면서 이들 분자들을 접합시켜 단단히 결속되도록 만든다. 온도가 더 올라가면 규산 알루미나가 많아지면서 유리질 물질과 혼합된다. 이러한 혼합으로 인해 점토로 만들어진 물체는 매우 단단하고 수정과 같은 구조를 갖게 된다. 이러한 화학적 구조 때문에 석기나 도기 제품을 때리면 특유의 울림 소리가 난다.

완성된 점토는 화학적으로 결합되어 있어서 늘어날 수 없다. 또한 점토 항아리를 불에 구우면 불꽃 위의 부분이 다른 부분보다 더 빨리 가열되어 가열이 고르게 이루어지지 않는다. 그 결과 내부 응력이 생겨서 도기가 부서질 수 있다. 아프리카의 도공들은 저온에서 도기를 구워서 규소와 알루미나가 결합되지 못하게 함으로써 그러한 문제를 해결한다. 이러한 저온 소성 방식 때문에 아프리카 도기는 불 위에서 고르지 않게 가열되어도 부서지지 않는다. 또한 이렇게 하면 도기에 더 많은 구멍이 생기기 때문에 열이 서서히 항아리에서 빠져나가서 점토가 식게 된다.

도기 유물의 출처와 시대를 정확히 알아내기 위해 고고학자들은 화학 분석법을 사용한다. 도기를 절단하는 방법에 비해 화학 분석법의 장점은 유물을 손상시키지 않고서도 아주 작은 샘플로 결과를 얻을 수 있다는 점이다. 화학 분석법에서 흔히 사용되는 기법 중 하나는 샘플을 산성 물질에 녹이는 것이다. 이 과정에서 방출된 원자를 분광사진기로 분석하면 도기에 포함된 원소들을 확인할 수 있다.

❶ water molecules

❷ 350 to 500

❸ impurities

❹ glassy substance

Exercise 4 1 ⓓ 2 ⓑ 3 ⓓ 4 ⓐ p.100

해석

알래스카의 에스키모 문화

알래스카 원주민은 크게 에스키모(54,761명), 틀링깃-하이다(22,365명), 아사베스칸(18,838명), 그리고 알류트(16,978명)의 네 집단으로 구분된다. 가장 큰 집단인 에스키모는 알래스카의 북극 지방의 수목 생장 한계선 위에서 사는 모든 부족을 가리키는 광범위한 용어이다. 여기에는 이누이트족과 유픽족이 포함된다. 에스키모라는 말은 "날고기를 먹는 사람들"이라는 뜻이다. 에스키모는 유목민으로서 카리부와 해양 동물들을 따라 계절마다 이동한다. 에스키모의 금기 사항 중 하나는 바다 동물과 육지 동물을 같이 두지 않는 것인데, 에스키모인들의 부엌에서 이들은 각각 따로 보관된다.

가혹한 환경 때문에 에스키모인들은 수준 높은 도구를 개발해야 했다. 운송을 위한 카약과, 눈 덩어리로 만드는 주택인 이글루를 발명했다. 대다수 에스키모들은 작은 마을에서 살며 식량을 얻기 위해 물고기를 잡는다. 실업률은 높지만 1960년대 이후 석유가 개발되면서 일부 에스키모인들에게 일자리가 생겼다. 하지만 그와 동시에 에스키모인들의 전통적 생활 방식이 위협을 받고 있다.

에스키모인들은 미국의 아메리카 인디언보다 동아시아인과 더 비슷하게 생겼다. 그 이유는 이들이 베링해의 육교를 건너 온 최초의 이주민들보다 훨씬 나중에 알래스카에 들어왔기 때문이다. 이 육교는 에스키모인들이 아시아에서 오기 전부터 이미 물에 잠겨 있었기 때문에 그들은 틀림없이 배를 이용해서 도착했을 것이다.

전통적인 에스키모들은 유럽인들이 카약이라고 불렀던 카자잇을 타고 고래, 물개, 그리고 바다코끼리를 사냥했던 사냥꾼이자 어부였다. 겨울에 물길이 얼어 붙으면 에스키모들은 얼음에 구멍을 내고 물개나 바다코끼리가 숨을 쉬기 위해 수면으로 나오기를 기다렸다. 육지에서는 허스키 개들이 끄는 개썰매를 타고 이동했다.

에스키모인들은 동물에 의존해서 생계를 유지했다. 동물은 식량을 제공해 주었을 뿐만 아니라 옷과 도구의 재료가 되었다. 에스키모 여성들은 동물 뼈로 만든 바늘과 동물 내장으로 만든 실을 이용해서 동물 가죽으로 옷과 신발을 만들었다. 무거운 외투는 파카였다. 여성들은 포대에 쌓인 아기를 등에 넣어 다닐 수 있도록 파카의 모자를 매우 크게 만들었다. 신발은 순록이나 물개의 가죽으로 만들었다. 남성과 여성의 역할은 명확하게 구분되어 남성은 사냥과 어업 활동을 했고 여성은 자녀 양육, 의복 및 도구 제작, 그리고 요리를 담당했다. 결혼이 항상 일부일처제였던 것은 아니어서 일부 남성들이 여러 명의 아내를 두기도 했다.

미국의 대중 문화에 존재하는 한 가지 잘못된 생각은 에스키모인들이 늙고 병든 친지들을 얼음 위에 내버려 두고 죽게 만든다는 것이다. 하지만 실제로 이러한 방식의 사망은 더 이상 일을 할 수 없어서 공동체에 기여할 수 없게 된 사람이 자의에 의해 때때로 선택했던 방법이었다.

---

❶ nomadic

❷ kayak

❸ whales, seals, and walruses

❹ clothes and tools

Exercise 5 1 ⓒ 2 ⓒ 3 ⓓ 4 ⓑ p.102

해석

은하 좌표계

지구상의 위치는 경도와 위도를 조합하여 확인할 수 있다. 동일한 방식으로, 우리 은하도 은하 좌표계로 위치를 나타낼 수 있다. 이는 1958년 국제 천문 연맹에 의해 만들어졌다. 고도와 방위각을 사용하는 시스템으로서, 보다 잘 알려진 지구의 좌표 시스템과 유사하다. 간단한 방정식을 통해 하나의 시스템을 나머지 하나의 시스템으로 바꿀 수 있다.

은하 적도가 위도 0도선에 해당된다. 이 선은 우리 은하의 면의 전체적인 방향과 평행을 이룬다. 따라서 은위 0도 근처에 있는 천체들은 은하계의 팔에 위치한다. 양의 은위를 가진 천체는 팔 위쪽 은하 북반구에 위치한다. 그리고 음의 은위를 가진 물체는 팔 아래쪽 은하 남반구에 위치한다.

은경은 임의적으로 정해지며 은하의 중심 방향을 가리킨다. 범위는 0도에서 360도까지이다. 은경은 은하구의 꼭대기에서 볼 때 반시계 방향으로 움직인다. 지구의 태양이 구의 중심에 위치하는데, 이 지점에서는 은위 0도가 은경 90도를 양분한다. 은하 북극은 은위 90도에 위치한다. 은하 남극은 은위 −90도에 위치한다.

우리 은하의 경계를 나타내는 가상의 구에 이러한 좌표값을 부여함으로써 천문학자들은 은경과 은위의 격자 시스템으로 천체를 찾을 수 있다. 예를 들어 지구의 하늘에서 가장 밝은 항성은 시리우스인데, 이 항성은 은위 227도, 은경 −8.4도에 위치해 있다. 이러한 표시의 도움을 받아 항성에 대한 연구를 할 수 있고 은하 내에서 이루어지는 천체의 움직임을 추적할 수 있다. 또한 은하 적도와의 거리에 따라 항성들의 밀도가 얼마나 다른지, 혹은 원반 모양의 은하계 끝부분이 얼마나 평평한지도 알 수 있다.

은하 좌표계는 태양계에서 멀리 떨어져 있는 천체의 위치를 표시할 때 유용하다. 지구와 태양 너머에 있는 항성들은 너무나 멀리 떨어져 있기 때문에 인간이 멀리 떨어진 천체의 위치를 인식하는데 지구가 태양을 공전한다는 점은 거의 영향을 끼치지 못한다. 하지만 동일한 공전 현상 때문에 태양계 내에 있는 천체들에 대해서는 은하 좌표계로 정확한 측정을 할 수가 없다.

우리 은하 바깥에 있는 천체들은 함께 회전하지 않는다. 따라서 사람들은 이들의 위치가 상당한 정도로 바뀐다고 인식한다. 하지만 은하 좌표와 관련해서는 예측 가능한 방식으로 바뀐다. 자전하는 우리 은하를 고려하여 측정할 경우 다른 은하들은 2억 2천만년마다 지구 주위를 한 바퀴씩 돌고 있다.

Summary Note

❶ location of stars

❷ 1958

❸ altitude-azimuth

❹ solar system

해석

전해 검파기

1800년대 말 우편 서비스를 제외한 유일한 장거리 통신 수단은 전보와 전화였다. 하지만 두 가지 모두 신호를 보내기 위해서는 전선을 필요로 했다. 무선 전송의 가능성은 공상 과학 소설에나 나올 법한 이야기였다. 하지만 1900년대 초반에 무선 방송은 현실이 되었다.

19세기에 무선 방송을 가능하게 만든 몇 가지 법칙들이 발견되었다. 최초의 획기적인 발견은 1831년 영국의 물리학자였던 마이클 패러데이에 의해 이루어졌다. 그는 전류가 한 전선을 통과할 때, 전선들이 서로 닿아 있지 않더라도, 다른 전선에 전류를 발생시킨다는 사실을 발견했다. 1864년 제임스 맥스웰은 전자기파로 이루어진 이러한 전류가 광속으로 이동한다는 것을 보여 주었다. 하인리히 헤르츠는 전자기파가 고체를 통과한다는 점을 입증했다. 이러한 발견들이 알려지자 무선 방송 시스템을 개발하기 위한 경쟁이 시작되었다.

경쟁자 중에는 캐나다 발명가인 레지널드 페센던이 있었다. 그는 음성 전송이 가능하다는 것을 보여 주기 위해 전파 탐지기로 실험을 하기 시작했다. 1900년 그는 최초로 자신의 음성을 전송하는데 성공했지만 파장이 지속적이지 않아 소리를 알아들을 수가 없었다. 그는 AM(진폭 변조) 신호를 수신하기 위해 *교환기*를 뜻하는 불어에서 이름을 딴 배레터 탐지기를 발명했으나, 이는 감도가 충분하지 못했다. 1901년 어느 날 그는 우연히 전선 한 가닥을 산성 물질에 너무 오래 담가 두었는데, 전선 끝 부분만 산성 물질에 닿게 되었다. 페센던은 전선을 산성 물질에 담그면 배레터가 근처의 지속적인 전파에 대단히 민감해진다는 것을 알게 되었다.

페센던은 자신의 발명품을 액체 배레터라고 불렀지만, 이는 전해 검파기로 알려졌다. 이 검파기는 하나의 전기 회로를 구성하는 몇 개의 연결된 부품들로 이루어졌다. 질산이나 황산으로 채워지고 땅에 연결시킨 작은 백금 컵에 은을 입힌 백금선을 담구었다. 전선과 산성 물질 사이에 배터리를 연결시켜 탐지기에 전류가 흐르도록 했다. 검파기에 연결된 헤드폰을 착용하면 쉿쉿거리는 소리를 들을 수 있었는데, 이 소리는 조절이 가능해서 다이얼을 돌려 멈추게 할 수도 있었다. 바로 그 지점에서 검파기는 유입되는 전파에 매우 민감하게 반응했다.

이러한 습식 장치는 산성 물질에 담근 노출 전선의 이름을 따서 노출 전해 검파기라고 알려졌다. 보다 발전된 디자인인 밀봉 전해 검파기는 유리로 밀봉되었기 때문에 보다 안정적이었다. 따라서 산성 물질이 엎질러지거나 증발하지 않았다. 페센던은 1903년에 자신의 검파기에 대한 특허를 얻었다. 이 장치는 초기 무선 수신기에 사용되었다. 이는 1915년 진공관에 의해 대체될 때까지 무선 수신기 감도의 기준을 마련해 주었다.

📝 Summary Note

❶ speed of light
❷ solid objects
❸ voice transmission
❹ electrolytic detector

Building Summary Skills   p.106

Exercise 1   Native American Indian Languages

Native American Indians spoke over a thousand languages.

But the European conquest of America began the slow extinction of most Native Indian languages. Today, just eight languages remain with more than a thousand speakers. The largest are Navajo, Cree, Ojibwa, and Cherokee. The languages are characterized by polysynthesis, in which a single word can express many ideas with endings or prefixes added to a root word. Many common English words, such as tobacco and chocolate, were borrowed from Indian languages.

Exercise 2   Mars and Earth

Earth and Mars share similar origins and compositions. They both condensed from a cloud of gas around the sun and are made of the same chemical elements. But Mars is much smaller, resulting in a weaker force of gravity, a thinner atmosphere, and a lack of water. While volcanic activity continues to shape Earth today, the Martian surface is no longer changed by tectonic movements. Without the kind of magnetic field that protects Earth, Mars is bombarded by electrically charged particles from the sun.

Exercise 3   The Chemistry of Pottery

Pottery is made by exposing clay to high temperatures. The process involves two stages. In the dehydration stage, clay is heated to between 350 and 500 degrees Celsius. As the clay heats, it dehydrates and hardens. In the vitrification stage, clay is heated above 500 degrees Celsius, which removes the impurities and gives clay its glassy surface. Pottery may shatter during heating as its chemical bonds hinder expansion. Heating at a lower temperature can avoid this problem. Chemical analysis can detect the age and the source of a pottery shard.

Exercise 4   The Culture of the Alaskan Eskimo

The Eskimo are the largest group of Alaskan Indians. They are nomadic, moving with the seasons to follow their food supply of caribou and sea animals. They have adapted to the harsh environment by inventing kayaks for water travel, dog sleds for land travel, and igloos for shelter. Men do the hunting and the fishing while women do the domestic chores and childcare. Animals provide not only food but also clothing and tools. Women sew outer garments called parkas, which are made from animal hides. Some men marry more than one wife.

Exercise 5   Galactic Coordinates

Celestial objects in the Milky Way Galaxy can be mapped with the galactic coordinate system, which was invented by the International Astronomical Union in 1958. Lines of latitude and longitude are imposed on an imaginary grid over the Milky Way. Using these lines, astronomers can assign locations to stars and track their movements through the galaxy. The system also permits the mapping of objects outside the Milky Way as they move in predictable ways relative to the galactic coordinates.

Exercise 6 The Electrolytic Detector

Radio transmission was made possible by the electrolytic detector, which was invented by Reginald Fessenden in 1901. The detector formed an electric circuit when a platinum wire was dipped in acid. The circuit could detect incoming radio waves. A person wearing headphones connected to the detector could hear the hissing sound of the radio waves. The device was used in early radio receivers until 1915.

Mini TOEFL iBT Practice Test   p.108

1 Ⓐ	2 Ⓓ	3 Ⓒ	4 Ⓑ	5 Ⓑ
6 Ⓒ	7 Ⓓ	8 ③, ④, ⑤		
9 Ⓒ	10 Ⓐ	11 Ⓐ	12 Ⓑ	13 Ⓓ
14 Ⓒ	15 Ⓐ	16 ①, ③, ⑥		

해석

[1-8]

화성 생명체 존재설

1700년대 중반 천문학자들이 화성 극지방의 만년설을 관찰했다. 윌리엄 허셜은 계절에 따라 만년설의 크기가 달라진다는 것을 발견했다. 지구에서 볼 수 있는 특징인 물과 계절이 존재한다는 사실은 화성에도 생명체가 존재할지 모른다는 추측을 낳았다.

19세기 망원경의 발달로 이러한 추측에 불이 붙었다. 망원경 덕분에 화성 표면의 특징들이 관찰되었다. 1877년에는 이탈리아의 천문학자인 지오바니 스키아파렐리가 22cm 망원경을 사용하여 최초로 화성 지도를 그렸다. 지도에는 기다란 선이 그려져 있었는데, 그는 이 선들을 이탈리아어로 "수로"를 뜻하는 *카날리*라고 명명했다. 하지만 그가 사용했던 용어는 영어로 옮겨질 때 실수로 "운하"라고 번역되었다. 수로는 보통 자연적인 것이고 운하는 인공적인 것이기 때문에, 이러한 실수로 이후 100년에 걸쳐 화성의 생명체에 대한 상상력 넘치는 이론들이 등장했다.

지적인 존재에 의해 운하가 만들어졌다는 견해를 지지한 주요 인물은 미국의 천문학자인 퍼시벌 로웰이었다. 애리조나 플래그스태프의 공기가 맑고 높은 곳에 위치한 로웰 천문대에서 로웰은 화성을 광범위하게 연구해서 화성 표면의 특징들을 자세히 그려 냈다. 그는 1906년 작인 *화성과 운하*, 그리고 1908년 작인 *화성, 생명체의 거주지*를 포함하여 화성에 관한 자신의 연구를 책으로 발표했다. 로웰은 이러한 운하들이 오래 전에 사라진 문명에 의해 정교한 관개 시설로서 건설되었다고 주장했다. 운하는 극지방의 물을 화성에서 생명체가 살고 있던 건조한 지역으로 가져다 주었다. 로웰의 아이디어는 대중 문화에 반영되었다. 영국의 소설가인 H.G. 웰스는 화성의 생명체를 묘사한 가장 유명한 소설인 우주 *전쟁*을 썼다. 그는 화성인들이 멸망하는 자신의 행성에서 벗어나기 위해 지구를 침공한다는 상상을 했다. 20세기의 보다 크고 우수한 망원경 렌즈들도 로웰이 실제로 관찰했던 형체가 운하라는 것을 확인시켜 주지 못했다. 사실 이들은 결국 착시에 의한 것으로 밝혀졌다.

1965년을 시작으로 화성 생명체 존재설은 보다 큰 타격을 입게 되었다. 미국

은 우주선 *마리너* 우주선들을 발사해 화성 표면에 접근하여 사진을 찍고 그곳 대기를 조사하도록 했다. 이 탐사선들은 화성에 주로 이산화탄소로 이루어진 얇은 층의 대기가 존재하며 극지방의 만년설은 물이 아니라 결빙된 이산화탄소라는 점을 밝혀냈다. 사진에서는 화성에 강, 해양, 혹은 기타 생명의 흔적이 전혀 존재하지 않는다는 점이 드러났다. 과학자들은 화성의 대기층이 얇고 자기장이 약해서 화성이 해로운 우주 방사선에 취약하다고 결론지었다. 1976년에는 *바이킹* 프로젝트에 의해 생물학적 조사와 토양 조사가 진행되었다. 과학자들에게는 놀라운 일이었는데, 조사에 따르면 화성 표면에는 유기물이 전혀 존재하지 않았다. 그 결과 현재의 견해는 화성의 역사상 초기에는 생명체가 존재했을 수도 있지만, 이들은 이후 멸종되어 현재의 화성에는 생명체가 살지 않는다는 것이다.

1996년을 시작으로 미국은 여러 차례 화성 착륙에 성공했다. 생명체를 발견하지는 못했지만, 이로써 화성의 지질과 화학에 대한 인류의 지식이 확대되었다. 2001년에는 로봇 탐사선이 화성의 지형을 찍은 웅장한 이미지들을 지구로 보내왔다. 다른 탐사에서는 수소와 메탄이 감지되었다. 2004년의 화성 탐사선들은 먼 과거에 물이 존재했다는 결정적인 증거를 제시해 주었다. 미국의 추가적인 탐사 계획이 현재 진행 중이다. 유럽 우주국은 2035년까지 화성에 인간을 착륙시키려고 한다. 그리고 2004년 미국 대통령은 화성에 우주 비행사를 보내서 화성을 탐사하겠다는 국가적인 목표를 발표했다.

[9-16]

미국의 조경 건축

조경 건축은 인간이 사용하고 즐길 수 있도록 토지를 설계하고 개발하는 것이다. 19세기 중반 이전에는 조경 건축이 일이 아닌 예술로서 행해졌다. 고대부터 이러한 예술은 부유층들의 전유물이었다. 로마인들에게는 안뜰이, 페르시아인들에게는 정원이, 이탈리아인들에게는 도시 광장이, 그리고 프랑스인들에게는 궁전이 있었다. 미국 식민지 시대의 상류층들은 영국의 조경 양식, 특히 정교한 정원을 받아들였다. 대부분의 조경 프로젝트에는 정원이 포함되어 있기 때문에 설계자들은 조경 정원사라고 불렸다.

조경 건축이라는 용어를 만든 사람은 영국인 학자 길버트 랭 메슨으로, 그는 1828년 발표한 책에서 이 용어를 사용했다. 그는 처음으로 자연 조경과 건축 디자인 원칙 사이의 연관성에 대한 관심을 불러일으켰다. 미국에서 이러한 문구는 최초로 그러한 명칭을 자신의 직업으로 표방한 프레더릭 로 옴스테드에 의해 도입되었다.

옴스테드와 건축가 칼버트 복스가 뉴욕의 센트럴 파크 설계 공모전에 참여하면서 이 분야에 혁명이 일어났다. 1800년대 초 뉴욕의 인구가 급증하면서 시 지도층들은 공원용 부지를 확보해야 할 필요성을 느끼게 되었다. 뉴욕 의회는 시 중심에 직사각형 형태의 대규모 공원을 설립하기 위한 예산을 승인했다. 1858년 옴스테드와 복스의 설계가 선정되었고, 이후 15년에 걸쳐 공사가 진행되었다.

옴스테드의 컨셉은 공원을 이상적인 민주주의 및 평등주의의 상징으로 만드는 것이었다. 그는 공원을 모든 계층의 사람들에게 열려 있고 이들이 일상의 압박으로부터 벗어나 명상과 휴식을 취할 수 있는 장소로 생각했다. 그의 새로운 설계 아이디어는 보행자, 말을 탄 사람, 그리고 마차에 탄 사람과 같은 각기 다른 계층의 사용자들을 위해 그가 "분리된 순환 시스템"이라고 부른 것을 만드는 것이었다. 풍경이 훼손되지 않도록 공원을 통과하는 차량들은 덤불로 가려지고 움푹 들어가 있는 도로로 그 모습이 감춰졌다. 오늘날 공원에는 달리기 코스, 아이스 스케이트장, 야생 생물 보호 구역, 야구장, 운동장 그리고 세계적으로 유명한 레스토랑인 태번 온 더 그린이 포함되어 있다.

옴스테드는 또한 워싱턴 D.C.의 미국 국회의사당 부지도 설계했다. 그는 의사당 건물 측면에 돌출되어 있는 대리석 테라스를 설치했다. 의사당을 찾는 일부 방문객들이 말에게 물을 먹일 장소가 없다고 불평했다. 이에 대응하여 옴스테드

는 야외 벽돌 건물인 서머 하우스를 설계했는데, 여기에는 말이 물을 마실 수 있는 샘이 있었다.

조경 건축가들은 1899년에 자신들의 조직인 미국 조경 건축가 협회를 설립했다. 현재 조경 건축가는 의사 및 변호사에 비견되는 직업으로 높은 학력과 자격증이 요구되는 직업이다. 이 분야는 여러 가지 전문 분야로 이루어져 있으며, 조경 건축가는 수학, 과학, 공학, 미술, 그리고 첨단 기술에 정통해야 한다. 또한 작업의 사회적 맥락을 이해해야 하며 정치인, 공공 단체, 그리고 정부 기관을 상대하는 일에도 능숙해야 한다.

이 직업은 점점 더 전문화되고 있다. 조경 설계사와 및 조경 기술자, 혹은 조경 엔지니어들이 프로젝트를 계획하고 실행에 옮긴다. 조경 관리사는 조경의 장기적인 관리를 담당한다. 이들은 조림이나 자연 보전, 혹은 부지 관리의 업무를 맡을 수 있다. 조경학자는 건축가들과 함께 토양, 수리학, 혹은 식물학과 같은 분야의 기술적인 문제들을 해결한다. 공공 정책 및 계획 전략은 조경 계획사의 도움을 받아 수립된다. 정원 설계사는 사유지의 정원과 관련된 일뿐만 아니라 역사적인 정원을 보존하는 일도 담당한다.

Vocabulary Check-Up   p.114

A 1 Ⓐ   2 Ⓒ   3 Ⓓ   4 Ⓒ   5 Ⓐ
       6 Ⓑ   7 Ⓒ   8 Ⓐ   9 Ⓓ   10 Ⓐ

B 1 Ⓓ   2 Ⓗ   3 Ⓔ   4 Ⓘ   5 Ⓙ
       6 Ⓐ   7 Ⓕ   8 Ⓑ   9 Ⓖ   10 Ⓒ

UNIT 05 Sentence Simplification

Basic Drill   p.118

Drill 1 Ⓐ

해석

해수면과 육지

해수면이란 육지와 비교한 바다의 평균 높이를 말한다. 바다의 경우 한 지점의 높이가 다른 지점에 비해 2미터 정도 더 높을 수 있어서 바다의 높이를 측정하는 일은 쉽지 않다. 또한 달의 위치에 따라 생기는 조수 때문에 해수면이 상승할 수도 있다. 만조는 육지에 비해 해수면이 높은 때를 말하며 이로 인해 해안가에서 해변이 거의 사라지는 반면, 간조는 육지에 비해 바다가 낮은 때로서 이 경우 해변의 크기가 증가한다. 빙산이 녹아도 해수면이 상승할 수 있다. 빙산은 지구에서 가장 차가운 바다에 떠다니는 거대한 얼음 덩어리이다. 날씨가 따뜻하거나 이들이 남쪽으로 떠내려가는 경우 빙하가 녹을 수 있는데, 그렇게 되면 전 세계의 평균 해수면이 상승한다. 녹아내리는 빙하 때문에 몇몇 섬들은 바다 속으로 가라앉게 될 위험에 처해 있다.

Drill 2 Ⓑ

해석

철새

가을과 겨울이 되면 새들은 남쪽으로 이동하기 시작한다. 이러한 장거리 여행을 하는 이유는 매우 다양한데, 예를 들어 먹이가 더 많은 곳, 보다 편하게 살 수 있는 곳, 혹은 안전하게 알을 낳을 수 있는 곳으로 가야 할 수 있다. 철새들은 종종 여름에는 북쪽 지방에 머무르다가 기온이 떨어지기 시작하면 남쪽으로 이동한다. 따뜻한 남쪽 지역에서 겨울을 나고 이후 기온이 너무 더워지기 시작하면 다시 북쪽으로 돌아온다. 이동의 장점으로는 북쪽에서의 긴 여름 동안 새끼들에게 먹이를 먹일 수 있는 시간이 더 많다는 점과 곤충과 같은 먹을 수 있는 먹이가 많다는 점을 들 수 있다. 날씨가 추워지기 시작하면 철새들은 보다 따뜻한 지역으로 돌아오는데, 이곳에서는 낮의 길이와 먹이의 양이 크게 달라지지 않는다. 단점으로는 이동이 위험한 여정이 될 수 있다는 점과 이동에 많은 에너지가 필요하다는 점을 들 수 있다.

Drill 3 Ⓒ

해석

사막의 날씨 변화

사막에서는 단 하루 사이에도 날씨가 급격히 변할 수 있다. 예를 들어 오후 2시에는 기온이 40°C까지 오르지만 같은 날 새벽 3시에는 영하 15°C까지 떨어질 가능성도 있다. 낮에는 모래가 햇빛을 반사하기 때문에 모래와 공기의 온도가 모두 크게 올라간다. 그 이면에 있는 원리는 더운 날 해변을 따라 걸으면 발 아래 모래가 타는 듯이 뜨겁게 느껴지는 것과 같은 원리이다. 사막에서도 동일한 원리가 적용된다. 밤에는 기온이 크게 내려가는데, 그 이유는 모래가 낮 동안 태양열을 전혀 흡수하지 않기 때문이다. 숲과 초원에서는 낮 동안 나무와 잔디가 태양열을 흡수하기 때문에 밤에도 사막만큼 기온이 내려가지 않지만, 사막에는 나무가 거의 없고 잔디도 매우 적다. 따라서 열기가 흡수되지 않기 때문에 극도로 더운 낮이 지나가면 엄청나게 추운 밤이 찾아온다.

Drill 4 Ⓑ

해석

초식 동물에 대한 식물의 방어 수단

식물은 여러 가지 방법으로 자신을 먹는 동물로부터 스스로를 방어할 수 있다. 이러한 다양한 방어 수단 덕분에 식물들은 초식 동물이 많은 곳에서도 살아남을 수 있다. 식물의 방어 수단에는 장미의 가시와 같이 식물 표면에 있는 보호 장치, 식물 내에 존재하는 동물이 소화하기 힘든 물질, 그리고 초식 동물을 죽이거나 아프게 만드는 독이 포함된다. 또한 식물들은 초식 동물을 사냥해서 잡아먹는 육식 동물을 유인함으로써 스스로를 보호하는 놀라운 방법들도 사용한다. 예를 들어 식물들은 초식 동물의 포식자들이 좋아하는 냄새를 만들어 내거나, 육식 동물에게 먹이나 보금자리를 제공하기도 한다. 방어 수단은 식물 내에 항상 존재할 수도 있고, 아니면 식물이 초식 동물로부터 피해를 입은 후에 발달할 수도 있다. 식물종들은 초식 동물로부터 자신을 보호할 수 있는 여러 가지 방어 수단을 가지고 있는 경우가 많기 때문에 수령이 수백만 년 된 종들도 많다.

Exercises with Long Passages

Exercise 1 1 Ⓑ   2 Ⓒ   3 Ⓐ   4 Ⓓ   p.120

해석

여러 종들의 눈 변이

인간의 정상 시력 기준은 스넬런 시력 검사표의 기준선들을 거침없이 읽을 수 있는 20/20이다. 점수는 개인이 약 6m 떨어진 곳에서 크기가 다른 글자들을 얼마나 잘 읽을 수 있는지에 따라 부여된다. 하지만 다른 종의 경우, 시력 검사표의 맨 아래 선을 읽는 정도로는 정상 축에도 끼지 못한다. 대부분의 새들은 인간들이 심각한 시각 장애를 겪고 있다고 생각할 것이다. 예를 들어 매는 엠파이어 스테이트 빌딩의 꼭대기에 앉아서도 인도에 떨어진 10원짜리 동전을 볼 수 있을 정도로 시력이 뛰어나다. 매의 망막에는 1평방밀리미터당 백만 개의 추상체가 있기 때문에 매는 미세한 것들도 식별할 수 있다. 그리고 물속에서 인간은 원시가 되지만, 공중에서 급강하해 물고기를 잡는 물총새는 두 개의 중심와, 즉 대부분이 물체의 구별을 가능하게 만드는 추상체로 이루어진 영역을 가지고 있기 때문에, 공중과 물속 모두에서 잘 볼 수 있다. 물총새는 공중에서 중심과 하나로 아래에 있는 물을 한쪽 눈으로 한 번에 훑어 볼 수 있다. 이것을 단안시라고 부른다. 물속으로 들어가면 나머지 중심와가 가세해 물총새는 쌍안경과 같이 양쪽 눈의 초점을 동시에 먹이에게 맞추게 된다. 개구리 시력의 특징은 물체들을 끊이지 않는 하나의 영상으로 인식하는 능력에 있다. 곤충 탐지기로 알려진, 개구리의 눈에 있는 고도로 발달된 세포들이 주로 움직이는 물체에만 반응하기 때문에, 곤충들 사체 위에 앉아 있는 개구리는 이들이 먹이인 줄 모르고 굶어 죽을 것이라고 말해진다.

벌은 겹눈을 가지고 있으며 이를 비행에 사용한다. 겹눈에는 눈에 보이는 것을 점 모양, 즉 모자이크 패턴으로 나타내는 15,000개의 개안이 있다. 벌은 이러한 시력으로 태양을 하나의 점으로 보는데, 이는 항상 기준점이 된다. 따라서 벌의 눈은 태양에 대한 비행선의 각도를 계속 측정해 주는 뛰어난 항해 도구가 된다. 벌의 눈은 또한 비행 속도를 측정한다. 인간의 정상 시력인 20/20을 무색하게 만들 만큼은 아니지만, 벌은 인간이 보지 못하는 자외선을 볼 수가 있다. 따라서 인간이 정상 시력이라고 간주하는 것도 사실 다른 종들을 연구해 보면 상당히 제한적인 것이다. 하지만 인간의 눈에 관해서는 여전히 할 말이 많다. 모든 포유류 중에서 인간과 일부 영장류만이 색을 인식하는 혜택을 누리고 있다.

📝 Summary Note

❶ high up
❷ foveae
❸ in motion
❹ compound eyes

Exercise 2 1 ⓑ, ⓓ 2 ⓒ 3 ⓐ 4 ⓒ p.122

해석

흰개미

흰개미는 터마이트라는 이름으로 더 잘 알려져 있다. 어느 정도 개미와 흡사하게 보이기 때문에 흰개미라는 이름이 붙여졌다. 하지만 식성과 생활 방식은 완전히 다르다. 흰개미들은 대부분 죽은 초목을 먹기 때문에 사람들이 나무로 집을 짓는 지역에서는 해충으로도 간주된다. 또한 농작물에 커다란 피해를 끼칠 수도 있다. 반면에 죽은 초목을 다시 생태계로 돌려보낸다는 점에서는 매우 유용한 동물이다. 이들은 죽은 초목을 먹고 미네랄이 풍부한 분비물을 배출함으로써 종종 숲 속 생물들에게 영양분을 제공해 준다.

흰개미는 보통 개미들과 크기 및 사회적 습성이 비슷하지만, 더 이상의 유사성은 존재하지 않는다. 이들은 개미보다 더 부드럽고, 희고, 다리가 짧고, 통통하며, 그리고 움직임이 훨씬 느리다. 놀랍게도 흰개미들은 사마귀나 바퀴벌레와 같은 종에 속한다. 흰개미는 입의 일부를 사용해서 죽은 나무를 씹기 때문에 이빨

이 상당히 튼튼하다. 보통은 어두운 보금자리나 굴속에서 살며, 새로운 굴이나 보금자리를 만드는 경우, 혹은 먹이를 찾기 위한 경우가 아니고는 사는 곳을 떠나지 않는다.

흰개미는 수백에서 수백만 마리씩 군락을 이루고 산다는 점에서 매우 사회적이다. 이들은 자신에게 필요한 먹이뿐만 아니라 군락 전체에 필요한 먹이를 찾고 모으기 위해 서로 협력한다. 또한 군락에서 각자가 수행해야 할 일 혹은 임무에 따라 조직화가 잘 이루어져 있다. 대부분의 흰개미들은 일개미이지만, 병정개미, 번식 역할만을 담당하는 수개미, 그리고 알을 낳는 여왕개미도 존재한다.

일부 지역에서는 흰개미가 만든 거대한 개미집들이 결국 둔덕을 이루어 하늘로 높이 솟아 있는 형태가 나타날 수도 있다. 많은 아프리카 국가에서는 때때로 높이가 6미터에 이르는 이러한 거대한 흙더미들을 곳곳에서 찾아볼 수 있다. 흰개미들은 수평보다 수직으로 집을 짓는 경향이 있다. 일부 과학자들은 그렇게 하는 이유가 커다란 개미집 안에서 공기가 더 잘 순환되도록 하기 위함이라고 믿는다. 공기 순환이 잘 되면 외부 기온과 상관없이 내부 기온이 하루 종일 거의 일정하게 유지된다. 이는 중요한 점인데, 온도가 크게 변하면 흰개미 알이 부화하기 전에 죽을 수 있기 때문이다. 또한 개미집 안의 복잡한 굴들은 흰개미들이 일을 보다 쉽고 조직적으로 할 수 있게 만든다. 대부분의 굴은 특정한 용도로 사용되며, 흰개미들은 특정한 일을 할 때 항상 어떤 터널을 이용하고 어떤 길로 가야 하는지 아는 것처럼 보인다. 일부 측면에서는 흰개미가 사람보다 더 똑똑해 보인다.

📝 Summary Note

❶ termites
❷ nourish forests
❸ shorter legged
❹ reproduction

Exercise 3 1 ⓑ 2 ⓒ 3 ⓑ 4 ⓐ p.124

해석

시조새 화석

시조새 화석은 고고학자들이 발견해 낸 매우 중요한 화석이었다. 이 화석은 독일 남부에서 발견되었는데, 이곳에는 보존 상태가 좋은 화석들이 많이 존재한다. 시조새 화석은 약 1억 5천만 년 전 고대 조류의 화석이다. 많은 과학자들은 시조새가 최초의 조류였을 것으로 믿는다. 하지만 오늘날 서식하는 조류들과는 그다지 유사하지 않다. 과학자들은 시조새가 깃털과 날개를 가지고 있지만 고대의 공룡들과 마찬가지로 파충류였기 때문에 시조새가 부분적으로는 조류이고 부분적으로는 공룡이었다고 생각한다. 오늘날의 조류와는 달리 시조새는 이빨을 모두 가지고 있었고, 가슴은 납작했으며, 기다란 골질의 꼬리를 가지고 있었고, 그리고 날개에는 세 개의 발톱이 있었는데, 이 발톱들은 먹이를 공격하거나 나무를 붙잡기 위해 사용되었을 것이다. 실제로 시조새 화석을 살펴 보면 이 고대의 생물은 조류보다 공룡에 더 가까워 보인다.

시조새의 깃털의 용도에 관해서 학자들 사이에 커다란 논란이 존재한다. 일부 학자들은 깃털이 체온 조절을 위해 사용되었을 것이라고 주장하는 반면 일부 학자들은 깃털이 비행에 사용되었을 것이라고 믿는다. 이는 과학자들에게 매우 중요한 문제로, 과학자들은 동물이 처음 어떻게 날기 시작했는지 알고 싶어한다. 최초의 비행에 관한, 그리고 시조새가 깃털을 어떤 용도로 사용했는지에 관한 두 가지 이론이 존재한다. 첫 번째는 트리 다운이라는 이론으로, 이 이론에서는 오늘날 날다람쥐들이 하는 것처럼 고대의 새들이 날개를 이용하여 나무에서 땅으로 활공했을 것으로 생각된다. 다른 이론은 그라운드 업이라는 이론인데, 이는 고대의 새들이 땅에서 살았으며 깃털을 이용할 필요가 있을 때마다 나무로 멀리 뛰어

24

올랐다고 주장한다. 예를 들어 포식자로부터 달아나야 하는 경우 이들은 먼 거리의 나무로 뛰어 올라 발톱으로 나무를 붙잡을 수 있었다.

학자들은 고대 조류들이 현대의 조류처럼 날개짓을 한 이유에 대해 궁금해한다. 그들은 일부 공룡들이 강력한 앞발을 이용해서 먹이를 움켜쥐고 붙잡는 방법과 관련이 있을 수도 있다고 생각한다. 만약 시조새가 이렇게 했다면 강력한 앞발로 날개를 퍼덕여 보다 오랜 시간 동안 공중에 머물러 있을 수 있다는 점도 알게 되었을 것이다. 수백만 년에 걸쳐 시조새와 친척 관계였던 동물들은 점점 더 오래 공중에 떠 있을 수 있었을 것이고, 마침내 현대 조류들처럼 날 수 있었을 것이다.

📝 **Summary Note**

❶ Southern Germany
❷ 150 million
❸ body temperature
❹ glide down

Exercise 4   1 ⓒ   2 ⓓ   3 ⓒ   4 ⓑ   p.126

해석

생태계

생태계는 *생태*라는 단어와, *계*라는 단어를 합친 말이다. 생태계는 자연의 일정 지역에 존재하는 모든 자연적인 것과 동물, 식물, 그리고 광물의 성질을 조절하는 과정을 가리킨다. 한 가지 예가 사막 생태계이다. 보통 밤에는 매우 추울 수 있지만, 주로 덥고 건조한 곳이다. 따라서 모든 동식물 및 기타 존재들이 이러한 환경에 적응해 왔다. 다시 말해 사막 생태계에서는 사막에 서식하거나 존재하는 모든 것들과 사막 환경이 조화를 이룬다. 생태계의 크기에는 제한이 없다. 조화가 존재하면 생태계도 존재한다.

전 세계의 많은 생태계들이 파괴되고 있기 때문에 생태계는 현대 정치 및 환경주의 단체 사이에서 중요한 이슈가 되고 있다. 최근에는 전 세계의 거의 모든 국가인 170국 대표들이 생물 다양성 협약이라는 국제 조약에 서명했다. 이 협약은 모든 국가와 개인들이 생태계와 자연 서식지를 보호하고 모든 생태계 내에 존재하는 동식물의 개체수를 유지하기 위해 노력해야 한다는 점을 명시하고 있다. 또한 한 생태계 내의 모든 부분은 조화를 이루어 하나로서 기능하기 때문에 생태계는 하나의 단위 또는 하나의 신체와 같다는 점을 밝히고 있다. 신체의 일부가 잘리거나 괴사하면 몸 전체가 죽거나 정상적인 기능을 못하게 될 가능성이 크다. 생태계의 어떤 부분이라도 파괴된다면 그 생태계는 파괴되거나 정상적으로 작동하지 못할 가능성이 높다.

생태계에서 어떻게 조화와 균형이 유지되는지를 아는 것이 중요하다. 균형은 생태계의 여러 부분 간의 여러 가지 다양한 상호 작용을 통해 유지된다. 예를 들어 숲에 모기가 너무 많은 경우에는 개구리가 모기를 많이 잡아먹는다. 개구리는 많이 먹어서 더 튼튼해지고 더 많은 새끼를 낳게 된다. 그러나 개구리의 수가 너무 많아지기 때문에 다른 동물들이 개구리를 더 많이 잡아먹기 시작한다. 생태계에 조화가 생길 때까지 이러한 순환은 반복된다. 일부 동식물들은 보다 쉽게 생존할 수 있도록 서로를 돕는다. 흰개미와 같은 곤충들은 죽은 나무를 분해시켜 토양에 영양분을 되돌려 준다. 이로써 토양에 양분이 많아지면 그곳 식물들이 더 잘 자랄 수 있다. 생태계에서는 수백만 가지의 일들이 일어나서 균형이나 조화를 유지시킨다. 하지만 인간이 환경에 영향을 미침으로써 생태계의 일부가 파괴되면 생태계에 끔찍한 결과가 나타날 수 있다.

📝 **Summary Note**

❶ plants, animals, and minerals
❷ in harmony
❸ destroyed
❹ maintain harmony

Exercise 5   1 ⓒ   2 ⓐ   3 ⓓ   4 ⓑ   p.128

해석

돌고래의 지능

많은 학자들은 돌고래가 커다란 뇌를 가지고 있고, 영리하게 행동하며, 창의적이라는 점에서 돌고래를 매우 지능이 높은 동물로 생각한다. 이러한 모든 요인들 때문에 돌고래는 학자들에게 대단히 매력적인 연구 대상이다. 일부 학자들은 돌고래를 연구함으로써 인간이 어떻게 그처럼 지적인 동물이 되었는지를 알아낼 수 있다고 생각한다.

돌고래의 뇌는 다른 동물에 비해 상당히 큰 편이다. 실제로 체중을 고려하는 경우 돌고래의 뇌는 인간보다도 더 크다. 하지만 전체적인 몸 크기와 뇌 무게를 비교해서 살펴보면 인간의 뇌가 약간 더 크다. 또한, 지적인 동물로 간주되며 많은 사람들이 인간과 관련되어 있다고 생각하는 침팬지와 비교했을 때, 병코돌고래의 뇌가 네 배 더 크다. 뇌의 한 부분인 대뇌 피질의 경우, 인간 보다 돌고래가 40% 더 크다. 이곳은 많은 학자들에 의해 여러 가지 복잡한 사고들이 일어나는 곳이라고 생각되는 뇌의 일부이다.

돌고래의 복잡한 행동은 이들의 지능이 매우 높다는 점을 보여 준다. 예를 들어 돌고래는 보통 6마리에서 12마리씩 소규모 떼를 지어 헤엄을 친다. 연구자들은 돌고래들이 무리 내에서 서로를 인식할 수 있다고 생각한다. 스코틀랜드의 몇몇 학자들은 두세 마리의 돌고래들이 서로 간에, 인간의 끈끈한 우정과 유사한, 긴밀한 유대감을 종종 형성한다는 점을 보여 주었다. 또한 돌고래는 하나의 단위로서 행동하면서 서로가 생존하고 잘 살 수 있도록 돕는다. 상어가 다가오면 돌고래들은 위험을 피하기 위해 정확히 같은 시간에 함께 움직인다. 심지어 일부 학자들은 돌고래들이 서로에게 경고를 하기 위해 딸깍하는 소리를 낸다고 믿는다. 이들은 함께 행동하며 항상 주변을 경계하는데, 이는 대부분의 사람들도 하지 못하는 일이다.

돌고래는 또한 창의성이 뛰어나다는 점에서도 특별하다. 캐런 프라이어라는 한 미국인 과학자가 포획 상태의 돌고래들을 대상으로 이들이 얼마나 독창적인지를 실험했다. 돌고래들은 여러 가지 재주를 배운 상태였지만, 프라이어는 이들을 창의적으로 행동하도록 만드는 것이 가능한지 알고 싶었다. 예를 들어 돌고래들이 독창적인 방법으로 재주를 부리면 더 많은 생선으로 보상을 했다. 하지만 전과 똑같은 재주를 부리면 보상이 주어지지 않았다. 돌고래들은 얼마 후 독창적인 재주를 부리면 보상을 받는다는 사실을 깨닫고서 보다 독창적이고 창의적인 재주를 선보이기 시작했다. 프라이어는 돌고래들이 자신에게 요구되는 것이 무엇인지를 깨닫는데 걸리는 시간을 측정했다. 이후 그녀는 사람들에게 간단한 재주를 가르친 후 이들이 창의적으로 재주를 선보이면 보상을 해 주었다. 흥미롭게도 사람들의 경우에도 돌고래가 자신에게 요구되는 것이 무엇인지를 파악하는데 걸렸던 시간과 동일한 시간이 걸렸다.

📝 Summary Note

❶ large brains
❷ cerebral cortex
❸ swim in groups
❹ creative behavior

Exercise 6   1 Ⓑ   2 Ⓓ   3 Ⓑ   4 Ⓐ   p.130

해석

규소

규소는 탄소와 유사한 매우 중요한 원소이며 지구의 거의 모든 곳에서 찾아볼 수 있다. 지각의 4분의 1이상이 규소로 이루어져 있기 때문에 규소는 지구에서 두 번째로 풍부한 원소이다. 규소는 단독으로 존재하지 않는다. 점토, 모래, 그리고 암석과 같은 광물질 안에 들어 있다. 암석, 모래, 그리고 기타 광물질에서 규소를 채취하면 규소는 진한 회색 빛깔을 나타내며 금속처럼 보인다. 쉽게 쪼개지고 부서질 수 있다는 점에서 유리와 비슷하다. 중요한 것은 규소가 전기 및 기타 형태의 에너지를 매우 쉽게 전달하기 때문에 반도체 생산에서 규소가 이용된다는 점이다.

규소는 컴퓨터 및 반도체와 같은 다양한 컴퓨터 부품의 제조에 사용되기 때문에 중요하다. 하지만 반도체 생산에만 사용되는 것은 아니다. 여러 가지 다양한 방면에서 사용된다. 실제로 훨씬 더 많은 양의 규소가 컴퓨터 제품이 아닌 알루미늄 생산을 위해 사용된다. 사실 자동차 부품에 들어가는 알루미늄 생산에 사용되는 규소의 양이 전 세계 규소 사용량의 55%를 차지한다. 두 번째로 많이 사용되는 경우는 실리콘 생산을 위해서인데, 실리콘은 내구성이 뛰어난 물질로 플라스틱이나 고무와 비슷하다. 세 번째로 많이 사용되는 경우가 반도체 생산을 위해서이다. 그 외에도 규소는 기타 수백 가지 제품에서 사용되고 있으며, 이로써 규소는 지구에서 가장 많이 사용되는 물질 중 하나가 되고 있다.

규소는 암석, 모래, 점토, 또는 기타 광물질을 매우 뜨거운 용광로 속에 넣어 얻는다. 용광로를 1,900°C 이상으로 가열하면 규소를 포함하고 있던 광물질이 타버리고 약간의 탄소가 들어 있는 액화 규소만 남게 된다. 용광로의 바닥에 규소가 모이면 이를 추출해 냉각시킨다. 규소는 식히면 고체로 변한다. 이때의 규소에는 탄소가 남아 있어서 98%의 순도를 나타낸다. 이 상태의 규소는 자동차 부품 제조에 적합하다. 하지만 고품질의 반도체를 만들기 위해서는 기술자들이 순도가 거의 100%인 규소를 사용해야 한다. 따라서 컴퓨터 부품에 사용되는 규소는 정제되어야 한다.

규소를 정제하는 과정은 복잡하다. 오늘날 과학자들과 기술자들은 화학 처리 과정을 통해 컴퓨터 부품 생산에 사용할 규소를 정제한다. 지멘스 프로세스라고 불리는 한 방법에서는 불순물이 섞인 규소를 고온을 이용하여 특수한 기체에 노출시킨다. 이 과정에서 규소 분자의 크기가 훨씬 더 커지고 탄소 분자의 크기는 상대적으로 작아지게 된다. 그 결과 거의 순수한 상태의 규소가 만들어진다.

📝 Summary Note

❶ carbon
❷ conduct electricity
❸ aluminum
❹ 1,900 degrees

Building Summary Skills   p.132

Exercise 1 Eye Variation Among Different Species

While humans consider 20/20 eyesight to be perfect, this is not true for members of the animal kingdom, which see in different ways. Hawks can see extremely small objects from distances high in the sky. The kingfisher has monocular vision, where it uses just one eye to see above and under the water. Frogs see things only when they move. And bees have compound eyes that see everything as a mosaic of dots.

Exercise 2 The White Ant

Termites are sometimes called white ants, but they are very different from ants. They are considered pests because they eat wood, which can bother humans. They do not resemble ants at all but are members of the mantis and cockroach family. They are social insects that live in communities of up to several million insects. They have enormous nests that can be up to six meters high.

Exercise 3 The Archaeopteryx Fossil

An Archaeopteryx fossil was first found in Germany. It was a bird that lived over 150 million years ago. It did not resemble modern birds, having a full set of teeth, a flat chest, a long, bony tail, and three claws on its wings. There are a couple of theories that attempt to explain how Archaeopteryx used its feathers. Scientists want to know about this so that they can learn how birds first learned to fly.

Exercise 4 Ecosystems

The ecosystem refers to all natural things and processes that control the behavior of plants, animals, and minerals in a certain part of nature. All living things must achieve harmony to survive in their own ecosystem. Environmentalists and countries are becoming more involved in caring about ecosystems. Many countries signed the Convention of Biological Diversity recently. It is important to know about the ecosystem in order to keep it functioning properly.

Exercise 5 Dolphin Intelligence

Scientists believe dolphins are intelligent because of their large brains and ability to be creative. In fact, dolphins have larger brains than humans and chimpanzees. They form bonds like friendship, and this helps when predators attack. Karen Pryor, a scientist, experimented with them and discovered that they have the ability to engage in creative behavior. Dolphins can also learn tricks at about the same rate as humans.

Exercise 6 Silicon

Silicon is a highly abundant and extremely common element that can be found almost everywhere on the Earth. It has many qualities, particularly its ability to conduct electricity, which makes it ideal for manufacturing. It has many different uses, including computers, computer parts like semiconductors, and aluminum parts in cars. It must be purified by heating it to extreme temperatures. After it hardens, it can be used to manufacture various items.

Mini TOEFL iBT Practice Test   p.134

1	Ⓑ	2	Ⓐ	3	Ⓒ	4	Ⓓ	5	Ⓑ
6	Ⓒ	7	Ⓓ	8	Ⓑ				
9	Ⓑ	10	Ⓑ	11	Ⓒ	12	Ⓒ	13	Ⓐ
14	Ⓒ	15	Ⓐ	16	**2**				

해석

[1-8]

생물학적 해충 방제

농사를 짓는 많은 사람들이 농지와 농장에서 해충 및 질병을 퇴치하기 위해 화학 살충제 대신 생물학적 방법을 이용하고 있다. 생물학적 해충 방제는 농작물에 피해를 입히는 기생충들을 사냥하고, 죽이고, 잡아먹는 포식 동물 및 곤충을 일정 지역에 투입시키는 방법이다. 또 다른 생물학적 해충 방제의 형태는 질병과 피해를 가져온다고 알려진 기생충을 자연적으로 막아 줄 수 있는 다양한 식물들을 농지나 농장에 심는 것이다.

이러한 방식의 해충 및 질병 방제는 유기농법의 원칙을 고려한다. 유기농법으로 농사를 짓는 사람들은 농사를 지을 때 화학 물질의 사용을 최소화하거나 이를 전혀 사용하지 않으려고 한다. 화학 물질을 사용하는 기존 농법들은 해로운 생물과 유익한 생물 모두를 무차별적으로 죽이는 것으로 알려져 있다. 하지만 전체를 고려하는 접근법을 사용함으로써 농사를 짓는 사람들은 농지 내 다양한 동식물 간의 복잡한 상호 작용을 이용할 수 있다.

이러한 방식의 농사는 농지의 생물 다양성 수준을 증가시켜서 전체적으로 농지의 질이 향상된다고 생각된다. 이러한 생각은 생물 다양성이 증가하면 지속 가능한 생태계가 조성됨으로써, 해충과 질병이 사라지지는 않지만, 관리가 가능한 수준으로 감소된다는 원리에 바탕을 두고 있다. 이러한 점에서 생물학적 해충 방제의 목적은 농지의 생태계가 자립해서 생태계의 번성을 가져오는, 견제와 균형에 의한 시스템을 구축하는 것이다. 이러한 자립 상태는 균형 상태라고 할 수 있다.

화학 살충제가 생태계에 야기하는 피해에 관한 한 가지 좋은 예는 모기를 죽이기 위해 일정 지역에 살충제를 분무하는 것이다. 그렇게 되면 살충제 때문에 잠자리도 죽게 된다. 잠자리는 모기와 모기 유충을 잡아먹는 중요한 생물학적 방제 곤충이다. 이러한 방식의 분무는 장기적으로 볼 때 모기의 개체수를 종종 증가시키는데, 그 이유는 부화 중인 모기 유충을 잡아먹을 잠자리가 주변에 없기 때문이다.

탁월한 생물학적 방제 곤충은 무당벌레와 무당벌레의 유충이다. 이 곤충은 농작물을 파괴하는 여러 해충들, 즉 진디, 초록진딧물, 진드기, 애벌레와 같은 곤충들을 사냥해서 죽이고 잡아먹는다. 농사를 짓는 많은 사람들이 이 유익한 곤충을 농지에 투입해서 농작물을 보호하고 있다. 심지어 무당벌레가 더 많이 서식하고

번식해서 그 수가 늘어날 수 있도록 무당벌레 제방이라는 덤불을 조성하기도 한다. 이 유익한 곤충들은 대부분의 원예용품점에서 구입이 가능하다.

일부 식물들 역시 농지 및 작물을 보호하기 위해 사용될 수 있다. 이 특별한 생물학적 해충 방제 식물들은 여러 가지 면에서 도움이 될 수 있다. 조절 식물을 농작물 근처에 심거나 농작물과 같이 심으면 해충으로부터 농작물을 보호할 수 있다. 그렇게 되면 해충이 혼란을 느껴서 중요한 농작물 가까이에 가지 못하게 된다. 또한 이 식물들은 후각적 억제제를 만들어서 해충을 유인하는 냄새를 바꿔 놓으며, 해충의 후각신경에 신호를 보내서 해충이 중요한 농작물로부터 떨어지도록 만든다. 이들 식물들은 또한 유익한 곤충이 번식할 수 있는 장소를 제공해 주기도 한다.

그와 같은 생물학적 방제 식물로 파리와 모기를 쫓아내는 바질, 뜀벼룩갑충을 내쫓는 개박하, 그리고 알풍뎅이가 오지 못하게 막는 마늘을 들 수 있다. 이러한 식물 가운데 가장 유익한 식물은 금잔화인데, 금잔화는 멕시코무당벌레, 민달팽이, 그리고 기타 해충들을 내쫓는다. 이러한 식물들을 이용하면 이들이 유익한 포식 곤충들과 함께 효과를 발휘함으로써 화학 물질을 전혀 사용하지 않고도 해충으로 인한 피해 수준이 최소화되는 안정 상태가 만들어진다. 생물학적 해충 방제는 매우 경제적인 것으로 입증되었다. 여러 해에 걸쳐 진행된 실험에 따르면 생물학적 해충 방제의 비용 대비 편익 비율은 32:1이었던 반면에 화학 살충제를 쓴 일반적인 경우의 비용 대비 편익은 13:1이었다.

[9-16]

툰드라 식물

툰드라는 지면 아래의 토양층이 영구적으로 얼어 있는 지역으로 분류된다. 짧은 여름 기간에는 지면이 녹지만, 하층토는 계속 영구 동토층 상태로 남아 있다. 이러한 토양과 기후 조건이 툰드라에서 자랄 수 있는 식물의 유형을 결정짓는다.

툰드라에서는 강한 바람이 불며 비가 거의 내리지 않는다. 대부분의 강수는 눈에 의한 것이다. 툰드라 지역의 강수량은 사막 기후와 비슷하다. 여름에는 일부 식물들이 성장하고 번식할 수 있을 정도로 영구 동토층이 녹는다. 하지만 지면 아래의 하층토는 계속 얼어 있기 때문에 물이 그 아래로 내려갈 수 없다. 하절기에는 갇혀 있는 물에 의해서 호수와 습지가 만들어진다.

툰드라의 하절기에는 지면의 눈이 녹을 정도로 기온이 오르지만 지하의 눈은 녹지 않는다. 기온이 낮고 생장철이 짧은 탓에 이곳에서는 나무가 거의 자라지 않는다. 수목 한계선이라는 자연적인 수목 장벽에 의해 툰드라와 산림 지대가 구분된다. 툰드라 지역에서 가장 흔히 볼 수 있는 식물은 풀, 이끼, 그리고 지의류이다. 이러한 식물들은 긴 혹한의 동절기에서 살아남을 수 있으며, 여름의 짧은 생장철 기간에 빠르게 성장할 수 있다.

툰드라의 명확한 특징 중 하나는 생물 다양성 수준이 매우 낮다는 것이다. 1,700종 미만의 식물과 48종의 육상 포유류를 이 지역에서 찾아볼 수 있다. 영구 동토층의 상부층이 녹아 습지가 만들어지는 하절기에만 수천 종의 곤충이 툰드라에 서식한다.

툰드라는 전 세계 여러 지역에 존재한다. 대부분은 남극과 북극의 극지방에서 발견되며, 고도가 높은 지역에서도 발견된다. 이러한 지역은 북극 툰드라, 남극 툰드라, 그리고 고산 툰드라로 구분할 수 있으며, 이들은 각각 고유한 특성을 지닌다.

북극 툰드라는 북반구 끝 타이가 지대의 북쪽에 있는 넓고 황량한 지역이다. 이곳은 거의 일년 내내 완전히 얼어 있다. 러시아 북부 및 캐나다의 광활한 지역뿐만 아니라 라플란드 북부도 여기에 포함된다. 이곳에서는 나무가 자랄 수 없다. 땅에는 초록이 거의 없고 바위가 많다. 이러한 바위에서 지의류 및 이끼가 자라며, 자갈과 돌멩이 사이에서는 가끔씩 약간의 풀이 자라나기도 한다. [이곳에는 동물의 먹이가 될 만한 것이 거의 존재하지 않는다.] 강인한 소수의 포유류 종들만이 많은 개체수를 유지할 수 있다. 순록, 북극여우, 북극곰, 레밍, 그리고

사향소 등이 여기에 해당된다.

남극 툰드라는 북극 툰드라의 지구 반대편에 있다. 남극 툰드라는 이곳 남극 대륙뿐만 아니라 남극 및 아남극에 있는 일부 섬에서도 찾아볼 수 있다. 남극 반도의 돌이 많은 토양 지대가 남극에서 생물이 서식할 수 있는 유일한 지역 중 하나이다. 이곳에서는 수백 종의 지의류, 이끼, 그리고 우산이끼를 찾아볼 수 있다. 많은 육상조류 및 해조류 또한 자랄 수 있다. 꽃을 피우는 식물은 단 두 종만 발견되는데, 남극 좀새풀과 남극 개미자리가 그것이다. 물개 및 펭귄과 같은 포유동물들도 이처럼 생물이 서식하기에 좋지 않은 툰드라 지역에서 서식한다.

고산 툰드라는 전 세계적으로 고도가 높은 산악 지대에서 찾아볼 수 있다. 이 툰드라에서는 나무가 자랄 수 없다. 고도가 낮은 일부 고산 툰드라의 경우 눈과 얼음이 산의 경사면 아래로 흘러 내려갈 수 있기 때문에 영구 동토층이 존재하지 않는다. 케아앵무, 마모트, 산양, 친칠라, 그리고 새앙토끼와 같은 동물들이 고산 툰드라 지역에서 발견될 수 있다. 하지만 전 세계의 여러 고산 툰드라 지역에서 다양한 종의 동식물들을 찾아볼 수 있다.

Vocabulary Check-Up
p.140

A
1 Ⓑ	2 Ⓓ	3 Ⓒ	4 Ⓑ	5 Ⓓ
6 Ⓐ	7 Ⓐ	8 Ⓒ	9 Ⓑ	10 Ⓓ

B
1 Ⓕ	2 Ⓙ	3 Ⓐ	4 Ⓖ	5 Ⓑ
6 Ⓘ	7 Ⓒ	8 Ⓔ	9 Ⓓ	10 Ⓗ

UNIT 06 Rhetorical Purpose

Basic Drill
p.146

Drill 1 1 Ⓒ 2 Ⓐ

해석

원숭이 무리의 사회적 그루밍

원숭이는 매우 사회적인 동물이다. 이를 잘 보여 주는 예가 그들이 서로에게 털 고르기를 해 준다는 사실이다. 사회적 그루밍은 서로 가까이 사는 동물들이 다른 개체와 유대감을 형성할 수 있는 방법이다. 이는 인간이 우정을 쌓는 것과 비슷하다. 사회적 그루밍은 또한 다른 원숭이에게 사과하는 수단으로, 혹은 싸움을 피하기 위한 수단으로도 이용될 수 있다. 뿐만 아니라 이 동물들이 청결을 유지하기 위해 사용하는 방법이기도 하다. 원숭이들은 털이 많기 때문에 종종 곤충, 나뭇잎, 흙, 그리고 나뭇가지 등이 몸에 잘 달라붙는다. 다른 원숭이들이 털을 골라 줄 때 이들은 흙, 벌레, 그리고 기타 물질들을 떼어 내는데, 이때 털이 골라지는 개체들과 중요한 유대감을 형성하게 된다. 이러한 유대감은 사회 생활에서 중요한 것으로, 이는 인간에게 우정이 중요한 것과 마찬가지이다.

Drill 2 1 Ⓐ 2 Ⓒ

해석

사회 집단의 정의와 종류

사회학에서 집단은 몇 가지 측면에서 유사하고, 상호 작용을 하며, 특정한 사회적 책임을 받아들이고, 공통된 정체성을 지니는 사람이나 동물들의 무리이다. 이러한 정의에 따르면 인류 문명은 하나의 사회 집단으로 간주될 수 있다. 사회학에는 세 개의 사회 집단, 즉 1차 집단, 2차 집단, 그리고 준거 집단이 있다. 1차 집단은 매우 긴밀한 관계로 이루어진 소규모 집단이다. 친한 친구 및 가족이 1차 집단의 구성원이다. 2차 집단은 규모가 큰 집단으로서 이들의 관계는 형식적이거나, 학교 친구나 직장 동료 사이의 경우와 같이, 특정한 사회적 환경에 기반한다. 학교 친구가 친한 친구가 되는 경우처럼 때때로 2차 집단에서 1차 집단이 형성될 수도 있다. 준거 집단은 실제 구성원을 가지고 있지는 않지만 개인들이 스스로 소속되어 있다고 생각하는 집단이다. 예를 들어 어떤 사람들은 어두운 색 옷을 입고 어두운 화장을 한 후 스스로를 "고트족"이라고 생각하지만, 그러한 사회적 집단은 공식적으로 존재하지 않는다.

Drill 3 1 Ⓑ 2 Ⓐ

해석

문학 비평

문학 비평은 문학 작품을 연구하고, 토론하고, 그리고 해석하는 것이다. 요즘에는 대다수의 문학 비평가들이 몇몇 문학 이론을 이용하여 소설, 시, 그리고 희곡을 평가한다. 문학 이론은 비평가들이 책이나 시를 논평할 때 활용하는 특정한 철학 사상에 기반해 있다. 이러한 철학 사상에는 마르크스주의, 페미니즘, 혹은 사실주의가 포함될 수 있다. 대다수의 전문적인 문학 비평가들은 대학 교수이거나 문학 잡지에 글을 쓰는 기자들이다. 마르크스주의 문학 비평가의 예로서 한 대학 교수를 들어 보면, 그는 경제학자이자 철학자였던 칼 마르크스가 만든 사회 이론에 기초하여 *어린 왕자*를 분석할 것이다. 따라서 이 교수는 모든 인간이 기본적으로 탐욕스럽기 때문에 어린 왕자가 여행 중에 만나는 모든 인물들이 탐욕스럽게 행동한다고 주장할 것이다. 이는 칼 마르크스의 개념을 단순화시킨 것이다.

해석

아일랜드 만담가 *셔나치이*

책이 존재하기 전 고대 아일랜드에는 *셔나치이*라고 불리는 사람들이 있었다. *셔나치이*는 아일랜드 게일어로 "이야기꾼"을 의미한다. 이들은 이 마을에서 저 마을로 옮겨 다니면서 이야기를 해 주고 돈을 받았다. 종종 고대 아일랜드 전설에 관한 이야기를 들려 주었다. 때로는 이전 마을에서 들었던 이야기를 전해 주기도 했다. 이후 영국인들이 아일랜드를 점령해서 아일랜드인들에게 아일랜드 게일어 대신 영어를 쓰게 했음에도 *셔나치이*는 계속 마을을 떠돌아다니면서 모국어로 이야기를 들려 주었다. 시간이 흐르자 이야기 자체보다 아일랜드 게일어를 말한다는 것이 더 중요해졌는데, 그 이유는 이로 인해 아일랜드어가 보존될 수 있었기 때문이었다. 오늘날 아일랜드 게일어를 말하는 원어민들은 많지 않지만 아일랜드의 특정 지역에 일부가 살고 있다. 게일어는 또한 학교에서도 가르쳐진다. *셔나치이*는 이 언어가 보존되는데 많은 역할을 했다.

Exercises with Long Passages

해석

프레리도그

프레리도그는 북아메리카의 초원에 사는 작은 설치류이다. 프레리도그는 매우 사회적인 동물로 가족을 이루고 살며, 가족은 보통 한 마리의 수컷과 2마리에서 4마리 사이의 암컷으로 구성된다. 초원은 곳곳에 야생 풀들이 자라는 넓고 평평한 지대이다. 이곳에서 프레리도그는 구멍과 굴을 파고 그 안에서 생활한다. 이들 설치류에게 작은 구멍과 굴은 완벽한 곳인데, 그 이유는 이들이 평균적으로 12에서 16인치까지의 길이로 자라지만 키는 4인치 정도밖에 되지 않는 기다랗고 마른 동물이기 때문이다. 프레리도그가 파는 굴들은 서로 연결되어 있으며, 프레리도그는 20년이나 30년 동안 종종 같은 굴을 이용한다.

이들의 굴은 매우 넓게 퍼져있다. 공동으로 사용하는 굴에는 잠을 자고, 먹이를 먹고, 그리고 새끼를 돌보는 방들이 구분되어 있다. 굴은 먼 거리까지 뻗어 있을 수도 있고 땅속 33피트까지 들어가 있을 수도 있다. 굴은 또한 포식자로부터 프레리도그를 보호해 준다. 프레리도그는 포식자가 오는지를 확인하기 위해 종종 굴 구멍의 주위에 있는 풀이나 잡초를 뽑기도 한다. 만약 포식자가 다가오는 것을 보면 날카로운 소리를 내서 다른 가족 구성원들에게 위험을 알린다. 실제로 일부 학자들은 마주하는 포식자의 종류에 따라 이들이 특별한 소리를 낸다고 생각한다. 소리가 들리면 지상에 있는 모든 가족 구성원들이 굴로 들어가서 위험으로부터 몸을 피한다.

농부들은 프레리도그를 유해 동물로 간주하고 있으며, 가능한 많은 프레리도그를 죽임으로써 농사와 관련된 문제를 예방하려고 한다. 특히 농기계나 소떼의 경우에 그러하다. 프레리도그의 굴은 지반을 약하게 만들기 때문에 땅을 가는 무거운 트랙터가 종종 손상되기도 하며, 프레리도그의 굴에 빠지기 쉬운 소들은 다리가 부러지는 부상을 입을 가능성이 높다.

그럼에도 불구하고 전문가들은 프레리도그가 초원의 생태계에 필수적인 존재라고 믿는다. 주요 먹잇감으로서 프레리도그를 사냥하는 많은 독수리, 매, 그리고 여우에게 이들은 중요한 피식 동물이다. 들소와 사슴과 같은 야생 동물들

은 프레리도그가 사는 초원에서 풀을 뜯어 먹는 것을 선호하는데, 그 이유는 그곳 야생의 풀들이 더 건강하고 무성하며, 소가 풀을 뜯어 먹어서 딱딱해진 땅이 프레리도그의 굴로 푹신하게 되기 때문이다. 게다가 굴 때문에 빗물이 땅속 깊은 곳까지 스며들게 된다. 이러한 굴은 홍수 및 초원 내 토양의 침식을 예방해 주기 때문에 중요하다.

📝 Summary Note

❶ small rodents
❷ flat, grassy lands
❸ farm machinery
❹ soften ground

해석

로스앤젤레스의 도시화

도시화는 시간이 지나면서 인구가 증가하거나 크고 작은 도시들의 크기가 증가하는 것이다. 비판가들은 도시화로 인해 많은 문제들이 발생하고 있으며, 도시에 사는 사람들의 삶의 질도 급격하게 떨어지고 있다고 주장한다. 미국에서는 도시화가 경제, 사회, 그리고 크고 작은 도시 주변의 생태계에 주로 부정적인 영향을 미쳐 왔다. 특히 캘리포니아의 로스앤젤레스시는 도시화에 의한 많은 문제들을 겪고 있다. 도시 쇠퇴 현상이 일어났으며 게토가 증가했다.

로스앤젤레스시는 그곳이 차지하고 있는 면적으로 볼 때 미국에서 가장 큰 도시이다. 이곳에서 나타난 도시화의 부정적인 효과로는 난개발을 들 수 있다. 난개발은 대도시 안이나 그 주변에서 무계획적이고 무질서한 개발이 확대되는 것이다. 로스앤젤레스를 비판하는 사람들은 난개발로 인해 보기에 좋지 않고 안전하지 못한 건물들과 구역이 만들어짐으로써 막대한 양의 오염 물질과 폭력 범죄가 발생했다고 지적한다. 로스앤젤레스의 도시 계획가들이 도시의 크기를 너무나 급하게 키우는 바람에 건물과 구역이 빠르고 싼값에 지어졌으며, 그에 따라 매력적이지 못한 구역과 환경이 조성되었다. 그 결과 매력적이지 못한 환경이 반영되어 주민들의 태도도 대체적으로 부정적으로 바뀌었다. 부정적인 태도는 폭력적인 갱단을 결성하고 마약과 알코올의 복용을 늘리는 것과 같은 부정적인 행동으로 이어졌다. 게다가 각 구역에 사는 사람들의 수가 증가하면서 오염 및 이러한 시내 구역을 특징짓는 비위생적인 주거 환경도 증가했다.

경제적인 측면에서 도시화 과정은 도시로 이주해 오는 모든 사람들에게 경제적인 기회를 제공하기 위한 것이었다. 미국의 도시 계획가들은 시민들이 보다 나은 일자리, 교육, 그리고 시장을 접하게 될 것으로 생각했다. 하지만 로스앤젤레스와 같은 도시에서는 도시 공간과 주택이 점점 부족해지자 일부 지역의 경우 주거비가 매우 높아졌다. 따라서 가난한 사람들은 좋은 지역에서 살 수 없게 되었고, 많은 이들이 게토라고 알려진 지역으로 이사를 했다. 일반적으로 게토에 사는 사람들은 경제적 능력이 없기 때문에 보다 좋은 교육을 받을 수가 없고, 그 결과 이후에도 보다 좋은 일자리를 구할 수가 없다. 게토에 사는 사람들의 경우, 스스로 삶을 개선시켜 그곳을 빠져나가기가 매우 힘들다. 아마도 이러한 점이 도시화의 가장 부정적인 측면일 것이다.

📝 Summary Note

❶ negative impact
❷ urban sprawl
❸ unsanitary conditions
❹ good educations

해석

신고전주의 연극

신고전주의 연극은 16세기에서 18세기까지 서유럽, 특히 프랑스에서 가장 중요한 형태의 극이었다. 신고전주의 연극에서는 정교한 장면과 의상이 대단히 중요했으며, 과장된 연기와 공통된 주제 및 연기 방식을 따르는 것도 마찬가지였다. 신고전주의 연극에서는, 오늘날의 연속극과 마찬가지로, 줄거리가 비슷했고 반복적이었다. 또한 소극과 비극을 많이 사용하는 경향이 있었다.

신고전주의 연극은 16세기 프랑스에서 발전해서 극작가들이 극을 쓰는 방식을 바꾸어 놓았다. 또한 제작 방식과 세트 디자인 방식도 바꾸어 놓았다. 프랑스의 신고전주의 연극은 대체적으로 일치성에 기초했다. 시간의 일치, 행동의 일치, 장소의 일치, 그리고 기타 일치들이 있었다. 다시 말해서 프랑스의 신고전주의 극작가들은 극의 시간, 장소, 그리고 행동이 일치되기를 원했고 극이 보다 현실적으로 보이기를 원했다. 따라서 신고전주의자들에 따르면 실제와 마찬가지로 일몰과 일출이 없이는 극에서 날짜가 바뀔 수 없었다. 또한 극의 행위가 이루어지는 장소가 바뀌면 배경도 바뀌어야 했다. 신고전주의 연극의 또 다른 중요한 측면은 중요한 상황이나 인물을 우스꽝스럽게 보이도록 만드는 방법인 소극을 사용했다는 점이었다. 소극의 반대인 비극 역시 신고전주의 연극에서 흔하게 사용되었다. 비극은 슬픈 상황을 더 슬프게 보이도록 만드는 극의 방법이다.

가장 인기가 높았던 세 명의 신고전주의 극작가는 피에르 코르네유, 장 라신느, 그리고 몰리에르였다. 이들은 모두 각자 다른 스타일의 극을 썼고, 같은 시기에 파리에서 활동했다. 파리의 관객들은 서로 다른 스타일의 희극을 관람하고 이 셋을 비교하는 것을 좋아했다. 코르네유가 제일 먼저 극을 쓰기 시작했는데, 작품의 내용 때문에 많은 논란이 일어났다. 1637년에 쓰여진 그의 가장 유명한 작품 *르 시드*는 기존 신고전주의 연극의 일치성을 따르지 않았기 때문에 인기도 많고 논란도 많았다. 오늘날에도 비평가들은 이 작품을 신고전주의 연극으로 분류해야 하는지에 대해 논쟁을 벌이고 있다. 장 라신느는 코르네유와는 달리 최대한 신고전주의 연극의 원칙을 고수하려고 노력했다. 1664년에 쓰여진 그의 가장 유명한 비극 *안드로마케*는 아마도 신고전주의 연극의 가장 좋은 예가 될 것이다. 한편 몰리에르는 소극의 왕이었으며, 가장 영향력이 컸던 신고전주의 극작가였다. 그의 극중 인물들은 실제 인물을 묘사하기 위해 사용되었고, 그는 인간의 약점의 실체를 최대한 많이 나타내려고 했다.

📝 Summary Note

❶ 16th-18th centuries

❷ similar and repetitive

❸ time, action, place

❹ Molière

해석

노인학

노인학은 노인 및 노화 과정을 연구하는 학문이다. 노인학에는 사회학적 연구, 생물학적 연구, 그리고 심리학적 연구가 포함된다. 이러한 연구에는 나이가 들면서 겪게 되는 신체적, 정신적, 그리고 사회적 변화에 대한 연구와 노령 인구가 사회에 미치는 영향에 대한 연구가 포함된다. 노인학자들은 자신들이 알게 된 점을 노령층을 지원하는 정부 정책 및 프로그램에 적용시킨다.

많은 노인학자들이 다양한 학력을 가지고 있다. 예를 들어 노인학자들은 사회

학, 의학, 심리학, 혹은 경영학 학위를 가지고 있을 수 있다. 더 나아가 이들은 병원, 대학, 그리고 정부 기관에서 일을 한다. 행정적인 차원에서는 노인들에게 도움이 될 프로그램 및 서비스를 개발하고 조정한다.

이러한 전문가들은 모두 노인들의 삶을 이해하고 향상시키기 위한 노력의 일환으로서 연구를 하고 있다. 이들은 개개인으로서 가족과 함께 사는 노인들, 혹은 비슷한 연령대의 다른 노인들과 함께 모여 사는 노인들을 상대로 연구를 하며, 이들과 직접 커뮤니케이션을 한다. 노인에 대한 연구 및 이들과의 대화를 통해 얻은 정보는 노인들의 삶을 향상시키기 위한 노인용 주택 및 여가 활동을 설계할 때 고려된다. 또한 노인학자들은 잡지에 글을 쓰고 책을 출판함으로써 다른 전문가들이 노인 및 그 가족의 특별한 관심사에 대해 더 많이 알 수 있도록 한다.

또한 노인학에는 생물 노인학과 생물 의학 노인학이라고 불리는 하위 분야가 있다. 이들은 의학적인 치료를 통해 노화 과정을 늦추거나 조절할 수 있는지에 관심을 갖는다. 이 분야의 노인학 전문가들은 특별한 의학적 지식과 목적을 가지고 있다. 이들은 생물 노인학자와 생물 의학 노인학자로 알려져 있다. 생물 노인학자들은 치매를 일으키는 노화의 생물학적 과정을 연구한다. 치매란 노인들이 더 이상 정확한 사고를 하지 못하고 때때로 다시 아이가 된 것처럼 행동하는 것이다. 이는 일종의 퇴행성 사고 방식 장애로 보인다. 반면 생물 의학 노인학자들은 사람과 동물의 노화 과정을 조절, 예방, 혹은 역전시키기 위해 연구하는 학자들이다. 이들 두 가지 유형의 전문가들은, 현재 대단히 인기가 높은, 노화 방지 분야에서 일한다.

오늘날에는 노화를 조절하고 역전시킬 수 있는 사람들에 대한 수요가 매우 높다. 이 분야에서 혁신적인 발전이 이루어지면 그러한 의학 전문가들에게 막대한 수익이 돌아갈 수 있다. 노화에 대한 치료제는 결코 존재하지 않을 수도 있지만, 생물 노인학자와 생물 의학 노인학자들은 자신들이 노화의 과정을 늦출 수 있다고 확신한다. 그렇게 되면 사람들이 고령에 이를 때까지 보다 길고 만족스러운 삶을 살 수 있을 것이다.

📝 Summary Note

❶ old people

❷ conversations

❸ Biogerontology

❹ slow down

해석

애리조나의 방울뱀

방울뱀은 북아메리카와 남아메리카 전역에서 찾아볼 수 있는 독사이다. 다른 파충류와 달리 방울뱀은 알 대신 새끼를 낳는다. 이 새끼 방울뱀들은 치명적인 독을 잔뜩 가진 채 태어난다. 몇 차례 허물을 벗은 뒤, 뱀에 방울이 생긴다. 방울은 죽은 피부 조직으로 만들어지며 뱀 꼬리의 끝 부분에 달려 있다. 방울뱀은 위협을 인식하면 방울을 흔든다. 또한 꼬리 흔들기라는 과정을 통해 방울을 이용해서 다른 방울뱀과 의사소통을 할 수도 있다.

방울뱀의 눈과 콧구멍 사이에는 피트라고 불리는 복잡한 피부막이 있다. 이 기관은 멀리 떨어진 곳에서의 움직임, 진동, 혹은 기온 변화를 탐지할 수 있다. 방울뱀은 귀를 가지고 있지는 않지만 피트를 사용해서 소리를 들을 수 있고, 혀를 이용해 공기 중의 입자를 수집함으로써 포식자를 감지할 수 있다.

방울뱀의 송곳니는 병원에서 사용되는 피하 주사기와 비슷하게 작동한다. 이는 자신을 공격할 공격자의 몸에 독을 주입하는 방어 수단이다. 이 독으로 상대방을 마비시키거나 때때로 죽일 수도 있는데, 그 효과는 독을 뿜는 방울뱀의 종

류에 따라 다르다. 치명적인 방울뱀에 물리고도 살아 남은 사람들은, 처음 물리고서 회복된 후에도, 종종 운동 능력을 상실하고 조직 손상의 문제를 겪게 된다.

애리조나에서는 17종의 방울뱀을 찾아볼 수 있는데, 가장 흔한 종은 서부다이아몬드방울뱀이다. 이 뱀은 위장용 무늬를 가지고 있으며 주변 환경과 섞이기 때문에 찾기가 매우 어려울 수 있다. 이로 인해 서부다이아몬드방울뱀은 하이킹을 하는 사람들과 이들의 서식지 주변을 돌아다니는 사람들에게 특히 위험하다. 많은 사람들이 자신도 모르게 이 뱀을 밟은 다음에 뱀에 물린다.

쓰리-스테퍼 혹은 그린백뱀으로도 알려져 있는 모하비방울뱀은 북아메리카에서 가장 강력한 독을 가지고 있는 방울뱀이다. 이 뱀의 독은 서부다이아몬드방울뱀과 같은 일반적인 다른 방울뱀의 독보다 20배나 강하며, 북아메리카에서 방울뱀에 물려 죽은 대부분의 사람들이 모하비방울뱀에 물려서 사망한다. "쓰리-스테퍼"라는 별명은 사람이 방울뱀에 물린 후 쓰러져 죽기까지 보통 몇 발자국을 걸어가는지 알려 준다.

한 종류의 방울뱀들만이 파란색 눈을 가지고 있다. 바로 애리조나점박이방울뱀이다. 이 뱀의 눈 색깔은 흰색, 회색, 그리고 파란색을 띄는 것으로 알려져 있는데, 붉은색 바위에 둘러싸이면 붉은색으로 바뀔 수도 있다. 이 뱀은 모하비방울뱀만큼 치명적이지는 않지만 서부다이아몬드방울뱀의 독보다 2배나 강한 독을 지니고 있으며, 박쥐를 잡아먹는 것으로 알려져 있다.

하지만 일반적으로 뱀은 사람을 먼저 공격하지 않고 기회가 있으면 거의 대부분 달아난다고 알려져 있다. 실제로 일부 전문가들에 의하면 방울뱀은 근처에 있는 사람들의 의도를 파악해서 그에 따라 반응한다고 한다. 예를 들어 한 대조 연구에서는 폐쇄된 공간 내의 방울뱀의 경우 자신을 해칠 가능성이 높은 농장주에게는 보다 방어적으로 반응하지만 자신을 좋아하고 위협을 끼치지 않는 파충류학자들에게는 보다 수동적으로 반응할 것이라는 점이 입증되었다.

📝 Summary Note

❶ born live
❷ temperature changes
❸ defensive
❹ Western Diamondback

Exercise 6 1 Ⓐ 2 Ⓒ 3 Ⓒ 4 Ⓓ p.158

해석

진 버코 글리슨의 워그 테스트

1958년 미국의 심리 언어학자인 진 버코 글리슨이 워그 테스트라고 하는 실험을 고안했는데, 이 실험은 *cats*, *dogs*, 그리고 *horses*와 같은 영어 명사의 복수형을 만드는 법을 아이들이 어떻게 배우는지를 연구했다. 아이들에게 가상의 단어를 단수 형태로 준 후 이 단어들을 복수형으로 바꿀 것을 요구했다. 영어에서 복수 명사 뒤에 붙는 "s"는 /z/, /s/, 혹은 /iz/의 세 가지로 발음된다. 가장 흔한 발음은 *dogs*에서와 같이 /z/ 발음이며, 그 다음은 *cats*에서와 같이 /s/ 발음이고, 마지막은 *horses*에서와 같이 /iz/ 발음이다.

실험에서 아이들은 상상 속 동물의 그림을 받았다. 그리고는 그 동물이 워그라는 말을 들었다. 실험자가 "이것은 워그예요."라고 말했다. 실험자는 또 다른 워그가 그려진 다른 한 장의 카드를 꺼내서 "이제 두 마리가 있군요. 이 두 마리는...?"이라고 말했다. "g"로 끝나는 명사의 복수형을 제대로 알고 있는 아이라면 /z/ 발음을 넣어 "두 마리의 워그들(two wugs)이에요."라고 말할 것이다. 종종 매우 어린 아이들은 이에 혼란을 느껴 "두 마리의 워그(wug)예요."라고 말했다. 일반적으로 4세 이상의 아이들은 질문에 올바른 대답을 했다. 연구자들은 또한 /s/ 발음과 /iz/ 발음으로 끝나는 복수형을 만들어야 하는 기타 실험들을 진행했

는데, 이들은 /z/ 발음만큼 일반적이지 않기 때문에 이러한 규칙은 아이들이 보통 나중에 알게 된다는 점을 밝혀냈다.

워그 테스트는 또한 아이가 동사의 올바른 사용법과 소유격의 용법을 이해하는지 알아보기 위해 "이것은 롭의 자전거입니다."와 같은 질문들을 포함하고 있었다. 소유격은 소유 사실을 나타내는 문법 파트이다. 더 나아가 아이들에게, 운전하는(drive) 사람을 운전사(driver)라고 하는 것과 같이, 접미사 −er을 사용해서 사람의 직업을 나타내도록 유도했다. 다시 한 번 아이들에게 의미가 없는, 이번에는 "zib"이라는 단어가 주어졌다. 연구자는 아이들에게 "집(zib)하는 사람은..?"이라고 물었다. 일부 어린 아이들은 "지버(zibber)예요."라고 답했지만, 다수의 어린 아이들은 "집맨(zibman)이에요."라고 답했다.

워그 테스트는 매우 어린 아이들도 전에 전혀 들어본 적이 없는 단어의 복수형, 소유격, 그리고 기타 형태들을 만들 수 있는 문법 체계를 지니고 있다는 점을 보여 주었다. 이 실험은 아이들이 문법 규칙을 배우지 않더라도 자연적으로 언어 능력을 습득한다는 것을 입증한 최초의 실험이었다.

📝 Summary Note

❶ plural forms
❷ imaginary words
❸ verbs and possessives
❹ grammatical systems

Building Summary Skills   p.160

Exercise 1 Prairie Dogs

Prairie dogs are small, slender social animals that burrow complex tunnels in the large flatlands of North America. Many farmers consider prairie dogs to be pests because their tunnels can cause damage to machinery and cattle. But scientists recognize that prairie dogs are important to the ecosystem. For example, prairie dogs are the food source for some predator species, and their intricate tunnels create the conditions needed to grow preferred grasses for cattle and keep grazer-tamped ground soft. Furthermore, the tunnels help channel rainwater that could cause erosion to the soil.

Exercise 2 Urbanization in Los Angeles

Urbanization is the spread of cities accompanied by the increase in population in those areas. The city of Los Angeles in the United States is a good example of urban sprawl. Urban sprawl is the uncontrolled and unplanned development that takes place in city areas. In Los Angeles, many neighborhoods were constructed cheaply and quickly. As a result, unattractive, unsafe, and crowded neighborhoods, called ghettos, gave rise to unsanitary conditions and violent crime among the poor. There, opportunities for better education and jobs are seldom seen.

Exercise 3 Neoclassical Theater

Neoclassical theater was the most important form of theater from the sixteenth to the eighteenth century in Western Europe, especially in France. French neoclassical dramatists wanted the time, place, and action of the play to be unified and to be more like real life. Playwrights used costumes and scenery to evoke a sense of real time and place in their productions, and they employed methods of farce to make important situations seem ridiculous or methods of tragedy to make sad situations even sadder. The most influential neoclassical playwright was Molière, who used farce to highlight human weaknesses.

Exercise 4 Gerontology

Gerontologists are scientists who are concerned with issues of the elderly. They come from various backgrounds. Many gerontologists research, study, and plan the day-to-day conditions and needs of the elderly, which include the development of old age homes and recreational activities as well as administrative services and the publication of related health information. Two particular types of gerontologists are biogerontologists and biomedical gerontologists. Biogerontologists study the aging process while biomedical gerontologists try to find ways to control, prevent, or even reverse the process of aging.

Exercise 5 Rattlesnakes in Arizona

Rattlesnakes can be found all over North and South America. Their unique physical characteristics such as pits and an ability to bear live young set them apart from other snakes and help them to adapt to their environments. Seventeen types of rattlesnakes have been identified in Arizona alone. Among them are the western diamondback, the Mohave, and the Arizona speckled rattlesnake. Although rattlesnake venom is often fatal to humans, studies have shown that rattlesnakes are not naturally aggressive. In fact, rattlesnakes only seem to attack humans as a defense mechanism.

Exercise 6 Jean Berko Gleason's Wug Test

In 1958, Jean Berko Gleason, an American psycholinguist, conducted experiments to find out how children learn language. One experiment was the Wug Test. In order to examine children's appropriate use of plurals, each child was shown a toy creature called a wug and then prompted to finish the sentence, "These are two . . . ?" In a separate experiment, each child was asked to change verb forms of words to noun forms as related to occupations. For example, a person who drives is a driver. The results of the experiment proved that children learn language naturally without being taught grammar rules.

Mini TOEFL iBT Practice Test p.162

1 Ⓐ   2 Ⓐ   3 Ⓑ   4 Ⓓ   5 Ⓒ

6 Ⓒ   7 Ⓓ   8 Ⓑ

9 Ⓑ   10 Ⓓ   11 Ⓑ   12 Ⓐ   13 Ⓒ

14 Ⓒ   15 **2**   16 Social Interactionism: ①, ④, ⑦

Critical Period Hypothesis: ②, ⑤

해석

[1-8]

막스 베버

막스 베버는 현대 사회학의 창시자 중 한 명으로 간주되며, 현대의 정치학과 경제학에도 큰 공헌을 했다. 베버의 경력은 종교 사회학 연구로 시작되었다. 그는 서양 국가들과 동양 국가들 사이에 문화적인 차이가 나타난 주요한 이유 중 하나가 종교 때문이라고 주장했다. 또한 종교와 문화가 국가의 정치 체제를 형성시키는 주된 요인이라고 생각했다. 그는 또한 특정 종교 집단에 속한 사람들의 공통적인 특성의 중요성을 강조했다. 예를 들어 베버는 많은 서유럽인들이 철저한 직업 윤리를 가지고 있다고 생각했다. 흥미롭게도, 베버는 일반화를 통해 전체 인종들을 규정했고, 특히 서유럽인의 직업 윤리를 "프로테스탄트 윤리"라고 명명했다. 베버의 연구에서 핵심적인 논지는 서양인들의 종교의 결과로서 서양에서는 자본주의가 탄생했으며, 같은 원리로 동양에서는 사람들의 종교 때문에 자본주의가 결코 성공하지 못할 것이라는 점이었다.

종교 사회학에 관한 베버의 연구는 자신의 가장 유명한 에세이가 될 *프로테스탄트 윤리와 자본주의 정신*으로 시작되었다. 이 책이 발표된 후 그는 다른 에세이에서 세계의 모든 주요 종교들에 대한 글을 썼다. 여기에서 그는 세 가지 주제를 설명했다. 종교 사상이 경제 활동에 미치는 영향, 사회 계급과 종교 사상의 관계, 그리고 서양 문명을 동양 문명과 다르게 만드는 서양 문명의 특징이 그것이었다. 그의 연구 목적은 왜 동양의 문화와 서양의 문화가 다르게 발전했는지 그 이유를 밝히려는 것이었다. 하지만 그는, 동료들이 그랬던 것과는 달리, 한 문명이 다른 문명보다 낫다고 생각하지 않았다. 그의 아이디어는 관찰에 기초해 있었다. 베버는 저서에서 프로테스탄트의 종교적 사고 때문에 서유럽과 미국의 경제 체제가 발전했다고 주장했다. 서구의 경제 체제를 형성시킨 또 다른 현상들도 있었다. 여기에는 과학적 그리고 수학적인 발견, 법체제의 수립, 정부 구성, 그리고 중소기업의 설립이 포함되었다. 베버는 사회 조직, 종교, 그리고 현대 경제 체제의 발달을 통해 서양인들이 원시적이고 미신을 따르는 믿음에서 벗어나고 있다고 생각했다.

그와 대조적으로 베버는 동양의 종교가 서양 종교와 근본적으로 다르며, 이러한 점 때문에 중국에서는 자본주의가 발달하지 못했다고 생각했다. 베버는 서양 종교가 원시적인 미신에서 벗어났던 반면, 유교, 도교, 그리고 힌두교와 같은 동양의 종교들은 그러한 믿음을 체계화시켰다고 믿었다. 이는 그 후 그들 종교의 중요한 부분이 되었다. 게다가 유교와 도교에서는 "군자"가 부자가 되려고 노력해서는 안 되었다. 최대한 사회에 봉사를 해야만 했다. 베버에게 이러한 점은 동양의 여러 국가에서 자본주의가 발달할 수 없다는 점을 의미했다. 그는 또한 동양의 국가에서는 교육을 받은 자와 교육을 받지 못한 자로 사회가 나뉘어져 있다고 생각했다. 교육을 받은 자는 끊임없이 선각자처럼 행동하려는 반면에 교육을 받지 못한 자들은 생계에만 매달리면서 주술을 믿었다. 이러한 이유로 그는 성공적인 경제 체제가 형성될 수 없다고 믿었다.

[9-16]

아동의 언어 습득

언어 습득은 제1언어이든 그 이후의 언어이든 사람들이 언어를 배우는 방식을 가리킨다. 요즘 언어학자들 사이의 뜨거운 논쟁거리는 아동이 선천적인 언어 습득 능력을 가지고 태어나는지 혹은 환경으로부터 언어를 이해하는 법을 배우는지에 관한 것이다. 이 논쟁은 생득론 대 경험론 논쟁으로 알려져 있다.

생득론을 지지하는 언어학자들은 아이들이 언어의 법칙을 조직할 수 있는 선천적인 능력을 통해 배운다고 생각한다. 하지만 대화를 나눌 다른 사람이 없는 경우에는 이러한 능력을 사용할 수 없다. 생득론에 따르면 태어나는 순간 아이들의 뇌는 언어를 학습할 준비가 되어 있기 때문에 아이들에게는 언어를 배우기 위한 어떠한 학습도 필요하지 않다. 생득론자들의 주장에 따르면 갓 태어난 아기는 자국어 문법이나 모국어 문법을 기본적으로 이해하기 때문에 언어를 이해할 수 있다. 아이는 성장하면서 타고난 문법 지식을 이용하여 세상을 이해하며 복잡한 방식으로 사고를 표현하고 해석하게 된다. 이 이론이 옳다면 아기였을 때부터 언어를 이해할 수 있게 만드는 기본적인 지식이 유전자 속에 존재해야 한다.

반면에 여러가지 다양한 경험론들이 존재한다. 여기에는 사회적 상호 작용론으로 불리는, 가장 인기 있는 경험론이 포함된다. 사회적 상호 작용론자들은 아이들의 언어 습득에 어른들이 중요한 역할을 한다고 생각한다. 이 언어학자들은 부모, 특히 엄마가 정규 언어 수업에서와 비슷한 방식으로 아이들에게 말을 시킨다고 생각한다. 그리고 아이들이 쉽게 언어를 배우는 것처럼 보이지만, 이들의 발전은 거의 항상 이루어지는 언어 수업을 받은 결과이다. 또한 사회적 상호 작용론자들은 십대나 성인에 비해 아이들이 훨씬 빠르게 학습하는 능력을 가지고 있다고 생각한다. 하지만 전 세계 많은 사회에서 어머니가 아이에게 그다지 말을 많이 하지 않아도 아이가 금새 말을 유창하게 하는 경우가 많기 때문에 이 이론은 도전을 받고 있다.

아동의 언어 습득에 관한 또 다른 중요한 이론은 결정적 시기 가설이다. 이 이론을 지지하는 언어학자들은 언어를 상당한 정도로, 그리고 주로 제1언어의 습득과 관련해서, 능숙한 정도로 깨닫는 아동들의 선천적 능력이 보통 12세 정도에 끝난다고 주장한다. 그 이후에는 누구도 언어를 완전하게 익힐 수 없다고 믿는다. 이 이론을 지지하는 사람들은, 야생 소녀라고도 알려진, 지니라는 여자 아이를 예로 든다.

지니는 고립된 상태에서 자랐다. 그녀의 아버지는 정신 장애를 겪고 있었는데, 그녀를 다른 사람들과 접촉하지 못하게 했고, 그녀에게 결코 말을 하지 않았으며, 그녀가 아무것도 배우지 못하게 했다. [실제로 지니는 빛이 거의 들어오지 않는 방에 감금되어 유아용 변기에 묶인 채 대부분의 시간을 보냈다.] 그녀는 13세에 발견되어 아버지로부터 격리되었다. 그녀의 상황은 매우 비극적이었지만, 언어학자들은 그녀를 통해 결정적 시기 가설, 그리고 생득론 또는 경험론을 실험해 볼 수 있었기 때문에, 소녀에게 언어를 가르칠 기회가 생겼다는 사실에 흥분했다. 지니는 언어를 어느 정도 배울 수 있었다. 하지만 일반적인 십대의 수준에는 결코 도달하지 못했다. 언어학자들은 지니의 사례가 결정적 시기 가설을 입증해 준다고 생각하지만, 이것이 생득론자나 경험론자의 주장을 지지하는지에 대해서는 여전히 논란이 있다.

Vocabulary Check-Up
p.168

A

| 1 | ⓑ | 2 | ⓒ | 3 | ⓐ | 4 | ⓐ | 5 | ⓑ |
| 6 | ⓒ | 7 | ⓓ | 8 | ⓒ | 9 | ⓐ | 10 | ⓐ |

B

| 1 | ⓗ | 2 | ⓔ | 3 | ⓐ | 4 | ⓕ | 5 | ⓙ |
| 6 | ⓘ | 7 | ⓑ | 8 | ⓒ | 9 | ⓖ | 10 | ⓓ |

UNIT 07 Inference

Basic Drill
p.172

Drill 1 1 ⓓ 2 ⓒ

해석

시베리아

환경 보호론자들은 지구 온난화의 원인과 영향에 관심을 갖기 때문에 시베리아의 황량한 경관을 주목해 왔다. 매서운 추위, 얼음, 그리고 눈으로 잘 알려져 있는 시베리아는 러시아의 절반 이상을 차지한다. 아시아 북동부 상단의 끝자락을 제외한 모든 지역을 둘러싸고 있다. 시베리아는 캐나다, 스칸디나비아, 그리고 알래스카의 일부 지역과 함께 북극 툰드라를 구성한다. 이곳에서는, 비록 나무는 없지만, 초목과 동물들이 수천 년 동안 전통적인 생업을 유지시켜 주었다. 이러한 생업에는 순록 방목, 사냥, 그리고 어업이 포함된다. 하지만 오늘날 그러한 환은 바뀌고 있다. 북극 지역은 대규모 산업 단지 및 그 주변 도시들의 본거지가 되고 있으며, 이로 인해 지구의 중위도에서 올라오는 오염 물질의 유입이 증가하고 있다. 이러한 증가는 북극 툰드라의 민감한 생태계에 심각한 영향을 미치고 있으며, 지구 전체에 중대한 위협이 되고 있다.

Drill 2 1 ⓒ 2 ⓐ

해석

야코브 레비 모레노

야코브 레비 모레노는 계량사회학, 사이코드라마, 그리고 집단 심리 치료의 아버지이다. 1889년 루마니아에서 태어났지만 비엔나에서 자란 그는 1925년에 미국으로 건너갔다. 모레노는 칼 융의 주장을 연구하고 확대시켰지만, 치료를 환자 개인의 개인적인 공상에만 국한시켜야 한다고 생각했던 지그문트 프로이드의 이론은 도외시했다.

모레노는 프로이드와 달리 대중적 혹은 사회적 치료에 초점을 맞추었다. 그는 학습과 생활을 사회적으로 구성되는 경험으로 보았다. 그는 환자들이 판단을 내리지 않는 안전한 그룹 환경에서 멀리 떨어져 있는 문제를 해결하는 방법을 배운다면 일상 생활에서 일어나는 실제 문제들을 보다 잘 해결할 수 있을 것이라고 생각했다. 만약 실제 문제들이 쉽게 해결된다면 환자들의 삶도 보다 행복해질 것이다.

Drill 3 1 ⓑ 2 ⓑ

해석

로제타 스톤

로제타 스톤은 1799년 이집트의 항구 도시인 로제타 인근에서 발견되었다. 이는 고대 문서의 해독에 필요한 결정적인 단서가 되었기 때문에 학계에 있어서는 귀중한 발견이었다. 기원전 196년에 만들어진 분홍빛을 띤 이 회색의 석판은 이집트의 파라오인 프톨레마이오스 5세에게 신관들이 경의를 표하기 위한 글을 새겨 넣은 진상물이었다.

신관들은 모든 사람들이 읽을 수 있도록 당시 널리 사용되던 세 가지 표기 방식, 즉 상형 문자, 그리스 문자, 그리고 민중 문자를 사용해서 자신들의 충성심을 이집트어와 그리스어로 기록했다. 상형 문자는 종교적 규범에 관한 것으로서 양식화된 그림으로 중요한 개념들을 나타냈으며, 그리스 문자는 지배층의 언어였고, 그리고 민중 문자는 대중들의 일상적인 말과 글에서 사용되었다. 그리스 문자와 민중 문자는 번성했던 반면에 상형 문자는 잊혀졌기 때문에 이집트 유물들의 이면에 들어 있는 의미들은 미스터리로 남게 되었다.

하지만 1822년 그리스어를 포함하여 여러 개의 언어를 구사했던 젊은 역사 강사 장 프랑수아 샹폴리옹이 동일한 내용이 적혀 있는 문서들을 비교해서 알기 힘든 상형 문자의 비밀을 풀어 냈다.

Drill 4 1 Ⓐ 2 Ⓓ

해석

애팔래치아산맥

애팔래치아산맥은 북아메리카 대륙에서 가장 오래된 산맥이다. 북쪽으로는 캐나다부터 남쪽으로는 미국까지 이어져 있으며, 그 길이는 19,884마일 정도이다. 산맥 전체는 크게 세 부분으로 나눌 수 있다. 북쪽 부분은 캐나다의 뉴펀들랜드에서 허드슨밸리까지 뻗어 있는 산들을 포함한다. 중간 부분은 허드슨 밸리부터 버지니아의 뉴리버밸리까지, 그리고 웨스트버지니아까지 뻗어 있는 산들을 포함한다. 남쪽 부분은 뉴리버밸리에서 시작해서 중부 앨라배마에 있는 산맥의 끝까지 이어져 있는 산들을 포함한다. 애팔래치아산맥은 대서양 해안과 나란히 뻗어 있기 때문에 미국의 동부 해안과 중서부 지역을 가르는 자연적인 경계선이 된다.

Exercises with Long Passages

Exercise 1 1 Ⓒ 2 Ⓐ 3 Ⓑ 4 Ⓐ   p.174

해석

장 피아제의 인지 발달 단계

스위스의 심리학자인 장 피아제는 인지 발달 단계를 네 가지 단계, 즉 감각 운동기, 전조작기, 구체적 조작기, 그리고 형식적 조작기로 구분했다. 이 단계들은 시간 순서로 일어나며 대체적으로 연령과 관련이 있다. 몇몇 단계의 특징들은 같은 시간대에서 중첩될 수도 있다. 하지만 각 단계에 해당하는 나이는 그 시기의 현실에 대한 대략적인 이해도를 반영한다.

감각 운동기는 감각 정보 및 운동 활동의 경험으로만 지식이 구성되는 유아기에 나타난다. 이때 중요한 두 가지 능력을 습득할 수 있다. 첫 번째는 자아와 타인을 구분하는 것이다. 두 번째는, 보이는지, 만져지는지, 혹은 들리는지와 상관없이, 물체와 사건이 존재한다는 점을 깨닫는 것이다.

2세와 7세 사이에는 전조작기가 나타난다. 이때는 언어 능력이 발달하면서 현실에 대한 상징적 표현이 중요해지는데, 이는 두 개의 연속적인 하위 단계로 구성된다. 바로 상징적 사고 단계와 직관적 사고 단계이다. 상징적 사고 단계는 2세와 4세 사이에 나타난다. 이름 붙이기와 자기 중심주의 및 애니미즘에 의해 제한되는 가상 놀이가 그 특징이다. 자기 중심주의는 타인의 관점에서 인식하는 것을 방해하며, 애니미즘은 무생물도 인간과 같이 느끼고 행동하는 특성을 지닌다고 믿는 것이다.

4세와 7세 사이에는 직관적 사고에 의한 상위 인지가 나타난다. 직관적 사고로 아이가 알 수 있다. 하지만 그러한 지식이 어떻게 도출되는지는 이해할 수 없다. 이러한 현상은 다른 모든 것을 배제시킨 채 하나의 측면이나 아이디어에만 집중한 결과이다. 이때의 특징은 사물의 형태가 변하는 경우 아이들의 머리 속에 사물의 고유한 특성이 보존되지 않는다는 것이다.

구체적 조작기는 7세에서 11세 사이에 나타난다. 구체적 조작기에 들어간 아이들은 정보를 논리적으로 해석하기 시작한다. 공통된 특징이나 연관된 특징에 따라 사물을 분류할 수 있다. 또한 서열화 및 이행성 순서를 바꿀 수도 있다. 서열

화는 연속적인 양에 따라 자극을 순서대로 배열하는 과정이다. 이행성은 구체적으로 표현된 '만약 그렇다면' 시나리오에서 사용되는 문제 해결 전략이다.

형식적 조작기는 11세에서 15세 이상까지의 시기에 나타날 수 있다. 이 시기의 특징으로는 추상적이고 관념적인 추론과 청소년 자기 중심성, 즉 자신과 타인에 대한 평가를 촉진시키는 고양된 자의식을 들 수 있다. 이 단계의 개인들은 추측과 가설을 검증하려는 경향을 보이며, 논리적인 결론에 도달하기 위해 광범위하고 체계적인 알고리즘을 만들고 작동시킬 수 있다. 이러한 능력 덕분에 청소년들은, 보다 확고한 선입관을 가지고 있는 구체적 조작기의 아동에 비해, 보다 많은 가능성을 탐구할 수 있다.

인지 발달 단계에 대한 피아제 이론은 1950년대에 소개된 이후로 각기 다른 발달 수준에 있는 아동들의 능력을 편협하게 평가한다는 점에서 비판을 받아 왔다. 이 이론이 한 단계에서 다음 단계로 넘어가는 속도와 정도에 있어서 사회적 담화, 문화, 그리고 교육이라는 요인을 고려하지 않는다고 비판하는 사람들도 있다. 게다가 최근의 연구들은 학습 영역에 따라서 몇 가지 단계가 동시에 나타나기 쉽다는 점을 보여 준다. 그럼에도 불구하고 피아제의 단계는 교육학계의 경향에 막대한 영향을 끼치고 있다.

📝 Summary Note

❶ Sensorimotor
❷ symbolic thought
❸ seven to eleven
❹ abstract and ideological

Exercise 2 1 Ⓒ 2 Ⓐ 3 Ⓐ 4 Ⓓ   p.176

해석

숫자 기호

수는 개념이다. 수는 추상적이다. 볼 수도, 들을 수도, 그리고 맛을 보거나 냄새를 맡을 수도 없다. 숫자는 수를 나타내기 위해 만든 기호로, 하나의 수는 여러 가지 방법으로 나타낼 수 있다. 수는 서수와 기수로 분류할 수 있다. 서수는 한정사의 역할을 하며 "어떤 것?"이라는 질문에 대한 답을 준다. 이는 또한 순서를 나타내기도 하는데, 이에 비해서 기수는 수량을 알려 준다.

숫자는 수를 나타내는 기호이며, 기수법은 수를 기호로 나타내는 방법이다. 기수법에는 단항 기수법, 승법적 기수법, 그리고 위치 기수법 세 가지가 있다. 단순 기수법에서는 밑수에 동일한 지수가 적용되며 각 숫자의 값이 더해진다. 예를 들어 여러 개의 줄을 더함으로써 총계를 낸다. 승법적 기수법에서는 밑수와 밑수의 기호를 정한 후 승수를 사용함으로써 단위 기호가 한 번 이상 쓰이지 않는다. 일반적으로는 하나의 승수 뒤에 단위 기호가 붙는 형태로 수들이 짝을 이루어 쓰인다. 밑수에 도달할 때마다 새로운 기호가 사용된다. 만약 밑수가 4인 경우, 줄표나 선을 사용해 1, 2, 3, 4를 나타내겠지만, 5는 새로운 기호 등으로 나타내게 된다. 배열된 기호들을 모두 더해서 총계를 낸다. 위치 기수법은 자리값 개념을 도입하여 승법적 기수법을 개선시킨 것이다. 자리값이 있기 때문에 기호는 다시 사용될 수 있지만, 단위 기호에서 차지하는 위치나 순서에 따라 각기 다른 수를 나타낸다.

역사적으로 고유한 기호 및 밑수로 수를 표시해 왔던 여러 문화에서 각기 다른 기수법들이 사용되었다. 예를 들어 초기 이집트 문명에서는 10진법에 기반한 단항 기수법이 사용되었다. 이집트 숫자를 읽기 위해서는 길게 늘어서 있는 기호들을 분류해서 더해야 했다. 반면에 중국-일본식 기수법에서는 승법적 기수법이 사용되었다. 이집트 기수법과 마찬가지로 10진법에 기반해 있었지만, 이 기수법은 승수로 한 가지 기호만을 사용하는 대신 서로 다른 9개의 기호를, 이집트 기수법에서처럼 좌우 방향이 아니라, 세로 방향으로 적어 나타냈다.

바빌로니아인들은 60진법에 기반한 변형된 위치 기수법을 사용했다. 1을 나타내는 기호와 10을 나타내는 기호에 대응하는 두 개의 승수 기호가 있었는데, 이들은 자리값에서만 쓰였다. 0을 나타내는 기호는 없었다. 바빌로니아 기수법의 단점은 각 숫자 배합마다 다수의 해석이 가능하다는 점이었다. 마야의 변형된 위치 기수법은 20진법에 기초해 있었다. 이 기수법에는 0이 있었고 세로로 표기가 되었다. 가장 밑의 숫자는 일의 자리를 표시했으며 올라갈수록 값이 커졌다. 하지만 세 번째 자리에서 20×20 표기가 20×18로 바뀜으로써 연속된 자리값들의 진행 방식이 바뀌었다.

힌두–아라비아식 기수법이 가장 발달된 기수법이다. 이 기수법은 10진법에 기초한 위치 기수법이다. 10개의 승수가 사용되며, 각 승수는 디지트라고 불린다. 10개의 디지트는 0, 1, 2, 3, 4, 5, 6, 7, 8, 그리고 9이다. 각 디지트는 하나의 기호로 표시될 수 있고 다른 디지트와 다르다. 하나의 디지트가 특정한 자리에 들어가면 그 자리값이 얼마를 나타내는지가 표시된다. 그래서 힌두–아라비아식 기수법은 보다 정교할 뿐만 아니라 사용하기에 보다 더 편리하다. 게다가 일정한 밑수를 가진 모든 위치 기수는 힌두–아라비아식 기수법으로 바꾸어 쓸 수 있다. 예를 들어 힌두–아라비아식 기수법은 오늘날의 컴퓨터 프로그래밍에 사용되는 2진법의 틀을 제공해 주었다.

📝 Summary Note

❶ abstract concepts
❷ symbols
❸ multiplicative system
❹ Hindu-Arabic

Exercise 3 1 Ⓑ 2 Ⓒ 3 Ⓑ 4 Ⓓ p.178

해석

슈피리어호

슈피리어호는 세계에서 가장 큰 담수호로 북아메리카에 위치해 있다. 이곳은 미국과 캐나다의 자연적 경계를 이룬다. 또한 휴런호, 온타리오호, 미시간호, 그리고 이리호와 더불어 오대호를 구성한다. 북쪽과 동쪽은 캐나다 온타리오와, 남쪽으로는 미시간주 및 위스콘신주와, 그리고 서쪽으로는 미네소타주와 경계를 이룬다. 오대호 가운데 슈피리어호가 가장 북쪽에, 그리고 서쪽 맨 끝에 위치해 있다. 이곳은 매우 외진 곳으로, 산림이 무성하고 인구 밀도가 낮다.

슈피리어호는 너무 커서 오대호의 나머지 호수들, 즉 휴런호, 온타리오호, 미시간호, 그리고 이리호와, 거기에 이리호 크기의 호수 세 개를 채울 수 있다. 이 호수에는 약 2,900입방마일, 즉 12,110조 리터의 물이 들어 있다. 슈피리오호의 길이는 350마일이고, 폭은 160마일이며, 최고 수심은 거의 1,333피트에 이른다. 표면 고도는 600피트이다. 300개 이상의 시내와 강으로 연결되어 있는 슈피리어호는 휴런호로 흘러 들어간다.

슈피리어호는 또한 거대한 크기와 깊이 때문에 오대호 중 가장 추운 곳으로, 항상 화씨 40도 정도의 온도가 유지된다. 호수의 온도가 주변 지역의 기후를 조절해서 여름 날씨는 더 시원하고 겨울 날씨는 더 따뜻하다. 또한 지구에서 가장 많은 눈을 내리게 만드는 호수 효과를 발생시킨다. 때로는 20에서 30마일 떨어진 내륙 지방에 눈이 내리기도 하며, 일부 지역에서는 16.5피트 높이까지 눈이 쌓이기도 한다.

슈피리어호는 면적으로는 가장 크고 부피로는 세 번째로 큰 담수호이다. 면적은 대략 32,000평방마일이다. 지구 전체 담수 공급량의 20%가 오대호에서 나오는데, 무려 10%가 슈피리어호에서 나온다. 이러한 점은 중요한데, 그 이유는 지구에 존재하는 물의 3%만이 담수이며, 그 가운데 3분의 2는 빙하와 만년설의 형태로 얼어 있기 때문이다. 다른 물에는 인간에게 해로운 염분이 포함되어 있고

인간을 포함하여 많은 종의 생존을 위해서는 담수가 필요하기 때문에 담수는 중요하다.

슈피리어호의 물은 주변 지역에 거주하는 4천 만 명 이상의 주민들에게 식수가 되고 있으며, 보다 최근에는 병에 담겨 해외로 수출되고 있다. 그 순도를 유지할 수 있도록 1972년에 미국과 캐나다 사이에 조약이 체결됨으로써 원치 않는 불순물이 제거되고 식수 공급이 원활해졌다. 현재 국제 슈피리어호 위원회가 수위를 측정하고 조절하고 있다.

📝 Summary Note

❶ freshwater lake
❷ Great Lakes
❸ water temperature
❹ ten percent

Exercise 4 1 Ⓑ 2 Ⓓ 3 Ⓑ 4 Ⓒ p.180

해석

기억 이론

기억에 관한 이론은 사람들이 어떻게 학습하는지를 설명해 주기 때문에 중요하다. 학습은 경험으로 정보를 얻은 후에 뒤따르는 행동, 지식, 그리고 사고 능력에 비교적 영구적인 영향을 끼친다. 그러한 경험은 사실이나 사건에 대한 신체적인 접촉 또는 관찰로 얻게 되는데, 이후 그러한 경험으로부터 얻은 정보가 기억이 된다.

기억은 세 가지 주요 과정으로 형성된다. 부호화, 저장, 그리고 인출이다. 부호화는 정보를 지각했을 때 정보를 흡수하는 과정이다. 저장은 그러한 정보를 머리에 저장하거나 그려 보는 과정이다. 그리고 인출은, 특정한 관련 과제에서 필요한 경우, 그러한 정보를 불러내는 과정이다.

부호화는 학습과 주의에 기반한다. 학습은 감각 기관이 경험을 해석하는 방식과 관련이 있지만, 주의는 특정한 과제에 초점을 맞추고 정신을 집중시키는 것이다. 주의에는 한 가지 활동에서 다른 활동으로 옮겨갈 수 있는 능력과, 서로 다른 능력을 사용하여 관련된 목표를 달성할 수 있는 능력이 포함된다. 예를 들어 문장 쓰기에 주의하기 위해서는 글자의 목적에 집중해야 할 뿐만 아니라 종이에 글자를 쓰고 정확히 철자를 적는 법에도 집중해야 한다. 이러한 과제를 완수하기 위해서는 대문자 표기, 문법, 그리고 구두점 표시가 올바르게 이루어져야 한다. 관련된 무언가에 주의를 기울이기 위해서는 노력이 필요하다.

저장은 단계적으로 진행될 수 있는 방식으로, 이때 이후의 인출을 위해 경험이 기억으로 분류된다. 기억이 저장되는 세 가지 유형은 감각 기억, 단기 기억, 그리고 장기 기억이다. 감각 기억은 순간적으로만 지속되며 정보를 원래의 형태로 소개해 준다. 예를 들어 뜨거운 냄비를 만지거나 천둥이 치는 소리를 들으면 감각 기억이 생길 것이다. 경험이 즉각적인 탓에 관련된 정보에 주의를 기울여야만 기억이 유지된다.

단기 기억은 보통 30초까지 지속된다. 이 기억은 개인이 한 번에 저장할 수 있는 정보량에 의해 제한을 받는다. 정보를 보다 오래 가지고 있기 위해서는 이를 기계적으로 반복 및 암기하거나 기존에 알고 있는 단서들과 연결시켜야 한다. 장기 기억은 비교적 영속적인 정보로서 다양한 스키마에 연결되어 기능한다. 스키마는 개인의 머릿속에 존재하는 개념이나 지식 체계이다. 이들이 정보를 조직하고 해석한다. 일련의 정보가 장기 기억이 되면 정보를 활용하고 정보의 배치를 강화시키는 거대하고 복잡한 아이디어의 네트워크와 연결된다.

인출은 관련된 정보를 검색하는 과정이다. 부호화와 마찬가지로 인출은 자동적으로 일어날 수도 있고 개인의 노력 및 주의를 요구할 수도 있다. 모든 경험이

기억으로 보존되는 것은 아니기 때문에 정보의 저장은 인출의 용이성 혹은 가능성에 영향을 미친다.

학자들에 따르면 기억은 개인에 의해 능동적으로 형성될 수 있다. 기억의 과정이 어떻게 이루어지는지 이해하는 것은 교육자 및 학생들에게 중요하다. 이는 새로운 개념을 배우는데 필요한 기초적인 지식을 습득하고 떠올릴 수 있게 해 주는 새로운 교수법 및 학습 전략의 수립에 도움을 준다.

Summary Note

❶ retrieval
❷ attention
❸ sensory memory
❹ automatic

Exercise 5　1 Ⓐ　2 Ⓑ　3 Ⓓ　4 Ⓒ　p.182

해석

쾌속 범선

쾌속 범선은 1800년대 초반부터 중반까지 전성기를 맞이했다. 동인도회사가 해체되고 캘리포니아주의 골드러시가 시작됨에 따라 쾌속 범선은 부패하기 쉬운 화물을 빠르고 효과적으로 수송해야 한다는 기대에 부응했다.

동양에서 온 상인들은 자신의 상품을 서쪽 캘리포니아로 가지고 가서 터무니없이 높게 오른 가격으로 이를 판매하고자 했다. 뉴욕에서 4달러인 밀가루 1배럴이 샌프란시스코에서는 40달러에 판매되었고, 넉 달이 지난 필라델피아의 신문 가격은 1달러였다. 가장 빨리 수송해야 하는 상품 중 하나는 중국산 차였다. 차는 인기 품목으로 신선할 때 더 맛이 좋았다. 중국의 항구에서 시작되어 뉴욕항에서 잠시 멈춘 후 케이프 혼을 돌아 미국 서해안에서 끝나는 느린 여정으로 인해 차는 사람이 먹을 수 없는 상태가 되었다. 미국인들은 차를 매우 좋아했고 기꺼이 그에 대한 값을 지불하려고 했다. 따라서 선주들은 새로운 선박의 설계에 얼마를 투자하더라도 그 돈은 수익으로 되돌아올 것이며 그 정도의 수고는 감수할 가치가 있을 것으로 확신했다.

많은 역사가들은 냇 팔머, 에드워드 콜린스, 도널드 맥케이, 그리고 존 윌리스 그리피스가 새로운 종류의 배를 발명했다고 생각한다. 경험이 풍부한 선원이자 선장이었던 냇 팔머는 당시 유행하던 V자 형태 대신 평탄한 바닥을 갖춘 범선을 최초로 고안했다. 이 프로젝트에 자금을 지원했던 에드워드 콜린스는 선박 회사의 소유자로서 기꺼이 새로운 구조에 대한 위험을 무릅쓰고자 했다. 실제로 배를 만들기 위해서는 뛰어난 기술자이자 조선소 소유자였던 도널드 맥케이가 고용되었고, 유명한 천재였던 존 윌리스 그리피스는 과학 및 고등 수학의 원리에 기반하여 설계도를 작성했다.

시간을 단축시키는 능력 때문에 그러한 이름이 붙여진 쾌속 범선은 물살을 쉽게 가르는 칼 모양의 선수, 배를 부드럽게 이동하게 만드는 좁은 선체, 그리고 배를 따라 지나가는 바람을 모두 모아 주는 높은 돛대를 갖추고 있었다. 그리피스는 갑판 위의 있던 모든 것을 제거해서 평소 선박의 속도를 늦추게 만들었던 공기 저항을 감소시켰다. 최종 결과는 멋지고 유선형 형태를 지닌 *레인보우*호였다. *레인보우*호는 진정한 최초의 쾌속 범선이었다. 이 배는 빠른 속도로 세상을 놀라게 만든 새로운 세대의 선박의 전형이 되었고, 이에 영감을 받은 시인들은 배의 우아한 선들이 만들어 내는 움직임을 낭만적으로 묘사하기 시작했다.

Summary Note

❶ mid-1800s
❷ Donald McKay
❸ wind resistance
❹ *Rainbow*

Exercise 6　1 Ⓓ　2 Ⓒ, Ⓓ　3 Ⓐ　4 Ⓒ　p.184

해석

미국의 북서 해안

미국의 북서 해안의 독특한 특징은 거대한 캐스케이드산맥이 있다는 점이다. 높은 활화산들로 이루어진 이 산맥은 하이 캐스케이드라고도 알려져 있으며, 캐나다의 브리티시 콜롬비아에서부터 워싱턴 및 오리건주 지역에 걸쳐 있다. 이 산맥은 캐나다와 미국의 국경을 가로지르며 태평양산계의 북쪽 3분의 1을 차지한다. 코스트산맥이라고도 알려져 있는 이 산계는 캐나다에서 미국으로 흘러 들어가는 형태를 띠며, 태평양 해안의 만곡을 따라 내륙으로 150마일에서 200마일까지 들어가 있다. 남쪽 캘리포니아로 들어가는 도중에 시에라네바다산맥과 합쳐진다. 시에라네바다는 베이슨 레인지와 연결되어 산맥을 완성시킨다.

캐스케이드산맥은 거대하고, 언제라도 폭발할 수 있으며, 꼭대기가 눈으로 덮인 화산들로 가장 잘 알려져 있다. 여기에는 베이커산, 레이니어산, 아담스산, 세인트 헬렌스산, 그리고 후드산이 포함된다. 베이커산, 레이니어산, 아담스산, 그리고 세인트 헬렌스산은 워싱턴주에 있다. 후드산은 오리건주에 위치해 있다. 이 거대한 자연 지형들은 보통 단독으로 솟아 있고 넓은 고원들에 의해 분리되어 있다. 이곳에는 지그재그로 깊게 파인 흔적들이 있는데, 이는 빙하가 남긴 흔적이다.

거대한 화산 이외에도 화산이 아닌 산들도 다수 존재한다. 이들 중 가장 유명한 것은 길이가 150마일에 이르는 고원 지대로, 이는 캐나다의 바로 아래쪽인 워싱턴 노스캐스케이드에 위치해 있다. 이 암석 산봉우리들은 화산의 산봉우리에 비하면 작다고 생각되지만, 이들은 높이가 서로 다른 수백 개의 정상으로 이루어져 있으며, 그 높이가 시에라네바다의 정상들의 높이를 종종 뛰어넘기도 한다.

북서 해안은 지형도 특이하지만 이곳 해안가 산맥 주변에서 기후들이 각축을 벌이고 있다는 점 때문에 더욱 유명하다. 캐스케이드산맥에는 거대한 빙하들이 있고 폭설도 내리지만, 이곳은 낮은 구름과 온대성 폭우로도 악명이 높다. 이러한 조건은 온대 우림의 형성에 도움이 된다.

두터운 우림층이, 특히 서쪽에서 시작되는, 산맥 주변의 깊고 좁은 계곡을 덮고 있는데, 이는 알래스카에서 시작되어 캐나다를 거친 후 캘리포니아 북부까지 이어져 있다. 뿐만 아니라 이 우림층은 지구에서 가장 큰 온대 우림 지대를 형성하는 북아메리카 태평양 온대 우림에 속한다. 해안가 산맥의 서쪽면에만 있는 이 우림에서는 세상에서 가장 큰 나무들이 자라는 경우가 많으며, 이곳은 북아메리카의 대부분을 둘러싸고 있는 신북구 생태계의 일부를 이룬다.

Summary Note

❶ active volcanoes
❷ Mount St. Helens
❸ glaciers
❹ temperate rainforests

Exercise 1 Jean Piaget's Stages of Cognitive Development

Swiss psychologist Jean Piaget introduced a theory about the four stages of cognitive development. They are the sensorimotor stage, the pre-operational stage, the concrete operational stage, and the formal operational stage. Each of the stages is roughly age related and occurs in chronological order. Although Piaget's theory gained wide acceptance in the 1950s, today it is criticized for its narrow view of children's competencies and its failure to address social and cultural influences on learning as well as the possibility that stages are apt to co-occur.

Exercise 2 Numeric Symbols

Because numbers are abstract concepts, different cultures have used distinct symbols and systems to represent them. The symbols that are used to represent the numbers are called numerals, and they are typically arranged in one of three kinds of numeration systems: simple, multiplicative, and positional. Of these, the positional Hindu-Arabic system is the most advanced. It is the simplest to use and can be adapted to any base.

Exercise 3 Lake Superior

North America's Lake Superior, a natural boundary between the United States and Canada, is the largest freshwater lake in the world. It was formed from the remnants of glaciers and provides a significant portion of the Earth's freshwater supply. Fresh water that is free of salts and other unhealthy pollutants is needed by humans and many other species for survival. For that reason, the United States and Canada work together to protect the lake from pollutants and to monitor and improve its water supply.

Exercise 4 Memory Theories

Memory theories focus on how experiences are encoded, stored, and retrieved. There are three types of memory storage: sensory memory, short-term memory, and long-term memory. Since the encoding and retrieval processes that surround memory storage can be controlled by the learner, understanding memory processes is influential in the development of teaching and learning strategies. Such strategies seek to engage learners so that new learning finds stable connections to past experiences.

Exercise 5 Clipper Ships

As a result of the breaking up of the East India Trading Company and the California Gold Rush, merchants sought a quick and efficient means to transport commodities to the west coast of the United States. This was particularly true for merchants who wanted to ensure that perishable items like tea reached the coast in a timely fashion. In answer to this unprecedented need, American innovators applied scientific and mathematical principles to create the first true clipper ship, the *Rainbow*. The *Rainbow* became a prototype for the new swift and streamlined merchant vessels.

Exercise 6 The Northwest Coast of the United States

The Cascade Mountain Range runs along the Northwest coast of the United States and into Canada. It makes up the northernmost third of the Pacific Mountain System and is comprised of volcanic and non-volcanic mountains. Although the Cascade Mountain Range is best known for its glaciers and heavy snowfalls, it also houses temperate rainforests that grow under the low clouds and heavy warm weather rains that are common in the mountain region.

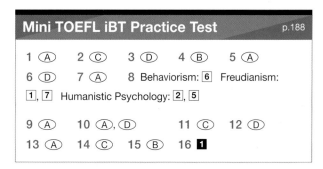

Mini TOEFL iBT Practice Test
p.188

1 Ⓐ   2 Ⓒ   3 Ⓓ   4 Ⓑ   5 Ⓐ
6 Ⓓ   7 Ⓐ   8 Behaviorism: ⑥ Freudianism:
①, ⑦ Humanistic Psychology: ②, ⑤

9 Ⓐ   10 Ⓐ, Ⓓ   11 Ⓒ   12 Ⓓ
13 Ⓐ   14 Ⓒ   15 Ⓑ   16 ❶

해석

[1-8]

에이브러햄 매슬로의 욕구 단계설

에이브러햄 매슬로는 1908년 브루클린에서 태어났다. 유대인 이민 가족의 장남이었던 그는 당시의 가장 위대한 사회 사상가들과 교류할 정도로 뛰어난 지성을 갖추고 있었다. 프로이드주의자들은 개인의 잠재 의식이 행동에 미치는 영향을 선전했다. 행동주의자들은 행동에 영향을 미치는 외적인 처벌과 보상을 강조했다. 그리고 게슈탈트 이론가들은 전체가 어떻게 다수의 요소로 구성되는지를 알아내려고 했다. 열띤 토론들로 지속적인 담론이 이어지자 이에 자극을 받은 매슬로는 그처럼 이질적이고 종종 충돌하기도 하는 학설들을 통합하여 인간의 동기화에 관한 새로운 개념을 정립하기로 결심했다.

매슬로의 관점은 인도주의적인 것이었다. 그는 개인들이 인격적으로 성장할 수 있는 선천적인 능력, 자신의 운명을 위해 선택하고 행동할 수 있는 자유, 그리고 삶의 질에 영향을 미치는 기타 긍정적인 특성들을 지니고 있다는 점을 강조했다. 1948년 매슬로는 사람들의 내적인 욕구와 그것이 어떻게 충족되는지를 다룬 두 편의 논문을 발표했다. 제목은 "특수성과 일반성의 인지"와 "기본 욕구 충족의 정치적 결과"였다. 이들 논문에서 매슬로는 당시 지배적이었던 프로이드 사상가들과 행태주의자들이 제시하는 생리적 욕구보다 더 큰 욕구가 있다고 주장했다. 또한 대립적으로 보이는 이들 학설들을 통합하여, 게슈탈트적 관점과 마찬가지로, 욕구가 충족된 개인들의 알려지지 않은 특성들을 밝혀냈다. 그는 기본적인 욕구가 충족된 개인들은 다른 사람들과 다르게 행동한다는 점을 관찰했다.

매슬로의 견해의 중심에는 욕구의 단계가 있다. 이는 삶의 지침이 되는 가치를 구분하기 위해 실시된 관찰에 기반한 것이다. 매슬로는 개인이 정치적인 생득권을 통해 얻을 수 있는 별도의 능력을 가지고 태어나는 것이 아니라는 점을 입증하고자 했다. 대신 개인에게는 위대함을, 또는 최소한 성공을 달성하는데 필요한 도구들이 주어지거나 주어지지 않는 것이다. 낮은 단계의 욕구에서 저지를 당하거나 좌절을 경험할 때 사람들의 모습이 어떠한지를 묘사했던 프로이드주의자나 신프로이드주의자와는 달리, 매슬로는 사람들의 욕구가 충족되었을 때의 최종 결과와 그렇게 되기까지의 과정을 살펴보고자 했다. 그는 정신적인 건강을 연구할 때에는 병에 걸린 사람들만이 아니라 건강한 사람들을 상대로도 연구를 해야 한다고 주장했다.

매슬로는 개인마다 기본적인 욕구를 가지고 있다고 주장했다. 여기에는 배고픔, 목마름, 그리고 잠과 연관이 있는 신체적인 건강, 피해로부터의 보호, 사회적 영역 내에서의 소속감과 사랑, 그리고 긍정적이고 바람직한 자존감이 포함된다. 그는 또한 이러한 욕구가 특별한 순서나 위계로 배열된다고 주장했다. 우선 음식과 수면에 대한 욕구가 충족되어야 하고, 그 다음에는 안전 및 사랑에 대한 욕구가 뒤따른다. 위계의 마지막 단계는 자아 실현이다. 자아 실현은 인간으로서 자신의 잠재력을 충분히 개발하려는 동기를 포함하고 있으며, 낮은 단계의 모든 욕구들이 충족된 후에야 이룰 수 있는 것이다. 매슬로에 따르면 대부분의 사람들은 높은 자존감이 생기면 더 이상 진전을 보이지 않기 때문에 자아 실현 단계에 도달하지 못한다. 실제로 매슬로는 일단 낮은 단계의 욕구들이 충족되면 스스로를 더 높은 자리로 끌어올리려는 동기가 약해진다고 주장했다. 그는 낮은 단계의 욕구들이 보다 강하고 맹렬한 동물적인 특성을 나타내는 반면, 높은 단계의 욕구들은 보다 약하고 인간적인 특성을 나타낸다고 생각했다.

[9-16]
영국 북아메리카 식민지의 해운업과 조선업

영국 북아메리카 식민지의 초기 선박 건조 기술은 조악하고 허술했다. 모든 판자들을 톱으로 잘랐고, 부피가 큰 부품들은 크고 작은 도끼와 대패를 사용해서 형태를 잡고 모양을 다듬었다. 번거로운 과정의 일부로서, 구덩이를 파고 거기에 작업대 혹은 받침대를 설치했다. 작업대 위에 통나무를 놓고 두 사람이 짝을 지어 함께 톱을 밀고 당기는 방식으로 톱질을 했다. 한 사람은 구덩이 안에 들어가고 한 사람은 작업대 위에서 통나무가 판자로 쪼개질 때까지 톱질을 했다. 이러한 일에 숙달하려면 매우 많은 기술이 필요했기 때문에 톱잡이는 인정 받는 직업이 되었다.

1600대 초기 정착지에서는 영국의 조선공들이 들어와서 견습생을 훈련시켰다. 제2수는 조선공을 돕는 조수였는데, 이 두 사람이 조를 이루었다. 제3수는 톱질이 받침대와 너무 가까운 곳에서 이루어지는 것처럼 보일 때나 톱질을 새로 시작할 때에 작업대에서 통나무를 치우는 일을 했다. 조선업 덕분에 돛, 로프, 못, 닻, 그리고 체인 제작을 위한 기타 산업들이 등장하기는 했지만, 목재를 유용한 판자로 만드는데 들어가는 비용이 너무나 커서 목재 산업은 한동안 발전을 하지 못했다. 또한 조선업자들은 선박을 건조할 때 다량의 생 재목을 사용했다.

[선박을 건조하는 일은 느리기는 했지만 꾸준히 이윤을 많이 남기는 방식으로 계속되었다.] 1650년대 중반 대다수의 식민지들은 3년에 한 번 이상 선박을 건조하지 않았다. 조선업자들은 선박이 출항해서 목적지에 도달하면 가득 실려 있던 화물뿐만 아니라 선박도 영국 또는 해외의 선주들에게 팔아 버렸다. 속도가 느린 이 배들은 400년 동안 유지된 전통적인 형태를 철저히 따르고 있었고 영국 및 덴마크 스타일을 띠었다. 배의 넓은 바닥에는 세 개의 돛과 정사각형 형태의 삭구가 있었지만, 보통 그 크기가 훨씬 작았다. 그럼에도 불구하고 1600년대 후반 식민지의 조선업자들은 조선업 및 해상 무역에서 강력한 경쟁자가 되었으며 대서양 횡단 무역의 활성화에 기여하였다.

식민지 보스턴은 영국의 상업적 업적 가운데 가장 빛나는 업적이었다. 청교도 방식으로 관리되는 보스턴의 항구와 풍부한 자원은 튼튼한 무역 경제를 보장해 주었고, 이는 미국의 신생 식민지들에게 당연한 일이 되었다. 모피 생산, 철 생산, 그리고 직물 생산에 필요한 자원을 제공해 주었던 해안 및 대륙의 자원들은, 신생 식민지의 고갈되지 않는 수출품으로 생각된 풍부한 목재 및 어업 생산량에 비

하면, 미미해 보였다. 수산업을 포함해서 어떤 무역도 지속적인 일자리를 제공해 주지는 못했지만, 이러한 자원들은 해운업과 조선업이 자리를 잡을 수 있도록 안정적인 경제 성장의 토대를 마련해 주었다.

1700년대 초반 보스턴 항구는 미국 제일의 항구이자 영국의 대서양 세력권 내에서 세 번째로 큰 항구가 되었다. 수익이 높은 소금에 절인 대구가 거래됨에 따라 조선업자, 어부, 그리고 상인들 사이에는 강력한 연대 의식이 형성되었다. 또한 그로 인해 악명 높은 삼각 무역의 항로를 열어 준 조선업의 혁명이 이루어졌으며, 보스턴은 1760년대에 미국에서 가장 크고, 가장 부유하며, 가장 영향력 있는 도시가 되었다.

UNIT 08 Insert Text

Basic Drill   p.198

Drill 1 1

해석
바우하우스 운동

바우하우스 운동은 모더니즘 건축 및 인테리어 디자인에 가장 큰 영향을 끼친 슈타틀리헤스 바우하우스라는 독일의 한 예술 학교의 이름을 따서 명명되었다. [이 운동의 철학은 사물이 가치를 지니려면 유용해야 한다는 믿음에 기반해 있었다.] 아이러니컬하게도, 이 학교는 1차 세계 대전과 2차 세계 대전 사이인 1919년부터 1933년까지의 비교적 짧은 기간 동안에, 그리고 미국에서는 1937년부터 1938년까지의 매우 짧은 기간 동안에만 운영되었다. 교내 운영진의 끊임없는 교체와 권력 투쟁으로 인해 학교의 주안점, 기법, 강사, 그리고 정책들이 끊임없이 바뀌었다. 이러한 실용주의 스타일의 운동을 촉진시킨 것은 1908년 비평가 아돌프 로스가 발표한 책이었다. 제목이 *장식과 범죄*였던 이 책은 표면 장식이 원시적이라고 주장했다. 학교의 창립자였던 건축가 발터 그로피우스는 창립 성명서에서 이 학교의 목표가 "장인과 예술가 사이의 오만한 장벽을 세우는 계급 차별을 없애고 새로운 장인 조합을 창설하는 것"이라고 선언했다.

Drill 2 2

시장 규제

시장 규제는 정부가 법 적용을 통해 특정 시장의 일부 또는 모든 측면을 조정하려고 할 때 이루어진다. 정부는 중앙 계획 시장을 만들거나 시장의 실패를 바로잡는 것과 같은 여러 가지 목적을 달성하기 위해서 시장을 규제한다. [그러나 이러한 조치들이 항상 민간 부문의 최선의 이익에 부합하는 것은 아니다.] 시장 규제는 부패한 정부가 연줄이 있는 기업이나 정치인들에게 특혜를 주기 위한 목적으로 실시되기도 한다. 흔히 규제를 받는 시장 중 하나는 공공 서비스 시장이다. 이는 수익 극대화와 공공 서비스 수요자들의 이익 극대화라는 상반된 이해관계의 균형을 맞추기 위해 이루어진다. 이에 대한 좋은 예는 주류 및 처방약 시장에서 이루어지는 정부의 규제이다. 대다수 국가들은 이러한 시장들을 규제하려고 한다. 그러면 제품들이 안전하다는 점과 적절한 고객들에게만 판매된다는 점이 보장될 수 있다.

Drill 3 **1**

해석

인지 과학

인지는 지성이나 지능이 작동하거나 사고하는 과정으로 정의된다. [여기에는 자각, 인식, 추론, 그리고 판단이 포함된다.] 인지 과학은 이러한 과정을 이해하기 위해 심리학, 신경 과학, 언어학, 철학, 컴퓨터 과학, 인류학, 그리고 생물학을 이용하는 학제간 연구 분야이다. 인지 과학은 인간의 뇌에 관한 연구와 동물의 뇌에 관한 연구로 구분할 수 있다. 인지 과학의 세 가지 주요 접근법은 기호주의, 연결주의, 그리고 역동 시스템이다. 기호주의 접근법은 기호로 이루어지는 연산을 이용해서 인지를 설명하려는 시도이다. 이러한 연산은 디지털 컴퓨터의 작동 방식과 유사하게 이루어지며, 명확한 계산주의 및 정신적 과정의 모드로 표현된다. 이러한 정신적 과정은 물리적인 뇌 수준에서는 고려되지 않는다. 연결주의 접근법은 물리적인 뇌의 특성을 갖춘 인공 신경망 모델을 통해 인지를 살펴본다. 세 번째 접근법은 역동 시스템 접근법이다. 이는 인지가, 모든 요소들이 서로 연결되어 있는, 지속적인 역동 시스템의 형태로 가장 잘 설명될 수 있다고 주장한다.

Drill 4 **3**

해석

알렉산드리아의 히파티아

알렉산드리아의 히파티아는 이집트의 철학자이자 수학자이며 천문학자였다. 그녀는 기원후 370년에 태어난 것으로 생각된다. 히파티아가 쓴 저작물 중 어떤 것도 남아 있지 않다. 그렇기 때문에 역사가들은 한 제자가 그녀에게 쓴 편지를 통해, 그리고 다른 작가들이 남긴 개인 기록물에서의 몇 가지 묘사를 통해서만 그녀에 대해 알 수 있다. 이들로부터 역사가들은 히파티아가 대단히 존경받는 학자였으며 알렉산드리아의 지성 공동체의 일원이었다는 점을 알게 되었다. [그녀의 관심 덕분에 많은 것이 발명되었다.] 히파티아는 플라톤 학파의 철학을 추종했으며, 별의 위치를 나타나는데 사용되었던 아스트롤라베와 지금도 액체의 비중을 알아내는데 쓰이는 액체 비중계를 발명한 것으로 알려져 있다. 415년 이교도였던 히파티아는 당시 성장 중이던 기독교 운동과 충돌하게 되었고 잔인한 폭도들에게 살해되었다.

Exercises with Long Passages

Exercise 1 1 Ⓑ 2 Ⓓ 3 **A1** 4 **B2**   p.200

해석

1973년의 석유 위기

1973년의 석유 위기는 당시 이집트와 시리아, 그리고 이스라엘 간에 발생한 욤 키푸르 전쟁 때문에 시작되었다. OPEC(석유 수출국 기구)의 회원국이었던 시리아와 이집트는 이 조직의 아랍 회원국들을 설득하여 이스라엘을 지원하는 국가에게 석유 공급이 중단되도록 만들었다. 이러한 수출 금지 조치는 즉각적으로 미국, 캐나다, 그리고 이들의 동맹국인 여러 서유럽 국가들에게 영향을 끼쳤다.

아랍의 산유국들이 서방 세계에 꼭 필요한 석유 공급량을 감소시킴에 따라 전 세계의 유가 또한 인상되었다. 이러한 급격한 인상은 전 세계 경제에 극적인 인플레이션 효과를 가져다 주었다. 특히 이스라엘의 든든한 지지자였던 미국과 네덜란드가 이러한 수출 금지 조치의 표적이 되어 즉각적으로 경제적인 영향을 받았다.

이러한 수출 금지 조치의 가장 즉각적인 효과는 배럴당 유가가 4배로 뛰었다는 점이었다. 석유를 관할하는 아랍의 정치인들과 기타 엘리트들은 순식간에 부자가 되었다. 이처럼 갑작스럽게 부국이 된 많은 국가들은 새로 생긴 부를 무기에 투자했고, 이로써 중동 지역의 긴장감이 더욱 고조되었다. [이러한 석유 파동은 결국 서구 사회에 대혼란을 일으켰다.] 휘발유의 갤런당 소매 가격이 폭등했고, 뉴욕 증권 거래소의 주가는 6주 동안 970억 달러가 떨어졌다. 아랍이 미국에 공급하던 석유량은 하루 120만 배럴에서 단 19,000배럴로 줄어들었다. 미국은 2차 세계 대전 이후로 최악의 연료 부족 현상을 겪게 되었다.

휘발유를 사기 위해 주유소에 늘어 선 줄과 이로 인한 바가지 요금을 규제하기 위해 미국 정부는 여러 가지 조치를 취했다. 그중 하나는 석유 탐사를 유도하기 위해 "새 석유"의 가격은 책정하지 않고 이미 발견된 "기존 석유"의 가격만 제한하는 것이었다. 또 다른 조치는 홀수 번호판 차량의 운전자는 그 달의 홀수일에만 휘발유를 구입할 수 있게 하는 것이었다. 대신 짝수 번호판 차량의 운전자는 그 달의 짝수일에만 휘발유 구입이 가능했다.

미국 정부는 또한 시민들에게 휘발유 사용량을 줄이고 최대한 에너지를 아껴 쓸 것을 권장하기 시작했다. 이를 위해 전국적으로 제한 속도가 시속 55마일로 하향되었다. 조명의 필요성을 줄이기 위해 서머 타임 제도도 시행되었다. 사람들의 에너지 사용량을 줄이기 위한 에너지 절약 표어 중 인기 있었던 것은 "에너지를 낭비하는 바보가 되지 마세요."였다. [그럼에도 불구하고 석유 위기의 충격은 광범위한 영향을 미쳤다.] 1974년 3월 욤 키푸르 전쟁이 끝나자 리비아를 제외한 OPEC의 아랍 회원국들은 미국에 대한 수출 금지 조치를 해제했다. 석유 공급이 늘어나고 유가는 떨어졌지만, 이미 시작된 일련의 경제 불황은 1980년대에 걸쳐 많은 서방 국가들에게 고통을 안겨 주었다.

📝 Summary Note

❶ Yom Kippur War
❷ price of oil
❸ stock exchange
❹ speed limit

Exercise 2 1 Ⓒ 2 Ⓑ 3 **A4** 4 **B1**   p.202

해석

철새의 이동

많은 철새들이 장거리를 이동하는 것으로 알려져 있다. 다수의 종들은 보통 북반구의 온화한 기후에서 여름을 보낸다. 그곳에서 번식을 하고 풍부한 먹이를 먹으며 살을 찌운다. 겨울철이 되면 이러한 철새들은 남쪽으로 날아가서 따뜻한 열대 지역 및 남반구 지역에서 겨울을 보낸다.

이처럼 이동하는 습성은 육지새들에게서 가장 흔히 찾아볼 수 있다. 다양한 종들이 엄청난 거리를 이동하는 것으로 알려져 있다. 이러한 새들은 가을과 겨울에 북반부에서 먹이를 구하기가 힘들기 때문에 먹이를 찾아 이동을 한다. 이러한 새들은 이동 불안감을 해소하기 위해 이동시 수반되는 위험을 무릅쓰는 유전학적인 경향을 보인다. 이러한 감정은 이망증이라는 뜻의 독일어인 *Zugunruhe*로 나타낸다.

이망증은 이동 충동을 일으킬 수 있는 환경적인 자극이 차단된 새장 속 새들에게도 존재하다는 점이 밝혀졌다. 이러한 본능적인 충동은 이들 포획 상태의 새들이 날고자 하는 방향에서 드러난다. 이는 야생 상태에 있는 같은 종의 새들이 이동하는 방향과 같다. 이들은 심지어 야생 상태에 있는 같은 종의 새들이 일년 중 이동하는 시기와 동일한 시기에 그러한 비행 방향을 선호하는 것으로 보여진다. 이러한 방향은 야상 생태의 새들이 비행 코스를 바꿀 때 같이 바뀐다. [관찰 가능한 자료는 날개 표식 조사, 가락지 부착 연구, 그리고 이동 경로를 알아내는 데 도움이 되는 개인적인 관찰을 통해 수집되었다.] 이러한 관찰을 통해 과학자들은, 철새의 이동을 완벽히 이해하지는 못하지만, 반복적으로 같은 이동 경로를 따르는 철새의 능력이 새의 유전자 안에 들어 있는 1년 주기의 내생적 프로그래밍 조합에 기반해 있다고 믿는다. 또한 새들이 가지고 있는 인지 능력 때문에 새들의 머릿속에는 랜드마크 및 서식지에 대한 기억에 기반한 단순한 형태의 지도가 그려진다고 믿는다.

이러한 이동 경로는 철새의 유전자 구조에 프로그래밍되어 있다. 하지만 다양한 이유로 경로가 변경된다고 알려져 있다. 이러한 이유에는 항공역학적인 효율성을 높이고, 날씨 변화에 대응하고, 그리고 포식자의 위험을 피하기 위한 것이 포함된다. 엘레오노라매라는 새는 번식기를 상당히 늦춤으로써 이동 패턴에 적응한 것으로 알려져 있다. 그 결과 이 새는 겨울에 남쪽으로 날아가는 연작류 철새들을 사냥할 수 있다.

[당연하게도, 과학자들은 보다 짧은 거리를 이동하는 철새들의 습성도 조사해 왔다.] 장거리를 이동하지 않는 철새로는 수리, 독수리, 말똥가리, 그리고 황새와 같이 날개가 큰 새들을 들 수 있다. 이러한 큰 새들은 따뜻한 상승 기류의 열기둥에 의해서만 날아오를 수 있다. 열기둥은 육지에서만 발생하므로 그와 같은 필수 조건은 이 새들이 광활한 바다를 건널 수 없도록 만든다. 이처럼 넓은 바다를 건널 수 없기 때문에 이 커다란 새들은 이동 주기 동안 육지 사이의 간격이 가장 좁은 곳을 횡단한다. 한 가지 예로 엄청난 규모의 육식조와 황새 무리를 들 수 있는데, 이들은 겨울을 보내기 위해 유럽에서부터 남쪽 아프리카로 가는 동안, 지브롤터 및 보스포러스 해협과 같이 지중해에서 가장 간격이 좁은 지점에서, 지중해를 건너는 모습이 관찰될 수 있다.

📝 Summary Note

❶ genetically inclined
❷ sense of restlessness
❸ caged birds
❹ genes and cognitive ability

| Exercise 3 | 1 ⓒ | 2 ⓑ | 3 **A2** | 4 **B1** | p.204 |

해석

조지아 오키프

조지아 오키프는 20세기 가장 영향력 있는 미국인 화가 중 한 명이었다. 오늘날 그녀는 추상 및 구상을 나타내기 위해 꽃, 바위, 조개, 풍경, 그리고 동물의 뼈와 같은 자연물의 이미지를 사용하여 그림을 그린 것으로 유명하다. 1928년, 오키프가 그린 여섯 점의 칼라 릴리 시리즈는 25,000달러에 판매되었다. 이 금액

은 당시 현존했던 미국 화가의 작품 시리즈에 지불된 금액 중 가장 높은 것이었다.

오키프는 1887년 위스콘신에서 7남매 중 둘째로 태어났다. 낙농업에 종사했던 그녀의 부모는 그녀가 어렸을 때 그녀의 예술적 재능을 발견하고 일찍부터 그녀가 미술 교육을 받게 했다. [실제로 오키프는 8세 때 화가가 되기로 결심했다.] 그녀의 첫 번째 선생님은 사라 만이라는 그 지역의 수채화가였다. 오키프는 고등학교를 졸업한 뒤 시카고 예술 대학을 다녔고, 나중에는 뉴욕의 아트 스튜던츠 리그를 다녔다. 그녀가 291이라는 이름의 미술관에서 열린 로댕의 수채화 전시회에 간 것도 그녀가 뉴욕에 있을 때였다. 이 미술관의 소유주는 알프레드 스티글리츠였는데, 몇 년 후 그는 그녀의 남편이 되었다.

그 후 몇 년 동안 오키프는 질병과 재정 문제로 힘든 시기를 보냈다. 1908년 그녀는 그림으로는 생계를 이어갈 수 없다고 생각하고 그림을 완전히 접었다. [대신 텍사스주 아마릴로에서 교사직을 수락했다.] 그러다가 1912년 버지니아 대학의 서머 스쿨에서 미술 수업을 받던 중 그녀의 창의력에 다시 불이 붙었다. 그곳 강사였던 알론 비멘트가 선, 형태, 색채의 조화로운 상호 작용을 거친 디자인에 관한 새로운 아이디어를 그녀에게 소개해 주었다. 이러한 아이디어로 인해 창의적인 예술적 과정에 대한 오키프의 생각이 큰 영향을 받아 바뀌게 되었다.

마침내 알프레드 스티글리츠가 화가로서의 그녀의 경력이 유지될 수 있게 도움으로써 그녀의 삶에 다시 들어오게 되었다. 그는 그녀가 뉴욕에서 살 수 있도록 그녀에게 아파트를 마련해 주었다. 그곳에서 그들은 깊은 사랑에 빠졌고 스티글리츠는 그녀와 결혼하기 위해 자신의 아내와 이혼했다. 결혼한 직후, 스티글리츠는 누드 사진을 포함해서 오키프의 사진을 찍기 시작했다. 이 사진들은 그의 회고전에 전시되었고 곧바로 대중의 관심을 불러일으켰다.

그 뒤로 여러 해 동안 오키프는 초기 미국 모더니스트 미술계의 일원이 되었다. 이 무렵 오키프는 기존의 수채화 그림에서 벗어나 유화로 그림을 그리기 시작했다. 그녀는 곧 대규모로, 마치 망원경 렌즈 아래에 놓인 것과 같이, 매우 클로즈업된 상태에 있는 자연 형태들을 묘사함으로써 새로운 스타일을 만들어 냈다. 그녀의 남편인 스티글리츠는 그녀의 작품을 자신의 미술관에 전시하기 시작했다. 오키프는 화가로서 빛을 발하기 시작하여 1928년 칼라 릴리 작품들의 판매와 같은 커다란 상업적인 성공을 거두었다.

이후 1929년 여름 오키프는 한 친구와 뉴멕시코를 방문해서 그곳의 독특한 건축 형태와 풍경을 접하게 되었다. 1929년부터 1949년까지 오키프는 매년 일정 기간 동안 뉴멕시코에서 작업을 하며 시간을 보냈다. 그곳에서 그녀는 자신이 수집한 동물 뼈에서 영감을 얻어 그곳에서 보낸 두 번째 여름에 그림을 그렸다. 소의 머리뼈, 광활한 푸른 하늘, 그리고 울퉁불퉁한 바위산의 이미지들이 그녀의 작품 속에 들어 있는 이미지들 중 가장 기억에 남는 것이 되었다. 마침내 그녀는 애비큐 북쪽에서 부지 한 곳을 찾아냈는데, 그 이름을 유령 목장이라고 지었다. 주변의 다채로운 사막 풍경과 이 지역에 있는 압도적인 절벽 및 언덕들이 이후 그녀의 예술 활동에 영감을 주었다.

📝 Summary Note

❶ natural images
❷ Wisconsin
❸ Alfred Stieglitz
❹ New Mexico

| Exercise 4 | 1 ⓐ | 2 ⓓ | 3 **A4** | 4 **B3** | p.206 |

19세기의 골드러시

1800년대 북아메리카에서는 금과 은 탐광자들이 막대한 부를 거두었다. 19세기는 금과 은이 풍부한 몇몇 광산 혹은 광맥들이 발견된 때였다. 이러한 발견이 공표되자마자 골드러시라고 불렸던 이주 열풍이 시작되었다. 러시는 수천 명의 탐광자들이 발견 지점의 인근 지역으로 가는 현상이었다. 그곳에서 그들은 직접 발견을 해서 부를 거두고자 했다. 이러한 과정으로 인해 캘리포니아, 네바다, 알래스카, 그리고 캐나다 북부의 유콘 준주와 같은 개척지에 백인들의 정착이 가속화되었다. 또한 이 때문에 이미 진행 중인 것보다 훨씬 빠른 속도로 원주민들 및 그들의 문화가 내쫓기게 되었다.

이러한 탐광자들은 교육 수준이 최저인 하층 계급의 노동자부터 부유한 사업가까지 그 범위가 다양했다. 모든 탐광의 핵심에는 부유해지고 싶은 깊은 욕망이 자리잡고 있었다. 많은 탐광자들이 막대한 부를 얻을 수 있었다. 하지만 그렇지 못한 사람들이 더 많았고, 탐광을 하다가 죽은 사람들도 매우 많았다. 부유하든 가난하든, 나이가 적든 많은 모든 탐광자들이 탐광 기간 동안의 엄청난 고난을 견뎌내야 했다. 음식과 물은 부족했고, 사막의 기온은 말과 노새를 쓰러뜨려 죽게 만들 만큼 더웠다. 겨울은 항상 더 가혹해서 탐광자들은 수족을 절단해야 하는 동상을 끊임없이 겪어야 했다.

미국 역사상 최초의 주요 골드러시는 캘리포니아 골드러시로, 이는 1848년에 캘리포니아 서터스 밀에서 금이 발견되면서 시작되었다. 1848년에 도착했던 초기의 이 탐광자들은 포티 에이터즈라고 불렸다. 이들 중 많은 사람들이 오리곤이나 캘리포니아 내 다른 지역과 같은 인근 지역 출신이었다. 이 행운의 탐광자들은 개울에서 매일 수천 달러의 가치가 나가는 금을 손쉽게 채취할 수 있었다. 하지만 1949년에 도착한 포티 나이너즈라고 불렸던 사람들의 경우, 쉽게 구할 수 있던 상당량의 금이 이미 채취된 상태였기 때문에 금을 채취하는 일이 보다 어려웠다. 1855년경에는 약 30만 명의 탐광자들이 미국 전역과 해외에서 캘리포니아로 모여들었다. 이들은 포장마차나 선박을 이용하여 캘리포니아로 왔으며, 많은 이들이 매우 단순한 방법을 사용하여 개울 바닥에 흐르는 물에서 금 조각을 채취했다. [이러한 사금은 풍화 작용의 결과로서 주광맥에서 자연적으로 떨어져 나온 것이었다.] 이 단순한 과정은 패닝이라고 불렸다.

북아메리카에서의 또 다른 골드러시는 1896년에 이루어졌다. 스쿠쿰 짐 마온이라고 하는 원주민과 그 일행이 캐나다의 북쪽 유콘 준주에 있는 클론다이크 강에서 풍부한 사금 광산을 발견한 때였다. 당시 유콘 준주는 혹독한 겨울로 인해 일년 중 대부분의 기간 동안 차가운 눈으로 덮여 있었기 때문에 백인들이 거의 거주하지 않았다. 다시 한 번 금이 발견되었다는 소식이 전해지자마자 탐광자들이 모여들기 시작했다. 이들은 패닝으로 부를 획득할 수 있기를 바라면서 경쟁적으로 이곳에 몰려들었다.

1898년 클론다이크강 주변의 인구는 수천 명에서 4만 명으로 증가했다. 이러한 급격한 증가 때문에 이곳은 기아의 위협과 오염된 식수로 인한 장티푸스의 위협을 받게 되었다. [하지만 이때에는 북서 기마 순찰대가 안전과 질서 유지를 위해 탐광자들의 활동을 감시했다.] 잭 런던의 *늑대개 화이트 팽*, *야생의 부름*, 그리고 그의 가장 유명한 단편 소설인 *불을 지피다*와 같은 클론다이크 골드러시 문학에서 묘사된 것처럼, 또 다시 많은 부가 축적되었다. 하지만 몹시 가혹한 기후 조건 때문에, 한 사람의 부자가 탄생하기까지 수백 명의 다른 사람들이 고통을 겪었다.

📝 Summary Note

❶ gold fever

❷ Yukon Territories

❸ California Gold Rush

❹ Jack London

Exercise 5　1 ⓑ　2 ⓓ　3 **A3**　4 **B3**　　　　p.208

원자로

최초의 원자로는 인간이 만든 것이 아니라 자연적으로 발생한 것이었다. 서아프리카의 가봉에 있는 오클로 광산의 우라늄 광상에서 15개의 천연 핵분열로가 발견되었다. 과학자들은 이 원자로들이 약 1억 5천만 년 동안 열, 빛, 그리고 기타 방사선들을 내뿜었다고 주장한다. 이 우라늄 광상은 오클로 화석 원자로라고 알려져 있다. 이들은 1972년 프랑스의 물리학자인 프랜시스 페랭에 의해 발견되었다. 활동 당시 평균적으로 100킬로와트의 전력을 생산해 냈을 것으로 추정된다.

현대의 원자로는 유용한 전력을 생산하기 위해 핵 연쇄 반응을 일으키는 장치이다. 이러한 일은 일정한 속도로 핵분열을 일으키고, 제어하고, 그리고 유지시킴으로써 이루어진다. [전력을 공급해 준다는 점에서 핵분열의 잠재적인 응용 분야는 많다.] 원자로의 주된 용도는 전력을 생산하는 것이다. 하지만 무기급 플루토늄과 방사성 동위 원소를 만들기 위해 빔라인 실험으로 연구를 할 때에도 사용된다. 심지어 핵추진 잠수함 및 선박을 나아가게 할 수도 있다.

핵분열은 안전하면서도 오염 물질을 배출하지 않는 전력 공급원으로 알려져 있기 때문에 오늘날 상업적으로 이용되는 유일한 핵반응 과정이다. 그와 반대로 핵융합은 현재 실험적인 단계에 있는 기술이다. 핵융합이 야기할 수 있는 건강 및 안전상의 잠재적인 위험성 때문에 많은 과학자들이 핵융합을 부정적으로 생각한다. [이러한 이유로 과학자들은 보다 안전한 방식의 전력 생산 방식을 선호한다.] 핵 반응을 제어할 수 있는 또 다른 방법으로 방사성 동위 원소 열전기 발전기와 원자력 전지가 있다. 이들은 모두 외부 자극에 의한 방사성 붕괴를 통해 열과 전력을 생산한다.

핵분열에 의한 상업용 전기를 생산하기 위해 몇 가지 서로 다른 방식의 원자로 기술들이 사용된다. 이는 두 가지 종류, 즉 고속 원자로와 저속 원자로로 구분할 수 있다. 이들은 중성자의 에너지에 기반하여 핵분열 연쇄 반응을 유지시킨다.

저속 원자로는 열중성자로라고도 알려져 있다. 이들은 느린 중성자들을 이용한다. 이 중성자들은 중성자의 움직임을 느리게 만드는 물질에 의해 감속이 되면 주변 입자들의 평균적인 운동 에너지와 비슷한 에너지를 갖게 된다. 이러한 과정을 열운동화라고 한다. 이는 전력 생산에 쓰이는 가장 일반적인 원자로 형태이다. 최초의 상업용 플루토늄 원자로들이 이러한 유형에 속했으며, 감속재로는 흑연이 사용되었다.

고속 원자로는 빠른 중성자를 이용해 필요한 핵분열 연쇄 반응을 일으키고 유지시키며, 저속 원자로에서 쓰이는 감속재를 필요로 하지 않는다. 이러한 종류의 원자로에는 무기급 플루토늄과 같이 상당히 농축된 연료가 필요하다. 이로써 우라늄 238의 양을 최소화할 수 있는데, 그렇게 하는 이유는 방사능 오염을 피하기 위해서이다. 초기의 일부 러시아 선박 및 잠수함 추진 장치뿐만 아니라 초기의 몇몇 원자력 발전소에서도 고속 원자로가 사용되었다. 하지만, 이러한 종류의 원자로가 계속 건설되고 있기는 하지만, 모든 분야에서 저속 원자로가 거둔 만큼의 성공은 이루어 내지 못하고 있다.

📝 Summary Note

❶ Oklo mine

❷ nuclear fission

❸ dangerous and unhealthy

❹ thermalization

[해석]

식민지 시대 미국의 위대한 초상화가

식민지 시대 미국에서 가장 유명한 초상화가 중 두 명은 존 싱글턴 코플리와 길버트 스튜어트였다. 카메라와 사진술이 등장하기 전인 이 시기에는 사실주의 초상화가들이 중요했는데, 그 이유는 이들만이 중요한 인물 및 장소들을 시각적으로 기록할 수 있었기 때문이었다.

존 싱글턴 코플리는 보스턴 태생의 화가로서 혁신적인 스타일로 유명했다. 그의 대부분의 초상화들은 식민지 시대 뉴잉글랜드의 중요한 인물들뿐만 아니라 중산층 남녀들을 그린 것이었다. 일반적으로 톱을 든 목수나 책을 들고 있는 교사와 같이 삶의 세세한 부분을 나타내는 물건을 들고 포즈를 취한 대상들을 보여주었다. 코플리가 그린 가장 유명한 초상화로 독립 전쟁의 영웅인 사무엘 애덤스와 폴 리비어의 초상화를 들 수 있다. 하지만 1774년에 독립 전쟁이 발발하자 코플리는 전쟁을 피하고 자신의 그림 실력을 높이기 위해 유럽으로 건너갔다.

이 시기의 또 다른 주요 화가는 길버트 스튜어트였다. 화가로서의 경력이 코플리만큼 순탄하지는 않았는데, 코플리는 스튜어트에게 큰 영향을 미쳤다. 하지만 결국에는 스튜어트의 그림이 코플리 그림보다 훨씬 더 높은 평가를 받고 있다. 스코틀랜드 화가인 코스모 알렉산더 밑에서 교육을 받은 뒤 스튜어트는 존 싱글턴 코플리의 선례를 따라 독립 전쟁을 피하고 그림을 계속 그리기 위해 유럽으로 건너갔다. 하지만 초기에 화가로서 자리를 잡으려는 스튜어트의 노력은 성공하지 못했다.

초기에 몇 차례의 실패를 경험한 후 스튜어트는 런던에서 벤자민 웨스트의 제자가 되었다. 1777년 스튜어트는 왕립 미술원에서 자신의 작품을 전시할 수 있었고, 마침내 성공과 찬사를 누리게 되었다. 스튜어트의 회화 작품의 가격은 곧 급격하게 올랐지만, 이러한 성공에도 불구하고 그는 성격상 금전 관리를 제대로 하지 못했다. 금전 관리에 부주의했던 탓에 그는 채무자 감옥에 가는 것을 피하기 위해서 1787년 아일랜드로 달아나야만 했다.

1793년 미국으로 돌아온 직후 스튜어트는 필라델피아에 스튜디오를 열었다. 여기에서 그는 미국 주요 인물들의 초상화를 그리면서 지속적인 명성을 쌓았다. [하지만 그는 구세계에서 온 인물들도 많이 그렸다.] 아마도 그의 작품 가운데 가장 유명한 작품은 조지 워싱턴의 초상화 시리즈일 것이다. 이 새로운 명성 덕분에 스튜어트는 수년 동안 바빴고 많은 돈을 벌었다. 조지 워싱턴 화상 중 가장 많은 찬사를 받는 작품은 아테나이온 두상이라는 것인데, 이는 현재 미국의 1달러짜리 지폐에 들어가 있다. 스튜어트가 그린 워싱턴 초상화 중 가장 유명한 작품은 백악관의 이스트룸에 걸려 있는 대형 그림이다. 이 초상화는 영국 군인들이 대통령 관저를 불태웠던 1812년 전쟁 당시 영부인이던 돌리 매디슨에 의해 위기를 모면했다.

스튜어트는 화가 생활을 접을 때까지 천 명 이상의 미국 정치인들의 초상화를 그렸다. 그의 스타일은 활기와 자연스러움 때문에 높이 평가되었다. 미국의 위대한 건국 아버지이자 대통령이었던 존 애덤스는, 보통 초상화가 앞에 앉으면 지독한 불편함을 겪게 되지만, 스튜어트 앞에 앉으면 그의 여유 있는 태도와 재미있는 대화 덕분에 즐거운 시간을 보냈다고 말한 것으로 전해진다. [실제로 스튜어트의 친근한 행동 때문에 그에게는 열성적인 추종자들이 있었다.] 스튜어트는 또한 스케치를 하지 않고 캔버스 위에 바로 그림을 그리기 시작하는 것으로도 유명했다.

Summary Note

❶ the middle class
❷ Samuel Adams
❸ Benjamin West
❹ George Washington

Building Summary Skills
p.212

Exercise 1 The 1973 Oil Crisis

In 1973, during the Yom Kippur War, Syria and Egypt tried to stifle support for Israel. They convinced the Arab members of the OPEC to withhold petroleum from the United States, Canada, and many of their allies in Western Europe. The U.S. government took many steps to ease the effects of the shortage while elite Arabs grew rich from their increased profits and invested much of their newfound wealth in the purchase of weapons. Meanwhile, although the Yom Kippur War ended in 1974, the ramifications of the oil crisis included a series of recessions in many Western countries throughout the 1980s.

Exercise 2 Bird Migration

Many land-dwelling bird species have migratory patterns. According to scientists, these patterns are the result of genetic programming as well as environmental factors. Both short and long-distance migration patterns have been studied. Although both types are generally associated with birds that take flight to warmer climates for food and other basic needs during cold weather months, short-distance migrators, like buzzards and vultures, which are typically broad-winged, must rely on thermal columns of air to travel. Migration is instinctual; the urge to migrate—known by the German word *Zugunruhe*—has been found even in birds raised in cages.

Exercise 3 Georgia O'Keeffe

Georgia O'Keeffe is one of the best-known painters of the twentieth century. Her works include natural objects and landscapes. She adopted a unique style of painting natural scenes close up as if they were magnified. Her career was aided by her husband, photographer Alfred Stieglitz, for whom she posed nude. Recognized as a great talent during her own lifetime, O'Keeffe reportedly garnered the highest compensation of that time for a set of six calla lily paintings that earned her 25,000 dollars. Later, inspired by the colorful images of New Mexico, she moved to reside there and reflected those images in her work.

Exercise 4 Gold Rush in the Nineteenth Century

During the mid-1800s century, discoveries of gold ore sparked the imaginations of thousands of prospectors. These greedy, courageous, and starry-eyed adventurers rapidly migrated to California and the Yukon Territories of North Canada. Suffering great hardships to overcome the insurmountable odds of striking it rich, great rushes of whites infiltrated sparsely populated areas and brought with them the threat of frostbite, famine, and plague. Author Jack London captured this period in his famous works that include *White Fang*, *Call of the Wild*, and *To Build a Fire*.

Exercise 5 Nuclear Reactors

Nuclear reactors can be natural or manmade. Natural reactors have been found in uranium deposits in West Africa. In order to generate electrical power, scientists have designed nuclear reactors that initiate, control, and sustain nuclear fission at a steady rate. Unlike nuclear fusion, nuclear fission is considered to be a safe and pollution-free source of power, and it is used commercially. Nuclear reactors are classified as fast or slow. This classification is based on the energy of neutrons employed in the reaction process. Although slow thermal reactors are the most common and successful, the construction of fast reactors still continues.

Exercise 6 The Great Portrait Painters of Colonial America

John Singleton Copley and Gilbert Stuart are recognized as the most outstanding portrait painters of the American Colonial Period. Although both men fled to Europe to avoid the trials of the American Revolution, each became renowned for his masterful portraits of the politically elite. Copley's subjects included Samuel Adams and Paul Revere. Stuart's included George Washington and John Adams. Although they were contemporaries and Copley was a major influence on Stuart, the painters never met. Ironically, Stuart's reputation for fine work eventually surpassed Copley's.

Mini TOEFL iBT Practice Test p.214

1 Ⓑ 2 Ⓓ 3 Ⓐ 4 Ⓑ 5 Ⓒ

6 Ⓒ 7 **1** 8 Pottery Wheel: **1**, **7**

Wood-fired Kiln: **2**, **4**, **5**

9 Ⓐ 10 Ⓐ 11 Ⓒ 12 Ⓓ 13 Ⓓ

14 Ⓒ 15 Ⓑ 16 **2**

해석

[1-8]

도기의 발달

전 세계의 원시 문화에서 도기가 출현한 것은 인류 역사상 중요한 이정표였다. 때때로 용기의 혁명이라고도 일컬어지는 도기는 원시인들이 음식을 끓이고 찔 수 있게 해 주었는데, 이는 또 다시 원시인들로 하여금 새롭고 보다 다양한 재료에서 영양분을 얻도록 만들었다. 또한 내구성이 뛰어나고 물이 새지 않는 도기 덕분에 빗물 혹은 깨끗한 강과 호수의 담수를 담아 저장할 수 있었다.

최초의 도기는 소수의 문명에서 그 기원을 찾을 수 있으며, 이들은 서로 독립적으로 발달한 것으로 보인다. 역사가들에게 가장 오래된 것으로 알려진 도기는 대략 기원전 10,500년경 일본의 조몽인들이 만든 것이다. 도기가 독립적으로 발달했다는 증거는 기원전 10,000년경 북아프리카에서 만들어진 도기와 기원전 7,000년경 남아메리카에서 만들어진 도기에서도 찾을 수 있다.

고고학자들이 수집한 도기 파편은, 특히 문자가 생기기 이전의 문명으로서 역사 기록을 남길 수 없었던, 고대 문화의 발전 수준을 확인할 수 있는 가장 좋은 방법 중 하나로 알려져 있다. 고고학자들은 다양한 지층에서 다양한 파편을 발굴해냄으로써 한 문화의 발전 단계의 시기를 쉽게 측정할 수 있다. 또한 도기 조각의 스타일과 장식을 살펴봄으로써 그렇게 할 수도 있다. 더 나아가 이들 연구자들은 미량 원소 분석을 통해 도기 제작에 사용된 점토의 출처를 정확히 알아낼 수도 있다.

초기의 도기는 수세공이라는 기술로 만들어졌다. 수세공 도기는 손으로 긴 띠 모양의 점토를 꼰 후 이를 감아서 그릇의 몸통을 만든다. 이러한 초기의 도기들은 수세공의 특징인 불규칙성 때문에 각각 세상에서 하나뿐인 것이었다. 이러한 원시 도기들은 손으로 모양이 빚어진 후 원시 가마에서 구워졌는데, 원시 가마는 오히려 장작불 형태와 비슷했을 것이다.

다음으로 중요한 도기의 발전은 기원전 6,000년에서 기원전 2,400년 사이 메소포타미아에서 물레가 발명되면서 이루어졌다. 이 장치는 도기 생산에 혁명을 가져왔는데, 그 이유는 도공들로 하여금 세계 최초의 도시들의 수요 증가에 부응할 수 있도록 제품을 대량 생산할 수 있게 만들었기 때문이었다. 돌림판은 발판으로 작동되며 매우 빠른 속도로 점토를 돌리는 회전 테이블로, 이를 통해 도공은 회전에 의한 대칭 형태의 도기를 만들 수 있었다. 그 결과 수세공 도기보다 훨씬 더 일정한 형태의 도기 제품들이 만들어졌다.

[유약의 도입도 도기의 품질 향상에 기여했다.] 기원후 800년 사마라와 바그다드의 이슬람 도공들은 납으로 만든 유약을 사용해서 도기의 마무리 작업을 했다. 이러한 유약 처리 과정은 로마에서 비롯된 것으로, 로마인들이 이를 지중해와 북아프리카에 전파했다. 이러한 도공들은 또한 당시 인기가 높았던 중국의 백자를 따라 만드는 과정에서 새로운 형태의 유약 처리법을 알아내기도 했다. 중국 자기를 매우 비슷하게 따라 만들 수 있었지만, 실험 결과에 의해 납 대신 산화 주석을 이용하는 새로운 유약 처리법이 알려졌다.

도기를 단단하게 굳히기 위해서는 도기를 고온 상태의 가마에서 구워야 한다. 중국인들은 도기 역사 초창기에 아나가마라고 불리는 매우 효율적인 장작 가마를 개발했다. 이 유용한 장치 덕분에 석탄을 쓰지 않고서도 필요한 온도가 유지될 수 있었는데, 이는 곧 한국과 일본에도 도입되었다.

진정한 대량 생산을 할 수 있는 도기 공장의 시대는 1785년 영국의 도시인 스토크온트렌트에서 시작되었다. 이곳은 도기 생산이 1차 산업이었던 최초의 공업 도시 중 하나였다. 이 도시에는 2만 명 이상이 고용된 도기 공장이 200개 이상 존재했던 것으로 알려져 있다. 이 도시는 도기로 너무나 유명해서 "더 포터리즈"라는 별명을 얻기도 했다.

프레더릭 윈슬로 테일러

프레더릭 윈슬로 테일러는 문제를 해결할 수 있는 "한 가지 최선의 방법"이 항상 존재한다고 믿었다. 그는 과학적 관리론을 만든 사람이었다. 효율성에 관한 그의 생각과 연구는 전 세계의 관리 방식과 관리자 및 노동자들의 작업 환경에 변화를 가져다 주었다. 그는 20세기 초 효율성 운동의 선봉에 섰던 미국인 엔지니어였다. 이 운동으로 인해 전 세계 강대국에서 산업주의가 등장하게 되었다.

공학적인 효율성에 대한 테일러의 관심은 좋지 않은 시력 때문에 하버드 대학의 진학이 불가능해지자 시작되었다. 그에 대한 대안으로서 그는 1874년에 견습 기계공이 되었다. 이 기간 동안 그는 공장의 상황을 직접 체험할 수 있었다. 공장 노동자로 일하면서도 그는 기계공학 학위를 받을 수 있었다. 그는 스티븐스 공과 대학의 통신 과정으로 공부를 해서 1883년에 졸업을 했다.

효율성에 관한 테일러의 신념의 핵심은 어떤 일에서도 주의 깊은 과학적 분석을 통해 "한 가지 최선의 방법"을 찾을 수 있다는 생각이었다. 그는 이러한 원칙에 기반하여 시간 동작 연구라고 불리는 자신의 가장 유명한 실험을 고안했다. 이 실험에서는 하나의 공정이 기본 구성 요소로 분해되었고, 각각의 작업은 초 단위로 측정되었다.

그러한 테일러의 연구 중 가장 유명한 것이 삽을 이용한 연구였다. [하지만 당시에 그는 이 연구로 어떠한 명성도 얻지 못했다.] 연구는 그가 노동자들이 각기 다른 재료에 동일한 삽을 사용한다는 점을 알았을 때 시작되었다. 그는 그들의 동작을 자세히 분석한 후 가장 효과적인 적재량이 약 10킬로그램이라는 점을 알아냈다. 그런 다음 각각의 재료를 정확히 그 양만큼 퍼 올릴 수 있는 삽을 만들었다. 그러나 아이러니컬하게도 테일러가 자신의 생각을 실제 공장에 적용시키면 성공을 거두는 경우가 별로 없었다. 그의 생각은 몇 년 후 그의 가르침을 따르는 추종자들이 그의 아이디어를 시행했을 때 인정받게 되었다.

자신의 원칙을 적용시키는데 실패하자 그는 자신이 일했던 대규모 철강 회사에서 해고되었고, 관리에 대한 자신의 생각을 책으로 쓰기 시작했다. 그는 당시의 일반적인 관리 방식이 아마추어적이라고 굳게 믿었다. 또한 경영이 하나의 학문으로 연구되어야 하며, 올바른 경영이 이루어지면 노동자가 관리자와 협력을 할 것이기 때문에 노동 조합이 필요 없을 것이라고 확신했다.

테일러는 1900년경 다트머스 대학의 턱 경영대학원의 교수가 되었다. 그곳에서 그는 자신의 주요 저작물인 *과학적 관리 원칙*을 발표했다. 이 책에서 그는 과학적 관리의 네 가지 주요 원칙을 설명했다. 그의 관리 원칙은 주먹구구식 작업 방식 대신 업무를 과학적으로 연구해서 얻은 방법을 채택할 것, 각 노동자들을 과학적으로 고용, 훈련, 개발시키고 노동자들이 혼자서 일을 배우게 하지 말 것, 노동자들과 협력해서 과학적으로 개발된 방법이 준수되도록 할 것, 그리고 관리자들이 전략을 수립할 때 과학적인 관리 원칙을 사용하고 노동자들도 자신이 하는 일에 같은 원칙을 사용할 수 있도록 관리자와 노동자 사이에 업무를 공정하게 분배할 것이었다.

1908년 하버드 대학은 테일러의 아이디어뿐만 아니라 그의 네 가지 과학적 관리 원칙에 기초한 경영학 수업을 대학원 과정에서 가르치기 시작했다. 헨리 포드가 소개한 대량 생산의 개념과 함께 테일러의 아이디어는 스위스, 프랑스, 그리고 특히 소련과 같은 나라들을 포함하여 전 세계에 커다란 영향을 끼쳤다. 테일러의 사고를 시행한 전 세계의 관리자들은 이를 테일러의 원칙, 그리고 때로는 경멸하는 의미로서 테일러주의라고 불렀다.

Vocabulary Check-Up
p.220

A
| 1 | ⓒ | 2 | Ⓐ | 3 | Ⓑ | 4 | Ⓐ | 5 | ⓒ |
| 6 | Ⓐ | 7 | ⓒ | 8 | Ⓓ | 9 | Ⓓ | 10 | Ⓑ |

B
| 1 | Ⓗ | 2 | Ⓙ | 3 | Ⓔ | 4 | ⓒ | 5 | Ⓘ |
| 6 | Ⓐ | 7 | Ⓕ | 8 | Ⓖ | 9 | Ⓓ | 10 | Ⓑ |

UNIT 09 Prose Summary

Basic Drill ···································· p.226

Drill 1 ① ② ④

해석

지진파의 종류

지진파는 지진의 한 가지 결과로서 땅속을 통과하는 파장이다. 지진파에는 두 종류가 있다. 하나는 지구 내부를 통과하는 "실체파"이고, 다른 하나는 지구의 바깥 부분 바로 아래를 통과하는 "표면파"이다.

지진 발생시 경험할 수 있는 초기 진동은 실체파 때문일 수 있는데, 실체파는 P파와 S파로 이루어진다. 이 두 파가 지나가는 경로는 땅의 조성과 밀도에 따라 달라진다. P파는 번갈아가면서 땅을 압축시키고 팽창시키는 반면, S파는 횡파 형태로 땅을 움직인다.

표면파는 낮은 주파수, 긴 지속 시간, 그리고 큰 진폭을 나타내며, 지진에 수반되는 피해를 일으킨다. 표면파에는 두 가지 종류가 있다. 레일파는 땅을 물결처럼 출렁거리게 만들며, 러브파는 땅을 수평으로 흔들리게 만든다.

Drill 2 ② ④ ⑤

해석

소행성 1989 FC

소행성은 태양계를 떠다니며 태양 주위를 도는 천체이다. 한 종류의 소행성은 지구의 공전 궤도와 매우 근접한 공전 궤도를 가지고 있기 때문에 NEA, 즉 근지구 소행성으로 알려져 있다. 일부 NEA는 지구와 교차하는 궤도를 가지고 있어서 이로 인한 충돌의 위험성이 존재한다.

1994년 3월 23일, 그러한 NEA 중 하나가 지구에 심각한 위협이 되었다. 나중에 1989 FC로 알려진 아폴로 소행성 4581 아스클레피우스가 400,163마일 차이로 지구와의 충돌을 피했다. 근소한 차이가 아닌 것처럼 보일 수 있지만, 정확히 이야기하면 소행성 1989 FC는 우주에서 지구가 불과 6시간 전에 있었던 곳과 같은 장소에 들어갔다. 소행성이 지구와 충돌했다면 인간이 알고 있는 가장 큰 폭발이 일어났을 것이다. 그 충격은 50일 연속으로 1초마다 대형 원자 폭탄이 폭발하는 위력과 같았을 것이다.

Drill 3 ① ④ ⑥

해석

식품과 탄수화물

살아남기 위해 사람은 다양한 음식물을 섭취해야 한다. 사람들이 먹는 모든 종류의 음식은 세 가지의 주요 영양소, 즉 단백질, 지방, 그리고 탄수화물로 분해될 수 있다. 각각은 신체 유지에 중요한 역할을 하지만, 인간의 주요 에너지원이 되는 것은 바로 탄수화물이다.

탄수화물은 체내에서 에너지 저장과 운반을 돕는 생체 분자이다. 탄수화물은 당 또는 당류라고도 알려져 있다. 탄수화물의 기본 단위는 단당류이다. 단당류는 무한한 방식으로 서로 결합하여 다당류 및 포도당과 같은 다른 탄수화물을 만든다.

음식에 대해 이야기할 때 영양학자들은 탄수화물을 두 가지 부류로 구분한다. 바로 복합탄수화물이 포함된 음식과 단순탄수화물이 포함된 음식이다. 복합탄수화물은 단순탄수화물에 비해 체내에서 분해되는 시간이 더 길다. 탄수화물 함량이 높은 식품으로는 쌀, 감자, 빵, 그리고 시리얼 등을 들 수 있다.

Drill 4 ① ② ⑥

해석

변성암

변성암은 다른 종류의 암석, 예를 들어 화성암이나 퇴적암 같은 암석이 극도로 높은 열과 압력을 받아 성분에 변화가 생길 때 만들어진다. 이러한 과정은 변성 작용으로 알려져 있으며, 열이나 압력이 가해지기 전에 존재했던 암석은 원암으로 알려져 있다. 예를 들어 대부분 퇴적암으로 이루어져 있던 섬에서 갑자기 화산 폭발이 일어난다고 하자. 화산이 폭발하면서 퇴적암, 즉 원암이 열과 압력을 받아 변하게 된다. 이제 이 퇴적암은 변성암으로 알려진다.

과학자들은 변성암을 연구함으로써 지각의 구조에 대해 많은 것을 알아낼 수 있는데, 그 이유는 변성암이 지구의 내부 온도 및 압력에 관한 소중한 정보와 지구가 지질학적 시간에 따라 어떻게 변했는지를 알려 주기 때문이다. 변성암의 두 가지 예로 점판암과 대리석을 들 수 있다.

Exercises with Long Passages

Exercise 1 1 Ⓐ 2 Ⓐ 3 ② ③ ⑥ ······ p.230

해석

지질 연대 측정법

지질 연대는 과학자들이 지구의 역사에서 일어났던 사건들 사이의 시간 및 관계를 설명하기 위해 사용하는 시간 단위이다. 지구의 나이는 45억 7천 만년 이상이기 때문에 인간이 시간을 표시하기 위해 사용하는 날, 년, 그리고 세기라는 단위는 너무 작아서 지구 시간을 측정할 때에는 쓸모가 없다. 지질 연대는 다양한 시기에 일어난 특정 사건들에 따른 단위로 나뉘어진다. 일반적으로 지질 연대표의 시기는 공룡의 멸종이나 인간의 출현과 같은 지질학적인 주요 사건들에 의해서 규정된다.

지질 연대는 또한 세 개의 주요 단위, 즉 누대, 대, 그리고 기로 구분된다. 누대가 가장 큰 시간 단위이다. 누대는 대로 나누어지며, 대는 또 다시 여러 개의 기로 나누어진다. 기는 일반적으로 상부, 중부, 하부로 구분된다. 상부와 하부라는 용어 대신 후기와 전기라는 용어를 사용할 수도 있다. 예를 들어 한 명의 고고학자와 한 명의 지질학자가 특별한 종류의 암석에 들어 있는 공룡 뼈를 발견했다고 하자. 고고학자는 실험실에서 공룡 뼈의 구조를 조사한 후 지질 연대표를 이용해서 뼈가 진화한 누대, 대, 기를 알아내고자 할 것이다. 아마도 지질학자에게 "이 공룡은 현생 누대에 해당하는 중생대 상부 쥐라기 때 만들어진 화석이다."라고 말할 수도 있다. 지질학자는 그 암석이 뼈와 동일한 기, 대, 그리고 누대에 형성된 상부 쥐라기 사암이라는 것을 알게 될 것이다.

지질 연대표는 17세기 말 덴마크의 지질학자인 니콜라스 스테노에 의해 최초로 고안되었다. 스테노는 지구에서 발견되는 암석층은 특정 기간에 만들어졌으며, 암석의 형성 과정 및 성분을 연구함으로써 지구의 연대표를 만들 수 있다는 결론을 내렸다. 또한 스테노는 특정 암석층이 그 위에 있는 것보다는 오래되고 그 아래에 있는 것보다는 오래되지 않았을 것이라고 주장했다. 스테노 이후 많은 과학자들이 귀중한 연구와 자료를 제공함으로써 지질 연대표가 만들어졌다. 영국의 지질학자들이 그러한 과정을 주도했는데, 몇몇 시기의 이름에서 그들의 영향을 확인할 수 있다. 캄브리아와 실루리아는 영국의 부족 이름이었고, 데본기는 영국의 마을 이름인 데본셔에서 비롯된 것이다.

결론적으로, 전 세계의 과학자들이 여러 종류의 암석층과 화석 사이의 관계에 기초하여 지질 연대표를 만들었다. 이러한 연대표 덕분에 과학자들은 지구 역사에 관한 정밀한 가설들을 세울 수 있었다.

📝 Summary Note

❶ big time increments
❷ eons, eras, and periods
❸ Nicholas Steno
❹ layers of rock

Exercise 2　1　Ⓐ　2　Ⓒ　3　1, 3, 6　　　　p.232

해석

플레이아데스 성단

플레이아데스 성단은 일종의 산개 성단으로, 같은 성간 구름에서 만들어지고 중력 때문에 서로 느슨하게 결합되어 있는 수천 개의 별로 이루어져 있다. 플레이아데스 성단은 특히 황소자리에서 찾을 수 있는 산개 성단을 가리킨다. 플레이아데스 성단은 또한 M45 또는 일곱자매별로도 알려져 있다.

플레이아데스 성단을 이루는 별들은 지난 1억 이내에 형성되었기 때문에 천문학적인 관점에서는 비교적 어린 편이다. 이 별들은 특히 청백색 별의 일종인데, 이는 이들이 은하계 가장 뜨겁고 강력한 별에 속한다는 점을 의미한다. 이들이 너무나 강력하기 때문에 플레이아데스 성단은 매우 빨리 타 버려서 짧은 기간 동안만 존재하게 될 것으로 추정된다. 이 성단은 2억 5천만 년 정도 더 존재한 후 다른 중력으로 인해 은하계 내에서 흩어질 것으로 생각된다. 거리에 대해 말하자면 플레이아데스 성단은 지구로부터 약 440광년 떨어진 곳에 있다고 알려져 있으며, 전체 직경은 12광년이다.

플레이아데스 성단은 별로만 이루어진 것이 아니라 반사 성운이라는 것도 포함하고 있는데, 반사 성운은 인근의 별에서 나오는 빛을 반사시키는 먼지 구름이다. 반사 성운은 또한 플레이아데스 성단의 전체적 밝기에 영향을 미친다. 한때는 플레이아데스 성단을 둘러싼 먼지 입자가 플레이아데스 성단을 만들어 낸 원래 성간 구름의 일부라고 생각되었지만, 현재는 플라이아데스 성단이 은하계에서 특히 먼지가 많은 부분을 통과하고 있는 것이라고 생각된다.

플레이아데스 성단은 역사상 여러 문화권에서 중요한 역할을 했다. 고대 그리스인들은 플레이아데스 성단을 별자리로 생각했고, 호머의 고전인 *일리아드*와 *오디세이*에서도 플레이아데스 성단이 언급되었다. 플레이아데스 성단은 성경에서 세 차례 언급되었으며, 그리스 신화 덕분에 일곱칠자매별이라는 이름을 얻었고, 힌두교 신화 덕분에 일곱어머니별이라는 이름도 얻었다. 고대 아즈텍인들은 플레이아데스 성단에 기초해 달력을 만들었으며, 아메리카 원주민들은 플레이아데스 성단에서 몇 개의 별을 볼 수 있는지에 따라 서로의 시력을 측정했다. 플레이아데스 성단을 둘러 싼 수많은 신화들은 밤하늘에서 이 성단이 얼마나 눈에 잘 띄고 밝게 빛나는지 알려 준다.

📝 Summary Note

❶ open star
❷ 440 light years
❸ Reflection nebulae
❹ Aztecs

Exercise 3　1　Ⓑ　2　Ⓓ　3　2, 3, 5　　　　p.234

해석

은판 사진술

은판 사진은 제작 과정이 매우 복잡하고 힘든 초창기 형태의 사진이다. 광택을 낸 은판 표면에 이미지를 직접 노출시키면 사진이 만들어진다. 이 사진술의 주된 단점은 음화가 없다는 것인데, 이는 하나의 정확한 이미지가 복제될 수 없다는 점을 의미한다.

은판 사진술, 즉 다게레오타입이라는 말은 은판 사진을 발명한 사람 중 한 명인 프랑스인 화학자 루이 다게르의 이름에서 비롯되었다. 그는 빛의 다양한 특성에 관심을 가졌던 화가이기도 했다. 다게르는 또 다른 프랑스인 발명가 니세포르 니엡스와 수년 간 공동으로 연구한 후 1839년에 은과 백악의 혼합물을 빛에 노출시키면 어두워진다는 점을 알아냈다.

은판 사진술은 광택을 낸 은판에 할로겐화은을 분사시킴으로써 시작된다. 그 후 렌즈를 통해 은판에 이미지의 초점을 맞춘다. 수은을 넣어 가열한 컵 위에 은판을 놓으면 이미지가 떠오른다. 열로 인해 수은 증기가 생기면 수은 증기가 은판에서 가장 많이 빛에 노출된 곳에 응결된다. 수은이 은판에 달라붙으면 사진이 현상된다. 은판 사진술의 마지막 단계는 소다라는 액체에 은판을 담금으로써 은판에 이미지를 고착시키는 것이다. 염화금으로 은판을 처리하는 것 또한 이미지를 강화시키는데 도움이 된다. 그러나 이미지가 손상되기 쉽고 사진을 다시 얻을 수가 없기 때문에 다게르와 그 이후의 사람들은 잊지 않고 유리 조각으로 영상을 덮어야 했다.

은판 사진술은 빠르게 전 세계로 퍼져나갔다. 은판 사진술이 인기가 높았던 이유 중 하나는 이전의 사진술에 비해 은판 사진술의 과정이 훨씬 더 빨랐기 때문이었다. 19세기 중반, 은판 사진술을 이용하여 사진을 찍는 사진사들이 이 마을 저 마을을 돌며 사람들의 초상 사진을 찍어 주었다. 역사상 최초로 사람들이, 화가의 눈으로 먼저 걸러진 이미지가 아닌, 자신과 똑같은 이미지를 소유할 수 있었다.

하지만 안타깝게도 시간이 흐르면서 보다 새로운 형태의 사진술이 발명되었고, 은판 사진술은 사진사에게 너무 힘들고 일반인들에게는 너무 비싼 것으로 판명되면서 잘 쓰이지 않게 되었다. 게다가 또한 은판 사진의 이미지는 복제가 불가능했기 때문에 음화를 만들어 내는 새로운 형태의 사진술이 훨씬 더 선호되었다. 음화를 만들어 냈던 후기 형태의 사진술 중 하나는 은염을 사용한 유리 조각에 이미지를 고착시키는 방식이었다.

📝 Summary Note

❶ negative
❷ Louis Daguerre
❸ silver halide
❹ mercury vapors

Exercise 4　1　Ⓑ　2　Ⓐ　3　1, 5, 6　　　　p.236

해석

사구

사구는 풍성 작용이라고 불리는 바람의 침식 작용으로 인해 형성된, 단순히 모래가 쌓여 있는 지형이다. 사구의 형태와 크기는 전적으로 바람에 의해 결정되며 인접한 사구들끼리도 모습이 다를 수 있다. 모습이 다를 수는 있지만, 모든 유형의 사구에 적용되는 몇 가지 표준적인 설명 용어들이 존재한다. 저지는 인접한 두 개의 사구 사이의 골짜기이며, 사구원은 사구가 가득한 지형을 가리킨다. 사구원이 특히 큰 경우에는 에르그라고 불린다. 사구의 측면은 사면이라고 한다.

사구를 찾아볼 수 있는 가장 흔한 장소로는 해안 지역과 사막과 같이 넓고 건조한 내륙 지방 두 곳을 들 수 있다. 해안을 따라 있는 사구는 폭풍이 이는 바다와 그로 인한 침식으로부터 육지를 보호해 준다. 조건이 상당히 열악해 보이지만, 많은 해초와 바다새들에게 해안 사구는 이상적인 서식지이며, 다양한 종의 선인장, 뱀, 그리고 거미에게는 사막 사구의 환경이 이상적이다.

사구의 형상은 다양하며, 각각은 부분적으로 바람의 세기 및 방향, 그리고 주변 지형에 의해 결정된다. 가장 흔한 사구 형상은 초승달 모양의 사구이다. 이러한 형상의 사구는 일반적으로 길이보다 폭이 넓으며 바람이 계속해서 한 방향으로 불 때 만들어진다. 별 모양의 사구는 매우 대칭적으로, 이 경우 높은 정상 부분에서 세 개 이상의 가지가 방사형으로 뻗어 있다. 이러한 유형의 사구는 사하라의 그랜드 에르그 오리엔탈 사막에서 흔하며, 바람이 여러 방향에서 불기 때문에 형성된다. 이러한 사구는 옆이 아니라 위쪽으로 커진다. 역전 사구는 주기적으로 바뀌는 바람의 방향 때문에 다양한 형상과 크기를 나타내는 사구이다.

사구의 형상에 상관없이 각각의 유형은 세 가지 형태, 즉 단순형, 혼합형, 그리고 복합형으로 구분될 수 있다. 단순형 사구는 기하학적 형상을 이루는 최소한의 측면, 즉 사면을 가지고 있는 사구이다. 혼합형 사구는 그 보다 큰 사구로, 그 안에는 그와 동일한 모양의 작은 사구들이 다수 포함되어 있으며, 복합형 사구는 두 가지 이상의 사구 유형이 섞여 있는 것이다.

사구는 특히 해안 지역과 같은 특정 서식지의 필수적인 부분으로, 사구는 해안 지역의 토양 침식을 막고 특정 야생 생물들이 살 수 있는 환경을 제공해 준다. 반면에 사구는 사막화로 알려진 문제를 일으킬 수도 있다. 사막화는 기후 변화로 인해 토양이 침식될 때 발생한다. 사구를 만들어 내는 것과 동일한 바람이, 건물 및 농작물에 큰 피해를 줄 수 있는 모래 폭풍이나 모래 사태의 형태로, 종종 인간의 주거지에 사구를 형성시키기도 한다. 해마다 아프리카 및 중동 지역과 같은 곳에서는 거주 지역으로 모래가 들어오지 못하도록 모래 방벽이 설치되고 있다.

📝 Summary Note

❶ the wind
❷ crescent shape
❸ many smaller dunes
❹ desertification

Exercise 5 1 Ⓑ   2 ⓒ   3 ①, ③, ⑥   p.238

[해석]

첨단 전파 망원경의 발달

전파 망원경은 전파를 "보는" 라디오 수신기이다. 빛을 보는 보통의 망원경과는 달리 전파 망원경은 천체에서 발산되는 전파를 감지할 수 있기 때문에 천문학 분야에서 주로 사용된다. 라디오 물체라고도 불리는 우주의 천체들은 다양한 원자와 분자들이 방출하는 고온의 기체, 저자, 그리고 파장과 같은 것일 수 있다.

최초의 전파 망원경은 1937년 그로테 리버에 의해 발명되었다. 그는 미국인이었고 공학 분야의 학위를 받았다. 그는 아마추어 무선 통신사로 일을 했다. 이후 그는 자기집 뒷마당에 자신의 전파 망원경을 설치하기로 결심했다. 리버가 처음에 만든 두 대의 라디오 수신기는 우주로부터 아무런 신호도 받지 못했지만, 1938년 세 번째 전파 망원경으로 우주에서 온 신호를 받아내는데 성공했다.

전파 망원경은 한 개, 혹은 두 개 이상의 거대한 접시형 안테나들로 구성된다. 접시 형태는 들어오는 전파를 하나의 초점에 모이도록 만든다는 점에서 중요하다. 이로써 신호가 최대한 강하게 수신될 수 있다. 접시 크기가 클수록 보다 많은 신호를 수신하고 초점에 모을 수 있다.

1950년대 후반과 1960년대 초반에 당시로서는 가장 큰 전파 망원경이 발명되었다. 76미터짜리 망원경이었다. 하지만 그 후 더 큰 망원경이 만들어졌다. 현존하는 세계 최대의 전파 망원경은 러시아에 있는 RATAN-600으로, 그 직경이 576미터에 이른다. 이 전파 망원경은 태양 전파 파장과 대기에 관한 귀중한 정보를 제공해 주고 있다. 유럽 최대의 전파 망원경은 독일에 있는 직경 100미터짜리 망원경이며, 미국 최대의 전파 망원경은 오하이오주에 있는 빅 이어이다. 가장 규모가 큰 전파 간섭계는 인도에 있는 거대 미터파 전파 망원경이다.

전파 망원경은 과학자들에게 우주에 관한 귀중한 정보를 제공해 준다. 전파 망원경의 가장 중요한 기능 중 하나는 과학자들로 하여금 우주에서 무인 우주 미션을 수행 중인 다양한 우주 탐사선의 경로를 추적할 수 있게 하는 것이다. 전파 망원경 때문에 화성 표면처럼 인간이 탐사하기에는 너무나 위험한 곳에도 우주 탐사선을 보낼 수 있다. 전파 기술이 없다면 과학자들은 우주에 존재하는 것들에 대해 많은 것을 알 수도, 그리고 볼 수도 없을 것이다. 전파는 우주에서 인간의 눈과 귀가 된다.

📝 Summary Note

❶ radio waves
❷ Grote Reber
❸ Big Ear
❹ unmanned

Exercise 6 1 ⓒ   2 ⓒ   3 ②, ③, ⑥   p.240

[해석]

원자 이온화

이온화는 원자에 들어 있는 양성자 수와 전자 수가 바뀜에 따라 원자가 하전된 이온으로 변하는 과정이다. 원자는 양 전하를 띨 수도 있고 음전하를 띨 수도 있다. 이는 한 개 또는 그 이상의 전자를 빼앗기느냐 혹은 얻느냐에 따라 달라진다. 전자를 빼앗기는 경우, 여분의 양성자가 존재하게 되어 원자는 양이온이 된다. 자유 전자를 얻는 경우, 원자는 음이온이 된다. 원자가 양이온 또는 음이온 중 어떤 것이 되느냐에 따라 이온화 과정은 약간 달라진다.

1913년 덴마크의 물리학자인 닐스 보어는 이온화 과정에서 원자가 다른 원자와 결합하거나 분리되기 위해 필요한 에너지는 그러한 장벽을 허무는데 필요한 잠재 에너지를 결코 초과할 수 없다고 가정했다. 예를 들어 보어의 이론에 따르면 어떤 사람이 2피트 높이의 바를 넘으려고 하면 그 사람은 공중으로 최소 2피트를 뛰어오를 수 있어야 한다. 이 이론에 따르면 전자가 원자와 결합하거나 원자에서 분리될 때 원자에 필요한 에너지는 결코 장벽의 잠재 에너지보다 낮을 수 없다.

물은 이온화 과정을 보여 주는 좋은 예다. 물은 +1인 양전하를 지닌 수소 이온 2개와, −2의 음전하를 가진 산소 이온 1개로 이루어져 있다. 두 개의 수소 원자와 한 개의 산소 원자가 접촉하면 (두 개의 전자를 잃었기 때문에) 수소의 양전하가 산소 원자의 여분의 전자 두 개와 붙게 된다. 원자는 가장 균형 있는 상태를 유지하려고 하기 때문에 그러한 일이 일어난다. 따라서 H_2O는 단단히 결속 상태를 유지하며, 에너지 전위가 보다 큰 다른 분자와 접촉하는 경우에만 이온화가 이루어진다.

실용적인 측면에서 보면 원자 이온화 과정은 과학자들로 하여금 플라스틱이나 화학 약품 같은 새로운 제품에 필요한 분자들을 만들고 조작할 수 있게 해 준다. 또한 이온화는 환경적인 측면에서 인기가 매우 높아지고 있다. 오늘날 기업들은 공기 청정기를 생산하는데, 이는 이온화 장치에 불과하다. 공기 청정기는 공기 중의 자유 라디칼 이온을 끌어당기고 전자들로 이들의 전하량을 다시 맞춤으로써 작동한다.

위에서 설명한 닐스 보어의 모델에 기초한 이온화 과정은 고전적 이온화로 알려져 있다. 또한 터널 이온화 및 비연속 이온화와 같은 보다 복잡한 이온화 과정도 존재한다. 하지만 이러한 과정들은 덜 보편적이며 종종 실험실에서 이루어진다.

📝 Summary Note

❶ protons and electrons

❷ Neils Bohr

❸ molecules

❹ tunnel ionization

Building Summary Skills
p.242

Exercise 1 How to Measure Geologic Time

Nicholas Steno devised the geologic time scale in the late seventeenth century. The time scale calibrates the history of the Earth according to major geological events. The scale is divided into eons, eras, and periods. These smaller increments allow scientists to categorize and reference historic artifacts and fossils within certain timeframes and to piece together a map of the Earth's history. Since its inception, many scientists have contributed to the time scale.

Exercise 2 The Pleiades

The Pleiades is found in the constellation Taurus. It is formed of the hottest and brightest stars in the galaxy as well as reflection nebulae that further enhance its overall shine. Estimated to be about 440 light years away from Earth and spanning twelve light years in diameter, scientists predict that it will burn itself out before gravitational forces can pull it apart. Meanwhile, its intense power and brilliance have won it a prominent role in the mythologies and advancements of many cultures.

Exercise 3 The Daguerreotype

The daguerreotype was invented by French chemist Louis Daguerre in 1839 when he discovered that a mixture of silver and chalk would darken an image exposed to light. This discovery made it possible to create exact images of people. Furthermore, although early methods of photography had been attempted, the daguerreotype process was less cumbersome than its predecessors and meant that early photographers could travel from town to town to take portraitures of their subjects. Unfortunately, the daguerreotype lacked the means to produce copies, and with the introduction of the negative, the daguerreotype soon lost favor.

Exercise 4 Sand Dunes

A sand dune is a mound of sand formed from wind erosion. Generally, dunes are created along coastal areas or in desert regions. The ferocity and the direction of the wind determines the type of sand dune that is formed. Although sand dunes provide ideal habitats for various plants and animals as well as prevent subsequent erosion, they also encroach on human habitats through a process called desertification. In desertification, sand storms and sand avalanches cause major damage to buildings and crops.

Exercise 5 The Development of Advanced Radio Telescopes

Radio telescopes are important to scientists because they are able to see and track information from space. First developed by American Grote Reber in 1937, radio telescopes are designed with a parabolic shape that concentrates signals into a strong focal point that can more easily be detected. A larger dish size determines a greater degree of concentration. Since then, the early 1960s saw the invention of a radio telescope with a 76-meter diameter, but today the largest radio telescopes exceed 100 meters in diameter with the largest having a diameter of 576 meters. Furthermore, radio telescopes can be found around the world.

Exercise 6 The Ionization of an Atom

Ionization is the process of changing the charge of an atom. It allows scientists to manipulate atoms into new products. Possibly because it is environmentally friendly, the process of ionization has become particularly profitable for companies that market air purifiers. Ionization enables the purifiers to attract free radical ions and to rebalance their charges with electrons. This type of ionization is called classical ionization and was first theorized by Neils Bohr in 1931. Although other types of ionization processes have been developed, they are less commonly used.

Mini TOEFL iBT Practice Test p.244

1 Ⓐ   2 Ⓐ   3 Ⓓ   4 Ⓑ   5 Ⓐ
6 Ⓐ   7 **2**   8 ①, ③, ⑥
9 Ⓒ   10 Ⓐ   11 Ⓑ   12 Ⓐ   13 Ⓑ
14 Ⓒ   15 **4**   16 ②, ④, ⑥

해석

[1-8]

금성의 대기

샛별과 저녁별로도 불리는 금성은 두 번째로 태양 가까이에 있는 행성이며 밤하늘에서 가장 밝게 빛나는 천체이다. 이 행성은 지구일로 224일마다 태양 주위를 한 바퀴 돈다. 금성은 때때로 지구의 자매 행성으로 불리기도 하는데, 그 이유는 이 둘의 면적과 부피가 비슷하기 때문이다. 하지만 금성의 대기는 지구의 대기와 비슷하지 않다.

금성의 대기는 지구 대기보다 훨씬 무거우며 밀도가 높다. 또한 금성의 대기는 지구의 대기보다 훨씬 높은 높이까지 뻗어 있다. 하지만 두꺼운 구름층이 금성 표면을 덮고 있기 때문에 레이더 매핑을 통해 관찰하지 않는 이상 금성의 표면을 보는 것은 거의 불가능하다.

금성의 상층부 대기의 압력과 온도는 지구의 경우와 비슷하다. 하지만 하층부 대기의 열과 압력은 용광로와 다를 바 없다. 금성의 대기는 매우 두꺼우며 주로 이산화탄소 및 소량의 질소로 구성되어 있다. 만약 인간이 금성 표면의 극도로 높은 열(400℃)을 견딜 수 있다고 하더라도, 인간은 지구 기압보다 90배 더 높은 지상 기압을 상대해야 한다. 금성의 극도로 높은 기온은 엄청난 양의 이산화탄소에 의해 일어나는 온실 효과 때문이다. 온실 효과란 태양의 적외선이 대기에 보다 쉽게 흡수되는 과정이다. 일년 내내 식물을 키우기 위해 사용되는 실제 온실에서와 마찬가지로, 다량의 이산화탄소가 복사열을 가두어 금성의 대기를 뜨겁게 만든다. 이러한 현상 때문에, 비록 금성이 수성보다 태양에서 두 배 더 멀리 떨어져 있지만, 금성의 대기 기온이 수성보다 높다.

하지만 과학자들은 금성의 대기가 항상 뜨거운 것은 아니었다고 생각한다. 연구에 따르면 금성 표면에는 한때 다량의 물이 있었지만, 결국 물이 모두 증발해서 쉽게 온실 효과가 나타났고, 이 온실 효과가 오늘날 금성을 지배하고 있다. [원인은 다르더라도 그 결과는 동일하다.] 따라서, 인류가 초기 단계의 온실 효과와 맞서기 시작했기 때문에, 금성은 현재의 과학자들에게 중요한 연구 대상이 되고 있다. 지구의 문제는 수원이 증발함으로써 발생하는 것이 아니라 기업 및 자동차가 배출하는 이산화탄소와 기타 온실 가스의 증가 때문에 발생하고 있다.

금성의 대기와 관련해서 주목할 만한 또 한 가지 흥미로운 특징은 금성의 낮과 밤의 기온이 그다지 큰 차이를 보이지 않는다는 점이다. 이는 기온 변화에도 불구하고 열을 가두는 물질의 능력인 열관성과 금성의 강력한 바람에 의한 열전달 현상 때문이다. 금성의 표면에서 부는 바람은 지구의 바람에 비해 속도가 느리다. 하지만 금성의 대기의 밀도가 너무나 높기 때문에, 그곳에서는 바람이 약하게 불어도 커다란 장애물이 움직일 수 있고 행성 표면에 있는 돌들이 날아갈 수도 있다.

1966년 인류는 최초로 금성 대기에 기록 장치를 보내려고 했다. *베네라 3호*가 금성 표면에 도달했다. 하지만 갑작스러운 충격으로 통신 시스템이 고장 나서 어떠한 피드백도 보낼 수 없었다. 1967년에 *베네라 4호*가 성공적으로 금성 대기에 진입을 해서 많은 정보를 보낼 수 있었는데, 그중 하나에는 금성 대기의 90%에서 95%가 이산화탄소라고 기록되어 있었다. 후속 *베네라* 탐사선들이 금성 대기로 보내졌지만, 대부분이 높은 기압의 벽을 뚫지 못했다.

[9-16]
대수층

대수층은 물을 통과시키는 암석 및 기타 용해되지 않은 물질로 이루어진 지하층으로, 이곳에서 우물을 이용하여 지하수를 퍼 올릴 수 있다. 대수층은 자유면대수층이거나 피압대수층 중 하나이다. 자유면대수층은 대수층과 지표면 사이에 압층이 존재하지 않는 대수층이다. 피압대수층에는 상부 경계로서 반대수층이 존재하며, 종종 그 위에 또 다른 비피압대수층이 존재한다. 반대수층은 한 대수층에서 다른 대수층으로의 지하수 흐름을 제한하는 지구상의 지역이다. 완전히 관통할 수 없는 대수층은 난투수층 혹은 비대수층이라고 불린다. 반대수층은 점토 또는 작은 구멍이 없는 암석과 같이 투수 계수가 낮은 물질들로 이루어져 있다.

지구의 얕은 표면 아래에서는 거의 어디에서나 지하수를 찾을 수 있다. 지각은 포화대와 불포화대 두 지역으로 나누어진다. 포화대에서는 모든 빈 공간들이

물로 채워져 있다. 이곳에서 대수층이 발견될 수 있다. 불포화대에서는 지하수가 도달하지 못한 일부 공간들이 공기로 채워져 있다. 포화대에서의 대수층의 압력은 대기압보다 크다. 지하 수면에서 물에 가해지는 압력은 대기압과 동일하다. 반면에 불포화대에서는 물이 음압을 받아 위로 빨려 올라가서 그 위에 있는 상부 경계에 머무르게 된다.

산이 없는 지역에서의 대수층은, 전형적으로 강이나 다른 유수에 의해 퇴적된 토양인, 충적토로 이루어진다. 충적토는 일반적으로 침니나 점토와 같은 작은 입자로 구성되며, 모래 및 자갈과 같은 보다 큰 입자들로도 구성된다. 강은 끊임없이 미세한 입자들을 옮겨 놓는다. 강물이 빠르게 이동하면 느리게 이동하는 경우보다 더 많은 입자들을 옮겨 놓는다. 짐작할 수 있듯이, 강에 있는 큰 입자들을 운반하기 위해서는 많은 에너지가 필요하기 때문에 보다 큰 암석 및 자갈들은 종종 수원 근처에서 발견되지만, 주로 수원에서 멀리 떨어져 있는 대수층은 보다 미세한 물질들로 이루어져 있음을 알 수 있다.

대수층은 거주지에 상관없이 사람들로 하여금 땅에서 물을 끌어올 수 있게 해 준다는 점에서 인간의 삶에 필수적이다. 당연하게도, 크고 오픈된 수원에 더 가까이 있을수록 땅을 얇게 파도 이용 가능한 대수층을 발견할 수 있다. 보다 건조한 지역이나 고도가 높은 곳에 사는 사람들은 더 깊게 땅을 파야 대수층을 발견할 수 있다. 또한 일부 대수층은 다른 대수층보다 크기가 더 크다. [대수층을 찾기 위한 굴착 계획을 세울 때에는 필요한 물의 양을 먼저 계산해야 한다.] 만약 우물을 파는 용도가 순전히 한 가정이 마실 수 있는 식수를 얻기 위한 것이라면 대수층은 작아도 된다. 하지만 대수층을 관개나 채굴 작업에 사용할 계획이라면 보다 큰 대수층이 필요할 것이다. 대부분의 천연 자원과 마찬가지로 매장량이 한정되어 있으므로 인간이 대수층을 지나치게 개발하지 않는 것이 중요하다. 특히 바로 마실 수 있는 물은 다시 채워지기가 힘들기 때문에 담수 대수층이 남용되어서는 안 될 것이다. 하지만 일부 대수층은 조만간 고갈될 위험이 거의 없다. 예를 들어 호주에 있는 그레이트 아티즌 베이슨은 세계에서 가장 큰 대수층이다. 이 대수층은 심지어 호주의 가장 외진 곳까지 물을 공급하고 있으며, 호주 대륙의 23%에 해당되는 지역의 아래에 존재한다.

Vocabulary Check-Up   p.250

A
1 ⓓ	2 ⓐ	3 ⓒ	4 ⓒ	5 ⓐ
6 ⓓ	7 ⓑ	8 ⓒ	9 ⓐ	10 ⓑ

B
1 ⓖ	2 ⓐ	3 ⓘ	4 ⓒ	5 ⓙ
6 ⓗ	7 ⓓ	8 ⓔ	9 ⓑ	10 ⓕ

Basic Drill ··· p.254

Drill 1　Life Stages of the Fruit Tree Leaf Roller: 1, 3, 5
Habitat of the Fruit Tree Leaf Roller: 4, 6

해석

과일나무잎벌레

과일나무잎벌레(*Archips argyrospilus*)는 캘리포니아 전역의 나무에 피해를 입히는 벌레이다. 이 해충은 낙엽수 및 떡갈나무와 같은 관상용 나무들의 잎을 시들게 만든다. 또한 버찌, 사과, 살구, 그리고 자두 나무의 열매에도 피해를 입힌다. 심지어 이 벌레는 땅으로 내려와서 나무 아래에 있는 풀과 식물의 잎도 시들게 만들 수 있다. 이 곤충은 네 개의 발달 단계를 거치며, 크고 작은 나무가지에 쌓여 있는 여러 개의 알 중 하나에서 태어난다. 새로 부화한 유충은 단단한 덩어리에서 나온 후 숙주 나무를 갉아 먹기 시작해서 성장을 마치면 모충이 된다. 충분히 먹이를 먹은 유충은 번데기라고 불리는 실크로 싸이고 감긴 나뭇잎 안에 몸을 말아 넣는다. 8일에서 11일이 지나면 번데기에서 성충이 나온다. 그 후 성충은 다음 라이프 사이클이 시작될 수 있도록 새로운 곳으로 가서 짝짓기를 하고 알을 낳는다.

Drill 2　Neolithic Humans: 2, 4, 5　Pre-Neolithic Humans:
1, 6

해석

신석기 문화

신석기 시대는 구석기 시대, 즉 초기 석기 시대와 청동기 시대 사이에 존재했다. 신석기 시대는 신석기 시대가 존재했던 시간이 아니라 그 시대에 나타났던 행태적 및 문화적 특성에 의해 규정된다. 그러한 특성 중 하나가 야생 식물과 농작물의 경작이다. 이러한 농경 문화로 인해 초기 인류의 유목 생활은 종말을 맞이했고, 인류는 농사를 짓는 터전을 만들어 평생 동안 그곳에 살면서 일하게 되었다. 또 다른 특징은 동물의 사육이다. 축산업의 출현은 과학에서 심리학에 이르기까지 인간의 모든 영역에 발전을 가져다 주었다. 화석 증거를 통해 신석기 시대로 판명된 최초의 문화 중 하나는 서남아시아와 중동에 존재했다. 그곳 아나톨리아 남동쪽과 메소포타미아 북쪽에서 기원전 10,000년 직후에 발전이 이루어졌고, 이는 동쪽과 서쪽으로 퍼져나갔다.

Drill 3　Characteristics: 1, 4　Benefits: 3, 5, 7

해석

맹그로브 숲

맹그로브 숲은 나무와 관목이 자랄 수 있는 바닷가 지역에서 찾아볼 수 있다. 전 세계적으로 바닷가의 맹그로브 숲에는 약 110종의 관목과 나무들이 자란다. 이러한 습지는 맹그로브의 뿌리가 자라기 좋은, 미세한 퇴적물이 풍부한 강과 해안 지역에 존재한다. 맹그로브는 또한 영양분을 공급해 주는 유기물 성분이 많은 지역에서도 잘 자란다. 또한 이 지역은 강한 파도의 작용으로부터 어느 정도 보호되어야 한다. 이 숲에 있는 식물들은 산소 결핍, 염분, 그리고 조수에 의한 잦은 범람과 같은 몇 가지 문제들을 성공적으로 해결해 왔다. 맹그로브의 수중 뿌리는 굴, 해면 동물, 그리고 심지어 게와 같은 해양 생물들의 은신처이다. 이러한 생물들에게 은신처를 제공해 주는 것 외에도 맹그로브는 해안 지역을 강타할 수 있는

폭풍 및 기타 자연 현상을 막아 주는 중요한 역할을 수행한다. 이 숲은 또한 침식을 늦추며 비정상적으로 큰 파도를 막아 주는 방벽 역할도 담당한다.

Drill 4　Positive Effects: 2, 7　Negative Effects: 1, 3, 4

해석

텔레비전이 미국 가정에 미치는 영향

텔레비전이 미국 내 가정의 구성원에게 미치는 영향이 면밀하게 연구되었다. 일부 학자들은 매일 텔레비전 프로그램에 노출되면 가족 간의 커뮤니케이션 패턴에 엄청난 영향이 미친다고 생각한다. 반면 어린이의 사고력이 향상된다고 믿는 학자들도 있다. 한 연구에서 다이애드라고 불리는 부모-아동 그룹을 대상으로 비교 설문지를 작성하도록 했다. 연구는 자녀들에게 텔레비전 시청을 허용한 부모들이 자녀들을 보다 효과적으로 통제할 수 있다는 점을 보여 주었다. 하지만 그들의 커뮤니케이션은 덜 효과적이었다. 다양한 종류의 텔레비전 쇼에 노출되면 부모와 자녀 간의 커뮤니케이션이 더 어려울 수 있다. 그 이유는 서로 다른 관점을 가지고 있기 때문이다. 텔레비전 속의 폭력은 관점을 좁게 만든다는 점이 입증되었다. 이는 또 다시, 특히 부모가 그러한 폭력적인 쇼는 현실적이지 못하다고 설명하지 않는 경우, 자녀가 도덕적 사고를 발전시키지 못하도록 만든다.

Exercises with Long Passages

Exercise 1　1 Ⓐ　2 Ⓓ　3 The Law of the Sea　p.258
Treaty: 1, 6, 7　The Traffic Light Color
Convention: 2, 3

해석

남획에 대한 해결책

남획은 상업적인 어업 활동으로 인해 어류 자원이 감소하면서 개체수가 자연적인 번식을 통해 유지되지 못하거나 기존 수준을 회복할 수 없을 정도로 번식이 느리게 이루어지는 상황에서 발생하는 문제이다. 인류가 먹을 수 있는 어류로 바다를 채워 주는 라이프 사이클 평형은 이윤을 바라는 어부들의 욕망 때문에 지속 불가능한 사이클에 갇혀 버렸다.

어류 자원의 붕괴는 이전에 관찰되었던 최대 존재량의 10% 미만으로 어류 자원이 감소한 상태로 정의된다. *사이언스*지에 발표된 한 국제 과학 연구 논문은 전 세계에 분포하는 모든 어류 자원량의 3분의 1이 붕괴되었다고 결론지었다. 만약 이러한 추세가 계속된다면 전 세계의 모든 어류 자원량이 향후 50년 내에 붕괴될 것이다.

남획의 예는 1970년대에 목격되었다. 이때는 페루 해안의 멸치 자원량이 고갈된 때였다. 동시에 과학자들은 페루 해안의 자연 멸치 자원량이 엘니뇨 효과로 인해 감소했다고 주장했다. 1971년과 1972년 사이 페루 어부들의 멸치 어획량은 전년 대비 60% 감소했다. 이러한 붕괴는 페루 경제에 막대한 손실을 야기했다.

이러한 문제를 우려했던 과학자들은 이 새로 발생한 문제를 해결하기 위해 예방 조치로서의 일련의 남획 원칙을 제시했다. 이들은 전 세계 수산업계에 어획 규제 관리 원칙을 소개했다. 신호등 협약이라고 불린 시스템을 고안함으로써 남획, 고갈, 그리고 어류 자원량의 붕괴에 맞서기 위한 규정들을 소개했다. 이는 조업 수역을 분류하는 단순한 협약이다. 초록색은 어업이 가능한 곳을 의미하고, 노란색은 어류 자원 수준에 경계를 해야 하는, 어업이 강하게 규제되는 곳을 나타낸다. 빨간색은 어류 자원량이 안정적이고 지속 가능한 수준으로 되돌아올 때까지 조업을 해서는 안 되는 지역을 의미한다.

신호등 협약 외에 UN 해양법 협약에도 남획 문제와 관련된 몇 가지 조항들이 존재한다. 이러한 문제가 처음 언급되어 있는 조항은 61조이다. 여기에는 남획으로 어종들이 멸종 위기에 처하지 않도록 모든 해안 국가들이 조업 지역의 생물 자원을 보존해야 한다고 명시되어 있다. 이 조항은 또한 심각한 위협을 받고 있는 종의 보존과 회복을 요구한다. 이 문제와 관련된 그 다음 조항은 62조이다. 여기에는 모든 해안 국가들이 자신의 경제 수역 내에 있는 상업적 생물 자원을 최대한 활용해야 한다고 적혀 있다. 마지막으로 65조는 상업적 이익을 위한 해양 포유류의 포획을 규제를 할 수 있는 권리를 해안 국가에게 부여하고 있다.

남획 문제를 해결할 수 있는 또 다른 해결책은 유전자 접합 기술이다. 이는 물고기의 번식 속도를 몇 배 더 높일 수 있다. 이 방법은 뉴펀들랜드에 있는 기업인 아쿠아 바운티 팜스에 의해 개발되었다. 기술이 더 발전하면 이 프로그램을 통해 어부들이 폐쇄된 수조 시스템을 이용하여 전 세계의 어류 수요량을 충족시킬 수 있을 것이며, 동시에 자연적인 어류 자원량은 영향을 받지 않고 계속 보존될 것이다.

📑 Summary Note

❶ ten percent
❷ fifty years
❸ Traffic Light Color Convention
❹ Gene splicing

Exercise 2	1 Ⓑ	2 Ⓑ	3 Dance Language	p.260

Theory: ②, ④, ⑥   Odor Plume Theory: ①, ③

해석

꿀벌의 커뮤니케이션과 학습

꿀벌은 학습과 커뮤니케이션이 가능한 매우 발달한 종의 벌로, 이들은 학습과 커뮤니케이션을 통해 먹이를 찾는다. 또한 이러한 능력을 사용해서 일벌을 배치하고 먹이를 모은다.

학습 과정이 꿀벌에게 중요한 이유는 이들이 각 벌집에 적합한 효율적이고 성공적인 채집 시스템을 만들기 때문이다. 먹이를 찾는 벌은 아침에 벌집을 나와서 꽃가루 및 즙을 제공해 주는 식물과 꽃을 찾는다. 만약 식물이나 꽃이 충분한 먹이를 제공해 주지 않으면 먹이를 찾는 벌은 다시 여기에 올 필요가 없다는 점을 빠르게 학습한다. 많은 먹이를 제공해 주는 경우에는 벌이 다시 여기에 와야 한다는 점을 학습하게 된다. 이러한 형태의 학습을 연상 학습이라고 부르며, 이는 보통 척추 동물에서만 찾아볼 수 있다.

과학자들은 간단한 Y자형 미로를 사용한 실험으로 꿀벌의 학습 능력을 연구했다. 먹이를 찾는 벌들을 훈련시켜 특정 색깔로 표시된 미로 안으로 들어가면 보상을 받도록 만들었다. 그런 다음 이 벌들에게 방향을 선택하도록 했다. 한쪽은 입구와 같은 색으로 표시가 되어 있었고, 다른 쪽은 다른 색깔로 표시가 되어 있었다. 벌들은 동일한 색으로 표시된 방향에 보상이 존재한다는 것을 빠르게 학습했다.

이 실험을 실시한 과학자들은 또한 벌이 새로운 조건을 또 다시 학습할 수 있는지 알아내기 위해 색깔을 바꾸고 미로의 길이를 연장시켰는데, 벌들은 이때에도 학습을 했다. 올바른 색깔 표시를 보기 위해 벌들이 이동해야 하는 거리를 늘임으로써 과학자들은 벌들이 최대 5초까지 색깔 표시 정보를 기억할 수 있다는 점을 입증할 수 있었다. 이는 꿀벌이 많은 조류의 기억력과 비슷한 단기 기억력을 지닌다는 점을 입증해 주었다.

가장 많은 보상을 주는 식물과 꽃의 위치를 파악한 후, 먹이를 찾는 벌들은 벌집으로 돌아와서 자신이 발견한 것에 대해 일벌들과 커뮤니케이션을 한다. 이렇

게 하는 이유는 같은 곳에서 꽃가루와 즙을 가지고 올 일벌을 모으기 위해서이다. 먹이를 찾는 벌들이 일벌을 어떻게 모으는지에 대해서는 두 개의 상충되는 이론이 있다. 이 두 가지 이론은 춤 언어 이론과 향기 발산 이론이다.

아리스토텔레스의 고대 그리스 시대 이후로 꿀벌은 꽃가루와 즙을 찾는데 성공하면 벌집으로 돌아와서 춤을 주는 것으로 알려져 있다. 그들이 추는 두 가지 춤은 원형 춤과 8자 춤이다. 원형 춤은 벌이 작은 원을 그리며 추는 춤이고, 8자 춤은 지그재그 모양을 그리며 추는 춤이다. 이 춤들은 먹이가 있는 식물 및 꽃의 존재와 위치에 대한 커뮤니케이션을 위한 것으로, 보다 많은 즙과 꽃가루를 얻기 위해 일벌들을 모아서 내보내는 것이 그 목적이다. 춤 언어 이론에 따르면 이러한 행동은 모인 꿀벌들에게 즙이 풍부한 장소를 알려 주는 기능을 한다.

향기 발산 이론은 꿀벌의 춤 언어가 단지 주의를 끌기 위한 것이며, 즙과 꽃가루를 찾기 위해 일벌들이 모이는 것은 즙에서 발산되는 향기 때문이라고 주장한다. 이를 입증하기 위해 과학자들이 실험을 했는데, 먹이를 찾는 벌에게 향기가 없는 당 성분을 주었더니 그곳으로 갈 다른 꿀벌들을 모을 수 없었다.

📑 Summary Note

❶ food sources
❷ by colors
❸ waggle dance
❹ Odor plume theory

Exercise 3	1 Ⓐ	2 Ⓑ	3 Direct: ④, ⑦	p.262

Forced: ②, ⑤   Indirect: ⑥

해석

문화 전파

문화 전파란 서로 다른 문화 간에 사고, 행동, 그리고 물체가 확산되는 현상을 가리킬 때 사용되는 용어이다. 이 용어는, 특히 인구 이동이나 사람들의 대규모 이주와 관계 없이, 그러한 움직임이 나타날 때 사용된다.

문화 전파의 개념과 관련된 이론은 인류학계에 종종 논란을 일으킨다. 그 이유는 이들이 종종 집단 이주에 관한 이론들과 상충되기 때문이다. 문화 전파와 집단 이주 간의 그러한 대립은, 북아메리카, 유럽, 그리고 아시아 대륙 북극권 주변의 동굴 곰 두개골과 관련이 있는, 유인원 매장지에 관한 이론에서 찾을 수 있다. 그럼에도 불구하고 많은 인류학자들은 일반적으로 이를 설명할 때 문화 전파, 즉 문화 간 특성들의 차용에 기초한 이론들을 더 많이 고려하는 경향이 있다.

인류의 역사와 선사 시대를 통틀어 문화들이 서로 완전히 고립된 상태로 존재했던 적은 없었다. 봉건 시대 일본의 고립주의 문화에서도 인도와 중국에서 온 불교의 종교 철학이 확산될 수 있었는데, 불교는 인도와 중국의 객승들로부터 유래되었다. 이는 어떻게 문화 전파가 대규모로 이루어질 수 있는지를 보여 주는 사례이다. 이러한 유형의 문화 전파는 오늘날에도 이루어지고 있다. 문화 전파의 경우 세 가지의 형태, 즉 직접 전파, 강제 전파, 그리고 간접 전파가 존재한다.

직접 전파는 두 문화가 지리적으로 가까운 위치에 있을 때 일어난다. 그 결과, 국제 결혼이 이루어지고, 무역이 발생하며, 그리고 물리적 충돌이 일어난다. 직접 전파의 예는, 멕시코인과 미국인처럼, 국경을 접하고 있는 두 나라의 국민들이 결혼을 하거나, 미국과 캐나다처럼, 인접한 두 국가의 선수들이 하키나 야구와 같은 스포츠를 함께 하는 경우이다.

강제 전파는 보다 강한 문화가 약한 문화를 정복하거나 노예 상태로 만들어서 자신의 문화를 정복당한 국민들에게 강요할 때 일어난다. 이에 대한 예는 미국으로 넘어온 아프리카 노예들에게 강제로 기독교를 믿게 한 것이다. 또 다른 좋은 예는 영국이 인도를 식민지로 삼으면서 많은 인도인들에게 강제로 영어를 배우

도록 만든 것이다.

간접 전파는 오늘날 가장 흔히 일어나는 전파 유형이다. 이 유형의 전파는 전파의 주체 및 객체가 되는 문화들이 직접 접촉하지 않은 상태에서 매개물 또는 중개인을 통해 문화 사이에 문화적 특성이 전해질 때 이루어진다. 이러한 일은 유럽인들이 미국을 방문해 스시라고 불리는 일본 음식을 알게 되었을 때 일어난다. 또 다른 예는 디즈니랜드에 한 번도 가본 적이 없는 아프리카 사람이 관광객으로부터 미키 마우스 티셔츠를 받아서 입는 경우이다.

이러한 문화 전파의 형태들은 역사적으로 각기 다른 시기에 우세하거나 열세한 경향을 보여 왔다. 고대에는 사람들이 서로 인접한 지역에서 거주했기 때문에 직접 전파가 매우 일반적이었다. 하지만 오늘날에는 매스 미디어와 인터넷의 출현으로 간접 전파가 가장 흔한 형태이다.

📝 Summary Note

❶ ideas, behavior, and material objects
❷ located nearby
❸ forced diffusion
❹ globalization

Exercise 4　1　Ⓓ　　2　Ⓒ　　3 Squirrel: ①, ⑤　　　p.264
Mouse: ②, ④　Prairie Dog: ⑥

설치류의 영소 습성

설치류는 2,000에서 3,000 사이의 종을 포함하는 포유류의 목으로서, 전체 포유 동물 중 40% 이상을 이들이 차지한다. 설치목은 크기가 작고, 번식 주기가 짧으며, 다양한 종류의 먹이를 먹고 생존할 수 있는 전반적인 능력 때문에 번성하고 있다.

대부분의 설치류는 크기가 작은 편이지만, 무게와 신체적 특징은 매우 다양하다. 이러한 다양성에 관한 확실한 예는 몸무게가 약 7그램인 아프리카피그미쥐와 현재 가장 몸집이 큰 설치류로서 몸무게가 최대 45킬로그램까지 나가는 카피바라 간의 차이에서 찾을 수 있다.

설치류의 종들 간의 일반적인 차이는 각기 다른 설치류들이 만드는 보금자리의 형태를 관찰할 때 명확히 드러난다. 예를 들어 아메리카비버는 나무를 갉아쓰러뜨려서 보금자리를 만드는 설치류이다. 비버는 그러한 나무뿐만 아니라 다양한 나뭇가지를 이용하여 강이나 개울에 댐을 만드는데, 이로써 결국 인공 연못이 만들어진다. 이 연못에서, 비버는 소굴이라고 불리는 반수생 보금자리를 만든다.

비버와 많은 차이를 보이는 설치 동물의 보금자리는 다람쥐가 짓는 보금자리이다. 다람쥐는 나뭇가지들 사이에 다람쥐굴이라고 불리는 보금자리를 만든다. 또한 다람쥐는 겨울철에 영양분을 공급해 줄 도토리 및 기타 견과류들을 보관하는 저장소를 보금자리 안이나 그 주변에 만드는 것으로 알려져 있다. 과학자들은 다람쥐들이 매우 단기적인 기억력을 지니고 있기 때문에 저장소를 기억하게 만드는 표시가 있는 곳에 열매를 저장한다는 점을 알아냈다. 예를 들어 다람쥐는 먹이를 저장한 장소를 기억할 수 있도록 나무의 북쪽 면에 견과류를 보관할 수도 있다.

보금자리를 만드는 방식이 매우 특이한 또 다른 설치류로 프레리도그를 들 수 있다. 프레리도그는 대규모의 프레리도그 가족이 사는, 매우 조직적인 군락 혹은 마을을 만드는 것으로 유명하다. 한 가족은 보통 한 마리의 수컷과 두 마리에서 네 마리에 이르는 암컷으로 구성된다. 이러한 마을은 사실 프레리도그가 지하에 판 거대한 굴이다. 이러한 굴은 신선한 공기의 유입을 극대화하고 빗물의 흐름을

조절할 수 있도록 만들어진다. 여기에는 심지어 잠을 자고, 먹이를 먹고, 그리고 새끼를 키우는 방이 따로 마련되어 있다. 또한 이러한 굴에는 포식자가 침입하는 경우 탈출할 수 있는 통로도 몇 개 포함되어 있다.

하지만 또 다른 설치류 동물인 쥐는 지상에 보금자리를 만든다. 대부분의 쥐는 잔디, 섬유, 그리고 조각난 물건들로 좁은 지역에서 보금자리를 짓는다. 이곳에서 쥐들은 잠을 자고, 짝짓기를 하고, 그리고 새끼를 키운다. 대부분의 쥐들은 작고 아늑한 지상의 안전한 곳에 보금자리를 만들지만, 일부 쥐들의 경우 깊이가 얕은 굴을 파는 모습도 관찰되었다. 또 다른 종류의 쥐들은 오래된 주택의 벽, 나무의 그루터기, 그리고 심지어는 폐차의 배기관 속에 보금자리를 만드는 것으로도 알려져 있다.

📝 Summary Note

❶ 2,000 to 3,000
❷ semi-aquatic
❸ two to four
❹ aboveground

Exercise 5　1　Ⓐ, Ⓓ　　2　Ⓒ　　3 Food Acquisition　　p.266
Skills: ②, ⑤　Service Skills: ④, ⑥, ⑦

카푸친원숭이의 지능

카푸친원숭이는 신세계의 원숭이종 중에서 가장 지능이 높은 종으로 생각된다. 이들은 중앙아메리카 및 남아메리카에서 찾아볼 수 있다. 이들은 숲에서 살며 하루의 대부분을 먹이를 찾으며 보낸다. 밤이 되면 나뭇가지 사이에 몸을 말아 넣은 채 나무에서 함께 모여 잠을 잔다. 크기가 큰 매, 뱀, 그리고 고양이와 같은 천적을 피하기 위해 나무 위에서 밤을 보낸다.

카푸친원숭이는 과일, 견과, 씨앗, 그리고 싹뿐만 아니라 곤충, 거미, 새알, 그리고 작은 설치류도 먹는 잡식성 동물이다. 또한 돌멩이를 이용해 게의 껍질을 갈라서 이를 먹는 모습도 관찰된 바 있다. 이 털이 많은 카푸친원숭이는 특히 지능이 높은 것으로 알려져 있으며, 장기간에 걸쳐 도구를 사용하는 모습이 관찰되었다. 이는 유인원을 제외하고 영장류가 도구를 사용하는 몇 안 되는 사례 중 하나이다. 이 카푸친원숭이들이 야자 열매를 먹을 때 마코앵무새가 열매를 쪼개는 행동을 따라하는 모습도 관찰된 바 있다.

카푸친원숭이는 가장 잘 익은 열매를 골라서 그 끝을 물어 뜯은 다음 즙을 마신다. 그 후에는 마치 열매를 버리는 것처럼 열매를 옆으로 치운다. 하지만 일단 이 버려진 열매들이 단단해지면 카푸친원숭이는 이들을 모아 크고 평평한 바위 위에 두는데, 이곳에서 원숭이들은 그전에 모아둔 강돌로 열매를 쪼갠 후 그 안에 들어 있는 견과류를 먹는다. 카푸친원숭이는 이전에 열매를 쪼갤 때 모아서 사용했던 것과 같은 돌을 사용하기 때문에 카푸친원숭이들이 사용하는 강돌은 장기적인 도구로 여겨진다. 새끼 카푸친원숭이들은 나이가 많은 원숭이들이 이처럼 행동하는 모습을 보고 마침내 그들로부터 배우게 된다.

카푸친원숭이의 지능 및 도구 사용에 관한 또 다른 예는 모기들이 활동하는 시기에 볼 수 있다. 이 시기가 되면 나이 많은 카푸친원숭이들이 노래기를 모아서 뭉갠다. 그런 다음 서로의 등에 뭉개진 노래기의 액을 문지른다. 이들이 만든 이 노래기 액은 천연 벌레 퇴치제의 기능을 한다.

카푸친원숭이에 관한 한 연구에서는 이 동물의 자기 인식 능력을 조사하기 해 거울이 사용되었다. 한 카푸친원숭이는 거울에 바친 자신의 모습을 보았을 때, 다른 원숭이로 보는 경우와 이미지를 그 자체로 인식하는 경우의 중간에 해당되는, 자기 인식 능력을 나타내는 방식으로 반응하는 모습이 관찰되었다. 이

실험은 카푸친원숭이들이 다른 여러 종의 영장류보다 훨씬 더 자기 인식 능력이 뛰어나다는 점을 보여 주었다.

수백 년 동안 이 원숭이들은 자신의 지능을 이용하여 인간에게 도움을 주었다. 이들은 과거의 음악가들과 함께 여행하던 풍금 연주 원숭이로 잘 알려져 있다. 또한 이동 서커스나 카니발에서 흥을 돋우는 역할을 하기도 했다. 오늘날 카푸친원숭이들은 도우미 동물로서 대마비 환자 및 척추 장애를 가진 있는 사람들을 돕고 있다. 이러한 환자들의 집에서 카푸친원숭이들은 음식을 전자레인지로 데우고, 환자의 얼굴을 씻기고, 그리고 병 뚜껑을 따는 것과 같은 단순한 일을 함으로써 도움을 주고 있다.

📑 Summary Note

❶ omnivores

❷ mosquito repellent

❸ self-aware

❹ paraplegics or injured

Exercise 6	1 Ⓑ 2 Ⓑ 3 Academic Theories: p.268
	①, ④, ⑦ Current Puebloan People's Theories: ②, ⑥

해석

푸에블로 문화

아나사지 문화권의 사람들은 기원전 약 1200년부터 밝혀지지 않은 이유로 자취를 감춘 기원후 1300년까지 미국의 남서부 지역에 거주했다. 지금은 사라진 이 문명이 남긴 가장 큰 건축 유적은 유타, 애리조나, 뉴멕시코, 그리고 콜로라도의 일부 지역을 포함하는 포 코너스 지역에서 찾아볼 수 있다.

현재 아나사지족의 후손들은 자신들이 푸에블로 문화의 구성원이라는 점에서 푸에블로인으로 불리는 것을 더 선호한다. 그 이유는 아나사지라는 단어가 서로 다른 언어를 사용하는 또 다른 부족인 나바호족에서 유래되었기 때문이다. 그들의 언어로 아나사지라는 말은 "적의 조상"을 의미한다. 예전부터 이 지역에 유적을 남긴 사라진 문화를 설명할 때 이 단어가 사용되었고, 그에 따라 오늘날에도 여전히 사용되고 있지만, 많은 사람들은 이 단어가 사용되지 않기를 바라고 있다.

고대 푸에블로 문화는 하칼, 어도비, 그리고 사암과 같은 돌과 점토로 만들어진 절벽 경사면에 거주지를 지은 것으로 가장 잘 알려져 있다. 이러한 고대 절벽 주거지 유적의 상당 부분은 차코 문화 역사 공원, 메사 베르드 국립 공원, 그리고 밴덜리어 국립 유적지와 같은 국립 역사 공원 내에서 찾아볼 수 있다. 이러한 거주지 가운데 일부는 로프를 이용하거나 암벽 등반을 통해서만 접근이 가능하다.

하지만 최초의 푸에블로 주택들은 절벽의 경사면에 있지 않았다. 이 주택들은, 바스켓메이커 문화라고 불린 많은 고대 문화권에서 일반적이었던, 구덩이 형태의 주택 설계에 기반해 있었다. 이러한 초기의 주택들은 작은 마을 내에 위치해 있었다. 구조는 단순했고 L자형, 반원형, 혹은 직사각형 형태를 띠었다. 시간이 흐르면서 점점 더 정교해지고 견고해졌다. 푸에블로 문화가 발전했던 1150년경에는 절벽의 경사면에 이러한 거주지가 지어질 정도로 건축 기술이 발전했다. 이 고대 푸에블로인들은 또한 이국적이고 독특한 스타일의 도기뿐만 아니라 암각화 및 그림 문자의 형태로 표현된 다수의 미술 작품으로도 유명하다.

고고학자들과 인류학자들은 푸에블로인들이 12세기와 13세기에 만들어진 절벽 거주지를 왜 남겨 놓았는지 모르고 있다. 여러 가지 가능한 이유들이 제시되었다. 그중 일부로 장기간에 걸친 가뭄, 표토 침식, 환경 파괴, 종교 또는 문화의 변화, 그리고 심지어는 새로 온 사람들의 적개심을 들 수 있다.

고대 푸에블로인들이 미스테리하게 사라진 이유에 대한 현재 학계의 의견은 기후 변화로 농업에 큰 차질이 빚어졌고 동시에 새로운 부족의 유입되어 이들을 몰아냈다는 것이다. 이러한 의견에 대해 현재의 많은 푸에블로인들은 이의를 제기하면서 고대의 조상들이 사라진 것이 아니라고 생각한다. 대신 그들이 보다 강우량이 풍부하고 더 좋은 시내가 있는 남서쪽 지역으로 이동했을 뿐이라고 믿는다. 또한 그들은 고대 푸에블로인들이 멕시코 원주민과 남서부의 부족과 같은 다른 부족들과 섞였다고 주장한다.

📑 Summary Note

❶ southwestern U.S.

❷ Puebloans

❸ pit house designs

❹ hostility

Building Summary Skills p.270

Exercise 1 Possible Solutions to Overfishing

The problem of overfishing has led to the decline and collapse of fish stocks. Several steps are needed to combat the problem. Fishing rules have been implemented to regulate fishing in depleted areas until their fish stocks return to safe and sustainable levels. The United Nations Convention on the Law of the Sea Treaty issued several articles that address related issues of exploitation, and methods of accelerating fish reproduction have been introduced.

Exercise 2 The Communication and Learning of Honeybees

Scientists are interested in how bees learn and communicate. They have investigated the memory capacity of honeybees and determined that honeybees have a short-term memory similar to that of birds. Scientists have also studied the ways and purposes that bees communicate through dances, particularly the round dance and the waggle dance. The study has led to debate on the odor plume theory because while some scientists argue that the dance is merely used to attract the attention of worker bees, which are cued to the existence of rewarding plants through their aromas, other scientists argue that the dance itself communicates the whereabouts of the desired plants.

Exercise 3 Cultural Diffusion

Although anthropologists do not agree on all aspects of cultural diffusion, they have identified three main forms: direct, indirect, and forced. Direct diffusion occurs when populations are geographically close enough to allow for interaction through activities that include trade or marriage. Indirect diffusion can occur from exposure brought through a middleman such as a traveling merchant who carries wares and stories from one culture to another. Forced diffusion is the imposition of one culture's values and customs on another through subjugation. Today, with the widespread use of mass media and the Internet, indirect diffusion is the most prevalent form.

Exercise 4 The Nesting Habits of Rodents

Rodents are a varied and hardy kind of mammal that make up more than forty percent of all mammal species. Included among the 2,000 to 3,000 rodent species are beavers, squirrels, prairie dogs, and mice. Although each is distinguished by the type of nest that it builds, rodents are usually characterized as relatively small animals that have short breeding cycles and the ability to eat many kinds of food for survival. Their high survival rate is owed to nests that are built in safety away from predators. Beavers build nests by felling trees, squirrels build them between tree branches, mice construct nests above ground, and prairie dogs dig tunnels.

Exercise 5 The Intelligence of Capuchin Monkeys

Scientists have taken an interest in the capuchin monkeys because they are sociable and demonstrate a high level of intelligence. For example, they sleep together at night, and during the day, they look for and process food with river stones. They have even learned to make a salve from millipedes to protect themselves from insect bites. In the past, capuchin monkeys were well known for their adeptness at entertaining, but today, scientists are more interested in training the monkeys to perform household and personal tasks for paraplegics and victims of spinal cord injuries.

Exercise 6 The Puebloan Culture

Known for their strong homes and exquisite artistry, the Anasazi cliff-dwelling people of southwestern North America mysteriously disappeared about 1300 A.D. Anthropologists and archaeologists, as well as the descendants of that culture, who prefer to be called Puebloans, speculate about the disappearance. Some of their explanations involve environmental changes that would have devastated an agricultural lifestyle while others suggest that the Anasazi people merged with other cultures. Still another explanation is that the emergence of a hostile tribe drove them from their territory.

Mini TOEFL iBT Practice Test p.272

1 Ⓐ 2 Ⓒ 3 Ⓑ 4 Ⓓ 5 Ⓒ
6 Ⓑ 7 Ⓑ 8 Causes: ②, ③, ⑥ Methods: ⑤, ⑦
9 Ⓒ 10 Ⓑ 11 Ⓑ 12 Ⓐ 13 Ⓒ
14 Ⓐ 15 Ⓓ 16 Phototropism: ③, ④
Heliotropism: ①, ② Hydrotropism: ⑥

해석

[1-8]

사막화

사막화는 아습 지대, 건조 지대, 그리고 반건조 지대의 한때 비옥했던 땅이 불모의 사막으로 변하는 과정이다. 이러한 변화는 기후 변화 및 인간의 활동 때문에 일어날 수 있다. 현대의 사막화는 주로 인구 증가에 따라 작물을 경작할 수 있는 토지와 가축을 방목할 수 있는 토지에 대한 수요가 크게 늘어나면서 생긴 결과이다.

사막화의 가장 큰 문제는 생물 다양성 및 생산 능력의 감소이다. 이러한 영향은 미국의 남서부에서 찾아볼 수 있는데, 이곳에서는 한때 주종을 이루었던 번치그래스가 사라지고 1900년대 초반부터 크레오소트 관목이 이를 대체하게 되었다. 이러한 변화가 뚜렷한 또 다른 지역은 마다가스카르의 중앙 고원으로, 마다가스카르의 전체 국토 중 10%가 사막화 과정을 겪고 있다. 이러한 초목과 농지의 막대한 소실은 토착민들이 사용하는 화전 농법 때문이다.

현대에 사막화를 일으키는 주요한 원인 중 하나는 한정된 땅에서 지속 가능한 한계 이상으로 가축들을 방목하기 때문이다. 예를 들어 소와 양들이 발굽으로 토양을 밟으면서 다니면 하층토가 단단해져서 수분을 흡수할 수 있는 능력이 감소된다. 또한 가축의 무게와 계속적인 발구름 때문에 토양이 더욱 미세한 입자들로 부숴진다. 이러한 모든 활동들은 토양을 바람 및 물에 의한 침식 작용에 보다 취약하게 만든다. 가축을 방목하는 행위뿐만 아니라 땔감용 장작을 모으는 일 역시 토양을 고정시키는 식물을 감소시키고 사라지게 만든다.

사막화의 또 다른 원인은 토양의 과다 경작이다. 비옥한 토지에 작물을 심으면 작물을 수확한 후 땅이 재사용된다. 결국 토지는 광물질과 수분을 빼앗기게 된다. 농부가 새로운 작물을 심기 위해 땅을 갈면 토양은 침식 작용에 노출된다. 이러한 좋지 못한 농업으로 1930년대 미국 중서부 지역이 사막화를 겪었다. 엄청난 인구로 하여금 생산력이 없는 토지를 버리고 집을 떠나게 만든 이러한 경제적 재앙은 더스트볼이라고 불렸다. 사막화는 또한 중국의 광대한 지역에서도 빠르게 진행되고 있다. 20세기 중반 이후 농촌 지역의 인구가 증가하고 보다 먹이를 많이 먹는 가축들이 도입되면서 사막화는 증가 추세에 있다.

사막화는 생물 다양성에 대한 주요한 위협 요인으로 인식되기 때문에 일부 국가들은 생물 다양성 사업 계획을 마련함으로써 이러한 악영향을 상쇄시키려고 한다. 이러한 계획은 위해 요소를 제한하고 또한 멸종 위기에 처한 동식물을 보호하기 위해 고안되었다. 사막화에 대응하기 위해 사용되고 있는 한 가지 방법은 콩과 식물을 심는 것이다. 이 식물들은 공기에서 질소를 추출하여 토양에 집어넣는다. 이러한 과정은 사막화가 진행되기 시작한 땅에서 생산력을 회복시키는 것으로 입증되었다. 또 다른 방법은 아침 이슬이 모여 토양의 수분이 유지될 수 있도록 나무 밑동 주위에 돌을 쌓아 표면적을 크게 만드는 것이다.

토양을 회복시키는 또 다른 방법은 땅에 인공 도랑을 파는 것으로, 이곳에 빗물이 남게 되면 바람에 날린 씨앗들이 도랑에 갇히게 된다. 이 도랑이 사막화로부터 토지를 보호해 준다. 이 방법은 약간의 노력만으로도 땅이 보호될 수 있다는 점을 보여 준다. 이란의 환경 보호주의자들은 작물을 심은 반건조 지역에 석유를 분사하는 새로운 방법을 시도했다. 이러한 과정은 수분이 증발하지 않도록 묘목에 막을 입혀 주며 이들이 바람에 날아가는 것을 막아 준다.

사막화를 방지하는 매우 간단하지만 성공적인 방법 중 하나는 모래가 해당 지역으로 들어오지 않도록 모래 방벽을 설치하고 바람에 의한 토양 침식을 막을 수 있는 바람막이를 설치하는 것이다. 사막화에 맞서기 위한 또 다른 중요한 제한 조치는 토양에 피해를 입히는 오프로드 자동차의 운행 지역을 제한하는 것이다.

[9-16]

굴성의 종류

과학자들은 굴성을 생물이 환경의 자극에 반응하여 몸을 틀거나 자라는 생물학적 변이 현상으로 간주한다. 생물이 자라거나 몸을 트는 방향은 자극의 방향에 따라 결정된다. 굴성의 반대 현상은 경성 운동으로, 이 경우 자극에 대한 반응의 방향성이 없는 것으로 간주된다.

굴성은 이를 일으키는 자극에 따라 이름이 지어진다. 굴성을 뜻하는 *tropism*은 "돌다" 또는 "변하다"라는 의미를 지니는 그리스 단어 *trope*에서 유래되었다. 굴성의 종류로는 굴화성, 굴지성, 굴수성, 향일성, 굴광성, 그리고 굴촉성을 들 수 있다. 굴성은 대개 식물이나 기타 고착 생물들과 관련이 있다. 만약 어떤 생물이 자신의 의지나 자동력에 의해 물리적으로 움직일 수 있는 경우, 자극에 대한 반응으로 나타나는 활동이나 움직임은 굴성으로 간주되지 않고 지향적 반응인 주성이나 무지향적 반응인 무정위 운동성으로 간주된다.

굴화성은 화학적 자극의 결과로 보통 식물이나 박테리아에서 나타난다. 이러한 움직임에 대한 좋은 예는 화분관이 성장할 때 뚜렷하게 나타난다. 이는 암술머리 표면에 지질이 존재해서 화분관의 성장이 가속될 때 관찰할 수 있다. 또한 이 관들은 꽃의 암술머리에 한 개 이상의 꽃가루가 있는 경우 자극을 받아 훨씬 더 빠른 속도로 성장할 수 있다.

식물이나 균류가 지구 중력에 대한 반응으로 몸을 틀거나 성장하는 현상인 굴지성 또는 향지성을 처음 밝힌 것은 찰스 다윈이었다. 이는 식물의 뿌리가 아래로 자라는 모습과 정글의 넝쿨 식물이 나무 꼭대기에서 아래쪽으로 자라는 모습에서 확인할 수 있다. 또한 바위의 지의류나 이끼류가 성장하는 방향을 면밀히 관찰함으로써 확인할 수도 있다.

굴수성은 물의 자극과 물의 이동 방향에 반응하여 방향성을 나타내는 성장이다. 굴수성이 존재하더라도 이를 식물의 뿌리에서 관찰하기는 매우 어려운데, 그 이유는 물이 토양에서 끊임 없이 흐르고, 이를 관찰하려면 실험 대상인 식물에게 피해가 갈 수도 있기 때문이다. 하지만 수분이 부족한 식물의 뿌리는 수분을 얻기에 가장 적합한 방향으로 뻗어서 자라기 때문에 그러한 과정을 상상하기는 어렵지 않다.

또한 향일성은 식물의 주행성 움직임을 가리킨다. 이 용어는 하늘을 가로지르는 태양의 이동에 직접 반응하는 식물의 움직임을 설명한다. 밤에는 꽃들이 아무 방향이나 향할 수 있지만, 동쪽에서 해가 뜨면 해를 향해 몸을 돌리고 해가 서쪽으로 지는 동안 해의 방향을 따른다. 이러한 움직임은 꽃의 바로 아래쪽 줄기의 유연한 부분 안에 들어 있는 운동 세포에 의해 이루어진다. 이들은 조직에 칼륨 이온을 보내 압력을 변화시킴으로써 그러한 일을 가능하게 만드는데, 그 결과로서 움직임이 나타난다.

굴광성은 햇빛에 국한되지 않는 빛의 자극에 반응을 보이는 식물의 움직임을 가리킨다는 점에서 향일성과 다르다. 광원 쪽으로 식물의 성장이 이루어지는 것은 양성 굴광성이고, 빛의 반대 방향으로 성장이 이루어지는 것은 음성 굴광성이다. 대부분의 식물들은 양성 굴광성을 나타내지만, 뿌리는 토양 깊숙이 뿌리를 내리면서 음성 굴광성의 경향을 보인다. 많은 이끼류 및 지의류는 굴광성을 띠며 태양에 노출된 바위의 면에서 자라는 모습이 관찰되지만, 사상균이나 곰팡이는 햇빛이 전혀 비치지 않는 곳에서 자란다. 덩굴과 같이 일부 기어오르는 식물들은 접촉 혹은 밀착 자극에 반응하는 굴촉성을 보인다. 이러한 방식으로 반응하는 식물에는 옥신을 만드는 세포가 들어 있는데, 이 옥신 때문에 식물이 벽, 화분, 그리고 막대 등의 표면에서 자라게 된다.

Vocabulary Check-Up
p.278

A

	1	2	3	4	5
	Ⓐ	Ⓒ	Ⓓ	Ⓑ	Ⓒ
	6	7	8	9	10
	Ⓐ	Ⓓ	Ⓐ	Ⓒ	Ⓑ

B

	1	2	3	4	5
	Ⓒ	Ⓖ	Ⓙ	Ⓐ	Ⓗ
	6	7	8	9	10
	Ⓑ	Ⓘ	Ⓕ	Ⓓ	Ⓔ

Actual Test

1 Ⓑ	2 Ⓒ	3 Ⓓ	4 Ⓑ	5 Ⓒ, Ⓓ
6 Ⓒ	7 Ⓒ	8 Ⓐ	9 **4**
10 **1**, **5**, **6**
11 Ⓒ	12 Ⓒ	13 Ⓐ	14 Ⓑ	15 Ⓑ
16 Ⓑ	17 Ⓒ	18 Ⓓ	19 **3**

20 Right-handedness: **1**, **3**, **5** Left-handedness: **2**, **6**

해석

[1-10]

지구형 행성과 목성형 행성

지구의 태양계에 있는 행성들은 태양을 중심으로 대략 동심의 타원형 궤도를 돌면서 거의 동일한 평면에 배열되어 있다. 하지만 태양과 가까이에 있는 행성들은 바깥쪽 행성들과 매우 다른 특징을 지닌다. 전자를 지구형 행성이라고 하며 −태양에서부터 순서대로 − 수성, 금성, 지구, 그리고 화성이 여기에 포함된다. 후자는 목성형 행성으로, 여기에는 목성, 토성, 천왕성, 그리고 해왕성이 해당된다. 지구형 행성에 비해 목성형 행성은 크기가 더 크고, 자전 속도가 더 빠르며, 자기장이 더 강력하다. 또한 목성형 행성은 모두 고리를 가지고 있으며, 그 주위를 도는 위성들이 다수 존재한다. 목성형(Jovian)이라는 말은 로마의 신 주피터, 라틴어로는 *Jovis*에서 유래되었다. 일반적으로 아홉 번째 행성이자 가장 바깥쪽에 위치한 행성이라고 여겨지는 명왕성은 양쪽 그룹의 특징을 모두 나타내기 때문에 두 카테고리 중 어느 쪽에도 속하지 않는다. 2006년 과학자들은 명왕성을 행성 리스트에서 제외시켰다.

두 카테고리 간의 주요한 차이점은 구성 성분에 있다. 지구형 행성은 주로 암석으로 이루어져 있으며, 핵은 금속철로, 그리고 표면은 규산염으로 구성되어 있다. 지구가 이러한 성분을 지니고 있기 때문에 이와 구성 성분이 비슷한 네 개의 행성을, 라틴어로 지구를 뜻하는 단어인 *terra*에서 이름을 딴, 지구형(terrestrial) 행성이라고 부른다. 그 표면이 암석으로 이루어져 있기 때문에 지구형 행성에는 산, 협곡, 분화구, 그리고 화산들이 산재해 있다. 핵이 고체라는 점에서 지구형 행성들은 판 이동의 영향을 받으며, 이로 인해 지구의 대륙 이동에서 볼 수 있듯이, 오랜 시간에 걸쳐 표면이 이동하게 된다.

이와 대조적으로 목성형 행성은 주로 수소와 헬륨으로 구성되어 있고 소량의 메탄, 물, 그리고 암모니아를 포함하고 있기 때문에 거대 가스 행성이라고 불린다. 거대 가스 행성의 핵은 액체 상태의 암석이나 금속으로 이루어져 있다. 하지만 핵은 단단한 덩어리가 아니라 철과 규소와 같은 무거운 원소들이 농축되어 있는 형태에 더 가깝다. 그리고 이들의 내핵은 목성형 행성의 부피 대부분을 차지하는 가스 혼합물에 의해서 작아 보인다. 가스는 엄청난 압력을 받고 있기 때문에 행성의 핵과 대기 사이에는 뚜렷한 경계가 없다. 따라서 목성형 행성에는 우주선이 착륙할 수 없다.

목성형 행성 중 처음 두 개에 해당되는 목성과 토성은 전형적인 거대 가스 행성인 반면, 천왕성과 해왕성은 주로 얼음으로 구성되어 있고 소량의 물, 메탄, 그리고 암모니아를 포함하고 있기 때문에 거대 얼음 행성이라는 하위 그룹에 속한다. 이들 목성형 행성에 얼음이 많은 이유는 태양으로부터 더 멀리 떨어져 있기 때문이다. 목성형 행성들은 지구형 행성보다 훨씬 더 크기가 크기 때문에 훨씬 더 강력한 자기장을 발산하며, 이는 또 다시 이들 대기의 밀도를 더 높게 만든다.

지구와 비슷한 행성들의 표면은 망원경과 우주 탐사선으로 관찰이 가능하지만, 목성형 행성의 핵은 가스로 이루어진 두꺼운 대기층으로 가려져 있다.

지구형 행성의 내부 온도가 훨씬 더 낮다. 지구의 표면 온도 때문에 지구는 인간이 살 수 있는 유일한 행성이다. 다른 지구형 행성들의 표면 온도는 수성의 경우 510℃이고 화성의 경우 영하 80℃이다. 태양으로부터 훨씬 더 멀리 떨어져 있는 목성형 행성들은 온도가 더 낮아서 목성의 온도는 영하 148℃, 해왕성의 온도는 영하 214℃이다.

자전 속도가 빠른 목성형 행성의 경우 바깥에 있는 가스층 주변에 띠나 줄 모양의 바람 무늬가 생긴다. 이 띠는 고기압과 저기압 지역으로, 고기압과 저기압 지역이 국지적으로 나타나는 지구와 달리, 빠른 속도의 자전으로 인해 행성 전체를 완전히 두르고 있다. 또한 네 개의 행성 모두 고리와 위성을 가지고 있으며, 지구에서는 토성의 고리가 가장 뚜렷하게 보인다. 고리는 얼음 결정 입자로 이루어져 있다. 고리의 기원은 알려져 있지 않다. 가장 가능성이 높아 보이는 설명은 토성의 위성들이 토성과 너무 가까워졌을 때 고리가 생겼다는 것이다. 토성의 조력 때문에 위성이 작은 조각들로 쪼개졌을 것이다. 이러한 조각들이 현재의 고리를 만든 것이다. 지구형 행성 중 고리를 가지고 있는 행성은 없으며, 위성은 단 세 개, 즉 지구에 한 개, 화성에 두 개가 있다. 토성에만 146개의 위성이 존재하며, 목성에는 95개, 천왕성에는 28개, 해왕성에는 14개의 위성이 존재한다. [추후 이처럼 멀리 떨어진 행성 주위를 도는 위성들이 더 많이 발견되면 그러한 숫자는 늘어날 가능성이 있다.]

[11-20]

우세한 오른손잡이

인간의 경우 균형이 맞지 않을 정도로 오른손잡이가 많다. 어느 손이 우세손인지 확인할 수 있는 기준이 없기 때문에 오른손잡이 대 왼손잡이의 정확한 비율에 관해 과학자들의 의견은 서로 일치하지 않는다. 예를 들어 오른손으로 글을 쓰거나 물건을 던지는 사람이 다른 일을 할 때에는 왼손을 쓰거나 공을 찰 때에는 왼발로 찰 수도 있다. 따라서 객관적인 기준이 없기 때문에 추정치의 범위가 넓다. 오른손잡이는 전체의 85%에서 95%를 차지하고, 왼손잡이는 5%에서 15%를 차지하며, 나머지 소수의 비율은 오른손과 왼손을 모두 능숙하게 사용하는 양손잡이가 차지한다.

아마도 오른손잡이가 우세한 점과 관련된 가장 특이한 사실은 그 원인이 거의 알려져 있지 않다는 것이다. 몇 가지 이론들이 제시되었다. 그러한 현상이 유전적이라는 증거는 존재하지만, 유전에 의해 우세손이 유전되는 과정에 대해서는 유전학자들의 의견이 일치하지 않는다. 교사나 부모가 선천적으로 왼손잡이인 아이에게 오른손을 사용하도록 강요하는 경우와 같이, 사회적 및 문화적 요인들도 특정 손에 대한 선호의 원인이 될 수 있다. 또한 인류학자들은 보다 엄격한 사회에서는 왼손잡이가 덜 흔한 반면 보다 관대한 사회에서는 왼손잡이가 더 흔하다는 점을 알게 되었지만, 어떻게 그럴 수 있는지에 대해서는 의견 일치를 보지 못했다.

가장 신빙성이 높은 설명은 뇌 내부의 기능에 초점을 맞춘다. 뇌의 두 반구는 신체의 반대쪽을 제어한다고 알려져 있다. 뇌 신경이 목 부분에서 교차되어 신체의 반대쪽으로 이어지기 때문에 뇌의 오른쪽 부분은 몸의 왼쪽 부분을, 뇌의 왼쪽 부분은 몸의 오른쪽 부분을 통제한다고 생각된다. 과학자들은 뇌의 왼쪽 부분이 진화를 해서 오른쪽보다 우세하게 되었다고 믿는다. 따라서 몸의 오른쪽 부분이 보다 우세한 좌뇌에 의해 통제됨으로써 오른쪽의 신체적 활동이 보다 능숙해진 것이다. 하지만 우뇌가 우세한 상태로 태난 사람은 왼손잡이가 될 것이다. 일부 학자들은 왼손잡이들에게 출생 시 뇌 손상에 따른 병리학적인 요인이 있을 수도 있다고 주장한다.

진화론에 기초한 한 가지 이론은 전사와 방패 이론이다. 이는 오른손잡이 전사가 왼손으로 방패를 들어 심장을 가리고 오른손으로는 무기를 잡을 수 있었기 때문에 오랜 세월에 걸친 진화를 통해 오른손잡이가 우세하게 되었다고 설명한다. 반대로 왼손잡이 전사는 왼손으로 무기를 잡고 오른손으로 방패를 잡아야 했기 때문에 자신의 심장이 노출되었다. 따라서 적의 공격으로부터 심장을 보호할 수 있었던 오른손잡이 전사들이 생존할 가능성이 더 컸다. 자연 선택의 과정에 따라 왼손잡이보다 오른손잡이가 더 선호되었다.

또 다른 이론은 자연적으로 비대칭적인 인체의 배치에 초점을 맞춘다. 그러한 비대칭성은 얼굴의 오른쪽 부분이 왼쪽과 약간 다르다는 점, 한쪽 다리가 다른 쪽 다리에 비해 보다 힘이 세거나 길이가 길다는 점, 그리고 한쪽 발이 다른 쪽 발보다 더 크다는 점을 보면 명확히 알 수 있다. 이 이론에 따르면 오른손잡이는 이러한 자연적 비대칭성의 한 가지 예일 뿐이다.

오른손잡이가 우세하기 때문에 대부분의 소비재들도 오른손잡이만을 위해 만들어지고 있으며, 왼손잡이들은 자신들을 염두에 두지 않고 만들어진 디자인에 적응하기 위해 분투하고 있다. 이러한 제품에는 가위, 손잡이, 자물쇠, 스크루드라이버, 자동차 조작 장치, 냉장고, 캔 따개, 옷 단추 및 잠금 장치, 그리고 악기가 포함된다. [왼손잡이들은 종종 이러한 제품들의 주문 제작 버전을 찾는다.] 이러한 디자인상의 편견은 불편함 이상을 가져다 줄 수 있다. 오른손잡이용으로 제작된 소총을 사용하는 일부 왼손잡이 군인들은 튀어나온 탄피 때문에 계속해서 눈과 머리에 부상을 입는다.

어느 손이 우세손인지에 대한 문제는 인간이 아닌 동물종에서는 일어나지 않는 것으로 보인다. 몇몇 동물들의 경우 다른 손에 비해 한쪽 손을 더 많이 사용하는 모습이 관찰될 수 있지만, 인간처럼 종 전체에 그러한 우세함이 일반적으로 나타나는 경우는 존재하지 않는다. 일부 과학자들은 동물에게서도 이러한 우세함이 관찰되었다고 주장하지만, 이는 동물원이나 연구소와 같이 통제된 공간에서만, 그리고 동물들이 손으로 하는 실험 과제가 야생에서 손을 사용하는 방식을 제대로 반영하지 못하는 경우에만 그러했다.

1 Ⓒ	2 Ⓑ	3 Ⓑ	4 Ⓒ	5 Ⓐ
6 Ⓑ	7 Ⓑ	8 Ⓓ	9 **2**	
10 **2**, **4**, **5**				
11 Ⓐ	12 Ⓑ	13 Ⓓ	14 Ⓑ	15 Ⓐ
16 Ⓑ	17 Ⓒ	18 Ⓑ	19 **4**	
20 **1**, **4**, **5**				

해석

[1-10]

사막의 물

사막은 연간 강수량이 25센티미터 미만인 지역이다. 사막은 보통 무더운 곳이라고 생각되지만, 남극과 같은 추운 지역에서도 찾아볼 수 있다. 사막은 강수량에 따라 분류된다. 가장 건조한 사막은 과건조 사막이라고 불리며, 이곳은 적어도 12개월 이상 계속해서 비가 오지 않는 곳이다. 건조 사막에서는 약간의 비가 내리기는 하지만 연간 강수량이 250밀리미터 미만이다. 마지막으로 반건조 사막은 강수량이 250에서 500밀리미터 사이인 곳이다.

사막에서는 장기간에 걸쳐 비가 내리지 않지만 가끔 엄청난 폭우가 퍼붓기도 한다. 이처럼 폭우가 내리는 동안에는 우곡이라고 불리는 말라 버린 강바닥이 빠르게 물로 채워져서 범람을 하면 때때로 위험한 분류성 홍수가 발생하기도 한다. 물이 산에서 빠르게 내려와 땅을 침식하면 자갈, 암석, 그리고 모래가 이동하여 우곡 바닥에 쌓이게 되는데, 이로써 충적 선상지라고 불리는 부채꼴 지형이 만들어진다. 또한 몇몇 사막의 경우 사막 외부에서 유입된 물로 채워지는 외래 하천

이라는 영구적인 강이 사막을 가로지르는 경우도 있다. 잘 알려진 외래 하천으로는 이집트의 나일강, 중국의 황하강, 애리조나의 콜로라도강을 들 수 있다. 또 다른 수원에는 지하의 샘이나 저수지가 포함되는데, 이들은 사막의 식물들에게 생명 유지에 필요한 수분을 공급해 준다. 사막에는 땅속 깊이 뻗어 있는 직근으로 아래쪽에 있는 물을 흡수하여 건조한 환경에 적응해 온 식물종들이 많다.

강우량이 충분한 경우에는 일시적인 호수가 만들어질 수 있다. 이러한 호수는 배출구가 없는 분지에 생긴다. 호수 바닥이 마르면 그 자리에 소금으로 평지가 나타나는데, 이는 플라야로 알려져 있다. 북아메리카의 사막 곳곳에는, 유타주의 그레이트 솔트 호수를 포함하여, 100개 이상의 플라야가 존재한다. 강수량이 적다고 해서 항상 사막이 만들어지는 것은 아니다. 강수량 대비 증발량의 비율, 즉 잠재 증발산량이라는 측정값이 높아야 한다. 이 수치는 일반적으로 이루어지는 증발과 식물에서 이루어지는 증발을 통한 수분 손실량을 합산한 값이다. 잠재 증발산량은 일정 지역에서 증발할 수 있는 물의 양이다. 이 수치가 실제 강수량을 초과하는 경우에 사막과 같은 환경이 형성될 수 있다.

따라서 잠재 증발산량이 강수량보다 크기만 하면 사막은 매우 더울 수도 있고 매우 추울 수도 있다. [이러한 현상은 가장 큰 두 개의 사막을 비교해 보면 알 수 있다.] 남극과 같이 추운 사막에서는 강수가 눈의 형태를 띠며, 이는 지면에 흡수되지 않는다. 그리고 사하라 사막과 같이 더운 사막에서는 비가 거의 내리지 않아서 강수량이 잠재 증발량보다 작다. 강수는 사막의 지표면 아래에 광상을 형성시킨다. 강수가 광물층을 통과하면 지하수면 근처에 광물질이 또 다시 퇴적되는데, 이곳에서는 채광 작업을 통해 쉽게 광물을 캐낼 수 있다. 광상은 또한 플라야의 수분 증발에 의해 가치가 높아지며, 이 경우 석고와 같은 광물과 질산나트륨 및 염화나트륨과 같은 염화합물이 만들어지기도 한다. 그러한 증발의 예는 미 서부의 그레이트 베이슨 사막에서 볼 수 있는데, 이곳에는 약품, 연수제, 유리, 그리고 다양한 농약의 제조에 반드시 필요한 붕소가 묻혀 있다.

사막의 형성에 있어서 수분의 역할은 남아메리카의 칠레 북부에 있는 아타카마 사막에서 확인할 수 있다. 이 사막은 서쪽으로는 태평양에서부터 동쪽으로는 안데스 산맥 사이에 있는 지역에 걸쳐 있다. 안데스 산맥 위쪽의 고기압으로 인해 건조하고 차가운 공기가 지면으로 내려온다. 이 공기는 수증기를 포함하고 있지 않고 태양에 의해 쉽게 데워지기 때문에 지면의 온도를 상승시키고 습도를 떨어뜨리는데, 이로써 사막이 형성되기 위한 완벽한 조건이 만들어진다. 아타카마에서는 비그늘이라는 현상 때문에 비가 잘 내리지 않는다. 아마존 열대 우림의 따뜻하고 습한 공기가 안데스 산맥에 막혀 아타카마까지 도달하지 못한다. 이 공기는 차가운 산 공기에 의해 냉각되고 응결되어서 산에서 비나 눈을 뿌리게 된다. 이 공기가 산맥의 서쪽을 따라 내려오면 데워져서 구름이 사라지기 때문에 땅에 비가 내리지 않는다. 따라서 안데스 산맥은 아마존강 분지를 극도로 습하게 만드는 동시에 산맥 반대쪽은 극도로 건조하게 만드는 특이한 효과를 만들어 낸다. 흥미롭게도 지구상에서 가장 건조한 지역과 가장 습한 지역이 거의 인접해 있는 것이다.

[11-20]

도시 열섬

도시는 보통 도시 주변의 교외 지역 및 시골 지역보다 화씨 10도 정도 더 따뜻한 경우가 많다. 과학자들은 이것이 도시 열섬 효과 때문이라고 생각하는데, 이로써 도시 지역의 몇 가지 특징들이 결합되어 주변 온도가 인위적으로 상승하게 된다.

도시 열섬의 주요 원인은 건축과 관련된 것이다. 도심지의 고층 건물에는 햇빛을 반사하고 흡수하는 많은 표면들이 노출되어 있다. 반사된 빛은 또 다른 건물에 도달하게 되며 주변 공기 속으로 들어가지 못한다. 주로 건물의 외부를 덮고 있는 어두운 물질에 흡수된 빛은 건물 자체를 데우게 된다. 콘크리트 및 아스팔트와 같은 이러한 물질들은 시골이나 교외 건물에 사용되는 자재에 비해 더 큰 열전도성과 반사 능력을 갖는다. 건물 사이에서 그리고 건물 주변에 열이 갇히게

되는 이러한 현상은 협곡 효과라고 불린다. 고층 건물의 또 다른 효과는, 주로 뜨거운 공기를 내보내고 남아 있는 공기를 식히는, 바람을 차단하는 것이다.

열이 빠져나가지 못하도록 만드는 또 다른 요인은 증발산이 이루어지지 않기 때문인데, 증발산은 지면과 식물의 잎에서 이루어지는 증발에 따른 수분 손실을 뜻한다. 이러한 현상은 냉각 효과를 가져다 주는 식물 및 웅덩이가 부족한 도시 지역에서 둔화된다. 사람들 역시 도시 열섬 효과를 만들어 내는데 일정한 역할을 한다. 도시의 인구 밀도는 곧 자동차, 버스, 그리고 기차와 같은 인간의 열 생산 과정 및 기술과, 에어컨 설비, 그리고 공장 생산 시설의 증가를 뜻한다. 이러한 모든 활동은 온실 효과로 이어지는 대기 오염을 유발하는데, 온실 효과는 대기 중의 오염 물질 때문에 지면의 뜨거운 공기가 대기로 빠져나가지 못하는 현상을 말한다.

도시 열섬 효과의 영향은 밤에 더 큰 것으로 보인다. 밤에는 복사 과정에 의해 지면 및 기타 표면들의 열이 위쪽 공기로 들어가게 된다. 하지만 도시에서는 이러한 상향 복사가 고층 건물에 의해 차단됨으로써 사람들이 거주하고 기온이 측정되는 높이에 열이 갇히게 되는 경향이 있다. 전 세계 인구의 거의 절반 정도가 도시에 거주하기 때문에 도시 열섬 효과는 30억 이상의 사람들의 삶에 영향을 끼칠 수 있다. 따라서 이는 인구 통계학자들 및 기상학자들에 의해 면밀히 연구되고 있다. 해마다 수천 명이 폭염으로 사망하고 있으며, 도시 열섬은 그러한 폭염의 강도와 기간을 증가시킨다. 도시에서는 밤이 되어도 도시 밖에서 일어나는 것과 같은 냉각 효과가 일어나지 않기 때문에 도시 열섬의 영향을 받는 지역에서는 밤이라고 해도 안심할 수가 없다.

도시 열섬의 또 다른 부작용은 에어컨 및 냉장고를 작동하기 위해 보다 많은 에너지가 필요하다는 점이다. 한 연구에 따르면 로스엔젤레스시의 경우 열섬 효과에 따른 에너지 사용량의 증가로 연간 1억 달러 이상의 비용이 들고 있다. 해당 지역의 날씨 또한, 예컨대 바람의 패턴이 바뀌고, 구름과 안개가 증가하고, 오염이 심각해지고, 번개가 잦아지고, 그리고 강수량이 증가하는 것과 같이, 영향을 받을 수 있다. 열섬 효과의 영향을 완화시킬 수 있는 한 가지 방법은 주택, 도로, 그리고 고속도로에 햇빛을 흡수하지 않고 반사시키는 자재를 사용하는 것이다. 또 다른 방법은, 많은 도시 주민들이 자신들의 아파트 및 사무실 지붕에서 하고 있는 것처럼, 보다 많은 식물을 심는 것이다.

열섬 효과가 지구 온난화에 영향을 미치는지에 관해서는 논란이 있다. 한 학파는 도시 지역과 비도시 지역 모두 장기적으로 거의 동일하게 온도가 상승하는 경향을 보이기 때문에 이 효과가 지역을 벗어난다는 증거는 없다고 주장한다. 이 견해는 바람이 불지 않는 밤과 바람이 부는 밤의 시내 온도를 비교한 2004년의 한 연구에 의해 지지를 받았다. 도시 열섬 효과 이론은 바람이 도시에서 뜨거운 공기를 밀어낼 것이기 때문에 바람이 부는 밤이 더 시원할 것이라고 예측했지만, 실제 온도 차이는 존재하지 않았다. 이 연구의 결론은 바람이 불지 않는 날과 바람이 부는 날 모두 전 세계적으로 기온이 상승했다는 점이었는데, 이는 전반적인 지구 온난화가 도시 개발에 의해서 일어난 것은 아니라는 점을 보여 주었다. 이와 다른 견해를 가진 사람들은 지구 온난화에 회의적인 입장을 보이는 사람들이다. 이들은 지상에 설치된 장비에서 측정된 거의 모든 온난화 현상은 도시 열섬에 의한 것이라고 주장한다. [또한 이들은 도시 지역에서 온도를 측정하는 것에 문제가 있다고 주장한다.] 하지만 이러한 소수 견해를 뒷받침할 만한 과학적인 연구는 아직까지 이루어진 적이 없다.

1 Ⓐ	2 Ⓐ	3 Ⓓ	4 Ⓑ	5 Ⓒ
6 Ⓒ, Ⓓ		7 Ⓐ	8 Ⓒ	9 **2**
10 ①, ④, ⑥				
11 Ⓐ	12 Ⓑ	13 Ⓓ	14 Ⓑ	15 Ⓓ
16 Ⓑ	17 Ⓐ	18 Ⓐ	19 **3**	

20 Pigeons: ①, ⑥　Robins: ②, ③, ⑦

해석

[1-10]

석회 동굴

동굴은 비어 있는 지하 공간으로, 주로 세 가지 방법 중 하나에 의해 형성된다. 해식 동굴은 해안가 바위에 물, 바람, 그리고 모래가 부딪쳐 만들어진다. 용암 동굴은 화산이 분출해서 용암이 굳으면 만들어진다. 모든 동굴 중에서 가장 수가 많은 석회 동굴은 빗물과 녹은 눈에 의해 석회암이 용해됨으로써 형성된다. 또한 전 세계 곳곳에서 만들어지는 석회 동굴은 이제까지 발견된 동굴 중에서 가장 깊고 가장 큰 동굴들이다. 가장 길이가 긴 동굴은 켄터키에 있는 매머드–플린트 리지 동굴로, 이곳의 길이는 306킬로미터가 넘는다. 그러한 동굴이 형성되기 위해서는 수백만 년이 넘는 기간이 필요하다.

석회암은 얕은 바다에 산호와 같은 죽은 해양 동물들이 서서히 쌓여 만들어진 암석이다. 해저에 쌓인 퇴적물은 수백만 년이 지나면 크고 단단한 석회암이 되어 결국 수면 위로 올라오게 된다. 빗물과 녹은 눈이 토양의 상층부 있는 틈과 굴 사이로 스며들면서, 유기 물질의 부패로 만들어진, 이산화탄소를 흡수한다. 물과 이산화탄소가 섞이면 탄산이 만들어지는데, 이것이 석회암의 용매가 된다. 이 탄산수는 틈이나 구멍 같이 석회암의 약한 부분으로 새어 나와 이 약한 부분 주위에 있는 석회암을 서서히 용해시킨다. 그 결과 광물 형태인 경우 방해석으로 불리는 탄산칼슘의 용액이 만들어지는데, 방해석은 석회석에 들어 있는 광물질이다.

그 후 탄산칼슘은 지구의 물을 머금고 있는 상한선인 지하수면까지 내려간다. 수천 년에 걸쳐 탄산칼슘이 이러한 과정을 반복하면 주위의 석회암을 침식시켜 결국 수로가 만들어진다. 용해 과정으로 인해 카르스트라는 특징적인 지형이 만들어진다. 동굴에서 지면까지의 연결부는 두 가지 방법으로 만들어질 수 있다. 동굴 위의 암석이 무너져 싱크홀이라고 불리는 수직의 통로가 만들어질 수도 있고, 혹은 하천이 동굴의 측면을 뚫고 들어와서 수평의 입구가 만들어질 수도 있다.

수로가 점점 넓어지고 길어지면 보다 많은 물을 수용할 수 있게 되는데, 그렇게 되면 또 다시 훨씬 더 많은 석회암이 용해된다. 그 결과 수로가 점점 커져서 동굴 크기를 갖게 되거나 인간이 들어갈 수 있을 정도로 커지게 된다. [새로 형성된 동굴은 그후 건조 과정을 거친다.] 동굴은 두 가지 방법으로 건조될 수 있다. 지하 수면이 낮아져 동굴이 공기에 노출될 수도 있고, 지진이나 기타 지각 변동에 의해 동굴이 융기할 수도 있다. 어느 경우이던 수분이 증발하거나 물이 빠져나감으로써 동굴 안은 공기로 채워지며, 그 결과 건조가 이루어진다. 지표면의 하천이 동굴을 관통하는 경우에는 동굴의 크기가 계속 커져서 더 많은 석회암을 용해시킬 수 있다. 그리고 탄산칼슘이 계속 동굴 천정에서 천천히 떨어지면 이것이 말라서 스펠레오뎀이라고 불리는 탄산칼슘의 퇴적물이 만들어진다. 가장 잘 알려진 스펠레오뎀은 종유석과 석순이다. 전자는 동굴의 천장에 매달린 고드름 같은 형태를 띠며, 후자는 바닥에서 솟아오르는 기둥이다.

자연광은 결코 동굴 내부로 들어올 수 없지만, 스펠렁커라고 불리는 동굴 탐험가들이 많은 동굴 내에 인공 조명을 설치함으로써 멋진 스펠레오뎀 지형이 모습을 드러내고 있다. 종유석과 석순 외에도, 천장에 붙어 있는 얇은 판 모양의 암석인 드레이퍼리, 동굴 벽과 바닥을 덮고 있는 얇은 광천수 층이 말라 있는 유석, 다공질 암석에서 뻗어 나온 나선형 결정인 석고석화, 그리고 암석에서 자라난 비틀린 원주 형태의 곡석도 스펠레오뎀에 포함된다. 가장 정교하게 장식된 동굴들은 인기 있는 관광 명소가 되어 통행로, 난간, 그리고 전기 조명을 갖추고 있다. 가장 흥미로운 동굴 두 개는 멕시코에 있는 칼즈배드 동굴과 버지니아에 있는 루레이 동굴이다.

동굴은 인간과 동물에게 보금자리와 피난처를 제공해 주었다. 네안데르탈인 및 크로마뇽인과 같은 선사 시대 사람들은 동굴에서 거주했다. 지금까지 알려진 가장 오래된 예술 작품은 동굴의 벽에서 발견되었다. 오늘날 동굴은 새, 박쥐, 귀뚜라미, 도마뱀, 그리고 쥐를 포함하여 여러 종의 동물들에게 보금자리를 제공해준다. 곰들은 종종 동굴에서 겨울잠을 자며, 박쥐는 낮 동안 동굴에서 잠을 자고 밤이 되면 밖으로 나와 곤충을 사냥한다. 구아노라고 알려진 박쥐의 배설물은 동굴에 서식하는 수많은 곤충들의 먹이가 된다.

[11-20]
철새가 이동 중에 길을 찾는 방법

철새의 이동은 가장 흥미로우면서도 가장 이해하기 힘든 자연 현상 중 하나이다. 매년 가을이면 북쪽 지방의 새들이 떼를 지어 따뜻한 남쪽 지방으로 날아갔다가 봄이 되면 다시 북쪽으로 돌아온다. 과학자들은 철새가 이동하는 주된 이유가 먹이를 찾기 위해, 그리고 가혹한 기후 조건을 피하기 위해서라는 점에 동의한다. 예를 들어 곤충들은 날씨가 추워지면 모습을 감추기 때문에 곤충을 먹는 새들은 곤충이 번식을 하는 따뜻한 남쪽 지방으로 이동을 하게 된다. 하지만 철새가 어떻게 길을 찾는지에 대해서는 그와 같은 의견 일치가 이루어지지 않고 있다. 최근 여러 차례의 실험에도 불구하고, 조류 전문가들은 아직까지 철새들이 어떻게 매년 같은 목적지에 도착하고 봄이 되면 다시 보금자리로 돌아오는지에 대해 알지 못한다.

일부 학자들은 철새들이 강과 산줄기와 같은 이정표를 이용해 길을 찾는다고 주장한다. 실험을 통해 일부 조류종들은 실제로 그러한 지형적 특징을 이용하는 것으로 확인되었다. 하지만 이 방법은 어떻게 새들이 야간에 이동을 하는지 설명하지 못한다. 또 다른 연구에서는 일부 야행성 조류들이 별을 보고 길을 찾는다는 점이 밝혀졌다. 하지만 이러한 설명은 낮에 이루어지는 이동이나 날씨가 흐린 경우의 이동을 설명할 수 없다. 현재 가장 널리 인정받고 있는 설명은 철새들이 지구의 자극에 의해 길을 찾는다는 것이다. 그러한 과정에 대한 메커니즘은 아직 밝혀지지 않았다. [하지만 학자들은 이를 곧 알아낼 수 있을 것으로 믿는다.] 한 이론은 일부 조류들의 뇌에 자철석, 즉 자연 발생적이면서 산화철로 이루어진 자성 물체가 들어 있다는 점을 지적한다. 자철석은 조류를 포함하여 많은 동물들에게서 발견된다. 뇌 속에 자철석을 가지고 있는 철새들은 남극과 북극의 자기장을 감지할 수 있을 것이다.

전서구를 대상으로 한 최근의 실험에서 자철석이 이동에 결정적인 역할을 한다는 증거가 발견되었다. 전서구는 수백 마일 떨어진 곳에서도 보금자리로 되돌아올 수 있는 능력을 지니고 있다고 알려져 있다. 학자들은 전서구를 훈련시켜 자기장의 변화를 인식하도록 만들 수 있다는 점을 알아냈다. 주변의 자기장이 정상적인 경우 전서구들은 새장의 한쪽 끝에 모여 있었다. 하지만 자기장의 극성이 바뀌자 새들은 반대쪽 끝으로 옮겨 앉았는데, 이는 새들이 자기장의 변화를 감지해서 그에 반응한다는 점을 암시한다.

또 다른 이론은 자극에 대한 이러한 민감성을 설명해 주는 것으로, 이 이론은 원자 내 입자들의 움직임을 연구하는 양자 역학에 기반해 있다. 양자 역학은 전자들이 쌍을 이루어 원자의 핵 주위를 돈다는 사실에 기초한다. 두 전자는 서로 반대 방향으로 회전하며, 이로써 서로의 극성을 상쇄시키는 두 개의 자석이 만들어진다. 하지만 분자가 쪼개져 다른 분자와 반응하여 화합물이 만들어지는 경우, 전자쌍은 더 이상 반대 방향으로 돌지 않는다. 대신 자석의 N극끼리 서로 밀어내는 경우와 같이, 서로를 밀어낼 수 있다. 두 전자가 서로의 극성을 상쇄시켜 아무

런 자기장이 나타나지 않는 안정된 상태에 도달하기 위해 전자들은 방향을 바꾸려고 한다. 위 이론에 따르면 새들이 빛의 변화에 노출되는 경우 이러한 전자쌍이 방해를 받는다. 남극과 북극의 인력에 미세한 차이가 존재하기 때문에 새들은 전자들이 안정 상태에 도달하려고 하는 것을 감지할 수 있다. 이러한 방식으로 새들은 비행하는 도중 남극과 북극의 방향을 알 수 있다.

이러한 효과를 확인하기 위한 실험에서는 인공 조명으로 유럽울새들을 속여 봄에 이동할 때가 되었다고 믿도록 만들었다. 이 새들은 열심히 북쪽으로 날아가려고 노력했다. 빛의 변화로 인해 위에서 언급한 전자쌍이 이동을 했고 울새들은 전자쌍을 수반하는 자기장에 노출되었다. 새들은 방향 감각을 잃고 사방으로 날아갔다. 실험에 사용된 모의 자기장은 너무 약해서 새들의 자연 자철석에 의해 감지될 수 없었는데, 이는 자철석이 아니라 전자쌍이 새들의 비행에 혼란을 일으켰을 것이라는 점을 암시한다. 따라서 현재의 견해는 빛이 철새의 길안내에 중요한 역할을 한다는 것이다. 이런 이유에서 새들이 비행을 시작하기에 앞서 좌우로 머리를 흔드는 것일 수도 있다. 눈으로 주변의 빛을 수집하는 것인데, 이를 통해 새들은 존재하는 자기장을 인식하고 분석할 수 있고 올바른 방향을 찾을 수 있다.

MEMO

How to
Master Skills for the

TOEFL® iBT

READING Advanced